palgrave macmillan law masters

medical law

jo samanta

Principal Lecturer, Department of Law,
De Montfort University, Leicester

ash samanta

Consultant Rheumatologist,
University Hospitals of Leicester NHS Trust
Part-Time Lecturer, Department of Law
De Montfort University, Leicester

palgrave
macmillan

© Jo Samanta and Ash Samanta 2011

All rights reserved. No reproduction, copy or transmission of this publication may be made without written permission.

Crown Copyright material is licensed under the Open Government Licence v1.0.

EC material is © European Union, http://eur-lex.europa.eu/. Only European Union legislation printed in the paper edition of the Official Journal of the European Union is deemed authentic.

No portion of this publication may be reproduced, copied or transmitted save with written permission or in accordance with the provisions of the Copyright, Designs and Patents Act 1988, or under the terms of any licence permitting limited copying issued by the Copyright Licensing Agency, Saffron House, 6–10 Kirby Street, London EC1N 8TS.

Any person who does any unauthorized act in relation to this publication may be liable to criminal prosecution and civil claims for damages.

The authors have asserted their right to be identified as the authors of this work in accordance with the Copyright, Designs and Patents Act 1988.

First published 2011 by PALGRAVE MACMILLAN

Palgrave Macmillan in the UK is an imprint of Macmillan Publishers Limited, registered in England, company number 785998, of Houndmills, Basingstoke, Hampshire RG21 6XS.

Palgrave Macmillan in the US is a division of St Martin's Press LLC, 175 Fifth Avenue, New York, NY 10010.

Palgrave Macmillan is the global academic imprint of the above companies and has companies and representatives throughout the world.

Palgrave® and Macmillan® are registered trademarks in the United States, the United Kingdom, Europe and other countries.

ISBN: 978–0–230–23532–8   paperback

This book is printed on paper suitable for recycling and made from fully managed and sustained forest sources. Logging, pulping and manufacturing processes are expected to conform to the environmental regulations of the country of origin.

A catalogue record for this book is available from the British Library.

10   9   8   7   6   5   4   3   2   1
20   19   18   17   16   15   14   13   12   11

Printed and bound in the UK by Thomson Litho, East Kilbride.

Edge Hill University
Learning Services

Barcode 244960

Contents

Preface

When we first considered writing a book on medical law, we gave much thought as to why there might be a need for yet another book on the subject. It has often been said that every book should have a good reason behind it. There are already several very good texts on this subject written by distinguished and highly regarded authors. What was it that a new book might add to these which was not already available? Colleagues cautioned that it might be quite a challenge to find a new angle. Nevertheless, after much consideration, we decided to go ahead for two principal reasons.

First, both of us have extensive experience of working in clinical settings and have witnessed first-hand how legal and ethical principles engage at the bedside. Prior to becoming an academic lawyer, Jo worked in senior positions in nursing and midwifery and then qualified in law and worked as a solicitor. Ash has always worked full-time in clinical practice after qualifying in medicine. He then took a law degree and developed a continuing interest in academic medical law. We believe that this blend of experience is distinctive and equips us to provide a different perspective from the approach adopted by many contemporary textbooks on medical law.

Second, we have included unique pedagogic features in this text. Each chapter (except the last) commences with a 'scenario'. The issues raised in these narratives are revisited at appropriate points to provide the reader with a focus for reflective consideration. The scenarios, and all characters, are fictitious. However, they are based upon incidents and experiences derived from clinical practice, and we hope that these might serve as a useful tool for translational learning. The last chapter, on Future Challenges, is intended to provide a flavour of the legal and ethical quandaries that might accompany key issues at the cutting edge of medical science and technology. Each chapter commences with a 'mind map' which is intended to assist the reader to navigate through the central concepts of each topic.

The purpose of this book is to provide an accessible introductory text suitable for a diverse range of readers. The book will interface with academic courses in law and combined law undergraduate programs. It will also be of interest to medical and health-care professional students and others who wish to gain insight into the subject area. The book is intended to give an up-to-date and clear explanation of medical law and its principles and consider how these can be applied in practical settings. The two standard caveats apply: the law is up-to-date as at the time of writing and any errors are entirely our own.

We are very grateful for the help received from a range of sources. We owe an (indirect) debt of gratitude to the many erudite authors who have produced texts on medical law and whose writing we have found inspirational. We are also very grateful to our legal and medical colleagues for their unstinting help and encouragement, as well as their comments, on earlier drafts. Thanks are given to our publishers for their constant support and for keeping us to timelines, as well as to anonymous reviewers for their feedback. Last, but by no means least, our thanks to Judith Wragg for her patience, bonhomie and meticulous secretarial assistance.

Jo and Ash Samanta
Leicester 2011

To our children
'our greatest inspiration'

Table of cases

Table of legislation

Chapter 1 follows overleaf.

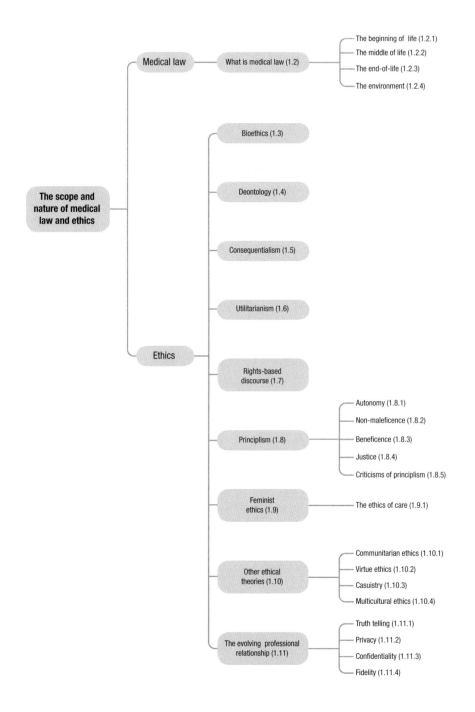

The scope and nature of medical law and ethics

Key Terms

▶ **Autonomy** – the principle of self-governance that promotes self-determination free from controlling influences and limitations (and in the current context the principle that underpins free choice in making health-care decisions for oneself).

▶ **Beneficence** – a moral obligation to act for the benefit of others.

▶ **Bioethics** – a branch of applied ethics used to determine the ethical implications of the biological and medical sciences, offering a framework of universal application for decision making on moral grounds.

▶ **Consequentialism** – an ethical framework that judges the right action to be that which produces an optimally good outcome, thereby identifying the consequences of an action as forming the basis for moral judgement.

▶ **Deontology** – an ethical framework that judges the rightness or wrongness of actions based upon adherence to rights, duties and obligations, rather than the perceived rightness or wrongness of the action's consequences.

▶ **Ethics** – a set of moral principles.

▶ **Feminist ethics** – a perspective aiming to address feminist and gender ethical issues in health care.

▶ **Justice** – moral correctness based upon fairness and equity.

▶ **Medical law** – the legal framework that pertains to the rights and duties of medical professionals and the rights of the patient.

▶ **Morals** – the motivations behind human action and character that are judged to be good or bad and differentiate between right and wrong.

▶ **Non-maleficence** – an obligation not to inflict harm on others.

▶ **Principlism** – a framework for ethical decision making in health care that incorporates the concepts of autonomy, non-maleficence, beneficence and justice.

▶ **Rights** – moral, social or legal claims that individuals (or groups) can make on other individuals or on society as a whole.

▶ **Utilitarianism** – a consequentialist theory that holds that an action is right according to its potential for providing pleasure and maximising the value of well-being.

Scenario

Emily is 78 years old and has chronic rheumatoid arthritis with severe pain in her joints and deformity. She also has substantial co-morbidity with mild respiratory failure, hypertension, heart failure and impaired kidney function. She has now developed a severe chest infection and is visited by her general practitioner (GP), who wants to admit her to hospital. She is fully competent and tells her GP that she does not want further treatment and would prefer to die at home.

Emily's GP insists that she is admitted because if she refuses the implications will be serious. She eventually acquiesces. The hospital consultant recommends a series of investigations to determine the cause of her infection. A junior doctor believes that the consultant has not fully taken account of Emily's wishes but decides not to voice her objection.

Emily is very unhappy at having to undergo further tests. She speaks to the nurses who, while sympathetic, consider that she should follow medical advice. She asks to be 'put down' and a nurse agrees that it is a pity that euthanasia is illegal for humans.

The results reveal that Emily's infection is caused by a virulent and resistant microorganism that requires treatment with a new, potent and very expensive drug. The clinical team seeks advice from a microbiologist, who considers, in the circumstances, that the use of this drug is inadvisable. Emily is now critically ill and the doctors record a 'do not attempt resuscitation' order in her notes.

Emily's condition improves and a decision is taken to transfer her to the Intensive Care Unit (ICU), where she can be monitored and given assisted ventilation if required. She will need to stay for at least a week. After 2 days the treating team is informed that she must be transferred to a low dependency ward because all the beds in the ICU are to be closed temporarily for the weekend on account of staff shortages. There is a need to maintain at least one bed for an emergency and this could only be achieved if Emily is transferred.

Emily is transferred and feels very much better. She asks one of the doctors whether she will be able to return home soon. Although her prognosis is poor, the doctor does not wish to upset her and misinforms her that she is fine. Emily makes a brief recovery and then deteriorates. She is placed on a ventilator, but 2 days later the ventilator is switched off and she dies.

1.1　Introduction

Medical law is firmly grounded in ethical and moral principles. This chapter provides an overview of medical law and its key ethical underpinnings. The relationship between doctor and patient is a fundamental component of good clinical care and this association is considered alongside the ethical principles that engage for contemporary health-care practice.

1.2　What is medical law?

Medical law conveys different meanings to different people and to some extent that meaning depends on one's own frame of reference. One of the authors conducted an informal survey during three separate teaching sessions in order to elicit perceptions about medical law. Respondent medical students felt that medical law was essentially about litigation and efforts to obtain redress and compensation when clinical care led to bad outcomes. Non-health-care respondents tended to perceive that medical law was primarily concerned with 'bad doctors' and 'bringing them to book'. Novice law students considered medical law to be an aspect of tort law. Such perceptions are perhaps unsurprising, particularly when one considers typical media reports of an increasingly litigious society and a compensation culture. However, although such straw poll views are not wrong, the scope of medical law encompasses far more than just negligence litigation or regulation. In fact, medical law is a pervasive subject that extends to a myriad of issues that span all stages of life. It is continually evolving and incorporates tenets and principles from tort law, family law, public law, criminal law, European law and human rights law.

In the next four sections we attempt to provide a general overview of the way the law operates in medicine and health care. This is intended to provide the reader with a 'flavour' of medical law, and the issues are examined in greater depth in subsequent chapters. Medical law has grown rapidly in recent years, as evidenced by the ubiquity and burgeoning size of core textbooks, monographs, articles and compendia, and it now exists as a specialist branch of law in its own right. In the way that health-care needs are apparent throughout life, medical law is all-encompassing.

1.2.1   The beginning of life

For many women pregnancy and childbirth represents a routine aspect of life. Yet for some, childlessness is for reasons other than personal and lifestyle choice. Infertility may be due to a specific cause although it is more often due to a complex interplay of factors such as the inability to produce gametes or difficulties with fertilisation or implantation and development of an embryo. Infertility may be due to male or female factors and can lead to significant emotional difficulties for individuals and couples with implications for society. A range of interventions are available to facilitate reproduction, and the United Kingdom was one of the first jurisdictions to appreciate the extent of the legal and ethical problems that are associated with the so-called reproductive revolution, particularly in the context of *in vitro* fertilisation. As a result, Parliament passed the Human Fertilisation and Embryology Act 1990 (HFEA) which established the Human Fertilisation and Embryology Authority. The main function of the Authority is to act as the statutory regulator for controversial and emotive issues such as assisted reproductive technologies, embryo research, and the storage and use of gametes and embryos (see 5.18.2).

Imagine the controversy caused when Mr Quintavalle brought an action claiming that embryos derived from somatic cell nuclear replacement were not provided for, and therefore not subject to, the terms of the 1990 Act (as in theory, this could mean that human cloning would be legally permissible). The Court of Appeal and the House of Lords took a purposive approach to this litigation and declared that the purpose of the legislation was to prohibit cloning (*R on the application of Quintavalle v Human Fertilisation and Embryology Authority* [2003] 2 All ER 105). Subsequent legislative changes have defined the offence of placing in a woman an embryo that has been created other than by fertilisation, thereby making human cloning for reproductive purposes unlawful, although 'therapeutic cloning' for the replacement of defective organs is permissible under licence (see 5.23.2).

One therapeutic approach to unwanted childlessness is artificial insemination, a technique rooted in antiquity. This intervention has led to considerable controversy in the circumstances of post-mortem use. Much publicity accompanied the Court of Appeal decision in *R v Human Fertilisation and Embryology Authority, ex p Blood*

[1997] 2 All ER 687. On the facts, Mr Blood contracted meningitis and lapsed into a coma. Once it became clear that he was not going to recover, Mrs Blood arranged for sperm samples to be obtained for artificial insemination. The Human Fertilisation and Embryology Authority refused to permit Mrs Blood to receive treatment with the samples on the grounds that Mr Blood had not given his consent for the removal, storage and use of his sperm. On appeal it was held that the Authority had no discretion to permit such use of the sperm in the United Kingdom but she was entitled to receive health care in another State. This meant that she was able to receive treatment in Belgium and now has (posthumously) two children by her late husband. The *Blood* case is a poor precedent for what the law should be in circumstances such as these, particularly in the twenty-first century and in the context of great advances in medical technology. The *Blood* litigation has since been followed by *L v Human Fertilisation and Embryology Authority* [2008] EWHC 2149 (Fam) (see 5.21.1).

Abortion is another controversial area that has generated polarised and protracted debate. Rights-based arguments are typically referred to alongside the right to reproductive choice and recognition of the woman's right to choose. Against these arguments are those that pertain to the interests of the unborn child and what has become loosely termed foetal rights to life. Foetal interests are created by establishing qualities of human personhood to early life and distinguishes a human being from human tissue. From the perspective of some, such as adherents of the Roman Catholic Church and certain other faith groups, human life ought to be protected by law from the time of implantation or, even more radically, from the point of fertilisation. In addition to abortion issues, these arguments have relevance to considerations of the legitimacy of embryo research. For abortion law, viability is considered to be a key point in foetal development since this represents the time following which the foetus would be capable of independent life outside the uterus. Viability is to some extent a context-specific concept that depends upon the availability of specialist neonatal staff and the existence of state-of-the-art health-care equipment. Whereas viability was traditionally considered to occur at 28 weeks' gestation, this has been brought back to 22 weeks in some centres of clinical excellence.

The concept of viability was recognised as a key determinant in the landmark decision in *Roe v Wade* [1973] 410 US 113 in the United States. In essence, the US Supreme Court divided pregnancy into three periods of time known as trimesters. During the first trimester (up to the first 12 weeks of pregnancy), the woman was considered to have the right to choose an abortion; during the second trimester, the State could intervene in a woman's right to choose, in the interests of the pregnant woman; in the third trimester, the foetus was presumed to be viable and the State could intervene to prevent the abortion taking place.

The precise point in time following which a foetus becomes viable is difficult to identify and has been left to the medical profession to determine. Modern technology has advanced greatly and the ability to maintain the lives of very early neonates has increased such that the time of viability is incrementally being pushed back. Inevitably this has created tensions in respect of late termination of pregnancy, particularly where an abortion is sought during the second trimester but still falls within the time limit of current legislation. In *C v S* [1987] 1 All ER 1230, a single woman who was pregnant with a foetus of between 18 and 21 weeks' gestation wished to terminate her pregnancy. The father sought to prevent the abortion on the grounds that the foetus was sufficiently mature to be born alive. The Court of Appeal held that although a foetus of this maturity was likely to show demonstrable signs of life, such a foetus would be incapable of an independent existence. This requirement that the foetus should be capable of an independent existence has the attraction of setting an anatomical and physiological point of development as a conceptual foundation for decision making. However, on the downside, this decision is perhaps questionable since nowadays it is relatively commonplace to sustain a neonate on a ventilator. If assistance was continued for 48 or 72 hours and to the extent that the foetus could rely on its own lungs, then justification argued on the basis of viability seems less persuasive. The father of the foetus has no right to veto a termination of pregnancy carried out in accordance with the law. *Paton v UK* (1980) 3 EHRR 408 clearly established that a pregnant woman's right to self-determined choice with regard to her body (and also that of her unborn foetus) trumped the rights of her partner and the prospective father of the unborn child (see 5.4.3). Within this jurisdiction, the unborn child has no right to action as long as it lies 'north of the vaginal introitus'.

1.2.2 The middle of life

Arguably, one of the most well-recognised areas of medical law is that of medical negligence. A key concept in negligence is whether or not the standard of care given by a health practitioner or health-care organisation, who owes a duty of care, has been breached. Traditionally the standard of care in a negligence action is according to the standard expected to be achieved in the circumstances by a reasonable man. However, for medical practitioners, the standard of care expected is according to the *Bolam* test. According to the *Bolam* standard, in situations where a special skill or competence was required, then the standard of care expected was not that of the proverbial reasonable man, since the reasonable man could not be expected to have the skills necessary to discharge the duty of care. The standard expected from a doctor will be that which accords with the practice accepted as proper by a responsible body of medical professionals who are skilled in that particular art. The test articulated in *Bolam v Friern Hospital Management Committee* [1957] 1 WLR 582 has survived for over half a century. There has been trenchant criticism that for medical negligence litigation, the standard has not been what ought to be done in practice, but is instead assessed according to that which is done in practice by the medical profession. For this reason, it is difficult for a claimant to prove that the standard has been breached, and the *Bolam* standard is considered to be deferential to the medical profession (see 3.3.1).

For a successful negligence action the claimant also has to prove that breach of the standard of care was the cause both in fact, and in law, of the damage. There is little dispute that a duty of care is owed once a health-care professional assumes the care of a patient but proof of causation can be a real challenge for a claimant since the damage suffered has to be shown to flow directly from the breach of the standard of care expected (on the balance of probabilities). If evidence shows that there was a 51% probability that the damage flowed from the breach, the claimant will be successful whereas if there is a 49% probability that the damage flowed from the breach, then the claimant is entitled to nothing. Furthermore, no claim is available in tort for 'loss of a chance' so a breach in the standard of care that may result in a 25% loss of a chance of a satisfactory outcome will attract no recovery in law, even if the outcome is adverse. Yet for the individual concerned, the personal loss in terms of human emotion, pain and suffering, can be considerable.

The adversarial system of negligence litigation means that only one party wins. In this jurisdiction there is no opportunity for a 'win-win' situation. This system of fault-based compensation has been criticised by several academics who have argued that a no-fault compensation is much fairer as it awards the victim some compensation, which is better than nothing. Those who support a fault-based system argue that a truly deserving victim gets 'full' compensation, which means the amount of damages that is sufficient to put the person back in the position that she would have been in had the breach and the ensuing damage not occurred. It will no doubt remain a moral and ethical debate as to whether it is better for all victims to have some compensation, or for some victims to receive full compensation.

The courts have not been blind or unsympathetic to the hurdles that claimants need to overcome in order to win their cases. *Bolitho v City and Hackney Health Authority* [1997] 4 All ER 771 was appealed to the House of Lords. Although the central issue was one of causation, Lord Browne-Wilkinson nevertheless went on to make *obiter* comments regarding the standard of care. On commenting that although the opinion in terms of the standard of medical care would align with mainstream medical opinion, this did not necessarily mean that a defendant doctor would automatically escape liability. Such an opinion would need to have a logical basis (see 3.3.3). Essentially these comments in *Bolitho* suggest that the courts would be prepared to take a more interventional stand in evaluating the professed standard of care in the appropriate circumstances, and a number of post-*Bolitho* cases indicate a subtle shift away from the traditional *Bolam* approach. This shift in judicial approach is also evident when applied to the principles of causation, for example, in *Fairchild v Glenhaven* [2002] UKHL 22, the House of Lords reaffirmed that a straightforward 'but for the negligent act the damage would not have occurred' approach was not justified in the circumstances. A more pragmatic approach was required and the question to be asked was whether the defendant's negligence had materially increased the risk of harm (see 3.4.2(b)). If the answer was yes then damages could be awarded, although being cognisant that the *Fairchild* exception is likely to apply in a very narrow range of circumstances. More interestingly, in *Chester v Afshar* [2004] UKHL 41, the surgeon's failure to warn the claimant of an inherent risk of injury in a procedure did not break the chain of causation even though there was evidence that the claimant would have consented to the same procedure (rather than never consenting to that procedure) at a future date (see 3.4.4). This decision does not align with conventional principles of causation but nonetheless can be supported on the grounds of a duty being vested upon a doctor to warn patients of the risk. Developments in the law of negligence can be seen to focus primarily on compensating those who are wrongfully injured by adopting a more pragmatic approach.

The law of consent is another area of central importance in medical law. In England and Wales there is no doctrine of informed consent, although valid consent requires that sufficient information has been provided to enable the individual to make an informed decision about whether to proceed with surgery or any other intervention. The obligations to disclose in jurisdictions that operate according to the doctrine of informed consent are far stricter than those that require consent with sufficient information. In the US case of *Canterbury v Spence* 464 F 2d 772 (D.C. Cir. 1972), disclosure of a risk was held to be mandatory in the circumstances that a reasonable person in what the physician knows to be, or should know to be, the patient's position would be likely to attach significance to that risk (see 4.6.2(a)). The onus of information disclosure in informed consent is upon the physician and is a high standard since it is assessed against what the physician should know to be the patient's position. The starting point is the assumption that doctors know what the hypothetical reasonable person in that position would want to know, which is arguably a difficult, if not impossible, requirement.

In the United Kingdom, valid consent is underpinned by sufficient information disclosure. The test to ascertain the amount of information that should be given to a patient was considered by the House of Lords in *Sidaway v Bethlem RHG* [1985] 1 All ER 643 (see 4.6.2). The outcome was that the level of disclosure (of risks of an operation) that should be made would be judged according to the *Bolam* standard, which was accepted as representing contemporaneous professional wisdom. Lord Scarman dissented in that the issue was of considerable significance and hinged upon the extent of the patient's right to know the inherent risks that accompanied medical intervention. In his judgement, the standard of information disclosure ought to be judged according to a patient-centred approach rather than a 'reasonable' or 'prudent' doctor approach. From a rights-based perspective, a patient has the right to self-determination which is founded on autonomy and, therefore, has the right to know what inherent risks he might be subjecting himself to in consenting to a particular procedure. The *Sidaway* decision has been criticised as being yet another example of the '*Bolam*-isation' of medicine with excessive deference being shown to the medical profession even where consent is concerned. Those who criticise the *Sidaway* judgement argue that it might be perfectly acceptable that the standard ought to be set by the medical profession where matters of *technical relevance* are concerned, but that this should not be the case with matters of patient consent, since the latter is based primarily upon the patient's right to know and accordingly make an informed choice.

The courts have not been altogether unsympathetic to the view that the standard of information disclosure ought to more closely align with the individual patient's perspective. In *Pearce v United Bristol Healthcare NHS Trust* [1999] PIQR P 53, Lord Woolf pronounced on risk disclosure and in doing so combined some of the views expressed in *Sidaway* and stated that if there was a significant risk that would affect the judgement of a reasonable patient, then it would be the responsibility of the doctor, in the normal course of events, to inform the patient of that significant risk (see 4.6.2(b)). While this approach does not reflect the requirements of the doctrine of informed consent, it nonetheless signifies a shift from the pure *Bolam* standard and represents the middle ground (although Lord Woolf's comments were *obiter*).

Another interesting development in the area of consent is the decision of *Chester v Afshar* (as above). The neurosurgeon's failure to warn was linked to causation. Ms Chester was not warned of a risk that subsequently materialised and on conventional causation principles would have needed to show that 'but for' the failure to warn, the damage would not have occurred. This would mean that she would have needed to show that not only would she not have undergone the operation at that particular time, but further that she would have never have undergone that operation at all since the risk was inherent in the procedure and was not due to negligence on the part of the defendant. Ms Chester could not prove that she would never have undergone the surgery, only that she would have delayed her decision in order to take a second opinion. Despite this the House of Lords held that causation was established and damages were awarded. The approach of their Lordships was more towards whatwas fair, just and reasonable for compensating a claimant who had been injured.

1.2.3   The end-of-life

The dying process is a significant part of one's life. Public opinion polls overwhelmingly indicate that most individuals would like to 'die with dignity' and have a 'good' death. Heroic medical intervention at the end-of-life can be intrusive and may adversely impact upon what is perceived to be a good death. Individuals with capacity can refuse even life-saving treatment but exercising the right to refuse can be problematic for those persons who lack (or are considered to lack) capacity.

In the absence of a valid and applicable prospective decision, or a *bona fide* proxy, treatment decisions for withholding or withdrawing treatment from a patient who lacks capacity can be made according to two models: substituted judgement or best interests. The substituted judgement approach is well established in United States jurisprudence but has been rejected within the United Kingdom. For a substituted judgement the decision-maker 'dons the mantle' of the patient concerned and makes a decision based on what that person would have done in the circumstances had that person the capacity to do so. It is, of course, impossible to consider every aspect that the individual might have considered and furthermore this type of approach will be inappropriate for the individual who has never possessed decision-making capacity (such as a very young child). A decision based upon best interests is one that is made on the overall best interests of the person at that time and in consideration of the section 4 criteria of the Mental Capacity Act 2005 which includes the previously expressed wishes and beliefs of the individual concerned (see 4.12.2).

There are certain situations where it will be apparent to doctors that treatment should not be initiated since to do so would be futile and health-care professionals have no duty to provide futile medical treatment. To a large extent the assessment of whether a treatment is futile will be a matter of clinical judgement made on the basis that the treatment being considered will serve no useful purpose. Equally, and importantly, decisions not to treat on grounds of futility may be based on covert or overt assessments of the anticipated quality of life following treatment. Although the law would be unlikely to criticise decisions not to commence treatment deemed to be clinically useless (such as attempts to resuscitate a corpse), the majority of futility determinations are likely to be less clear cut. The concept of futility is a complex notion that to some degree is determined according to the anticipated quality of outcome and extends to decisions about withholding or withdrawing treatment (see 10.10). Judicial guidance can be found in the Court of Appeal decision in *Re J (a minor) (wardship: medical treatment)* [1990] 3 All ER 930. The infant J was severely and permanently brain damaged. Although his quality of life was poor, he was not dying. The hospital was granted a declaration that it would not be unlawful to withhold further treatment. The court held that the primary issue to be considered was not about termination of life but whether to withhold treatment that was designed to prevent death from natural causes. For this determination the child's anticipated quality of life was an important and relevant factor (see 6.4.4(a)).

Withdrawal of treatment from a patient who lacks capacity is often justified on the grounds of best interests, of which the principle of futility is an accepted determinant (see 10.10). The alternative basis of decision making under such circumstances, that is substituted judgement, may be the preferred approach, as in *Cruzan v Director, Missouri Department of Health* (1990) 110 SCt 2841. The US Supreme Court indicated that they had convincing evidence that Ms Cruzan's purported wishes were necessary in order to make a substituted judgement decision on her behalf. However, if one were to equiparate best interests (on the basis of what others think is best) and substituted judgement (where others attempt to ascertain what the person would have wanted), arguably there may be little difference between the two. The Mental Capacity Act 2005 establishes (in line with the common law) that best interests are to be the basis of decision making for those who lack capacity, although the Code of Practice, in emphasising that the patient's previous beliefs and wishes should be taken into account, seems to reflect a slight shift towards a substituted judgement approach.

An alternative approach that arguably better respects patient autonomy is prospective decision making by way of advance decision to refuse treatment or the appointment of a proxy decision-maker acting under a health-care and welfare lasting power of attorney. An advance decision must be valid (in compliance with the requirements of the Mental Capacity Act 2005) and applicable (having direct relevance to the immediate health-care circumstances). The principal criticism of advance health-care decisions to refuse treatment is their tendency to fail on grounds of applicability since this depends upon clinical circumstances at the time the decision has to be made. Assessment of clinical circumstances will be determined by the clinical team in respect of either commencing or withholding treatment or continuing or withdrawing treatment (see 4.13). A lasting power of attorney is a more sophisticated power by which another previously appointed person may either consent to or refuse treatment on behalf of the incapacitated adult according to that individual's best interests in the circumstances (see 4.14.1).

Advance decisions to request treatment are not binding on health-care professionals. In *R (on the application of Burke) v General Medical Council* [2005] EWCA Civ. 1003, Leslie Burke, who suffered from a progressive neurological disorder, wanted to be assured that following his almost inevitable loss of capacity at the end of his life, artificial nutrition and hydration would not be withdrawn on the basis of futility. In the first instance, Munby J provided a powerful rights-based discourse to justify the decision that artificial nutrition and hydration would not be withdrawn. This decision was subsequently overturned by the Court of Appeal which criticised the first instance decision as going far beyond the concerns of the claimant and creating the danger that the court would be asked to pronounce on propositions of principle in future applications without full appreciation of the specific circumstances at that future time. Arguably, however, not all forms of artificial nutrition and hydration represent complex medical intervention and could represent an aspect of basic care. If artificial nutrition and hydration could function to prolong life in a patient with an underlying progressively deteriorating condition, such as Mr Burke's, extension of life would seem unlikely to be achieved for any prolonged period of time. It would seem, therefore, that the appellate decision was based on policy.

1.2.4 The environment

So far we have looked at aspects of the law as they apply to the life of the individual. This, however, cannot be considered in isolation or for society generally and must be considered in the context of a publicly funded health-care regime and the contemporary challenges of fiscal constraints.

Resource allocation has always played a central role in health-care delivery within the National Health Service and especially during the current period of financial austerity and cutbacks. The National Institute for Health and Clinical Excellence (NICE) was created principally to avoid the situation of a postcode lottery, where access to care is dependent upon residential location, and to provide clinical guidance based on robust clinical and scientific evidence. However, to achieve the latter, NICE has to consider the clinical and cost-effectiveness of interventions and rely upon health economics for its reasoning and decision-making processes. One method for determining cost-effectiveness is that of quality adjusted life years (QALYs). This is not without its problems and the principal objection is that it is not possible to determine or to translate a person's quality of life into pure monetary considerations; furthermore, QALYs may not adequately protect the interests of older persons and those with severe disabilities (see 2.22.2).

The approach towards financial constraints and resources within the NHS has been that of considering due process by way of judicial review. In an early case on resource allocation, *R v Cambridge DHA ex p B* [1995] 2 All ER 129, the Cambridge DHA took a decision not to fund further treatment of a 10-year-old girl with leukaemia. Her father applied for judicial review of the decision. Although successful at first instance, the decision was overturned on appeal. The Court of Appeal emphasised that the court would simply be shutting its eyes to the real world if it did not recognise that financial constraints were an unfortunate reality and that it would be up to each health authority to decide how best to use its limited resources. In more recent decisions, the courts have focused upon the decision-making processes used by commissioning bodies in restricting or refusing treatment in that the existence of blanket policies and procedures that do not operate on a rational basis for distinguishing between individual situations are likely to fall foul of the court. However, it is unlikely that the court will intervene in individual rationing decisions, and the onus of making the decision will revert to the original decision-making body (see 2.19).

The approach of the court is that the welfare of individual patients is the paramount consideration, although individual patients cannot demand treatment if the commissioning body has reasonable grounds for refusal, such as resource constraints. What the courts have been prepared to scrutinise is whether the Authority, in relying upon the defence of limited resources, has acted outside its powers or has arrived at an irrational decision. Health authorities must set out the reasons for their decisions clearly, for otherwise the policy might be deemed unreasonable and unlawful.

Medical law must remain aligned to societal mores. A typical example is provided by that of transsexualism. A transsexual is an individual whose biological sex remains undisputed but nonetheless is convinced that he or she has been provided with the wrong physical sexual attributes. This compares with transvestitism whereby heterosexual males obtain arousal through dressing in female clothes. Transsexualism is now accepted as a genuine psychiatric condition that merits treatment and, therefore, the legitimate use of NHS resources. Conventional treatments in the manner of psychotherapy tend to be less effective than gender reassignment surgery and supportive hormonal therapy.

Consider for example, the transsexual's right to extensive surgical and hormonal therapy with the lack of Leslie Burke's right to be assured that artificial nutrition and hydration would not be withdrawn at the end of a life ridden by a progressive degenerative neurological condition. Perhaps this piquant contrast usefully illustrates what medical law is about. Medical law provides a legal framework whereby ethical and moral issues relating to health care have to be balanced in the interests of all relevant parties and against a background of a changing and evolving society.

1.3　Bioethics

The *Oxford Dictionary* defines the word 'morals' as pertaining to human character or behaviour considered to be good or bad, or pertaining to the distinction between right and wrong, or good and evil, in relation to actions, volitions or character of responsible beings. 'Ethics' is defined as representing a set of moral principles. Medical ethics is principally concerned with how difficult issues surrounding medical practice are resolved in terms of what is 'right' and what is 'wrong' in specific circumstances. By way of example, medical ethics may engage in end-of-life decision making, euthanasia, abortions, genetic engineering and self-determination with regard to consent for treatment. Traditionally, medical ethics was physician-centred and focused on how doctors ought to treat their patients according to their judgement and what would be best for their patients. Relatively little regard was given to broader social issues of health care, as well as the patient's perspective, which typically engages in issues around self-determined choice of medical care. Wider social issues may engage in terms of the way in which health care is provided in the contemporary National Health Service (NHS), particularly with respect to the limits of care that can be provided free at the point of delivery. A further dimension of the social context of medical ethics arguably lies in the obligations of patients and the extent to which those who depend upon health-care services ought to have a moral obligation to take preventative measures to protect their health and reduce recognised risk factors for disease such as smoking, excessive alcohol intake, obesity and lack of exercise.

The term 'bioethics' has a wider remit than traditional medical ethics, and advances in biotechnology as well as challenges to medical paternalism have been the principal drivers for its development. Bioethics, as a concept, was independently conceived in the early 1970s by Van Rensselaer Potter and Andre Hellegers who recognised an ethic to incorporate society's obligations to other individuals and the biosphere as a whole. More commonly it is used to describe the study of ethical issues that arise on account of biological medical sciences.

By tradition, medical ethics focused on the doctor and patient relationship and, in particular, upon the virtues of being a good doctor. Bioethics is more critical and reflective and aims to promote a better understanding of the issues in health care by establishing principles that move away from subjectivism and relativism to a position that is of universal application. This means that if an ethical judgement is made according to hypothetical as well as actual circumstances, and if one could be transposed into the position of the parties affected, the test would be to determine whether one would still be able to accept that particular judgement as valid. Many people have an intuitive reaction to ethical dilemmas and a gut reaction as to what is right and what is wrong. It is, however, important to maintain a coherent framework of reasoning based on moral principles which would justify the ethical stance that one takes. Bioethics aims to provide such justification on a systematic analysis of moral rules, thereby providing ethical principles of universal application to health-care and biomedical developments.

The principal components that underpin bioethical debates include religious perspectives and secular ethics theory. Religious perspectives include respect for the sanctity of life, treating all human beings equally, emphasising the right or wrong of certain actions and considerations on the meaning of life and death. It is beyond the scope of this work to discuss theological ethics in any detail. Secular ethical theories include (amongst others) deontology, consequentialism, the four principles approach (or principlism), virtue ethics and feminist ethics. These are considered below.

1.4 Deontology

Deontological theories (derived from the Greek word *deontos* meaning duty) hold that certain choices are right or wrong, irrespective of their consequences, and that the 'correctness' depends upon whether or not it is consistent with moral principles and norms. The morality of a choice or an action is determined by the underlying motivation rather than the outcomes of that choice or action. Deontologists typically consider that there are several distinct types of duties and that certain choices or types of action are intrinsically morally wrong. Two important classes of duty are recognised. First, there are those that arise from social and personal relationships in respect of particular persons; for example, parents have duties to children, children owe duties to their parents, an employee has a duty to his or her employer and so forth. Second, there are those duties that arise by way of general and pervasive constraints such as the duty not to cheat, torture or murder another.

Key to the deontological approach is the principle that a breach of duty cannot be justified simply by reference to its consequences, no matter how beneficial that consequence might be. One school of deontological thought is that all or at least some deontological principles are absolute and can never be breached. Others argue that an act might breach a constraint principle, but such a breach could be overcome if there was a sufficiently pressing duty on the other side. Thus, if a deontological duty is not absolute, then a conflict between two duties must be settled by determining which is the more pressing under the circumstances.

A leading exponent of deontological thinking was Immanuel Kant. His ethic, based upon the 'categorical imperative', is that in judging the morality of an action one has to ascertain the principle that an action is based on and whether that principle could legitimately be extended as a universal law. By way of example, consider lying to an individual in order to avoid risk of offence. Since the liar's motive was 'good', this action could satisfy the first principle. Applying the categorical imperative as to whether lying could be extended as a universal law, difficulties are readily apparent. Since the effect of lies depends on deception, knowledge that all persons were habitual liars would mean that people would be deceived. On this analysis from a Kantian perspective, the inviolable rule would be never to tell a lie. Another tenet of Kant's perspective of deontology is the notion of personhood and the respect owed by virtue of an individual's innate dignity. This principle extends to Kant's inviolable maxim to always treat others as ends in themselves and never as means to an end.

Linked to the theory of deontology is the concept of moral rights. It is important to note that moral and legal rights are distinct entities. Legal rights are often grounded in ethics. For example, the legal right to life is a way of lawfully enforcing the moral right to life. A rights-based approach focuses on the interests of the individual. It is designed to protect the individual from improper claims and harm which could be justified in the interests of others or in the interests of society. Rights put a limit as to what can happen and when it can happen.

An understanding of deontology may be furthered by considering this theory in relation to consequentialism (see 1.5).

1.5   Consequentialism

Consequentialism is a group of moral theories based on the premise that the correct action, or choice, is that which produces the best overall consequence or outcome. Some degree of consideration of the consequences of actions represents part of all moral theories, although the emphasis varies considerably. Even within deontology (which is principally duty based), if there is conflict between two duties that are not absolute, then the right action is determined according to which duty is more pressing in the circumstances. In doing so, some account of consequences will inevitably be taken into consideration. A similar example can be seen through the application of a deontological approach to the doctrine of double effect (see 10.3.3). According to this premise, in certain circumstances, it is morally permissible to risk or bring about an act that is undertaken for its good effect, but which may also have foreseen, but unintended, bad effects. Consequentialism, however, differs from deontology (and other forms of moral thinking) because within this construct, it is nothing but the consequences that matter.

McNaughton (1998) explains that consequentialism assesses the rightness or wrongness of actions depending upon the outcomes and the value of these consequences. The most predominant form of consequentialism is 'act-consequentialism' which states that all actions are open to an individual but the correct action is that which produces the most beneficial outcome. Contrast this to the deontological approach which holds that certain kinds of actions are intrinsically wrong while others are right, and are unconnected to the goodness or the badness of their consequences. In its simplest form, act-consequentialism holds that the right action is that which produces the greatest balance of good over bad consequences. Where there are two or more actions that are equal in terms of consequences, then there is a legitimate choice between the two. If there are different kinds of good which fall under different categories (so-called pluralistic good outcomes), then in order to determine which possible action is the right one, a person would have to rank the outcomes of each action from the worst to the best.

It is worth contrasting consequentialism with deontology since these are two of the oldest and most ascribed to secular moral theories:

▶ As previously noted, the word 'deontology' derives from the Greek word *deontos* meaning duty, or *deon*, meaning 'one must', and is based upon several distinct duties that can be either in the form of positive performances (those that must be done) or constraints on action (those to be avoided). Consequentialism is described as being a teleological theory (derived from the Greek word *telos* meaning consequences) because it is a moral theory that sets a goal (the greatest good) that one should strive to achieve.

▶ A second distinction between deontology and consequentialism is that the former is described as 'agent-relative', whereas the latter is 'agent-neutral'. For deontology this means that the agent (the person) is in a role that is ineliminable within the specification of that duty. For example, parents have a duty to help their drowning child but may have no duty to help another unconnected drowning person. This duty represents the basis of the 'duty of care' principle in the law of negligence. For consequentialism, agent-neutrality means that the identity of the person who does the act makes no difference since the rightness or wrongness of the action is determined according to the best outcome.

▶ A third distinction between the two theories is that deontology adopts a stance of moral integrity whereas consequentialism is more aligned to 'doing what is best in the circumstances'. This can be seen, for example, particularly with regard to constraints that are imposed on certain actions. The biblical prohibition of 'thou shalt not kill' means that a deontologist ought not to kill a murderer even though that single killing might prevent the murder (by the murderer) of two or more other persons. From a consequentialist perspective, if murder in itself is a bad thing, then how can it be rational to forbid the killing of one person (the hypothetical murderer in question) if this would save two or more potential future victims from being murdered by the felon.

Emily develops a life-threatening infection, but refuses to receive further treatment or be admitted to hospital. Her GP insists she is admitted on the grounds that if she refuses, the implications for him will be serious. She eventually acquiesces.
Consider the duties owed by Emily's GP:

▶ To what extent has the doctor acted according to deontological principles?
▶ What are the consequentialist issues if the doctor admits Emily for treatment?
▶ Consider the entire scenario from a deontological and consequentialist perspective. In your opinion which is the most persuasive?

A junior doctor believes that Emily's consultant has not acknowledged Emily's wishes but refrains from expressing her objection. To what extent does the doctor owe a moral duty to express these thoughts?

At first sight, consequentialist theory appears attractive as having practical value. Some argue that within the context of transplantation, and in an attempt to overcome the acute shortage of organs, consequentialist theory has, from a utility point of view, extended the boundaries of death from being 'cold, stiff and blue' to that of brain death (see 8.3.2(c)). However, act-consequentialism could be criticised for running counter to moral intuition. First, it seems excessively onerous as there is a requirement to maximise good and therefore virtually all energy and resources should be devoted to making the world a better place, and allowing individuals little or no time to pursue their own interests and goals. This situation seems at odds with common morality, which allows the pursuit of self-interest provided that this does not breach any fundamental duties. Second, act-consequentialism leaves no scope for special duties, particularly in respect of those who are close, such as family and friends. Since act-consequentialism is agent-neutral, this means that in relation to family and friends, there would be no option but to perform the act that gives the most beneficial overall outcome even if that action is detrimental to a family member or friend, as this particular relationship is irrelevant. Third, arguably, act-consequentialism is too permissive as it does not impose any restraint on prohibitions. In the example above, a consequentialist might view that it would be perfectly acceptable to kill one individual if this would prevent that individual from killing two others because preventing two deaths is better in the overall scheme of 'goodness'. Thus, in a sense the end would justify the means. This is in sharp and stark contrast to the Kantian imperative (see 1.4) that each person should be considered as an end and not as a means to an end.

As act-consequentialism may generate outcomes that are counter-intuitive, the pure consequentialist theory has been amended in two ways. The first approach is indirect act-consequentialism. This theory retains the claim that the ultimate goal is that which has the best consequences but a person need not be guided solely by consequentialist thoughts when deciding how to act, or which choice to make. In other words, the action that produces the best consequences may not necessarily be the best way to act in the circumstances, and a better consequentialist outcome may be achieved by following alternative moral rules. The second approach is rule-consequentialism. Rule-consequentialism holds that an action is right if it accords with a set of rules and such rules would bear a resemblance to what are currently regarded as moral rules. These variations on direct act-consequentialism are theories that endeavour to eliminate possible outcomes that could be perceived as being at odds with common morality, particularly if moral prohibitions are used to obtain a 'good' consequentialist result.

Consequentialism and deontology represent two very different theories and neither in isolation can satisfactorily address all the ethical dilemmas that pervade health-care practice and the health services. Although philosophical purists may baulk at the concept, it appears that medical legal and ethical dilemmas may require a combined approach. Singer (1993), a leading proponent of consequentialism, takes the view that the starting point should be a consequentialist approach, and alternatives should be adopted only if there are legitimate reasons for doing so. Morrison (2005) proposes a hybrid approach that involves looking at the consequences of the action, as well as the rights and duties of those involved and striking a reasoned balance between them. If one is prepared to accept the concept of meta-ethical relativism (which holds that there is no single true or most justified morality) and that moral propositions are true only in conforming to the relevant societies, conventions and attitudes, then in a pluralistic and multicultural society, one would need to accept that there would be no single theory that would adequately answer all health care and related dilemmas.

1.6   Utilitarianism

One of the most widely recognised branches of consequentialism is utilitarianism, a theory by which the moral worth of an action is determined according to its overall utility in providing well-being, such as pleasure, happiness, welfare, satisfaction and preference. The fundamental underlying premise is that utility, represented by values, happiness or pleasure is of paramount importance. One expression of this view is Bentham's utility rule of producing the greatest good for the greatest number.

Utilitarianism emerged as an alternative to secular Christian ethics, mainly through the work of Jeremy Bentham in the eighteenth century and John Stuart Mill in the nineteenth century. In their view an action was 'right' if as a result of that action there was a greater surplus of happiness over pain and suffering by all those affected by that action. Maximisation of human welfare or, where this is not possible, minimisation of human pain and suffering is the fundamental tenet that underpins utilitarianism. This view is striking, particularly in two ways. First it is egalitarian and according to Bentham value is universal. The inherent value of happiness is unaffected by the identity of the individual concerned and hence 'each counts for one and none for more than one' meaning that the happiness of a commoner was as much value as the happiness of a person of noble birth. The second feature of utilitarianism is that it has been advanced as a universal principle, cutting through the confines of ethical subjectivism and cultural relativism. This means that the moral theory of utilitarianism is of application even if morality is held to be a relative construct that operates to reduce ethical constructs to factual beliefs and irrespective of whether different cultures apply differing moral standards for evaluating actions as right or wrong.

John Stuart Mill (1859) in his essay 'On liberty' opined that the concept of utility held the ultimate appeal to all ethical dilemmas. However, such utility had to be construed in the larger sense grounded on the permanent interests of man, as a progressive being. The only justification for interfering with personal liberty would be for self-protection, and there is a case for punishing anyone committing a harmful act to another, either through legal mechanisms or by general disapprobation. The Millian concept of liberty is grounded on freedom of the conscience in its most comprehensive sense, encompassing liberty of thought, feeling and opinion. This principle requires respect for freedom of tastes, pursuits and planning of one's life to suit one's own character without external impediment, as long as exercise of this freedom does not harm anyone. A society in which such liberties are not respected is not a free society. The only freedom worth the name

> is that of pursuing our own good in our own way, so long as we do not attempt to deprive others of theirs, or impede their efforts to obtain it. Each is the proper guardian of his own health, whether bodily, or mental and spiritual. Mankind are greater gainers by suffering each other to live as seems good to themselves, than by compelling each to live as seems good to the rest. Mill JS, On Liberty, Watts and Co, London, 1929 (first published 1859) 15.

As Bentham and Mill conceive utility as happiness or pleasure, they can be regarded as hedonistic utilitarians. However, what counts as utility to one person may not be shared by others. For one person, there may be great utility in exercising every evening after work, whereas for another the preference might be to socialise with friends and enjoy a good meal. Furthermore, there are some human activities such as researching or working almost to the point of exhaustion which would not appear to produce any direct personal happiness. Utilitarian philosophers therefore argue that a diverse set of values contributes to well-being and this is related to individual preferences. In attempting to maximise preferences generally, however, there needs to be some mechanism by which consequences can be ranked to allow a principled, rather than intuitive, conclusion to be reached as to whether one particular consequence is to be preferred over another.

Critics have argued that utilitarianism can be problematic in several ways (Beauchamp and Childress, 2009). Utilitarianism demands that the moral worth of an action is determined by its overall good outcome, which is a quantitative approach to welfare. How is this quantification to be judged? For example, would it be justified on utilitarian grounds to kill one 60-year-old individual in order to use each healthy kidney, as well as the heart and the lungs, for four potentially life-saving transplants in four 20-year-olds? On grounds of common morality such a situation is repugnant and one could argue that on Millian principles, it would be wrong to harm the 60-year-old individual. But what if that person was fully competent and protests that this is her firm and considered preference and within her framework of 'utility' since the knowledge that she will sacrifice her life to benefit those of four others is of value. The fundamental point of this controversy is whether the utilitarian principle pertains to acts in particular circumstances, or instead to general rules. As discussed previously in consequentialism (see 1.5), one branch of the theory is rule-consequentialism. Similarly, some utilitarian apply the principle of rule-utilitarianism.

Act-utilitarianism provides that the moral worth of a judgement is ascertained according to the likely consequences of each specific act or decision. The fundamental question concerns the utility value of each particular judgement. If the utility value is good, then the judgement is right. Rule-utilitarians start by looking at potential rules of action in order to determine their moral worth. Whether a rule should be followed is determined by considering the likely consequences if that rule was constantly followed. Thus, in the above example (killing an individual to harvest the organs for the benefit of others), the pure act-utilitarian may consider this to be justified. The rule-utilitarian would be expected to argue that the moral rules against taking human life would not justify the killing because overall happiness and pleasure would not be maximised if this rule was constantly followed.

Purist act-utilitarians might well consider that rule-utilitarianism is at odds with the principle of utility that aims to maximise value. The middle ground between these two schools of thought is one of sometimes obeying rules. Consider this option in the context of truth telling. A previously fit and well individual is taken to hospital and diagnosed with widespread cancer. The dilemma for the doctor is whether to tell the whole truth to the patient *immediately*. From a utilitarian perspective the benefits of immediate truth telling could be perceived to outweigh the benefits of deception. However, not divulging the whole truth, immediately, might arguably lead to a better overall therapeutic outcome in the specific circumstances and would still comply with the general rule of truth telling. Alternatively, for the example provided, the rule that hope should be sustained could be used to justify the decision not to declare the truth. While this line of argument might seem at odds with the tenor of 'pure' utilitarianism, those who advocate the rule-based or middle ground approach accept the principle of utility as being unabsolute and, therefore, no derogative rule is either absolute or unrevisable.

The problem of an immoral act as being obligatory in order to maximise utility (as in the example of killing for organs) is one of the principal criticisms of pure act-utilitarianism, and it is apparent that application of the rule theory is way of potentially circumventing this particular problem. Other criticisms of the theory are that utilitarianism demands too much of individuals and can also result in injustice. Beauchamp and Childress (2009) in their analysis argue that moral ideals run along a continuum. At one end of the spectrum of moral obligation are those concepts that are strictly obligatory. This encompasses the core principles and rules of common morality. The next level is those principles that have weaker moral obligations and exist at the periphery of the ordinary expectations of common morality. Beyond these levels exists the level of supererogation, being those morally good acts considered to be 'beyond the call of duty', which categorises those obligations that are considered to be 'virtuous'.

This ranges from ideals that are beyond the obligatory and include high levels of charitableness or generosity to those at the far end of the spectrum of obligations which include saintly and heroic ideals. One particular problem with utilitarianism is the difficulty in maintaining a distinction between actions that are morally obligatory and those that are supererogatory. In the example of organ donation above, if a utilitarian holds that the heroic donation of bodily parts to save another person's life is obligatory, then this would sit uncomfortably with common morality on account of the value placed on human life and the prohibition against killing. Furthermore, even if one were to simply consider the principle that utilitarianism demands maximising welfare, then this leaves little room for undertaking those actions that afford personal pleasure (without necessarily maximising the overall welfare of others). From the perspective that utilitarianism should maximise the pleasure and happiness of everyone, it has been argued that individuals are forced to act in a saintly manner without consideration of personal interest and goals.

A further problem is that by concentrating on majority interests, utilitarianism does not protect adequately against minority interests and is a situation that could lead to injustice. Those who belong to a group that is already prosperous may have more value added to their lives through the overall benefit principle of utilitarianism; however, there is no independent weight accorded to justice or to minority interests. Beauchamp and Childress (2009) state that in the medical context this constraint may engage where cost-effectiveness in medical research indicates that it is more beneficial to target a specific group, for example, those already diagnosed with hypertension, compared with screening for hypertension. The effect would to be to divert funds away from the population in need who may well reap considerable benefit from early intervention.

Although utilitarianism is recognised as a consequential theory, its method of operation to achieve its goal of promoting welfare is beneficence based. According to Sen (1987), 'Consequentialist reasoning may be fruitfully used even when consequentialism as such is not accepted. To ignore consequences is to leave an ethics story half told'.

Emily's infection requires treatment with a new and expensive antibiotic.

▶ Consider the extent to which the proposed treatment can be justified on principles of utilitarianism and justice.
▶ To what extent might the microbiologist's opinion be based upon a quality of life assessment?
▶ Consider the extent to which the 'do not resuscitate' order and the antibiotic issue align to the principle of justice.

1.7 Rights-based discourse

Rights are justified claims that individuals and groups can make on other individuals or on society. Sumner (2000 at 288) states that

> Of all the moral concepts, rights seem most in tune with the temper of our time. At their best they evoke images of heroic struggles against oppression and discrimination. At their worst they furnish the material for lurid tabloid stories of litigious former spouses and lovers. Whatever the use to which they are put, they are ubiquitous, the global currency of moral/ political argument.

According to Sumner there are three components of every right. First, a right has a subject recognised as the holder or bearer of the right. Second, it has an object, that is to say, the person against whom that right is held. Third, it has content, namely that which the right should do or should have done. Subjects of rights are usually persons, although they could be other entities, such as corporations, animals and so forth. The object of a right is an agent capable of having duties or obligations and the content of a right is always some action on the part of either the subject, or the object, of that right.

While the above represents the basic constituents of a right, it must be remembered that in practice rights could engage the interests of multiple parties simultaneously. Consequently, a horizontal correlation exists between the rights of parties, as well as a vertical correlation between individual rights and obligations. Beauchamp and Childress (2009) provide a medical illustration. A 5-year-old child is in need of a kidney transplant and the father is a potential donor. The father has rights of autonomy, privacy and confidentiality that operate to protect his bodily integrity. He has a right to receive information about the risks and benefits, as well as alternatives, to donating one of his kidneys. It could be argued that the child has a right to receive a kidney from her father due to parental obligations, or medical need. The father might exercise his right of autonomy and self-determined choice in allowing tests to ascertain whether he would be a compatible match as a donor. Having found such compatibility, the father may then wish to exercise his right to confidentiality to prevent disclosure of this information. If the child is in urgent need of a kidney transplant, to what extent does the doctor have a right to reject the father's right to confidentiality? Does the child's mother have the right to access the tissue compatibility information by virtue of her relationship with the father and child? These problems are complex and contentious and the conflicting rights of each individual have to be balanced against one another. Much of medical law engages in such a balancing act against the backdrop of rights-based discourse.

Rights are justified or exist because of a normative structure that pertains to what should or ought to be, and allows or disallows, the moral or legal claim in question. More often than not, rules are derived from rights, and moral rights are often the precursors of legal rights. Apart from the normative theory that substantiates rights, the philosophy of liberal individualism represents another important justification. This standpoint emphasises the central importance of personal freedom and choice and the presumption that a just political and societal system permits individuals to pursue their personal goals. Respect for liberal individualism has been instrumental in the development of specific freedoms, such as the freedom of speech and religious expression. Contemporary liberal society is replete with such rights, such as those of children, ethnic minorities, women, employees and so forth.

Rights may be categorised as being either positive or negative. Positive rights allow or oblige an action, whereas negative rights permit or oblige freedom from action. In the biomedical context a positive right might, for example, be the right to health care (if such a right exists). This would mean that an individual would be entitled to health-care services on the basis that such a right is grounded in a claim of justice. Most rights, however, are negative rights, for example, the right to refuse consent for a medical procedure which is grounded on the principle of autonomy and self-determined choice. Yet it is recognised that rights are not absolute claims. Rights generate a *prima facie* claim, meaning that the starting point is that a claim exists. According to rights-based discourse (as advanced by Ronald Dworkin), the starting point of decisions as to whether or not rights should be upheld is based principally on the projected social utility of what would be the position if the rights in question did not exist. In situations where the claim of public utility is very high, an individual's rights may be overridden. This is referred to as an infringement of rights whereby justified action is taken in overriding a right, as opposed to violation of a right where there is unjustified action against a right.

Within the context of medical law, the Human Rights Act 1998 has had a major impact through the incorporation of the articles of the European Convention for the Protection of Human Rights and Fundamental Freedoms (Samanta and Samanta, 2005). The Articles that have had a significant impact on health care are Articles 2 (the right to life), 3 (the prohibition of torture and inhuman or degrading treatment), 5 (the right to liberty and security) and 8 (the right to respect for private and family life). Article 3 represents an absolute prohibition and cannot be interfered with by the State; Articles 2 and 5 are subject to limited qualifications; Article 8 is a qualified obligation that requires a balance to be struck between the interests of the individual and the wider interests of society. Article 8(1) underpins autonomy and the right to self-determined choice, although this right may be contravened through the derogation under Article 8(2) in consideration of the public interest. For example, the right to refusal of vaccination may be overridden in the event of an infectious pandemic and in the interests of public health.

A further consideration is the relationship between rights and duties. These fundamentally deontological concepts are connected although their actual connections are complex and difficult to unravel. In a straightforward example, if X has a claim against Y to do something, then that could be equivalent to a duty on Y's part towards X. However, matters become more difficult since not all duties are relational and rights cannot simply be reduced to a duty as they may contain elements that are not definable as such. Beauchamp and Childress (2009 at 353) state that there is an untidy correlativity between obligations and rights because

> at least one use of the words requirement, obligation, and duty indicates that not all obligations imply corresponding rights. For example, although we sometimes refer to requirements or obligations of charity, no person can claim another person's charity as a matter of right. If such norms of charity express what we 'ought to do', they do so not from moral obligation but from personal ideals that exceed obligation.

As a result some commitments are generated as self-imposed 'oughts' and are not required by common morality. In the example above where the child requires a kidney transplant, the mother may argue that she has a right to know what the prospects are with regard to medical treatment for her child. However, would it be morally justifiable for her to generate a rights claim that she could go behind the duty of confidentiality owed to the father (which is protected by his right to privacy and enshrined within Article 8 of the European Convention of Human Rights) in order to determine his compatibility status as a donor?

An example of how the courts deal with multiple correlative obligations arising from rights can be seen in *Re A (children) (conjoined twins)* [2000] 4 All ER 961. Article 2(1) of the European Convention of Human Rights states: 'Everyone's right to life shall be protected by law. No one shall be deprived of his life intentionally save in the execution of a sentence of a Court following his conviction of a crime for which this penalty is provided by law.' Thus, Article 2 imposes a positive duty to safeguard life, as well as a negative duty not to deliberately take life. Although the Human Rights Act 1998 was not in force at the time of the decision, the Court of Appeal considered the human rights implications and took the view that Article 2 imposed a duty to protect the stronger twin and not merely a negative duty to prevent the death of the weaker twin. In so doing, the court did not interpret 'intentionally' as 'virtually certain', but instead using a natural construction of language meaning 'specific purpose', which in this case meant causing death. In applying this meaning, the court concluded that separation would be lawful in order to save the life of the stronger twin, and not with the intention of depriving the weaker twin of life.

Correlativity does not determine whether rights or obligations are the more fundamental moral theory. According to Gewirth (1996) burdens are principally for the sake of benefits as opposed to the other way around. Therefore, obligations which are burdens are for the sake of rights. Rights therefore rank above obligations in the order of justifying purpose. Thus, correlative obligations arise because subjects have certain rights and these rights form the justificatory basis of obligations. Perhaps this is why some writers use the language of rights robustly, particularly with regard to the critical interests of persons. The language of human rights is very much the currency of contemporary moral discourse and refers to individual entitlements that have become the substantive basis of much of medical law.

> Emily's GP admits her to hospital despite her preference to 'die at home'. The hospital consultant recommends investigations in full knowledge that this is against Emily's wishes.
>
> ▶ Consider the scenario from a rights-based perspective. To what extent does her admission represent a violation of her autonomy?
> ▶ To what extent could the consultant's actions form the basis of a subsequent legal action?

1.8　Principlism

Principlism is an influential bioethical approach that relies upon the application of principles, as opposed to moral theory, to guide ethical decision making. This approach emerged in the 1970s and 1980s, led by key proponents Tom Beauchamp, James Childress and Robert Veatch. Beauchamp and Childress provided a detailed analysis in their 'Principles of biomedical ethics', which has been revised several times to accommodate biomedical developments, most recently in 2009. Essentially, principlism incorporates four principles that represent basic statements about accepted moral values: autonomy, non-maleficence, beneficence and justice. These principles act as a framework to guide ethical decision making for health-care dilemmas particularly in situations in which competing obligations exist. Although the principles seem fundamentally deontological, the framework can also use a consequentialist philosophy in maximising positive outcomes. Beauchamp and Childress have emphasised that the four principles approach does not necessarily provide a method for *choosing* between complex health-care dilemmas. What it does is to form 'a set of ordered rules' (we would respectfully suggest a preferred term of 'framework' rather than 'ordered rules') for ethical decision making in the health-care context by giving attention to these principles' scope of application.

Principlism is perhaps the most widely recognised bioethical approach applied in contemporary health-care decision making. It has been championed in the United Kingdom by Raanon Gillon who has used this as a simple, accessible and culturally neutral approach to thinking about ethical issues in health care. In Gillon's (1994 at 184) view, the 'four principles plus scope' approach is of universal applicability and 'that whatever our personal philosophy, politics, religion, moral theory, or life stance, we will find no difficulty in committing ourselves to four *prima facie* moral principles plus a reflective concern about their scope of application. Moreover, these four principles, plus attention to their scope of application, encompass most of the moral issues that arise in healthcare. ... What the principles plus scope approach can provide, however, is a set of moral commitments, a common moral language and a common set of moral issues'. While some aspects of these statements might appear somewhat sweeping and open to challenge, nonetheless principlism offers some apparent advantages over the more conventional philosophical and moral theories in that it is relatively easy to understand and apply and is perceived as being more 'user friendly' by health-care practitioners in the context of practical application to real-life clinical dilemma.

Clouser and Gert (1990), in their critique of principlism, state that at best principles operate as checklists and at worst they obscure and confuse moral reasoning by their eclectic and unsystematic use of moral theory. They state that the appeal of principlism is that it tends to make use of features of each ethical theory that has most support. Thus, autonomy acknowledges the Kantian imperative in emphasising the importance of the individual, beneficence acknowledges Millian theory and avoidance of harm is a consequentialist approach that necessitates taking into account both benefits and harms.

Beauchamp and Childress (2009) acknowledge that the cluster of principles does not constitute a general moral theory, and the framework is sparse and contains insufficient content to address perplexities of many moral circumstances. They contend that in applying the principles it is important to consider specification and balancing. Specification involves the creation of more context-specific norms, and balancing consists of deliberation, evaluation and judgement of the relative weights and strengths of specific norms in the context of other competing moral principles. Both these methods are required in applying principlism because they address different issues. Specification addresses the dimension of moral principles and their scope, and balancing addresses their relative weight or importance. Using these methods within the principlism framework provides a way forward through some of the health-care issues encountered in practice. In the next section, each of the four principles will be considered in general terms and a more in-depth exploration will be found in other areas of this text.

1.8.1 Autonomy

The word 'autonomy' derives from the Greek words *autos* (self) and *nomos* (rule). Autonomy as applied to individuals encompasses the repudiation of controlling interference from others and permitting individuals to make self-determined choices. Respect for autonomy is a moral obligation to acknowledge each individual's right to choose and take action according to that person's own values and belief system. It reflects the Kantian principle of the importance of the individual and treating others as an end in themselves and never merely as a means to an end.

Within the health-care context, respect for autonomy pervades a range of areas and includes informed consent based on adequate provision of information prior to medical interventions, confidentiality, the need to be truthful to patients, to work in partnership with patients in terms of health-care decisions and good communication. In clinical practice this list encompasses some examples although there are many other situations where respect for autonomy engages.

There are a number of theories that pertain to autonomy. Virtually all, however, require satisfaction of two fundamental and essential conditions. These are independence from controlling influences and the capacity for intentional action. Some theories focus on the ability, skills or traits of the person making the choice and this requires that the individual has capacity for understanding, reasoning, deliberating and choosing independently. In the medical context, this has relevance for those who lack decision-making capacity. A person who lacks capacity by definition may not be able to exercise autonomous choice and action. However, decision-making capacity is seldom an all or nothing concept and at any one time decision-making ability may vary. This has been recognised in the Mental Capacity Act 2005 and respect for autonomy is reflected in the spirit of the Act which requires that efforts are made to involve the individual who lacks capacity to the fullest extent possible, according to guidance in the Code of Practice.

Beauchamp and Childress (2009) maintain the view that consequential decisions can never be truly autonomous, but at best are substantially autonomous. In their view in order for an action to qualify as autonomous, a *substantial degree* of understanding and freedom from constraint is required, as opposed to a full understanding or complete absence of influence. In fact, full understanding and complete lack of influence is often illusory, and the appropriate criteria for exercise of significant autonomy are best addressed within a particular context and framework of reference. This view might better reflect reality since within the medical context, although one speaks of 'informed consent', meaning consent with information, how that information is actually received and used by an individual depends much upon how that information is processed, as well as the level of understanding. For the purpose of medical law, the central issues include the meaning of informed consent and the standards required for information disclosure (see 4.6). Likewise, the concept of substantial autonomy is better aligned to the reality of medical decision making since competence and incompetence are not absolute states and tend to exist along a continuum so that levels of competence required for decision making are event and intervention specific.

The principle of respect for autonomy can be stated as being a negative and positive obligation. As a negative obligation it should not be constrained or controlled by others, and as a positive obligation requires respectful treatment and actions that enhance and facilitate autonomous decision making. This includes obtaining valid consent prior to treatment, providing sufficient information and respecting privacy and confidentiality.

1.8.2 Non-maleficence

Non-maleficence imposes the duty not to inflict harm on others and underscores the maxim *primum non nocere* (above all (or first), do no harm). According to the principle of non-maleficence, harmful actions are *prima facie* wrong, unless that harm is justifiable in the circumstances subject to a lawful excuse, or reason. For example, although killing is *prima facie* wrong, it can be justified in the circumstances of legitimate self-defence, where it will not be wrongful.

In biomedical ethics, the principle is applied in several areas and particularly in respect of the doctrine of double effect, killing and letting die, withholding and withdrawing treatment, futility arguments and quality of life debates. The norms that pertain to non-maleficence are refraining from inflicting evil or harm, preventing evil or harm, eradicating evil or harm, and doing or promoting good (beneficence). Some philosophers bring non-maleficence and beneficence under a single umbrella but retaining their separation helps to preserve the inherent distinctions and obligations.

An important aspect of non-maleficence, particularly with respect to beneficence, is that it advocates against harming one person in order to help another. To this end its application can be illustrated by the American case of *McFall v Shimp* (1978) 10 Pa D and C 3d 90. McFall was dying of aplastic anaemia, and receiving a bone marrow transplant from a genetically compatible donor was expected to enhance his short-term survival. His cousin, Shimp, underwent preliminary tissue compatibility tests, but thereafter refused to undergo tests for genetic compatibility on the basis that he had changed his mind about donation. McFall's lawyer asked the court to compel Shimp to undergo the second test and to donate bone marrow if he was found to be a good match. McFall's argument was that Shimp owed him an obligation of non-maleficence, which required that he did not make McFall's condition worse. The court ruled that Shimp did not violate any legal obligation in refusing to undergo further tests and to donate. It would be wrong, in law, to compel Shimp to undergo tests and donate bone marrow against his will, even though the likely harm to Shimp was minimal and would be of considerable advantage to McFall. The judge commented, however, that Shimp's refusal was morally indefensible.

The principle of non-maleficence underpins several moral rules, which include do not kill, do not cause pain or suffering, do not incapacitate, do not cause offence and do not deprive others of the benefits of life. Thus, the principle of non-maleficence includes not only the obligation not to inflict evil or harm, but also the duty not to impose risks of harm. Beauchamp and Childress argue that limits apply to these principles which are not absolute. In their view, non-maleficence is a *prima facie* obligation, which means that it must be fulfilled unless it conflicts with an equal or stronger obligation. If this view is accepted, then in the case above it could be argued that since the expected harm to Shimp, in undergoing tests and donating marrow, was relatively minor compared to the likely benefits to McFall, then there is a moral argument that Shimp should have been compelled to undergo testing and donate. However, according to the principle of autonomy, this approach is unsustainable. The decision-making process that is required to reach a conclusion in such a dilemma would be made using the method of specification and balancing (see 1.8) within the framework of autonomy and non-maleficence. Balancing, however, inevitably includes a subjective evaluative component. Some will consider that, taken in the round, Shimp's autonomy would be unacceptably violated by forcing him to proceed with donation. Others might feel that any infringement to Shimp's autonomy would be justified on account of the beneficial outcome of prolonging McFall's life, particularly if the principle of non-maleficence is not considered absolute. Looking at the scenario from an alternative perspective, a deontologist would uphold a verdict in favour of Shimp, while a consequentialist or utilitarian would be expected to uphold a verdict in favour of McFall.

As noted, the principle of non-maleficence engages in application of the doctrine of double effect. This principle is based upon the assertion that a moral distinction exists between the intended effects of an action and its foreseen, yet unintended, effects and can be applied where an action has two inextricably connected effects: one ethically justifiable and the other more problematic. The classic example is that of a patient with terminal cancer who is in considerable pain. Substantial amounts of morphine-based analgesia are necessary in order to control the pain. It is believed that administration of medication at the levels required to control pain is likely to lead to respiratory depression and death. The dose of morphine is gradually escalated to control the patient's pain and the patient finally dies. According to the doctrine of double effect, although the morphine may well have hastened the patient's death, this was not wrong since it was given with the intention of pain relief as opposed to ending the patient's life.

In the classical formulation, four conditions must be satisfied for an act with a double effect to be justified. First, and independent of its consequences, the nature of the act must be good, or at least morally neutral. Second, the agent's intention should be to achieve the good effect and not the bad effect. The bad effect may be foreseen, permitted or tolerated, but cannot be intended. Third, a distinction is made between means and effects. The bad effect should not be the means to the good effect. Fourth, proportionality demands that the good effect must outweigh the bad effect. The bad effect will be justified only for tolerating the bad effect if a proportionate reason exists. Although each of these four conditions are controversial and have been criticised (Botros, 1999), the doctrine of double effect remains an accepted ethical principle of medical law (see 10.3.3).

The principle of non-maleficence also engages in the distinction drawn between killing and letting die. The distinction drawn between killing and letting die has been used to separate permissible and unacceptable practice. Withdrawal and withholding of treatment is generally classified as 'letting die' whereas assisting in suicide is 'killing' (see 10.6). Letting die is *prima facie* acceptable in health-care situations in the event that continued intervention is reasonably considered to be useless, or that it is futile to persist with treatment. Letting die will also be legitimate in the event of a valid refusal of life-sustaining treatment.

A further division is sometimes made between acts and omissions in the killing and letting die distinction, in that 'letting die' is considered to be passive whereas killing is active. However, where medical treatment has been started and continuation is considered to be futile, then withdrawal of treatment is likely to entail an act, be it switching off a ventilator or instigating an order that no further treatment is given. The distinction between letting die and killing can be subtle and involve more that categorisation of passive or active. Labelling an act as killing or letting die does not necessarily determine which action is morally better or worse. Killing by brutal murder may be worse than allowing someone to die by withdrawing treatment from a person in a permanent vegetative state. However, from a moral perspective, not resuscitating a patient who could potentially have been saved could be worse than a particular instance of 'mercy killing' carried out at the patient's request. Therefore, judging whether letting die or killing is ethically defensible requires knowledge about the actor's motive, the patient's preferences and the consequences of the act or omission (see 10.6.2(a)).

1.8.3   Beneficence

The principle of beneficence refers to the moral obligation to act for the benefit of others. Positive beneficence requires the provision of benefit to others and extends to acts of mercy, kindness, charity, altruism, love and humanity.

Positive beneficence encompasses a number of duties such as protecting and defending the rights of others, preventing harm from occurring to others, removing conditions that might cause harm to others, helping persons or rescuing those in danger. The rules of beneficence can be distinguished from those of non-maleficence since beneficence requires positive action and generally does not provide reason for retribution since they do not always need to be followed impartially. In contrast, the principle of non-maleficence refers to prohibitions on action and obligations to be followed impartially. Non-maleficence can provide the moral grounds for legal prohibitions that pertain to certain forms of conduct. Beneficence is often justified on the grounds of social interaction and as benefits are received from society, it follows that individuals ought to promote societal interests. According to Beauchamp and Childress (2009), obligations of 'specific' beneficence arise from special relationships that give rise to duties, such as those that parents owe their child or doctors owe their patient.

Recognition of beneficence as a primary obligation owed by doctors to their patients is not new. Fundamentally, clinicians will want the best for their patients, although determination of what was best for the patient was typically considered from a medical perspective. Over the last decades this view has been considerably challenged by assertions of patients' rights to make independent judgements about their own health care. Thus, the balance between 'patient autonomy' and 'medical paternalism' has been brought to the forefront of health-care services.

1.8.3(a) Medical paternalism

The term 'medical paternalism' describes the perspective that beneficence overrides the principle of autonomy and is derived from the view that a father acts in a beneficent manner, according to his own perception, to safeguard the interests of his children. In the health-care context, paternalism is viewed as the beneficent approach assumed by a health-care practitioner with specialist skills and knowledge, in determining what decision lies best in a patient's interests. Beauchamp and Childress (2009) pose a normatively neutral definition of paternalism as 'the intentional overriding of one person's preferences or actions by another person, where the person who overrides justifies this action by appeal to the goal of benefiting or of preventing or mitigating harm to the person whose preferences or actions are overridden' (at 208). They assert that this definition is preferred for the medical context as it does not presume that paternalism is either justified or unjustified, and it does not prejudge the beneficent act as justified or misplaced.

At least three forms of paternalism are recognised: soft, hard and passive. Soft paternalism describes interventions of the health-care professional on the grounds of beneficence or non-maleficence in order to prevent significantly non-voluntary conduct. A typical example is provided by the patient who has drug addiction or depression to the extent that this interferes with his or her autonomous decision making. A soft, or weak, paternalistic approach would be apparent in the recommendation of choices or actions which the doctor believes that patient would make, but cannot do so on account of his or her limited self-control. The principal issue here is that the patient has limited decision-making capacity which effectively constrains his or her ability to act in a substantially autonomous manner. The clinician who intervenes will rely upon beneficence and non-maleficence as the justificatory basis for such intervention. Hard paternalism describes those interventions that are intended to prevent or reduce harm or to benefit a person, on the grounds of what the doctor considers being correct and in so doing overrides a person's (risky) choice, even though that choice was informed, voluntary and autonomous. In soft paternalism the patient's choice is deemed to be unreasonable in light of the individual's own standards in the context of the particular circumstances of the case. In hard paternalism, the individual's choice is deemed to be unreasonable (from the standpoint of the physician acting on the grounds of beneficence or non-maleficence). The individual's values used to define his or her interests are not accepted and are overridden.

From a moral stance, both soft and hard paternalism violate an individual's choice, and soft paternalism may pave the way for hard paternalism. In clinical settings, however, doctors may find themselves in a position where they are invited to adopt a paternalistic approach. This can occur in situations where after having provided information to a patient, the patient then asks the question 'What would you advise me to do?' In these circumstances, in providing an answer after disclosing all relevant information, the question could be used to further elicit the salient considerations that are most relevant to the patient, and to discuss possible outcomes of different approaches and treatment decisions as relevant to that individual patient. Information disclosure is likely to be accompanied by benefits and risks, what might be considered optimal from a clinical perspective, and then to assist the patient to balance these factors in the round. In considering whether to adopt a paternalistic approach, some factors that the physician may wish to consider include whether the patient is at risk of significant preventable harm; whether a paternalistic approach could, in all likelihood, prevent the harm; the projected benefits and risks of such an action; any reasonable alternatives to limitation of autonomy and finally the alternative that is least restrictive in respect of autonomy.

A third form of paternalism is passive paternalism. This is apparent when a health-care professional refuses, on grounds of patient-centred beneficence, a patient's positive preference for an intervention. Note the distinction between this and that of conscientious objection where a clinician or nurse may refuse to carry out an intervention, such as an abortion, on the grounds of their conscience. Passive paternalism is central to debates on medical futility where the anticipated benefits of an intervention are perceived to be virtually non-existent or negligible and (usually) the potential side effects or harms are expected to be greater. Passive paternalism also engages in debates about quality of life where the intervention may have some benefit but is unlikely to produce any significant improvement in the overall quality of life. Passive paternalism is justified on the grounds that physicians are not obliged to carry out patients' requests when these are incompatible with accepted standards of clinical practice, or when the desired intervention is unlikely to produce any clinical benefit. Often, although not always, cost benefit and cost-effectiveness analyses enter the equation. In law, a competent person may refuse even life-saving treatment, but as the *Burke* litigation (see 10.9) has shown, there is correlative right to demand treatment. With this in mind, it seems likely that the court would view passive paternalism as a matter to be settled by doctors on medical grounds.

1.8.4   Justice

Justice is often expressed as being what is fair, equitable or reasonable. Gillon (1994) considers that within the health-care context, justice falls into three main categories: fair distribution of scarce resources (distributive justice), respect for people's rights (rights-based justice) and respect for morally acceptable laws (legal justice).

At the heart of justice lies equality but it remains problematic as to how to determine whether two people are equal and how to determine if treatment is equal. The debate about the morally relevant criteria for regarding people as equals is ongoing.

A clinical decision is taken to transfer Emily to ICU for at least a week. Two days later the clinical team is told that she must be transferred to a low dependency ward due to resource constraints.

▶ What are the inherent issues in transferring Emily out of ICU? To what extent can this decision be justified on the grounds of utilitarianism and justice?
▶ What are the right-based arguments that could be advanced?
▶ Is it more worthwhile for Emily to be on a low dependency unit compared with another patient? Is there a value judgement here?
▶ What competing obligations exist, if any, in the clinical team's duty to Emily in the context of limited resources and their duty to the organisation?

Emily's condition deteriorates. She is placed on a ventilator but 2 days later the ventilator is switched off and she dies.

▶ Apply the concepts of quality of life, utilitarianism and non-maleficence. To the decision to switch off the ventilator, consider whether this action is morally justified.

Justice underlines the system for distributing health-care resources and constructive reflection on health policy. Although the principle can be supported on egalitarian and utilitarian theoretical grounds, no single theory satisfactorily supports policies of equitable access to health care, strategies to promote health-care efficiency, and the need to reduce health-impairing conditions. In the current era of austerity, society must ration its resources, including those that are diverted into health care. Justice demands, however, that the NHS provides a minimum level of quality provision that is available and accessible to all, including vulnerable groups such as the infirm, the disabled, the elderly, those of low socio-economic status and ethnic minorities. Principles of distributive justice are underpinned by fairness and 'giving to each that which is her due'.

1.8.5   Criticisms of principlism

Without doubt, principlism represents one of the most influential bioethical approaches in recent years, although it is not without its critics. The general principles approach, such as that advocated by Beauchamp and Childress, is superfluous since specific moral rules amply provide for all bioethical dilemmas. Clouser and Gert (1990) argue that principlism is fundamentally flawed since it does not represent a true guide for ethical conduct and action but instead offers a 'checklist' of factors to be considered when confronted with an ethical dilemma. Furthermore, lack of strong moral theories means that it is not possible to resolve conflicts among opposing principles. According to Beauchamp and Childress (2009), the principles operate as a framework for considering and reflecting upon moral considerations, as opposed to representing a moral theory.

Emily is 78 years old and is severely ill. She is competent to make decisions and makes a general statement to refuse further treatment and wishes to die at home.

▶ In the circumstances, to what extent can Emily refuse to be admitted to hospital?

> ▶ Is it relevant that admission to hospital and antibiotic therapy might save her life?
> ▶ To what extent is Emily's refusal an application of her autonomous rights?
> ▶ Consider the duties of the GP. How might the ethical principles of beneficence and non-maleficence engage?
> ▶ How might the principle of justice engage with the scenario?

1.9 Feminist ethics

Feminist ethics spring from the observation that much of academia, including medical academe and ethics, is male-dominated and hence the conclusions to a large extent are biologically determined. One feminist perspective considers that medical ethics explicitly fails to acknowledge the apparent differences in approach between the sexes, and that much of bioethics represents a deeply entrenched male-dominated view that fails to consider gender roles. Women have a right to live in a society that is not constrained by potential avenues of success, and their parts played in society are frequently complex and inadequately portrayed. In consequence, many of the conclusions of traditional ethical theories represent outdated biological determinism and there is a need for a fresh approach that incorporates an enhanced balance of gender perspectives. Sherwin (1996 at 48) states that bioethicists

> think of themselves as involved in an activity that helps to undermine some of the subtle effects of sexism. But even among these sympathetic bioethicists, gender is seldom raised as a relevant consideration in the topics explored, or viewed as significant in the context addressed. Feminists, however, are unlikely to be comforted by these omissions, having learned elsewhere that invisibility is no assurance of irrelevance in matters of oppression.

Questions about (gender) dominance and oppression represent dimensions of feminist ethics, one of which is concerned with the need to address inequality. An example of inequality is the relative difference in the number of women recruited into research trials. Such exclusion means that the results of the trials may not be readily extrapolated to women when such medications are used in practice. Feminists also point to manifest inequalities in health-care provisions and lack of research into diseases that affect women in particular. A further dimension of feminist ethics considers the extent to which male norms can be used to disempower, and exercise control over, women. The medicalisation of childbirth has resulted in women losing control over the birthing process and likewise doctors control the gateway to obtaining lawful abortion, resulting in doctors making critical decisions rather than women themselves.

Much of feminist critique has arisen from the seminal work of Gilligan (1982). She notes that the majority of ethical discourse is male-dominated, rooted in an ethic of justice and defined by its commitment to abstract universal principles. One of these principles is that of autonomy. Many feminists are critical of the perspective of persons as autonomous self-asserters since no individual emerges fully grown and complete to the world to perform such actions. Furthermore, the concept of autonomy is perceived as exclusionary and designed to protect those who are already well situated. Women, in line with members of oppressed groups and children, are often denied autonomous respect and may be regarded as emotional and improperly treated as incompetent, thereby being subject to medical treatment against their will. Examples can be found in common law where women in labour have not been regarded as competent to make decisions about treatment in relation to pregnancy and have been treated against their will, for example, being compelled to undergo caesarean section.

1.9.1   The ethics of care

Gilligan (1982) concludes from her empirical work that the psychology of women is such that it is more orientated towards relationships and interdependence, thereby bringing a perception that is different to typical male perspectives of priorities and human experience. Women are considered to be more likely to develop an ethic of care. An ethic of care considers the particular needs of patients and the health professional's special relationship towards them by adopting a holistic approach to treating people with dignity and respect. Care is an intermittent ongoing process and ethical dilemmas are ubiquitous in commonplace and routine events. This distinguishes it from medical activity, which focuses mainly on diagnosis, treatment and prognosis. Care ethics focuses on the importance of interpersonal relationships, although this normative ethical theory has been criticised on the grounds that it could be harmful to women. If women are seen mainly as carers, this could lead to further repression and subordination. However, a more preferred view might be to regard care ethics as an adjunct to traditional ethics rather than being antagonistic towards it.

Emily speaks to the nurses who advise her to follow medical advice. She asks whether she can be 'put down'.

▶ What is the extent of the nurses' duties in these circumstances, particularly in the context of the ethics of care?
▶ Is it ethically and legally permissible for Emily to be 'put down'?
▶ Consider the competing moral arguments between the deontological obligation to preserve life and the consequentialist act of putting Emily out of her misery. To what extent do the four principles engage in this scenario?

1.10   Other ethical theories

There are several other ethical theories that may have relevance for medical practice and health-care dilemmas.

1.10.1   Communitarian ethics

Communitarianism is considered to be a derivation of virtue ethics (see below) and asserts that too much weight is attached to the rights and interests of individuals. Individuals, as members of society, share common obligations since a good society is the key to a good life. For this reason, the good of the community can at times legitimately override individual interests. Communitarians therefore permit certain actions to be undertaken without individual consent in the interests of society in general. One example of practice underscored by communitarianism is the compulsory donation of organs from the deceased for the purposes of transplantation, as is compulsory immunisation of children that is required in certain jurisdictions. The essence of communitarianism is that greater good in certain instances can be more important than individual interests. The risk of this approach is that communitarianism could work against the interests of vulnerable minority groups.

1.10.2   Virtue ethics

The origins of virtue ethics go back to the ancient Greek philosophers and serves to emphasise the moral virtues and attitudes of the agent as more important than the outcomes or consequences of actions. A virtue is considered to be a trait, or character, deemed to be a valued attribute for a good moral person. From the perspective of a virtue ethicist, a health-care professional should have virtues of compassion, honesty, fairness, empathy and loyalty. However, how one determines appropriate virtues is problematic. Furthermore, it is quite possible that an action motivated by virtue yields to a bad outcome. If motivation is the only factor in judging the moral worth of an action, then a well-meant act can never be wrong regardless of the consequences, a position that aligns uneasily with common morality and the law.

1.10.3   Casuistry

Casuistry is case-based reasoning and is used to resolve moral dilemmas by applying theoretical rules. Most ethical theories represent a top-down approach and begin with application of broad and abstract principles. Casuistry represents a bottom-up approach that considers the ethical and moral issues that arise from difficult cases. On the face of it, it might seem logical to look at similar situations and dilemmas and appraise how they have been handled in the past. However, casuistry may not always provide an answer when faced with a difficult dilemma. In casuistry, decision making is guided not only by general principles but also by careful analysis of the specific facts of the case. Bioethicists frequently tend to use imaginary scenarios in their attempts to develop ethical and moral reasoning.

1.10.4   Multicultural ethics

In a pluralistic society, multicultural ethics is likely to play a considerable part in health-care services. A person who believes in *karma* (fate or destiny) may not wish to attach great weight to consequentialist theories. In understanding the eternal cycle of reincarnation a duty- and virtue-based stance takes precedence in determining what action (if at all) needs to be taken, and for that matter the choice that an individual might make. For some cultures, non-secular philosophical principles and theories, as well as the interdependence of familial relationships, are ascribed far greater accord than the more secular Western European concepts of autonomy and utility. An understanding of peer ethics within a population of increasing diversity and multiculturalism is undoubtedly of emerging relevance given the demographic shifts of society.

The cultural norms of ethnic communities may impact upon health-care services in several ways, and of central importance is freedom of belief and tolerance of the convictions of others. Religious beliefs may have an impact upon biomedical ethics particularly with respect to death rites. The Buddha's theory, for example, involves an eight-fold path that incorporates the precepts of prohibitions on killing, lying and drinking intoxicants. Many cultures, including ancient Chinese and Islamic cultures, set out the rules of conduct that a physician must follow. Deeply ingrained cultural and religious convictions need to be considered for contemporary ethical frameworks involving health care.

1.11 The evolving professional relationship

The professional relationship between the doctor and the patient has evolved into one that is multifaceted, with complex moral and ethical interactions. All the above ethical concepts may engage in this relationship at varying levels. The doctor–patient relationship has more recently resulted in some areas of practice as posing sharper contemporary ethical challenges.

1.11.1 Truth telling

Honesty, truthfulness and candour are expected traits of health-care professionals. The trait of veracity, or truth telling, refers to accurate, objective and comprehensive information being transmitted from the doctor to the patient. This concept is based upon the principle that respect is owed to others. It is also based upon an expectation of trust between the doctor and the patient, and the belief that health-care professionals will be frank and truthful. However, non-disclosure, limited disclosure and even frank deception can at times be perceived as justifiable where there is a conflict of obligations.

A typical example of non-disclosure, or limited disclosure, might occur where a diagnosis of cancer is made, or when the prognosis is particularly poor, especially with regard to imminent death. An interesting study was undertaken by Oken in 1961. Eighty-eight percent of clinicians surveyed indicated that they would not disclose a diagnosis of cancer to their patients. However, this attitude had changed dramatically less than two decades later. In 1979, Novack reported that 98% of physicians surveyed would disclose the diagnosis of cancer to patients. There are several reasons why physicians choose not to tell patients the truth, particularly in relation to diagnosis of a dread disease. One reason could arise from a sense of beneficence and the attempt to avoid news or information that might be harmful to the patient. However, there is an argument that ultimately the patient may benefit if the truth is disclosed as early as possible. This shift in thinking might account for some of the change in the attitudes of physicians towards truth telling under such circumstances. Another reason for the change in attitude emanates from the greater respect for autonomy and self-determined choice. Individuals have a right to know the truth about their own health. Frank communication may be hindered by friends and relatives who do not want the patient to know. This is seen in certain cultural groups where relatives feel that it would be detrimental to their loved one to know that he or she has cancer. Families provide important care and support for patients and therefore families' views need to be respected. However, by what right can a physician inform the family first of the diagnosis of cancer without informing the patient? Furthermore, is it correct that the family should veto the patient's right to know the truth? Another argument for non-disclosure is that physicians can really never know the 'whole truth' when a patient asks 'What is going to happen to me?' The most that the doctor can do under these circumstances is to provide the best clinical opinion as informed by evidence and experience. A further reason for non-disclosure, or at least limited disclosure, is the rationale of staging the disclosure of bad news. In certain specific circumstances this might be considered beneficial for promoting adjustment to the news.

Disclosure of medical errors represents an aspect of breaking bad news. On one level, there is a moral responsibility to disclose specific medical errors to patients and their families. However, as Beauchamp and Childress (2009) indicate, adequate disclosure does not occur and is rarely documented. Evasive formulations are commonly used, as well as euphemistic and ambiguous language. One principal reason for non-disclosure is fear of litigation, and other reasons include concern about damaging patient and public trust and bringing the institution and its staff into disrepute. Non-disclosure of medical errors has been described as a 'collusive silence that often surrounds medical mistakes [and] is a troublesome feature of medical cultures' (Beauchamp and Childress, 2009 at 294).

Deception by doctors has been known to occur in relation to insurance claims. Studies have shown that physicians may exaggerate the severity of their patients' medical conditions and even alter the diagnosis or alter reported signs and symptoms with the intention of helping patients obtain adequate financial compensation. The argument that may be used to justify such actions is that patients have paid their premiums and are therefore entitled to benefit. Physicians face dissention between their traditional role as patient advocate and their role to control and use financial resources most effectively. This is a difficult dilemma and doctors might consider alternative approaches, such as formal appeals in order to make the systems less restrictive.

> Emily is transferred to a low dependency ward and feels more optimistic. She asks if she can return home soon. However, her prognosis is poor and the doctor falsely reassures her that she is fine.
>
> ▶ Consider the extent to which the doctor's actions are morally justified?
> ▶ What are the possible benefits and potential harms of the doctor's action?

1.11.2 Privacy

The concept of privacy embraces a range of issues and includes liberty, autonomy, the right to enjoy life, the right to be left alone and the right to be free from interference. An intrusion into privacy has to be balanced against competing interests. Within the medical context this might occur as part of public health ethics involving screening to ensure effective treatment. Policies for anonymous screening (e.g. for HIV) and others for coercive treatment (e.g. treatment of tuberculosis) can be justified in terms of the overall benefit for public health. However, such policies should always be least restrictive and least intrusive.

1.11.3 Confidentiality

Confidentiality is closely related to privacy. The fundamental difference is that in medical confidentiality, personal information is disclosed either by the doctor or the institution undertaking medical care of the person. By comparison, if such information is obtained by a third party without authorisation, then the individual's privacy is violated (and at the same time confidential information about the individual becomes known to the third party). The standard exceptions for breach of confidentiality are discussed elsewhere in this text (see 2.23). However, a tension may arise between the physician's duty to respect his patient's confidentiality and information disclosure. This might, for example, occur with regard to disclosure of HIV status to a spouse or sexual partner. Breach of confidentiality in this regard is often justified on the grounds of preventing harm to at-risk individuals. Generally, in these circumstances, the physician should try to persuade the infected person to allow disclosure to cease endangering the lives and health of other individuals. However, if this fails, then disclosure in breach of confidentiality needs to be considered, either through policies that have been devised for such purposes or through direct action on the part of the doctor. Similar tensions in the physician's duty to protect confidentiality and protect a third party from harm might occur with regard to disclosure of genetic information, particularly where sharing that information with at-risk relatives may then enable the relatives to take action to reduce harm to themselves.

1.11.4 Fidelity

The obligation of fidelity arises when a physician or health-care professional establishes a significant relationship with a patient, and abandoning the patient would amount to disloyalty. Fidelity to patients may come into conflict with allegiance to colleagues, an institution, corporations or the State. Furthermore, fidelity may come into conflict in the case of a doctor who is a manager where the doctor has a duty to the patient but also owes a duty towards the institution or organisation of which he is manager. Care of the individual may come into conflict with institutional objectives in the case of medical assistance in prisons and other correctional institutions.

Summary

1.1 Medical law is underpinned by ethical principles. The doctor and patient relationship is central to good medical practice and ethical issues engage at all levels.

1.2 Medical law issues are pervasive throughout the life of individuals and can extend from before birth to after death. Medical law provides a framework whereby moral and ethical issues are balanced while taking into account the interests of parties and has evolved in response to societal change.

1.3 Morals are the motivations behind human actions and choices and distinguish between right and wrong and good and bad. Ethics refers to a set of moral principles that apply to a particular situation. Bioethics is 'applied' ethics to situations that arise from the biological and medical sciences, and aims to provide a structure of universal applicability to decision making in health care. Bioethics is grounded upon religious and secular ethical theories.

1.4 Deontology holds that there are several distinct duties and that the intrinsic rightness or wrongness of an action depends upon whether it is consistent with basic moral principles (as opposed to the outcome of the act). Immanuel Kant was a proponent of deontological moral theory. The Kantian maxim to treat others as an end (in themselves) and not just as the means to an end is often cited in health-care law. This forms the basis of respect for autonomy. Rights theories act as the basis of protection for individuals.

1.5 Consequentialism is the ethical theory that assesses the moral worth of an action by the consequences of that action. Act-consequentialism holds that the right action is one which produces the most good. The principal criticisms of act-consequentialism are that it imposes onerous requirements to make the world a better place, that it leaves no place for duties

Summary cont'd

towards family and friends and that it can at times produce results that are counter-intuitive to common morality.

1.6 Utilitarianism is a consequentialist-based theory that determines the moral worth of an action by the utility it produces. An action is judged as correct if it maximises utility and has been formulated as doing the greatest good for the greatest number. Like consequentialism, a strict application of pure utilitarianism may produce outcomes that are counter-intuitive. A branch of this theory, known as rule-utilitarianism, aims to circumvent this outcome by considering utilitarian consequences of a particular action or judgement within the framework of certain rules.

1.7 Rights-based discourse underpins much of medical law. Moral rights are justified by normative structures in morality, and legal rights are justified by normative structures in law. Moral and legal rights are distinct although moral rights may underpin legal rights. Within the context of medical law, rights are not absolute and may be infringed, meaning that justified action could be taken in overriding a right. The language of rights is used more robustly when it comes to protecting the critical interests of persons.

1.8 Principlism is an approach to health-care ethics based upon autonomy, non-maleficence, beneficence and justice. This approach provides an analytical framework within which ethical issues related to health care may be analysed. The four principles encompass self-governance, self-determined choice and respect for the individual (autonomy); the obligation to do no harm (non-maleficence); the obligation to do good (beneficence); and fair and equitable distribution of health resources with equal access to all to provide a decent minimum level of health care (justice). Principlism is a commonly used ethical framework within the practical health-care setting.

1.9 Feminist ethics provides a feminist critique of moral theory and aims to address gender inequalities. Ethics of care is a branch of feminist ethics that focuses on interdependence of persons, such as between the patient and carer and emphasises a holistic approach to patient care.

1.10 A range of other ethical theories are relevant to health-care ethics. This includes communitarianism (overriding individual interests in specific cases for societal benefit); virtue ethics (acts being judged as right on the basis of being motivated by good virtues); casuistry (case-based reasoning representing a bottom-up approach to ethical problems and moral questions) and multicultural ethics (cultural diversity of secular and non-secular philosophical concepts and ethical principles).

1.11 The evolving doctor–patient relationship has more recently resulted in some areas of practice as posing sharper ethical challenges. Truth telling refers to a comprehensive, accurate and objective transmission of information by a doctor. Non-disclosure, limited disclosure or deception can occur where bad news has to be broken to patients. The concept of privacy embraces a number of elements but essentially refers to freedom of the individual from intrusion. Within the medical context, intrusion of privacy engages in public health policies such as screening and treatment for communicable diseases. Confidentiality remains a fundamental duty of the physician. However, this obligation may be breached when balanced against preventing harm to third parties; for example, disclosure of HIV to spouses and partners and disclosure of specific genetic information to relatives. An obligation of fidelity arises when a physician establishes a significant relationship with a patient. This obligation may conflict with regard to third party or institutional interests.

Exercises

1.1 What do you understand by bioethics? Why do you think bioethics is relevant to practising health-care professionals and medical lawyers?

1.2 'Bioethical theories are at best abstract and at worst confusing. In the final analysis ethical issues are resolved by the conscience of the individual practitioner'. Critically evaluate this statement.

1.3 'The four principles approach to bioethics provides a simple, accessible and culturally neutral approach to most of the moral issues that arise in health care'. Critically evaluate this statement.

1.4 Consider whether or not feminist ethics (and other related ethical concepts) are an attractive alternative to 'mainstream' or 'traditional' ethics?

1.5 What do you consider as key ethical issues in contemporary health care?

Further reading

Beauchamp TL, Childress JF. *Principles of biomedical ethics*. Oxford University Press, Oxford, 2009.

Gillon R. Medical ethics: four principles plus attention to scope. *British Medical Journal* 1994; 309: 184.

Kuhse H, Singer P. *Bioethics: an anthology*. Edited by Helga Kuhse and Peter Singer. Blackwell, Oxford, 2006.

Morrison D. A holistic approach to clinical and research decision-making. *Medical Law Review* 2005; 13: 45.

Woolf S. (Ed.). *Feminism and bioethics*. Oxford University Press, Oxford, 1996.

Links to relevant websites can be found at: http://www.palgrave.com/law/samanta

Chapter 2 follows overleaf.

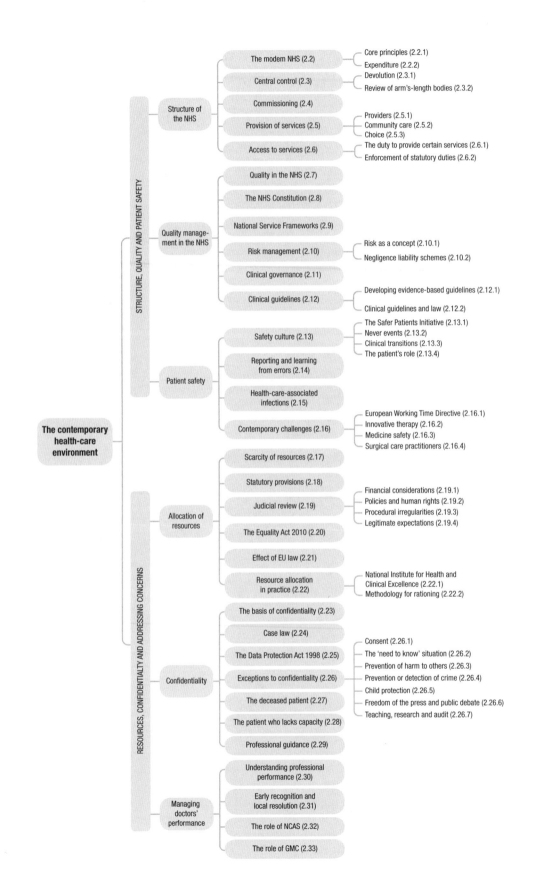

The contemporary health-care environment

STRUCTURE, QUALITY AND PATIENT SAFETY

Structure of the NHS
- The modern NHS (2.2)
  - Core principles (2.2.1)
  - Expenditure (2.2.2)
- Central control (2.3)
  - Devolution (2.3.1)
  - Review of arm's-length bodies (2.3.2)
- Commissioning (2.4)
- Provision of services (2.5)
  - Providers (2.5.1)
  - Community care (2.5.2)
  - Choice (2.5.3)
- Access to services (2.6)
  - The duty to provide certain services (2.6.1)
  - Enforcement of statutory duties (2.6.2)

Quality management in the NHS
- Quality in the NHS (2.7)
- The NHS Constitution (2.8)
- National Service Frameworks (2.9)
- Risk management (2.10)
  - Risk as a concept (2.10.1)
  - Negligence liability schemes (2.10.2)
- Clinical governance (2.11)
- Clinical guidelines (2.12)
  - Developing evidence-based guidelines (2.12.1)
  - Clinical guidelines and law (2.12.2)

Patient safety
- Safety culture (2.13)
  - The Safer Patients Initiative (2.13.1)
  - Never events (2.13.2)
  - Clinical transitions (2.13.3)
  - The patient's role (2.13.4)
- Reporting and learning from errors (2.14)
- Health-care-associated infections (2.15)
- Contemporary challenges (2.16)
  - European Working Time Directive (2.16.1)
  - Innovative therapy (2.16.2)
  - Medicine safety (2.16.3)
  - Surgical care practitioners (2.16.4)

RESOURCES, CONFIDENTIALITY AND ADDRESSING CONCERNS

Allocation of resources
- Scarcity of resources (2.17)
- Statutory provisions (2.18)
- Judicial review (2.19)
  - Financial considerations (2.19.1)
  - Policies and human rights (2.19.2)
  - Procedural irregularities (2.19.3)
  - Legitimate expectations (2.19.4)
- The Equality Act 2010 (2.20)
- Effect of EU law (2.21)
- Resource allocation in practice (2.22)
  - National Institute for Health and Clinical Excellence (2.22.1)
  - Methodology for rationing (2.22.2)

Confidentiality
- The basis of confidentiality (2.23)
- Case law (2.24)
- The Data Protection Act 1998 (2.25)
- Exceptions to confidentiality (2.26)
  - Consent (2.26.1)
  - The 'need to know' situation (2.26.2)
  - Prevention of harm to others (2.26.3)
  - Prevention or detection of crime (2.26.4)
  - Child protection (2.26.5)
  - Freedom of the press and public debate (2.26.6)
  - Teaching, research and audit (2.26.7)
- The deceased patient (2.27)
- The patient who lacks capacity (2.28)
- Professional guidance (2.29)

Managing doctors' performance
- Understanding professional performance (2.30)
- Early recognition and local resolution (2.31)
- The role of NCAS (2.32)
- The role of GMC (2.33)

The contemporary health-care environment

Key Terms

- **Access to health services** – a statutory duty imposed upon the Secretary of State to enable public access to health care.
- **Caldicott Guardian** – a senior person within the NHS or local authority who is responsible for protecting confidentiality of patient information and who enables appropriate information sharing.
- **Clinical governance** – a system through which NHS organisations are accountable for continuously monitoring, improving and safeguarding high standards of care and services.
- **Commissioning** – the purchasing of health-care services from providers.
- **Confidentiality** – a duty upon medical practitioners (based on the confidential relationship between doctor and patient) that precludes the disclosure of medical information (subject to certain exceptions).
- **Data Protection Act 1998** – the enabling legislation that permits the collection and processing of sensitive medical information within the health-care context.
- **Decentralisation** – the devolution of power to local health-care organisations with regard to the provision of health-care services.
- **National Service Frameworks** – policies set by the NHS to define standards of care and reduce variations in specific health-care services.
- **NHS Constitution** – a framework for quality within the NHS which sets out the key rights and responsibilities of patients and staff.
- **NHS core principles** – accessibility, choice and high quality services based on clinical need and aimed at reducing health inequalities.
- **Providers** – those who provide front-line care of patients within the NHS.
- **Resource allocation** – a decision to limit some forms of investigations and treatment to certain people based on limited resources.
- **Risk management** – an approach taken to identify and minimise clinical risk, thereby improving patient safety.
- **Root cause analysis** – a comprehensive dissection of a medical error to expose underlying causes.

Scenario

Javed, a 55-year-old immigrant from Pakistan, has been living and working in England for several years. He is employed as a manual operative and speaks little English. He has chronic arthritis and recently developed severe pain and swelling in his right knee. His attempts to contact his GP have been unsuccessful. The GP surgery operates a telephone triage system whereby urgent cases receive priority appointments and non-urgent cases are allocated a routine appointment. Since Javed was unable to explain his situation fully to the receptionist, he received a routine appointment to see his doctor 10 days later.

At the appointment, Javed is diagnosed with acute infection in his knee and is immediately admitted to hospital. He is prescribed a relatively new broad-spectrum antibiotic. It is a potent medication that carries a high risk of an allergic reaction, particularly for persons who are prone to allergies. Unfortunately, due to linguistic barriers, Javed's previous history of eczema, asthma and hay fever was not discovered by the doctor. A nurse gave the antibiotic intravenously and within minutes Javed developed a severe allergic reaction with acute respiratory difficulties. There was no junior doctor on the ward because of a new shift pattern and by the time a clinician arrived from a different part of the hospital, Javed was seriously ill and had to be transferred to the ICU, where he remained for 2 weeks.

Javed is finally discharged from hospital. The infection has resolved but his arthritis remains severe. A new biologic therapy is available and although Javed qualifies for treatment on clinical grounds, his doctor is unable to prescribe the drug due to the high cost of treatment. Javed is informed that the medication has not yet been approved by NICE although specialist bodies strongly advocate the new medication as a first-line therapy for arthritis.

Javed attends an NHS conference on arthritis which is attended by patients and health-care professionals. A junior doctor gives a presentation on the new antibiotic which Javed had previously been prescribed and its potential side effects and refers to a case study to illustrate the potential risks of allergic reaction. Javed is mortified when he realises that his own case is being discussed and that his first name appears on one of the slides. Javed is very upset and would like to obtain some form of redress.

2.1 Introduction

Contemporary health-care environments are complex, expensive and frequently bureaucratic. The NHS, in particular, has undergone massive and unrelenting changes driven by politics and societal pressure. Increasing demands due to demographic shifts and an increasing population of older persons have compounded this effect. Opportunities and challenges have accompanied progress in medical technologies and the development of new therapies that have significantly changed the landscape of clinical practice since the NHS was founded just over 60 years ago.

Several issues are central to understanding how the contemporary health-care system works. These include awareness of the structure of the NHS and its overriding commitment to quality and patient safety. Irrespective of political rhetoric, resources are of central importance and must be allocated according to need in the most cost-effective way. Health-care delivery has witnessed a fundamental shift in the doctor–patient relationship, and medical paternalism, no matter how benign, is no longer acceptable. Even so, the shift to a more patient-centred approach means that to some degree the balance of power has shifted in the dyadic relationship between doctor and patient. This change requires a different ideological approach to clinical practice compared to the one just 20 years ago. A further influence is that regulation of the medical profession has considerably altered with greater control and accountability being imposed upon all health-care professionals with the imperative to demonstrate practice that is commensurate with set standards. These pervading themes are explored in this chapter.

A The structure of the NHS

2.2 The modern NHS

The modern NHS is a complex organisation with an enormous remit. The NHS Information Centre (July 2007) reported that 289.8 million general practice consultations took place in 2006 and the overall consultation rate was 5.3 visits per person per year. During 2008 to 2009, there were 11,012,063 admissions for procedures and interventions in NHS hospitals (NHS Information Centre, 2010). More than 1,100 million NHS prescriptions are issued annually (The Association of British Pharmaceutical Industry, 2009). The NHS is the largest employer in the United Kingdom, and in April 2010 there were 1,216,149 staff members (NHS Information Centre, 2010). This section considers some of the issues around the structure of this massive organisation and selects key features that are relevant to the delivery of contemporary health-care.

2.2.1 Core principles

The NHS is underpinned by several core principles (Department of Health, 2010):

- ▶ Provision of a comprehensive service available to all
- ▶ Access to NHS services is based upon clinical need rather than the ability to pay
- ▶ The highest standards of excellence and professionalism
- ▶ Reflection of the needs and preferences of patients, their families and their carers
- ▶ The need to work across organisational boundaries and in partnership with other organisations in the interest of patients, local communities and the wider population
- ▶ Commitment to provision of best value for taxpayers' money and the most effective, fair and sustainable use of finite resources
- ▶ Accountability to the public, communities and the patients it serves.

The Department of Health has prioritised choice as a means of empowering patients, to be achieved by facilitating diversity of provision and allowing providers to innovate and improve service provision alongside financial incentives to improve care and maximise efficiency (Department of Health, 2006a). National standards have been agreed upon to regulate service provision and guarantee quality, safety and equity by using information management to achieve better and safer clinical service.

The modern NHS aims to provide an equitable service that permits consumer choice according to clinical need. Monitoring the effectiveness of safety, quality and consumer satisfaction initiatives is carried out by routine national surveys; for example, annual patient choice surveys have been used for monitoring patient awareness of choice of NHS providers (Department of Health, 2010).

Nonetheless, the NHS faces considerable challenges. There is an ever-increasing expectation of shorter waiting times alongside enhanced service provision. Patients quite rightly demand more from health services and have greater expectations of what medicine can deliver. Demographic changes are apparent with an ageing population, cultural diversity and the increased prevalence of chronic conditions. These factors merge to increase the demands upon service provision and the public purse.

Medical technology and its capabilities are rising at an exponential rate and are changing disease management strategies in the context of heightened public expectations all of which operate to impose further demands upon resources and service configuration.

2.2.2 Expenditure

The costs of the NHS are astronomical. In 2007 to 2008 the total expenditure was in the region of £90 billion (Her Majesty's Treasury, 2007), and £99.5 billion has been allocated for 2010–2011 (Budget Report, June 2010). This increase in expenditure follows several trends in sociological shifts such as increasing prosperity and better public health. Diseases of poverty have tended to be replaced with illness of affluence and longevity, and massive strides in medical technology are often very expensive. Recent sociological drivers of change include the prevalence of 'lifestyle disorders' such as anxiety and obesity, and the extent to which the expense of modern medicine can be met by a publicly funded health system is unclear.

The deficit in the NHS budget for the year 2005 to 2006 was approximately £1.2 billion. Palmer (2006) notes that the annual spend for 2007 and 2008 was approximately 40% higher than the previous 5 years and yet, despite this increase in funding, the NHS budget remains in serious deficit. In view of recent and imminent cutbacks it seems likely that this shortfall will increase possibly leading to reductions in staff, service cutbacks and ward closures. More positively, the financial reviews and intended reforms might operate to reduce duplication of services and enhance professional, managerial and fiscal accountability.

2.3 Central control

The NHS has always been funded through general taxation to meet the laudable aim of providing health care that is free at the point of delivery and irrespective of the patient's ability to pay. The Secretary of State for Health is accountable to Parliament for the performance of the NHS. Parliamentary Select Committees produce regular reports on NHS performance and the Health Committee examines expenditure, administration and policy making. The Public Accounts Committee is responsible for ensuring that the NHS is run in an economic and efficient manner, and the Public Administration Committee scrutinises reports from the Health Service Commissioner. Policy making and centralised planning is the function of the Department of Health, which is also responsible for the overall direction of the NHS. The Department of Health works with key partners to set national standards to improve health-care service quality. Its principal aim is to improve public well-being through better overall health.

2.3.1 Devolution

A key feature of the modern NHS is devolution of power from the centre to provider organisations. The strategy is based on the notion that the public ought to be instrumental in shaping the future direction and development of the NHS. There is a duty to local organisations, such as strategic health authorities and trusts, to make arrangements for involving and consulting patients and the public pursuant to section 11 of the Health and Social Care Act 2000. Public consultations and input are achieved through patient and public interest forums that canvass opinions on health-care service provision to ensure that these are consumer responsive and that these meet the needs of society.

Decentralisation means that local NHS organisations are vested with greater control to meet the health needs of specific localities. The primary purpose of the centre is to provide adequate resources to permit the delivery of necessary NHS care while operational implementation is the function of local organisations. One advantage of this approach is that health service provision ought to be more in tune with local requirements, although potential disadvantages are apparent. Decentralisation can lead to service inequalities due to resources being allocated according to different priorities for health care in different localities. While such differentials might be due to genuine differences in the clinical needs of populations, factors such as local policies and politics will undoubtedly be influential, possibly leading to disparities within the NHS from one area to another.

2.3.2　Review of arm's-length bodies

A number of functions of the NHS are carried out by arm's-length bodies (ALBs). A review of ALBs has been proposed by the Coalition Government in the recently published White Paper 'Equity and Excellence: Liberating the NHS' (available at http://www.dh.gov.uk). Over the next 4 years, the Government is committed to reduce NHS spending by 45% by simplifying the number of ALBs. In total the ALBs employ approximately 18,000 staff, and in 2009 to 2010 the sector as a whole spent in the region of £1.6 billion. A number of ALBs will be dissolved and their functions subsumed within existing parts of the central system. Those that remain will be expected to work within a tight governance and accountability framework, as well as take full advantage of commercial opportunities to enhance value for money in the delivery of services.

The proposals set out in this document plan to abolish 10 Strategic Health Authorities and replace Primary Care Trusts (PCTs) and practice-based commissioners with GP commissioning consortia. There will be an expanded role for NICE putting it on a more solid statutory footing and extending its remit into social care. The roles of Monitor and the Care Quality Commission (CQC) are to be expanded and an independent NHS board is to be established. The MHRA, NHS Blood and Transplant, and Health and Social Care Information Centre have a clear future. The functions of the Human Fertilisation and Embryology Authority and the Human Tissue Authority will be transferred to other organisations to achieve greater synergy. The NHS Litigation Authority will be subject to commercial review by industry experts to identify and achieve cost-benefit opportunities.

Many of the changes will require either primary or secondary legislation and it is expected that they will come into effect by 2013–2014. It is hoped that the changes will bring about the advantages of a streamlined sector, less bureaucracy and greater efficiency through contestability. The precise impact and shape of these proposals remain to be seen, and the following section(s) in this chapter (and others) describes the NHS as it functions at the time of writing.

2.4　Commissioning

Service commissioning is the process of purchasing and managing services from a range of providers to ensure that health-care services effectively meet the needs of the population being served. In addition to purchasing, it requires precise assessment of population requirements to accurately prioritise local health needs. Primary care providers in the NHS include general practitioners, opticians, dentists and pharmacists and these are usually managed by PCTs. It also includes NHS Direct, which is a telephone helpline and interactive online service. Secondary care includes hospitals and the acute sector, and tertiary care includes specialist centres. The more complex services are usually undertaken in hospitals whereas the majority of services may be carried out in the community.

Strategic health authorities ensure that the health-care needs of individuals within a locality can be met. They are responsible for the development of plans for health improvement, making certain the quality and capacity of local services and ensuring the implementation of national priorities.

Primary Care Trusts (PCTs) currently receive around three-quarters of the NHS budget. It is their duty to identify the specific health needs of the community being served to ascertain how needs can best be met and to commission appropriate services from providers. The rationale behind NHS commissioning is based upon the provider and purchaser concept. The purchaser is the body with the resources to purchase health services whereas the provider supplies the required services in return for payment. There are intrinsic incentives upon providers to offer excellent quality services in order to ensure their continued viability, particularly where there is competition amongst several providers. In the 1990s, part of the Conservative manifesto was to promote competition amongst providers to operate as a driver to enhance the quality and cost-effectiveness of care. The subsequent Labour Government gave less emphasis to competitiveness and leaned more towards a model of partnership between commissioner and providers to meet local need. Only if any particular provider could not deliver the necessary services to the required standard would commissioners look elsewhere.

To some extent, all of these approaches have led to a degree of confusion since the same body can act as commissioner as well as provider. For example, PCTs often have commissioning arms and provider arms. It is not unusual for the commissioning arm of a PCT to purchase the services of the provider arm of the same PCT. It is therefore arguable that the purchaser–provider split is nothing more than an elaborate mechanism to circulate money around a single organisation and that there is insufficient real competition to positively enhance the quality of service provision. In fact, the system could be criticised as wasteful of scare resources due to increased managerial activity and bureaucracy.

The process of disbanding PCTs and replacing them with groups each made up of a number of general practices ('GP Consortia') that will take over many of the functions of PCTs including commissioning is being undertaken. It is believed that this re-structuring will achieve a greater degree of patient-centred services that have direct relevance to local health-care needs.

2.5 Provision of services

Service provision of the NHS is overseen by the Secretary of State for Health. NHS care has been subject to continual evolution since its inception, and the concept of the internal market was introduced by the NHS and Community Care Act 1990 which was later consolidated into the National Health Service Act 2006.

2.5.1 Providers

Primary care serves as the usual first point of contact with the health-care system and is typically delivered within the community. General practitioners (GPs) tend to work with teams of health-care professionals and the majority of NHS work is carried out in primary care. There is a trend towards more flexible care arrangements that includes enhanced care provision in community hospitals, such as diagnostic scans and minor surgery. A particular emphasis has been placed on practice-based commissioning, which means that PCTs and GP practices share the role of commissioning hospital services.

Secondary care, in the form of acute services and specialist care, is typically provided in hospitals through NHS trusts which are accountable to the Secretary of State for the provision of effective and efficient services. The relationship between PCTs and NHS trusts is contractual, a system introduced by section 4(3) of the NHS and Community Care Act 1990 and provided for by section 9(5) of the consolidating National Health Service Act 2006. Section 9(5) states that 'Whether or not an arrangement which constitutes an NHS contract would, apart from this subsection, be a contract in law, it shall not be regarded for any purpose as giving rise to contractual rights or liabilities'. Section 9(6) clarifies that 'if any dispute arises with respect to such an arrangement, either party may refer the matter to the Secretary of State for determination under this section'. It therefore appears that section 9(5) excludes an action from being brought in contract and dispute resolution ought to be resolved at the local level. Where this is not possible, the disagreement could be referred for statutory dispute resolution under the NHS Contracts (Dispute Resolution) Regulations 1996 (SI 1996/623) for an adjudicator to find for one party or the other.

The creation of foundation trusts was part of the Labour Government's drive to decentralise health care to promote a patient-responsive NHS. In June 2010 there were 130 NHS foundation trusts which had been granted enhanced levels of autonomy and accountability by the National Health Service Act 2006. Foundation trusts are run by boards of governors comprising of managers, staff and the public. They are public-benefit co-operatives rooted in local ownership, with considerably more financial and organisational freedom than NHS trusts. Members of the local community can apply to become members of the board of local foundation trusts, as can patients and staff. Monitor (an independent regulator) oversees quality assurance for foundation trusts.

The White Paper 'Equity and excellence: Liberating the NHS' states that all NHS trusts will become foundation trusts by 2013. Foundation trusts will be able to introduce strategies for improved services following removal of the current restriction on private income generation in order to enhance the range of services offered to patients. Monitor is set to become the economic regulator for all foundation trusts, and the Care Quality Commission (CQC) will regulate quality of service provision. It remains to be seen how democratic these foundation trusts will be in practice and whether minority interests and the interests of the local community will be adequately represented.

2.5.2 Community care

NHS care is provided free at the point of delivery, although certain services such as the provision of wigs, drugs, optical or dental appliances are charged for on the basis of statutory mandate. Individuals have legitimate expectations of the availability and provision of NHS services and one area of dispute has been over the provision of community care. The NHS and Community Care Act 1990 requires local authorities to prepare and publish plans for community care provision and includes the accommodation and care of persons who are unable to care for themselves, the elderly, those with certain disabilities and persons who have been discharged from Mental Health Services. Under section 47, persons have a right to be assessed for community care, although there is no guarantee of service provision. An exception is made for those who are severely disabled with permanent handicaps through illnesses, severe injuries or congenital disabilities. Under the Chronically Sick and Disabled Persons Act 1970 the local authority has a duty to provide necessary services. There is no overriding duty to others, however, and there may be a requirement for payment.

Two points need to be considered in respect of community care services. First, what can the client expect from the local authority with respect to service provision and second, will the service incur a charge. In *R v North Devon Health Authority, ex p Coughlan* [2000] 3 All ER 850, these matters were considered by the Court of Appeal. A decision had been taken in 1998 to close an NHS residential home that provided for the needs of the chronically disabled. Ms Coughlan, a resident with severe disabilities, had initially agreed to being transferred from hospital to the residential home after being assured that she could live there for as long as she chose. One implication of the decision to close was that Ms Coughlan's care would be transferred from the NHS to local authority services. This meant that she would be liable for the costs of her care according to her means. The decision to close the residential home was quashed following judicial review on the grounds of Ms Coughlan's and others' legitimate expectations following the assurances previously given. The court held that the Secretary of State was at liberty to exclude certain nursing services from those provided by the NHS and these services could then be provided as part of a social services package provided by the local authority. Each case had to be considered on its merits. The approach in *Coughlan* was that a legitimate expectation could be constrained by whatever policy was in force at that time, and equally a legitimate expectation could emanate from what had been promised. In considering the latter, the court would take into account procedural as well as substantive aspects. A procedural aspect, for example, might include a requirement to be consulted prior to a decision being taken, and in the absence of an overriding reason for it, the court would judge the adequacy of the reasons behind such a change of policy, being mindful of the requirements of fairness. In considering a substantive legitimate expectation, the court would decide whether frustration of the expectation would be so unfair as to amount to an abuse of power.

With regard to nursing care in the context of *Coughlan*, the court's view was that the NHS was not responsible for all aftercare. Patients with requirements above and beyond the level of basic care or those whose needs were so great that they should be regarded as the responsibility of the health authority rather than Social Services should be entitled to NHS care. Part IV of the Health and Social Care Act 2001 provides for the manner in which long-term health care is provided and funded in England and Wales, and section 49 specifically excludes nursing care from community care services that are given, planned or supervised by a registered nurse.

A local authority cannot charge for such nursing care unless such care is considered unnecessary for the health needs of the patient. The NHS Ombudsman criticised the extent to which the *Coughlan* judgement has been complied with by local authorities. Services provided in response to health needs should not be charged for by local authorities. However, the criteria used to distinguish between health-care and social care needs are somewhat arbitrary and inconsistent, a situation that has caused uncertainty of outcome as well as delays and difficulty in interpreting eligibility, with some being wrongly denied funding (Newdick, 2005).

2.5.3 Choice

The rise of the consumer ideology in the NHS has been accompanied by an enhanced emphasis on choice for patients. In setting out its vision for creating a patient-led NHS, the Department of Health (2005) placed patient choice as centre stage to empower patients to personalise their care by choosing the time and place of their care according to their convenience. This right to choose, supported by information to support that choice, is expressly provided for in the NHS Constitution (2010).

It remains to be seen whether real patient choice can be achieved, or indeed whether it is something that should be aspired to. In resource-constrained times, patient choice might not represent a premier consideration. Patient choice inevitably costs money and its cost-effectiveness is uncertain. Given the current economic climate it could be argued that choice for individual patients does not weigh heavily against other competing public interests, although the White Paper 'Equity and excellence: Liberating the NHS' (July 2010) restates the government's commitment to providing patients with high quality information and current data on NHS health care. Dr Foster Intelligence, a main provider of health and social care information, is currently being reviewed with the aim of developing such provision.

The extent to which information can enhance patient care remains to be seen and it is unclear as to whether choice will benefit those outside the educated middle classes. The convenience of being seen sooner may be at the expense of having to travel further, particularly since many general practices offer electronic bookings through the 'Choose and Book' system. A speedy time to consultation at a specialist provider has to be balanced against the inconvenience of travelling further and possibly to an unfamiliar environment. The premise that increased choice leads to increased satisfaction is still to be tested, and whether this is an achievable objective in the current economic climate remains to be seen.

2.6 Access to services

The Secretary of State has a duty to provide certain medical services, and patients have a right to enforce this duty.

2.6.1 The duty to provide certain services

Section 3(1) of the National Health Service Act 2006 provides that

> The Secretary of State must provide throughout England, to such extent as he considers necessary to meet all reasonable requirements –
>
> (a) hospital accommodation,
> (b) other accommodation for the purpose of any service provided under this Act,
> (c) medical, dental, ophthalmic, nursing and ambulance services,
> (d) such other services or facilities for the care of pregnant women, women who are breastfeeding and young children as he considers are appropriate as part of the health service,

(e) such other services or facilities for the prevention of illness, the care of persons suffering from illness and the after-care of persons who have suffered from illness as he considers are appropriate as part of the health service,

(f) such other services or facilities as are required for the diagnosis and treatment of illness.

> Javed has developed an acutely inflamed knee and his attempts to contact his GP have been unsuccessful. He receives a non-urgent appointment in error.
>
> ▶ Consider whether, in the circumstances, Javed has had appropriate access to NHS care?

Over and above these provisions are a range of services that are provided by local authorities. These include

- ▶ Accommodation for adults who cannot look after themselves
- ▶ Services for those who are blind, deaf, dumb or substantially or permanently handicapped by illness, injury or congenital disability
- ▶ Adaptation of homes
- ▶ Provision of meals
- ▶ Provision of special equipment
- ▶ Promoting welfare of elderly people
- ▶ Aftercare services, including for those discharged from mental health services.

2.6.2　Enforcement of statutory duties

Enforcement of statutory duties is principally through judicial review of decisions to refuse care although an aggrieved individual may claim compensation if damages are suffered due to failure to provide services to which he or she was entitled. Those who have sought to enforce the statutory duty have been singularly unsuccessful. Access to services is usually denied on the grounds of scarce resources and the courts tend to be reluctant to scrutinise economic decisions of health-care organisations. In *R v Secretary of State for Social Services, ex p Hincks* (1980) 1 BMLR 93, plans had been approved to extend a Staffordshire hospital's facilities for orthopaedic surgery. These plans were subsequently postponed and later abandoned since the lowest tender was considerably greater than the available funds. The Court of Appeal refused the judicial review application of four patients who brought proceedings against the Secretary of State for the decision to abandon the plans. According to Lord Denning MR (at 98),

> ...it is impossible to pinpoint any breach of statutory duty on the part of the Secretary of State. If he is entitled to take into account financial resources, as in my judgement he is, then it follows that everything that can be done within the limit of financial resources available has been done in the region and in the area. ... the Secretary of State says that he is doing the best he can with the financial resources available to him: and I do not think that he can be faulted in the matter.

The Secretary of State is not obliged to meet every demand for health services and can achieve only what is possible with the resources available.

In *R v Central Birmingham HA, ex p Walker* (1987) 3 BMLR 32 at 38, parents sought judicial review after being informed that their child's cardiac surgery was to be postponed due to lack of specialist nursing staff. The High Court refused leave to apply since it was not possible to determine any substantive or procedural illegality in the decision. The Court of Appeal held that it was not the court's function to substitute its own judgement for that of those responsible for resource allocation unless such allocation was *Wednesbury* unreasonable. Sir John Donaldson MR explained:

> ... if the court is prepared to grant leave in all or even most cases where patients are, from their points of view, very reasonably disturbed at what is going on, we should ourselves be using up National Health Service resources by requiring the authority to stop doing the work for which they were appointed and to meet the complaints of their patients. It is a very delicate balance. As I have made clear and as Mr Bailey has made clear, the jurisdiction does exist. But it has to be used extremely sparingly.

The court is reluctant to intervene in matters relating to access to health care. In these situations it would not be sufficient to persuade the court that a better decision could have been made unless the decision was *Wednesbury* unreasonable, meaning that the health authority's decision was one which no other reasonable health authority would have taken in the circumstances.

B   Quality management in the NHS

2.7   Quality in the NHS

Prior to 1999, health-care providers in England and Wales had a common law duty to exercise reasonable care and skill in service provision. Section 45 of the Health and Social Care (Community Health and Standards) Act 2003 requires every NHS body to ensure that arrangements are in place for monitoring and improving the quality of care that it provides for individuals. This obligation is enhanced by section 8 of the Health Act 2009 that requires NHS organisations, including foundation trusts, to provide specific information relevant to the quality of service provision.

2.8   The NHS Constitution

The plan for NHS services to become more personalised, effective and safe was apparent in 'Our NHS, our future: NHS Next Stage Review' (Department of Health, 2008), and a clear focus on quality is evident in the NHS Constitution which enshrines the values of the NHS and the rights and responsibilities of patients and staff. The enabling legislation for these initiatives is the Health Act 2009. Part 2 chapter 1 of the Act describes the powers of the Secretary of State with respect to failing NHS providers, and of particular note are those with respect to foundation trusts that have considerably enhanced autonomy and flexibility in how they organise their services and utilise resources. The financial regulator of foundation trusts, Monitor, has the ability to intervene in circumstances of failure by removing trust directors pursuant to powers conferred by sections 52 and 54 of the National Health Service Act 2006. The Health and Social Care Act 2008 gives statutory force to the quality agenda to enhance the regulation of health-care services. The CQC was established by Part 1 of the Act and also creates a system of registration for service providers. Section 139 amends section 23 of the National Health Service Act 2006 to impose a duty on PCTs to make sure arrangements are in place to ensure continual improvements in the quality of health-care provision.

> The GP surgery operates a triage system to prioritise urgent cases. However, despite his acute condition, Javed receives a standard appointment because he was unable to explain his condition.
>
> ▶ To what extent does Javed's experience reflect a quality service?
> ▶ What are Javed's rights, if any, through the NHS Constitution?
> ▶ To what extent should the Constitution and the quality framework provide for diversity?

Section 2 of the Health Act 2009 requires Monitor and the CQC to have regard to the NHS Constitution. The CQC regulates the quality of health and social care in England by ensuring that providers will meet requisite standards. All providers must be registered with the CQC, and the Commission has the power to levy fines to ensure that service provision meets the requisite standards.

While the Constitution purports to confer rights to service users there is an argument that the system is insufficiently robust. The Patients' Rights (Scotland) Bill (2010) has a strong patient-centred focus and emphasises the need to provide optimum benefit and information with a central feature of guaranteeing that patients receive hospital treatment within 12 weeks following agreement to treat. This is of particular note in the present political climate where targets are being abolished in England and Wales. The Constitution also fails to endorse redress mechanisms through the NHS Redress Act 2006 (which has yet to be implemented).

2.9 National Service Frameworks

National Service Frameworks (NSFs) are policies that set out defined standards of care with the aim of reducing variations in NHS service provision. NSFs identify service models for specific care groups, alongside strategies, implementation and quality indicators. Topics are chosen according to their relevance to the government's agenda for health improvement and to date include diabetes, heart disease and mental health. Doctors have input into the drafting of NSFs through their professional collegiate bodies as well as acting as individually commissioned experts. The concept of NSFs was first introduced in 'The new NHS: Modern, dependable' (Department of Health, 1997) and there is a rolling programme to introduce a new framework each year. The programme has received considerable publicity and has raised the expectations of the public and health-care staff with respect to quality standards. They operate as policy documents principally and do not bestow rights on patients. Quality assurance mechanisms, such as NSFs and nationally developed guidelines, rely upon local action to audit and maintain standards. There is an argument that this might deflect standard setting issues that are tangential to the central effect of regulation and might simply mirror image what happens in current practice, thereby resulting in no actual uplift of standards. Consultation with representatives of patients and carers represents one safeguard against this.

2.10 Risk management

Risk management is a key aspect of NHS service provision and aims to improve patient safety by identifying and minimising areas of potential risk.

2.10.1   Risk as a concept

The concept of clinical risk is complex and pervasive and applies to all health-care organisations. Wilson and Tingle (1999) define clinical risk as circumstances where there is a variance with intended treatment, care, therapeutic intervention or diagnostic results irrespective of an untoward outcome. The salient point of this definition lies in the notion that there either may or may not be an untoward outcome. The presence of risk is commonly perceived only after an untoward event has occurred. In fact, 'near miss' situations offer vital learning opportunities for patient safety education. Information and experiences must be disseminated to ensure that preventative action can be taken to avoid future adverse clinical outcomes.

Risk management places particular emphasis on improving the quality of care through minimised risk. This involves harnessing information, using the expertise of key personnel within the organisation and translation of that information into action to develop a safer clinical environment. Risk management programmes provide a framework for safe clinical practice and are based upon identification of risk using data from incidents and near misses, organisational audits, reporting and analysing adverse patient outcomes and developing positive action to avoid or minimise the future occurrence of such risks.

2.10.2   Negligence liability schemes

The principal negligence scheme used by trusts is the Clinical Negligence Scheme for Trusts (CNST) run by the National Health Service Litigation Authority (NHSLA). The NHSLA is a special health authority by section 28 of the National Health Service Act 2006 and indemnifies NHS organisations through a risk-pooling scheme that is managed by a central fund.

The CNST requires trusts to meet standards of clinical risk management set by the NHSLA and contributions are levied according to these standards. Trusts therefore have economic incentives to comply with risk management systems to receive discounted premiums that are dependent upon the level achieved by the trust. Discounts are set at three levels, namely 30%, 20% and 10%. A large trust, for example, that has met the highest level of standards would be eligible for a 30% discount and in real terms this could amount to more than £1,000,000.

2.11   Clinical governance

Clinical governance has been defined by Scally and Donaldson (1998) as the 'system through which NHS organisations are accountable for continuously monitoring and improving the quality of their care and services, and safeguarding high standards of care and services'. Clinical governance operates to promote and maintain patient safety and high quality care in health and social care organisations. The framework that incorporates other business components of health-care organisations and corporate governance is encompassed by integrated governance (Department of Health, 2006).

There are several different components of clinical governance. In clinical practice there are two main strands: audit and managing complaints. Audit is the process by which clinical practice is measured against set standards. It is an iterative process that uses audit findings to implement change followed by a system of re-audit to demonstrate improvement. Clinical audit is a central feature of medical practice and doctors of all grades are required to demonstrate audit of personal and clinical activity to enable the monitoring of clinical performance.

Effective complaints handling is fundamental to successful quality management. If complaints are not dealt with appropriately this can negatively affect any existing tensions in the doctor–patient relationship and more generally can detrimentally affect the public perception of the NHS. Patients have 12 months in which to lodge a complaint and this is dealt with principally through local resolution. Local resolution requires that a complaint is referred to the management team or medical professional. The complaint is then investigated and a response is sent back to the complainant with reflections on learning points and suggestions for future improvement. If the complainant remains dissatisfied, the health-care organisation has a duty to revisit its investigation and response in order to meet the specific issues raised by the complainant. Ultimately, the complaint can be referred to the Ombudsman. The health service ombudsman is independent of the NHS and government and is able to provide an independent view with recommendations regarding the complaint. The current emphasis is geared towards local resolution wherever possible. Health-care organisations are encouraged to be flexible in complaints resolution and to seek early clarification of what went wrong, why and how matters can be resolved for the future.

2.12 Clinical guidelines

Clinical guidelines aim to provide health professionals with information on best practice for the management of specific conditions. The purpose of these guidelines is to provide uniform high quality clinical care and to reduce inconsistencies and variations in clinical practice.

2.12.1 Developing evidence-based guidelines

Clinical guidelines are guidelines for care based upon evidence-based principles. They are typically commissioned or developed by working groups that consist of clinicians with expertise in the area, other health-care professionals, experts in information technology and statistics, and include patient and public representation. The development of guidelines is a protracted process and involves data collection, collating according to the weight of the evidence, development of draft guidance, obtaining feedback from potential professional user groups and refinement. Guidelines may be developed by any organisation but those used in practice tend to have been developed by the National Institute of Clinical Health and Excellence (NICE), the Royal Colleges and specialist societies.

The majority of clinical guidelines across all clinical specialities are those produced by NICE which has a remit for publishing guidance on treatment as well as technology appraisal. It aims to provide guidelines by a process that is thorough, transparent and inclusive. NICE also has the remits of considering the cost-effectiveness of the guidance it produces, as well as the technologies it approves. This has led to criticism that NICE acts to control financial spending within the NHS (see 2.17).

Another criticism of clinical guidelines is that there is not always suficiently robust evidence behind them on account of lack of evidence in the scientific literature. Furthermore, even if guidelines are produced on the basis of robust evidence, the highest standard being the randomised control trial, the inclusion criteria of such a trial may not always make such guidance transferable into clinical care. Medical practice is dependent upon the unique circumstances of individual patients, and clinicians sometimes work within uncertainty where experience and intuition apply. It has been argued that prescriptive guidelines are incompatible with situations that require intuitive clinical thinking. Guidelines however are here to stay, and there is a growing tendency to measure clinical practice against established guidelines. The result of audits against guidelines is fed into managerial processes and those that govern individual clinicians' performance and that depart from established guidance are expected to be minimal and justified on clinical grounds.

> Javed is informed that the medication has not yet been approved by NICE although specialist bodies strongly advocate the new medication as first-line therapy for arthritis.
>
> ▶ What is the remit of NICE?
> ▶ What methodologies are used by NICE?

2.12.2 Clinical guidelines and law

Clinical guidelines have attracted much attention in the medical literature and one concern is the extent to which they could be used in medical litigation as a determinant of the standard of care. Since the inception of NICE and the development of clinical guidelines processes, it is possible that guidelines from NICE may take on a more indicative role in cases of alleged clinical negligence.

Samanta et al. (2006) conducted a questionnaire-based survey to ascertain the views of solicitors and barristers in the United Kingdom on the extent to which clinical guidelines could be used or are used in medical litigation and the expectation for potential future use. Briefly, 372 lawyers practising in clinical negligence in England and Wales were surveyed and of the respondents, 80% were familiar with clinical guidelines (particularly those from NICE and the medical Royal Colleges); 89% reported that their team had used guidelines in their cases handled in the past 3 years; 40% believed that guidelines had been influential in the Court's decision. The majority of respondents felt that there would be an increased use of guidelines by the court in the future.

The traditional test in law with regard to the standard of care is the *Bolam* test, which is a measure of the standard of care against what is done (rather than what ought to be done) in medical practice. With the advent of evidence-based guidelines, there is a likelihood that they may impact upon the standard that governs legal liability and a departure from guidelines could possibly be perceived adversely by the court, particularly in the absence of clear justification.

c Patient safety

2.13 Safety culture

The NHS has been subject to considerable organisational change to implement effective and sustained patient safety policies. Implementing change requires action, and altering organisational culture can be difficult.

McCarthy and Blumenthal (2006) have shown that change can be achieved principally in two ways, either by a 'top-down' or 'bottom-up' approach. A top-down approach is driven by policy initiatives and government dictats to senior officials through to front-line staff. This is an effective strategy but requires considerable investment of time and resources particularly to ensure necessary senior management commitment.

A bottom-up approach is one that is based essentially upon integrated managed care. This type of approach, as exemplified by that of the Kaiser Permanente Institution, aims to enhance teamwork and communication skills. This has been shown to be an effective and efficient method of implementing change when supported by physician involvement and strong managerial leadership, particularly in high risk specialities such as obstetrics.

2.13.1 The Safer Patients Initiative

The World Health Organisation (2005) World Alliance for Patient Safety sought to prioritise the urgent and global need to reduce the incidence of medical error. The Safer Patients Initiative was a top-down system-based approach to focus executive attention on the need to ensure patient safety as a central and overriding priority (Safer Patients Initiative, the Health Foundation). A number of hospital-based sites were involved and a range of positive outcomes occurred. These included a reduction in the number of emergency crash calls following the use of an effective early warning system, a reduction in the prevalence of hospital-acquired infections and enhanced surgical care due to better communication within teams.

2.13.2 Never events

The concept of 'never events' was introduced in the Darzi Report 'High quality care for all', and derives from the United States experience whereby some private medical insurers refuse to pay health-care providers for costs arising from such incidents. 'Never events' include wrong side surgery (such as amputation of an arm rather than a leg); retained instruments following surgery; wrong route chemotherapy; non-detected misplaced feeding tubes; in-patient maternal death from post partum haemorrhage after elective caesarean section; escape of prisoners from medium high-secure mental health hospitals; suicide of in-patients by non-collapsible bedrails and the administration of concentrated potassium chloride.

2.13.3 Clinical transitions

A key aspect of a patient's experience of hospital care is that of transitions which reflect necessary changes that confront patients during their hospital stay. Typical transitions include admission to or discharge from hospital, handover of staff to ensure continuity of care and transfer from theatre to ward. Transitions represent pinch points that expose patients to heightened risk of harm if not adequately managed.

The common types of errors that occur with clinical transitions include drug errors, such as omissions, mistakes in frequency and duplication (Tam et al., 2005). Errors often take place when transfers take place at night on the basis that such transfers tend to be driven by resource constraints and bed shortages. Receiving wards may not have sufficient capacity to offer the necessary staff-to-patient ratio required by the patient's condition.

Discharge from secondary care presents a period of heightened risk, particularly for the elderly and those with complex care needs. Adverse events following discharge tend to be caused by drug errors, hospital-acquired infections and complications of procedures or errors in therapeutic management. A third of patients who suffer an adverse event on discharge are likely to be readmitted or might even die (Forster et al., 2003).

2.13.4 The patient's role

The majority of patient safety initiatives target the environments where adverse incidents are caused by the interaction of the health-care environment and the recipients of care. Only recently have agencies such as the National Patient Safety Agency (NPSA) actively encouraged patient involvement. One example of a patient-focused initiative was the 'clean your hands' campaign (NPSA, 2004) which encouraged patients and relatives to adopt a 'clean hands' approach themselves and also to challenge the health-care team.

In the United States, public access to reliable health-care and performance data has had a positive influence on patient safety. Patients who can access such information are in a stronger position to make informed decisions which can positively drive clinical and organisational standards. Patient health records are a useful and reliable strategy to enhance self-management in certain areas, for example, maternity care, diabetes and cancer. However, patient involvement programmes are only effective in organisations that value and support consumer input.

2.14 Reporting and learning from errors

Investigation into errors often reveals a number of underlying factors, such as systems failure, that are the root cause of the mistake. One approach to addressing systems failures involves the early reporting of incidents, root cause analysis and learning through implementation of action plans. The NPSA (2004) published 'Seven steps to patient safety', which includes building a safety culture, leading and supporting the workforce, integrating risk management committees, promoting the reporting of adverse incidents and near misses, involving and communicating with patients and the public, learning and sharing safety lessons and implementing solutions to prevent harm.

Root cause analysis involves the comprehensive dissection of an error to expose all relevant facts while searching for the underlying cause. The concept of root cause analysis can be misleading since it implies that errors have a single root cause, whereas in reality causation is likely to be multifactorial. Root cause investigations are often only a preliminary step in the investigative process and further deliberations are necessary to expose any inadequacies within the host environment. Proactive prevention of error requires that weaknesses within the system are corrected to avoid repetition of the index event and systems analysis needs to be balanced with organisational factors as well as individual and team accountability.

The National Reporting and Learning System (NRLS) was established by the NPSA. Its database is a voluntary and anonymous open access system that allows reporting by patients, the public and health-care staff. The purpose of the system is to collect and collate as much data as possible about adverse events and to analyse its cause in order to promote learning. Through analysis of patient safety reports, the NRLS issues Patient Safety Alerts that span a range of topics from surgical swab retention, vaccines and patient identification. Although a significant body of data has been collected, most of the reports have tended to concentrate on relatively minor incidents and senior clinicians have been reluctant to make use of the system. The charity Action Against Medical Accidents has reported that a large number of trusts do not comply with NPSA alerts despite a reminder from the Department of Health (AvMA, 2011).

> Javed is given a broad-spectrum antibiotic and is unable to disclose his previous medical history.
>
> ▶ Should the hospital have arranged for an interpreter?
> ▶ To what extent does Javed's situation fall within the quality framework of the NHS?

A further approach to facilitating the delivery of patient safety is through the National Patient Safety Forum, which escalates patient safety by providing high quality information on patterns, trends and underlying causes of harm to patients.

2.15 Health-care-associated infections

Health-care-associated infections (HCAI), such as methicillin-resistant *Staphylococcus aureus* and *Clostridium difficile*, are important issues on the patient safety agenda (House of Commons Public Accounts Committee, 2009). HCAI are broadly due to auto-infection caused by the patient's own microbial flora and commensals, cross-infection from others and inadequate decontamination of equipment. Since the CQC assumed regulatory responsibility, it is empowered to take remedial action where patients are at risk. NHS trusts must be registered with the CQC which requires compliance with regulations that pertain to HCAI.

A number of preventative measures can reduce the risk of infection, for example, self-infection can be reduced by preventative antimicrobial agents. Cross-infection is typically caused by failure of staff to adequately clean their hands before and after contact with patients, and cleansing with alcohol and other antiseptic lotions is advised. Clinical governance arrangements need to ensure clear lines of accountability and responsibility for preventive strategies.

For organisations that fail to comply with CQC regulations, the Commission is empowered to take enforcement action. This can include issuing a warning, the imposition, variation or removal of conditions, prosecutions and financial penalties and ultimately cancellation of registration.

2.16 Contemporary challenges

A range of issues in the modern NHS can pose a challenge to patient safety. Some of these issues are discussed below.

2.16.1 European Working Time Directive

> Following Javed's allergic reaction there was no doctor on the ward because of a new shift pattern. The delay meant that Javed had to be transferred to the ICU.
>
> ▶ Was this incident reported and linked to reporting and learning from errors?
> ▶ What can be done to prevent recurrences in the future?
> ▶ What are the clinical governance implications?

The European Working Time Directive has the potential to negatively, or even positively, impact upon patient safety and the training junior doctors in the NHS. The main effect of the directive on health and safety legislation is an entitlement to a 11-hour break in each 24-hour cycle, and junior doctors must work for no more than an average of 48 hours per week. There is a genuine concern that doctors in training may not receive adequate practical experience. Conversely, there is an argument that allowing reasonable breaks at work will avoid over fatigue of doctors and thereby enhance the safety of care.

Nettleship v Weston [1971] 3 All ER 581 provides authority that lack of experience will not reduce the standard of care expected from a trainee. The duty of care can be discharged by a trainee who lacks expertise by referring to a more experienced practitioner. However, even knowing when to refer requires a certain degree of skill and expertise. Nonetheless, more frequent referrals will require greater manpower at senior staff levels which may not always be available. Some of these challenges have been addressed by using a mixture of shifts and on call from home rotas, particularly for surgical trainees.

2.16.2   Innovative therapy

The demand for less invasive surgical techniques and new interventions is increasing. This requires the development of novel techniques and surgeons will necessarily embark on a personal learning curve to develop proficiency. Therapeutic innovation and novel surgical techniques have implications for the standard of care in the event of a negligence action. The usual test of the standard of care that is expected is according to the *Bolam* principle (see 3.3.1). However, by definition, innovation is likely to be at the forefront of medical practice. Since the *Bolam* standard is that which is endorsed by a responsible body of professional opinion, there might be insufficient experience available to make such a judgement. In *Simms v Simms* [2003] 1 All ER 669, it was established that moving away from approved practice would not necessarily amount to negligent care since it would not be in the public interest to impede medical progress.

The Declaration of Helsinki states that patients should be informed of all risks and benefits inherent in innovative procedures although this might well be very difficult to satisfy due to the limited knowledge available. Harm that results following an innovative procedure could lead to civil litigation, damage to the organisation's reputation and possibly challenge under Articles 3 and 8 of the European Convention of Human Rights.

2.16.3   Medicine safety

Boseley (2006) reported that almost 40,000 drug errors had occurred in NHS trusts in England in a single year. Patients are often prescribed complex medication regimes, and those taking hypoglycaemic agents, anticoagulants and corticosteroids had a significantly increased likelihood of suffering an adverse event. Adverse events tended to be related to newly prescribed medication or changes in dosage or frequency. Patient education programmes are considered an essential component of error reduction.

2.16.4   Surgical care practitioners

Surgical care practitioners are playing an increasingly important role in many surgical teams. These practitioners perform surgical interventions under the direction and supervision of consultant colleagues particularly for procedures at the lower end of complexity. Since it is unusual for them to hold medical qualifications (although they are professionally qualified in their own right) concerns have been raised about patient safety. The Royal College of Surgeons of England has tried to address this concern by creating the National Association of Assistants in Surgical Practice, its purpose being to establish professional standards for this group of practitioners.

D Allocation of resources

2.17 Scarcity of resources

Since its inception, allocation of NHS resources has always presented a challenge. When it was created, the NHS was resourced by allocating funds to the hospitals that the service inherited. Since 1971 resource allocation was prioritised to distribute funds to geographical regions, and more recently according to the size and age of local populations. Recently, more sophisticated models have been developed using capitation formulae to take into account the relative health needs of different populations and the attendant costs of health-care provision. Resources are now allocated to PCTs according to the relative needs of each population according to a weighted capitation formula to enable the purchase of similar levels of services for populations of similar need. An organisation known as the Advisory Committee on Resource Allocation is responsible for overseeing the development of new weighted capitation approaches and makes recommendations for change to the Secretary of State.

Despite the complex calculations that are undertaken to facilitate equitable resource allocation, the NHS is unable to fund every treatment that might be clinically indicated. It is inevitable that funding certain treatments means that other forms of treatment cannot be resourced. Politicians have tended to skirt the issue of inevitable NHS resource constraints by focusing on cost improvements, efficiency savings and targets.

In contemporary health-care practice, resource allocation decisions are made principally with respect to some of the newer therapies and technologies that are often expensive. It is easy to understand why decisions not to fund treatment can lead to social outcry and legal challenge.

2.18 Statutory provisions

Section 1 of the National Health Service Act 2006 obliges the Secretary of State to provide 'a comprehensive health service designed to secure improvement –

(a) in the physical and mental health of the people of England, and
(b) in the prevention, diagnosis and treatment of illness'.

This duty is usually discharged through the PCTs who arrange for general practice, ophthalmic, dental and pharmaceutical services. Primary care services are mostly provided by the GP who also refer patients to secondary and tertiary care.

It is highly unlikely that the Secretary of State would be found to be in breach of the statutory duty under section 1 of the National Health Service Act 2006. In *Re HIV Haemophiliac Litigation* (1990) 41 BMLR 171, the Court of Appeal accepted that the predecessor to section 1 (section 3 of the National Health Service Act 1977) did not provide the basis of an action for breach of statutory duty. Furthermore, in *R v Secretary of State for Social Services ex p Hincks* (1980) 1 BMLR 93, the Court of Appeal clearly stated that the duty of the Secretary of State for Health was to the extent considered necessary to meet all reasonable requirements and which could be provided within the resources available. Resource constraints can therefore be taken into account when deciding whether or not to offer a particular treatment to an individual patient or group of patients.

2.19 Judicial review

It is clear that financial considerations and resource availability can be taken into account in the decision whether to offer treatment to a patient. However, a challenge to a rationing decision may be brought in the courts by way of judicial review on the grounds that the decision is illegal (meaning that the decision-maker did not have power to make that decision) or that the decision was irrational (meaning that the decision was so unreasonable that no reasonable decision-maker would have arrived at it), or that there was an error in the procedure used to reach that decision. A number of reasons may underlie a consideration of judicial review.

2.19.1 Financial considerations

One of the earlier cases of judicial review was *R v Cambridge DHA ex p B* [1995] 2 All ER 129. B was a 10-year-old girl with leukaemia and her father applied for judicial review of the decision of Cambridge district health authority not to fund further treatment. She had previously had a bone marrow transplant and chemotherapy. Medical opinion was divided in that her doctors in Cambridge believed that B had only a few weeks to live and that any further treatment would be futile. However, other doctors in London and the United States felt that further treatment would be of benefit. Her father sought judicial review of the health authority's refusal to pay. He was successful in the High Court but lost in the Court of Appeal, and the arguments are instructive.

At first instance Laws J emphasised B's right to life under Article 2 of the Convention, which meant that compelling reasons had to be provided to justify the needs of other patients over hers. In his view, 'where the question is whether the life of a 10-year-old child might be saved by however slim a chance, the responsible authority must...do more than toll the bell of tight resources. They must explain the priorities that have led them to decline to fund treatment. They have not adequately done so here'. Laws J therefore quashed the health authority's decision and required them to re-examine the question (although he did not order treatment to be funded). The authority appealed to the Court of Appeal using the standard test for reasonableness of the decision based on *Wednesbury* principles of whether the decision was so unreasonable that no reasonable decision-maker could have made it. On this basis the first instance decision was overturned. While the Court of Appeal showed great sympathy to B's position, Sir Thomas Bingham MR (at 136) remarked that in a perfect world, any treatment which might offer any chance of survival would be provided. However, it would be

> shutting one's eyes to the real world if the court were to proceed on the basis that we do live in such a world. It is common knowledge that health authorities of all kinds are constantly pressed to make ends meet...difficult and agonising judgements have to be made as to how

a limited budget is best allocated to the maximum advantage of the maximum number of patients. That is not a judgement which the court can make.

It remains unclear as to how the Court of Appeal would have disentangled funding issues from those concerning conflict of medical opinion. Interestingly, B went on to have treatment in the United States (funded by an anonymous benefactor) and survived until May 1996, more than a year longer than had been expected by medical opinion in Cambridge.

In *R (Rogers) v Swindon NHS Primary Care Trust* [2006] EWCA Civ. 392, Mrs Rogers sought judicial review of the PCT's decision to refuse to fund her breast cancer treatment with Herceptin (an unlicensed drug). Initially she had self-funded her treatment but when her savings ran out she applied to the PCT. The PCT justified its refusal on the grounds that their policy was to fund treatment in exceptional circumstances only and determined that none existed in her particular situation. The Court of Appeal found that there was no rational basis in such cases for distinguishing between exceptional and non-exceptional circumstances. Such a policy would be legal only if the policy-maker had envisaged the types of case that would be exceptional. Since the PCT had not done this, its policy was irrational and unlawful. It is noteworthy that the PCT had declared that costs were not a relevant factor. This finding was of central importance to the Court's reasoning and it seems that had the PCT openly declared that financial considerations were an essential factor in the funding decision, then it would have been legitimate to deny medication on the grounds of cost.

In *R (Otley) v Barking and Dagenham NHS PCT* [2007] EWHC 1927 (Admin), Ms Otley sought judicial review of the trust's refusal to fund treatment using an anticancer medication known as Avastin. The Panel (of the trust that rejected Ms Otley's case) had received reports in favour of the drug, but had noted that Avastin had not been used as part of a cocktail of medication. The court found that the Panel had failed to give sufficient weight to the fact that the regime of drugs was the only one available and that the possibility that Avastin could extend Ms Otley's life by a few months was an important opportunity that she should be allowed to have. The court had emphasised that the decision in Ms Otley's case was not one that was decided on arguments of resources.

It appears that an application for judicial review is more likely to succeed where there are procedural irregularities and if proper reasons for the determination have not been given. It therefore seems necessary that an authority accurately assesses the nature of the illness and the effectiveness of treatment. Proper weight should be given to the effectiveness of treatment as part of the assessment to determine whether or not treatment should be resourced. In *Rogers* and *Otley* the trusts' decisions to decline funding had not been justified on the basis of lack of resources. The reported decisions appear to imply that if decision-making bodies are frank about resource factors, the courts are less likely to interfere with the decisions in recognition that difficult resource allocation decisions have to be made.

A new biologic therapy is clinically indicated and available for Javed's arthritis but his doctor is unable to prescribe the drug due to the high cost of therapy.

▶ Consider the basis of lawful resource allocation decisions.
▶ Is it likely that Javed would be successful in an application for judicial review of the decision not to provide treatment?

2.19.2 Policies and human rights

At first instance in *R v Cambridge DHA, ex p B* (see 2.19.1), Laws J considered the application of Article 2 in delivering judgement in favour of the claimant even though this decision predated the Human Rights Act 1998. The extent to which human rights legislation might impact upon applications for judicial review of resource allocation decisions can perhaps be gleaned from *R v North West Lancashire Health Authority ex p A* [2000] 1 WLR 977. The applicants applied for judicial review of the health authority's decision to refuse access to gender reassignment surgery. Two of the claimants had confirmed diagnoses of clinical need, and the third was awaiting confirmation.

The health authority had a policy in relation to gender reassignment surgery and it was deemed that the effectiveness of the procedure was equivocal. Exceptions were provided for on the basis of overriding clinical need, although it had been anticipated that such exceptions would be rare, unpredictable and based upon circumstances that could not be envisaged at the time the policy was brought into force. On judicial review of the health authority's decision to refuse, the first instance decision was in favour of the claimants and was subsequently upheld by the Court of Appeal.

A policy that is predetermined and is unresponsive to individual needs will not be lawful. In *R v North West Lancashire Health Authority*, the policy against funding of gender reassignment surgery was unlawful since it had the effect of fettering the discretion of the health authority and failed to take into account the individual facts and needs of each particular person. The Court of Appeal acknowledged that in establishing its priorities, each health authority would give greater priority to life-threatening and other grave illnesses, and that the allocation and weighting of such priorities was a matter of judgement for each Authority. Auld LJ explained that a policy to position trans-sexualism low in the order of priorities of illnesses for treatment and to deny treatment except in exceptional circumstances, such as overriding clinical need, was not in principle irrational. Such policy would, however, genuinely need to recognise the possibility of there being an overriding need and the health authority gave no indication as to what might amount to an overriding need or of any other exceptional circumstances. According to Auld LJ (at 996) the policy was flawed in two important respects:

> First, it does not in truth treat trans-sexualism as an illness, but as an attitude or state of mind which does not warrant medical treatment. Second, the ostensible provision that it makes for exceptions in individual cases and its manner of considering them amount effectively to the operation of a 'blanket policy' against funding treatment for the condition because it does not believe in such treatment.

Accordingly, since this was effectively a blanket policy, the health authority was asked to reformulate its guidelines in order to allow for exceptions in individual cases.

At the time that *R v North West Health Authority* was decided, the Human Rights Act 1998 had been enacted but was not yet in force. Nonetheless, the court considered the possible impact of Articles 3 and 8 of the Convention. With regard to Article 3, Buxton LJ stated that this addresses positive conduct (by public officials) of a high degree of seriousness and opprobrium, and any attempt to bring the present case under Article 3 would strain both language and common sense and trivialise the Article in respect of the very important values that it protects. The situation with Article 8 was less straightforward. Since a person's sexual behaviour and orientation is an important aspect of private life, Buxton LJ considered that on the facts of the case Article 8 would undoubtedly engage, although this had not been invoked in argument because the Human Rights Act 1998 had not yet been brought into force.

A blanket policy will inevitably be declared unlawful on judicial review. However, policy based on cogent reasons would be likely to succeed, as seen in *R v Secretary of State for Health ex p Pfizer Ltd* [1999] Lloyds Med Rep 289. In this case, the Secretary of State had issued a health service circular aimed at limiting the prescription of Viagra by general practitioners, a decision that was challenged by the drug company Pfizer. The terms and conditions for NHS GPs provide that a doctor shall order drugs or appliances which are necessary for the treatment of any patient to whom she is providing treatment. The action for judicial review succeeded. The court held that a doctor is entitled to give such treatment as necessary and clinically appropriate. The Secretary of State subsequently issued regulations to restrict the prescription of Viagra on the basis of cost. Pfizer's ensuing challenge failed, the Court of Appeal finding that the restrictions were objective, verifiable and based upon the legitimate aim of improving the economic situation of the health system. This rationale is in alignment with the subsequent decisions in *Rogers* and *Otley* where explicit economic restrictions were lawfully provided that these were legitimately reasoned (Syrett, 2004).

It appears that Article 3 did not engage in the aforementioned rationing decisions because of the high threshold. While Article 8 might be considered to engage, the *North West Lancashire* case indicates that it cannot be relied upon to found a right to receive treatment. One possibility would be for a challenge to be brought against a resource allocation decision under Article 2, for instance where there has been a refusal of life-saving treatment. The Article 14 right to protection from discrimination might be persuasive if an applicant can claim that resource allocation was discriminatory on the grounds of race, sex or religious belief, although this seems unlikely. However, there may be grounds to base a claim on age or disability. Although these factors are not expressly mentioned as examples under Article 14, the courts might be willing to give these matters greater attention.

2.19.3 Procedural irregularities

A successful action in judicial review can be brought if the NHS body has either failed to take into account relevant considerations or has taken into account irrelevant considerations in its decision making. In *R v North Derbyshire HA ex p Fisher* (1997) 38 BMLR 76, the applicants successfully challenged the North Derbyshire Health Authority's refusal to fund the drug beta-interferon. The court found procedural irregularities in the decision-making process of the health authority in that it had failed to follow an NHS circular without explanation as to why it had done so. The health authority operated a blanket policy not to fund beta-interferon unless there were clinical trials being undertaken. In the circumstances there were no trials being undertaken and this decision was also against existing Department of Health guidance.

2.19.4 Legitimate expectations

A successful application for judicial review can be brought if an NHS body has created a legitimate expectation and then alters its policy so that it disadvantages those who have relied upon that expectation (*R v North and East Devon Health Authority ex p Coughlan* – see 2.5.2).

2.20 The Equality Act 2010

It remains unclear as to how the Equality Act 2010 will impact upon resource allocation decisions. The Act prohibits discrimination on the basis of disability. Section 6(1) provides that a person (P) has a disability if (a) P has a physical or mental impairment, and (b) the impairment has a substantial and long-term adverse effect on P's ability to carry out normal day-to-day activities. An impairment is one that affects the ability of the person concerned to carry out normal day-to-day activities if it affects mobility, manual dexterity, physical co-ordination, continence, the ability to lift, carry or move everyday objects, speech, hearing or eyesight, memory or ability to concentrate, learn or understand, or perception of the risk of physical danger. It would be unlawful for a health-care organisation not to allocate resources purely on the basis of a physical problem, or a physical problem if that person also suffered from a mental illness. This might have particular relevance for those with long-term disabilities, such as chronic arthritis. It seems likely that an NHS body in allocating resources will circumvent the disability issue and create policies based on prioritisation due to financial constraints, backed up by verifiable reasons and evidence.

2.21 Effect of EU law

Resource allocation in the NHS needs to be considered in the context of European law as illustrated by *R (on the application of Watts) v Secretary of State for Health* [2004] EWCA Civ 166.

In 1998, the European Court of Justice (ECJ) ruled that citizens of Member States have the right to obtain planned health care in a Member State other than their home State. Article 56 of the Treaty pertains to the free movement of services (formerly Article 49 of the EC Treaty) and prohibits restrictions on the freedom to provide services across Member States. Article 56 provides: 'restrictions on the freedom to provide services within the Union shall be prohibited in respect of nationals of Member States who are established in a Member State other than that of the person for whom the services are intended'. Health care is a service covered by Article 56 and Member State citizens may exercise their free movement rights in order to access health services of other Member States.

Medical treatment falls within this category as above (*Luisi and Carbone v Ministero del Tesoro (cases 286/82 and 26/83)* [1984] ECR 377). Article 22 of Regulation 1408/71 allows Member State nationals to travel to other Member States for health care at the expense of the home State provided that they are authorised to do so by their home State. Article 22(2) (as amended by Council Regulation 2793/81) provides that authorisation may not be refused

> where the treatment in question is among the benefits provided for by the legislation of the Member State on whose territory the person concerned resides and where he cannot be given such treatment within the time normally necessary for obtaining the treatment in question in the Member State of residence taking account of his current state of health and the probable course of the disease.

Taken together, Articles 56 and 22 permit free movement between Member States for the purposes of health care and that this can be reimbursed subject to prior authorisation. Refusal to reimburse the costs of treatment has been subject to legal challenge in two principal decisions, *Geraets-Smits and Peerbooms* C157–99 [2001] and

Müller-Fauré and *van Riet (Case C-385/99)* [2003]. In *Geraets-Smits*, the ECJ held that medical services that fell within the EC Treaty applied to hospital services that had been paid for. Furthermore, any limitations that Member States could impose on individuals' ability to access services in other Member States must be proportionate in the context of an overriding public interest. In *Müller-Fauré* it was suggested that as far as hospital services were concerned, treatment without prior authorisation would fundamentally undermine the planning of hospital services. Notwithstanding this, the ECJ would be prepared to scrutinise what amounted to an undue delay. An undue delay could be because of long waiting lists and these situations were subsequently confirmed by the ECJ in *Inizan v Caisse primaire d'assurance maladie des Hauts-de-Seine (Case C-56/01)* [2003]. In *Inizan* the ECJ confirmed that some restrictions which Member States might impose would be justifiable in order to prevent any subsequent instability within their own national health systems provided that such restrictions were necessary and proportionate.

The case of *Watts* (as above) concerned a 72-year-old woman with severe osteoarthritis who required a bilateral hip replacement. There was a 12-month waiting time and her case was allocated to the routine waiting list. She applied to have surgery in France on the basis of an E-112 form under Article 22 of regulation 1408/71. Her request was refused by the PCT on the basis that the 12-month wait did not amount to an 'undue delay' (one of the criteria for authorisation). On application for judicial review her situation was considered to be more urgent and a revised waiting time of 3–4 months was given. In the meantime Mrs Watts proceeded with treatment in France and attempted to claim the costs of surgery on her return. Her claim was rejected.

At first instance Munby J held that the principles of free movements were applicable in relation to services on the NHS. However, on the facts Mrs Watts had not been subjected to an undue delay as required by Article 22 since treatment would be available within the normal waiting time for this type of treatment in a Member State. On appeal, May LJ, held that determination of whether an undue delay was involved was a matter of clinical judgement and the impact of the delay had to be considered in the context of the current state of health and the probable disease progression in each individual patient. Therefore, if clinical judgement, according to further orthopaedic opinion, was that a 3 or 4-month waiting period was acceptable, then this was what a court would normally ratify. Nonetheless, the Court of Appeal was of the view that given the wide-ranging policy implications of the decision, there was a need for a preliminary ruling from the ECJ to clarify the application of Articles 49 and 22 in this instance.

The ECJ provided a detailed judgement (Case C372/04 *Watts v Bedford Primary Care Trust* [2006] ECR I-4352). However, the crucial aspect was framed as the 'seventh' question which was: 'Are Article 49 EC and Article 22 of Regulation 1408/71 to be interpreted as imposing an obligation on Member States to fund hospital treatment in other Member States without reference to budgetary constraints...' In answer, the ECJ stated that there must be an obligation on the competent institution (under Articles 22 and 49) to authorise a patient registered with the NHS to obtain at that organisation's own expense hospital treatment in another Member State where the waiting time exceeds an acceptable period. Interpretation of the word acceptable had to be considered with regard to an objective medical assessment of the patient's condition, to include factors such as clinical history, the likely cause of the illness, the degree of pain and suffering, the nature of the disability and the outcome if there was a delay. Economic factors and budgetary constraints were not relevant considerations.

The impact of the ECJ's decision in *Watts* is that there is a need for NHS bodies to establish a system of prior authorisation for cross-border treatments. The system should be non-discriminatory, impartial, accessible and capable of being challenged by judicial review. The reason for having treatment abroad will principally depend upon clinical judgement and is not to be determined by economic factors.

There are several implications of this decision. One possibility is that those who are able to travel abroad may bypass NHS waiting lists and this could offer a possible solution for the middle classes. In theory, this could undermine national policy by encouraging low priority patients to receive treatment abroad. Treatment of patients in Member States would mean that patients had to be given information about this possibility; second, that this may give rise to difficulties in terms of litigation should something go wrong while they are treated abroad; and third, that cross-border purchasing and provision of health care may need to be included as an aspect of service commissioning.

2.22   Resource allocation in practice

In the past, rationing decisions have tended to be covert and made on the basis of either insubstantial evidence to support a treatment modality or alternatively by declaring that an intervention is not clinically indicated in a patient's particular circumstances. The thrust was principally to discourage front-line NHS staff from being wasteful of resources and the process of resource allocation was fragmented into individualised transactions between doctors and patient to maintain the fiction that the NHS could meet all requirements at all times. Over the past decade, resource allocation decisions have become more overt through the remit of NICE.

2.22.1   National Institute for Health and Clinical Excellence

NICE was created in 1999 to reduce what is colloquially known as the 'postcode lottery', meaning that the place where people live defines the availability and quality of the health care they can expect to receive. Nowadays, NICE is responsible for setting standards to ensure uniform and consistent high quality health care throughout the country. One of its principal roles has been the development and dissemination of evidence-based guidance for the management of diseases and conditions and to disseminate these to front-line staff and patients (Samanta et al., 2003). Health economics and cost–benefit assessments of its advice have been taken into account in its recommendations. Professor Sir Michael Rawlins (2004), the Chair of NICE, explains that 'The Institute will have to take into account the NHS's broad clinical priorities and the broad balance between benefits and costs. The Institute will have to take into account guidance from ministers on the resources likely to be available; and the Institute will have to ensure that the technology represents an effective use of available resources'. NICE has accordingly used health economics and the impact of resources in its reasoning and decision-making processes. NICE's processes are expected to be transparent and could be subject to judicial review. In considering whether or not to recommend a treatment or intervention, NICE takes into account the clinical needs and the evidence base for the available technology, the priorities of the NHS, the balance between benefits and cost, the impact upon other NHS resources and guidance from the government in terms of the availability of resources. Smith (2000) has been critical of NICE and its decision-making processes in that many decisions are made on the basis of data and a computer. However, evidence alone cannot make the decision and patient and community values must be an integral part of the outcome. NICE produces clinical guidelines for health care which by definition means that this is guidance rather than mandatory orders. Nonetheless, there is some evidence to suggest that guidance from an influential body such as NICE may be instrumental in influencing the legal standard of care (Samanta et al., 2006).

The National Audit Office (2005) examined compliance with NICE guidance and reported that a third of responding trusts stated that they were not able to fully fund NICE recommendations and that NICE guidance was not integrated into financial planning decisions taken by NHS organisations. This finding raises a host of issues that can be categorised into three main areas: management, whether poor management is the root cause within such organisations; the impact of cost constraints and persistent variations in clinical care between different geographical locations.

2.22.2 Methodology of rationing

The most commonly used methodology for determining the cost-effectiveness of treatment is the quality adjusted life year (QALY) which is a crude indicator that assesses the additional quality and quantity of life that can be expected following specific health-care interventions, and the cost of such treatment. A treatment that provides 1 year of perfect health will be worth one QALY, whereas death will be equivalent to zero. Less than a perfect year can range anywhere between 0 and 1. A relatively inexpensive intervention that offers a high number of QALYs would be considered highly cost effective. Thus, cervical cancer screening for women aged between 20 and 59 years amounts to £200 per QALY and is considered highly effective. A breast cancer screening programme amounts to around £7,000 per QALY and hospital dialysis for end-stage renal disease in a patient aged between 55 and 64 would amount to £45,000 per QALY.

The use of QALYs is not without its problems. A principal objection is that it is not possible to determine or translate a person's quality of life into pure monetary terms. Furthermore, it is believed that QALYs might discriminate against older persons and those with disabilities. An older person, or one who is disabled, is likely to require a greater sum of money per QALY when compared to a younger person who was previously fit. QALYs may have the effect of assessing the 'worth' of a person through value judgements. According to Quigley (2007), using QALYs to undertake cost–benefit analyses means that one is effectively balancing the quality of one person's life against that of another, using a mathematical formula approach. As a result, QALYs make a value judgement about the worth of patients' lives by determining a numerical score that forms the basis for assessing which people should be treated from limited resources.

An alternative approach to resource allocation is to allow unlimited access and availability for all, although this utopian ideal is impossible for any publicly funded service. Society might take a collective view as to how health-care resources ought to be allocated. Alternatively, each individual might agree that after a certain age there should be a decrease in the availability of certain services because there comes a point when it might be right to focus on the health-care needs of those who have yet to reach their normal lifespan, especially for those who have already enjoyed a full life. Another possibility would be for a list to be drawn up that prioritises cost-effective treatments, and funding could be allocated to those ranked at the top. It seems inevitable that resource allocation in health care will always be controversial.

E Confidentiality

2.23 The basis of confidentiality

The origin of the confidential relationship between doctor and patient and the doctor's duty to respect this relationship is found in the Hippocratic Oath. Matters that pertain to a patient's health are private to that individual. From a duty-based perspective, confidentiality serves to emphasise the patient's right to privacy. From a consequentialist point of view, effective care can only be provided if a patient can be honest with the doctor and the foundation of this honesty is based upon the tacit understanding that the doctor will not disclose personal information. This can be particularly important and relevant when ascertaining sexual history, psychological and familial factors that pertain to health. Some medical enquiries can be intrusive on a person's private life but nevertheless necessary within that particular context, and patients would be unlikely to disclose such information unless they were assured of confidentiality.

From a utilitarian perspective, the confidential doctor-patient relationship serves to encourage individuals to seek medical advice. The absence of confidentiality would deter some patients from seeking treatment, and the duty of confidentiality could be justified on this basis alone. However, this relationship must be considered within the context of close relationships and some patients may prefer not to keep information secret from their immediate relatives or close friends. This is often seen in clinical practice where a patient arrives for a consultation with a relative or a friend, and this can be particularly relevant in situations where the doctor has to break bad news or where there is an underlying serious medical condition.

The duty of confidentiality, however, is not absolute. To provide adequate medical care, aspects of the patient's medical condition will need to be shared with other health-care professionals. Furthermore, while there is an obvious advantage in maintaining confidentiality for the patient, there may be circumstances where the duty of confidentiality can be overridden in the public interest.

2.24 Case law

The duty of confidence is well established in the common law. In *AG v Guardian Newspapers* (2) [1990] 1 AC 109 (the Spycatcher case), the court explained that the duty of confidence arises from an obligation in good conscience. Lord Goff stated that a duty of confidence arises 'when confidential information comes to the knowledge of a person (the confidant) in circumstances where he has notice, or is held to have agreed, that the information is confidential, with the effect that it would be just in all the circumstances that he should be precluded from disclosing the information to others'. Medical information is generally treated as confidential information. Within the context of medical law, confidentiality is also protected by Article 8(1) of the Convention whereby everyone has a right to respect for his private life, which will include medical matters. However, the duty to respect confidentiality is not absolute and, as per Lord Goff, can be trumped in the event of a weightier public interest in the disclosure. Likewise, the derogation under Article 8(2) of the Convention serves to qualify the Article 8(1) right if interference with the right is in accordance with the law and necessary in a democratic society. Thus, establishing that disclosure is justifiable would prevent a claim based on breach of confidentiality.

From a human rights perspective, justification under Article 8(2) was apparent in *Z v Finland* (1997) 25 EHRR 371. Z was married to a HIV positive man who had been charged with a number of sexual offences. The police sought and gained access to Z's medical records to determine when her husband had become aware of his HIV status. The European Court of Human Rights held that seizure of Z's medical records did not violate Article 8 because of the legitimate aim being pursued and the proportionate measures that were being used. The court accepted that the interests of patients and the community in protecting confidentiality of medical data could be outweighed by public interests in the investigation and prosecution of crime. This principle was again tested in *Szuluk v United Kingdom* (2009) 108 BMLR 190. The applicant had been sentenced to 14 years' imprisonment for conspiring to supply Class A drugs. On return to prison following cranial surgery he required continued monitoring and biannual hospital check-ups. He subsequently applied for judicial review of the prison authority's decision to refuse to allow him to correspond with his consultant in confidence, on the grounds of interference with his rights to privacy as protected by Article 8(1) of the Convention. The European Court of Human Rights considered that in the circumstances the applicant's Article 8 rights had been violated. It was considered significant that he had been suffering from a life-threatening disorder that required continuous medical supervision. In the circumstances monitoring his medical correspondence had not struck a fair balance with his right to privacy.

Stone v South East Coast SHA [2006] EWHC 1668 concerned the issue of confidentiality with respect of medical treatment. Michael Stone was a convicted murderer who sought to suppress publication of the homicide enquiry which included reference to his medical treatment. The judge concluded that a redacted version of the report would not be appropriate and might also be perceived to be a 'cover up'. The judge accepted that the most persuasive argument in favour of Mr Stone was his entitlement to the right of privacy as protected by Article 8 of the Convention. The force of that claim was, however, outweighed by other considerations such as the genuine public interest in knowing of the actual care and treatment that had been given in order to reach an informed assessment of the case. On undertaking a balancing exercise between his right to confidentiality and the public interest, disclosure of the medical information was justified.

It is possible that Articles 6 and 10 might also engage in the context of the Article 8 right to privacy. In *Campbell v MGM Ltd* [2004] UKHL 22, supermodel Naomi Campbell accepted that the media was entitled to disclose that she was a drug addict. However, she sought to prevent publication of her attendance at Narcotics Anonymous alongside photographic evidence on the grounds that this amounted to a breach of her privacy. The newspaper sought to publish this information under the freedom of expression provision of Article 10 of the Convention. In balancing the rights of Article 10 against Article 8, Baroness Hale stated that in this particular instance, publication would cause Ms Campbell harm and that it was the risk of harm that mattered at that stage, rather than proof that actual harm had occurred. Those attempting to recover from drug addiction needed dedication and commitment, along with positive reinforcement from others. Organisations such as Narcotics Anonymous could do much good and media interference at a stage when the patient was acknowledged to be 'fragile' could cause a considerable set back.

In *R (on the application of B) v Stafford Combined Court* [2006] EWHC 1645 (Admin), B was a 14-year-old girl who was the main witness in the trial of the defendant, who was accused (and subsequently convicted) of sexually abusing her. The defendant's advisors sought to access B's psychiatric records on the grounds that these were relevant to her credibility as a witness. In balancing B's right to confidentiality under Article 8 and the defendant's right to a fair trial under Article 6, the judge concluded (at first instance) that the right to a fair trial outweighed the right to confidentiality and ordered disclosure of the girl's records. This decision was trenchantly criticised on appeal on the grounds that it was unacceptable for a 14-year-old schoolgirl with a history of attempted suicide to be brought to court at short notice with the apparent choice of agreeing to disclosure of her psychiatric records or to delay a trial which was already causing her distress. B had not been given due notice of the application for the witness summons, nor had she been given the opportunity to make representations before the order was made. The Court of Appeal concluded that interference with her rights (of confidentiality) was not necessary within the derogation of Article 8(2) and in fact that the lower court had acted in a way that was incompatible with B's Convention rights.

2.25 The Data Protection Act 1998

The Data Protection Act 1998 (DPA) implements the European Directive 95/46/EC and provides for the regulation of the processing of information, including personal data, and the obtaining, holding, use or disclosure of such data. Under the first principle of data protection, all personal data must be processed fairly and lawfully. This is stated in Schedule 1 as follows:

> Personal data shall be processed fairly and lawfully and, in particular, shall not be processed unless –
>
> (a) at least one of the conditions in Schedule 2 is met, and
> (b) in the case of sensitive personal data, at least one of the conditions in Schedule 3 is also met.

Schedule 2 outlines the conditions that are relevant for the purposes of processing personal data fairly and lawfully. Such data may be processed by the data controller if the subject has given his consent, although even in the absence of consent certain exceptions may apply:

▶ For the performance of a contract to which the data subject is a party
▶ To comply with any legal obligation to which the data controller is subject
▶ To protect the vital interests of the data subject
▶ Processing is necessary for the administration of justice
▶ For the exercise of functions of the Houses of Parliament
▶ For the exercise of any functions conferred on any person by or under any enactment
▶ For the exercise of any functions of the Crown, a minister of the Crown or a government department
▶ For the exercise of any other functions of a public nature exercised in the public interest by any person
▶ For the purposes of legitimate interests pursued by the data controller or by the third party or parties for whom data is disclosed
▶ The Secretary of State may by order specify particular circumstances.

In the context of health care, processing of data might be necessary where the patient's life is in danger and this might fall within the exception for protecting the vital interests of the data subject. Data processing might also be necessary for promoting a comprehensive health service through registries, such as cancer registry, registries of procedures such as prosthetic joint replacement, and registries for innovative interventions, such as the use of biologic therapies for inflammatory conditions. Data processing might also be considered necessary for the purposes of the data controller's legitimate interests, for example, processing data for training, and audit purposes.

Data processing of sensitive personal data, such as ethnic origin, political opinions, religious beliefs and medical history, requires that the person has given explicit consent. Processing can also be lawful if necessary to protect the vital interests of the data subject or another person if consent cannot be given, is likely to be unreasonably withheld in compliance with Schedule 3. With regard to data for health-care purposes, Schedule 3, paragraph 8 provides that

(1) The processing is necessary for medical purposes and is undertaken by –
    (a) a health professional, or
    (b) a person who in the circumstances owes a duty of confidentiality which is equivalent to that which would arise if that person were a health professional.
(2) In this paragraph 'medical purposes' includes the purposes of preventative medicine, medical diagnosis, medical research, the provision of care and treatment and the management of healthcare services.

Schedule 3 is comparatively broad and allows sensitive personal data to be processed by a health-care professional, or another, who owes an equivalent duty of confidentiality. It permits data processing as necessary to protect the vital interests of individuals and where the consent of the data subject cannot be given or is likely to be withheld by data subject. Such information can be disclosed without consent in order to protect the health of a third party.

Breach of the DPA requires the data subject to serve a notice requiring cessation or refraining from possessing personal data; or the data subject may apply for a court order that the data controller rectifies or destroys the inaccurate data; it is also possible for the data subject to seek compensation.

2.26 Exceptions to confidentiality

Breaches of confidentiality may be inadvertent and might typically arise through indiscrete conversations, from leaving medical records in unsecure environments, from failing to log out of computer programmes that include medical information or during teaching and training when identifiable information may be inadvertently released. However, the duty of confidentiality is not absolute and there are circumstances where disclosure of medical information can be legitimate.

2.26.1 Consent

Explicit consent is perhaps the most obvious way by which a doctor can be relieved of the duty of confidentiality. The issue becomes more contentious in the event that it is alleged that a patient has given implied consent to disclosure. Many would generally accept that medical information will be shared within the health-care team although it is good practice to highlight this likelihood with patients, particularly if identifiable information is being shared. The patient's understanding of the implications ought to be checked and this is particularly apposite where a patient may have initially given consent for disclosure and subsequently withdraws this, or *vice versa*.

If a patient undergoes a medical examination on behalf of a third party, for example, for insurance purposes or for employment, then it is a moot point as to whether there is implied consent for disclosure of the medical report to the employer. In *Kapadia v London Borough of Lambeth* [2000] 57 BMLR 170, this issue was considered by the Court of Appeal and *dicta* provides that the report should be 'disclosed by the doctor to the employers. No further consent was required from the claimant. By consenting to being examined on behalf of the employers the claimant was consenting to the disclosure to the employers of a report resulting from that examination'. While this most certainly represents one approach, an alternative perspective is that the doctor who discloses such information has breached the duty of confidentiality, if not in law then certainly in terms of professional ethics and could therefore be subject to disciplinary action by the medical regulator. In these specific circumstances, disclosure of information to the employer that is directly related to the impact of work upon their health or the impact of health upon the workplace might be relevant, but disclosure of other medical information might be very hard to justify.

> Javed attends a conference and recognises that his case is being discussed and that his first name appears on one of the slides.
>
> ▶ What are Javed's rights here, if any?
> ▶ Can the presentation be considered educational?
> ▶ What legislative provisions, if any, apply given that Javed's name appears on the presentation?
> ▶ What exceptions exist to confidentiality?
> ▶ What should the doctor have done if he wanted to present this case?

2.26.2　The 'need to know' situation

A general exception to the duty of confidence is where disclosure is required to another professional in order to hand over, or share, that patient's care and as is the norm in team-based NHS care. In addition to health professionals, administrative staff might well also need access to information to process medical records and to liaise with other agencies such as Social Services in readiness for discharge and possibly care in the community. In *R v Department of Health, ex p Source Informatics Ltd* [2000] 1 All ER 786, the Court of Appeal held that disclosure of anonymous patient information for market research purposes would not necessarily represent a breach of confidence even if patients had not given express consent. The reasons for this decision are not entirely clear but might be based upon public interest and to ensure that health services can operate.

The Confidentiality and Disclosure Health Information Toolkit (BMA, 2009) provided by the British Medical Association (BMA) states (at 12):

> In the absence of evidence to the contrary, patients are normally considered to have given implied consent for the use of their information by health professionals for the purpose of the care they receive. Information sharing in this context is acceptable to the extent that health professionals share what is necessary and relevant for patient care on a 'need to know' basis.

Schedules 2 and 3 of the DPA (see 2.25) include the broad category of 'medical purposes' as being within the public interest and justifies the processing of data without the subject's consent. However, the 'need to know' exception is narrowly interpreted by the BMA as information that is 'both necessary and relevant for patient care' and cannot therefore be considered as an all-inclusive justification for sharing information.

2.26.3   Prevention of harm to others

Prevention of harm to others represents one circumstance where the public interest in disclosure of medical information may trump the duty of confidentiality. In *W v Egdell* [1990] Ch 359, W had killed five people and had been detained in a secure hospital. He applied for release and his solicitor asked for an independent psychiatric opinion, which indicated that he was still a risk to the public. This report was disclosed by Dr Egdell to the Secretary of State. W applied for an injunction on the basis of breach of confidence and failed. Bingham LJ (at 424) indicated that the balancing exercise in *Egdell* was relatively straightforward in that while there was a strong public interest in maintaining the duty of confidence, such a duty was not absolute. This duty could be overridden where there is a stronger public interest in disclosure since

> [w]here a man has committed multiple killings under the disability of serious mental illness, decisions which may lead directly or indirectly to his release from hospital should not be made unless a responsible authority is properly able to make an informed judgement that the risk of repetition is so small as to be acceptable. A consultant psychiatrist who becomes aware, even in the course of a confidential relationship, of information which leads him, in the exercise of what the court considers a sound professional judgement, to fear that such decisions may be made on the basis of inadequate information and with a real risk of consequent danger to the public is entitled to take such steps as are reasonable in all the circumstances to communicate the grounds of his concern to the responsible authorities.

Egdell illustrates that the duty of confidentiality can be overridden in the interests of protection of the public. *Tarasoff v Regents of the University of California* 551 P. 2d 334 (Cal. 1976) shows that this duty can extend to the need to warn an individual who is not a patient. The patient had confided to a psychotherapist that he intended to harm a fellow student, Tarasoff, who had rejected his advances. The therapist informed the police but did not inform Tarasoff herself, who was subsequently murdered. The Supreme Court of California held that the University psychotherapist was under a duty to protect Tarasoff by disclosing the threats to her. An obligation arises to protect an intended victim from violence and although there is a public interest in safeguarding the duty of confidentiality, this must yield to disclosure in order to prevent harm to others. In a dissenting judgement, however, Clarke J stated that imposing a duty to warn a third party significantly increases the risk of commitment of those who are mentally ill since the number of patients who make threats is considerable even though few of these threats are ever executed. It is unlikely that a case like *Tarasoff* will pose a legal duty to warn in the United Kingdom because of lack of proximity between the intended victim and the confidante.

2.26.4   Prevention or detection of crime

Medical records are classified as 'excluded material' to which the police would not normally be allowed access under sections 11 and 12 of the Police and Criminal Evidence Act 1984. An exception is provided where there is an investigation for a 'serious arrestable offence', in which case the police may obtain a special procedure warrant which requires the disclosure of such records.

Disclosure in order to detect crime is considered to be in the public interest. However, what is classified as serious crime is not entirely clear. Evidently, serious crime includes murder, manslaughter, rape, treason, kidnapping, child abuse or other cases where individuals may suffer serious harm. Serious harm may also occur through crime involving the security of the State or public order. Generally the detection of crime of such sorts would warrant a breach of confidentiality (Department of Health, 2003a). In contrast, crime such as theft, fraud or damage to property would generally not warrant a breach of confidence.

Under section 172 of the Road Traffic Act 1988, a person can be required to give information which may lead to the identification of a driver alleged to have committed an offence, a duty that could extend to a doctor who is treating a patient. In *Hunter v Mann* [1974] QB 767, a doctor had treated two people involved in a road traffic accident. The doctor later refused to disclose the names and addresses of the persons he had treated to a police officer on the grounds of confidentiality. As a result he was convicted under the (then applicable) Road Traffic Act 1972 and this was upheld on appeal. The court recognised the conflict that the doctor had faced with respect to breaching confidentiality on one hand and providing information to the police for a legitimate purpose on the other. However, in these circumstances the doctor had only to disclose information pertaining to the identification of the individuals and the duty would not extend to matters that relate to the individual's medical history.

2.26.5 Child protection

Re M [1990] 1 All ER 205 has established that when evidence comes to light in confidential circumstances that a person may be abusing a child, then a breach of confidence would be lawful provided that the welfare of the child is protected. It could be argued that there is an obligation to disclose information relating to child protection. Health authorities are obliged to co-operate with local authorities to assist them with carrying out their functions under section 27 of the Children Act 1989, although it is unclear whether this extends to a duty in law. It is also apparent that the duty to assist engages in relation to Part III of the Children Act 1989, which does not pertain to child protection functions. If steps have been taken to avoid breaching the duty of confidentiality owed to a child, and if this has failed to provide an adequate safeguard, then disclosure may be justified and legitimate. In *G v G* [1990] 1 FLR 395, the Court of Appeal indicated that where it became clear that a child might be at risk, the court should consider alerting the Social Services Department. This implies that the courts may be moving towards a duty to disclose when a risk to children is considered.

2.26.6 Freedom of the press and public debate

Maintaining confidentiality of medical information needs to be balanced against the public interest in the freedom of expression of the media. In *X v Y* [1988] 2 All ER 648, a newspaper reported that two general practitioners were continuing to practice medicine despite having contracted HIV. The health authority successfully obtained an injunction to restrain publication of doctors' identity. The court held that while there was some public interest in knowing this information, the risk of a GP transmitting HIV to his patients was negligible. The benefits of publishing such information would have been substantially outweighed against the public interest of protecting the doctor's identities.

In *H (a healthcare worker) v Associated Newspapers Ltd* [2002] EWCA Civ 195, H had been identified as being HIV positive and had notified his employers who then wanted to carry out a 'look back' exercise in order to notify H's patients and offer them advice and diagnostic testing. H claimed that this was unlawful. In the meantime a newspaper wanted to publish the story, and H obtained an injunction from the Court of Appeal restraining the publication of information about his and the health authority's identity. The court stated that the consequences to H would be devastating if his identify were to be disclosed and furthermore if confidentiality was not maintained in these circumstances, this would discourage health-care workers from self-reporting their HIV status.

The court has, however, justified disclosure to the General Medical Council (GMC) on account of matters pertaining to medical practitioners that may have a regulatory impact, as in *Woolgar v Chief Constable of the Sussex Police* [1999] 3 All ER 604. The court held that the police were entitled to release material to a regulatory body on the basis that this could be used for the purposes of its own enquiry if this was considered to be in the public interest. If the police came into possession of confidential information which in their reasonable opinion ought to be considered by the GMC in the public interest, then the police would be free to pass that information on to the Regulator for its consideration.

2.26.7 Teaching, research and audit

Access to medical records and patient information is necessary for teaching, research and audit. For research and teaching purposes, data is usually anonymised. In *R v Department of Health ex p Source Informatics* [2001] QB 424, it was decided that use of anonymous medical information did not represent a breach of confidence. On the facts the applicant processed information received from pharmacists and GPs about medication prescribed for anonymous patients. This information was sold to pharmaceutical companies for marketing purposes. The applicants applied for judicial review of the Department of Health's subsequent policy guidance that disclosure of anonymous patient data would not relieve GPs and pharmacists of the duty of confidence owed to patients and who could incur liability. According to the court, the privacy of the patients was protected in the circumstances, and patients had no proprietary claim to the prescription form or the information that it contained provided that privacy was not at risk.

The DPA requires that processing of data is done fairly and lawfully (see 2.25). If consent for the use of anonymous sensitive personal data has not been given, this must be 'necessary' (Schedule 2) for 'medical purposes' (Schedule 3). It is also of note that under the second principle of data protection, data should be obtained for specific purposes and not used for others, although this requirement is qualified by section 33 which provides that the principle will not be breached where further processing is done for 'research purposes'. In the *Source Informatics* case, the information was obtained for treatment purposes and had then been used for commercial gain. The tension that arises was whether Source Informatics' primary interest in the data was for research purposes or whether it was for commercial exploitation. One possible way to avoid this particular problem would be to obtain patients' consent for anonymisation and further use of data although patients with diseases that are perceived to carry stigma (e.g. sexually transmitted disease) may not be prepared to give consent. The Source Informatics raises several problematic issues. Use of anonymous data should be both necessary and for medical purposes in order to comply with the first principle of the DPA which requires sensitive personal information to be done fairly and lawfully. It also raises problematic issues for the second principle of the Data Protection Act: that it should be used for a specific purpose and not for others, as qualified by the research provision (section 33). Exactly what constitutes a research purpose is unclear, and ambiguity could represent a significant obstacle to epidemiological and other public health research studies. Section 251 of the National Health Service Act 2006 provides for the control of patient information and permits the Secretary of State to make regulations to authorise the disclosure of confidential patient information in the absence of consent where this is necessary to support essential NHS activity. This statutory provision perhaps follows-on from Simon Brown LJ's *obiter* comments in *Source Informatics*. However, the exception created by section 251 has been criticised on the grounds that the therapeutic relationship between doctors and patients could be at risk and patients who are aware of the possibility of disclosure of their records to government departments may be less than frank with their doctors about the information they choose to disclose (Case, 2003). Furthermore, section 251 has been considered as being contradictory to the protection of individual rights and at odds with legislation such as the Human Rights Act 1998 and the DPA, both of which have a protective jurisdiction.

2.27 The deceased patient

There are several reasons why the duty to maintain confidentiality extends after death. It is in the interests of all patients to know that the information they disclose will remain confidential and such a rule is premised on the notion that it will produce the best consequences. Maintaining confidentiality also protects the interests of other groups such as blood relatives and third parties since the release of confidential information can result in very real harm, a view maintained in *Bluck v The Information Commissioner* (2007) 98 BMLR 1 and confirmed in *Lewis v Secretary of State for Health* [2008] EWHC 2196. In *Lewis* the judge stated that there was no doubt that a professional obligation was owed by the doctor to maintain the patient's medical confidences after the patient's death. However, this obligation can be overridden in the public interest and the duty of confidence has to be balanced against what truly lies in the public interest.

GMC professional guidance on confidentiality (2009, at paragraph 71) describes some of the situations where information may be legitimately disclosed following a patient's death. Examples given include assisting a coroner with disclosure required by section 251, participating in national confidential enquiries or for local clinical audit, production of death certificates for public health surveillance, parental request for information about their child's death, or when a partner, close relative or friend asks for the circumstances of the death of an adult.

2.28 The patient who lacks capacity

The duty of confidentiality extends to the adult who lacks capacity and is protected by law. In *R (on the application of Stevens) v Plymouth City Council* [2002] EWCA Civ 388, a case decided prior to implementation of the Mental Capacity Act 2005, the court stated that it was all too easy for professionals to consider those who lacked capacity as having no independent interests. Yet the importance of that duty could not be overestimated, and is augmented by the Mental Capacity Act 2005 and the need to act in the patient's best interests.

GMC guidance (2009, at paragraphs 59 and 60) states that when taking a decision whether to disclose information about a patient who lacks capacity, the patient should be supported and encouraged to be involved to the fullest extent possible. Doctors should consider the views of anyone that the patient asks should be consulted, as well as previously expressed preferences. It is also important to consider whether lack of decision-making capacity is permanent or temporary, and if temporary whether the decision to disclose could reasonably be deferred until after capacity is regained.

2.29 Professional guidance

Most breaches of confidentiality by health-care professionals are inadvertent and tend to be brought before the regulatory bodies rather than in a court of law. The areas where issues of confidentiality arise include the inaccurate determination of what lies in the public interest, details of sexually transmitted diseases and the secondary use of medical information. Professional guidance is available for practitioners from several sources. The BMA (2008) states that the public interest can only be determined definitively by the courts; however, when considering whether disclosure of information might be in the public interest, medical practitioners must

▶ Appraise the benefits of disclosure against the harms associated with breach of confidentiality
▶ Assess the urgency for disclosure
▶ Persuade the patient to disclose voluntarily
▶ Inform the patient prior to disclosure and seek consent
▶ Disclose information promptly to the appropriate body
▶ Reveal the minimum information necessary to meet the intended objectives
▶ Seek assurance that information will be used only for the purposes for which it is disclosed
▶ Document the steps taken to seek or obtain consent
▶ Be able to justify the decision
▶ Document the extent of, and the grounds for, the disclosure.

The GMC (2009) has issued very similar guidance.

In clinical circumstances much will depend upon the urgency of the need to disclose. When time is at a premium, and opportunities for complying with the above steps are limited, the early involvement of the Caldicott Guardian may be appropriate. Caldicott Guardians are senior officials in NHS organisations and local authorities who are responsible for protecting the confidentiality of patient information and who enable appropriate information sharing. Doctors employed in managed environments should follow organisational information governance and confidentiality policies.

Difficulties may arise in relation to communicable diseases, such as HIV and AIDS. The question as to whether a doctor should alert the partner of a person who is HIV-positive remains challenging. From an ethical perspective, the advantages of alerting the partner are clear although there is a risk that disclosure might discourage others from seeking medical advice and treatment for fear of repercussions. The GMC (2009) suggests that non-consensual disclosure can be justified if the doctor believes that the patient has not informed the partner and cannot be persuaded to do so. Again, the general advice is that every effort should be made to encourage the person to voluntarily disclose and that all efforts made are appropriately documented. Nevertheless, compliance with guidance would not preclude the patient from reporting non-consensual disclosure to the GMC, which would then be duty bound to conduct an investigation, even if the doctor is ultimately absolved.

Disclosure of data for secondary use should ideally be anonymised or coded (GMC, 2009). Where this is not possible, disclosure under section 251 of the National Health Service Act 2006 should be considered and advice may be sought from the National Information Governance Board, or the Privacy Advisory Committee in Northern Ireland and Scotland. If data is identifiable, then it could be sent to a 'safe haven' with facilities for the safe management of information. Again, while this advice is sound in principle, the practicalities of achieving this can be complex and a doctor would be well advised to consult a Caldicott Guardian or an information governance team so that disclosure can be made according to defined policies. For the purposes of research, disclosure must be in accordance with what has been approved by a research ethics committee. The Caldicott Guardian would need to balance secondary use against patient confidentiality and the public interest. A range of factors are likely to be taken into account, including the potential for distress or harm to the individual whose information is being disclosed, the nature of the information as well as the use and scope of circulation of the information.

Javed is very upset that his confidential medical details have been presented and he wishes to obtain redress against the doctor.

▶ What professional guidance is available on the duty of confidentiality?
▶ What would be the possible outcomes of a successful complaint to the Trust?
▶ Could Javed complain to the GMC?

F Managing doctors' performance

2.30 Understanding professional performance

Doctors' professional performance has been subjected to considerable public scrutiny in recent years. Although there is a common assumption that doctors are competent, recent events have raised concerns, and the medical profession has begun to address problems about poor performance to achieve effective solutions (Smith, 1998).

A range of factors may operate to affect a doctor's performance. These include physical and mental health issues, personality traits, attitudes, values and beliefs. Additional factors that can impinge upon professional performance include heavy workloads, organisational culture, teamwork, managerial issues and life events. Poor performance amongst doctors in the hospital workforce is around 6% (Donaldson, 1994), although only a minority are considered to be incompetent. A complex interplay of factors typically impacts upon performance, and Finucane (2003) has identified three levels for assessing a doctor's performance:

▶ Level 1 involves screening of the entire population of doctors;
▶ Level 2 targets the 'at risk' group;
▶ Level 3 involves assessment of individual practitioners whose performance is poor.

Evidence from Canada indicates that assessments at Levels 1 and 2, namely screening and targeted assessment, are extremely valuable for the early detection of performance issues. In the United Kingdom, although in-depth assessment at Level 3 is extremely well developed, assessments at Levels 1 and 2 are insufficiently robust. These levels are currently being addressed through systems of enhanced appraisal, and efforts are directed to tackling concerns locally with local resolution. A further factor is recognition that good doctors need more than clinical competence, skills and knowledge, but also several non-clinical attributes that are embedded in good practice such as team working, leadership, communication skills and appropriate work place behaviours.

In 1995 the GMC, being the body responsible for regulation of the medical profession, was given the necessary legislative framework to allow the assessment of a doctor's performance. The work undertaken by the regulator concentrates mainly on performance issues and has a disciplinary rather than developmental remit.

In 2001 the National Clinical Assessment Authority, part of the National Patient Safety Agency and now known as the National Clinical Assessment Service (NCAS), was created to help manage the poor performance of doctors. NCAS carries out not only assessments of performance but also acts to clarify concerns and make recommendations to employing bodies. Its assessments and processes are informative rather than disciplinary. In undertaking assessments, NCAS relies upon clinical assessments of competence and performance and also carries out behavioural and occupational health assessments for purposes of remediation.

Cox et al., (2006) consider that poor performance broadly falls into two categories: individual factors and those associated with work. Individual factors include physical and psychological ill health, personality and attitudes, education, training and continuing professional development. Factors associated with work include climate and culture, team working, leadership and organisational difficulties. There is also evidence that ethnicity and diversity impact professional performance and this represents an area that requires further research. Appreciation of these factors helps towards remediation which, to be effective, needs the support of an educational framework together with organisational buy-in. Two essential components of remediation are a shift away from the traditional approaches to learning through a didactic culture to one based upon reflective learning and strong empowering leadership to facilitate effective team work.

2.31 Early recognition and local resolution

Good clinical performance and safeguarding patient safety requires doctors to have a range of essential competencies: knowing (knowledge and skills), ability to do (competence), actually doing (performance), and demonstrating (a positive affirmation of knowledge, skills, competence and performance). A mechanism for checks and balances is also required for each of these stages. The Chief Medical Officer's review in 'Good doctors, safer patients' proposes processes for the modern management of doctors' performance (Samanta and Samanta, 2007a). At local level this will include the appointment of GMC affiliates who will bridge the gap between the employer and regulator. Responsible officers, who are expected to be medical directors, will recommend doctors for revalidation by the GMC on 5-year cycles.

Information for revalidation is expected to be gained through an enhanced appraisal system whereby each doctor will need to positively demonstrate good practice through continuing professional development, evidence of clinical performance, multisource feedback, reflective learning from complaints, participation in clinical audit, an affirmation of health and probity, and an agreed personal development plan that must be achieved on an annual basis. Performance issues are expected to be resolved locally with only the more serious cases being referred to NCAS or the GMC for a performance assessment. These local initiatives are expected to enhance Levels 1 and 2 assessments, and referral being required only for Level 3 assessments.

Local management and resolution is, in principle, an attractive idea and in theory should assist with the development of bespoke rehabilitation, remediation and re-skilling packages. Medical directors will have enhanced regulatory responsibility and concerns are expected to be addressed through a line management structure. A potential risk might be managerial overreaction, particularly where doctors may be working in suboptimal environments. Questions remain about a 'dual' role taken on by the responsible officer with a possible conflict of interest between remediation objectives and employer loyalty. The implications and benefits of these initiatives remain to be seen and the legislative provisions that will enable revalidation have been delayed.

Whistle blowing represents another method for the early detection of concerns and this has been encouraged through local policies as well as statutory protection for the whistleblower. Whistle blowing is defined as the spontaneous reporting outside normal channels by individual members of staff and is intended to draw attention to unsafe practice. There are, however, ethical dilemmas for those seeking to balance personal loyalty to colleagues and organisations and the wider public interest. Protection for whistleblowers exists under the Public Interest Disclosure Act 1998, although NHS staff remain concerned about potential negative repercussions for their careers. The Department of Health requires every NHS Trust and Health Authority to have in place policies and procedures that are compliant with the Act, as well as guidance for staff for raising concerns.

2.32 The role of NCAS

The NCAS is part of the National Patient Safety Agency. Employers have a duty to consult with NCAS at key stages of investigatory and disciplinary proceedings if the case involves the exclusion of a medical practitioner from the workplace, if an assessment of capability is required or if a capability hearing is being considered. NCAS provides expert advice and support to the employing body although the final decision-maker is the employer.

NHS organisations require procedures for dealing with performance, conduct and health of medical personnel and local procedures must be in accordance with the Restriction of Practice and Exclusion from Work Directions 2003 and the Directions on Disciplinary Procedures 2005. NHS employers are expected to comply with the standards in 'Maintaining high professional standards in the modern NHS', which has introduced a framework for screening of concerns about the conduct and performance of medical and dental employees. The standards provide guidance for the processes to be followed for the investigation of concerns, reviewing and reporting on exclusions, disciplinary processes, capability hearings and health-related matters. Local policies should reflect the framework set out in the standards.

A key feature of the framework includes separation of the investigatory process from the decision-making process and the role of remediation, together with the need to avoid exclusion from the workplace wherever possible by considering the use of alternatives such as restricted or non-clinical duties.

NCAS (2009) has reported that referrals have increased over the past few years and are being received from all parts of the United Kingdom broadly in proportion to the workforce size. The trends that have been noted are that there are fewer referrals for women practitioners and above-average rates for psychiatrists. More than half of excluded practitioners from secondary care eventually return to work in the same organisation and around two-thirds of practitioners undergoing NCAS assessment are still in employment. NCAS has made a demonstrable improvement in avoiding unnecessary or unduly lengthy suspension or exclusion, as well as implementing remediation.

2.33 The role of the GMC

The role of NCAS is principally to determine fitness of purpose with regard to the medical practitioner. The role of the GMC is to determine fitness to practise.

Referrals to the GMC are investigated by two case examiners, one of whom is medical and the other lay. The purpose is to provide a rapid response to the complaint although if this is not possible the case is referred to the Investigation Committee of the GMC. In some instances a very rapid response is necessary, in which case the doctor may be asked to appear before the Interim Orders Panel. Dependent upon the nature of the case, the Panel may impose conditions upon the doctor's registration or suspend the doctor while the investigation is continuing in order to protect patients and the public. On completion of the investigation the case is put before a Fitness to Practise Panel and a full hearing is conducted. The case is heard by a Panel of at least three members, and generally there is a lay preponderance. A legal assessor will be present throughout to advise on matters of law. The sanctions available to the Panel are to take no action, to give a warning, impose conditions on registration, impose a period of suspension, or to erase the doctor from the Register. At all stages the Panel is required to give reasons for its decision and the overriding interest is patient safety and the public interest.

The GMC processes and regulations have been strengthened considerably in recent years and are intended to maintain and sustain the confidence of the public that a robust regulatory system is in place. The standard of proof that is applied is the civil standard, being the balance of probabilities. The previous standard was that of the criminal standard, being beyond reasonable doubt. This alteration of the burden of proof has led to speculation that more doctors are likely to be found 'guilty' by the Panel, although an alternative view is that this is unlikely to be the situation. The more serious allegations will require evidence, the quality of which would need to be more robust and more persuasive than that required for allegations at the lower end of the scale.

Revalidation is another important initiative to safeguard patient safety in the public interest. Previously doctors would automatically continue to stay on the medical register (in the absence of reasons for not being allowed), revalidation will require positive evidence of a doctor's fitness to practise to be given every 5 years. This will include evidence from a range of sources through an enhanced appraisal system.

Summary

2.1 Contemporary health care is complex and has changed considerably since the inception of the NHS. The key themes of the NHS include quality, patient safety, the dynamics of the doctor–patient relationship, accountability and professional regulation.

2.2 The modern NHS is a vast organisation. Its core principles are to provide a universal and comprehensive service with equity of access, the right to choose, high quality services dependent upon clinical need and irrespective of the ability to pay. A major challenge will be in embodying these principles in a climate of financial restraint.

2.3 Parliament is responsible for allocating funds to the NHS, and the Secretary of State is accountable to Parliament for the performance of the NHS. The Department of Health has a role in setting the direction for the NHS. There is a growing impetus for greater patient and public involvement with power being devolved to local health-care organisations to shape services according to the needs of local communities. In its recent White Paper, the Coalition Government is proposing a radical overhaul of a number ALBs (which have undertaken a range of functions within the NHS) with a view to decreasing bureaucracy and enhancing effectiveness through accountability.

2.4 The commissioning of health-care services is usually by those who receive the NHS budget, and to date has been the PCTs. Services are commissioned from providers, such as primary, secondary and tertiary care services.

2.5 Provision of services is through providers such as general practitioners, NHS trusts and foundation trusts. Community care is provided by local authorities and essential nursing care cannot be charged to the patient.

2.6 The Secretary of State has a statutory duty to provide a comprehensive health service. Access is usually constrained by limited resources. The duty of the Secretary of State is enforceable through judicial review although the courts have been reluctant to intervene.

2.7 There is a statutory duty on NHS providers to monitor and improve the quality of health-care services and to provide specific information relevant to the quality of service provision.

2.8 The NHS Constitution enshrines the values of the NHS for setting out the key rights and responsibilities of patients and staff. The Health Act 2009 is the enabling legislation that implements these aspects. Regulators such as Monitor and the CQC have a statutory duty to have regard to the NHS Constitution when carrying out their regulatory functions.

2.9 National Service Frameworks are policies set by the NHS to define standards of care and reduce variations in health-care services. They have raised legitimate expectations of the public and staff and operate at the level of guidance without bestowing additional enforceable rights to patients.

2.10 Risk management is the process used by trusts to identify areas of clinical risk in order to implement preventative action. A robust risk management programme requires identification of risks through a range of sources with preventative measures. The NHSLA is a special health authority that operates a risk pooling scheme managed through a central fund. Trusts are required to meet CNST standards and have a financial incentive to attain higher standards which would make them eligible for discounted contributions.

Summary cont'd

2.11 Clinical governance is a system through which NHS organisations are accountable for continuously monitoring, improving and safeguarding high standards of care and services. Clinical governance is part of the overarching framework of integrated governance within the NHS. Within the clinical area the two main strands of clinical governance include clinical audit and complaints management.

2.12 There is a growing proliferation of clinical guidelines. Clinical guidelines inform best practice through evidence-based medicine. The majority of guidelines are produced by NICE, the Royal Colleges and specialist societies. Clinical guidelines may impact by informing the standard of care in medical litigation.

2.13 The imperative to promote patient safety is central to the modern NHS. Emphasis is given to organisational cultures to implement sustained patient safety policies. There has been a growing recognition of 'pinch points' that may adversely affect patient safety, such as clinical transitions. A number of initiatives have been developed to enhance patient safety through organisational culture as well as by consumer input.

2.14 Reporting and learning from errors is an approach towards the remedy of systems failure. The National Patient Safety Agency has provided a seven-step framework to build a safety culture. An important factor is root cause analysis that dissects clinical error to unravel underlying causes and facilitate the development of learning strategies. The NRLS is a reporting system designed to facilitate data collection.

2.15 HCAIs are an important item on the patient safety agenda. Infections can be caused by the patient's own microbial flora, cross-infection from others or inadequate decontamination of equipment. A number of strategies have been developed to reduce infections. Part of the remit of the CQC is to monitor HCAI and the CQC is empowered to take action against those health-care organisations that do not comply with preventative strategies.

2.16 The contemporary health-care environment is evolving rapidly. Developments that may adversely impact upon patient safety include reduced junior doctor training time due to the European Working Time Directive, the development of modern technology and innovative therapy, the expanding role of non-medical health-care practitioners who are now beginning to take on more medicalised roles, including surgery, and the administration of multiple and complex medication. While such initiatives have definite advantages, the potential challenges in respect of patient safety need to be recognised and addressed.

2.17 Resource allocation, or rationing, is a system by which certain investigations and treatment are not offered to certain groups of patients. This is not because such interventions are clinically ineffective but because of limitations in resources. In contemporary practice, this is often seen with regard to newer and high cost therapies.

2.18 Under the National Health Service Act 1977, the Secretary of State has a duty to provide a comprehensive Health Service. However, this in itself does not form the basis for an action for a breach of statutory duty and furthermore, in discharging this duty the Secretary of State can provide such services that are considered necessary to meet reasonable requirements within available resources.

2.19 A decision regarding resource allocation or rationing can be challenged through judicial review. A successful challenge will be made if it can be proved that the decision was illegal, or that the decision was unreasonable or that there was procedural impropriety in making that decision. Actions are brought mainly on the basis of financial considerations, policies being inflexible, procedural irregularity and the frustration of legitimate expectations. An

Summary cont'd

action will usually be successful if it can be shown that the NHS body operated a blanket policy or a policy that fettered discretion.

2.20 The effect of the Equality Act 2010 on rationing decisions remains to be seen. However, it would seem that it would be unlawful for an NHS body not to allocate resources on the grounds of a person's physical problem or mental illness.

2.21 Under European law, freedom of movement permits medical services and reimbursement to be claimed from a host Member State provided that the waiting time for home state funded treatment or care exceeds an acceptable period. In theory this could undermine the moral choices that form part of resource allocation decisions in this country and could have implications for cross-border commissioning.

2.22 Rationing and resource allocation in the NHS has always been in existence, although historically this tended to be covert. This process has become more overt through the creation of NICE, which provides guidance and recommends treatments and interventions on the basis of evidence and cost-effectiveness. The principal methodology used to determine cost-effectiveness is the QALY. This is not without its problems and it has been argued that this indicator imposes a value judgement on life.

2.23 Confidentiality protects the confidential nature of the doctor–patient relationship. The duty of confidentiality is not absolute and can be overridden in certain circumstances.

2.24 At common law, the duty of confidentiality arises from an obligation in good conscience. With regard to medical information, this is protected under Article 8(1) of the European Convention of Human Rights. However, this protection needs to be balanced against factors such as the public interest in accordance with the law and necessary in a democratic society, as well as the rights conferred by other Articles, such as the right to freedom of expression and the right to a fair trial.

2.25 The Data Protection Act 1998 provides for the processing of sensitive medical information. In the absence of consent, medical data may be processed if it is necessary to protect the vital interests of the data subject, or for the purposes of legitimate interests pursued by the data controller and it is necessary for medical purposes, which includes medical diagnosis, medical research, preventative medicine and the provision of care and treatment, and management of health-care services.

2.26 Explicit consent for disclosure relieves the doctor of the duty not to disclose confidential medical information. Consent is implied where such information needs to be shared with other health-care professionals for continuation of care. Exceptions to the confidentiality requirement include prevention of harm to others, prevention or detection of crime, child protection, and teaching, audit and research.

2.27 A duty of confidentiality is owed to the deceased patient, although this may be overridden in certain circumstances, such as the public interest, when disclosure is required by law, when a person has a right of access to medical records, to assist a coroner, for national confidential enquiries, on death certificates and for public health surveillance.

2.28 The duty of confidence applies to adults who lack capacity. In determining whether to disclose information, all efforts should be made to engage the patient and determine current or pre-stated wishes, and consideration should be given as to whether disclosure can be delayed if lack of capacity is temporary.

2.29 Breaches of confidentiality tend to be inadvertent and complaints are usually brought before the professional Regulators. In considering non-consensual disclosure, every effort should be taken to engage the individual about whom data is being disclosed and where that is

Summary cont'd

not practicable, to document carefully the steps that were taken for such engagement and reasons why non-consensual disclosure has been undertaken. Advice and guidance may be obtained through information governance policies within a managed environment, as well as a Caldicott Guardian.

2.30 Poor performance in organisations can be up to 6% although only a small minority of doctors are actually incompetent. A range of individual or organisational factors may contribute to poor performance. Identification and resolution of these issues is essential for effective remediation.

2.31 Emphasis is given to early detection of concerns and local resolution. Doctors are expected to revalidate with the General Medical Council on a five yearly cycle by demonstrating good clinical practice as evidenced by enhanced appraisal procedures. There has been an emphasis on remediation of performance concerns at an early stage through a developmental rather than a disciplinary approach.

2.32 NCAS has an advisory role in advising employing organisations about concerns that may be raised about a medical practitioner. NCAS undertakes assessments and offers remediation through action planning. Recent figures have shown that there has been a reduction in exclusion from the workplace with a greater number of practitioners being able to get back to work once the concerns have been addressed.

2.33 The GMC is the regulator of the medical profession. In recent years the GMC has altered its processes to make the regulatory process more robust to enhance patient safety and sustain public confidence.

Exercises

2.1 'Rationing has always been prevalent in the NHS, but this should be overt.' Critically consider why rationing is necessary and how this is achieved within the contemporary health-care environment.

2.2 'Patient safety is a fundamental aspect of contemporary health-care systems.' Critically consider how patient safety is being addressed in the NHS and how this can be further enhanced.

2.3 Medical information is confidential. How is this balanced against disclosure in the public interest?

2.4 The sharing of medical information is essential for the purposes of teaching, audit and research. Critically consider whether current regulations hinder or promote these worthy causes.

2.5 Critically consider recent developments in managing concerns about doctors' performance and whether these are sufficient to sustain public confidence.

Further reading

Cox J, King J, Hutchinson A, McAvoy P. *Understanding doctors' performance*. Radcliffe Publishing, Oxford, 2006.

Department of Health (2010) The NHS Constitution for England (Department of Health) Available at http://www.dh.gov.uk/

Further reading cont'd

McCarthy D, Blumenthal D. Stories from the sharp end. Case studies in safety improvement. *Millbank Quarterly* 2006; 84: 165–200.

Newdick C. *Who should we treat?* Oxford University Press, Oxford, 2005.

Syrett K. Impotence or importance? Judicial review in an era of explicit NHS rationing. *Medical Law Review* 2004; 67: 289.

Links to relevant websites can be found at: http://www.palgrave.com/law/samanta

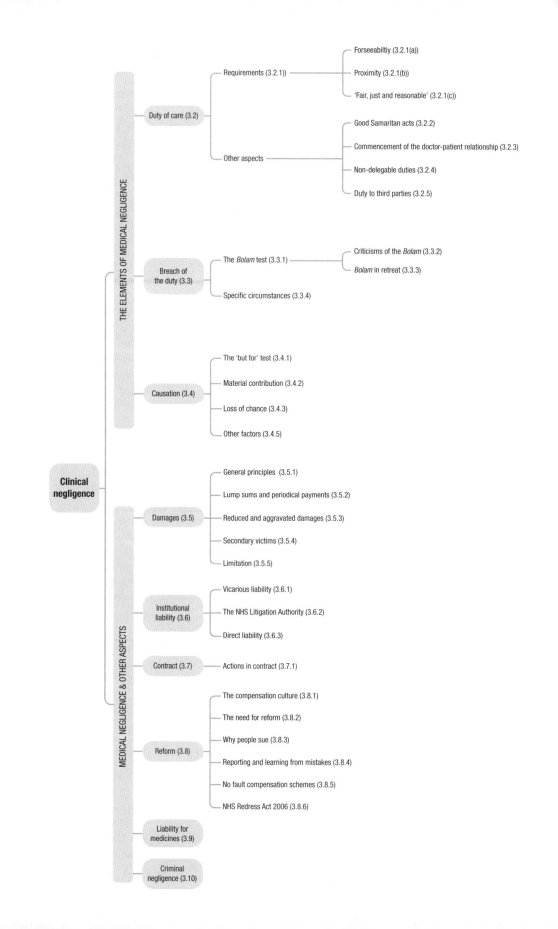

Key Terms

- ▶ **Bolam test** – a doctor is not guilty of negligence if he or she has acted in accordance with a practice accepted as proper by a responsible body of medical professionals skilled in that particular art.
- ▶ **Breach of duty** – failure to meet the requisite standard of care as measured against the *Bolam* test.
- ▶ **'But for' test** – the basic test in law for factual causation.
- ▶ **Causation** – to prove on the balance of probabilities that actionable damage was caused by the negligent act.
- ▶ **Duty of care** – a legal obligation imposed on individuals or organisations that they take reasonable care in the conduct of acts that could foreseeably result in actionable harm to another.
- ▶ **Elements of negligence** – duty of care; breach of duty and causation.
- ▶ **Vicarious liability** – an employer's liability for the negligence of its employees while acting in the course of their employment.

Scenario

Simon, who was 2 years old, was on holiday with his parents at a hotel on a remote island of Scilly. The day before the family was to return home, Simon became irritable. He developed a high temperature accompanied by a diffuse rash of pinprick spots. His parents called upon one of the guests, a retired doctor, for advice. The doctor examined Simon and advised regular pain relief and, if symptoms did not subside, to consult with his general practitioner on returning home. The doctor had considered the possibility that Simon might have meningitis but had ruled this out since Simon did not display any apparent sensitivity to light. Whilst a skin rash is a recognised characteristic of meningitis the doctor had felt that in the circumstances Simon's rash was most likely caused by heat.

On their return home on Saturday, Simon's condition had deteriorated and he was referred by his general practitioner to the paediatric unit of a large hospital. On arrival, Simon was seen by a junior doctor, Preeti, who had recently joined the department. She immediately suspected meningitis on account of Simon's condition and cold extremities and felt that an urgent lumbar puncture was required. She made several attempts to contact the consultant without success. Eventually, Preeti was able to hand over Simon's care to a locum who had been employed through a medical staffing agency.

Preparations were made for an urgent lumbar puncture. On insertion of the needle the pressure was found to be very high, and withdrawal of fluid led to Simon's collapse requiring emergency resuscitation. During resuscitation the doctor who attempted intubation (insertion of a tube down the wind pipe to help breathing) had difficulty performing the procedure and took longer than usual. Simon was left with permanent brain damage.

Expert evidence suggests that Simon would have had a 40% chance of recovering if referral and diagnosis to a specialist unit had occurred within 12 hours of the initial onset of symptoms. The locum doctor asserts that even if he had not performed the lumbar puncture Simon would have suffered brain damage as a result of the infection in any event.

3.1 Introduction

Clinical negligence describes the law that applies when a patient is harmed by medical care in circumstances where a health-care practitioner or organisation has failed to take reasonable care. In *An Organisation with a Memory*, the Department of Health (2000) reported that adverse events occur in approximately 10% of hospital admissions and cost the NHS around £2 billion a year on account of additional care alone. In 2005, 484,441 incidents were reported to the National Reporting and Learning Services, a figure which included 1804 deaths, of which death was directly attributable to a patient safety incident in 576 cases. Between 1 October 2009 and 31 March 2010, the number of patient safety incidents that resulted in severe harm or death was 3509. The most common categories were patient accident (30%), medication (11%) and treatment or procedure (10%).

A Special Health Authority known as the NHS Litigation Authority (NHSLA) is responsible for managing clinical and non-clinical negligence cases on behalf of the NHS. The NHSLA operates a collective risk-pooling indemnity scheme under which NHS trusts in England pay an agreed sum in return for cover. Although liability remains with the defendant Trust, the NHSLA provides administrative and financial services. Between 2008 and 2009 the NHSLA received 6088 claims (including potential claims) under its clinical negligence schemes. Specialties such as surgery, medicine and obstetrics and gynaecology generate the highest numbers of claims. While the proportion of adverse incidents that lead to litigation is relatively low, expenditure on settlements is high, and between 2007 and 2008 the NHSLA paid out £633.3 million in connection with these claims. To date, the NHSLA allows only membership of NHS bodies, although special arrangements are in place for the indemnity of independent sector providers when treating NHS patients who have been referred by their Primary Care Trust (PCT).

In 2001, figures from the National Audit Office revealed that health authorities in England had provided for potential liabilities of £3.9 billion, and for the accounting year 2006 to 2007, this figure had risen to £9.2 billion and in 2007 to 2008 was £11.95 billion (NHSLA Reports and Accounts, 2008). The 2009 Reports and Accounts state a figure of £13.5 billion and at 31 March 2010 this was £15.066 billion. These figures reflect the potential costs of outstanding claims which are expected to have a greater that 50% chance of succeeding, and bear little resemblance to the actual compensation paid out by the NHS on account of negligence claims. Legal costs are exorbitant and between 2009 and 2010 the NHSLA paid over £163 million in legal costs of which 74% was paid to claimant lawyers. A very significant number of adverse events occur in health-care practice yet only 4% of cases handled by the NHSLA are settled in court (NHSLA

Reports and Accounts, 2010). Forty-two per cent are settled out of court, but most are abandoned by the claimant.

Clinical negligence tends to be an emotive topic for patients and providers of care. It can bring tragic outcomes for patients and their loved ones whose lives may be shattered and their faith in health care destroyed. Likewise, litigation is likely to be distressing and stressful for health-care practitioners for two main reasons. First, the principal aim of medical care is to benefit the patient, and failure leads to professional regret. Second, the system of fault liability means that consequences for the defendant can be manifold. A civil action for compensation on account of negligence is likely (or possibly for breach of contract where private care has been received). A criminal prosecution for battery might be the outcome of performing a procedure on a patient without that person's valid consent. If the patient dies, a charge of gross negligence manslaughter could be brought (*R v Adomako* [1995] 1 AC 171). Futhermore, negligent acts or omissions might form the basis of disciplinary proceedings being brought against a practitioner by an employer or professional regulatory body.

Clinical negligence cases are often complex and difficult to resolve. There is a perception that the law is protective of practitioners at the expense of patients, largely on account of the difficult and potentially unassailable hurdles of the *Bolam* standard and the need to prove causation (section 3.4). Clinical negligence liability in English law is based upon general principles which operate under the tort of negligence. The focus in this chapter is on mistakes made by doctors as opposed to those of other health-care professionals. This is because clinical litigation is predominantly against doctors although the same principles can be extended to other professional groups.

In addition to individual tort liability, the underlying causes of clinical negligence may be direct, or indirect, organisational factors such as inadequate staffing ratios, efficiency initiatives and inadequate risk management strategies all of which operate to create a working environment that is not conducive to safe working practice. In negligence it is easier to bring an action against an identifiable individual rather than an organisation, even though system failures might be the root cause.

For a claimant to succeed in a civil action of negligence, three requirements must be proved:

1. The defendant owed the claimant a duty of care.
2. The defendant's performance was below the standard expected, thus resulting in a breach of duty.
3. The injury suffered by the claimant was caused by the defendant's breach of duty.

3.2   Duty of care

To succeed in an action of negligence a claimant must establish that, in the circumstances of the event, the defendant owed the claimant a duty of care. In typical health-care situations this requirement is usually satisfied and is based upon an assumption of responsibility, for example, by a doctor for a patient. Once the doctor and patient relationship is established it is foreseeable that lack of care could cause harm to the patient. The duty of care arises from tort law principles and whether, under the circumstances, a duty of care should be owed (*Caparo Industries plc v Dickman* [1990] 1 All ER 568 at 574). The relationship between the doctor and patient who has suffered harm must be of sufficient proximity that the harm caused by the practitioner's actions or omissions was reasonably foreseeable in the circumstances (*Goodwill v British Pregnancy Advisory Service* [1996] 2 All ER 161). The central question is how directly the actions of the clinician might have led to injury of the patient. If the likelihood of harm is apparent, then subject to the fairness and reasonableness of imposing such a duty, it is likely that a duty of care will be found.

3.2.1 Three requirements for the duty of care

In most circumstances, a duty of care will automatically arise once a general practitioner accepts a patient onto his or her list. Likewise, a duty will arise once a patient is admitted to an NHS hospital. In the private sector, a duty arises by virtue of a contractual relationship between patient and doctor. In certain situations establishing the existence of a duty of care can be more difficult, for example, in emergency first aid situations or whether a duty of care owed to a patient can be extended to a relative. In these circumstances issues related to foreseeability of harm, proximity of relationship and whether imposition of a duty would be fair, just and reasonable will be relevant (*Caparo Industries plc v Dickman* [1990] 2 AC 605). Ultimately, the definitive answer as to whether a duty of care arises is when a court makes a positive affirmation that in the circumstances a duty arises.

3.2.1(a) Foreseeability of harm

Foreseeability of harm is one of three factors that the court will consider in determining a duty of care. The question that is asked is whether it was reasonably foreseeable that the doctor's actions or omissions could result in harm to the injured person? If the answer is negative, it is unlikely that there will be a duty of care. An example of this situation is the doctor who prescribes medication for a patient. In these circumstances it is implicit that the doctor's lack of care could cause harm to the patient and therefore a duty of care will arise. If, however, the patient gives this medication to a friend who then suffers harm, this chain of events will not have been reasonably foreseeable by the prescribing doctor, and under these circumstances no duty to the patient's friend will be expected to arise.

3.2.1(b) Proximity of relationship

The second question relates to proximity. Was the relationship between the injured person and the practitioner sufficiently close that a duty of care ought to arise? The answer will depend to some extent upon whether the relationship is such that carelessness on the part of the practitioner could cause the person harm. In the case of a doctor treating a patient it is apparent that a close, or proximate, relationship is likely to exist. The court, however, tends to take a more restrictive view in establishing whether such a relationship extends between the practitioner and the patient's relative. In *Fairlie*, for example, a question arose was to whether a father was owed a duty of care by a Health Board (*Fairlie v Perth and Kinross Healthcare NHS Trust* 2004 SLT 1200 (OH)). The patient's father had suffered distress after being accused of abusing his daughter, who had undergone allegedly negligent treatment for a psychiatric condition. In the opinion of the court, there was nothing at any stage to indicate that a special or proximate relationship existed between the father and psychiatrist to the extent that a duty of care ought to arise. Similarly, in *MK (a child) v Oldham NHS Trust* [2003] Lloyds Rep Med 1, the court held that an insufficient degree of proximity existed between the claimant's parents and defendant Trust sufficient to impose a duty of care. In this case, there had been disruption of family life as a result of a prolonged investigation of the child's injuries by medical and social services during which the child had been separated from the parents.

In certain circumstances the type and effect of treatment, as well as a possible indirect effect of that intervention on a spouse or family member, may be sufficient to deem that a proximate relationship exists between the doctor and third party (*Goodwill v BPAS* [1996] 2 All ER 161). A doctor who gave contraceptive advice to a patient was held not to owe a duty of care to those persons who might engage in future sexual relations with the patient. In these circumstances, however, the doctor might owe a duty of care to the patient's spouse because in giving such advice, the doctor, knowing that the patient was married, could reasonably be expected to have that spouse or partner in mind at the time of the consultation.

3.2.1(c) 'Fair, just and reasonable'

The third factor that has been used by the courts to determine whether a duty of care is owed is based upon whether it would be 'fair, just and reasonable' to impose a duty in the circumstances. This requirement permits the court a wide discretion as to whether to permit, or reject, a duty of care. Within the medical context once a doctor has accepted a patient, a close (proximate) professional relationship automatically arises and it seems almost self-evident that it will be considered fair, just and reasonable that a duty of care will arise. Outside the typical doctor and patient relationship the court is generally reluctant to find that a duty of care extends to the public on grounds of public policy (*Palmer v Tees Health Authority* [1999] Lloyds Rep Med 151). The case concerned a woman who claimed nervous shock following the death of her daughter at the hands of a mentally disordered patient who had a history of paedophilia and violence. The issue that arose was whether or not the Health Authority owed a duty of care to the mother of the victim and more widely to the public at large on the basis that at the time of discharge the Health Authority was aware of the patient's violent nature. The Court of Appeal found that although the harm caused to the child had been foreseeable, the issue concerned proximity. The Health Authority owed no duty of care under the circumstances because the identity of the victim was unknown and unascertainable, and it could not be foreseen that the patient would have harmed a particular member of society. A salient point concerned what the defendant could have done to avoid the danger if suggested treatment or precautions were of doubtful effectiveness. Stuart-Smith LJ reserved judgement as to what would be an appropriate test if the victim had been known, or at least identifiable.

3.2.2   Good Samaritan acts

In first aid situations, such as the provision of assistance at a road traffic accident, a medical practitioner owes no legal duty to offer assistance unless this is required by the doctor's contract of employment. An employment-based contractual duty could, however, arise where a general practitioner is assisting at the road side and the injured party is a patient on the practitioner's list. Furthermore, the GP contract states that emergency care should be offered to all persons who may not be on the list, but nonetheless reside within the doctor's practice area, provided that the patient's own doctor is unable to provide immediate treatment (the National Health Service (General Medical Services) Regulations 1992) (SI 1992/635 Schedule 2, paragraph 4 (H)).

For all doctors, however, failure to offer first aid or emergency assistance might be grounds for a disciplinary hearing before the General Medical Council. This compares with many European jurisdictions where criminal and civil sanctions may be brought against even lay members of the public who fail to offer emergency assistance particularly in circumstances where assistance would be relatively straightforward to provide.

> The retired doctor is approached by Simon's parents. In agreeing to examine Simon and give advice in his capacity as a doctor,
>
> ▶ Has the doctor voluntarily assumed a duty of care for the child?
> ▶ If he had refused to assist for any reason whatsoever, could legal action have been brought against him even if such assistance might have saved Simon's life?
> ▶ Could he have been called before the General Medical Council on account of his conduct if he had refused to see or examine Simon?

3.2.3 Commencement of the doctor–patient relationship

Doctors have a duty to treat patients who are under their care although this does not extend to strangers. The duty of care is established once the doctor–patient relationship commences.

A stranger becomes a general practitioner's patient when that person is registered on the doctor's list and a duty of care is established at that stage (NHS (Choice of Medical Practitioner) Regulations 1998, SI 1992/635). In hospitals, such a relationship commences once there is an undertaking to provide treatment or medical care to that person. This assumption of duty need not necessarily be explicit, but can be implied from the relationship since an NHS hospital provides a public service and the doctor is employed by the hospital to provide that care and service. Once a patient is accepted by the hospital for advice and treatment services, then a duty of care will be owed. For this reason the duty of care might exist even before a patient is seen by a member of the health-care team. In *Barnett v Chelsea and Kensington Hospital Management Committee* [1969] 1 QB 428, the court found that a close and direct relationship between the hospital and the (deceased) patient imposed a duty of care on the hospital which transferred to those health-care practitioners who were employed to provide services at that time.

3.2.4 Non-delegable duties of care

A primary duty of care may be owed to a patient by a person or organisation other than a doctor. National Health Service Trusts and Health Authorities have a primary duty to provide a safe and reasonable standard of care to patients. This non-delegable duty extends to the provision of skilled medical staff and premises that are adequate and fit for purpose (*Wilsher v Essex AHA* [1986] 3 All ER 801) (CA)). Although a named individual does not necessarily need to be found, proof of causation will still be required to bring a successful claim. Several successful cases have been brought such as *Bull v Devon AHA* [1993] 4 Med LR 117 (CA), where the system in place for summoning doctors to provide emergency obstetric care was inadequate, and *Robertson v Nottingham Health Authority* [1997] 8 Med LR1. More recently, in *Farraj v King's Healthcare NHS Trust (KCH)* [2009] EWCA Civ 1203, the Court of Appeal held that the non-delegable duty of care owed by a hospital to its patients can, in certain circumstances, be discharged by delegating performance of a task to a competent independent contractor. The case concerned a Jordanian couple who both carried a gene for a very severe blood disorder. Because of this known risk, Mrs Farraj underwent prenatal genetic screening in Jordan. The sample was sent to the Kings Healthcare NHS Trust in London to determine whether the foetus had inherited the gene. Trusts tend to outsource specialities such as laboratory and radiology services, and Kings sent the sample to an independent laboratory which failed to identify that the sample contained maternal, rather than foetal, cells and as a result provided an erroneous negative result. The court at first instance held that the independent laboratory was two-thirds to blame and the NHS Trust, one-third. This was reversed on appeal in that the laboratory was 100% to blame.

The Secretary of State owes a statutory duty of care under the common law. In *Re HIV Haemophiliac Litigation* [1996] PNLR 290, the Secretary of State was held liable for negligence after blood purchased from the United States led to haemophiliac patients being infected following transfusions with a blood product contaminated by HIV. The case was settled out of court and did not proceed to a full hearing. Although the action brought in was negligence, it is arguable that judicial review might have been more appropriate in this instance.

3.2.5 Duty owed to third parties

The fundamental difficulty in establishing that a duty of care is owed to a person who is not a patient arises from the *Caparo* principles that are used to establish whether a duty of care is owed in the circumstances. It is difficult to establish the existence of a proximate relationship between a doctor and a third party or a secondary victim (*Palmer v Tees Health Authority* [1999] Lloyds Rep Med 359) (see 3.2.1 (c)).

In certain circumstances, however, a duty of care might arise between a doctor and a third party who suffers post-traumatic stress disorder as a result of witnessing negligent medical care. The principles established by *Alcock v Chief Constable of South Yorkshire* [1992] 1 AC 310 and *White v Chief Constable of South Yorkshire* [1999] 2 AC 455 require that the injured person must

(a) have a close relationship with the victim;
(b) be close to the incident (in terms of time and space);
(c) witness the incident, or its aftermath (with unaided senses) and
(d) suffer recognisable psychiatric illness as a result of witnessing the event.

In *X (minors) v Bedfordshire County Council* [1995] 2 AC 633, the House of Lords held that a doctor examining a child for suspected child abuse had no further duty beyond that which was not to injure the individual during the examination. Later, in *Phelps v Hillingdon LBC* [2000] 4 All ER 504, the House of Lords held that a doctor employed by a local authority could owe the patients he or she examines a duty of care in certain circumstances.

3.3 Breach of the duty of care

The second step in a case of alleged clinical negligence is for the claimant to prove, on the balance of probabilities, that the doctor has breached the duty of care. This is on the basis that the doctor did not provide the requisite standard of care that would have been expected in the circumstances.

3.3.1 Standard of care: the *Bolam* test

Traditionally, for an action in negligence, the standard of care is set by the court on the basis of what the reasonable man would have done under such circumstances. Where care has been delivered by a medical practitioner, however, the standard of care is set by the medical profession as evidenced by medical expert witness testimony. The yardstick for the standard of care expected of doctors has become known as the *Bolam* test from the case of *Bolam v Friern Hospital Management Committee* [1957] WLR 582. Mr Bolam suffered from a depressive illness for which his psychiatrist prescribed electroconvulsive therapy (ECT). One effect of ECT is convulsive shaking and twitching of the body, and as a result there is a small risk of fracture. Mr Bolam was not warned of this risk. He was not prescribed muscle relaxant drugs nor was he restrained during the procedure. During his treatment he sustained a fractured hip which led to serious complications. Medical opinion at that time was divided on the benefits of using relaxant drugs during ECT, as well as use of physical restraint and the need to warn patients of the risk of fracture. Mr Bolam brought an action in negligence arguing that the defendants were negligent in not prescribing relaxants, for not restraining him and further for not warning him about the risks of the procedure. He lost the case.

The *Bolam* case was decided by a jury (as medical negligence cases were at that time) and although this was a first instance decision, the effects of this judgement and the test have survived more than five decades. McNair J, in his direction to the jury, said that in a situation which involves the use of some special skill or competence, the test for negligence is not based on what the proverbial 'reasonable man' (i.e. the man on top of the Clapham omnibus) would have done, since that man would not have possessed that special skill. The test would be the standard expected of the ordinary skilled man who professes to have and exercises that special skill. He went on to state that a doctor is not guilty of negligence if he has acted in accordance with a practice accepted as proper by a responsible body of medical men skilled in that particular art. Thus, the test for the standard in medical negligence is different to that in other forms of negligence, where the standard is set by the court based upon the actions of the reasonable man. In medical negligence, the standard is essentially set by doctors on the basis of what a body of medical opinion would regard as being proper practice. The *Bolam* test is perceived by many as erecting an almost insurmountable hurdle for claimants to clear before they can succeed in a negligence action.

3.3.1(a) Endorsement of the Bolam standard

The *Bolam* test, or standard, applies not only to doctors but to health-care professionals more generally. The test has been approved by the House of Lords in *Maynard v West Midlands RHA* [1985] 1 All ER 635, in *Whitehouse v Jordan* [1981] 1 All ER 267 and *Sidaway v Board of Governors of Bethlem Royal Hospital* [1985] 1 All ER 643.

The effect of *Bolam* is that it is not easy for a claimant in a clinical negligence action to prove a breach of the duty of care. Introducing evidence from an expert to the effect that the procedure should not have been carried out in the manner that it was will not be sufficient. In fact, as McNair J stated, a doctor is not negligent if he acts in accordance with accepted practice merely because there is a body of opinion that takes a contrary view. To avoid liability the defendant would need to show evidence that a responsible body of medical opinion supports the way in which the defendant had acted. The standard expected is that of acceptable practice rather than the 'gold standard' of care (*Bellarby v Worthing and Southlands Hospitals NHS Trust* [2005] EWHC 2089). Doctors are not expected to have read every article or all published material that pertains to their practice. In *Crawford v Board of Governors of Charing Cross Hospital* (1953) (*The Times*, 8 December), this particular point was raised by a claimant who sued following the development of brachial palsy after his arm had been positioned awkwardly for an extended period during an operation. The risks of brachial palsy had been described in an article in a medical journal known as *The Lancet* 6 months previously, but the defendant anaesthetist had not read this. Lord Denning pronounced that it would be too high a burden to expect doctors to have read every article that appeared in the current medical press. However, *Crawford* was a pre-*Bolam* decision and it seems likely that with the rapid escalation of accessibility of information that the standard of knowledge expected of doctors might well be determined according to the *Bolam* test. Doctors of today are expected to keep abreast of recent developments in their fields of expertise as part of their professional responsibilities and continuing obligation to keep their practice under review.

In *Maynard v West Midlands RHA* [1985] 1 All ER 635, the claimant's symptoms could have been attributed to either tuberculosis or Hodgkin's disease (a form of blood cancer). Because of clinical doubt, it was recommended that she undergo a test for Hodgkin's disease. The diagnostic procedure carried an inherent risk of damage to her vocal cords, an injury that later materialised. In fact, the claimant had tuberculosis. In bringing an action, she presented expert evidence that the likelihood of her symptoms *not* being tuberculosis was so small that it did not justify the risk inherent in the diagnostic procedure used to rule out Hodgkin's disease. The trial judge found for the claimant but the decision was reversed on appeal. In the House of Lords, Lord Scarman stated that a judge's preference for one body of professional opinion to another was insufficient to establish negligence and that the courts should defer to expert opinion if this was truthfully expressed and honestly held. Negligence was not to be established by a preference for the opinion of one respected body as against that of another.

A further issue concerns the extent to which the opinion of the defendant actually represents that held by a 'substantial body', since much depends upon the interpretation of the word 'substantial'. In *De Freitas v O'Brien* [1995] 6 Med LR 108, expert evidence for the defendant showed that only a small minority of neurosurgeons would have endorsed the conduct of the defendant. Nevertheless, the Court of Appeal accepted this opinion as *Bolam*-compliant, and found for the defendant.

3.3.2 Criticisms of the *Bolam* standard

Several objections have been raised against the *Bolam* test. A major criticism is that the standard of care required of doctors is set by the medical profession, rather than by the courts. In an action of clinical negligence, if the conduct of a doctor accused of negligence is supported by a body of peers then that sets the standard against which the doctor is judged. It has been argued that such a test is self-serving and that the standard should be set more objectively by law. The archetypal example is a car driver charged with negligent driving. The driver's defence that other respectable drivers would have done the same in the circumstances would not be persuasive. In fact, the driver would be judged according to the expected standard as objectively viewed rather than by what other drivers in his or her position might have done. For these reasons, there is a perception that the courts have been excessively deferential to the medical profession (Woolf, 2001).

The *Bolam* test is considered to impose a high and arguably unattainable burden on claimants in order to prove their case. Sheldon (1998) argues that a responsible body of medical professionals could, in certain circumstances, be a single person and if indeed this does constitute a responsible body of opinion, then there is little or no chance of a claimant succeeding in a case of medical negligence. There is a perception that the law is more concerned with the reputation of the medical profession and its protection thereof (Montgomery, 1989).

The requisite standard of care that the doctor must meet is that which ought to be achieved as opposed to that which is actually achieved by other ordinary professionals practicing that particular art. Although adherence to accepted professional practice confers a large degree of protection on the defendant, it is not necessarily sufficient to avoid an allegation of negligence (*Edward Wong v Johnson Stokes and Master* [1984] AC 296). It is arguable that, particularly in health-care circumstances, a yardstick akin to the *Bolam* standard cannot reflect the reasonable and justifiable expectations of the public and a more objective criterion ought to be applied that is better able to withstand objective external scrutiny.

3.3.2(a) Does medical expert opinion reflect 'medical opinion'?

A further reason for moving away from the *Bolam* standard is the basis by which a body of responsible medical opinion is obtained for the purposes of adjudication. Determination of the standard is generally based upon expert medical testimony. It has been argued that such opinion is not necessarily reflective of mainstream opinion, since these experts may be 'hired hands' and instructed solely for the purposes of defending an action (Teff, 1998).

The results from an empirical study indicated that as many as two-thirds of expert witnesses were asked to modify their reports by the commissioning lawyer, and one-third of this group had done so as a result of this request (Teff, 1998). This finding raises questions as to the extent to which expert evidence presented to the court is truly 'independent'. It has been suggested that some experts have highly tuned presentational skills and that this alone could influence the court more than the actual content of the written report. This finding, if accurate, plus the known tendency for legal firms to 'shop around' until a sympathetic expert is found, would tend to favour institutional defendants. Ultimately, however, the *Bolam* test is a rule of evidence rather than a principle of law.

3.3.2(b) The Bolam standard and the Human Rights Act 1998

Prior to implementation of the Human Rights Act 1998 it was anticipated that clinical negligence actions might change considerably and that the *Bolam* standard would become of lesser effect, since the judiciary would be expected to pay greater attention to claimant's rights. However, this expectation has failed to materialise. It seems therefore that a claim brought under the Human Rights Act 1998 would need to be a free-standing and additional course of action rather than the incorporation of an additional principle into the determination of the standard of care (*Re Organ Retention Group Litigation* [2004] EWHC 644).

3.3.3   *Bolam* in retreat

There is an argument that clinical negligence litigation should be conducted in a more independent manner particularly in the context of the appraisal of the standard of care, as determined by expert evidence, and that this role ought to be undertaken by the court. This approach was apparent in the *dicta* of the appellate decision of *Bolitho v City and Hackney Health Authority* [1997] 4 All ER 771.

3.3.3(a) The new Bolam standard

The facts of *Bolitho* were that a 2-year-old boy, who had recurrent respiratory problems, suffered severe brain damage during an attack of croup and as a result suffered a cardiac arrest and subsequently died. Evidence was accepted that the on-call paediatric registrar had negligently failed to attend. The defendant's argument was based on causation in that even if she had attended she would not have intubated (inserted a tube down the wind pipe to help breathing) the patient, on the grounds that the procedure itself was not without significant risk for a child of that age. The judge was required to consider two issues. First, what would the doctor have done, or instructed others to do, had she attended, and second, to what extent was it negligent to arrive at a decision not to intubate. Expert evidence on the matter was diametrically opposed. The case was appealed to the House of Lords and was eventually dismissed on grounds of causation (see 3.4.1). However, the *obiter* comments of Lord Browne-Wilkinson are considered important for understanding how the courts may take a more interventionist stance with regard to the standard of care.

Lord Browne-Wilkinson's view was that although a defendant doctor might lead evidence from a number of medical experts who were honestly and truly of the opinion that the care received was in accordance with mainstream medical opinion, this would not necessarily mean that the defendant doctor would automatically escape liability. It would have to be shown that such an opinion had a logical basis. In developing this theme, he went on to say that it was a matter of weighing risks against benefits before the judge could accept the body of opinion as being demonstrative of the standard of care. If professional opinion is not capable of withstanding logical analysis, then that body of opinion cannot be regarded as reasonable or responsible, even though it might emanate from respectable personages.

The effect of *Bolitho* is that the House of Lords has indicated in *obiter* comments that the *Bolam* standard ought not to be unquestioningly accepted as being equivalent to the expected standard of care, and that more is required. In essence it is for the court rather than the medical profession to determine what is 'reasonable' since the *Bolam* test is a rule of practice or evidence. As Lord Bridge in *Sidaway* recognised about the application of the *Bolam* test in the context of information disclosure,

> ...I do not see that this approach involves the necessity 'to hand over to the medical profession the entire question of the scope of the duty of disclosure, including the question whether there has been a breach of that duty'. Of course, if there is a conflict of evidence whether a

responsible body of medical opinion approves of non-disclosure in a particular case, the judge will have to resolve that conflict.

The court as impartial adjudicator is expected to take a proactive role and examine the logical basis of expert testimony. Empirical data on the perception of lawyers with regard to the standard of care indicates that the judgement in *Bolitho* may continue to effect a shift away from the *Bolam* standard (Samanta et al., 2006). It seems possible, however, that the court's role as ultimate decision-maker might be weakened, in all but the most straightforward of instances, due to the need of the Court to consult even more experts in order to fully exercise its discretion.

3.3.3(b) Post-Bolitho *jurisprudence*

The *Bolitho* approach of scrutinising evidence that forms the basis of the standard of care and whether or not it withstands logical analysis can be seen in subsequent decisions. In *Wisniewski v Central Manchester Health Authority* [1998] *Lloyds Rep Med* 223, expert witnesses disagreed about the reasonableness of the defendant's failure to carry out a procedure which, if it had been performed, would have detected that a baby's umbilical cord was wrapped around its neck during its birth. In scrutinising the evidence, the court took the step of evaluating which expert's evidence was sustained on a logical basis.

In *Reynolds v North Tyneside Health Authority* [2002] All ER (D) 523, an infant was born with cerebral palsy due to cord prolapse. Evidence of the midwife's failure to examine the claimant's mother properly was scrutinised closely and disregarded. Bruce J stated that the only reason articulated in support of not conducting a vaginal examination was the risk of infection. On the evidence, this decision did not withstand scrutiny and, having taken all matters into consideration, the evidence for the defendant's practice was regarded as being neither logical nor defensible.

In *Marriott v West Midlands Regional Health Authority* [1999] *Lloyds Rep Med* 23, the Court of Appeal scrutinised the evidence of the defendant's experts and concluded that this could not be logically supported. In essence, Mr Marriott had suffered a head injury and had been unconscious for between 20 and 30 minutes. He was taken to hospital and discharged the following day. The following week he consulted his general practitioner on account of headache and lack of appetite. The doctor advised him to contact him again if his condition deteriorated. Four days later the claimant lost consciousness and had to undergo surgical removal of a large blood clot and was left permanently disabled. The claimant's case was that the general practitioner was negligent in failing to refer him back to hospital. Although there was a body of expert evidence to support the actions the doctor had taken, the trial judge concluded that in the circumstances where there was a risk of an intracranial lesion the only reasonable and prudent course of action was to admit the patient for further neurological investigations. In reaching this decision, the court took a more critical view of expert evidence and rejected the evidence provided on behalf of the defendant as being neither logical nor defensible.

Nowadays the court is in a stronger position to challenge the views of medical evidence. Better information is now readily available. The burgeoning of medical literature as well as the plethora of clinical guidelines from respected authorities means that there is a readily available source of clinical standard for what is regarded as good practice. The development of concepts such as evidence-based medicine and guidelines from eminent institutions such as NICE have helped to provide accessible barometers of good clinical care. Brazier and Miola (2000) have argued that the development of nationally promulgated guidelines alongside the judgement in *Bolitho* is likely to cause a shift away from the *Bolam* standard. Empirical work examining the perceptions of lawyers suggests that these factors, together with societal changes and greater expectations of the medical profession, may further lead to a move away from the traditional *Bolam* standard to one that is undertaken by the court in a more enquiring and scrutinising fashion (Samanta et al., 2006) with the overall potential for challenging the bulwark of *Bolam*.

3.3.3(c) Deference to the medical profession?

Lord Woolf (2001) has suggested, extra-judicially, that since *Bolitho* there has been a move away from the standard of care perceived by many as excessively deferential to the medical profession. He suggests that a more objective approach is being adopted largely on account of the courts' experiences in setting aside decisions of judicial review on behalf of the Crown in public affairs. In comparison to the latter, challenging the medical profession was relatively 'small beer'. The courts have also been influenced by recognition of the difficulties that claimants confront in bringing successful clinical negligence actions in circumstances where actionable harm has occurred. Other factors include the growth of the rights-based culture, as well as the perceived tarnishing of the medical profession's beneficent approach which has been vitiated by escalation of media reports that have served to highlight the perceived deficiencies of doctors, individually and collectively. Some reports have suggested that there is something fundamentally amiss with the health services and medical care. There has been an increasing awareness of patients' rights and as a result, the public expectation of all health-care professionals has grown exponentially.

The scale of medical litigation has increased substantially, even though the proportion of successful claims remains relatively small. The insurance industry has changed its approach to claims handling to a strategy that every case is worth fighting.

The courts of some jurisdictions, such as Canada and Australia, are progressively rejecting the approach of the English courts. In *Rogers v Whittaker* (1992) 109 ALR 625, the Australian Court concluded that the standard of care adopted by the medical profession is not solely, or primarily, determined according to practice supported by a responsible body of opinion and has instead adopted a more interventionist approach. Incorporation of the European Convention of Human Rights into English domestic law is also a factor that is encouraging the move away from the more traditional approach of accepting that the standard of care in clinical negligence is one that is primarily supported by a responsible body of medical opinion.

3.3.4 The standard of care in specific circumstances

Determination of the standard of care in specific circumstances and situations is illustrated by a range of judicial decisions as illustrated below.

3.3.4(a) Innovative techniques

For the use or application of medical innovation, the court has endorsed experimental techniques in circumstances where the alternative is serious harm or death as evidenced by the pragmatic approach in *Simms v Simms* [2002] 2 WLR 1465 and *A v A* [2003] 1 All ER 669. Whether application of a new technique might amount to negligence is assessed with respect to its potential risks and hazards and the patient's previous response to other mainstream therapy as assessed against the prognosis and seriousness of the patient's condition. In *Cooper v Royal United Hospital Bath NHS Trust* (2004) (unreported), it was held that the Trust had breached its duty of care in implementing an alternative technique without adequately informing the patient of its inherent risks. The standard of care expected in the delivery of new therapies would be that of the doctor who is reasonably competent in using such treatment. By its very nature, this might be difficult especially where a medical or surgical technique is original or innovative. Surgical techniques, in particular, require skilled operation, much of which is gained through repetition and practice, and a recognised 'learning curve' for the development of skills is apparent. The need to develop proficiency raises issues as to when it is ethically justifiable to continue with the learning curve that is a necessary precursor to safe practice during the development and perfection of new techniques (Healey and Samanta, 2008).

For new and experimental treatment and techniques, the claim might be brought under the Compensation Act 2006, for example, where a promising new treatment turns out to be ineffective. Section 1 allows the court, in considering a claim in negligence for breach of statutory duty may, in determining whether the defendant ought to have taken particular steps to meet the standard of care (by taking precautions against a risk or otherwise), have regard to the potential deterrent effect of such precautions on practitioners from undertaking desirable and pioneering activities.

3.3.4(b) Scarce resources

The NHS has finite resources and, as a result, the care that can be provided is limited. This factor can at times make judging the standard of care in negligence actions all the more difficult. Section 1 of the National Health Service Act 2006 does not impose a statutory duty to provide specific health-care services, and the court has traditionally been reluctant to find against resource allocation decisions unless a decision is irrational or interferes with the principle of proportionality with respect to a Convention right (see 2.18). It would not be reasonable to impose liability on NHS employees for failing to provide what is perceived to be an adequate standard of care if they do not have the resources or ability to change their practice. It has been argued that under such circumstances attribution of fault to hospital trusts or clinical staff is unreasonable and that the standard of care ought to be modified where there is evidence of underfunding (Witting, 2001).

In *Knight v Home Office* [1990] 3 All ER 237, insufficient resources were considered to be relevant to the standard of care that could be expected in a prison hospital. The prisoner, who had been detained under the Mental Health Act 1959, received care that was not commensurate with that which he would have expected in a psychiatric hospital. Although the patient was known to have suicidal tendencies he was not under continual watch. He committed suicide by hanging, and it was argued that the Home Office had failed to provide appropriate care. In giving judgement Pill J said that he was unable to accept that practices in a prison hospital ought to be judged by the standard appropriate in a specialist psychiatric specialist hospital, and that in a prison hospital there could be circumstances where the standard was below what might be expected in an NHS unit. This would not necessarily mean that the prison hospital had been negligent. However, a prison hospital did have a duty to provide a basic minimum level of care.

Knight is an old case and whether this view would prevail seems questionable. The case of *Brooks v Home Office* [1999] 2 FLR 33 (QBD) concerned the antenatal care of a prisoner who had a high risk pregnancy. As a result of not receiving immediate referral following an ultrasound scan which revealed that the pregnancy was at risk, the weaker twin died prior to birth. Garland J rejected *Knight v Home Office* as authority that a lesser level of care would apply and *Brooks* now appears indicative of the standard expected. In *Bull v Devon Area Health Authority* [1993] 4 Med LR 117, the Court of Appeal stated that a certain minimum and fixed standard of care is necessary as the benchmark for what should be provided irrespective of resource and other constraints. While this might seem a harsh and unrealistic approach, it is arguably justified on the basis that a variable standard of care would inevitably deny compensation to worthy claimants and lead to unfair disparities between NHS trusts.

3.3.4(c) Emergency situations

There is no legal duty for doctors to offer assistance in medical emergencies if they are off duty, although failure to offer such assistance might result in disciplinary action by the regulator (see 3.2.2). Once a doctor undertakes to provide assistance in an emergency, a duty of care arises and the practitioner could potentially be liable for negligent conduct.

On grounds of public policy, and the need to encourage emergency assistance, the standard expected is that of 'reasonable care'. It has been suggested that liability should arise only if the victim's medical condition is made worse as a result of the first aid. An application of the *Bolam* test assessed against a standard of care expected in a more conducive health-care environment would be unfair since the realities of most emergency situations are such that it would be almost impossible for a doctor to offer the same level of care as could be offered in a well-equipped hospital or a surgery. As recognised by Mustill LJ in *Wilsher v Essex Area Health Authority* [1986] 3A11 ER 801, in an emergency situation a doctor might well be working under 'battle conditions', and that in these circumstances 'allowances' had to be made.

3.3.4(d) Inexperienced practitioners

The extent to which a health-care professional's inexperience ought to reduce the standard of care expected arose in *Wilsher*. A premature infant was negligently given excessive oxygen and as a result developed a condition of the retina that led to almost complete loss of vision. The error occurred while the child was treated in the Special Care Unit where an inexperienced doctor inserted a catheter (a small tube) into a vein, rather than an artery. The mistake was not spotted by a middle grade doctor, who later repeated the error and following which the infant received an excessive amount of oxygen. The court recognised that a junior hospital doctor would not have the same level of experience as a senior doctor, and that junior doctors need to gain practical experience without the threat of litigation. Nonetheless, the law requires the trainee or novice to be judged by the same standard of care expected as that of a more experienced colleague, for several reasons. If a lesser standard was applied, then lack of experience could be used as a defence to a negligence claim. Furthermore, a patient entering the health-care system has a legitimate expectation of receiving a level of care appropriate to the condition being treated or the intervention undertaken. According to Mustill LJ and Glidewell LJ, expectation of a lower standard of care from an inexperienced practitioner would have a negative impact on patient care and confidence (see 3.4.1).

Sir Nicholas Brown-Wilkinson dissented in that since junior doctors need to gain experience it was unfair to hold them at fault in the event that they lacked the specific skills that were necessary. However, the exacting standard imposed by the court on the learner doctor has been justified on the grounds that the junior, as part of the learning process, should be able to identify when help is required and must ask for assistance from more experienced colleagues in order to discharge the duty of care.

> On arriving at the paediatric unit, Simon was seen by a junior doctor, Preeti. On the facts it can be assumed that Preeti owed Simon a duty of care.
>
> ▶ What is the standard of care expected from an inexperienced doctor who has only recently joined a specialist department?
> ▶ What does the law require a junior doctor's standard of care to be measured against?
> ▶ How can the duty of care that is owed by an inexperienced person be discharged if the person feels 'out of her depth'?
> ▶ Comment on Preeti's decision to contact the consultant.
> ▶ What can Preeti do to ensure that she's taken all reasonable steps?

3.3.4(e) Misdiagnosis

Liability may be incurred on account of misdiagnosis or failure to diagnose. In *Chin Keow v Government of Malaysia* [1967] 1 WLR 813, the defendant was liable for failing to take a proper medical history. Likewise, in *Langley v Campbell* (1975) *The Times*, 6 November, the defendant was liable for failing to diagnose malaria in a patient who had recently returned from East Africa. A relative gave evidence that the family had suggested the diagnosis to the doctor, who nonetheless failed to investigate. In *Tuffill v East Surrey Area Health Authority* (1978) *The Times*, 15 March, failure to diagnose amoebic dysentery in a patient who spent many years in a tropical environment was considered negligent. In situations of clinical doubt, the patient should be referred for specialist opinion since failure to do so might result in actionable harm. In *Official Solicitor v Allinson* [2004] EWHC 923, the general practitioner had negligently failed to diagnose breast cancer despite finding a localised lump in the breast and had failed to refer the patient to a specialist.

In recent years investigative and diagnostic techniques such as radiology and other forms of non-invasive imaging have improved greatly. Patient expectations have increased on account of self-diagnosis often informed by media portrayal and Internet-informed expectations of innovative, and frequently expensive, treatment modalities. While patient education and awareness is undoubtedly a beneficial and positive development, this can at times lead to unrealistic expectations and mistrust of health-care professionals. Enhanced information can lead to proliferation of the 'worried well' syndrome and contribute to over investigation and demand for non-evidenced-based care. Since most medications and investigative procedures carry some risk of side effects and iatrogenic harm, health-care professionals have a duty to counsel and advise as necessary. Although the law is clear that doctors have no duty to provide non-clinically indicated treatment (*Re J (a minor) (Wardship: Medical Treatment)* [1990]

3 All ER 930), the temptation to satisfy the demands of vociferous and well-informed patients might be acute, particularly where chronic illness is concerned. Where there is clinical doubt, or on request, patients are entitled to a specialist or second opinion. It seems likely, therefore, that liability arising from misdiagnosis, or harm caused through over-investigation, might well increase.

3.3.4(f) Alternative medicine

The standard of care expected from an alternative health-care practitioner was examined in *Shakoor v Situ* [2001] 1 WLR 410 where the defendant was a practitioner of traditional Chinese herbal medicine. The patient had consulted the defendant for a skin condition and after taking the prescribed herbal medicine suffered acute liver failure and died. The practitioner stated that on the basis of his knowledge based on Chinese medical textbooks and periodicals, he had believed that the remedy was completely safe. The literature from orthodox medical journals, however, indicated that the ingestion of similar compounds gave risk of liver damage.

The claim failed on the basis that the practitioner had practiced his 'art' according to the prevailing standard. In line with the *Bolam* approach the defendant could not be judged by the standard of a practitioner of orthodox medicine since he did not hold himself out as such. However, the *caveat* to this defence is that the claimant might wish to take an approach that the prevailing standard of skill and care of the practitioner was deficient on the basis that it failed to take into account publicised evidence of side effects and that the standard of care provided by the practitioner was deficient, compared to the standard expected in this jurisdiction.

3.3.4(g) Information disclosure

The leading case for negligent information disclosure is *Sidaway v Board of Governors of the Bethlem Royal Hospital* [1985] 1 All ER 643 (HL), which involved a patient who had surgery to relieve persistent pain. The surgery carried a small but inherent risk of damage to the spinal cord in the region of 1–2%. Mrs Sidaway was not informed of this risk which unfortunately materialised and following which she became severely disabled. She subsequently brought an action in negligence on the grounds that she had been given insufficient information to give valid consent. The question for the court concerned how much information should she have received in the circumstances.

The majority opinion of the House of Lords (Lords Diplock, Keith and Bridge) felt that a *Bolam* standard ought to be applied to ascertain the level of information disclosure required. Lord Templeman's view was that the amount of information should be that which would enable the patient to make a balanced judgement and that it was for the doctor to decide what information should be given. Lord Scarman dissented by rejecting the *Bolam* approach. According to Lord Scarman, the question for the court is whether, under the circumstances, the claimant received the level of information that a reasonably prudent patient would expect to receive in order to make an informed decision of the risks and benefits. The implications of *Sidaway* are that material risks of a procedure must be disclosed but the level of disclosure is essentially a medical determination assessed according to the *Bolam* standard. However, the validity of this approach in the context of current practice has been questioned (see 4.6.2).

3.4 Causation

To succeed in an action of clinical negligence, once it has been established that the claimant was owed a duty of care that was breached, the next step is to prove that the breach caused damage recognised in law. This means that the claimant must prove on the balance of probabilities that actionable damage was caused by the negligent act. It is insufficient to show that the health-care professional was negligent.

The need to prove causation is often perceived to be an unfair and unjust requirement. For the claimant lawyer the need to prove causation can be difficult particularly in the context of health care. The reasons are manifold. The patient who receives health care will often have a pre-existing condition which might complicate the ability to demonstrate the required causal link between the negligent act and the damage sustained. Where there are multiple causes of injury or damage, proving causation on the basis of a single negligent act is likely to be problematic. Furthermore, there might well have been an anticipated deterioration in health due to the natural history of the claimant's pre-existing disease and it might not be easy to tease out the difference between natural progression of the patient's pre-existing ill-health and the supervening effect of the negligent act or omission.

3.4.1 The 'but for' test

The standard used to establish causation is known as the 'but for' test. In effect, this means that 'but for' the negligent act the claimant's condition would have been diagnosed, or the claimant would not have suffered the injuries in question. A straightforward application of the test can be seen in *Barnett v Chelsea and Kensington HMC* [1968] 1 All ER 1068. In this particular case, a doctor refused to see a man who attended Casualty complaining of abdominal pain. The man died shortly afterwards due to arsenic poisoning. Evidence was available that although the doctor had negligently refused to see the patient, arsenic poisoning was rare and there was very little chance that an effective antidote would have been given even if he had attended the patient. Thus, although refusal to examine and admit the patient was negligent, the breach of duty of care did not cause the death of the patient who would have died in any event.

> Simon sustained permanent brain damage following the lumbar puncture. Even though the care received by Simon during the procedure did not meet the standard expected according to the *Bolam* test, causation must still be proved. If Simon's injury would not have occurred 'but for' the defendant's negligence, then that negligent act or omission is the cause of the injury.
>
> ▶ 'But for' the negligent act or omission would the damage have occurred?
> ▶ If the answer is 'no' then factual causation is proved.
> ▶ If the answer is 'yes' then other filters may need to be applied before causation can be proved.

The reality of many clinical situations is that a patient is usually suffering from a pre-existing condition or else may have other operative factors which complicate the causal link between the negligent act and the damage. Difficulties typically arise where there is more than one causative factor that has contributed to the injury in question. These problems, which are common, has led to modification of the 'but for' principle in certain circumstances.

In *Wilsher v Essex* [1988] 1 All ER 871, a premature infant was negligently given excess oxygen therapy and as a result developed a condition that led to blindness in one eye and seriously impaired the vision of the other. In evidence, it emerged that the negligent administration of oxygen was one of five possible causes that might have led to retrolental fibroplasia, or at least could have materially contributed to the development of the condition. On the balance of probabilities, it could not be proved that the harm had been caused by the negligence of the defendant, and therefore the action failed. On the face of it, this seems a harsh decision but in the view of Lord Bridge, only Parliament could change the required proof of fault that caused damage as the basis of liability in tort. In fact, it would be a disservice to society if the process was made unpredictable by distortion of the law in order to try and accommodate sympathetically the exigencies of 'hard' cases.

> Simon is known to have meningitis, a serious condition with inherent complications including death and brain damage. The locum doctor alleges that even if he had not performed the lumbar puncture Simon would have suffered brain damage in any event.
>
> ▶ What defence has the locum doctor raised?
> ▶ What is the law of multiple causative factors?
> ▶ If an action is brought, what is likely to be the outcome on the basis of *Wilsher*?
> ▶ Does it seem likely that the claim will succeed?

The potential difficulties of proving causation can be illustrated by the House of Lords decision of *Bolitho* (see 3.3.3(a)) where the case was argued on the basis of the doctor's failure to attend the child rather than a breach on account of failure to intubate. Although the doctor admitted that her failure to attend had been negligent, she argued that even if she had attended she would not have intubated on account of the inherent risks of the procedure, and that the symptoms of the child at that stage did not justify the taking of such risks. The expert evidence for the justification of intubation was equivocal. On a straightforward application of the 'but for' test, based upon the defendant's admitted negligent failure to attend, the claim failed on causation.

The approach of the appellate courts was to ask two questions: first, would the doctor have intubated the child if she had attended (this was answered in the negative on account of the evidence); second, was it negligent to decide not to intubate? If the evidence was such that she should have intubated, then causation would be established; however, since the evidence was inconclusive, the claimant lost the case. According to Grubb and Jones (Grubb, 2004), the approach of the House of Lords was unexpected on at least three grounds. First, it seems undesirable and counter-intuitive to base causation on an approach where there may be evidence to suggest that failure to carry out a procedure (in this case the defendant's admission that she would not have intubated even if she had attended) which in itself might amount to a further breach of duty. It is strange to allow a defendant to avoid liability by pleading that she would have compounded the original breach by a further breach. Second, what the doctor should (or should not) have done relates to his or her duty of care to the patient. Third, there is a danger that in cases where breach of duty is based upon a negligent omission to act, the legal enquiry into causation is converted into an investigation of what the defendant ought to have done.

3.4.2 Causation as a material contribution

A slightly different approach has, at times, been taken for the determination of causation in the event that a direct causal link cannot be demonstrated between the negligent act and the harm. In certain circumstances the courts have been willing to accept causation where the negligence has made a material contribution.

3.4.2(a) Material contribution to harm

In *Bonnington Castings v Wardlaw* (1956) AC 613, the claimant had been exposed to silica dust during the course of his employment. This led to a severe respiratory condition known as pneumoconiosis. Prior to his illness the claimant had been exposed to two sources of dust: one from a pneumatic hammer and the other from swing grinders. The defendant was liable only for the dust from the grinders in failing to provide an extractor fan. According to Lord Reid in the House of Lords, 'the source of his disease was the dust of both sources, and the real question is whether the dust from the swing grinders materially contributed to the disease'. The claimant did not have to prove that the dust from the grinders had been the sole cause on a balance of probabilities.

The decision of *Bailey v Ministry of Defence* [2008] EWCA Civ 883 also concerned cumulative causation. During a procedure to diagnose and treat a gall bladder obstruction, the claimant suffered a severe haemorrhage and, unknown to the health-care team, developed pancreatitis. Following the procedure the claimant received negligent care and inadequate resuscitation which left her in a seriously weakened condition. Since it was not clear whether the procedure had unblocked the gall bladder, a further diagnostic procedure was carried out during which the claimant's liver was damaged, a known complication that can materialise. Following emergency surgery the claimant aspirated vomit which led to cardiac arrest and severe brain damage. The claimant brought proceedings in negligence on the grounds that the negligent treatment had left her so significantly weakened that this had caused, or materially contributed to, the cardiac arrest. The defendant argued that the case failed on causation since there was insufficient causal link between the negligence and cardiac arrest which led to the injury.

Although the negligent breach of duty was proved, the decision turned on causation. At first instance it was held that although the defendant's negligence was not the sole cause of the injuries, this had materially contributed to the damage and a causal link could therefore be established between the negligence and injuries following the cardiac arrest. On appeal, the defendant submitted that the claimant must prove her case on the 'but for' principle, in that 'but for' the defendant's negligence the damage would not have occurred. The claimant could not do this since her underlying condition was the cause of the vomit and her inability to clear her airway. The Court of Appeal found in favour of the claimant applying *Bonnington Castings* in that it was sufficient to establish that the negligent care she received had made a material contribution to her weakness and that in these circumstances she could succeed.

The decision in *Bailey* has been followed in *Dickens v O2 Plc* [2008] Civ 1144 where a claimant succeeded in an action for psychiatric injuries caused partly by stress during the course of her employment.

3.4.2(b) Material contribution to risk of harm

An approach to causation that linked the claimant's injury to a risk or increased risk created by the defendant's tort was initially seen in *McGhee v National Coal Board* [1972]

3 All ER 1008. The claimant developed an inflammatory skin condition (dermatitis) following exposure to brick dust and because of his employer's breach of duty in failing to provide washing facilities. This meant that the claimant had to cycle home caked in dust which was a causative factor of his skin condition. The nature of dermatitis, however, is such that it could not be proved that 'but for' the lack of showers the claimant would not have developed the condition, and for this reason the claimant's action failed at first instance. The House of Lords allowed the appeal on the basis that the negligent failure to provide showers had 'materially increased the risk of harm', which was considered to be equivalent to a material contribution to the injury.

The approach of the House of Lords in *Wilsher* (see 3.4.1) fits uneasily with *McGhee*. Although *Wilsher* did not overrule *McGhee*, it was justified on a 'but for' analysis and on the grounds that the four other potential causes of the infant's loss of vision had not been due to the defendant's breach of duty. According to Lord Bridge, the decision was robust and pragmatic with respect to the undisputed primary facts, although on balance it seems likely that the decision was influenced strongly by policy.

In *Fairchild v Glenhaven* [2002] UKHL 22, the *McGhee* approach was revisited. In *Fairchild* several employees suffered mesothelioma after being negligently exposed to asbestos during the course of several employments. Expert evidence was available that the fatal condition could have been precipitated by a single asbestos fibre and it was not possible to identify when or where that trigger had occurred. For this reason it could not definitively be proved, on the balance of probabilities, which employer had been at fault, since each had materially contributed to the risk of the injury. The House of Lords held that all the employers who had negligently exposed the claimants to asbestos fibres should be held liable since they had all materially increased the risk of harm. Again, it seems likely that this decision was driven by policy and perhaps the inevitable fatality of the condition.

It is noteworthy that in *Fairchild* Lord Hoffman indicated that the courts were influenced by the financial constraints faced by the NHS, and that the political and economic arguments involved in imposing liability in such circumstances was invariably more complex than the reasons given in *McGhee* which concerned an employer who had failed to take simple preventative precautions. In *Fairchild* specific conditions were identified whereby the *McGhee* and *Fairchild* exceptions might apply, thereby reining in the principle from slipping into a causation approach of wider application. Whilst the compensation needs of the claimant are undoubtedly important, it appears that the test for materially increasing the risk of harm would have precedence in situations where liability is due to an employer's negligence, rather than that of the NHS. Nevertheless, the NHS is the largest employer in the United Kingdom as well as the provider of publicly funded health-care.

It is difficult to identify the circumstances where the *Fairchild* exception will apply. According to Lord Bingham, the exception applies to narrowly defined cases of mesothelioma. Lord Nicholls felt that the exception was limited to specific and exceptional situations and could extend to other eventualities. Lord Hoffman attempted to identify the conditions which would have to be satisfied before the *Fairchild* exception could apply. Lord Roger concurred that the exception would apply only to those cases in which it was impossible for the claimant to satisfy the 'but for' test, but where it could be established that the defendant's negligence had increased the risk of injury. It would be for the claimant to prove (on the balance of probabilities) that the injury suffered resulted from the kind or magnitude of risk created by the defendant's tort.

The *Fairchild* exception has been applied in *Novartis Grimsby Limited v John Cookson* [2007] EWCA Civ 1261. The claimant had developed bladder cancer after being exposed to carcinogenic compounds when employed by Novartis. He had smoked 20 cigarettes a day, which is also a known risk factor for this disease. The Court of Appeal found that the negligent exposure by the employer had been a material contribution to the risk.

In *Transco Plc v Griggs* [2003] EWCA Civ 564 an attempt was made to extend the *Fairchild* exception to a case of personal injury caused through vibration. On the facts the claimant sustained palmar arch disease which was considered to be 80% likely due to negligent exposure to vibration during his employment. Causation was complicated by the fact that non-negligent vibration had also played a role. At first instance, the court held that the claimant could not prove that 'but for' the negligent exposure, he would not have developed the injury, but then found for the claimant by applying the *McGhee* exception, since the negligent exposure had materially increased the risk of damage. On appeal, Hale LJ and Wilson J found that on the facts, the 'but for' test could be satisfied on the balance of probabilities, and therefore there was no need to invoke *Fairchild*.

> It appears that Simon's injuries were due to multiple causative factors.
>
> ▶ Which factors might have operated as causative agents?
> ▶ What factors, if any, might have acted as 'material contributions' to Simon's injuries?
> ▶ On the evidence and due to the multiplicity of causative factors, is the claimant likely to succeed?

3.4.3 Loss of chance

The general rule of causation is that the claimant must establish that on a balance of probabilities the negligent act or omission either caused, or materially contributed to, the injury. The claimant who succeeds is entitled to full compensation. On a mathematical framework the claimant must establish that there is a 51% probability that the damage sustained was caused by the negligence. However, in certain circumstances, a further cause of action is pleaded based upon 'loss of chance' on the grounds that the defendant's breach of duty deprived the claimant of the opportunity to either obtain a benefit or else avoid a loss. These actions, based upon loss of an expectation or chance, have been compensated in contract law but have tended to be unsuccessful in tort law.

In *Hotson v East Berkshire* [1987] AC 750 a boy of 13 fell out of a tree and injured his hip. He suffered avascular necrosis resulting in disability of the hip joint, and it was almost certain that he would develop osteoarthritis in later life. Had he been diagnosed and given appropriate treatment after his injury he would have had a 25% chance of a full recovery, and accordingly the trial judge awarded him a *pro rata* award of damages of 25%.

The first instance decision was overruled by the House of Lords on the basis that in order to succeed, the claimant would have to prove that had it not been for the negligence, then on the balance of probabilities the boy would not have developed avascular necrosis. In other words, the claimant would need to show that in the absence of the defendant's negligence there was a greater than 50% chance that he would not have suffered the (secondary) injury of avascular necrosis. On the evidence, there was only a 25% chance that this would not have happened and therefore the claim failed.

On the face of it, this appears a harsh and seemingly illogical judgement. After all, there was a 25% chance of a successful outcome, and the negligence had deprived the boy of this chance. The reasoning adopted by the court was as follows. Since there was a 75% chance that the secondary injury had already initiated at the time of admission (as opposed to a 25% chance that it had not), the claimant should receive nothing by way of compensation because on legal principles the negligence could not be shown to have 'caused' the loss (of a chance of recovery).

The issue of 'loss of a chance' in a personal injury claim was re-examined in *Gregg v Scott* [2005] UKHL 2 where the defendant's negligent misdiagnosis that a lump was benign resulted in a 9-month delay to the start of treatment for the claimant's tumour. As a result, the claimant's chance of survival (meaning survival for longer than 10 years) was reduced from 42% to 25%. The trial judge and the majority in the House of Lords considered that the claimant could not recover based on *Hotson*, namely that he would have to prove on the balance of probabilities that the injury would not have occurred, or that he had already not suffered the harm for which he was claiming, had there been no negligence. The decision was justified on the grounds that allowing a claim for loss of a chance would be a fundamental change in tort law and, as evinced by the majority, would have considerable implications with respect to compensation payments. Lord Hoffman felt that such a change, if necessary, ought to be made by Parliament rather than judicial decree. Baroness Hale voiced the concern that a loss of a chance approach would enable a claim to be made even where no harm had actually occurred (on the basis that such an occurrence might never actually happen). As a result, those with a less than 50% chance of succeeding would be winners, whereas those with an 80% chance of recovery would lose out since they could only claim 80% rather than the full recovery. In Lord Phillips' view the matter was simply one of causation: had the negligence caused the loss? In this case it had not. Although he accepted that the balance of probabilities approach might seem unfair in that the winner takes all, it was nonetheless a robust test (and produced rough justice) and could be justified on the grounds of public policy as well as maintaining coherence in the common law.

As it stands, the law allows a claimant to succeed if there is evidence, on the balance of probabilities, that the defendant's act caused the loss. Any likelihood of less than a 50% chance of a causal link would fail *(Hotson)*. Furthermore, after *Gregg v Scott*, it appears that any reduction in the chance of recovery can only succeed if it can be shown that in the absence of the negligent action, the chance of recovery was greater than 50%. The actual loss or reduction may be only of secondary importance.

The difficulty can be illustrated by two scenarios. In the first, the patient's chance of recovery is *reduced by 10%* on account of the defendant's negligent act or omission. If, in the absence of negligence, the chance of recovery would have been 51% (reduced to 40% on account of the negligence), then the claimant is likely to succeed. This is because in the absence of negligence it would have been more likely than not that the claimant would have recovered from the initial injury. In the second scenario, where the chance of recovery was hypothetically *reduced by 40%* and the original chance of recovery (without the defendant's negligence) was 49%, this action would fail even though the claimant has not only suffered a greater loss of chance, but has only a 9% chance of recovery which is considerably lower than that of his fellow victim. This concern was raised in *Gregg* by Lord Nicholls in his dissenting judgement in that if a doctor could show that the chance of recovery was less then 50%, even with proper treatment, then no compensation would be payable. This situation appears to make the doctor's duty of care to the patient somewhat hollow. Lord Hope (also dissenting) referred to several cases where the loss of a chance (such as the prospect of promotion) was recoverable in tort law and he argued that where there was a significant reduction in the prospects of a successful medical outcome, then compensation ought to be payable.

The cause of the quandary is the court's attempt to grapple with a trilemma: working within an artificial framework which requires a hypothetical consideration of what might, or could, happen in the future from a medical perspective; the need to consider what would be a fair outcome for the claimant; and the need to balance these factors in the context of public policy considerations. According to Lord Hope in *Gregg*, a distinction ought to be drawn between the *Hotson*-type case and the *Gregg*-type situation. In *Hotson*, the fall was the root cause, or at least the point from which the secondary injury originated, and the negligent act occurred after this event. In the *Gregg*-type scenario, the injury is one that might occur in the future due to negligently delayed commencement of treatment. Lord Phillips (whilst concurring with the majority) seemed to leave the door ajar for a situation where the defendant's negligence meant the loss of a chance of a cure, and where the claimant had subsequently developed the illness.

Evidence suggests that Simon would have had a 40% chance of recovering if he had been diagnosed and referred to a specialist unit within 12 hours following onset of symptoms. According to tort-based principles, a claimant will only succeed if the defendant caused the loss on a balance of probabilities:

▶ Is Simon likely to succeed according to *Hotson* and *Gregg*?
▶ Do you consider this to be a fair outcome?
▶ Are there opportunities for reform of the law in this area?

3.4.4 Failure to warn and causation

Some judicial sympathy for the claimant with respect to recovering for damages is seen in the House of Lords' decision of *Chester v Afshar* [2004] UKHL 41 (see 4.7). In brief, Ms Chester suffered persistent back pain and was referred for surgery. The neurosurgeon failed to warn her of the 1–2% risk of significant nerve damage which was an intrinsic and unavoidable risk of this type of spinal surgery. Although the operation was performed with all due care and attention, significant nerve damage occurred and the claimant was left partially paralysed. The trial judge found for the claimant. On her own evidence, had she been informed of the risk she would not have consented to surgery at that particular time but would have sought a second opinion. Nevertheless she would have consented to the procedure, probably with the same surgeon, albeit at a later date. On the evidence, therefore, the same injury might have materialised at that later date.

The House of Lords dismissed the defendant's appeal and ruled that in the event that a patient had not been warned of the risks of injury, and in consequence of that failure underwent the operation which she would not have undertaken at that time, she could still receive compensation. It was not necessary to show that she would *never have consented to that kind of operation at any time in the future*. While it was accepted that this decision was somewhat tenuous on the basis of conventional causation principles, it was nevertheless supported on the grounds that the duty is vested upon the doctor to warn patients of risks since this protects the patient's right to make an informed choice. According to Lord Steyn, 'In modern law medical paternalism no longer rules and a patient has a *prima facie* right to be informed by a surgeon of a small, but well established, risk of serious injury as a result of surgery'. The point of *Chester* is the link between 'but for' causation and failure to warn. The risk was within the scope of the duty of the surgeon to warn and therefore the defendant was liable; otherwise, the duty would be rendered worthless where it was needed most.

Tort law is concerned with compensating those who are wrongfully injured as opposed to punishing the defendant wrongdoer. Yet in *Chester* one gets a sense that the House of Lords was attempting to castigate the wrongdoing of the doctor primarily because failure to warn compromised the patient's autonomous right to make an informed choice. This infringement of rights was perceived by the House to be sufficient to justify a departure from conventional causation principles. Yet curiously the right to receive a non-negligent and timely diagnosis in *Gregg* was not deemed as serious. Arguably, *Gregg* could be characterised as one where the claimant received insufficient information of the risks of treatment or non-treatment, and that accordingly there was no justifiable basis for denying the claim.

3.4.5   Intervening factors

A further hurdle for the claimant is to prove causation in law, although some commentators consider that factual and legal causation are one and the same. If there is more than one independently sufficient cause of harm, the court will need to determine whether the defendant's negligent act was the cause of the damage in law.

3.4.5(a) Novus actus interveniens

A complicating factor occurs in the event that another person's conduct intervenes, thereby constituting a *novus actus interveniens* (an independent act of another) which might, in certain circumstances, break the chain of causation. An example of a *novus actus* can be given in relation to surgical sterilisation. If a pregnancy occurs following a negligently conducted sterilisation operation and the patient refuses to terminate the pregnancy, the claimant's refusal will not amount to a *novus actus* (*Emeh v Kensington and Chelsea Area Health Authority* [1985] QB 1012). However, the claimant's decision to have sexual intercourse knowing that a sterilisation operation has failed might constitute a *novus actus* (*Sabri-Tabrizi v Lothian Health Board* (1998) SLT 607).

A patient's action in deliberately taking his own life has been rejected as a *novus actus* in *Kirkham v Chief Constable of Greater Manchester* [1990] 2 QB 283, a case that concerned a clinically depressed prisoner. Likewise, in *Reeves v Commissioner of Police of the Metropolis* [2001] AC 360, another action brought following the suicide of a prisoner, the court dismissed the argument that the decision to take his own life constituted a *novus actus* since the suicide was a precise event against which the duty was directed and as a result, the *actus* was neither *novus* nor *interveniens*.

3.4.5(b) Remoteness

It is also necessary to establish that the type of damage caused was not too remote according to the *Wagon Mound* principles (*Wagon Mound* [1961] AC 388). The test for remoteness is whether the type of damage sustained was reasonably foreseeable in the circumstances. In clinical negligence actions damage or injury is reasonably foreseeable and it is rare for an action to be defended on these grounds. However, in *R. v Croydon Health Authority* (1997) BMLR 40, the claimant, who had undergone a pre-employment chest x-ray, had not been alerted to an abnormality that had been revealed, namely primary pulmonary hypertension which is a condition that could be exacerbated by pregnancy. She argued that had she been aware of this problem she would not have become pregnant. Her appeal was dismissed on the grounds that a claim for costs arising from the birth of a child was too remote. However, psychiatric injury caused by a defendant doctor's negligent act might not be too remote. In *Page v Smith* [1996] AC 155, the House of Lords held that since the claimant's physical injuries were foreseeable, the defendant could also be liable for any concomitant psychiatric injury as a result of the negligent act. What this means is that a doctor could be liable for psychiatric injury, even in the absence of physical injury, provided that the latter was reasonably foreseeable.

3.5 Damages

Compensation for clinical negligence injury is based upon tort liability, and fault of the wrongdoer must be proved on a balance of probability. For a successful action the principle of compensation is the award of monetary damages which are assessed at a level that puts the claimant back into the position that he or she would have been in prior to the wrongful act (*Livingstone v Raywards Coal Co* (1880) 5 App Cas 25). Rarely, awards of compensation are reduced or aggravated.

3.5.1 General principles

Ascertaining the extent of a claimant's injury in a clinical negligence action is frequently complicated by the existence of a pre-existing condition. This means that the claimant would be expected to have a level on ongoing injury despite the occurrence of the actionable negligence, a situation that significantly reduces the level of compensation awarded.

Compensation payments are intended to be 'fair, just and reasonable' on account of the injury suffered. They are separated into two elements: general damages (to compensate personal, non-economic losses which can only be subjectively estimated amounts) and special damages (which include more readily calculable pecuniary losses). General damages represent several heads of injury such as pain, suffering, and loss of amenity and may also include factors such as handicap on the labour market, loss of enjoyment and even marriage prospects. The Judicial Studies Board, *Guidelines for the assessment of general damages in personal injury cases* (2010, 10th edition) is used as the starting point for assessment of damages, which is invariably a complex determination. The guidelines aim to promote consistency between claimants and their awards.

Special damages such as past economic losses are more easily quantifiable and include all pecuniary losses that have been caused by, or have flowed in a foreseeable way from, the negligent injury. Such damages typically include lost earnings, costs of private health care and gratuitous care provided by the next-of-kin, travel expenses which have arisen following the injury, and necessary purchase of equipment. Future losses are included in this category, even though these are subjective approximations. Calculation of future losses requires a forecast to be made with respect to anticipated loss of earnings, pensions and possibly child care allowances. The Ogden Tables set out actuarial tables for the calculation of future loss and are used as the basis of calculation for all heads of future losses.

3.5.2 Lump sums and periodical payments

Until 2005 the courts tended to award compensation in the form of lump-sum payments. These amounts were final and could not be altered even where circumstances materially changed which led to a real possibility of over or under compensation particularly due to the uncertainty of life expectancy forecasts. Lump sum payments tended to be popular with claimants on account of their control over the monies received.

Parliament has since reviewed the lump sum principle by permitting provisional damages to be ordered (section 32A of Supreme Court Act 1981). Awards of provisional damages allow claimants to return to court to apply for further amounts after judgement has been given provided that there is a chance that they might develop a serious deterioration to their condition which was on account of the negligence that formed the basis of the claim. A claim for provisional damages must be pleaded and the requirements of CPR Part 41 must be complied with.

In *Wells v Wells* [1999] 1 AC 345, the lump sum approach was criticised in circumstances where the claimant had long-term injuries, mainly due to the lack of certainty for the claimant's future. Lord Steyn proposed that the court should have power to award periodical payments where appropriate which catalysed an amendment to the Damages Act 1996 to permit payment of future losses by instalments. Such payments reduce the uncertainty of life expectancy and ensure that compensation is available for as long as required. It also avoids the need for complex investment strategies to ensure that an income can be provided. Since 1 April 2005, the court has had power to order periodical payments (the Damages Act 1996 (as amended)).

3.5.3 Reduced and aggravated damages

In certain circumstances the level of damages awarded to claimants may be reduced on account of contributory negligence. A patient will be expected to cooperate with the health-care team, for example, with the need to disclose an accurate personal history since lack of compliance might negatively affect the doctor's ability to reach an accurate diagnosis. In *Pidgeon v Doncaster Health Authority* [2002] Lloyd's Rep Med 13, a claimant developed cervical cancer. She underwent a cervical smear test which was negligently reported as negative. Despite being sent several reminders she failed to present for further tests and her damages were reduced by two-thirds on account of her failure to attend. From tort principles, damages may be reduced if patients fail to mitigate their losses by taking reasonable steps that would reduce or limit the harm that has been caused. The patient negligently exposed to infection who fails to take prescribed antibiotics could received a reduced award.

In certain circumstances a claimant may be entitled to receive enhanced damages where there are aggravating characteristics of the defendant's conduct. The Law Commission (1997) in Aggravated, Exemplary and Restitutionary Damages (LC247) considered that to establish a claim for an aggravated award it was necessary to prove exceptional conduct or motive by the defendant against the victim. Such awards are extremely rare in this jurisdiction.

3.5.4 Secondary victims

The law is reluctant to allow a claim to be brought by a third party who was not directly injured as a result of the alleged negligence, but who has been affected by witnessing the injuries of those by the defendant's negligent conduct. The general law is that a third party cannot claim damages to compensate for the damage caused by what has happened to another. If, however, what has been witnessed is exceptionally awful, or if the third party has been informed in a negligent manner and this has led to a psychological injury, then in those circumstances compensation may be payable.

3.5.5 Limitation

Statutory rules govern the time period during which clinical negligence claims may be brought. For civil claims for personal injuries arising as a result of negligence the limitation period is 3 years from the date on which the injury occurred or the date of knowledge (if later) of the injury. For claims that allege negligence during the birth of a child, the date of the cause of action is the child's birth date. Where the injured person is a child, the 3-year limitation period does not commence until the child's 18th birthday since a child is deemed to be a person under a disability and time does not run until that disability ceases. If a person dies while continuing to pursue a claim, his or her personal representatives can bring a claim within 3 years of the date of death. The court has discretion to allow a claim outside the statutory limitation period and in exercising this discretion must take account of all relevant circumstances to ensure that no unfair prejudice arises as a result of such discretion.

3.6 Institutional liability

A health-care provider, such as an NHS trust, owes a vicarious duty of care to its patients. Institutional providers also owe a direct duty of care to patients, as stated by Denning LJ in *Cassidy v Ministry of Health* [1951] 2 KB 343 at 360:

> In my opinion authorities who run a hospital, be they local authorities, government boards, or any other corporation, are in law under the selfsame duty as the humblest doctor; whenever they accept a patient for treatment, they must use reasonable care and skill to cure him of his ailment. The hospital authorities cannot, of course, do it by themselves: they have no ears to listen through the stethoscope, and no hands to hold the surgeon's knife. They must do it by the staff which they employ; and if their staff are negligent in giving the treatment, they are just as liable for that negligence as is anyone else who employs others to do his duties for him...I take it to be clear law, as well as good sense, that, where a person is himself under a duty to use care, he cannot get rid of his responsibility by delegating the performance of it to someone else, no matter whether the delegation be to a servant under a contract of service or to an independent contractor under a contract for services.

Although liability does not require an individual to be identified, proof of causation is still necessary.

3.6.1 Vicarious liability

Under the doctrine of vicarious liability an employer is liable for the negligence of its employees who are acting in the course of their employment. It is a form of secondary no fault liability that arises out of the employer–employee relationship, and which can be imposed without the need to show that the employer was in any way negligent. The rationale for vicarious liability is based on public policy in that all economic activities, including health care, carry a risk of harm to the public. The concept of fairness and justice requires that those in control of activities are liable to those who suffer harm as a result of those activities. This means that injured persons will have recourse to organisations that are usually better placed to meet compensation than individual employees. A further advantage is that imposition of strict liability on employers encourages risk management strategies to maintain best practice and a risk adverse organisational culture. The NHS is responsible for the costs of litigation, settlements and compensation payments with respect to liability of its medical and other health-care staff under the NHS indemnity scheme introduced in 1990. Since 1995 the Clinical Negligence Scheme for Trusts (CNST) has operated a voluntary risk-pooling scheme for clinical negligence claims for NHS trusts, Foundation trusts and Primary Care Trusts, in order to meet this liability.

3.6.2   The NHS Litigation Authority

In 1999 the NHS Litigation Authority (NHSLA) was set up. It is a Special Health Authority with overarching responsibility for handling negligence claims against NHS organisations in England. It has an active risk management programme designed to raise standards of care in the NHS to reduce the number of incidents that lead to claims being made. A similar scheme, the Welsh Health Legal Services, operates in Wales. The purpose of the NHSLA is to encourage early admission of liability and provide other requirements that patients want, such as apologies, explanations and assurances that lessons have been learnt. The NHSLA uses a specialist panel of solicitors and the organisation's involvement has led to a reduction in the time taken to settle claims.

The NHSLA has promoted the wider use of mediation and other types of alternative dispute resolution. The overwhelming majority of clinical negligence cases are now settled out of court. For most forms of alternative dispute resolution, a third party will attempt to facilitate non-adversarial negotiations between the parties in order to arrive at a consensual solution.

3.6.3   Direct liability

An institutional health-care provider may have direct liability on account of its negligence as an employing body if, for example, it fails to ensure sufficient numbers of adequately trained staff, or fails to ensure safe working conditions. As a result there has been a growth in risk management strategies developed by Trusts in order to reduce their potential liability. The standard by which a Trust will be judged is an objective one. In *Bull v Devon AHA* [1993] 4 Med LR 117, the standard was not whether a Trust was acting at a level of other hospitals but whether those standards were reasonable in the circumstances. Direct liability of the hospital was also established in *Robertson v Nottingham Health Authority* [1997] 8 Med LR 1 where the system for summoning emergency obstetric care was found to be inadequate. However, in *Garcia v St Mary's NHS Trust* [2006] EWHC 2314 (QBD), the claimant's case of institutional liability failed following the delayed arrival of a suitably experienced cardiothoracic registrar, and each case will turn on its facts as in *Farraj v King's Healthcare NHS Trust (KCH)* [2009] EWCA Civ 1203 (see 3.2.4).

> Simon's lumbar puncture was carried out by a locum doctor employed through an agency. This practice is becoming more prevalent on account of acute staff shortages in certain specialities. If, in the circumstances that the agency doctor is found to have been negligent in the course of providing treatment, the question arises as to whether the Trust would be vicariously liable for the acts of an agency worker. The guideline HSG (96)48: NHS indemnity arrangements for handling clinical negligence claims against NHS staff applies where the health-care professional is employed under a contract of employment and also where the person was contracted to an NHS organisation to provide health-care services.
>
> ▶   What are the implications here?

General practitioners and doctors who engage in private practice are responsible for meeting their own costs and for this reason must maintain insurance cover. A Primary Care Trust could also be sued since it owes a primary duty of care to provide a reasonable level of service for all patients in its catchment area. In *A (a child) v Ministry of Defence* [2004] EWCA 641, it was stated that the NHS Trust owed a duty of care to provide a safe and satisfactory medical service to a patient.

3.7   Actions in contract

Reynolds v The Health First Medical Group [2000] *Lloyd's Rep Med* 240 established that there is no contract between a patient and the NHS, or its staff. An NHS patient can therefore only sue in negligence. A private patient may have an additional cause of action in contract. If a breach of contract can be established, then it is likely that negligence could also be established. However, a contract for medical care may be difficult to reconcile with other types of civil contract, where a range of remedies might be available following a breach, including specific performance. This aspect was demonstrated in *Thake v Maurice* [1986] 1 All ER 497 where the courts were reluctant to interpret a contract as a guarantee that a surgical procedure would be a success.

3.8   Reform of clinical negligence

3.8.1   The compensation culture

Media headlines frequently proclaim the existence of a 'compensation culture' in the United Kingdom on account of the rising number and value of clinical negligence actions. At the same time, data from bodies such as the NHSLA, the National Audit Office and the Department of Health suggests that only a percentage of those with a complaint actually make a claim for compensation, which seems to suggest that many victims may be 'under-compensated'. Furthermore, a compensation culture, if it does exist, may operate in a positive manner by improving risk management strategies and promoting safer practice within health services. Conversely, litigation is recognised as time consuming and a drain on scarce resources and may encourage defensive practices and stress for health-care providers. However, few would argue that those who suffer injury through negligent care must receive adequate compensation.

Where death ensues following actionable negligence, the husband, wife, civil partner, or parents of a child under 18 may recover statutory compensation under the Fatal

Accidents Act 1976 to the sum of £10,000 in respect of bereavement costs, a sum that would inevitably fail to compensate for such loss. If a stillborn results from negligent mismanagement of a woman in labour it is unlikely that the parents will receive any compensation at all. But to what extent can any amount of damages really compensate a parent for the loss of a child?

The calculation of special damages with respect to a person's occupation can significantly affect the level of compensation payable, irrespective of the injury sustained. Likewise, in the calculation of future pecuniary losses, the claimant's socio-economic background is a factor taken into consideration to arrive at a level of damages. In effect, this means that an award to a permanently injured child born to affluent middle-class parents would likely be greater than that to a child born to an unemployed single parent.

3.8.2   The need for reform

Following adverse events patients may well be dissatisfied with the outcome, the lack of an apology and explanation and even less with the lack of reassurance that appropriate measures have been taken to prevent any repeat of the event. In 2004 the now defunct Commission for Health Improvement revealed pervasive inadequacies throughout the NHS such as staff shortages, reliance on agency staff, poor teamwork, inadequate incident reporting, lack of training and supervision of staff, and financial constraints all of which play a role in the occurrence of medical error (Healthcare Commission, 2004).

The system of tort liability for clinical negligence is widely perceived as unsatisfactory in many respects. Claimants expect to receive compensation for injuries or damage caused by the negligence of health-care professionals, yet in fact many are denied monetary damages even after complex, protracted and stressful legal process. In 1999, of the last six clinical negligence cases to reach the House of Lords, the claimants won none and the defendants won all six (Jones, 1999). Now, however, the score is one in favour of the claimant following *Chester v Afshar* (see 3.4.4).

Despite major change to the process of civil litigation, the clinical negligence system remains complex, slow and exorbitantly expensive. It is clear that clinical negligence law and procedure has developed piecemeal and in view of the perceived deficiencies in the system, is due for change. A reform to the civil justice system was prompted by Lord Woolf's report, *Access to justice* (Lord Woolf, 1996). The Civil Procedure Rules 1998 (CPR), which were prompted by the report, have applied to the County Courts, the High Court and the Court of Appeal since April 1999 and were intended to improve access to justice. The pre-action protocol encourages openness by describing the steps that each party must take to seek and provide information prior to legal action and is aimed at reducing adversarial litigation by encouraging early settlement and use of mediation. There are sanctions for failing to keep to a defined timetable. Furthermore, the new CPR (pursuant to the Civil Procedure Act 1997) encourages the use of a joint expert wherever possible to avoid the tendency for the expert witness to be used as a 'hired gun' of the commissioning party, and instead ought to provide impartial evidence to assist the court in reaching its decision.

3.8.3   Why people sue

The motivation for bringing a civil action following negligent health care is complex, and the need for financial compensation is recognised to be only one of the drivers

(Morris, 2007). A national survey has demonstrated a multifactorial basis for bringing a claim (Mulcahy, 2003). A high proportion of claimants sought an acceptance of fault by the defendant. They also wanted reassurance that lessons had been learnt and that mistakes would not be repeated, as well as an explanation and an apology. Only a relatively small proportion admitted that financial compensation had been the principal reason for suing. Despite these findings which, arguably, suggest an altruistic basis for bringing an action, claimants often seek compensatory damages. Complaints or actions brought against doctors are often perceived by professionals as being slurs on professional competence and might well lead to defensive responses which can further complicate already delicate situations.

At an individual level, patients may want an explanation and reassurance that there has not been a cover up (Vincent, 1994). Patients also want sensitive handling and empathy. Good communication takes on a special significance when things have gone wrong, and the blame apportioned to doctors is not only for the mistake but also for what is perceived by many as a lack of openness or willingness to provide full and adequate explanations.

3.8.4 Reporting and learning from mistakes

In 2001 the National Patient Safety Agency (NPSA) was set up. The purpose of this organisation is to provide a streamlined approach to dealing with mistakes and ensuring that lessons are learnt, as well as disseminating good practice throughout the health services. The NPSA has three divisions, namely the National Clinical Assessment Services, aimed at dealing with and supporting doctors and dentists whose performance gives cause for concern; the National Reporting and Learning System, whose principal function is root cause analysis of mistakes, developing learning action points and disseminating this information; and the National Research and Ethics Services (NRES) which deals with applications for ethical approval for research studies that involve staff or patients of the NHS. The Coalition Government has recently announced a review of these arm's-length bodies (see 2.3.2).

One approach to prevent future risk is to analyse mistakes and to learn from them by ensuring that adequate and effective safeguards are put in place. However, an open reporting system is essentially a move away from the traditional blame culture which is promoted by the traditional adversarial tort system which requires the identification of a tortfeasor. The Department of Health's expert group, in formulating *An organisation with a memory* (2000) made several recommendations. The principal approach was to focus on systems, rather than individuals, and to accept that humans are fallible. Robust systems are therefore required to identify early warning signs for potential errors. The emphasis has been on developing a reporting system to provide information for developing solutions to specific hazards, relevant not only to actual mistakes but also near misses, the analogy being drawn from the aviation industry where pilots have a duty to report near misses, since this information is useful to prevent serious accidents in the future. The Bristol Royal Infirmary Inquiry found that institutional blame leads to defensiveness, cover-ups and denial which is counter-productive and works against patient interests. The Inquiry recommended full and open reporting within the NHS.

3.8.5 No fault compensation schemes

A no fault compensation scheme aims to remove the need to prove liability and compensates those who suffer injury or damage following health-care treatment irrespective of whether damage has been caused by actionable negligence. In New Zealand and Sweden the need to prove fault has been eliminated, at least for certain types of compensatable injury. No fault schemes also exist in Finland, Denmark and Norway. In Sweden, no fault compensation is available for avoidable injury caused by treatment, examination or drug injuries. The New Zealand scheme is administered by the Accident Rehabilitation and Compensation Corporation and records high rates of consumer satisfaction (ACC, *Annual report*, 2009). The scheme covers negligent medical error or rare and severe treatment outcomes and does not allow the injured patient to bring an action, unlike the Swedish system, which still permits this, although few patients choose to do so.

A no fault compensation scheme tends to mean that compensation is provided more effectively and efficiently to victims and reduces some of the stress and tension that accompanies adversarial process. There is a further attraction of simplicity, and one of corrective justice. For example, if two persons were to suffer the same injury as a result of clinical negligence it cannot be guaranteed that both will receive equivalent compensation under an adversarial system. One may succeed and the other may not. In a no fault scheme, however, both would receive equal compensation.

The principal argument against a no fault scheme is cost. The Chief Medical Officer concluded that even with a 25% reduction in the current level of compensation, a true no fault scheme would cost at least £1.6 billion a year and that this would be substantially more than the £400,000,000 spent on clinical negligence in the year 2000 to 2001 (*Making amends*, 2003). There is also concern that this type of scheme could be unfair since it would only compensate those who were ill as a result of medical treatment, and not those who were equally ill due to other reasons. This could create lack of parity, disputes and a sense of lack of justice. Another concern is that if compensation and blame are separated, then alternative systems of accountability will be required. The aggrieved patient would still want an explanation, apology and reassurance for the future. There would still be a need to ensure that lessons had been learnt and that remedial action has been taken to avoid a repeat occurrence of the same event.

3.8.6 NHS Redress Act 2006

The existing medical negligence system is commonly perceived as unduly expensive and potentially unfair for litigants. The appropriateness of the tort-based system has been subjected to on-going criticism as exemplified by the response to the Chief Medical Officer's Consultation paper *Making amends* (Chief Medical Officer, 2003). During the consultation process, evidence was presented that for the majority of claims under £45,000 the legal and administrative costs tended to exceed the value of compensation paid and an inversely proportionate relationship existed between the values of claims compared with the costs involved. *Making amends* acted as the catalyst for the enactment of the NHS Redress Act 2006 (not yet in force) to reform the manner by which lower value clinical negligence cases are dealt with to achieve appropriate and proportionate redress including non-compensation outcomes such as investigations, explanations and apologies, and to avoid litigation wherever possible. The statutory provisions permit a scheme to allow experts to decide on the appropriate level of compensation for claims for damages that do not exceed £20,000 and avoid the need for civil proceedings.

The Act has received a mixed reception and stakeholders have expressed concerns with respect to its independence, the availability of legal advice for those who choose to enter the scheme and transparency of process. It is quite possible that application of the Act may be challenged under the European Convention. Furthermore, since the Act is limited to cases where the alleged negligence has occurred within a hospital, and due to the cap on compensation levels, it may make little difference for many claimants.

The scheme will apply to liability for injuries or loss arising in consequence of proven medical negligence by a health-care professional and will be administered by the NHSLA. At present it is not anticipated that the scheme will apply to primary health care.

3.9 Liability for medicines

Before medicines are licensed, most are tested on animals. The next stage of the licensing process involves trials using healthy volunteers. This stage of development is to determine the effects of the drug on the human body (Phase 1 trials). Next, the drug is administered to patients with relevant conditions to establish safety and efficacy data and finally, clinical trials are used to compare effectiveness with other available treatment modalities and options. Trials on patients require special licences which are obtained from the Medicines and Healthcare Products Regulatory Agency (MHRA). More discussion on the law and ethics of clinical research is found in Chapter 7.

If a manufacturer produces a drug that causes harm to patients, an action in negligence can be brought. In these circumstances it must be proved that the manufacturer failed to take reasonable care during production and further that the drug was the cause of the patient's injuries. In order to prove this, it is simpler to bring a claim under the Consumer Protection Act 1987 (rather than in negligence) where the patient would need to show that the product was defective and that the defect caused the damage. Section 3(1) of the Act requires a defect to be present in the product and that the safety of the product is not such as persons generally are entitled to expect. There is no need to show that the producer was negligent.

Medical treatment in the form of medication will most often carry unavoidable side effects but that does not necessarily make the drug defective. In determining whether a drug is defective, a court will weigh the intended benefits against the potential side effects in a risk–benefit analysis. The manufacturers may have a defence under section 4(1)(e) of the Act which states 'that the state of scientific and technical knowledge at the relevant time was not such that a producer of products of the same description as the product in question might be expected to have discovered the defect if it had existed in his products while they were under his control'. In essence the producer must show that the scientific knowledge at the time of production was such that they could not have reasonably have been expected to discover the defect. This defence is known as the 'development defence'.

The scope of the development defence was tested in *A v National Blood Authority* [2001] 3 All ER 289. The claimants were patients who had been infected with hepatitis C virus following blood transfusions and proceedings were brought against the National Blood

Authority (now known as NHS Blood and Transplant) under the Consumer Protection Act 1987. The defendants argued that it was not always possible to test the blood for contamination. They also relied on the development defence and argued that at the relevant time there had been no effective tests to screen blood for hepatitis C. These arguments were rejected by the court and the ruling went in favour of the claimants. It was held that patients had a legitimate expectation that blood used for transfusions was clean, and that if the public was not informed of the risks of contaminated blood they were entitled to assume that it was safe. The main advantage of relying on the Act is that the claimant does not carry the burden of proof in having to show that the producer was negligent; instead the burden of proof shifts to the producers to show that they were not at fault.

3.10 Criminal negligence

A criminal action might be justified where death results following a grossly negligent (although otherwise lawful) act or omission. A prosecution might be more appropriate than civil liability where, on the facts, the 'negligence of the accused went beyond a mere matter of compensation between subjects and showed such disregard for the life and safety of others as to amount to a crime against the State and conduct deserving punishment' (*R v Bateman* [1925] All ER 45).

The leading authority for gross negligence manslaughter is the House of Lords decision in *R v Adomako* [1995] 1 AC 171. Dr Adomako was an anaesthetist. In the process of anaesthetising a patient the endotracheal tube (a tube inserted into the wind pipe) that delivered oxygen became disconnected. He failed to notice this for over 4 minutes and as a result the patient suffered a cardiac arrest and died. The standard of care was described by a prosecution witness as being abysmal, and another witness stated that a competent anaesthetist should have noticed the disconnection within 15 seconds. Dr Adomako conceded that he had been negligent but he denied criminal negligence. His conviction was upheld by the House of Lords where Lord Mackay stated that what amounted to criminal negligence in a doctor's conduct was a matter for the jury. The jury would have to consider the extent to which the conduct departed from the proper standard of care that it was incumbent upon the doctor to provide, involving as it must have done a risk of death to the patient. It was for the jury to decide whether the conduct was such that it should be regarded as criminal. There is an element of circularity in this. In order to ascertain whether the standard of care fell so low that it was extreme or gross, the jury had to first decide whether it was a crime that had been committed and then if so, determine the standard of care as being grossly below what was expected. In other words, the negligence was gross when it was so bad that it should be criminal.

This circular definition was used by the Court of Appeal in *R v Becker* (unreported, 19 June 2000), where Tuckey LJ said that the

> judge told the jury four times that they had to find the negligence criminal. Further definition of gross was not required as *Adomako* makes clear...[t]he jury had to face the crucial issue which, as the judge said, was for them and not for the doctors to decide. That is to say, whether the mistake which the appellant made was so bad, that they could characterise it as a crime.

The Court of Appeal in *R v Adomako* [1994] QB 302 (at 323) gave four examples of situations where criminal negligence could be found. These situations were where a doctor:

(a) displays an indifference to an obvious risk of injury to his patient;
(b) displays an awareness of a risk but decides to run it in any event;
(c) attempts to avoid a known risk but does so with such a high degree of negligence so as to deserve to be punished;
(d) displays inattention or failure to avert a serious risk, going beyond mere inadvertence.

Situations (a) and (b) encompass a degree of subjective wrongdoing but situations (c) and (d) do not and arguably these could occur due to a high degree of professional incompetence. There is an argument that criminal liability should be confined to those situations where there is a degree of culpability rather than an issue regarding competence, and that incompetence ought to be dealt with in some other way, for example, through regulatory action. More recently in *R v Misra* [2004] EWCA Crim 2375, it was argued that the crime of gross negligence manslaughter was contrary to Article 6 (the right to a fair trial) and Article 7 (the prohibition of criminal conviction in the absence of a pre-existing criminal offence) of the Convention rights. This argument failed in the Court of Appeal.

It is for the jury to decide whether the doctor's negligent act amounts to a criminal act. If they so find, then a doctor can be convicted. There has been a marked increase in the number of prosecutions against doctors for manslaughter. Seventeen doctors were charged with manslaughter in the 1990s compared with 2 in each of the preceding two decades (Ferner, 2000).

Summary

3.1 Clinical negligence cases are often complex, difficult to resolve and expensive. The number of claims and the cost of settlement have increased greatly in recent years. For a claimant to succeed in a civil action of negligence three requirements must be proved: that the defendant owed the claimant a duty of care; that the defendant's performance was below the standard expected, thus resulting in a breach of duty; and that the injury suffered by the claimant was caused by the defendant's breach of duty and was not too remote.

3.2 A legal duty of care will arise if it was reasonably foreseeable that the doctor's actions or omissions would cause harm to the injured person, if the relationship between the injured person and the practitioner was sufficiently close, and if it would be 'fair, just and reasonable' to impose a duty in the circumstances. Almost invariably, a duty of care will be found once a practitioner accepts clinical responsibility for a patient. A duty of care may also arise when a doctor is engaged by another party and a direct clinical relationship does not exist between the doctor and the victim. Generally, a duty of care does not arise between a doctor and an injured third party. An exception is when a third party suffers post-traumatic stress disorder as a result of witnessing negligent medical care.

3.3 The traditional test in medical negligence is the *Bolam* test: a doctor is not guilty of negligence if he has acted in accordance with a practice accepted as proper by a responsible body of medical men skilled in that particular art. The *Bolam* test has been approved by the House of Lords on several occasions and is the accepted standard for diagnosis, treatment and information disclosure. Several commentators have criticised the *Bolam* standard as being overly protective of doctors. *Obiter* comments in *Bolitho* have emphasised that the court should take a more scrutinising view of whether the proclaimed standard is satisfactory in the circumstances.

Summary cont'd

3.4 The claimant must prove, on the balance of probabilities that actionable damage was caused by the negligent act. The basic test for causation in fact is the 'but for' test. Its application may be particularly problematic where multiple factors are involved. Recent judicial decisions indicate a willingness of the court to move away from a strict application of 'but for' in determining causation. The legal test for remoteness is that the type of damage sustained was reasonably foreseeable in the circumstances.

3.5 Clinical negligence is compensated the award of monetary damages which are assessed at a level to put the claimant back into the position that he or she would have been in prior to the wrongful act. An amendment to the Damages Act 1996 allows the court to award payment of future losses by instalments. For civil claims for personal injuries arising as a result of negligence the limitation period is 3 years from the date on which the injury occurred or the date of knowledge (if later) of the injury.

3.6 Under the doctrine of vicarious liability, an employer is liable for the negligence of its employees who are acting in the course of their employment. It is a form of secondary liability which arises out of the employer–employee relationship, and a type of no-fault liability which can be imposed without the need to show that the employer itself was negligent. Institutional health-care providers may have direct liability on account of its negligence as an employing body if it fails to ensure sufficient numbers of adequately trained staff, or fails to implement procedures to ensure safe working conditions.

3.7 There is no contract between a patient and the NHS or its staff. An NHS patient can therefore only sue in negligence. A private patient may have an additional cause of action in contract. If a breach of contract can be established, then it is likely that negligence could also be pleaded.

3.8 There is a perception that a 'compensation culture' exists in the United Kingdom on account of the rising number and value of clinical negligence actions. It is also apparent that only a small percentage of those with a complaint actually make a claim for compensation. Evidence suggests that patients are frequently dissatisfied with the outcome of medical litigation. Several initiatives such as the National Patient Safety Agency have been set up in order to provide a streamlined approach to dealing with mistakes and ensuring that lessons are learnt and disseminating good practice throughout the health services. The NHS Redress Act 2006 (when implemented) aims to reform the way in which lower value clinical negligence cases are dealt with proportionately and avoid expensive and time-consuming litigation.

3.9 If a manufacturer produces a drug which causes harm to patients, an action in negligence might be appropriate. In these circumstances it must be proved that the manufacturer failed to take reasonable care during manufacture of the product and further that the drug was the cause of the patient's injuries. It is simpler to bring a claim under the Consumer Protection Act 1987 (rather than in negligence) where the patient would need to show that the product was defective and that the defect caused the damage.

3.10 A criminal action might be justified in circumstances in the event that death results from a grossly negligent (although otherwise lawful) act or omission. The Court of Appeal in *Adomako* gave four examples of situations where criminal negligence could be found. These are where a doctor displays an indifference to an obvious risk of injury to his patient *or* displays an awareness of a risk but decides to run it in any event *or* attempts to avoid a known risk but does so with such a high degree of negligence so as to deserve to be punished *or* displays inattention or failure to avert a serious risk, going beyond mere inadvertence.

Exercises

3.1 'The *Bolam* test is outdated and overly protective of doctors.' Discuss this statement in the context of contemporary case law.

3.2 Consider whether the *Bolitho* 'gloss' represents any real change to the standard of care expected in health-care situations.

3.3 'The "but for" test is unfair to claimants and poses an almost insurmountable hurdle'. Discuss this statement in the context of decided case law with an emphasis on recent judgements.

3.4 Lack of resources for staff, beds and equipment is an enduring characteristic of the NHS. To what extent is evidence of lack of resources a legitimate defence against a negligence action? To what extent should the standard of care be adapted according to the availability of resources? Is this fair for patients?

3.5 Critically consider the proposals for reform of medical negligence in England and Wales.

Further reading

Brazier M, Beswick J. Who's caring for me? *Medical Law International* 2006; 7: 183–199

Brazier M, Miola J. Bye-bye Bolam: A medical litigation revolution? *Medical Law Review* 2000; 8: 85

MacLean A. Beyond Bolam and Bolitho. *Medical Law International* 2002; 5: 205

Samanta A, Mello M, Foster C, Tingle J, Samanta J. The role of clinical guidelines in medical negligence litigation: A shift from the *Bolam* standard? *Medical Law Review* 2006; 14: 321

Teff H. The standard of care in medical negligence – moving on from *Bolam*? *Oxford Journal of Legal Studies* 1998; 18: 473–484

Links to relevant websites can be found at: http://www.palgrave.com/law/samanta

Chapter 4 follows overleaf.

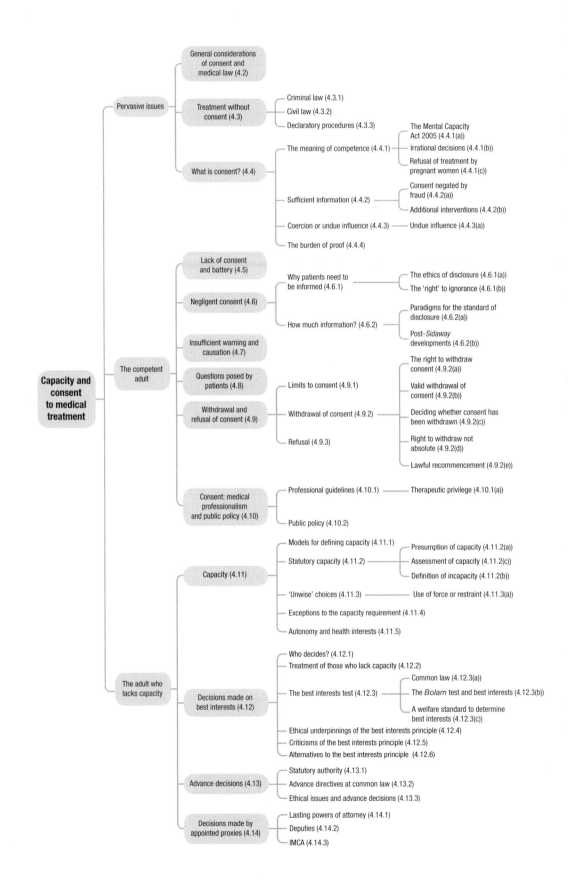

Capacity and consent to medical treatment

Pervasive issues

General considerations of consent and medical law (4.2)

Treatment without consent (4.3)
- Criminal law (4.3.1)
- Civil law (4.3.2)
- Declaratory procedures (4.3.3)

What is consent? (4.4)
- The meaning of competence (4.4.1)
  - The Mental Capacity Act 2005 (4.4.1(a))
  - Irrational decisions (4.4.1(b))
  - Refusal of treatment by pregnant women (4.4.1(c))
- Sufficient information (4.4.2)
  - Consent negated by fraud (4.4.2(a))
  - Additional interventions (4.4.2(b))
- Coercion or undue influence (4.4.3)
  - Undue influence (4.4.3(a))
- The burden of proof (4.4.4)

The competent adult

Lack of consent and battery (4.5)

Negligent consent (4.6)
- Why patients need to be informed (4.6.1)
  - The ethics of disclosure (4.6.1(a))
  - The 'right' to ignorance (4.6.1(b))
- How much information? (4.6.2)
  - Paradigms for the standard of disclosure (4.6.2(a))
  - Post-*Sidaway* developments (4.6.2(b))

Insufficient warning and causation (4.7)

Questions posed by patients (4.8)

Withdrawal and refusal of consent (4.9)
- Limits to consent (4.9.1)
- Withdrawal of consent (4.9.2)
  - The right to withdraw consent (4.9.2(a))
  - Valid withdrawal of consent (4.9.2(b))
  - Deciding whether consent has been withdrawn (4.9.2(c))
  - Right to withdraw not absolute (4.9.2(d))
  - Lawful recommencement (4.9.2(e))
- Refusal (4.9.3)

Consent: medical professionalism and public policy (4.10)
- Professional guidelines (4.10.1)
  - Therapeutic privilege (4.10.1(a))
- Public policy (4.10.2)

The adult who lacks capacity

Capacity (4.11)
- Models for defining capacity (4.11.1)
- Statutory capacity (4.11.2)
  - Presumption of capacity (4.11.2(a))
  - Assessment of capacity (4.11.2(c))
  - Definition of incapacity (4.11.2(b))
- 'Unwise' choices (4.11.3)
  - Use of force or restraint (4.11.3(a))
- Exceptions to the capacity requirement (4.11.4)
- Autonomy and health interests (4.11.5)

Decisions made on best interests (4.12)
- Who decides? (4.12.1)
- Treatment of those who lack capacity (4.12.2)
- The best interests test (4.12.3)
  - Common law (4.12.3(a))
  - The *Bolam* test and best interests (4.12.3(b))
  - A welfare standard to determine best interests (4.12.3(c))
- Ethical underpinnings of the best interests principle (4.12.4)
- Criticisms of the best interests principle (4.12.5)
- Alternatives to the best interests principle (4.12.6)

Advance decisions (4.13)
- Statutory authority (4.13.1)
- Advance directives at common law (4.13.2)
- Ethical issues and advance decisions (4.13.3)

Decisions made by appointed proxies (4.14)
- Lasting powers of attorney (4.14.1)
- Deputies (4.14.2)
- IMCA (4.14.3)

Capacity and consent to medical treatment

Key Terms

- **Advance decision** – an anticipatory decision made by an adult with capacity intended to refuse a specified proposed treatment in the event of future incapacity.
- **Best interests** – the test for decision making for the health care and treatment of those who lack capacity.
- **Capacity** – mental status of a person that is necessary to make a self-determined choice regarding a health-care intervention.
- **Competence** – the ability to understand, retain and weigh relevant information, and to be able to communicate that decision.
- **Consent** – the voluntary decision of a competent patient to undergo any form of medical intervention.
- **Independent Mental Capacity Advocate** – a person appointed by a health authority to support an individual who lacks capacity where no relatives or friends are available to consult regarding best interests.
- **Lasting power of attorney** – the legal instrument that empowers a trusted or willing person over the age of 18 to be appointed by an adult to make health-care decisions in the event of future incapacity.
- **Negligent consent** – negligent failure to provide information necessary for valid consent in the circumstances.
- **Non-consensual treatment** – treatment that is unlawful and could lead to a criminal charge of assault, or to a civil action in battery or tort.
- **Valid consent** – a voluntary decision made by a competent person based on sufficient information.

Scenario

Francine was a professional dancer who had developed a lower back complaint which was becoming progressively worse to the extent that she was no longer able to follow her vocation. She sought an opinion from a private neurosurgeon who, following a full series of investigations, advised spinal surgery to alleviate the condition.

Francine was sent home to consider her options. She had been given a prescription for pills, which Francine believed to be pain killers. She was provided with a clearly written and comprehensive set of information leaflets to read at home. These contained diagrams and details of the surgery, typical patient experiences and outcomes, and comprehensive details of possible complications.

After a few days, Francine decided to go ahead with the surgery. Shortly following admission, the surgeon told her about the most common risks of the intended procedure. She was not informed of the 1 per cent risk that surgery could lead to paralysis due to nerve damage and that such an injury could materialise even if the procedure was carried out with all due care and attention. She was also informed that her prescription pills were for anxiety rather than for pain.

Prior to the operation, Francine signed a consent form for the operation which was subsequently performed. During surgery Francine's nerves were damaged resulting in bilateral lower limb paralysis even though there was no negligence or want of care in the performance of the operation.

Francine is now confined to a wheelchair. She has had to give up her promising career. She claims she was unaware of the inherent risk of the operation, and that surgery could have been postponed. She also alleges that prior to admission she had specifically enquired whether surgery was dangerous but had been reassured by the neurosurgeon. She also wishes to bring a claim in battery on account of the medication she was given. She contends that her consent was for painkillers and not for pills for alleviation of anxiety.

The neurosurgeon contends that Francine was so fearful of surgery that he did not wish to further alarm her. It was for this reason that she was given the preoperative medication. In any event she would inevitably have required surgery in the future. Expert medical opinion is such that most other neurosurgeons would not have informed a patient of such a small risk prior to surgery.

4.1 Introduction

Consent lies at the heart of medical law and has pervasive application. This chapter considers the ethical and legal issues that pertain to capacity and consent to medical treatment. It is divided into three sections:

A. Pervasive issues
B. The competent adult
C. The adult who lacks capacity.

The chapter commences with an outline of the principles of consent before considering the law as applied to the competent patient followed by the adult who lacks decision-making capacity. To some extent this division is artificial and merging of the issues is readily apparent in health-care situations. Two illustrative scenarios are provided: one for the competent patient, the other for the incompetent adult. The law of consent as applied to children is examined in chapter 6.

A Pervasive issues

4.2 General considerations of consent and medical law

The rationale for consent to medical treatment was epitomised by Cardozo J in *Schloendorff v Society of New York Hospital* (NY, 1914) 105 NE 92 as: 'Every human being of adult years and sound mind has a right to determine what shall be done with his own body ...' Patients consult their doctors to receive skilled medical attention, although the ultimate decision as to whether to undergo a particular treatment rests with the person concerned. The principle of consent is underpinned by autonomy and a decision made by a patient to undergo a treatment must be made freely after receiving sufficient information to reach a considered decision. Consent may be expressed or implied (inferred from conduct) and must be valid. Failure to obtain valid consent prior to treatment could amount to the crime of assault, or form the basis of an action in tort.

Contemporary health-care practice and medical law increasingly emphasise the need to respect patient choice and self-determination. The dominant role of autonomy in the context of information disclosure prior to treatment has not always been evident, even among eminent ethicists. Buchanan (1979), for example, in his thesis against full disclosure of risk advanced three main arguments. First, a doctor has an overarching duty to do no harm. It is conceivable that some forms of disclosure might lead to harm. The paradox is that the doctor cannot know whether information will cause harm unless and until it is disclosed, in which case the psychological damage will have already occurred. Second, in the context of the therapeutic relationship, the patient 'cedes' to the doctor by allowing the doctor to reach a clinically appropriate decision. This type of argument is of historical significance only and seems untenable in present-day therapeutic relationships. Buchanan's third and final contention is that a full explanation given to a patient who lacks technical knowledge might further obfuscate decision making for the patient. While aspects of these arguments might be persuasive, for modern clinical practice they reflect a bygone age of paternalism. A better view might be that clinical care requires good communication skills such that appropriate information can be readily understood by its intended recipients.

Paternalism in the context of therapeutic relationships is believed to have stemmed from the Hippocratic Oath, traditionally sworn by doctors to practice ethical medicine on principles of beneficence and non-maleficence. A paternalistic approach conflicts with respect for autonomy and contemporary rights-based approaches to clinical care (see 1.8.3 (a)). In the context of consent, the arguments that support frank disclosure of risks and benefits of clinically indicated treatments, alternatives and refusal of care are founded on respect for self-determined choice. Appropriate and sensitive disclosure of information can be expected to enhance trust in the therapeutic relationship and bring ancillary benefits such as better participation of patients in clinical decision making. Nonetheless, limited resources, as well as other constraints, might operate to prevent full disclosure of all known benefits and risks. To confound matters further, philosophical obscurity surrounds the meaning of 'full' as applied to the therapeutic context: does this mean full in the manner of encompassing all known information; that which the individual patient might wish to know, or perhaps the information that is pertinent to the specific therapeutic circumstances? The later interpretation might invoke outrage amongst rights-based protagonists as being an antiquated relic of paternalism. It needs to be remembered, however, that most clinical situations are ones of uncertainty and clinical reasoning and decision making has to remain fluid with capacity to evolve. A pragmatic balance informed by ethical professional discretion has to be reached.

4.3 Treatment without consent

4.3.1 Criminal law

A doctor who merely touches a patient without consent could be guilty of assault, and surgical procedures often involve a level of harm which amounts to the affliction of 'grievous bodily harm'. For criminal law, voluntary and informed consent cannot provide a defence against this level of injury. Nonetheless, reasonable and proper medical care is lawful on the grounds of public interest (*Attorney-General's Reference (No 6 of 1980)* [1981] QB 715). In *Airedale NHS Trust v Bland* [1993] AC 789 at 891, Lord Mustill asked:

> How is it that, consistently with the proposition just stated, a doctor can with immunity perform on a consenting patient an act which would be a very serious crime if done by someone else? The answer must be that bodily invasions in the course of proper medical treatment stand completely outside the criminal law. The reason why the consent of the patient is so important is not that it furnishes a defence in itself, but because it is usually essential to the propriety of medical treatment.

It is for this reason that 'reasonable' and 'proper' surgical intervention lies outside the criminal law.

4.3.2 Civil law

Civil law actions can be brought in battery, or more commonly in negligence. To succeed in an action of battery, the claimant must prove on the balance of probabilities that the doctor carried out a non-consensual intervention. The civil wrong is committed by the physical contact itself and is actionable *per se*: proof of harm as a result of the touching is not required. In health-care contexts successful actions in battery are rare since the majority of disputes about consent are about its nature or quality. A successful action in battery requires that the patient gave no consent at all, or at least had not been told in broad terms of the nature of the proposed intervention. *Chatterton v Gerson* [1981] 1 All ER 257 established that for a case to be considered in battery the principal issue was whether or not the patient had consented in 'broad terms to the nature of the procedure'.

The majority of disputes about consent are brought in the tort of negligence. The claimant must prove that the health-care professional was negligent in securing consent prior to the intervention concerned. Typical actions include the alleged failure to provide sufficient information about the intervention since lack of information will compromise the patient's ability to reach an informed decision. Where the amount of information disclosed is disputed, the burden of proof is on the claimant to show that the level of disclosure did not reach the level expected according to a reasonable body of medical opinion (*Bolam v Friern Hospital Management Committee* [1957] 1 WLR 582). To succeed in negligence, the claimant must show that harm occurred as a result of the negligent disclosure of information and that, furthermore, had the allegedly missing information been provided she would not have undergone that procedure or treatment and thus would have avoided that injury. The actions of battery and negligence are considered in greater detail in Section B 'The competent adult'.

4.3.3 Declaratory procedures

A development of considerable importance for the law of consent and its application to health-care has been the ability of the family division of the High Court to declare that an intended intervention would not be unlawful if this was to be carried out in the best interests of a person who lacked capacity to consent. The inherent jurisdiction of the High Court operates as a safeguard to protect the welfare interests of the incompetent patient (*Re F (mental patient: sterilisation)* [1990] 2 AC 1 at 13 *per* Lord Donaldson of Lymington MR). The purpose of a declaratory order is for the court to declare the legal position in advance of an intended intervention, rather than wait for the conduct to occur and then adjudicate on its legality. Since October 2007, the Court of Protection has jurisdiction to declare on the lawfulness, or otherwise, of any act done or yet to be done, to an adult who lacks decision-making capacity (section 15(1)(c) Mental Capacity Act 2005).

In contrast to providing declaratory relief, the courts are reluctant to impose mandatory injunctions against doctors. The Court of Appeal in *Re J (a minor)* [1993] Fam 15 stated that in no circumstances would the court order a doctor to treat contrary to clinical judgement. At first instance, an interim injunctive order was given directing that life-prolonging treatment be provided to the infant concerned, which was against clinical opinion. The decision was overturned on appeal, although by that time the treating clinician was prepared to give life-prolonging treatment to the infant on clinical grounds (see 6.4.4 (a)).

4.4 What is consent?

The issue at the heart of many disputes in medical law is whether a patient's consent is valid. There are three elements to valid consent. The person who gives consent must:

- be competent;
- have received sufficient information to reach a decision;
- not have been influenced by coercion or manipulation.

Satisfying these elements will not provide a defence for the doctor who acts contrary to public policy. Patient consent will not exonerate a health-care professional who assaults a patient and causes actual, or grievous, bodily harm, outside therapeutic circumstances, or who kills a patient. Valid consent may be implied (inferred from the patient's conduct) or expressed, and there is no common law requirement for consent to be evidenced by writing. In certain circumstances specific legislation, such as the Human Tissue Act 2004 and the Human Fertilisation and Embryology Act 1990, require consent to be in writing and a signed consent form is usually required by organisational policy. However, 'It is not enough to get a patient to sign a pro forma expressing consent to a procedure with no explanation. The doctor must explain the implications of the procedure' (*Chatterton v Gerson* [1981] 1 All ER 257). In therapeutic relationships consent is perhaps best viewed as an ongoing process and part of good clinical care.

4.4.1 The meaning of competence

A competent adult in law is one who has the mental standing to make a health-care decision for himself or herself.

4.4.1(a) The Mental Capacity Act 2005

There is a statutory presumption that an adult has decision-making capacity (section 1(2) of the Mental Capacity Act 2005). Section 2(1) states that: '... a person lacks capacity in relation to a matter if at the material time he is unable to make a decision for himself in relation to the matter because of an impairment of, or a disturbance in the functioning of, the mind or brain'.

Inability to make a decision is explained further through provisions in section 3(1) of the Act (see 4.11.2(b)). The key components required for competence in decision making are the ability to understand and retain the relevant information, to weigh and use this, and to be able to communicate the decision that is made.

The Mental Capacity Act 2005 has codified the common law principles of assessment of competence with the additional requirement that persons must be able to communicate their decision. Determination of capacity is central in that a competent person has the unassailable right to refuse, or consent to, clinically indicated treatment. The principle of autonomy underpins the right to self-determined choice. Patients who lack capacity may receive clinically indicated treatment given in their best interests, a concept grounded on the basis of beneficence (see 1.8.3).

4.4.1(a)(i) The common law as the basis for codifying competence

The statutory presumption of capacity is rebuttable, which reflects the common law as exemplified by *Re C* [1994] 1 All ER 819. C was an in-patient at Broadmoor. His condition of paranoid schizophrenia was characterised by delusions that he was a great and infallible physician. Following a foot injury he developed gangrene and his clinicians believed that C had an 85 per cent risk of death if his foot was not amputated. C refused consent, stating that he preferred to die with two feet rather than live with one, a decision based on religious conviction. The declaration that surgical amputation would be lawful, and in C's best interests, was refused on the grounds that C was competent to refuse surgery. In giving judgement, Thorpe J stated (at 824):

> I am completely satisfied that the presumption that C's right of self-determination has not been displaced. Although his general capacity is impaired by schizophrenia, it has not been established that he does not sufficiently understand the nature, purpose and effects of the treatment he refuses. Indeed, I am satisfied that he has understood and retained the relevant treatment information, that in his own way he believes it, and that in the same fashion he has arrived at a clear choice.

Despite the fact that the amputation did not go ahead, C's foot eventually recovered. The test for competence proposed by Thorpe J was a three stage test: can the person comprehend and retain the relevant information, does the person believe the information, and can the person weigh the information in the balance in order to arrive at a choice. (See 4.11.2(c) for a further discussion on *Re C* and the two-limb statutory test for capacity.)

The *Re C* test was confirmed and applied by subsequent courts including the Court of Appeal in *Re MB* [1997] 2 FLR 426. Butler-Sloss LJ stated that the inability to arrive at a decision will be apparent when '(a) the patient is unable to comprehend and retain the information which is material to the decision, especially as to the likely consequences of having or not having the treatment in question; (b) the patient is unable to use the information and weigh it in the balance as part of the process of arriving at the decision'.

4.4.1(b) Irrational decisions

The right to decide is not limited to those decisions which others might regard as sensible and the right to decide persists notwithstanding the reasons for that choice, irrespective of whether these are rational, irrational, unknown or even non-existent (as objectively assessed) (*Re T* [1993] Fam 95). According to Butler-Sloss LJ, a decision to refuse medical treatment did not necessarily have to be sensible or well considered.

Staughton LJ stated: 'An adult whose mental capacity is unimpaired has the right to decide for herself whether she will or will not receive medical or surgical treatment, even in circumstances where she is likely or even certain to die in the absence of treatment. Thus far the law is clear.' This position is underpinned by human rights jurisprudence in particular by the right to respect for private and family life (Article 8 of the European Convention for Human Rights) as well as the right to life and the right not to be subjected to degrading treatment (Articles 2 and 3).

Although the right of a competent patient to make an objectively irrational decision with regard to medical treatment is protected, a framework is necessary to facilitate rational and critical decision making by the patient. A clinician committed to good medical care should use her best endeavours to enhance rational decision making by patients (Savulescu and Momeyer, 1997). According to Lord Donaldson what matters 'is that the doctors should consider whether at that time he had a capacity which was commensurate with the gravity of the decision which he purported to make. The more serious the decision, the greater the capacity required' (*Re T* [1993] Fam 95). The need for a level of capacity commensurate with the risk of death or irreversible harm was reiterated by Butler-Sloss LJ in that the 'graver the consequences of the decision, the commensurately greater the level of competence required to take the decision' (*Re MB* [1997] 2 FLR 426).

In *Re T* (at 113) Lord Donaldson explained that doctors

> faced with a refusal of consent have to give very careful and detailed consideration to the patient's capacity to decide at the time when the decision was made ... What matters is whether at that time the patient's capacity was reduced below the level needed in the case of a refusal of that importance, for refusals can vary in importance. Some may involve a risk to life or of irreparable damage to health. Others may not.

This suggests that the court might consider a sliding-scale approach to the determination of capacity dependent upon the implications of a context specific refusal. It implies that even if there is no formal requirement for a greater degree of capacity for a refusal, rather than giving consent to a clinically indicated intervention, this will in reality be applied. In fact, the trigger for a capacity assessment in most situations will be where a patient refuses treatment that a doctor considers appropriate under the circumstances (Gunn et al., 1999). The other practical consequence of such an approach might be that in the context of a 'serious' decision (as objectively assessed) autonomous self-determination is denied since the threshold for capacity becomes a 'moving goalpost'. Such a situation would without doubt allow the pendulum to swing away from autonomy and back towards beneficent paternalism.

4.4.1(c) Refusal of treatment by pregnant women

Situations where a pregnant woman's refusal of treatment could have a detrimental effect on a viable foetus have lead to several controversial decisions. The law is clear that a competent person (including a pregnant woman) can refuse even life-saving treatment. In the context of abortion, the life of an unborn foetus does not have priority against the rights of the pregnant woman (*Paton v United Kingdom* (8416/78) (1981) 3 EHRR 408). The morality is complex and irresistible. Irrespective of foetuses' legal or moral rights to life, the viable foetus is a vulnerable form of human life with potential to develop into a future person to be accorded the full protection of the law. The question arises as to whether foetal, paternal or even wider public interests can, or should, operate to override a pregnant woman's autonomy.

In *Re T* [1993] Fam 95, Lord Donaldson advanced a possible exception to the right to refuse treatment in that 'The only possible qualification is a case in which the choice may lead to the death of a viable foetus…if and when it arises, the courts would be faced with a novel problem of considerable legal and ethical complexity'. This decision was followed by *Re S (adult: refusal of treatment)* [1992] 4 All ER 671. S, who was fully competent, refused a caesarean section. An application was made to the court and a declaration was granted that surgery would be lawful. The approach taken by the court was one that was primarily duty-based towards the foetus. While in recent years the court has more expressly moved towards articulation of a position founded on the autonomy of the pregnant woman and her right to refuse, robust application of this principle seems doubtful.

In *Re MB (adult: medical treatment)* [1997] 2 FLR 426, Butler-Sloss LJ stated that 'a competent woman who has the capacity to decide may, for religious reasons, other reasons, for rational or irrational reasons, or for no reason at all, choose not to have medical intervention, even though the consequence may be the death or serious handicap of the child she bears, or her own death'. Although the court rejected Lord Donaldson's approach in *Re S*, MB lost her case. On the facts, MB was found to be incompetent to refuse a caesarean section. The court considered that her marked needle phobia was sufficient to have deprived her of decision-making capacity. The Court of Appeal upheld the High Court declaration that the caesarean section had been lawful.

In *St George's Healthcare NHS Trust v S* [1999] Fam 26, a woman who refused consent to an induced delivery, despite being told that this would endanger her unborn child, was sectioned for assessment under the Mental Health Act 1983. A declaration was applied for in that a caesarean section would be in her best interests. In the Court of Appeal, Judge LJ defended the pregnant woman's right to refuse treatment and stated that she should not have been forced to submit to bodily invasion, irrespective of whether her own life, or that of her unborn child, was at risk. The court's robust assertion in support of the pregnant woman's autonomy is reassuring, although translating sentiment into practice might not be straightforward.

The case law is firmly underscored by the morality of the rights and duties that characterise the maternal-foetal conflict in the circumstances of treatment refusal by a pregnant woman. It is apparent that the cases described were decided in a manner seemingly distinct from other treatment refusal cases in a way that failed to respect pregnant women's bodily integrity and rights of self-determined choice. The state has an overarching interest in the preservation of life (*Re T (adult: refusal of treatment)* [1993] Fam 95) (CA) which operates as a further confounding factor in these situations. In the clinical environment it seems likely that situations such as these will be managed by making every attempt to persuade and counsel, although the overriding principle that the body is inviolate means that the ultimate decision is with the competent woman alone.

4.4.2 Sufficient information

Information is the second key element of valid consent. The commonest type of claim brought under the tort of negligence is not that the individual did not consent to the procedure, but that the doctor was negligent for not adequately informing the patient of the inherent risks of the procedure (discussed in 4.6).

In *Chatterton v Gerson* [1981] 1 QB 432, it was established that an action in battery will be defeated if the patient understands in broad terms the nature of the procedure. The specific details are not required. Bristow J stated that 'once the patient is informed in broad terms of the nature of the procedure which is intended, and gives her consent, that consent is real, and the cause of the action on which to base a claim for failure to go into risks and implications is negligence, not trespass'. If trespass is to be pleaded, then the nature of the procedure undertaken has to be fundamentally different from what was originally envisaged. As an example, Bristow J referred to a case in the 1940s where a boy was admitted to hospital for a tonsillectomy and due to an administrative error was circumcised instead. In cases where there is such a gross divergence or error, it is more than likely that this would be settled out of court.

4.4.2(a) Consent negated by fraud

Consent can be negated by fraud, or by misleading a patient in terms of the 'nature and quality of what is being done'. In *Appleton v Garrett* (1995) 34 BMLR 23, a dentist deliberately misinformed his patients to coerce them to agree to treatment that was unnecessary for their dental health but led to financial gain for himself. Their consent was not real because had the patients been aware of the true situation (namely that treatment was unnecessary) they would not have given consent. In *R v Tabassum* [2000] Lloyds Rep Med 404, the deception related to the nature and quality of the act. A woman agreed to a breast examination under the misrepresentation that this was for educational purposes. In fact it was carried out for the defendant's own sexual gratification. However, in *R v Richardson* [1999] QB 444, evidence that the dentist was not registered with the General Dental Council did not vitiate the patient's consent to treatment. The case of *Tabassum* was distinguished on the basis that Tabassum's lack of medical qualifications affected the nature of the act whereas in *Richardson* the dentist's registration was considered to be a matter of attribute, rather than identity. These decisions seem difficult to reconcile on the facts. The principle from the common law is that apparent consent can be vitiated by evidence of mistake, fraud or misapprehension, although the rules are not always consistently applied.

4.4.2(b) Additional interventions

As a general rule an additional procedure carried out on an anaesthetised patient will be unlawful unless it can be justified on the doctrine of necessity (since the patient, being under an anaesthetic, lacks decision-making capacity at the relevant time). In *Devi v West Midlands RHA* [1980] CLY 6087, the patient had been admitted for repair of a perforated uterus. During the operation the surgeon decided to perform a sterilisation as well as he considered this procedure to be in the woman's best interests. The surgeon was held liable since consent had not been given for sterilisation. In *Bartley v Studd* (1995) 2 (8) Medical Law Monitor 1, a surgeon was liable for the non-consensual removal of ovaries during a hysterectomy, even though the surgeon considered this to be indicated on medical grounds.

An additional procedure on an unconscious patient, and which is outside the ambit of the consent provided, could nonetheless be lawful if performed on grounds of necessity. This argument was not raised in *Devi* or *Bartley* since neither additional procedure had been life saving. There is no direct English authority but Canadian jurisprudence suggests that necessity might be invoked as a successful defence. In

Marshall v Curry [1933] 3 DLR 260, the patient was admitted for a hernia repair during which his left testicle was removed since the surgeon considered this necessary due to the risk of gangrene. The Supreme Court of Nova Scotia accepted this defence, as it was necessary to protect the patient's life and health, both of which could have been compromised had the surgery been postponed to a later date. In *Murray v McMurchy* [1949] 2 DLR 442, the Supreme Court of British Columbia in Canada drew a distinction between surgery that was necessary for the protection of life, or even to preserve the health of the patient, as opposed to that which was merely convenient. In *Murray*, the patient had been admitted for a caesarean section during which the surgeon had carried out a sterilisation on the grounds that the uterus was in such a position so as to make any future pregnancy dangerous. On the facts, the court ruled that the sterilisation was unnecessary at the time at which it occurred, even though this was expedient. It follows that mere convenience does not preclude the need to obtain further consent.

4.4.3 Coercion or undue influence

The third requirement for valid consent is that it must be voluntary and freely given without coercion or undue influence. The absence of a written consent form is not definitive evidence of lack of voluntary consent. In *Freeman v Home Office* [1984] QB 524, a patient who was a prisoner argued that he had no option but to submit to the prison medical officer's proposed treatment, and that his consent was therefore invalid. It was further argued that consent had not been voluntary because of the absence of a written consent form. The Court of Appeal held that undue influence was a question of fact; a finding of undue influence did not necessarily follow from the mere absence of a document.

4.4.3(a) Undue influence

Re T (adult: refusal of treatment) [1993] Fam 95 is the leading authority for consent based on undue influence. T was pregnant and had been badly injured in a road traffic accident. Her mother was a practising Jehovah's Witness. Although T had been raised as a Jehovah's Witness she was not officially a member of that religion. Following an emergency caesarean section she required a blood transfusion on clinical grounds. Prior to surgery she had refused a blood transfusion. Her father and boyfriend sought a declaration that it would be lawful to administer blood since her pre-operative refusal had been due to pressure from her mother. Her prior refusal was set aside by the Court of Appeal on three principal grounds: that T had been incapacitated at the time of refusal; that she had not been properly informed; and that on the facts her mother had exerted undue influence. Since T's refusal had not been valid, the court declared that it would be in T's best interests to receive a transfusion. On the issue of undue influence Lord Donaldson stated: 'The real question in each such case is "Does the patient really mean what he says, or is he merely saying it for a quiet life, to satisfy someone else or because the advice and persuasion to which he has been subjected is such that he can no longer think and decide for himself?" ' In deciding this question, it is important to balance the will of the individual against the will and relationship of the person who was supposedly exercising the influence. Such pressure may be subtle, pervasive, insidious and powerful, particularly when religious beliefs are involved.

Determining whether or not undue influence has been imposed upon a patient by a health-care professional may be problematic. In *U v Centre for Reproductive Medicine* [2002] EWCA Civ. 565, Mr U agreed to the posthumous storage of his sperm, but subsequently withdrew his consent. Following his death, Mr U's wife brought an action against the clinic on the grounds that undue influence had been the cause of his withdrawal of consent. On the facts it emerged that following a meeting with a nursing sister at the clinic, Mr U was coerced to alter his position regarding consent to the posthumous use of his sperm on the basis of the clinic's ethical policy. At first instance, and on appeal, Mrs U could not establish that the pressure placed on her late husband amounted to undue influence. According to Butler-Sloss P, 'When one stands back and looks at the facts of this case, it seems to me that it is difficult to say that an able, intelligent, educated man of 47, with a responsible job and in good health, could have his will overborne so that the act of altering the form and initialling the alterations were done in circumstances in which Mr U no longer thought and decided for himself'. Butler-Sloss P attached great weight to Mr U's education, his standing in society, and the fact that he held a responsible position, all pointing to the likelihood of his ability to think for himself and assert his will. These characteristics played a major role in the court's finding that the nurse had not exerted undue influence. It is apparent, however, that patients are often vulnerable in clinical situations and may also believe and accept as correct the advice offered by health-care professionals. The burden of proof falls on the party alleging undue influence, and it appears that factors such as a high level of education, maturity, health and holding a position of responsibility will weigh against a finding of coercion.

4.4.4 The burden of proof

For a criminal charge brought on the basis of lack of consent, the prosecution bears the burden of proof. In negligence actions, it is less clear whether the claimant must establish that consent was invalid, or alternatively whether it is for the defendant to prove valid consent in order to rely upon this as a defence.

In *Freeman v Home Office* [1984] 1 QB 524, McCowan J stated that the burden of proving lack of consent would be for the claimant, a requirement that could be particularly harsh in some situations. Since it is for the defendant to take consent and record this, it is arguable that the onus of proving consent should lie upon the defendant. According to Kennedy and Grubb (2000), consent represents a defence and the obligation is therefore on the health-care professional to prove valid consent in the eventuality of a dispute.

B The competent adult

4.5 Lack of consent and battery

For competent patients, consent refers to their state of mind about the proposed violation of bodily integrity (*Sidaway v Bethlem Royal Hospital Governors* [1985] 1 All ER 643). If an individual agrees to treatment without understanding the nature and purpose of the intervention, an action may lie in battery. Alternatively, if the 'broad nature' of the intervention is known, then an action in battery is unlikely to succeed. *Chatterton v Gerson* [1981] 1 QB 432 provides authority that as long as a patient understands the nature of the proposed intervention in general terms, it is likely to be sufficient to absolve the practitioner of battery.

Francine wishes to bring an action in battery on account of the fact that she did not give real consent for the medication prescribed. In the circumstances she will not be able to recover damages. Even though Francine might prove that she had been misinformed about the nature and characteristics of the medication, the prescription of medication does not involve the requisite physical contact required for the tort.

4.6 Negligent consent

In an action brought on grounds of negligent consent, the claimant's case is that the doctor negligently failed to obtain appropriate permission prior to carrying out the intervention concerned.

An essential prerequisite of valid consent is sufficient information. The doctor's duty is a positive one: to ensure that the patient's entitlement to adequate information is satisfied. The majority of disputes arise on account of the claimant's perception that the doctor negligently failed to provide sufficient information upon which to base a decision and, in particular, that insufficient information was given about inherent risks. A person who knows nothing of the risks that accompany a procedure cannot validly consent and yet, equally, it is impossible and impractical to inform every patient of every known risk. Some information might be of a highly technical or scientific nature, and even if such information was provided it might not necessarily be understood. Equally, all efforts must be taken to ensure that technical jargon is interpreted in a manner that is comprehensible to a patient. Before examining how much information is sufficient, some of the ethical and moral arguments will be considered as these provide the bases of patients' rights to be informed.

4.6.1 Why patients need to be informed

Since the validity of consent often hinges on the amount of information provided, it might seem appropriate to give the fullest information about the intervention, its risks and the possible implications of refusal. In clinical situations this utopian ideal may not be possible, and clinical judgement will be necessary to ascertain which risks need to be disclosed in the context of each patient's unique circumstances. Even in an ideal health-care encounter and without pressure of time, attempts to disclose all known information about a proposed intervention could detrimentally impact upon the therapeutic relationship and might be counterproductive to a person attempting to make a considered decision about prospective treatment.

For elective procedures, printed information and brochures provide useful additions to augment, though not replace, patient-specific clinical information and advice. Although barriers such as literacy, language and ethnicity might be apparent, printed material that signposts sources of further information and support are a useful supplements to personalised care.

4.6.1(a) The ethics of disclosure

From a moral perspective there are several reasons why patients should be informed about the procedure they are contemplating, particularly in respect of possible risks. The fundamental justification lies in respect for patient autonomy and self-determination, grounded on a deontological basis (see 1.4). Respect for persons underscores the need to allow patients to make their own decisions and the principle of self-determination underpins access to information.

The contemporary ethos of good clinical care involves a partnership with patients who have the right to know about medical interventions that pertain to their health-care needs. From a consequentialist ideology, the 'patient as partner' approach enhances patient empowerment and personal involvement in their care. From a utilitarian perspective, appropriate disclosure might promote compliance and better clinical and patient-reported outcomes. For the 'virtue' purist, while there may be no absolute duties of conduct in this regard, it would appear that a moral responsibility lies with the doctor to provide as much information as possible since such practice would be considered 'virtuous'.

Over the years, critics have advanced numerous arguments against information disclosure. Merely providing information to a patient is, in itself, insufficient and does not necessarily equate with understanding. Furthermore, there is no clear consensus of how much information ought to be provided, and it seems likely that fear of litigation, in the form of defensive practice, might be what is behind the drive to deliver ever increasing amounts of information. Provision of vast quantities of non-individualised information can lead to lack of clarity and dissuade patients from agreeing to relatively low-risk procedures that could offer significant improvements to their quality of life. One example is hip replacement surgery. For the majority of patients without coexisting morbidity, this is a relatively low-risk procedure that offers considerable benefits. The orthopaedic surgeon, who informs every patient of all known risks including death, might be doing his patient a disservice. Conversely, withholding such information deprives the patient of the ability to take a personal decision based upon evidence. A middle path might be to present accurate information, using meaningful statistics and illustrations of risk-benefit.

Prior to surgery Francine was given a range of reading material about her proposed surgery and was informed of the most common risks of the procedure.
   Assuming that Francine is a competent adult:

▶ Consider the ethical basis for information disclosure.
▶ Explain the human rights basis for information disclosure.

The presentation of comprehensive information to every patient about all procedures is aspirational, rather than achievable. Doctors have been criticised for being poor communicators of information and risk. However, the reality of clinical practice is that much remains unknown and most clinical decisions are accompanied by some degree of uncertainty. Patients often seek definitive answers or solutions, and are interested in what might happen to them as individuals rather than the generality of statistical predictions. Individual patient outcomes are difficult to predict and often the best that can be offered is a broad indication of general risks, data on an individual practitioner's complication rates and a rough estimate of probability for that particular patient. If a person is unfortunate enough to have a particular risk materialise, then that could lead to a challenge as to whether or not the level of disclosure was in fact sufficient (such disclosure itself being based on an unavoidable degree of uncertainty).

4.6.1(b) The 'right' to ignorance

The extent to which patients have the right to refuse receiving information prior to giving consent is ethically controversial and this question has yet to be addressed in law. It is arguable that if competent patients voluntarily insist on maintaining their ignorance, then that is their right. Nonetheless, a person cannot be regarded as having given true consent without being informed of the rationale and potential risks and benefits of a proposed treatment. At a bare minimum, some information has to be given to patients (Harris, 1985).

Invariably, a few competent, educated patients will insist that they 'do not want to know'. Their doctors are asked to go ahead with whatever treatment they consider to be best for them at that time and for their particular circumstances. While this does not condone the view that 'doctor knows best', it nonetheless reflects one aspect of contemporary clinical care. Management requires sensitive communication and allowing the patient to have time to consider and reflect on the decision. Invitation of a trusted friend or relative to attend pre-operative consultations can be useful although the need to respect confidentiality is apparent. Provision of information booklets and resources can offer a useful adjunct to care but cannot replace patient-specific advice. It remains apparent that in a society that upholds the need for self-determined choice, patients may still insist that decision making is, at least notionally, left in the hands of a doctor they trust.

4.6.2   How much information?

The doctrine of informed consent requires that patients are made aware of *all* relevant and necessary information to make an informed choice and give consent. On strict legal analysis English law does not recognise this doctrine, although the term 'informed consent' is used loosely to mean that (some) information has been provided. The question of how much information is necessary to avoid liability is determined on the House of Lords authority of *Sidaway v Bethlem RHG* [1985] 1 All ER 653.

Following surgery to relieve a trapped nerve, Mrs Sidaway was left paralysed due to spinal cord damage. She brought an action against the hospital on the basis that she had not been informed of the inherent risks of surgery. The case hinged upon the surgeon's alleged failure to disclose the risks of paralysis, and if so, whether he had been negligent for not having conveyed this possibility. There were several evidential problems in *Sidaway*, augmented by the considerable time that elapsed between the operation and the case coming to trial and during which time the surgeon had died. The appeal to the House of Lords took place 10 years after the operation. Expert evidence indicated that at the time of the operation some neurosurgeons would have considered it appropriate not to inform a patient about the relatively remote risk of paralysis. In effect, there was a respectable body of professional opinion that supported the surgeon's decision not to disclose the risk. A key issue was whether the standard for disclosure of risk should be according to the *Bolam* standard, being that supported by a respectable body of professional opinion, or possibly a higher standard. The case failed on appeal and the legal standard for information disclosure was accepted as a *Bolam* standard. A doctor providing information according to the level of a 'reasonable doctor' in such circumstances would not be considered negligent. In arriving at this consensus, their Lordships provided markedly different justifications and reasoning.

Lord Diplock's view was that the required level of information disclosure ought to be determined according to *Bolam* (in accordance with contemporaneous accepted wisdom as in cases of disputes regarding diagnosis and treatment). Whether failure to disclose information was negligent ought to be judged according to the standard of the 'prudent doctor' or 'reasonable doctor' test. In his view, the *Bolam* standard encompassed information disclosure and the court could not second guess or put itself in the surgeon's shoes to ascertain the appropriate level of explanation. Determination of the appropriate level of information disclosure for purposes of consent, required exercise of professional skill and judgement and represented part of the doctor's comprehensive duty of care owed to the patient. As such the standard expected was appropriately measured against the standard set by a responsible body of skilled professionals. A doctor would only be negligent if failure to disclose the information would be unacceptable to responsible professionals within that particular speciality at that particular time.

Lord Scarman (who concurred with the majority because of evidential reasons) rejected the *Bolam* approach. He considered the instant case as being of considerable significance and addressed a question never before considered by the House, namely the extent of the patient's right to know, and the extent of the doctor's duty to disclose inherent risks. Lord Scarman's reasoning was based upon the scope of the doctor's duty, and his starting point was the right of patients to make their own self-determined choice. For the proper exercise of autonomous decision making the patient had a right to know, and therefore the doctor had a duty to disclose. Two caveats were applied: first, the duty was confined to disclosure of material risk; and second, the doctor would not be liable if, upon a reasonable assessment of the patient's condition, a view was formed that a warning of risks would be detrimental to the patient's health. The key to the application of these principles was the determination of a material risk, and the test for that would be according to the 'prudent patient' rather than the perspective of the 'reasonable' or 'prudent' doctor. The test of materiality was whether, in the circumstances of the case, the court was satisfied that a reasonable person in the patient's position would be likely to attach significance to the risk.

Somewhere between these opinions are the judgements of Lord Bridge (with whom Lord Keith agreed) and Lord Templeman. Lord Bridge held that *Bolam* applied, subject to two qualifications. First, this approach did not mean that the law was relinquishing its responsibility in handing over the standard for the scope of disclosure to the medical profession. The court would determine whether or not there was a body of opinion that approved non-disclosure in the circumstances, and in the presence of disagreement among the experts it would be for the judge to decide which view was preferable. Second, even if the established body of medical opinion was in favour of non-disclosure, it was nonetheless open for a judge to hold it as unacceptable and therefore not responsible. The conclusion was that failure to disclose a serious risk could be negligent, even if such non-disclosure was acceptable and supported by a respectable body of medical opinion, the example being given of a 10 per cent risk of stroke. However, in the instant case, since the risk was very small and non-disclosure was supported by a responsible body of opinion, the doctor had not been negligent.

Lord Templeman also opted for the middle course. In his view a doctor ought to draw attention to a danger that was special in kind or magnitude, or special to the patient concerned. After having informed the patient of such risks, it was for them to raise any further concerns. On the facts, since Mrs Sidaway had chosen not to elicit further information, the surgeon had no duty to provide this. Too much information could impair patients' ability to reach a decision in the same way as too little. In the final analysis, it would be for the doctor, cognizant of the best interests of the patient and her right to know, who would have to make a balanced judgement and decide on the amount of information to be provided, and how such information ought to be couched. Thus, again it appears that Lord Templeman was advocating what might be viewed as a modified *Bolam* approach. Whereas the general *Bolam* principle would apply, this would be subject to disclosure of information that might be 'special' to the individual concerned as informed by specific questions and concerns raised by the patient. Lord Templeman's approach moved slightly away from the traditional *Bolam* test towards that of a rights-based approach to information disclosure, but perhaps not as far as Lord Scarman's standard. Lord Templeman's approach is one that is subjective with regard to each individual patient in terms of disclosing what might be special or relevant to that particular individual. It is suggested that the latter approach most closely aligns with contemporary clinical practice.

> Prior to surgery, Francine was informed of the most common risks of the intended surgery. She was not informed of a 1 per cent risk that surgery could lead to paralysis due to nerve damage and that such an injury could materialise even if the procedure was carried out with all due care and attention. Consider the surgeon's conduct in light of the approaches taken by their Lordships in *Sidaway*.

4.6.2(a) Paradigms for the standard of disclosure

Although *Sidaway* endorsed the *Bolam* standard as that against which allegedly negligent disclosure ought to be measured, the judgement nonetheless raised three potential paradigms for the standard of information disclosure. Lord Diplock's approach fully endorsed the 'reasonable doctor' test (the *Bolam* standard); Lord Scarman's judgement raised the possibility of the objective 'prudent patient' test; and the judgements of Lords Bridge and Templeman raised the concept of the modified *Bolam* approach. In Lord Bridge's view, the *Bolam* test ought to apply subject to scrutiny by the court, whereas in Lord Templeman's view, the *Bolam* test was the starting point and encompassed any matters that were of particular importance to the patient, as well as any specific questions that the patient might raise. While Lord Templeman's view fits more closely with a subjective standard, the view expressed by Lord Bridge can be regarded as a modification of the benchmark, meaning that although the standard expressed by the defendant might be *Bolam*-endorsed, it was at the court's discretion to determine what *should be* normative within those specific circumstances rather than what *might be* normative. There are parallels here with *dicta* in the subsequent decision of *Bolitho*. Lord Bridge's view is the more objective approach and more closely aligns with the standard set by what *ought to be* normative rather than one that is set by what is normative based upon current practices.

The reasonable doctor test reflects the more traditional model whereby decision-making power is left the hands of doctors who purportedly possess the most relevant knowledge and expertise. The principal criticism is that the test does not sufficiently respect the patient's right to autonomous choice. To reach an informed decision there are two principal considerations: first, the technical knowledge base, and second, that patient's unique and individual values. In the exercise of self-determined choice, patient values play a significant role and informed choice is not limited only to technical knowhow and expertise. One stark example of how a patient's values can represent an essential part of the decision-making process is the decision between a prolongation of life compared with a shorter though enhanced quality of life. According to Teff (1985), the 'relative importance which patients attach, for example, to quality as against length of life, and to physical integrity or appearance as against a diminution of pain, may reflect personal values, circumstances and priorities of which the surgeon, in particular, is initially unaware and may never become sufficiently apprised.' The emphasis on the 'reasonable doctor' test is predominantly paternalistic, whereas informed choice is patient-centred and respects autonomy and personal values.

The 'reasonable doctor' test arguably creates a tension between a paternalistic approach to information provision and the irrefutable right of a competent patient to refuse medical treatment, be it rational, irrational or for no reason at all (*Re T (adult: refusal of treatment)* [1993] Fam 95). Furthermore, the 'reasonable doctor' test emphasises that which the doctor has offered by way of information disclosure, as opposed to what might have been required, relevant or even understood by that particular patient. A patient's lack of understanding may be due to factors which include the doctor's communication skills, the complexity of the explanation, the patient's capacity to understand, the way in which the information has been given, and its format whether verbal, written or audiovisual (Lesser, 1991).

Kennedy (1991) considers that the concept of a professionally set standard is nonsense, since the medical profession has not got together to develop a consensus as to which risks should be disclosed to which patients and under which particular circumstances. Practice varies among clinicians and what might be considered a cautious or even defensive approach to one doctor might well be another's idea of exemplary practice. In the absence of clearly defined professional standards, a body of opinion affirming a particular doctor's conduct could be seen as nothing more than professional solidarity and as such might operate to erode patient trust and confidence.

The 'prudent patient' test should, in theory, address the deficiencies of the 'reasonable doctor' test. In the US case of *Canterbury v Spence* (DC, 1972) 464 F 2d 772, it was stated that a risk must be disclosed 'when a reasonable person, in what the physician knows, or should know to be the patient's position would be likely to attach significance to the risk or cluster of risks in deciding whether or not to forgo the proposed therapy'. The fundamental problem with the 'prudent patient' test is the assumption that doctors know what the hypothetical reasonable patient would want to know in the circumstances. In using the 'prudent patient' approach, the standard of care has to be determined by the courts retrospectively in the event of subsequent litigation. It is almost impossible for a doctor to second guess what might be regarded as the proper standard in the event of future litigation and it seems likely that a health-care professional would seek guidance from colleagues in the field. The content of a patient-orientated standard could be especially burdensome for physicians since this standard is hypothetical compared to a professional standard that is empirically determinable. To determine what a reasonable patient would find relevant and material for the purposes of decision making, doctors would need to invest more time to ascertain each patient's unique values (Appelbaum et al., 1987). The practicalities of this proposal are moot, as is the more fundamental question as to whether this approach would actually improve patient outcomes and care. However, it seems more than likely that enhanced communication will indicate which patients are more concerned with the 'graver' risks (as perceived by doctors), compared with those who consider that the supposed 'lesser' risks to be of greater personal significance.

It has been argued that the subjective patient standard of disclosure is the optimum means of protecting patient autonomy. This standard acknowledges the highly variable needs of persons with regard to information disclosure and imposes a duty whereby the level of disclosure is bespoke to each individual's needs. It has been suggested that this standard requires the physician to individualise the information-giving process so that it is aligned to the obligation to individualise diagnostic and therapeutic care, and would be based upon what is known about each individual patient rather than the hypothetical prudent (or reasonable) patient (Capron, 1974 at 306). This could be effected into practice through enhanced communication since the

> key to effective communication is to invite active participation by patients or subjects in the context of an informational exchange...professionals would do well to end their traditional preoccupation with disclosure and instead ask questions, elicit the concerns and interests of the patient or subject, and establish a climate that encourages the patient or subject to ask questions. This is the most promising course to ensure that the patient or subject will receive information that is personally material. (Faden et al., 1986)

4.6.2(b) Post-Sidaway developments

In the immediate aftermath of *Sidaway*, the court tended to accept Lord Diplock's judgement as definitive of the level of information disclosure required. In *Gold v Haringey Health Authority* [1987] 2 All ER 888 the claimant underwent a sterilisation but subsequently gave birth to her fourth child. She alleged that she had not been warned of the potential failure rate of female sterilisation surgery and that had she been made aware, her husband would have undergone a vasectomy. Medical evidence was such that at this particular time a substantial body of responsible doctors would not have given this warning. At first instance it was found that the defendants had been negligent, but their appeal was allowed. In the Court of Appeal, Lloyd LJ stated that in *Sidaway*, 'the House of Lords applied the (*Bolam*) test to a case in which a doctor, before carrying out an operation, failed to warn his patient of a very small risk of a very serious injury. It would have been open to the House of Lords to hold that the *Bolam* test applied to negligent diagnosis and negligent treatment, but not negligent advice...' and '[It] is clear from Lord Diplock's speech in *Sidaway* that a doctor's duty of care in relation to diagnosis, treatment and advice, whether the doctor be a specialist or a general practitioner, is not to be dissected into its component parts'. In *Gold*, a direct and straightforward application of the *Bolam* test was applied in the context of information disclosure. This decision has been criticised for allowing too much discretion to the medical profession on the grounds that such an approach fails to protect patient choice and self-determination. While medical training might qualify doctors to diagnose and carry out treatment, it cannot qualify them to decide what patients need to know.

In *Bolitho v City and Hackney Health Authority* [1998] AC 232, the *Bolam* test was revisited in the light of the court taking a more interventionist approach towards scrutinising the logical basis of the professed responsible body of medical opinion. This, together with Lord Bridge's speech in *Sidaway* (where he espoused a more enquiring approach by the court) was reconciled by Lord Woolf as factors in shaping the judgement in *Pearce v United Bristol Healthcare NHS Trust* [1999] PIQR 53. On the facts Mrs Pearce was two weeks overdue for the birth of her sixth child and had begged her doctor for induction of labour or a caesarean section. The consultant considered medical induction of labour to be inappropriate and high risk and that recovery would be prolonged following a caesarean section. A few days later the baby died *in utero*. The two questions raised at the trial were (a) should Mrs Pearce have been informed of the small increased risk of stillbirth as a result of delayed delivery, and (b) had Mrs Pearce been so advised, would this have altered her decision to have a natural birth? The claim was dismissed at first instance and on appeal, even though Lord Woolf stated (in agreement with Roch and Mummery LJJ) that 'if there is a significant risk which would affect the judgement of a reasonable patient, then in the normal course it is the responsibility of a doctor to inform the patient of that significant risk... [In] the *Sidaway* case, Lord Bridge recognises that position'. Thus, on the facts, the defendant had not been negligent in failing to disclose the small additional risk, since it was not a 'significant' risk. There are two points worth noting. First, despite the verdict being against the claimant, Lord Woolf's assertions indicate a judicial willingness to move away from an unquestioning application of *Bolam* as far as information disclosure is concerned. The doctor has a duty to inform the patient of a significant risk that would affect the judgement of a reasonable patient. This is an explicit step towards patient-centered information disclosure and whilst perhaps not going approaching the 'prudent patient' test, it nonetheless implies an ascending degree of scrutiny by the court. This approach was developed in *Wyatt v Curtis* [2003] EWCA Civ 1779 in which Sedley LJ (at para 16) suggested that the *Pearce* approach refined Lord Bridge's judgement in *Sidaway*:

> Lord Woolf's formulation refines Lord Bridge's test by recognising that what is substantial and what is grave are questions on which the doctor's and the patient's perception may differ, and in relation to which the doctor must therefore have regard to what may be the patient's perception. To the doctor, a chance in a hundred... may well be an insubstantial chance... To the patient, a new risk which... doubles, or at least enhances, the background risk of a potentially catastrophic abnormality may well be both substantial and grave, or at least sufficiently real for her to want to make an informed decision about it.

The second point from *Pearce* is in relation to what might be considered a significant risk although unfortunately this detail was not explored by the court. While Lord Woolf's statement in *Pearce* indicated a more robust approach towards the patient's right to information, nevertheless in deciding whether the 0.1–0.2 per cent risk of stillbirth ought to have been disclosed, he stated that the medical expert witnesses called on behalf of the defendants did not regard this level of risk as significant. Once again, therefore, the court appeared to rely upon the doctor's judgement of whether the risk was significant, rather than Mrs Pearce's own perception of that risk, and how knowledge of that level of risk would have affected her decision to have a natural birth in accordance with medical advice.

In *Sidaway*, Lord Bridge did not consider a risk of 1 per cent of damage to the spinal cord, and about 2 per cent of damage to either the spinal cord or nerve roots, as significant. In *Pearce*, Lord Woolf did not consider a 0.1–0.2 per cent risk of stillbirth to be significant. Yet a risk of about 1 in 14,000 may be significant as adjudged by the High Court of Australia in *Rogers v Whittaker* (1992) 109 ALR 625. This was the level of risk that surgery on a patient's blind right eye carried in terms of rendering the patient totally blind, when the patient clearly feared damage to the good eye as a result of surgery to the other. Despite the surgeon's actions being supported by a body of medical opinion, the Federal Court in Australia found the surgeon negligent. Exactly how one aligns what a reasonable doctor feels to be significant to a particular patient will perhaps always be debatable.

Consider Francine's preoperative situation in the context of the above paradigms. Which standard do you think could best be applied to Francine's situation and why?

4.7 Insufficient warning and causation

If a patient is not warned about an inherent risk of a procedure and this outcome fails to materialise then there is no issue in respect of litigation. If, however, the risk does occur then a claim in negligence could be brought. The claimant may succeed in proving that the doctor's failure to warn had been negligent. However, there is an additional hurdle. The claimant must prove that the defendant's failure to warn was the cause of the damage. The claimant must therefore prove that the undisclosed risk resulted in the injury; that the injury left the claimant in a worse situation than she would have been in had the procedure not been performed; *and* that had she been informed of this risk or outcome, she would not have consented to the procedure (thereby avoiding the risk of the injury). With regard to having the procedure, the crucial point is this: if the claimant had been warned would this have prevented the claimant from undergoing the procedure? If the claimant would have undergone the procedure in any event even after being warned, then causation will not be proved. This was the central issue in *Chester v Afshar* [2004] 4 All ER 587.

In *Chester*, a journalist (Ms Chester) experienced persistent low back pain for which she consulted Mr Afshar, a consultant neurosurgeon. He advised surgery to remove three lumbar spinal discs that were the source of her discomfort, and she agreed to undergo the operation at the next available opportunity a few days later. Ms Chester voiced concerns about risks of surgery and these were allegedly dismissed by Mr Afshar, who said that he 'had not crippled anybody yet'. It was accepted by both parties that there was a 1–2 per cent inherent risk of developing a complication following surgery by some degree of functional motor impairment in the lower limbs. Following surgery Ms Chester suffered from severe pain and motor impairment. There was no dispute about the way in which the operation had been carried out, which was entirely appropriate. At first instance it was accepted that Ms Chester, had she been told of the risks, may have sought a second or third opinion, but would have still consented to the surgery at a future time. As this risk was inherent within the procedure and unavoidable, this meant she would have still faced the same risk of injury whenever she had the operation. Her claim therefore failed on conventional causation principles that must satisfy the 'but for' test or the 'material contribution' to the injury requirement. Mr Afshar had not operated without due care and attention and although he had negligently failed to inform her of the risk. Even if he had informed her of such a risk, she would still have undergone the same operation either at that time or probably later (according to her own evidence). Therefore her position, as a result of the failure to inform, was arguably no worse than it would have been had she been told of all the risks. The point of causation was the key issue on appeal to the House of Lords.

The majority of the House of Lords rejected the defendant's argument, and accepted that there was a specific loss for Ms Chester, and found in her favour. This departure from conventional causation principles would appear to be mainly to vindicate her right to autonomy as protected by Article 8 of the European Convention of Human Rights. It was held that she had the right to be informed of the risks and had suffered damage in the context where the doctor had breached his duty to inform her of those risks. The focus was on a policy issue that doctors should be liable if they fail to respect a patient's right to know about risks that were attendant or inherent upon a particular procedure. Traditional causation principles were applied only by the minority (Lords Bingham and Hoffman) who did not accept that Ms Chester was any the worse as a result of the negligent failure to inform her of the risks. The real loss to Ms Chester was loss of the opportunity to make an informed decision. Within the context of patient autonomy, such a loss is significant and needs to be recognised and marked by an award in damages. However, to award damages for all losses that flowed from this seems excessive.

Chester is fundamentally a policy decision, at the heart of which is protection of patient rights (to choose whether or not to undergo treatment). This was succinctly emphasised by Lord Hope: 'If it is to fulfil that function it must ensure that the duty to inform is respected by the doctor. It will fail to do this if an appropriate remedy cannot be given if the duty is breached and the very risk that the patient should have been told about occurs and she suffers injury.' The pro-claimant, patient-centred approach in *Chester* was heavily influenced by the leading Australian case of *Chappel v Hart* [1998] HCA 55, which recognised the difficulty that a claimant has in proving that she would *never* have consented to a particular procedure in the future. *Chester* shifts the bar towards maximising patient autonomy for making an informed choice.

It has been argued that it would be difficult to go against the majority reasoning in *Chester* and it would be unjust to require a patient to show that she would never have had a particular procedure in the future. Grubb (2004) states:

> It is also counterintuitive to think that because the patient may run the risk in the future – by agreeing to and having the procedure – the negligence is not connected to her injury. At worse, she will be exposed to a small risk of injury which is unlikely *then* to eventuate. ... She had in a real and immediate sense suffered injury that she would not otherwise have suffered. That should be sufficient to establish a causal link.

However, against this is the notion that the decision in *Chester* effectively abolishes the need for a claimant to prove causation. In Foster's view (2004):

> This is Alice in Wonderland stuff. Causation is not established but, since this should be, it will be deemed to be. ... [The] House of Lords has stretched the rules of causation before – notably in *Fairchild v Glenhaven Funeral Services*. But *Chester* goes much further: it abolishes the requirement for causation in any meaningful sense ... [We] have always thought of causation as a logical, or as a mathematical, business. To intrude policy into causation is like saying that 2+2 does not equal 4 because, for policy reasons, it should not. After *Chester*, nothing seems unthinkable.

Additional issues raised by Chester are that coincidental consequences unfold and should be judged within the scope of liability for a defendant. Furthermore, a defendant could be causally responsible if it is fair, just and reasonable that the defendant rather than the claimant should bear the loss.

What do you think would be the surgeon's position following Chester? What do you think are the relative benefits and potential problems in applying the Chester principle in Francine's case?

4.8   Questions posed by patients

Until now, we have considered the duty of doctors to inform their patients of the risks and benefits of clinically indicated procedures. In particular, the focus has been on the standard against which the medical practitioner's actions are measured. A question that arises is whether the duty to disclose ought to be enhanced in circumstances where the patient asks specific questions about the proposed treatment. In *Sidaway v Bethlem Royal Hospital* [1985] AC 871, Lords Diplock and Bridge indicated that if a specific question was asked, then the duty to disclose would be different compared to situations where no enquiries had been made. Lord Bridge said that the physician would have a duty to 'answer both truthfully and as fully as the questioner requires'. The inference appears to be that the *Bolam* test would have no application in situations where a patient has asked for specific information. These comments in *Sidaway*, however, were *obiter* and specific disclosure might be constrained to some degree by therapeutic privilege. If there is a reasonable belief that disclosure would be likely to cause psychological harm to the patient, then this information could be justifiably withheld.

The common law with regard to the legal standard for information disclosure required following questions is somewhat obscure. In *Blyth v Bloomsbury HA* [1993] 4 Med LR 151, Kerr LJ asserted that what should be told in response to 'a general enquiry cannot be divorced from the *Bolam* test any more than when no such enquiry is made'. Even when a specific enquiry is made, the *Bolam* test would still apply as a general proposition. On this analysis, even if a specific question has been asked, a cursory answer that was not full and complete might nonetheless satisfy the standard required if that response was considered appropriate by a responsible body of medical opinion. The problematic issue here is that if in such cases the *Bolam* standard were to apply, then arguably patients could be given limited information if that was endorsed by a responsible body of professional opinion as being the norm in practice, a position which clearly undermines patient autonomy and right to make an informed choice. In *Pearce*, Lord Woolf's (*obiter*) comments again seem to indicate that the court's likely approach would be more in line with *Sidaway* rather than *Blyth* (although this case was not specifically referred to) when he asserted that counsel for the claimant was correct in his submission that if a patient asks the doctor about the risk, then that doctor is required to give an honest and specific answer.

4.9   Withdrawal and refusal of consent

The law imposes limits on the extent to which consent may be given and on the types of procedure that a person may consent to. Consent may be refused or withdrawn by a competent person.

4.9.1   Limits to consent

The common law approach to the limits of consent is grounded in public policy. Criminal law places a limit on the degree of harm that a person may validly consent. The *prima facie* position is that in English law a person may not consent to anything that is intended to cause or that causes more than actual bodily harm (*R v Brown* [1994] 1 AC 212). Many forms of medical intervention, even though intended to benefit the patient, operate to cause considerably more than this level of injury. In *Brown*, the House of Lords accepted this as an exception to the general rule as stated by Lord Lane CJ in the *Attorney-General's Reference* (No 6 of 1980) [1981] 2 All ER 1057 in that 'reasonable surgical interference' falls outside the criminal law. Lord Mustill in *Airedale NHS Trust v Bland* [1993] AC 789 at 889 articulated this attitude more explicitly in that

> proper medical treatment stand[s] completely outside the criminal law. The reason why the consent of the patient is so important is not that it furnishes a defence in itself, but because it is usually essential to the propriety of medical treatment. Thus, if consent is absent, and is not dispensed with in special circumstances by operation of law, the acts of the doctor lose their immunity.

Whether or not a procedure falls within the medical exception rule depends principally upon whether it is intended to be of therapeutic benefit to the patient, with 'benefit' being widely interpreted to include physical or mental health. In *Bellinger v Bellinger* [2003] 2 All ER 593 (HL), it was held that a person may consent to serious injury in the form of gender reassignment surgery provided that there is a therapeutic basis for the intervention. Other procedures that may not necessarily have a therapeutic effect for the individual but which are nonetheless considered socially acceptable may also fall within the medical exception, for example, the donation of organs and tissue, cosmetic surgery, abortion and sterilisation.

4.9.2 Withdrawal of consent

The inviolability of a person's bodily integrity is the basis that provides the right to withdraw consent. If consent has been validly withdrawn, then continuation of treatment is unlawful. While there is no direct English authority, this issue was considered by the Canadian Supreme Court in *Ciarlariello v Schacter* (1993) 100 DLR (4th) 609 (Can SC). The claimant was undergoing a cerebral angiogram during which she experienced severe discomfort and asked for the procedure to be stopped. She subsequently asked the doctor to continue and thereafter suffered a rare allergic reaction to the dye. The Supreme Court dismissed the action for battery. With regard to the right to withdraw consent, however, the court accepted that there was such a right but only if the person was capable of doing so in law. Withdrawal of consent was a matter of fact. The right to withdraw consent was not absolute, and on the evidence the procedure had been lawfully recommenced.

4.9.2(a) *The right to withdraw consent*

In *Ciarlariello*, Cory J stated that a person's right to decide what surgical procedures were acceptable must include the right to terminate a procedure, and that a person's right to self-determination provided the basis for withdrawal of consent even if a procedure is underway. Once consent is withdrawn, the procedure must be terminated.

4.9.2(b) *Valid withdrawal of consent*

A patient must have capacity in order to withdraw consent, a situation that can be constrained by clinical circumstances. In *Ciarlariello*, the judge stated that if medication has been administered to the patient, then it must be determined whether or not the patient's decision-making capacity had been affected by the medication. The question as to whether a patient is capable of withdrawing consent therefore depends on the circumstances of each situation.

4.9.2(c) Deciding whether consent has been withdrawn

Situations where a patient indicates withdrawal of consent might be vague in certain circumstances and the words or behaviour of a patient could be difficult to interpret. A doctor might well consider that the words used by a patient are indicative of anxiety or pain rather than a withdrawal of consent, as recognised in *Ciarlariello*.

4.9.2(d) Right to withdraw not absolute

The right to withdraw consent is not absolute, even for a person with decision-making capacity. This means, for example, that if the effect of terminating a procedure could have life-threatening implications or might seriously compromise the patient's condition, then withdrawal would not be valid on grounds of public policy. The doctor owes an overriding duty of care to the patient, and this would be breached if serious harm was to occur.

4.9.2(e) Lawful recommencement

In recommencing a procedure after consent has been withdrawn, there are two issues to consider. First, has valid consent been given prior to recommencement, and, second, has sufficient information been given prior to continuation. This is similar to English law, where any procedure requires valid consent, and there is a duty to provide information relevant to the decision the patient must make at that particular point. In *Ciarlariello*, and with regard to lawful recommencement, Cory J found in favour of the claimant on both these questions.

4.9.3 Refusal

An adult with capacity has the absolute right to refuse consent to treatment. This was articulated unequivocally by Lord Donaldson MR in *Re T (adult: refusal of treatment)* [1993] Fam 95 (at 102):

> An adult patient who…suffers from no mental incapacity has an absolute right to choose whether to consent to medical treatment, to refuse it or to choose one rather than another of the treatments being offered…This right of choice is not limited to decisions which others might regard as sensible. It exists notwithstanding that the reasons for making the choice are rational, irrational, unknown or even non-existent.

There are, however, certain exceptions to this principle. Section 63 of the Mental Health Act 1983 provides that 'The consent of a patient shall not be required for any medical treatment given to him for the mental disorder from which he is suffering, not being a form of treatment to which section 57, 58 or 58A above applies, if the treatment is given by or under the direction of the approved clinician in charge of the treatment'. (Section 57 applies to psychosurgery and the surgical implantation of hormones given to reduce male sex drive; section 58 applies to electroconvulsive therapy.) Section 63 provides a broad exception to the common law rule that consent is required for medical treatment. It applies to persons detained under the 1983 Act and applies to treatment for mental disorders, although more recently the scope of section 63 has been extended. In *B v Croydon HA* [1995] 1 All ER 683 (CA) the Court of Appeal accepted that section 63 applied not only to the treatment of the mental disorder but also to other symptoms, such as refusal to eat. The basis of this extension was that a particular symptom being treated was a manifestation of the mental disorder *per se* and was therefore regarded by the court as being within the class of treatment 'for the mental disorder' as required by section 63. However, in *Thameside and Glossop NHS Trust v CH* [1996] 1 FLR 762 this principle was further extended for a pregnant paranoid schizophrenic patient detained under the Mental Health Act 1983, and whose foetus had evidence of intrauterine growth retardation. An application for a declaration was granted that it would be lawful to carry out a caesarean section on the basis that a successful outcome to the pregnancy was a necessary part of the overall treatment for her mental disorder. This is a controversial decision in that interpretation of treatment for a mental disorder has been unduly stretched. The Mental Health Act 1983 is examined in greater depth in Chapter 9.

Other exceptions to the tenet that treatment cannot be carried out without consent may be justified under the principle of necessity at common law on the basis of public policy. A patient could not, for example, refuse basic care and hygiene. In certain circumstances the refusal of clinically indicated treatment by a competent child or a parent of a child may be overridden by the court unless such a refusal is in the patient's best interests. Refusal of consent by competent minors is considered in chapter 6.

4.10 Consent: medical professionalism and public policy

Although consent is founded on autonomy and self-determined choice, it is to some extent qualified by policy and guidance from the professional bodies.

4.10.1 Professional guidelines

Several professional organisations and learned societies have published position statements and guidance as to how informed consent ought to be obtained. The Department of Health publication 'Good Practice and Consent' (Department of Health, 2001), states that patients have a fundamental legal and ethical right to determine what happens to their bodies. For this reason, valid consent is a prerequisite to all forms of health care ranging from provision of personal care to major surgery. The Department of Health's position is strongly reflective of a rights-based approach to patient care.

The emphasis for consent has been on the amount of information provided and its relevance to the particular procedure being proposed, as well as its format and accessibility. Guidance from the British Medical Association states that patients need to feel confident about the information and its relevance to them, that they should be able to understand the information and be in a position to seek clarifications where necessary (British Medical Association and The Law Society, 2009). Likewise, the Royal College of Surgeons (2002) has stated that patients require information about their proposed intervention as well as the main risks, side effects and complications, and any alternatives.

Since consent is a key aspect of good clinical care the General Medical Council (GMC, 2008) has published relatively detailed guidance for its members. The approach reflects the shift away from a beneficent attitude to one of a therapeutic partnership. The guidance includes a non-exhaustive list of issues to be covered, such as the likely prognosis of the untreated condition, uncertainties about diagnosis, alternative options and management including the decision to do nothing at all. The patient should be informed of the identity of the doctor with overall clinical responsibility and whether, and the extent to which, doctors in training are likely to be involved. Patients should be reminded of their right to a second opinion and the right to change their minds about their care, and information must be presented in way that can be understood to facilitate informed decision making. Professional guidance sets a high standard for information disclosure that forms the basis of valid consent.

4.10.1(a) Therapeutic privilege

Therapeutic privilege is the reasonable withholding of information from a patient on the grounds that such disclosure could be positively harmful to the patient. It represents a paternalistic approach to care.

To what degree must openness and honesty be adhered to by clinicians and to what extent is there a role for clinical discretion in respect of information provision, for example, in circumstances where a doctor suspects that frank disclosure could lead to serious psychological harm, particularly where the patient is extremely frail or terminal? Their Lordships in *Sidaway* seemed to consider that there was a role for such discretion. Exercise of this discretion is 'a therapeutic privilege' in that this is clearly a unique privilege offered only to doctors.

Guidance from the GMC (2008) states that doctors should not withhold information unless it is reasonably believed that 'serious harm' will result. The notion of therapeutic privilege is strongly opposed by rights-based protagonists. Therapeutic privilege perhaps can only be relied upon in tightly circumscribed circumstances where the individual is so frail that disclosure could cause the patient great harm. The heavy burden of proof would be on the doctor to prove that non-disclosure was justifiable in the circumstances.

The fundamental criticism of therapeutic privilege is that it is essentially paternalistic and the more widely it is applied the greater the encroachment upon patient autonomy. The GMC guidance requires doctors not to withhold information *unless* (our emphasis) it is thought that such disclosure would cause serious harm. On the face of it, this appears to run counter (at least to some degree) to the *obiter* statements of Lord Bridge in *Sidaway* and Lord Woolf in *Pearce* (see 4.8) which taken together require that if a patient asks questions, these need to be answered fully and truthfully. Nonetheless, the obligation and duty of veracity is not absolute and medical information has to be carefully conveyed. Limited disclosure, non-disclosure, deception and even outright lies may on occasion be justifiable in those very limited circumstances where the duty of veracity conflicts with other obligations, although the weight of competing obligations may be difficult to determine (Beauchamp and Childress, 2009).

Each patient encounter must be decided on its relative merits and unique circumstances. Conveying bad news might need to be tempered according to the individual's needs and there are several arguments to support this. First, if a patient is hopeful of recovery, bad news at an early stage might overwhelm the good news that some chance of recovery remains. Second, each patient is unique and one can never know the whole truth. It is impossible for any doctor to give a prognosis with absolute certainty. Third, even if the professional is best placed to provide an educated guess, timing the disclosure might be everything, and persons often need time to fully comprehend information and its implications. Initial reassurance might better pave the way for later frank and open discussion (Beauchamp and Childress, 2009).

While therapeutic privilege appears to run counter to the modern ethic of patient autonomy, it is suggested that there may be a role for such privilege in very limited circumstances perhaps when the patient is psychologically very fragile or when the patient is incompetent. This privilege can temporarily extend to family members. The counter-argument is that use of therapeutic privilege deprives or reduces the ability of the patient, and possibly that of their loved ones, to make fully informed decisions. Needless to say, the extent to which one can make truly informed decisions in extreme cases of distress and fragility is certainly moot.

4.10.2 Public policy

Public policy imposes limits on the degree of bodily harm for which a person can lawfully give consent, particularly in respect of surgical interventions. The boundaries dictated by public policy depend upon the relative interaction of patient autonomy and the public interest in maintaining the non-maleficent basis of medical practice. However, these boundaries are not absolute as perhaps best exemplified by apotemnophilia, a psychological identity disorder that manifests in the desire for the amputation of one or more healthy limbs, and gender reassignment surgery. The conflict between a rights-based approach against that of non-maleficence was well illustrated by the attempted separation of the conjoined twins, Ladan and Laleh (Pattinson, 2006). The greatest desire of the competent twins was for separation even though their brains were anatomically fused. Following surgery the twins died. While autonomy-based theories would support the decision being left to the individuals concerned, the practicalities may dictate that at times the outcome will be unsuccessful.

Policy considerations may also limit the extent to which treatment can be refused, for example, with regard to the spread of highly infectious and possibly fatal diseases. To what extent would it be justified for someone to refuse treatment in such a situation (on the grounds of autonomous self-determination), thereby increasing the risk of spreading the disease and its possible complications. It is likely that a rights-based autonomous refusal in such a situation would be curtailed and justified under the derogation provided by Article 8(2) of the Human Rights Act 1998.

C The adult who lacks capacity

Mary, aged 67 years, has mild dementia. She lives alone but is frequently visited by close family. During the last three months, due to a worsening of her condition, she has been visited by a church volunteer, Jenny. This morning on arrival at Mary's home, Jenny discovers Mary at the foot of the stairs in great pain. It appears that Mary may have fallen down the stairs prior to Jenny's visit. Jenny calls for an ambulance, and suspects a fractured arm. Mary is very confused and her speech is incoherent. Jenny escorts Mary to the hospital where the diagnosis is confirmed. Clinical opinion is that surgical reduction of the fracture is urgently necessary to prevent possible deformity, disability and complications (including loss of function of her arm) as well as alleviation of pain. It is felt that pain might be contributing to her current confusion.

Mary becomes increasingly distressed and agitated when attempts are made to explain the proposed surgery. At intervals she becomes more lucid and compliant and seems to understand where she is and what has happened. Shortly afterwards

Mary attempts to bite the staff when they attempt to dress her for theatre. She strongly resists all attempts to give her pain relief, and it is apparent that she does not want surgery.

Mary's brother, Albert, arrives. Jenny and Albert attempt to calm Mary but without success. A junior doctor asks Albert to sign the consent form on behalf of his sister. He refuses and explains that Mary had always been terrified of health-care environments and has always been a devotee of natural health care. He is adamant that non-surgical external immobilisation should be tried and that she should be allowed to return home as soon as possible. He tells staff that he and Mary and often discussed health-care issues. Mary had given birth to her four children at home and had always used herbal remedies for herself and her family. Jenny disagrees with Albert. Surgical reduction is carried out on Mary's arm, on the basis that the operation was in her best interests and was necessary.

4.11 Capacity

An adult who lacks capacity cannot give valid consent. In these circumstances, treatment can be lawfully provided under the doctrine of necessity, or in the best interests of the individual. The presumption is, however, that an adult has decision-making capacity unless proved otherwise. If a person is competent to make a decision about a particular health-care decision, then that person's consent, or refusal, is decisive. The decision as to whether or not a person has capacity is vital.

4.11.1 Models for defining capacity

Broadly, there are two approaches to the definition of capacity. The first is referred to as the 'status' approach by which certain categories of persons are presumed not to have capacity due to their status. A typical example is a child (subject to certain exceptions, see chapter 6). The second is the 'functional' approach which is based upon an assessment of the cognitive functions and decision-specific capability of an individual.

The status approach can be relatively easy to apply with children, where age is the determining factor. However, childhood spans a considerable period and a considerable difference in decision-making capability exists between a very young child and a mature 16-year old. While both are categorised as children, considerable differences are likely to be apparent in their mental abilities, maturity and individual specific traits and characteristics. As Kennedy (1988 at 57–58) suggests,

> The fundamental flaw in the status approach is that it takes no account of the individuality of each person. Respect for autonomy, however, involves respect for each person's individuality. It demands, therefore, that any criteria intended to determine when someone is incapable of being autonomous should, equally, be respectful of that person's individuality. Merely placing them in a class is far too gross a test of incapacity.

A more valid test for capacity would need to take into account each individual's ability to understand the nature and consequences of proposed treatment. The functional approach to capacity offers a more effective way to protect patient autonomy although it is invariably more complex and application depends upon two principal factors: first, the individual's ability to communicate, and, second, the assessment of the individual's capability of making that particular health-care decision at that particular time.

Some ability to communicate, whether verbal or non-verbal, is necessary in order to take into account an individual's decision. In clinical conditions such as the 'locked-in' syndrome, individuals can be mute and physically unresponsive and yet still retain their cognitive abilities. If the health-care practitioner is to take into account their decisions and act upon those, then some vestigial ability to communicate is necessary. It would be impossible to act upon the wishes of a person with no ability to communicate, even if that person retains his or her cognitive ability, since their views cannot be expressed.

Assessment of an individual's capacity for making decisions needs to focus on the decision-making process rather than the content of the decision. If the individual meets the required criteria for decision-making ability, then that individual is regarded as competent irrespective of the actual decision made. Gunn (1994) believes that 'Capacity and incapacity are not concepts with clear *a priori* boundaries. They appear on a continuum which ranges from full capacity at one end to incapacity at the other end. They are, therefore, degrees of capacity. The challenge is to choose the right level to set as the gateway to decision-making, and respect for persons and autonomy'. It follows, therefore, that if an individual meets the threshold criteria for capacity and makes a decision which appears to others to be irrational, then that should not necessarily be taken as evidence that the individual lacks capacity to make that particular decision.

It is unlikely that a person's decision-making capacity would be challenged when she agrees to a proposed treatment. A challenge is more likely those situations where treatment is refused contrary to medical advice. Empirical evidence has shown that nearly 50 per cent of acutely ill medical in-patients lack decision-making capacity but since they did not refuse treatment, their decision-making capacity was assumed and treatment was provided without valid consent being given (Raymont et al., 2004). This study suggests that in routine clinical practice, doctors fail to identify patients with significant cognitive impairment. The authors suspected that a substantial proportion of patients who had difficulties with decision-making passively acquiesced with medical treatment plans that had been proposed. The inference was that a considerable proportion of in-patients on a general medical ward, who did not have decision-making capacity and were not able to make informed treatment decisions, were treated on the basis that they had given consent, inferred from their passive acceptance of treatment plans.

4.11.2 Statutory capacity

The Mental Capacity Act 2005 has, among other things, codified, supplemented and replaced the common law rules that pertain to capacity. The first part of the Act deals with 'persons who lack capacity.' The statutory provisions are exercisable only in relation to those aged 16 or over (section 2(5)) and guidance on implementation and interpretation of the Act is provided in a detailed Code of Practice.

4.11.2(a) Presumption of capacity

Section 1 of the Mental Capacity Act 2005 incorporates the common law presumption of capacity, as well as the principle that an unwise decision does not necessarily equate with lack of capacity: Section 1(2) states 'A person must be assumed to have capacity unless it is established that he lacks capacity'. Section 1(4) states: 'A person is not to be treated as unable to make a decision merely because he makes an unwise decision.' It may be difficult to draw a distinction between a person's irrational wish which must be respected on the basis that the person has made an autonomous choice and the person's inability to come to a reasoned decision due to lack of capacity. In *Re T*, Lord Donaldson suggested that an unusual or bizarre decision could be grounds for questioning the patient's competence, and a choice that is contrary to what might be expected from the majority of adults might be relevant to determining capacity, particularly if there are other grounds for doubting the individual's decision-making capacity. This view was echoed by Butler-Sloss LJ in *Re MB* [1997] 2 FLR 426), when she stated, 'Although it might be thought that irrationality sits uneasily with competence to decide, panic, indecisiveness and irrationality in themselves do not as such amount to incompetence, but they may be symptoms or evidence of incompetence'.

> Mary has dementia. Can it be therefore assumed, without more, that she lacks decision-making capacity? What factors will be relevant in the determination of whether Mary has capacity? Who makes the decision?

4.11.2(b) Definition of incapacity

Incapacity or lack of capacity is defined by section 2(1) (see 4.4.1(a)) as a person's inability to make a decision for herself in relation to a matter (at a material time) because of an impairment or disturbance in the functioning of the mind or brain. The cognitive disability requirement includes temporary states of impairment and is easier to satisfy than the 'mental disorder' requirement of section 1 of the Mental Health Act 1983. Impairment in the functioning of the mind or brain may be caused by a long-standing physical illness that leads to chronic pain. It can also be caused by the influence of medication. These factors, if they result in transient impairment, might render the patient as one lacking capacity and in these circumstances treatment could be administered on the principles of best interests. This situation might arise in an environment where patients are acutely ill.

Section 3(1) provides that:

For the purposes of section 2, a person is unable to make a decision for himself if he is unable –

a) to understand the information relevant to the decision,
b) to retain that information,
c) to use or weigh that information as part of the process of making the decision, or
d) to communicate his decision (whether by talking, using sign language or any other means).

The Code of Practice of the Mental Capacity Act 2005 non-exhaustibly states that conditions involving impairment or disturbance of the functioning of the brain might include some forms of mental illness, learning disabilities (if significant), long-term effects of brain damage, delirium, dementia, conditions that cause confusion, drowsiness or loss of consciousness.

It cannot be assumed that a person with impaired decision-making capacity invariably lacks competence. Attempts must be made to enhance the patient's ability to make a decision by use of appropriate language or by presenting information in different formats. The Mental Capacity Act 2005 emphasises that a person should not be treated as lacking capacity 'unless all practical steps to help him' achieve capacity 'have been taken without success'. Section 2(2) states: 'A person is not to be regarded as unable to understand the information relevant to a decision if he is able to understand an explanation of it given to him in a way that is appropriate to his circumstances (using simple language, visual aids or any other means)'.

Section 2(3) provides that 'A lack of capacity cannot be established merely by reference to –

(a) a person's age or appearance, or
(b) a condition of his, or an aspect of his behaviour, which might lead others to make unjustified assumptions about his capacity'

The purpose of this provision is to avoid potential discrimination on the basis of outward appearance. Bartlett (2005), however, argues that use of the word 'merely' is surprising. In his view, this suggests that such characteristics can be one of the factors taken into account in the assessment of capacity, although they cannot be used by themselves.

4.11.2(c) Assessment of capacity

The Code of Practice suggests that assessment of capacity can be undertaken by doctors, health-care professionals or even family members who care for the individual. The inclusion of carers is useful in that they might be best placed to know the patient. It is, however, quite possible, for any assessor of capacity to arrive at an erroneous decision. Any subsequent intervention undertaken in the 'best interests' of the person could therefore, if the patient was in fact competent, theoretically amount to an assault.

Section 5(1) of the Mental Capacity Act 2005 introduces an objective standard in that acts done in connection with the care or treatment of a patient will not incur liability where the person had 'reasonable grounds' for deciding that the patient lacked capacity, even if that assessment was incorrect. Good practice requires that a record is kept of the reasons for the decision that the patient lacked capacity.

There are two limbs to assessment for lack of capacity under the Act. The first is the 'functional limb' which requires that a person must be suffering from an impairment or disturbance in the functioning of the mind or brain. This is prerequisite for proceeding to the second limb of the test. The functional limb could be satisfied by factors such as alcohol or drug misuse, head injuries and effects of medication, as well as primary causes such as learning difficulties and mental illness.

The second limb of the test is decision specific and focuses on the ability of the person to make a particular decision. This is defined in section 3(1) of the Act and in essence codifies the *Re C* test, with the addition of a 'communication' requirement (see also 4.4.1(a)(i)).

Re C [1994] 1 All ER 819 concerned a 68-year-old patient who developed gangrene of his foot and without amputation his prospects for survival were around 15 per cent. He suffered delusions that he had a very promising medical career. C refused to give consent to surgery, stating that he would rather die with two feet than live with one. The key question was whether he was competent to refuse such treatment. He had a diagnosed mental illness, with a background of paranoid schizophrenia and delusions. Nevertheless, Thorpe J felt that C had capacity to refuse consent to amputation. In reaching his decision, Thorpe J relied heavily on the view of the expert witness that there were three stages to the decision-making process: (a) can the person understand and retain the information regarding treatment; (b) can he believe it; and (c) can he weigh it in the balance to arrive at a choice.

Section 3(1)(a) requires that the individual can understand the information relevant to the decision. According to the common law, a difference can be drawn between the ability to understand and actual understanding. In *R (Burke) v GMC* [2004] EWHC

1879, Munby J stated: 'Essentially capacity is dependent upon having the ability, whether or not one chooses to use it, to function rationally: having the ability to understand, retain, believe and evaluate (i.e. process) and weigh the information which is relevant to the subject matter.' This suggests that competence requires the ability to understand, rather than actual understanding. Kennedy and Grubb (2000) consider that actual understanding is dependent upon what the patient is told by the doctor. For example, if the information is provided in a straightforward and clear fashion, then this would be easier to understand compared with information provided in a complex and obscure manner. This could mean that the section 3(1)(a) requirement might be more easily satisfied dependent upon the way information is presented to a patient. This argument has been used against utilising 'actual understanding' as opposed to the 'ability to understand' for the determination of capacity since actual understanding is a malleable concept and dependent upon information presentation. Gunn et al. (1999) have argued that there is in reality very little difference between the ability to understand test and the actual understanding test since the only way by which ability to understand can be determined is to look for evidence of actual understanding. For the purposes of determining capacity a decision that an individual lacks capacity should only be made if that individual is unable to understand simple and clearly presented information.

The 'understanding' and 'retention of information' requirements of the decision-specific limb of the test are further elaborated. Section 1(3) provides that 'A person is not to be treated as unable to make a decision unless all practicable steps to help him to do so have been taken without success'. Section 3(2) provides that 'A person is not to be regarded as unable to understand the information relevant to a decision if he is able to understand an explanation of it given to him in a way that is appropriate to his circumstances (using simple language, visual aids or any other means)'.

Section 3(3) provides that 'The fact that a person is able to retain the information relevant to a decision for a short period only does not prevent him from being regarded as able to make the decision'. This provision might be relevant to those with fluctuant capacity or perhaps in the early stages of Alzheimer's disease where only short term memory is compromised. Such persons can be expected to retain capacity to exercise control over their decisions and treatment options provided that appropriate support is given.

The spirit of the Mental Capacity Act 2005 is to protect an individual's right to self-determined choice in respect of treatment and welfare decisions. The Act leans heavily in favour of supporting and maintaining an individual's decision-making capacity wherever possible. In order to be protected from a charge of battery, a doctor who provides treatment in an incompetent person's best interests would need to hold a reasonable belief that the person lacks capacity. Treatment without consent of someone who has capacity, or someone in whom there are no reasonable grounds for believing that capacity is lacking, could result in an action in tort, or even a criminal prosecution.

4.11.3   'Unwise' choices

Section 1(4) provides that a person is not to be treated as unable to make a decision merely because he makes an unwise choice. This position reflects the common law principle that an irrational decision does not necessarily mean that a person lacks capacity to make that decision (*Re T* [1993] Fam 95) (see 4.4.1(b)).

In health-care situations, if a patient wishes to refuse potentially life-saving treatment, the decision-maker (whether the doctor or court) tends to scrutinise decisions and enquire more stringently into reasons behind a refusal. In *NHS Trust v T (adult patient: refusal of medical treatment)* [2004] EWHC 1279 (Fam), T had attempted to execute an advance directive refusing a blood transfusion. She required regular transfusions because of her tendency to self-harm. Her reason for refusal was that she believed that her blood was evil, carrying wickedness all around her body. Charles J in giving judgement emphasised that a bizarre decision in itself was not sufficient to make a finding of incapacity but on the facts of the case, T's belief that her blood was evil amounted to a disorder of the mind that rendered her incompetent. Similarly, in *South West Hertfordshire Health Authority v Brady* [1994] Med L Rev 208, the court found that a patient with anorexia nervosa was incompetent and non-consensual force feeding was authorised on the grounds that her condition impacted upon her ability to understand, believe and weigh information regarding treatment.

The line between the right to make a competent unwise choice and having capacity questioned is not clear. One possible reason for the court's approach in the above cases might be justified on the basis that a higher level of competence is required in respect of a decision that carries graver consequences (as Butler-Sloss LJ affirmed in *Re MB*). Buller (2001 at 93) questioned this approach since

> It appears arbitrary to demand that the riskier the decision, the higher standard of competence required ... Perhaps the underlying problem (with a risk-relative standard of competence) is that risk is being asked to do work for which it is not suited. ... The goal of protecting the wellbeing of questionably competent patients is a laudable one and there may be good paternalistic reasons for demanding a higher standard of competence for a patient to choose to reject life-sustaining treatment than to accept it; however these reasons, legitimate or otherwise, for overriding a patient's decision, rather than reasons for determining whether the patient is competent or not.

The concept of decision-relative competence operates on a sliding scale that is proportionate to the perceived risk as viewed from the medical perspective. The greater the potential harm of the choice, the higher the standard of competence required. This risk-relative standard of competence is supported by Buchanan and Brock (1989) who cite by way of example that consent to a low-risk life-saving procedure by an otherwise healthy individual ought to require only a minimal level of competence, whereas refusal of the same procedure should require the highest level of competence. In contrast, Beauchamp and Childress (2009 at 117) challenge this view and state: 'The level of *competence to decide* does not rise as the risk of an outcome increases. It is confusing to blend a decision's complexity or difficulty with the risk at stake. No basis exists for believing that risky decisions require more ability at decision-making than less risky decisions'. If a good outcome for the patient is to be ensured by avoiding a risky decision, then in their view, it is not the level of competence that should vary, but the level of evidence required for the determination of competence. The National Bioethics Advisory Commission, for example, recommends that a higher standard of evidence of competence is required to consent to participate in clinical research than to object to participation. The Commission states, whereas 'Brock and Buchanan propose that in the level of decision-making *competence in itself* belongs on a sliding scale from low to high in accordance with risk, we recommend patients only require *standards of evidence* for determining decision-making competence on a sliding scale'.

4.11.3(a) *Use of force or restraint*

The common law established that reasonable force could be used in carrying out treatment for an incapacitated person. In *Re MB* [1997] 2 FLR 426, Butler-Sloss LJ said that if 'a patient is not competent to refuse treatment, such treatment may have to be given against her continued objection if it is in her best interests that the treatment be given despite those objections'. Furthermore 'the extent of force or compulsion which may become necessary can only be judged on each individual case by the health-care professionals'. The extent of force used must be balanced against Article 3 of the Human Rights Act 1998 which prohibits inhuman and degrading treatment, although in *Herczegfalvy v Austria* (Applications 10533/83) (1992) 15 EHRR 437, the European Court of Human Rights clarified that Article 3 would not be breached if the force used was a 'therapeutic necessity', although the court 'must nevertheless satisfy itself that the medical necessity has been convincingly shown to exist'.

4.11.4 Exceptions to the capacity requirement

In exceptional circumstances, the capacity requirement may be waived. An example is where a person lacks capacity at the time treatment is required, but is almost certain to regain capacity at some time in the future. According to section 4(3) of the Mental Capacity Act 2005, this factor needs to be taken into account when deciding on the treatment of a person who lacks capacity. In emergency situations, treatment of the incompetent person can be provided under the doctrine of necessity. In *Re F* [1990] 2 AC 1, Lord Goff explained the basic requirements applicable in these cases: 'not only (1) must there be a necessity to act when it is not practicable to communicate with the assisted person, but also (2) the action taken must be such as a reasonable person would in all the circumstances take, acting in the best interests of the assisted person...'

A second type of emergency can arise during the course of an anaesthetic. While the patient is unconscious it becomes apparent that something unconnected with the index condition requires attention. To what extent should medical intervention go ahead, even though the patient did not consent to the secondary procedure? The issue that arises is whether the secondary condition ought to be treated in the patient's best interests. Although the patient's consent would extend to treatment necessary to save life whether or not the second intervention will be lawful will depend upon the level of risk that the patient would be exposed to if that intervention was not undertaken at that specific time. If the potential risk was life-threatening, then the likelihood is that the second intervention would be justified. If not, it is unlikely that the court find the non-consensual treatment to be lawful. As per Lord Goff in *Re F* (at 77) where

> a surgeon performs an operation without his consent on a patient temporarily rendered unconscious in an accident, he should do no more than is reasonably required, in the best interests of the patient, before he recovers consciousness. I can see no practical difficulty arising from this requirement, which derives from the fact that the patient is expected before long to regain consciousness and can be consulted about longer term measures.

Although Lord Goff's comment related to an accident, it seems likely that this general principle would extend more widely.

Mary indicates that she does not want surgery although the clinical team believes that surgery would be in her best interests. Assuming that Mary lacks decision-making capacity:

▶ Explain how a decision as to whether to treat Mary should be reached by the clinical team.

▶ Would the team have a duty to consult others? If so, who ought to be consulted and why?

▶ Explain the ethical and moral rationale for going ahead with treatment.

▶ In the event of uncertainty about whether the proposed surgery would be in Mary's best interests, what should the clinical team be advised to do from a legal perspective.

▶ What are the implications if Mary is found to be competent?

A third situation might arise when a patient refuses consent to treatment that doctors consider to be life saving, or where in the absence of treatment there is a risk of serious or irreparable damage to health. Although the law is clear that a competent patient can refuse any treatment at all, in these situations it is likely that the patient's capacity will be questioned.

4.11.5 Autonomy and health interests

Respect for autonomy is a paramount consideration in contemporary medical law and clinical practice. Kennedy (1988) states that doctors should respect and give effect to patients' decisions that are based on their (patients') beliefs and values. This is because such values are often long-standing and would have formed the basis of those persons' decisions about their lives, and to do otherwise would be to rob them of their right to individualism.

Beauchamp and Childress (2009 at 105) report that some writers lament the triumphs of autonomy. In their words

'Carl Schneider claims that the proponents of autonomy, whom he labels "autonomists", concern themselves less with what patients *do want* than with what, from the point of view of autonomy, they *should want*. He attempts to correct these views by appealing to human experience and empirical research'. He concludes that, "while patients largely wish to be informed about their medical circumstances, a substantial number of them [especially the elderly and the very sick] do not want to make their own medical decisions, or perhaps even to participate in those decisions in any very significant way"

Beauchamp and Childress quote two studies: in the first, researchers examine the differences and attitudes of elderly subjects from different ethnic backgrounds in relation to disclosure of diagnosis and prognosis of terminal illnesses in end-of-life decision making. Wide differences were found. Korean Americans and Mexican Americans were significantly less likely than European Americans and African Americans to believe that a patient should be told about the diagnosis of metastatic cancer. Unlike European Americans, Korean Americans and Mexican Americans tended to believe that the family should make decisions about use of life support. In another study of Navajo values, the researchers reported frequent conflicts emerging between autonomy and traditional Navajo concepts in that thought and language are believed to have power to shape reality and control events.

These ethnically based studies serve to emphasise that patient autonomy is not a universal ideal. There are several models of decision making such as the 'person-centred' approach of traditional Western white models, compared with those models that are 'family-centred' or 'belief-centred', that are characteristic of some ethnic groups. For health-care practice, the vexed issue is how best to inform patients of their rights to be informed and make a self-determined choice without bringing in unintended tensions with their views and beliefs.

4.12 Decisions made on best interests

Health-care treatment may be given to those who lack decision-making capacity where such treatment is their best interests.

4.12.1 Who decides?

Therapeutic decisions for those who lack capacity are usually made by the doctor with clinical responsibility, although other health-related decisions are often made by the wider health-care team. Decision makers have duties to consider an array of factors in making that decision including the past wishes, beliefs and values of the incompetent person, and to consult a range of non-medical persons to arrive at that decision. In the event of a dispute, recourse can be had to the Court of Protection.

Fann and Teo (2004) have persuasively argued that patients' relatives are often in a comparatively good position to decide what would be in the best interests of their next-of-kin since they would be expected to know that individual the most. This may be apparent in certain instances, and certain cultures may accept and promote decision making by relatives to a greater extent than others. This assumption, however, may not always be accurate and there is a danger that conflicts of interest can exist. Financial issues, for example, might conceivably operate to influence judgement. An alternative decision maker could be a neutral committee, such as an ethics committee. However, the practicalities of such an arrangement in terms of logistics and resources could make this unworkable.

> The junior doctor asks Albert to sign the consent form. If Mary lack's capacity, can Albert give consent on Mary's behalf? Are there any circumstances where Albert could give consent on Mary's behalf? (See discussion below on welfare attorneys)

4.12.2 Treatment of those who lack capacity

Section 1(5) provides that, 'An act done, or decision made, under this Act for or on behalf of a person who lacks capacity must be done, or made, in his best interests'.

This statutory provision is based upon the previous common law but has extended the principle in two ways. First, is that a range of factors have been given that must be considered when determining a person's best interests. Second, it employs what is known as the 'least restrictive alternative principle'.

Section 4 provides the factors to be considered in determining a person's best interests:

(2) The person making the determination must consider all the relevant circumstances and, in particular, take the following steps.

(3) He must consider –

a) whether it is likely that the person will at some time have capacity in relation to the matter in question, and
b) if it appears likely that he will, when that is likely to be....
(6) He must consider, so far as is reasonably ascertainable –
   a) the person's past and present wishes and feelings (and, in particular, any relevant written statements made by him when he had capacity),
   b) the beliefs and values that would be likely to influence his decision if he had capacity, and
   c) the other factors that he would be likely to consider if he were able to do so.
(7) He must take into account, if it is practicable and appropriate to consult them, the views of –
   a) anyone named by the person as someone to be consulted on the matter in question or on matters of that kind,
   b) anyone engaged in caring for the person or interested in his welfare,
   c) any donee of a lasting power of attorney granted by the person, and
   d) any deputy appointed for the person by the court, as to what would be in the person's best interests and, in particular, as to the matters mentioned in subsection (6).

Sections 4(3) and 4(6) are potentially challenging requirements for treating clinicians. Section 4(3) requires that regard is given to whether or not the person might regain capacity and if so, that particular decision regarding the person's treatment ought to be deferred (provided that it can wait) until the person regains capacity and can decide for him- or herself. This requirement is reinforced by section 4(4) which encourages the person's participation and requires that all steps are taken to improve the person's ability to participate as described in section 3(2) by way of using simple language, visual aids or any other means to enhance communication and understanding.

Section 4(6) specifies that it is necessary to take into account the person's wishes, feelings, beliefs and values which operate to clarify the strong subjective component of the best interests test. This is further supported by subsection 4 that requires consultation to be made with others to determine the person's best interests with a particular emphasis on matters specified in subsection 6. Taken together, subsections 6 and 7 function to emphasise patient subjectivity of best interests to the extent that this arguably borders upon a substituted judgement standard.

The Code of Practice sets out the criteria for the decision-maker, which for medical and related treatment is the person responsible for carrying out that treatment or procedure. The decision-maker needs to apply the statutory criteria in a flexible manner to ascertain the patient's best interests and ensure that the person who lacks capacity is central to the decision-making process. Clearly recorded decisions are required supported by reasons.

> Assuming Mary lacks capacity in respect of the decision whether to undergo surgery, consider the factors on the basis of statutory best interests assessment that would apply. Consider how this aligns with case law (as discussed below), in respect of providing greater empowerment to Mary's wishes.

In practical terms, the decision-maker should consider whether the decision can be postponed if it is more likely than not that the person will regain capacity and could make the decision at a later stage. The decision-maker should also permit and encourage, and try all means to improve the ability of the person to participate in the decision-making process, as well as take into account evidence of the person's past and present wishes, feelings and beliefs, and the views of anyone named by the person as someone to be consulted. The spirit of the Act is designed to empower and protect patients lacking capacity over the age of 16 who are unable to make their own decisions about particular health-care and welfare issues.

4.12.3 The best interests test

The statutory best interests test is based upon the common law doctrine of necessity.

4.12.3(a) Common law

Re F [1990] 2 AC 1 concerned a 36-year-old woman who was a voluntary in-patient at a mental hospital. She subsequently embarked upon a sexual relationship with a patient which led to concern that she would not be able to cope with the effects of pregnancy or motherhood. No form of reversible contraception was considered suitable for her circumstances and for this reason it was felt that sterilisation would offer the most appropriate option (even though it was clear that F could not give valid consent). This view was supported by hospital staff and F's mother. The House of Lords granted the declaration that sterilisation would be lawful on the grounds that the procedure would be in her 'best interests'.

In *Re F* it was recognised that circumstances could arise where adult patients would be unable to give or refuse consent to treatment and that the law would be seriously defective if it failed to provide a solution. It was held that following implementation of the Mental Health Act 1959, the ancient *parens patriae* jurisdiction (literally meaning 'parent of the country' authority) could not be exercised by the court. This meant that no-one could consent on behalf of an incapacitated adult and medical intervention would be lawful only if justified on the doctrine of necessity if provided in the patient's 'best interests'. In Lord Brandon's opinion an intervention would be lawful provided it was in the best interests of an incompetent patient. He went on to state: 'The operation or other treatment will be in their best interests if, but only if, it is carried out in order either to save their lives, or to ensure improvement or prevent deterioration in their physical or mental health.' It can be seen, therefore, that best interests can pertain to a range of factors and is not necessarily limited to those interventions that are aimed at the preservation of life. Interventions to improve health or prevent deterioration of physical or mental health could be captured within the concept of best interests. This was echoed by Lord Bridge in *Re F* who stated that it would be lawful to undertake treatment to 'preserve the life, health or wellbeing' of the individual who was unable to make a competent decision.

An intervention that is carried out to preserve life is one matter. The factors that engage in making such a decision are likely quite different to those that might engage in decisions related to the improvement of, or prevention of the deterioration of, the physical or mental health of persons who lack capacity. Graphic examples of the problematic issues that can arise in making decisions under the best interests principle can be seen in cases of treatment refusal in late pregnancy, and in cases of compulsory sterilisation.

While it is axiomatic that an adult with capacity has the absolute right to refuse medical treatment, the possible qualification which Lord Donaldson mentioned in *Re T*, that is where treatment refusal could lead to the death of a viable foetus, has been evident. In *Re S* [1993] Fam 123, the facts concerned whether a caesarean section could be lawfully performed on a woman who refused consent on religious grounds. On the basis of medical evidence that the operation was necessary to save the life of the woman and foetus, a declaration was granted that the intervention would be lawful. In *Re MB* [1997] 2 FLR 426, although the Court of Appeal reiterated the general principle that an adult with capacity can refuse any treatment, and confirmed that this applied with equal force to women in late pregnancy, the claimant nonetheless lost her appeal. On the evidence, MB was considered incompetent to refuse a caesarean section on account of her needle phobia, and the court declared that the intervention had been in her best interests. In *St George's Healthcare NHS Trust v S* [1999] Fam 26, a woman refused consent to an induced delivery. It was accepted that she understood the risks and yet still preferred a natural birth. Nevertheless, she was sectioned under the Mental Health Act 1983 and the court declared that a caesarean section would be in her best interests. In *Bolton Hospitals NHS Trust v O* [2002] EWHC 2871, a woman suffered post-traumatic stress disorder following four previous caesarean sections and she withdrew her consent moments prior to her fifth operation. If the caesarean section did not go ahead there was a 95 per cent chance that she and the foetus would die. The court declared that she was temporarily incapacitated because of panic. These cases taken together raise questions as to whether the decision-making process under the best interests principle is specifically focused on the individual's best interests or whether a decision is influenced by other factors and in these cases, those of the foetus.

4.12.3(b) The Bolam *test and best interests*

In *Re F*, Lord Goff, speaking of the incapacitated person where the mental state might be permanent or at least semi-permanent, stated that there would be no point in waiting to obtain the patient's consent since 'The need to care for him is obvious; and the doctor must then act in the best interests of his patient, just as if he had received his patient's consent to do so. Were this not so, much useful treatment and care could, in theory at least, be denied to the unfortunate'. It is not clear exactly what intervention might fall within the category of 'useful treatment and care' and in *Re F* it appears that there was a blurring between essential life-saving treatment and non-essential treatment aimed at the promotion of well-being. Lord Bridge (at 52) explained:

> It seems to me to be axiomatic that treatment which is necessary to preserve the life, health or well being of the patient may lawfully be given without consent. But if a rigid criterion of necessity were to be applied to determine what is and what is not lawful in the treatment of the unconscious and the incompetent, many of those unfortunate enough to be deprived of the capacity to make or communicate rational decisions by accident, illness or unsoundness of mind might be deprived of treatment which it would be entirely beneficial for them to receive.

What is the standard by which beneficial treatment is then to be measured when deciding on the best interests of the incapacitated person? In *Re F*, the House of Lords said that the doctor must give treatment that is considered to be in the best interests of the patient and the standard of care required would be that of the *Bolam* standard. However, while the *Bolam* might be necessary for determining medical treatment, it cannot decisively establish whether that treatment is in a particular person's best interests and subsequent cases have shown that a broader view may be required.

4.12.3(c) A welfare standard to determine best interests

In *Re S (adult patient: sterilisation)* [2001] Fam 15 (at 27), Butler-Sloss P stated:

> I would suggest that the starting point of any medical decision would be the principles enunciated in the Bolam test…The duty to act in accordance with responsible and competent professional opinion may give the doctor more than one option since there may well be more than one acceptable medical opinion. When the doctor moves on to consider the best interests of the patient, he or she has to choose the best option, often from a range of options.

The Court of Appeal has indicated that there are two duties in the determination of best interests. First, the treatment options that are on offer must accord with proper standards and satisfy the *Bolam* test. Second, what is chosen from among the treatment options must be in accordance with the best interests of that particular patient. Thus, the *Bolam* test may suggest several courses of action as being within the acceptable range of clinical judgement but the best interests test should logically give only one answer, that is, what is best for that particular person. Accordingly, Butler-Sloss P went on to state: 'The *Bolam* test was, in my view, irrelevant to the judicial decision, once the judge was satisfied that the range of options was within the range of acceptable opinion among competent and responsible practitioners.' Thorpe LJ in *Re S* reinforced this view stating that the *Bolam* test was to be applied only at the outset in order to ensure that the treatment proposed was recognised as proper by a responsible body of medical opinion skilled in delivering that particular treatment. However, in deciding what was best for that particular patient 'the judge must have regard to the patient's welfare as the paramount consideration. That embraces issues far wider than the medical. Indeed it would be undesirable and probably impossible to set bounds to what is relevant to a welfare determination'. The standard by which best interests are to be determined, therefore, is a welfare standard that incorporates a range of issues that are wider than purely medical matters. The starting point, namely the determination of relevant medical options, must be based on the *Bolam* standard. The second part of the decision as to which option is in the best interests has to be made by the doctor, or decision maker, according to a welfare standard. These two duties should not be conflated. McLean (1999) emphasises the need to distinguish between the appropriateness of a medical procedure and its lawfulness. The *Bolam* test uses acceptable medical practice as a measure of the competence of the procedure, but is not designed as a test of the lawfulness of the procedure, which would depend upon a welfare standard to determine what is in that particular person's best interests, at any particular time.

4.12.4 Ethical underpinnings of the best interests principle

One particular issue that arises in the application of best interests approach is the level of importance or weight to be given to the interests of the individual, the views and values of friends, family, health professionals and the wider society. One approach is that if the patient had expressed particular views while previously competent, then these ought to be considered decisive, as with an advance decision. However, advance decisions are by no means decisive and can be challenged on substantive grounds: that the decision was not applicable to the specific clinical circumstances; or that the person had not envisaged the particular set of factors that had come into being. The net effect of the statutory best interests test is, therefore, that decision making should be more greatly influenced by the views of third parties and, in particular, the views of health-care professionals.

The best interests test ought (in theory) to focus entirely on the interests of the incompetent person and not influenced by the value of that person's life for others. According to Beauchamp and Childress (2009), 'Quality-of-life judgements also concern only the individual's best interests, not his or her worth to enhance another's quality of life. Unfortunately, the best interests standard has sometimes been interpreted in highly malleable ways, thereby permitting consideration of values irrelevant to the individual's benefits or burdens. ... Such considerations should be greeted with scepticism ...'

A possible reason for this is the tension that exists and the moral justification that proceeds on the basis of a top-down (deductive model) and one that proceeds bottom-up (inductively).

In the top-down model of ethical decision making, moral judgements are rationalised through a structure of normative precepts that cover the decisions that have been made. This type of approach has been inspired by those disciplines that use a logical or deductive approach to justify an assertion by starting from a set of credible premises. Using best interests as an example, if every intervention that was in a patient's overall best interests was obligatory for a patient's doctor, and if the act of resuscitation is in the patient's best interests, then resuscitation is obligatory. Using a bottom-up model (the inductive model), the starting point for decision-making uses existing social practices, comparative case analyses, evolving moral life and experiential involvement (Beauchamp and Childress, 2009). According to this approach an intervention such as resuscitation may be a factor in the patient's best interests, but in the overall view, and taking everything into account, an attempt to resuscitate might not be in the best interests of the person at that particular time.

In theory, therefore, a test that is wider than best interests could be used, namely the test of overall interests. Under this umbrella, all competing interests would have to be balanced, which would include the interests and views of others, as well as the public interest. One potential problem with this type of approach is that a person who lacks capacity might be treated in a way that could not be considered to be in that person's best interests. It would be difficult to justify such a test on moral grounds and strict criteria would be required as to which interests needed to be considered and how much weight these should be accorded.

4.12.5 Criticisms of the best interests principle

The best interests principle has been criticised on two principle grounds. First, it suggests that treatment can be undertaken in what is regarded as a patient's best interests by a decision made by a judge or doctor alone. Best interests determinations might, due to necessity, be determined solely according to objective criteria rather than the patient's own subjective values, which admittedly may be impossible to determine in certain circumstances. This can be a particular issue in quality-of-life determinations or in circumstances where a patient's previously competent subjective values (e.g. a Jehovah's Witness refusal of blood products) might not be considered as being in the best interests of the now incompetent person.

The second major criticism lies in whether or not the best interests test can promote the previously competent individual's altruistic choice. Altruism is generally regarded as beneficial for society and by extension might be considered beneficial or even within the best interests of the incompetent person. In *Re Y (adult patient) (transplant: bone marrow)* [1997] Fam 110, it was held that it could be lawful to find a benefit for an incompetent person under the best interests principle by allowing that person to make a sacrifice. If, for example, the incompetent person has a close relationship with a sibling, then the sacrifice could make the incompetent person feel 'good'. Furthermore, the incompetent person may secure additional benefits, such as gratitude, from the family or wider society. However, this approach cuts two ways and there could be potential for abuse when using the altruistic motive approach in application of the best interests principle.

4.12.6 Alternatives to the best interests principle

Beauchamp and Childress (2009) state that biomedical ethics hold that an ordered set of standards for surrogate decision making that run from (a) an autonomously executed advance directive to (b) substituted judgement to (c) best interests, with advance decisions holding priority over the alternatives. Furthermore, advance decisions and substituted judgement ought to have priority over best interests in a situation of conflict. Advance decisions are discussed later (see 4.13), but substituted judgement is an alternative approach to best interests.

Using the substituted judgement standard, the decision maker has to make decisions on the basis of what persons lacking capacity would have wanted had they been able to make decisions. This has been described as requiring the decision maker to 'don the mantle' of the person lacking capacity. Thus, previously expressed opinions, religious and ethical views and other components that may have formed part of the incapacitated person's character while he had capacity, would represent factors of influence in the decision-making process. This approach has been highly influential in the United States.

Critics of the substituted judgement standard argue that this is an insufficiently robust test, as it places great weight on previous comments and views of the previously competent individual which may well have been 'off the cuff' and given without serious consideration. It can also encourage relatives to 'recall', either erroneously or otherwise, the wishes of the formerly competent person. The substituted judgement approach never really gained currency in the United Kingdom. In *Airedale NHS Trust v Bland* [1993] AC 789, Lord Mustill regarded the test as 'simply a fiction'. The Mental Capacity Act 2005 has not adopted this test but instead takes the best interests approach as the primary criterion for deciding on treatment for the person who lacks capacity. For the substituted judgement standard to be truly applicable, two criteria must be met. First, a person must have had capacity in the past in order to have expressed autonomous wishes. Second, there must be evidence at a required level that the views and values that are being taken into account in the individual's incapacitated state were his views while competent.

An arguably more flexible approach to best interests decision-making would be to allow intervention provided it is not against the interests of the incapacitated person, although it may not definitively be in the *best* interests of the person. This approach was adopted, for example, in *S v S* [1972] AC 24 in the context of paternity testing of children. The overall interests standard is another alternative, but again one that is not used because of the difficulties in moral justification. The concept of 'overall interests' could be widely interpreted, for example, Pattinson (2009 at 163) states that 'communitarians and utilitarians would require a patient's welfare autonomy interests to be balanced against societal interests. Even rights-based theorists could adopt an approach that is not restricted to the patient's interests where the rights of others potentially outweigh those of the incapacitated patient. Virtue ethicists will simply seek to foster and facilitate virtuous conduct...'

4.13 Advance decisions

Advance decisions can be made by competent adults to refuse or consent to medical treatment in the event of their future incapacity. Kennedy and Grubb (2000) assert that in almost every situation where a person gives consent prior to a procedure that decision is 'advance or anticipatory'. An advance refusal of medical care that complies with the provisions of the Mental Capacity Act 2005 will be binding in the event of that person's loss of capacity. In the context of a particular treatment decision, where a valid and applicable advance refusal exists, treatment cannot be given under the doctrine of necessity since the clinician will be dealing with the prospective decision of a competent person.

Prior to the statutory provisions being brought into force advance directives were enforceable under common law (*Re T* [1993] Fam 95). Thompson et al. (2003) suggest that on the basis of a vignette study, advance directives have seldom been consulted or followed in critical care situations. Bartlett (2005 at 76) asserts that there are no reported cases of an English court upholding a written advance directive to refuse life-sustaining treatment for a person who lacked capacity at the time of the hearing, although such refusals have been respected when the person has been competent.

4.13.1 Statutory authority

Sections 24 and 25 of the Mental Capacity Act 2005 govern advance decisions. An advance decision is defined in section 24(1):

a) an 'advance decision' is a decision made by a person ('P'), after he has reached 18 and when he has capacity to do so, that if – at a later time and in such circumstances as he may specify – a specified treatment is proposed to be carried out or continued by a person providing healthcare for him, and

b) at the time he lacks capacity to consent for the carrying out or continuation of the treatment

the specified treatment is not to be carried out or continued.

Several points arise from this definition. First, in order to be valid, the person making an advance decision must be competent and over the age of 18. Second, the advance decision is relevant or engages only in those situations where the person lacks capacity to consent to treatment. Third, an advance decision is binding in respect of refusals of care, as opposed to positive requests for treatment. An advance request might be relevant in a determination of what is in the person's best interests, but would not be decisive.

Section 24(2) provides that an advance refusal can be drafted in layman's terms, which means that precise technical language is not essential and failure to use such language will not necessarily undermine the legality of an advance decision. Except for refusal of life-saving treatment, an advance decision does not need to be in writing. In this respect the statute requires compliance with greater formalities than the previous common law. Section 24(3) provides that a person is able to withdraw or alter her advance decision at any time provided that she has capacity to do so, and subsections 4 and 5 state that these withdrawals and alterations do not have to be in writing, unless the alteration pertains to life-sustaining treatment.

To be effective an advance decision must be valid and applicable to the treatment proposed (section 25(1)). By section 25(2) an advance decision is not valid if P –

a) has withdrawn the decision at a time when he had capacity to do so,

b) has, under a lasting power of attorney created after the advance decision was made, conferred authority on the donee (or, if more than one, any of them) to give or refuse consent to the treatment to which the advance decision relates, or

c) has done anything else clearly inconsistent with the advance decision remaining his fixed decision.

The Code of Practice (paragraph 9.40) provides guidance on the application of the statutory provisions.

To satisfy the applicability requirement, the advance decision must apply to the specific situation in the context of current circumstances. An advance decision will only be applicable if the patient lacks capacity to give or refuse consent to the treatment in question at the relevant time (section 25(3)). Section 25(4) states that an advance decision is not applicable to the treatment in question if –

a) that treatment is not the treatment specified in the advance decision,
b) any circumstances specified in the advance decision are absent, or
c) there are reasonable grounds for believing that circumstances exist which P did not anticipate at the time of the advance decision and which would have affected his decision had he anticipated them.

Section 25(4)(c) seems particularly broad and could, in theory, be widely interpreted to extend to almost any set of circumstances where an advance decision has been executed by an individual in a state of 'relative' ignorance or lack of knowledge about precise medical circumstances in the event of future incapacity. This tension is further heightened by the potential defences available for decision makers who ignore or fail to act in accordance with an advance decision. Section 26(2) provides that 'A person does not incur liability for carrying out or continuing the treatment unless, at that time, he is satisfied that an advance decision exists which is valid and applicable to the treatment'. Together with section 25(4)(c) this provision gives wide scope for an advance decision to be ignored on grounds that it is not applicable to the circumstances in question. It arguably offers more latitude to continue treatment despite the existence of an advance decision to the contrary. While the statute does not explicitly state that if there is lack of clarity as to whether the advance decision is applicable that there should be a presumption in favour of preserving life, the drafting of these sections appears to imply such interpretation.

If the person has capacity, his or her contemporaneous consent or refusal will apply and will override any advance decision. Section 25(5) provides that an advance decision is not applicable to life-sustaining treatment unless evidenced by the person's written and witnessed statement. Section 26(1) confirms that if an individual has made an advance decision which is valid and applicable to the treatment being considered then that decision will have the same effect as if the competent individual had made it at the time the treatment decision arises.

Section 24(3) allows the person with capacity to withdraw and alter an advance decision and section 25(2)(c) operates to invalidate an advance decision if the person has done something 'clearly inconsistent' with the advance decision remaining his fixed decision. This appears slightly at odds with section 24(3) and seems to suggest that any inconsistent behaviour might operate to invalidate an advance decision.

Section 26(3) states that 'A person does not incur liability for the consequences of withholding or withdrawing a treatment from P if, at the time, he reasonably believes that an advance decision exists which is valid and applicable to the treatment'. Together with section 26(2) the statute is drafted to protect health-care professionals from liability whether or not they choose to respect an advance decision. However, it would seem to be easier to continue with treatment on the grounds that the advance decision is not applicable as the test is one of being *satisfied* of the existence of an advance decision that is applicable. The 'bar for the avoidance of liability for the continuation of treatment is therefore that of (a simply) subjective satisfaction on the part of the treating physician. On the other hand, protection from liability due to withholding or withdrawing treatment is founded on a reasonable belief and is therefore a more objective standard' (Samanta, 2009). Michalowski (2005) expresses concern that section 26(2) gives inadequate protection to advance treatment refusals and argues that the courts should not be too willing to overrule advance decisions refusing life-saving treatment.

If there is doubt about the validity or applicability of an advance decision, an application can be made to the court for a declaration (section 26(4)). In the interim, while advice is sought, section 26(5) permits the provision of life-sustaining treatment or steps necessary to prevent a deterioration of the person's condition.

4.13.2 Advance directives at common law

The statutory provisions that govern advance decisions have codified the previous common law with additional requirements in respect of refusals of life-sustaining treatment and minimum age. Consideration of the common law provides a useful illustration of the operation of advance decisions as well as the court's likely interpretation of the statutory provisions.

Re AK (2000) 58 BMLR 151 concerned a man of 19 who suffered progressive motor neurone disease, an incurable and fatal condition. He required 24-hour nursing care, provided at home by his family and professional carers. His condition gradually deteriorated and his only means of communication was by a very tiny movement of one of his eyelids, by which he could answer 'yes' or 'no' to questions. His intellectual ability was unaffected and he therefore retained the decision-making capacity of a competent adult. Using the laborious and only method of communication that he had, namely movement of one of his eyelids, he informed the nursing team in the presence of his mother that he wished to make an advance directive with regard to his future treatment. He indicated that he wanted doctors to remove the ventilator two weeks after he lost his ability to communicate. This eventuality was inevitable. He was fully aware that removal of the ventilator would lead to his death. He confirmed this wish on several occasions in the presence of his doctor, parents and care team, and indicated that he fully understood the consequences of his decision. The Health Authority applied to the High Court for a declaration that it would be lawful to discontinue life-sustaining treatment in accordance with AK's advance directive, in the certain eventuality of his losing the ability to communicate. The High Court granted the declaration. Treatment refusal by an adult with capacity must be observed in law and an advance directive made by a patient with capacity was legally binding.

Re AK reinforced the principle that a competent adult has the right to make an anticipatory decision to refuse treatment even though this will inevitably lead to that person's death. In giving judgement, Hughes J reaffirmed the principle of autonomy articulated by the House of Lords in *Airedale NHS Trust v Bland* [1993] AC 789. In particular, Lord Goff's observations that '...the principle of self-determination requires that respect must be given to the wishes of the patient, so that if an adult patient of sound mind refuses, however unreasonably, to consent to treatment or care by which his life would or might be prolonged, the doctors responsible for his care must give effect to his wishes, even though they do not consider it to be in his best interests to do so'.

Hughes J justified the rationale of the consequences of an advance directive, namely treatment refusal ending in death, as being different from taking active steps to end life or to kill, even with the consent or encouragement of the patient. In his view the cessation of ventilation was an 'omission', and he was fortified by the words of Lord Goff in *Bland* (at 886):

> I agree that the doctor's conduct in discontinuing life support can properly be categorised as an omission. ... But discontinuation of life support is, for the present purposes, no different from not initiating life support in the first place. In each case, the doctor is simply allowing his patient to die in the sense that he is desisting from taking a step which might, in certain circumstances, prevent his patient from dying as a result of a pre-existing condition ...

The ethical justification for the distinction between acts and omissions remains somewhat dubious (see 1.8.2). From a consequentialist perspective, there is no real difference between the two since both lead to the same outcome, namely death of the patient. From a deontological perspective, however, the doctor performs his duty owed to the patient by complying with the autonomous refusal of the person with capacity, since to do otherwise would be a breach of duty. However, an omission to act might conceivably still require a physical action (such as removing a tracheostomy tube, or switching off a ventilator). In the view of Lord Goff in *Bland*, a clear distinction can be drawn as to whether the physical movement or act is performed by an interloper or doctor. The act of an interloper would constitute interference of clinically administered life-prolonging treatment, whereas the act of the doctor would be to allow the patient to die of her pre-existing condition. Whether such a difference is justifiable, is moot.

Albert informs the staff about Mary's views, giving evidence by way of example. Is it possible that Mary has made an advance decision?

▶ If so, is the advance decision likely to satisfy the requirements of validity and applicability?
▶ What are the implications of Jenny's thoughts? Could this be evidence that Mary had revoked her advance decision?

4.13.3 Ethical issues and advance decisions

Although the law is now settled, a plethora of ethical and moral arguments are raised to reject or support the ethical and moral legitimacy of advance health-care planning, as a way of ensuring that a competent person's decision-making ability is retained and respected in the event of incapacity.

The principle of autonomy underscores the ethical legitimacy of advance refusals made at the time that an individual is competent to make decisions. Autonomy, however, is not always rationalised on the basis of protection of personal welfare. Nonetheless, autonomy is respected as the basis of protection of the integrity of an individual, and as recognised by Dworkin (1993) allows each to lead their lives according to their own individualism. The importance of autonomous decision making has been recognised in law on multiple occasions.

The anticipatory fear and sense of loss that can accompany introspective contemplation of personal future incapacity is all too real for many, particularly those of advancing years or newly diagnosed with conditions such as dementia, mental illness and certain physical ailments. While technological advances in medicine may prolong life, such advances do not always restore previous levels of quality of life and functioning. In these circumstances some may choose to avoid confronting the uncomfortable issues that might be associated with their failing health and inevitable mortality. Others, however, will attempt to influence their future fate by means of advance planning to refuse health care in defined circumstances in order to avoid existing in a state in which they perceive to be a life not worth living. They may consider that a life devoid of specific qualities would not be worth extending by heroic means on the grounds that quantitative extensions of life may add little in respect of qualitative value. To these individuals, advance health-care decision making is vitally important.

The ethical principles that engage in advance health-care planning for treatment refusal need to be evaluated within the context of specific situations that are likely to arise. Typical situations where individuals might seek to avoid life-sustaining care being given include persistent vegetative states and prolongation of life where advanced and terminal conditions are accompanied by pain and reduced quality of life as perceived by the individual. Thus, the diagnosis of a progressive or incurable condition characterised by dementia or a degenerative neurological condition, such as motor neurone disease, might operate as the trigger for advance health-care planning.

Several commentators have expressed concern about the moral legitimacy of advance decisions. Dworkin (1993) argues that people's lives are guided by the need to promote two kinds of interests, namely experiential and critical. On this analysis, a distinction must be drawn between 'experiential' interests, being those interests grounded on positive or negative experiences, and 'critical' interests that represent a person's critical judgements as opposed to his or her experiential preferences. Critical interests tend to include personal convictions about what makes a life worth living. Dworkin argues that in certain circumstances experiential interests can be legitimately overwritten in order to safeguard an individual's previously expressed critical interests.

Parfit (1984) believes that the individual who makes an advance directive is not the same person as the person who subsequently becomes incompetent (the personhood argument). Thus, for example, in the case of a patient with dementia, although the body remains the same, the loss of memory and the loss of connectivity with other persons, relatives and friends, as well as life's events, mean that this is no longer the same person as the previously competent individual who made the advance decision. On this premise the moral legitimacy of advance health-care planning is dubious. Robertson (1991) states, 'The values and interests of the competent person no longer are relevant to someone who has lost the rational structure on which those values and interests rested.... If the person is no longer competent enough to appreciate the degree of divergence from her previous activity that produced the choice against treatment, the prior directive does not represent her current interests merely because a competent directive was issued'. There is an argument that determining how the final chapter of one's life is written is a critical interest and therefore ought to be given precedence through a previously competent state. The degree of weight that should be accorded to these decisions is another matter.

A further argument against advance decision making is the primary societal obligation towards persons who lack capacity to show beneficent compassion to determine their best interests, and to treat them as such. This argument has been put forward principally by Dresser (1994), where she argues that the law must also ensure that the present person does not simply disappear in the shadow of the person that she once was. She goes on to state that the best interests standard shines the brightest light on the present person and that it is a tyranny for competent persons to try and exercise control over their future incompetent selves.

Advance decisions can present serious ethical dilemmas for those charged with the care of incompetent persons, on account of professional and personal conscience. Health-care professionals who hold the sanctity of life as paramount might consider that compliance with a contemporaneous or advance refusal is morally repugnant, even though such decisions have been fully informed and considered. In a contemporaneous situation, a clinician might be able to provide full or even 'fuller' information and discuss the likely implications of a decision. However, once an advance decision has been made and the person no longer lacks capacity, provision of information becomes irrelevant. It is therefore vital that sufficient information is available for individuals at the time that they enter into advance decisions. In the event of a conscientious objection by a doctor, there may be a possibility of discharging a duty of care by transferring the patient to a colleague, although in practice time constraints and human resource factors may make this option a theoretical rather than a real possibility.

The ability to revoke an advance decision may also represent ethical dilemmas for health-care professionals. Changes in personal circumstances and life events may influence a person to change their perception of the value of life during periods of fluctuant capacity. Views may also change on account of the ageing process, diagnosis of a terminal or irreversible medical condition, marriage, the death of a spouse, pregnancy, the birth of a child and the family, all of which might act as influences to an individual to revisit and revise their former intentions. The ethical difficulty that is likely to ensue is where the competence of the person concerned is in question. However, in all the debate over advance decisions, it should not be forgotten that at present only a few people make them, although this position might change in the future.

4.14 Decisions made by appointed proxies

The Mental Capacity Act 2005 permits the instruction of a proxy decision maker to make health and welfare decisions for the individual, in the event that they lack decision-making capacity. The authorising instrument is known as a welfare lasting power of attorney (LPA).

4.14.1 Lasting powers of attorney

Adults with capacity may select a trusted or willing person over the age of 18 to make welfare decisions on their behalf in the future should they lose capacity (section 9(1)(a) of the Mental Capacity Act 2005). The attorney is only permitted to take decisions about life-sustaining treatment if the donor has included a clear statement to this effect in the document.

The appointment of an LPA requires compliance with a range of formalities set out in the Mental Capacity Act Code of Practice. The document must be written, witnessed and registered with the Office of the Public Guardian. The purpose of the LPA is to enable maximisation of autonomy while that person has capacity by appointing a proxy who can take decisions on behalf of that person when or if he loses capacity.

The strict regulations and the formalities surrounding an LPA are set out in schedule 1 of the Mental Capacity Act 2005, and unless complied with, the power will be ineffective. The attorney's powers are defined in section 9(4) and require compliance with the principles of schedule 1. Attorneys must make decisions that are in the best interests of the incompetent person (section 4) and pursuant to section 4(3) must take into account whether the likelihood of the person regaining capacity, as well as past and present wishes and feelings (section 4(6)). The attorney has no power to 'authorise the giving or refusal of consent to the carrying out or continuation of life-sustaining treatment, unless the instrument contains specific provision to that effect' (section 11(8)).

Although the LPA is a new power within this jurisdiction and is expected to usher in a new era for protecting the interests of the incompetent person, its exact use and role remains to be determined. Samanta (2009) argues that the provisions that 'operate and legitimise the powers of welfare attorneys are overly restrictive and that the attorney's decision ought to be an emanation of the donor's previous autonomous choice'. The principal criticism that has been offered is that the attorney's powers must operate according to a standard that is essentially objective and do not extend as far as a substituted judgement or subjective approach might do. Thus, 'the benefit to be gained from such an appointment conflicts with the enabling potential of the LPA. Pragmatic difficulties for proxy decision makers can be envisaged.' It is possible that the health-care team may not be satisfied that the attorney is acting in the person's best interests and circumstances where the proxy decision does not align with medical wisdom and the net effect might be that only those decisions will be considered correct where a proxy is concerned where 'best interests' concurs with that of the clinical team.

4.14.2 Deputies

If a person lacks capacity in relation to a matter concerning personal welfare, a decision can be made on that person's behalf by the court, or alternatively the court may appoint a deputy to make such a decision (section 16(2)). These decisions have to be made in the person's best interests (section 4). The court must consider whether a decision by the court is preferable to the appointment of a deputy (section 16(4)(a)). If a deputy is appointed, the powers conferred on that individual should be limited in scope and duration as far as reasonably practicable (section 16(4)(b)). If decisions will have to be made on a regular basis, then the appointment of a deputy might be more suitable than circumstances where a one-off decision has to be made.

The deputy acts in accordance with the best interests of the person, and may not refuse consent to continuation of life-sustaining treatment. He or she may not act on behalf of that person if there are reasonable grounds for believing that the person has capacity in relation to particular decision. Provided that these requirements are met, a deputy may either give or refuse consent to medical treatment.

4.14.3 Independent Mental Capacity Advocates

Section 35 of the Mental Capacity Act 2005 CA creates the role of the Independent Mental Capacity Advocate (IMCA). IMCAs are appointed by health authorities. Their precise role is defined in section 36 and they are relied upon in circumstances where no other person is available to consult regarding the incapacitated person's best interests, besides a professional caregiver. The role of the IMCA is principally to support the person who lacks capacity. They have a right to ask for further medical opinions relating to the person, as well as make requests for further information. An IMCA may challenge a health-care decision if it is believed that any particular decision is not in the incapacitated person's best interests.

Summary

4.1 Consent to treatment lies at the heart of clinical practice and medical law.

4.2 The need for consent is underpinned by the principle of autonomy. A decision made by a patient to undergo specific health care must be made freely after being given sufficient information to reach a decision. Consent may be expressed or implied (inferred from conduct) and must be valid.

4.3 Failure to obtain valid consent prior to treatment could amount to the crime of assault or form the basis of a civil action in tort or battery.

4.4 There are three elements to valid consent: the person must be competent; he or she must have received sufficient information to reach a decision; consent must be voluntary and decision making should not be influenced by coercion or undue influence. Competence is the ability to understand and retain relevant information, and use that information to arrive at and communicate a self-determined choice regarding medical treatment.

4.5 Treatment without valid consent may result in a charge of battery. If it can be shown that a patient understood the medical intervention proposed in general terms then that would be sufficient to absolve the doctor of battery.

4.6 The majority of disputes about consent arise because of alleged negligence in providing sufficient information for valid consent. In this jurisdiction the question as to how much information should be provided in order to avoid liability is determined on the basis of the House of Lords decision of *Sidaway*. The standard for information disclosure is the *Bolam* standard.

4.7 If negligent consent (consent obtained by negligently failing to disclose sufficient information) is proved, the claimant still would have to prove on the balance of probabilities that had she known of the risk she would have had that particular medical intervention in order for her claim to succeed (on traditional principles of causation). The House of Lords decision in *Chester v Afshar* has altered this. *Chester* is a policy decision that imposes liability on a defendant for negligently obtaining consent and has moved the traditional boundaries of causation towards one that is more aligned to a patient-centred approach to information disclosure.

4.8 As per *obiter* statements from *Sidaway* and *Pearce* the duty of information disclosure ought to be enhanced in the event that the patient asks specific questions after having heard about the proposed treatment.

4.9 In English law a person may not consent to anything that is intended to or that causes more than actual bodily harm, but reasonable surgical interference falls outside this rule. Canadian jurisprudence shows that consent can be validly withdrawn during a procedure provided that it does not have life-threatening implications or pose immediate and serious threats to health.

4.10 Several professional organisations have published position statements and guidelines as to how consent should be obtained in practice. Professional guidance sets a high standard for information disclosure. Public policy imposes a limit as to what degree of bodily harm a person can lawfully consent to within the medical context. The boundaries are dependent upon the relative interaction of patient autonomy and public policy, as well as maintaining the non-maleficence principle of medical practice.

4.11 Section 1 of the Mental Capacity Act 2005 provides the rebuttable presumption of capacity in an adult. An unwise health-care decision does not necessarily equate with lack of capacity. Incapacity is defined by section 2(1) as the inability to make a decision in relation to a matter because of an impairment or disturbance in the functioning of the mind or brain. There are two limbs to the test for capacity under the Act. The first is the 'functional' limb which requires that a person must be suffering from an impairment or disturbance in the functioning of the mind or brain. The second limb is 'decision-specific' and is defined in section 3(1) of the Act which provides that a person must understand, retain, use or weigh that information as part of the process of making the decision, and be able to communicate his decision.

4.12 Health-care treatment may be given to individuals who lack decision-making capacity where such treatment is their best interests in accordance with section 1(5) of the Mental Capacity Act 2005. The factors to be considered in determining best interests are wide and are found in section 4.The Code of Practice sets out the criteria for the decision-maker, who should apply this in a flexible manner to ascertain the patient's best interests and ensure that the person who lacks capacity is central to the decision-making process. The statutory best interests test is based upon the common law doctrine of necessity.

4.13 An advance decision is an anticipatory decision made by a person aged 18 or above with capacity in respect of the continuation, discontinuation or refusal of a specified proposed treatment in the event of future incapacity. The advance decision engages only in those situations where the person lacks capacity. An advance decision must be valid and applicable to the treatment proposed. Advance decisions are governed by sections 24 and 25 of the Mental Capacity Act 2005.

4.14 Adults with capacity may select a trusted or willing person over the age of 18 to make welfare decisions on their behalf in the future should they lose capacity. This is through the appointment of a welfare attorney and is governed by section 9 of the Mental Capacity Act 2005. The appointment of an attorney requires compliance with a range of formalities set out in the Mental Capacity Act Code of Practice. The Act also creates a new role called the Independent Mental Capacity Advocate who may be appointed by health authorities in circumstances where no other person other than a professional caregiver is available to consult regarding the incapacitated person's best interests.

Exercises

4.1 Consider the judgement in *Sidaway* and the reasons given by the Law Lords for arriving at their decisions. What are the relative merits and problems with each view?

4.2 'The Mental Capacity Act 2005 has codified the common law and developed a statutory test for capacity. It would be more appropriate to develop a scale of competence, with a higher level of competence being required for more complex decisions or decisions that have a greater consequence.' Critically discuss the above statement.

4.3 The law recognises the right of the competent person to refuse any form of treatment. How far do you think this is applied in practice? Is it fair to be allowed the right to refuse but not the right to ask for a medically accepted intervention that may be applicable in the circumstances?

4.4 To what extent does an advance decision truly protect prospective autonomous decision making?

4.5 The new provision of the health and welfare lasting power of attorney is intended to enhance or protect future autonomous decision making. Consider this in the context of the potential limitations and benefits.

Further reading

Donnelly M. Best interests, patient participation and the Mental Capacity Act 2005. *Medical Law Review* 2009; 17: 1–29.

Gunn MJ, et al. Decision-making capacity. *Medical Law Review* 1999; 7: 269–306.

McLean A. Advance directives and the rocky waters of anticipatory decision-making. *Medical Law Review* 2008; 16: 1–22.

Samanta J. Lasting powers of attorney for healthcare under the Mental Capacity Act 2005: enhanced prospective self-determination for future incapacity or a simulacrum? *Medical Law Review* 2009; 17: 377–409.

Wrigley A. Proxy consent: moral authority misconceived. *Journal of Medical Ethics* 2007; 33: 527–531.

Links to relevant websites can be found at: http://www.palgrave.com/law/samanta

Chapter 5 follows overleaf.

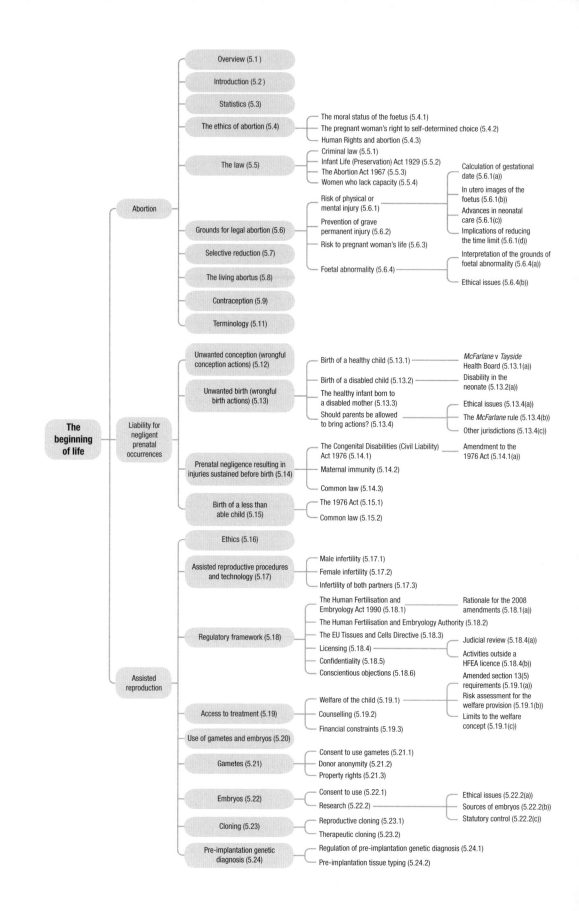

The beginning of life

Key Terms

- **Abortion** – the intentional destruction of a foetus in the uterus or the premature termination of a pregnancy with intent to cause death of the embryo or foetus.
- **Cell nuclear replacement** – involves removing the nucleus of an ovum and replacing it with the nucleus from an adult cell and stimulating it to undergo cell division thereby producing embryonic stem cells without the need for fertilisation.
- **Cloning** – the production of an exact genetic replica of an organism.
- **Embryo** – the first 8 weeks of life after which the term 'foetus' is used.
- **Foetal rights** – refer to the legal and moral rights of the foetus.
- **Gametes** – reproductive cells that unite during fertilisation.
- **Grounds for abortion** – the basis on which an abortion may be lawfully carried out under the provisions of the Abortion Act 1967.
- **Infertility** – the failure to conceive after frequent unprotected sexual intercourse for one to two years in couples in the reproductive age group.
- **Pre-implantation genetic diagnosis** – screening of embryos for genetic conditions prior to implantation during *in vitro* fertilisation.
- **Pre-implantation tissue typing** – screening of embryos to ascertain their tissue type prior to implantation during *in vitro* fertilisation.
- **Prenatal injury** – prenatal negligence that leads to injuries before or after birth.
- **Selective reduction** – the termination of one or more foetuses of a multiple pregnancy.
- **The Human Fertilisation and Embryology Act 1990** – the legal framework that regulates infertility treatment and research.
- **The Human Fertilisation and Embryology Authority** – the statutory independent regulator of treatments that use gametes and embryos.
- **Wrongful birth** – prenatal negligence that results in an unwanted birth.
- **Wrongful conception** – prenatal negligence that leads to an unwanted conception.
- **Wrongful life** – prenatal negligence leading to impairment of the life of the child.

Scenario

Lucy, who was 45, had been trying to conceive for 10 years following her marriage to Steve. The couple had undergone several investigations with inconclusive results. Lucy received three cycles of fertility treatment at her local NHS Trust but the Primary Care Trust would not fund further cycles. Steve and Lucy have remortgaged their home to fund private treatment.

Lucy was aware that her family had a genetic predisposition to cystic fibrosis. This is a rare, heritable disorder that can cause life-threatening lung conditions and reduced life expectancy. She informed her consultant who recorded this and assured the couple that pre-implantation screening will be carried out prior to implantation and storage of surplus embryos.

Three embryos were created and two implanted in the hope that at least one would be successful. The transferred embryos had negligently not been screened for cystic fibrosis, and one of the embryos had a genetic disorder known as Down's syndrome.

At the 18th week of pregnancy, routine screening tests revealed high levels of serum markers, a recognised indicator of Down's syndrome. The consultant reassured the couple that this was because Lucy was carrying twins. A 'quadruple test' was carried out and a positive result was received 2 weeks later.

Steve and Lucy were initially devastated, and Lucy seriously considered selective reduction of pregnancy. However, she changed her mind on learning of the inherent risks to the pregnancy. Lucy was now 24 weeks pregnant, calculated from the date of implantation.

At 36 weeks pregnancy, Lucy gave birth to twins. One was diagnosed with Down's syndrome, the other tested positive for cystic fibrosis. Lucy and Steve wish to bring an action on behalf of themselves and their children.

5.1 Overview

This chapter considers the ethical and legal issues that pertain to the beginning of life. It is divided into three sections:

▶ Abortion
▶ Liability for negligent prenatal occurrences
▶ Assisted reproduction.

A Abortion

5.2 Introduction

This section concentrates on issues around abortion, and to a lesser degree contraception and sterilisation. Abortion, in particular, attracts considerable and protracted debate that tends to focus on the value of unborn human life against the autonomous choice of pregnant women. For the purpose of this chapter, an abortion represents the intentional destruction of a foetus in the uterus or the premature termination of a pregnancy with intent to cause death of the embryo or foetus. Abortions that occur spontaneously (miscarriages) are not considered here. The term 'pregnant woman' is used to describe the woman who carries the pregnancy. An 'embryo' represents the first 8 weeks of life after which the term 'foetus' is used.

The status of the foetus is a central issue at the heart of the abortion debate and has profound implications for the rights and moral liberties of pregnant women. The moral legitimacy of abortion is questioned by many on the basis of the rapid and unrelenting pace of technological advances in neonatal intensive care medicine, and the ability to keep alive foetuses of less than 24 weeks gestation. The legitimacy of allowing abortion up until birth, in circumstances where there is a substantial risk that a child will be born with physical or mental abnormalities that amount to a serious handicap, has been criticised on the grounds of eugenics.

5.3   Statistics

It is apparent that a great many abortions take place. The Department of Health reports that in the year after the Abortion Act 1967 came into force approximately 50,000 abortions were notified. By 2008 this figure had risen to 195,296, of which 91% were funded by the NHS. In 2009 the total was 189,100 (a reduction of 3.2%) and the highest rates were for women aged 19 and 21 years. In 2009, 94% were funded by the NHS (DoH, 2010b). According to Stauch (2001) a considerable variation exists in the number of abortions performed in different parts of the United Kingdom. Higher rates tend to be found in areas with better family planning provision and higher percentages of women general practitioners, whereas lower rates tend to be found in socially disadvantaged areas. In 2009, 91% of abortions were carried out on pregnancies of less than 13 weeks' duration and 75% took place in the first 10 weeks. A total of 2085 abortions were carried out on the grounds that the child would be born handicapped.

5.4   The ethics of abortion

Abortion is a contentious topic with sharp divisions between those who support women's right to choose (pro-choice) and those who strongly support foetal rights (pro-life). The extent of this divide is graphically illustrated by reports of anti-abortion violence most of which emanate from the United States.

5.4.1   The moral status of the foetus

Philosophers and ethicists have long argued about whether or not the foetus has a moral status, and the extent to which a foetus is a person. Finnis (1973) believes that a foetus is a person from the point of conception and hence ought not to be discriminated against. From this perspective, abortion is always morally wrong.

At the other extreme is the view that the foetus holds no intrinsic value or status until birth. Moral status is dependent upon personhood, and therefore a foetus cannot have moral status since it is not a person. Warren (1973) considers that the central traits of personhood include self-awareness, consciousness and the capacity to feel pain, the ability to reason and carry on self-motivated activity, and the capacity to communicate. Accordingly, a foetus is not a person and therefore cannot have full moral rights. She further argues that even if a foetus is a *potential* person with some *prima facie* right to life, this could not outweigh the woman's right to obtain an abortion since she is an actual person, and the rights of an actual person must always prevail over those of a potential person.

Arguments based upon the moral status of a foetus and justified on personhood criteria can be problematic since on these grounds, children or incapacitated adults might also be classified as 'non-persons'. Certain categories of individuals (such as infants and the comatose) may be able to experience pain but not reason or communicate and could therefore be relegated to the status of 'non-persons'.

A middle ground exists in the form of a 'limited status' position and means that foetal worth rests somewhere between nil and full status. According to this theory, the moral standing of the foetus increases with gestational age until it obtains full status at birth, or shortly beyond. This approach of bestowing the foetus with a level of moral status proportional to gestational age serves as a utilitarian justification for abortion. Moral status is granted to those capable of sentience, and the permissibility of abortion depends upon the distress the act of abortion may inflict upon the foetus. Therefore, abortion is permissible during the earlier stages of gestation, rather than the latter.

According to Singer (1993) one must be sentient (i.e. have consciousness and self-awareness) to be ascribed moral status. Thus, it is only after the foetus is capable of feeling pain, considered to be around 18 weeks, that it has any moral interests. On these grounds, an abortion carried out before 18 weeks will be morally neutral and even after 18 weeks, can still be justified. Although the foetus may have moral status, in terms of proportionality this would be less than that of the pregnant woman. The abortion could be justified in that this would prevent the far greater suffering of the pregnant woman on account of the physical invasiveness of the pregnancy and the degree of self-sacrifice which would be forced upon her if she were compelled to continue with the unwanted pregnancy.

The law is clear that rights are recognised after birth and not before, yet the moral basis for this is obscure. A child has a right to life on being expelled from the uterus and yet has no such right immediately prior to birth. Gillon (2001a) has termed this a 'biological geographical distinction' since a foetus has no right to life if it lies north of a vaginal introitus but has a legally recognised right to life once it has moved south and has (entirely) emerged from the woman's body. Gillon questions the moral basis for attributing this momentous change in foetal moral worth in its transit from inside to outside its mother's body. Yet in England and Wales, and other jurisdictions, it is apparent that a foetus does not share equivalent rights with a born child, including the right to life. One reason for this distinction might be that the moment of birth serves as a practical and legal convenience.

The moral significance of the foetus is one of limited status that is proportionate to gestational age and development. The grounds for therapeutic abortion become more restrictive after 24 weeks and a foetus obtains full legal personality at birth. Prior to implantation, however, the embryo can be destroyed without recourse to the abortion legislation. For these reasons it is convenient to consider the law of abortion in three stages: pre-implantation, implantation to 24 weeks and 24 weeks to birth.

5.4.2 The pregnant woman's right to self-determined choice

The abortion debate is polarised by two competing interests: (a) the moral status of the foetus and its right to life and (b) the pregnant woman's right to terminate the pregnancy on grounds of her autonomous choice. The right to reproductive autonomy, as the decision to reproduce or refrain from procreating, is central to women's rights. The physical and psychological invasiveness of pregnancy upon a woman's body is profound and has implications irrespective of whether it is considered 'high risk' or 'normal' by the medical profession. If a foetus is perceived to have no moral status, the decision to abort is straightforward on ethical grounds. If, however, the foetus is ascribed a limited moral status, at which point should foetal interests that are proportionate to gestational development be allowed to override (if at all) the pregnant woman's right to self-determined choice?

Some commentators look upon the obligation of a woman to carry on with pregnancy as being 'fault based'. They argue that a pregnant woman has run the risk of pregnancy on a voluntary basis (notwithstanding rape) by consenting to sexual intercourse. McDonagh (1999) argues, however, that even though a woman may have consented to sexual intercourse, her consent does not automatically extend to subsequent 'injury' (such as pregnancy). In addition, even where a woman has negligently contributed by creating the risk of a pregnancy, she nonetheless retains a right of self-defence to prevent the foetus from inflicting harm on her body.

Feminist theorists assert that the abortion issue impacts more directly on women than it would ever impact upon men. Judith Thomson asserts that a woman has no moral obligation or duty to carry a foetus (Thomson, 1971). She provides a striking illustration of a person who wakes up one morning to find herself in a hospital bed connected to an unconscious man with kidney disease who is a world famous violinist. The violinist's only hope of survival is to be connected to someone of the same blood type for 9 months and that person is the only individual with that particular blood type. The person has been put in that position after being abducted by the Society of Music Lovers. The central issue concerns whether the person should be compelled to give up his or her liberty for 9 months in order to save the life of the violinist? Thompson asserts: 'Is it morally incumbent on you to accede to this situation? No doubt it would be very nice of you if you did, a great kindness. But do you have to accede to it? What if it were not nine months but nine years? Or longer still?' 'Why should the violinist's right to life (and all persons have a right to life) outweigh one's right to decide what happens in one's own body?' Intuitively, this seems outrageous and Thompson invites us to extend the analogy to a pregnant woman who carries a foetus. Thomson's analogy has been challenged on grounds of consent, that a foetus is not a 'stranger' in the sense that the violinist is, the distinction between killing and letting die, and that the scenario is all too artificial. Singer (1993) adopts a utilitarian stance in that no matter how outraged the person might be at having been kidnapped, if the consequences of disconnection are, on balance, and taking account of all interests of society, worse than the consequences of remaining connected, then the person ought to remain connected. This approach contrasts with an alternative utilitarian perspective, in that it would be of greater utilitarian benefit for the individual to disconnect herself rather than stay connected to the violinist (or foetus). In the context of the morality of abortion, a virtue ethicist would reject abortion where there is no virtuous reason for terminating the pregnancy. However, for practical purposes the law demands some degree of closure.

5.4.3   Human Rights and abortion

In *Paton v British Pregnancy Advisory Service* [1978] 2 All ER 987, it was observed that the foetus could not have rights of its own until it had a separate existence from its mother. On appeal to the European Court of Human Rights it was declared that even if the foetus had a right to life (which the court declined to find) this right would necessarily be constrained where the woman's life was in jeopardy (*Paton v UK* (1980) 3 EHRR 408).

The tragic facts of *Vo v France* (2005) 40 EHRR 12 involved the death of a foetus due to negligence. The European Court of Human Rights decided that there was no consensus on the moral status of the foetus. The foetus was a member of the human race but the extent to which its right to life was protected by Article 2 was indeterminate. The Council of Europe (2008) has reaffirmed its position that abortion must be avoided as far as possible and efforts made to reduce the number of unwanted pregnancies.

Concern was expressed that conditions and restrictions imposed by certain member states meant that some women were discriminated against in accessing safe, affordable and appropriate services. Member states were invited to decriminalise abortion (within reasonable gestational limits) and guarantee access to safe and legal abortion. The Abortion Act 1967 (as amended) does not give women a positive right to abortion and the question arises as to whether this could be challenged under Article 8 of the European Convention of Human Rights. The derogation provided by Article 8 (2) permits State interference with exercise of the right where this is in accordance with the law, necessary in a democratic society, and in order to safeguard interests such as the protection of health and morals, or the rights and freedoms of others. It remains to be seen whether a challenge will be brought.

5.4.4 Rights of others

Abortion debates typically focus on the foetus and pregnant woman. The birth of a baby or a decision to terminate a pregnancy will, however, usually have implications for others such as the potential father, close family and the woman's partner, whether male or female.

One situation is where the potential father wants the pregnant woman to have an abortion against her wishes. In these situations, following birth, the father will retain financial responsibility for the child. Alternatively, the woman may elect for an abortion against the wishes of the potential father. Although the law is relatively clear an abortion could be considered morally wrong since this decision would deny another's rights.

5.4.4(a) Fathers

In *Paton v Trustees of the British Pregnancy Advisory Service* [1979] QB 276, an application for an injunction to prevent an abortion was made by the pregnant woman's husband on behalf of the foetus. The application was rejected by Sir George Baker on grounds that the abortion was lawful (two doctors had given a certificate in good faith) and that the matter was essentially one between the woman and the doctors. The husband had 'no legal right enforceable in law or in equity to stop his wife having this abortion or to stop the doctors from carrying out the abortion'.

Mr Paton argued that he had legal standing to protect the foetus' right to life. The claim that his Article 8 rights of respect for private and family life had been violated was rejected (*Paton v United Kingdom* [1980] 3 EHRR 408). According to the Commission, the pregnant woman's right to private life (under Article 8) prevailed. Interestingly, in an earlier German decision the Commission held that 'Article 8(1) cannot be interpreted as meaning that pregnancy and its termination are, as a principle, solely a matter of the private life of the mother' (*Bruggemann v Germany* [1981] 3 EHRR 244). If this is correct then an interference with the woman's right to private life in this context could be justified on the grounds that this particular aspect of privacy has a shared commonality with the partner. Arguably then a husband or partner should have a say as to whether an abortion ought to take place. Evidently, each case will turn on its facts.

5.4.4(b) Conscientious objection

Section 4 of the Abortion Act 1967 provides that no person will be under a duty to participate in any treatment authorised by the Act, unless performance of an abortion is necessary to save the life or prevent permanent injury to the physical or mental health of a pregnant woman. The decision of *Janaway v Salford AHA* [1989] AC 537 established that the conscientious objection provision in section 4(1) applies to those actually participating in treatment for the purpose of terminating a pregnancy. Mrs Janaway, who held strong anti-abortion views, had been dismissed from her post as secretary at a health centre when she refused to type abortion referral letters. Her challenge against dismissal failed since typing a letter of referral could not be regarded as participating in the termination.

Although a doctor could rely on section 4(1) to avoid performing an abortion, it is unlikely that conscientious objection would extend to a refusal to refer a woman to another clinician. Termination of pregnancy is part of a comprehensive clinical service and by refusing to refer a pregnant woman the doctor might be in breach of contract. A doctor invoking the conscientious objection clause ought to immediately refer the patient if termination of pregnancy is a recognised medical option (*Barr v Matthews* [2000] 52 BMLR 217).

There is, perhaps, a moral argument that a doctor who holds a conscientious objection ought to be able to refuse to refer. However, the utilitarian need to ensure freedom of access to services prevails since the moral judgements of clinicians could detrimentally affect the care of women and ultimately the wider society.

5.4.4(c) Other parties

The Society for the Protection of the Unborn Child (SPUC) is strongly anti-abortion and campaigns on several issues including the protection of human life from conception. This pressure group sought a court injunction to prevent a woman from having one of her twins aborted. It was believed that the woman's request had been prompted by financial difficulties, and SPUC offered her a substantial sum for her to continue with the pregnancy. This information was not passed on by the hospital. SPUC applied to the High Court for an injunction but the abortion had already occurred before the hearing could take place (Sheldon, 1997).

From one perspective, SPUC's success in obtaining an injunction might have had a profound impact upon access to abortion services. Pro-life protagonists, however, might argue differently. Where decisions are based upon factors such as dire financial situations there is certainly an argument that this could certainly operate to constrain freedom of decision making.

5.5 The law

The statutory provisions that pertain to termination of pregnancy is found mainly in sections 58 and 59 of the Offences Against the Person Act 1861, the Abortion Act 1967, the Mental Capacity Act 2005 (for those who lack decision-making capacity) and the common law that assists with the interpretation of statutory provisions. Several unsuccessful attempts have been made to amend the Abortion Act, particularly to reduce the time limit included in section 1(1)(a).

5.5.1 Criminal law

Until the early nineteenth century, abortion was governed by the ecclesiastical courts. It was a criminal offence to carry out an abortion after 'quickening', being the stage at which the woman first became aware of foetal movement at around 16 to 18 weeks. In 1803, Lord Ellenborough's Act put the crime of inducing an abortion of a woman 'quick' with child on a statutory basis. The penalty for inducing an abortion after quickening was death and before quickening was transportation to a penal colony. The death penalty, as well as the 'quickening' distinction, was abolished in 1837.

Most abortions will be an offence under section 58 of the Offences Against the Person Act 1861, unless there is a legally recognised defence. Section 58 provides that:

> Every woman, being with child, who, with intent to procure her own miscarriage, shall unlawfully administer to herself any poison or other noxious thing, or shall unlawfully use any instrument or other means whatsoever with the like intent, and whosoever, with intent to procure the miscarriage of any woman, whether she be or not with child, shall unlawfully administer to her or cause to be taken by her any poison or other noxious thing, or shall unlawfully use any instrument or other means whatsoever with the like intent, shall be guilty of a felony.

A distinction is drawn between a woman who intends to procure her own abortion compared with anyone else. If the woman is charged it must be proved that she was actually pregnant at the time of the offence, which could be difficult to confirm. The *actus reus* of the offence is the unlawful administration of poison, use of an instrument or other noxious thing. Proof that the abortion was caused is not required. The *mens rea* is the intention to cause a miscarriage.

Section 59 provides that 'Whosoever shall unlawfully supply or procure any poison or other noxious thing, or any instrument or thing whatsoever, knowing that the same is intended to be unlawfully used or employed with intent to procure the miscarriage of any woman, whether she be or be not with child, shall be guilty of a misdemeanor ...'

The key elements of these offences are that someone must perform an act with a poison or instrument (or other noxious thing); that there must be an intention to procure a miscarriage; and the poison or instrument is used unlawfully. The term 'unlawfully' is important because it creates an exception for terminations of pregnancy that are undertaken for lawful purposes, such as in order to preserve a pregnant woman's life.

In *R v Bourne* [1939] 1 KB 687, the surgeon was charged with procuring a miscarriage on a 14-year-old who became pregnant following a violent rape. The surgeon's defence was that the abortion was not unlawful, since continuation of the pregnancy would have had a devastating effect on the girl's mental health. McNaughton J (at 694) agreed that the exception provided by the term 'unlawful' not only included imminent danger of death but also the wider health of the pregnant woman. He directed the jury that the words of the statute should be construed in a reasonable sense and that if

> the doctor is of the opinion, on reasonable grounds and with adequate knowledge, that the probable consequence of the continuance of the pregnancy will be to make the woman a physical or mental wreck, the jury are quite entitled to take the view that the doctor who, under those circumstances and in that honest belief, operates, is operating for the purpose of preserving the life of the mother.

Bourne was acquitted and the case established the common law defence that an abortion can be lawfully performed on grounds of necessity, although this has been superseded by the Abortion Act 1967.

5.5.2 Infant Life (Preservation) Act 1929

Section 1(1) of the Infant Life (Preservation) Act 1929 provides that

> any person who, with intent to destroy the life of a child capable of being born alive, by any wilful act causes a child to die before it has an existence independent of its mother, shall be

guilty of felony ... provided that no person shall be found guilty of an offence under this section unless it is proved that the act which caused the death of the child was not done in good faith for the purpose only of preserving the life of the mother.

Section 1(2) clarifies that 'for the purposes of this Act, evidence that a woman had at any material time been pregnant for a period of twenty-eight weeks or more shall be prima facie proof that she was at that time pregnant of a child capable of being born alive'.

The effect of section 1 is that it set a time limit for lawful abortion. Under the Act, it would be an offence to destroy the life of a foetus that might be 'capable of being born alive', with an exception where the abortion is carried out in good faith for the purposes of preserving the life of the mother. At the time that the 1929 Act came into force, it was assumed that the foetus would be capable of being born alive at around 28 weeks. In *Rance v Mid Downs HA* [1991] 1 QB 587, Brooke J held that the meaning of being capable of being born alive was when the foetus could breathe 'through its own lungs alone without deriving any of its living or power of living by or through any connection with its mother'. The 1929 Act is of little significance today and the Abortion Act was amended in 1990 to set a time limit of 24 weeks for abortions carried out on the grounds of section 1(1)(a).

5.5.3 The Abortion Act 1967

The principal purpose of the Abortion Act was to stamp out unsafe and unregulated backstreet abortions that resulted in considerable mortality and morbidity, as opposed to having been enacted to enhance women's reproductive autonomy. The Act provides (limited) statutory defences to the crime of abortion proscribed by sections 58 and 59 of the Offences Against the Person Act 1861. The Act allows lawful abortions to be carried out by medical practitioners, provided that certain statutory criteria are met.

Section 1(1) of the Abortion Act provides that a person shall not be guilty of an offence in undertaking an abortion when the pregnancy is terminated by a registered medical practitioner if two registered medical practitioners are of the opinion formed in good faith:

(a) that the pregnancy has not exceeded its 24th week and that the continuation of the pregnancy would involve risk, greater than if the pregnancy were terminated, of injury to the physical or mental health of the pregnant woman, or any other existing children of her family; or

(b) that the termination is necessary to prevent grave permanent injury to the physical or mental health of the pregnant woman; or

(c) that the continuance of the pregnancy would involve risk to the life of the pregnant woman, greater than if the pregnancy were terminated; or

(d) that there is a substantial risk that if the child were born, it would suffer from physical or mental abnormalities as to be seriously handicapped.

5.5.4 Women who lack capacity

Treatment decisions for those who lack decision-making capacity will depend upon a best interests test, governed by the Mental Capacity Act 2005. In determining whether an abortion is in a woman's best interests account needs to be taken of a range of factors including her values, beliefs and feelings (section 4(6) Mental Capacity Act 2005). Provided that the abortion meets the requirements of the Abortion Act 1967, a judicial declaration of best interests will not automatically be required unless there is doubt as to the capacity or best interests of the woman, there is division amongst health-care professionals as to what lies in the best interests of the patient, where immediate family members, or the foetus' father, object to termination, or if there are other exceptional circumstances. In these situations a declaration should be sought (*D v An NHS Trust (Medical Treatment: Consent: Termination)* [2003] EWHC 2793).

In *Re SS (medical treatment: later termination)* [2002] 1FLR 445, the judge declined to make an order to permit a late-term abortion for a woman who lacked decision-making capacity, even though she repeatedly insisted on an abortion. The pregnancy was at an advanced stage of 24 weeks and Wall J, in balancing the potential detrimental effects of continuing the pregnancy against termination concluded that although the evidence was finely balanced, continuation of pregnancy carried less likelihood of detriment to the applicant, and termination was therefore not in her best interests. He admitted that his decision would have almost certainly have been different had the hearing taken place as soon as the hospital had become aware of the woman's request. This decision has been regarded as troubling with regard to its ethical basis, especially as the woman had fluctuant capacity.

The ethical tension between the moral status of the foetus (and any right to life which flows from this) and the woman's right to self-determination becomes even more acute where the woman is a *Gillick*-competent minor. It would seem that a girl who is under 16, but nonetheless *Gillick*-competent, could give valid consent to an abortion (*R (on the application of Axon) v Secretary of State for Health* [2006] EWHC 37(Admin) (see 6.4.3). Yet in *Re W (a minor)* [1993] Fam 64, Lord Donaldson in *obiter* comments stated that it may be possible (as a matter of law) for an abortion to be carried out on a 16-year-old girl with the consent of her parents, despite her own objection. However, this statement was qualified in that the likelihood of this eventuality was low, unless the abortion was truly in the best interests of the pregnant woman.

For a girl who is not yet *Gillick*-competent, her wishes may be relevant but not decisive. In *Re B (wardship: abortion)* [1991] 2FLR 426, B was aged 12 with normal intelligence and understanding and wanted an abortion. Her decision was supported by her grandparents, with whom she lived (as well as the local authority and her 16-year-old boyfriend). However, her mother, who disapproved of abortion, objected. B was made a ward of court and an application was made to have her pregnancy terminated. The court came to the 'clear conclusion' that termination would be in the girl's best interests. Continuation of the pregnancy would involve risk to B that would be greater in terms of the deleterious effect upon her physical and mental health, than if the pregnancy was terminated. In giving judgement, Hollis J was influenced by two factors. First, the wishes of B which, as he said, were not decisive but were in his view influential. Second, due to B's personal circumstances, it would be impractical for her to keep the baby.

From an ethical perspective, it would seem important to take into account any views expressed by a woman (who lacks capacity) in deciding whether or not an abortion should take place. The Mental Capacity Act 2005 requires this as part of the best interests determination and yet the degree to which such wishes are considered may lead to different outcomes. On the facts of the case, *SS* vociferously demanded an abortion. She had fluctuant capacity (and it is therefore questionable as to whether she expressed these views while she was competent). Notwithstanding this, it was clear that she wanted an abortion. In law, both *SS* and *B* were deemed to lack capacity, yet in one an abortion was obtained and in the other it was not. It seems that other factors, such as possibly the right to life of the foetus (which was 24 weeks in *SS*) and a utilitarian perspective (the impracticality of bringing up a child and the need for arranging an adoption) might have been significant factors.

5.6 Grounds for legal abortion

5.6.1 Risk of physical or mental injury

The overwhelming majority of abortions are undertaken on the grounds of section 1(1)(a) of the Abortion Act 1967 which provides for pregnancy that has not exceeded its 24th week. A woman has no automatic right up until this time and it can be difficult to find a doctor willing to perform an abortion on these grounds after 16 weeks gestation.

Section 1(1)(a) provides two alternative justifications. The first is that continuation of pregnancy would involve risk to the woman's health (greater than if the pregnancy was terminated). The grounds for risk to physical or mental health are wide, and in many instances of an unwanted pregnancy, two doctors might easily come to the conclusion that the anguish created by an unwanted pregnancy would create a greater risk of mental ill health than if the pregnancy were terminated. According to the World Health Organisation, 'health' represents a state of complete physical and mental well-being and not just the absence of disease or infirmity. This means that the health requirement is relatively easy to satisfy. Similarly, on statistical grounds, continuation of a pregnancy represents a greater risk to the health of a woman than an abortion carried out in the first 12 weeks. The second justification involves risk to the existing children of the woman's family. The grounds under section 1(1)(a) are sometimes referred to as the 'social grounds' for abortion.

The 24-week limit has been traditionally linked to the concept of 'viability', being the stage of development after which a foetus could survive outside the uterine environment. However, its continued validity has been questioned on grounds such as the difficulties of ascertaining exact dates of gestation, '4D' visualisation of the foetus, and technological developments in neonatal care that have on occasion allowed foetuses from 21 weeks to survive.

5.6.1(a) Calculation of gestational date

Although section 1(1)(a) is subject to a 24-week limit, no guidance is given for its calculation. By convention, gestational age is calculated from the first day of the woman's last menstrual period, even though the woman would not be pregnant at this time. Ovulation typically occurs 14 days after the first day of the woman's last menstrual period. Fertilisation and implantation, which arguably are processes rather than specific points in time, occur a few days later. For the purpose of the Abortion Act, therefore, the time limit if taken from the first day of the woman's last menstrual period is based upon a fiction. For these reasons borderline cases of ambiguity ought to be construed in favour of the pregnant woman and her doctor.

Some countries have adopted a lesser time limit for abortion on 'social grounds'. The period of gestation in France, Denmark and Germany is up to 12 weeks; in Finland it is up to 16 weeks; and in Sweden an 18-week limit exists. However, these countries tend to emphasise women's rights of access to abortion to a greater degree than in England, Scotland and Wales.

5.6.1(b) In utero images of the foetus

Technological advances (such as sophisticated ultrasound imagery) reveal foetal movements in very great detail at very early stages of pregnancy. Pro-life and pro-choice campaigners have focused strongly on these developments to argue for a reduction in the time limit of abortion. Some of these images appear to show complex movement and animation. Kirklin (2004) suggests that the 'smiling foetus, who appears to coyly smile and then relax its mouth before coyly smiling again, is also an illusion. We do indeed see the foetus draw back its lips but instead of seeing what happens next, the illusion of smiling is created by loop presentation of the images'. In her view, a rapidly changing sequence of images and looped video clips are open to misinterpretation.

Foetal movements, demonstrated by such technology, have evoked strong emotion, and suggestions have been made that this reflects foetal sentience and perception of pain. Nevertheless, there is some consensus that the anatomical structures necessary for the perception of pain are unlikely to be in place before 26 weeks gestation (Lloyd Thomas and Fitzgerald, 1996). Pain is a subjective experience dependent upon a range of factors, predominantly cognitive brain functions, memory and anxiety. Such cognitive brain functions require a certain level of anatomical brain development and therefore the suggestion that pain can be experienced in the early stages of gestation has been rejected. There is, however, a possibility that the foetus might experience pain at a stage earlier than is currently believed by medical science. The ethical and legal implications of an abortion that is undertaken at a time when the foetus is sentient are profound. To address this issue, the Department of Health and the Royal College of Gynaecologists have produced guidelines that relate to all aspects of abortion (including options for gestational bands) (RCOG, 2004).

5.6.1(c) Advances in neonatal care

Neonatal medicine has witnessed enormous advances in recent years to the extent that 22-week-old foetuses have, on occasion, survived. The juxtaposition of these in the context of the time limit in section 1(1)(a) has precipitated considerable moral conflicts and unease for some health professionals.

Wyatt (2001) argues that the establishment of neonatal ICUs are testimony to the belief that even very premature infants who are uniquely vulnerable deserve the very best of care. Professionals have no legal duty to act in unborn foetus' best interests until birth after which the infant is bestowed with the full protection of the law. In terms of morality, the process of birth is arguably devoid of such profound significance. Wyatt's arguments resonate with reality. The concept of viability is obscure, and it is unclear whether this refers to the ability to live (even though the baby, having been born, may die within a few minutes or hours) or perhaps the ability to survive the neonatal period, or even longer. Furthermore, the lower the gestational age at birth, the more viability depends upon the availability of, and access to, sophisticated medical intervention to the extent that its meaning is determined by the environment.

5.6.1(d) Implications of reducing the time limit

Samanta and Healey (2005) suggest that a reduction in the time limit could have profound implications for women and society and will not remove the need for late-term abortion. Amongst these reasons, neonatologists will be under greater pressure to keep alive very premature infants. Resource allocation issues could be particularly acute if infants subsequently developed mental and physical disabilities. Women denied late-term abortion might feel compelled to give their child for adoption or alternatively seek termination in a more liberal jurisdiction, which would inevitably lead to discrimination in favour of those with knowledge and resources at their disposal.

5.6.2 Prevention of grave permanent injury

Section 1(1)(b) of the Abortion Act provides that an abortion can be carried out to prevent the 'grave permanent physical or mental injury' of the pregnant woman. No time limit is included and where serious dangers to the woman's health are apparent, this section may be relied upon up until birth.

The test for grave and permanent injury to the physical or mental health of the pregnant woman is a stringent test to satisfy. Although 'grave and permanent injury' is not defined by the statute, Lord Mackay LC, suggested that this might arise where a woman suffered severe pregnancy-induced hypertension which could lead to permanent kidney, brain or heart damage unless the pregnancy is terminated. Termination of the pregnancy must be 'necessary' and a last resort in that all other possibilities have been considered and a mere 'risk' of grave permanent injury would be insufficient.

5.6.3 Risk to the pregnant woman's life

Section 1(1)(c) permits a lawful abortion if two doctors concur that continuance of the pregnancy would involve risk to the life of the pregnant woman greater than if the pregnancy was terminated. The purpose of the abortion would be to reduce the risk to the woman's life (relative to continuation with the pregnancy), and not necessarily to eradicate the risk entirely. Therefore, an abortion carried out on a pregnant woman with hypertension and renal failure, must reduce the risk from the pregnancy on her life, but not necessarily remove the underlying medical condition that might also pose a threat to her life. Section 1(1)(c) requires greater risk to the woman's life compared with section 1(1)(a). In the Irish Supreme Court decision of *Attorney General v X* [1992] 1 IR 1, Finlay CJ stated that satisfaction of section 1(1)(c) would require evidence of a real and substantial threat to the life, as distinct from the health, of the pregnant woman.

5.6.4 Foetal abnormality

Section 1(1)(d) provides that termination of pregnancy is lawful if two doctors are of the opinion formed in good faith that there is a substantial risk that if the infant is born it will be seriously handicapped due to physical or mental abnormalities. This ground applies until birth and is relied upon in approximately 1% of abortions. Advances in medical technologies, such as amniocentesis and chorionic villous sampling, means that genetic profiles that are causative or indicative of disease susceptibility can be identified before birth.

5.6.4(a) Interpretation of the grounds of foetal abnormality

Interpretation of the factors 'substantial risk' and 'seriously handicapped' can be a difficult and potentially imprecise medical judgement. Proof of certainty is not required. Guidance of the Royal College of Obstetricians and Gynaecologists (RCOG) 2010 suggests that consideration is given to the following factors when reaching a decision:

(a) the potential for effective treatment, either in the uterus or after birth;
(b) the infant's probable degree of self-awareness and ability to communicate with others;
(c) the suffering that could be experienced;
(d) the extent to which actions performed by individuals without disabilities that are essential for health, would have to be provided by others;
(e) the probability of being able to live alone and be self-supportive as an adult.

Not all of these factors will be relevant in every situation and an authoritative definition of 'seriously handicapped' has not been provided. In *Jepson v The Chief Constable of West Mercia Police Constabulary* [2003] EWHC 3318, the question was raised as to what might constitute a serious handicap sufficient for section 1(1)(d) to apply. Reverend Joanna Jepson asked the West Mercia police to investigate the circumstances of an abortion carried out on a 28-week foetus with bilateral cleft lip and palate. She argued that the 1990 amendments to the Abortion Act had intended that late abortions would only be justified for more serious conditions than cleft lip and palate. Jepson was granted leave to apply for judicial review after the police decided not to prosecute whereupon the case was reopened. The Crown Prosecution Service concluded that the doctors had formed their opinion in good faith that the child would be seriously handicapped and that there was insufficient evidence for a realistic prospect of conviction.

It is relatively straightforward to justify an abortion on these grounds where a serious handicap at birth can be predicted with reasonable certainty. Decisions are more complex for late onset conditions such as Huntington's disease that is likely to materialise in adulthood. Prenatal genetic diagnosis may reveal genetic susceptibility to a condition that may, or may not, materialise in the future which raises disturbing questions as to whether a foetus ought to be aborted.

5.6.4(b) Ethical issues

Termination of pregnancy on grounds of foetal abnormality is controversial and has generated considerable discussion amongst commentators. Parents typically look forward to the birth of a perfect baby, and social and cultural factors often contribute to this expectation. If the foetus is potentially disabled, then this is outside the accepted norm and an abortion may be sought. According to Vehmas (2002), it is ethically unacceptable for a woman to reject a particular foetus on the grounds of negative characteristics, once she has made a decision to have a baby.

A further ethical issue arises from the fact that the foetal abnormality ground provides less protection for a 'seriously handicapped' unborn child when compared to one that is non-handicapped. From this perspective the law discriminates against foetuses at substantial risk of a serious handicap with those that are unaffected. On moral grounds there is a strong argument that no distinction should be drawn. Public opinion polls tend to suggest that abortion is more acceptable where there is evidence of serious disability. Three arguments have been proposed to support termination on grounds of foetal abnormality: foetal interests, replacement arguments and parental interests. The foetal argument is based on the notion that not being born would be best for the child in that it will prevent a life of suffering. However, this argument is likely to be persuasive in very few situations of where a child will have a negative quality of life (e.g. an infant with Tay-Sachs) since in many circumstances there would seem to be arguments that most lives have some positive qualities and are therefore worth living. A more prevalent genetic condition is that of Down's syndrome which is diagnosed on routine ante-natal testing. Termination may be offered on grounds of section 1(1)(d) even though those with the condition may lead happy and positive lives. For other conditions that may provide grounds for an abortion under section 1(1)(d), such as the mucopolysaccharidoses, the child may have a markedly reduced quality of life, yet in many instances it may nonetheless be positive and a life worth living. Arguably this section of the Abortion Act does not align with established case law of newborn infants. In *Re B (A minor) (Wardship: Medical Treatment)* [1981] 1 WLR 1421, the court held that it would be unlawful to withhold life-sustaining treatment from an infant with Down's syndrome since there was no evidence that it was in the child's best interests to die.

According to the replacement argument, one utilitarian perspective is that abortion of a disabled foetus is not wrong if it can be replaced by a non-afflicted one, since this offsets the loss of a foetus likely to have an afflicted life with another with greater prospects (Savulescu, 2001). Such arguments are premised on the assumption that non-handicapped life is expected to contribute to greater happiness in society, which is certainly a contentious premise.

The third, and arguably the most persuasive, ethical justification for termination of pregnancy carried out on these grounds is that it primarily protects the interests of the woman and her partner. Raising a child with physical or cognitive impairments, particularly where this is severe, is likely to be more costly and difficult. The most vociferous objection to this argument is based upon discrimination. Many of the difficulties experienced by mothers are on account of hostile societal factors rather that the child's disabilities *per se*.

Lucy was considering a selective reduction of pregnancy at 24 weeks, calculated from the date of implantation.

- Section 1(1)(a) of the Abortion Act is subject to a 24-week limit although no guidance is given for its calculation. Lucy is aware of the date of implantation and arguably this would be more accurate than in many other situations. What alternative date calculations could be made? What are the implications, if any?
- If Lucy had decided to go ahead with an abortion, which grounds, if any, might be satisfied?

5.7   Selective reduction

Multiple pregnancies are a risk to the health of the pregnant woman and the foetuses. This risk can be lessened by 'selective reduction' which is the termination of one or more foetuses of a multiple pregnancy. The procedure can also be carried out where there is a substantial risk of a serious handicap in one or more of the foetuses. It is a complex procedure that may involve injection of potassium chloride into the amniotic sac, or the heart of the foetus, and has been made possible by specific advances in ultrasonography. The foetus can be expelled after death, or alternatively its remains are expelled on delivery.

Prior to April 1991 it was not clear whether the abortion legislation covered selective termination. Section 58 of the Offences Against the Person Act 1861 pertains to the criminal offence of procuring a miscarriage, to which the abortion legislation provides a defence in certain circumstances. However, if the foetus is not expelled following selective reduction then it is arguable that no miscarriage has occurred. A further complication is that following selective reduction, the woman remains pregnant in that one or more live foetuses are retained following the procedure, which means that the abortion legislation could arguably not provide a defence to the potential crime of section 58. Following amendment of the Abortion Act 1967 by section 37(5) of the Human Fertilisation and Embryology Act 1990, section 5(2) of the Abortion Act states:

> For the purposes of the law relating to abortion, anything done with intent to procure a woman's miscarriage (or, in the case of a woman carrying more than one foetus, her miscarriage

of any foetus) is unlawfully done unless authorised by section 1 of this Act and, in the case of a woman carrying more than one foetus, anything done with intent to procure a miscarriage of any foetus is authorised by that section if –

(a) the ground for termination of the pregnancy specified in Subsection (1) (d) of that section applies in relation to any foetus and the thing is done for the purpose of procuring a miscarriage of that foetus, or

(b) any of the other grounds for termination of the pregnancy specified in that section applies.

Application of the grounds in section 5(2) are unproblematic except where a non-handicapped foetus is terminated in order to improve the chance of survival of the remainder. In these circumstances an abortion would be lawful by application of section 1(1)(a) of the Act, if the requirements are satisfied and the focus is on averting the risk to the woman's mental and physical health.

> The couple were devastated to hear the news that prenatal screening had revealed potentially serious conditions.
>
> ▶ What are the ethical and legal issues that pertain to selective reduction of pregnancy?

5.8 The living abortus

In the majority of abortions, at the time the procedure is performed the foetus is incapable of surviving outside the woman's body and hence dies immediately on removal. Rarely, however, the foetus may survive as a living abortus. The abortion legislation is silent on this point and in theory killing a living abortus could amount to manslaughter or even murder. To avoid this situation, efforts are made to ensure that the foetus is killed prior to removal in pregnancies of a gestational age of 21 weeks 6 days or more.

The ethical dilemma here is that a living abortus represents a premature unwanted infant and a tension arises with respect to the justification for ensuring that the foetus is dead. Advances in neonatal medicine mean that some extremely premature infants are capable of surviving. Generally the foetus' lungs remain solid until about 21 weeks gestation and until this time breathing outside the uterine environment is impossible. The only means of survival would be for the living foetus to be matured in an artificial uterus. If this was possible, it would be questionable as to whether abortion could be justified on its current grounds. Although a woman might have the right to remove the foetus she might not have the right to bring about its death, a situation that resounds with Judith Jarvis-Thompson's violinist scenario.

According to Jackson (2008) ectogenesis would create ambiguity for the meaning of viability. If a foetus could be transplanted to an artificial nurturing environment at a certain time in its gestational age, then an abortion after that point would not be legitimate. If transfer was carried out immediately following fertilisation, then it is doubtful whether an abortion could ever be lawfully undertaken.

5.9 Contraception

Pregnancy occurs when the fertilised ovum implants in the woman's uterus, which is normally a few days (usually six) after fertilisation. Around 75% of fertilised eggs fail to implant and are lost. This situation is not a miscarriage since a miscarriage occurs only after implantation. There is no statutory definition of miscarriage, and for the purposes of the law it is taken in its ordinary and natural sense. In *R v Dhingra* (unreported, 25 January 1991), a doctor was charged under the Offences Against the Person Act 1861 after fitting a woman with an intrauterine contraceptive device (IUD) 11 days after having sexual relations with her. On the evidence, the judge held that at the time of fitting the intrauterine device, there could not have been a miscarriage and therefore no offence had been committed.

A post-coital contraceptive pill (the morning after pill) can prevent a fertilised egg from implanting into the uterus. In *R (on the application of Smeeton) v Secretary of State for Health* [2002] EWCA 610, SPUC sought to challenge regulations that were introduced to allow the morning after pill to be dispensed by pharmacists. The SPUC's argument was that the pill is an abortive agent and in dispensing this, as well as taking this, offences would be committed under the 1861 Act. Munby J rejected SPUC's claim, stating that miscarriage should be interpreted in its ordinary sense. Some other contraceptives, such as intra-uterine contraceptive devices that also work by inhibiting implantation of the fertilised egg, would have to be rejected since these might involve the commission of a criminal offence. He noted that if this argument applied to all forms of contraception (except use of a condom), then preventing implantation of a fertilised egg meant that around 34% of all women between the ages of 16 and 49 in Great Britain would potentially be guilty of an offence.

Smeeton is now settled law. Keown (2005) has criticised the decision on the basis that no clear consensus exists as to exactly when fertilisation occurs. Furthermore, Munby J, in arriving at his decision, placed far too much emphasis on the potential negative social consequences of making a finding that the morning after pill is an abortive agent.

B Liability for negligent prenatal occurrences

5.10 Introduction

Liability for negligent prenatal occurrences is perhaps best considered as a reproductive or pregnancy-related tort. Actions may be brought by (or on behalf of) a live-born infant or the parents of the child. Parental actions include wrongful conception and wrongful birth. Actions by (or for) the child include prenatal injury and wrongful life.

Wrongful conception actions encompass those situations where parents have lost the opportunity to avoid a pregnancy. A typical example is where a negligently performed sterilisation or vasectomy procedure precedes an unplanned birth. Wrongful conception actions also extend to those situations where pregnancy is sought but the parents have lost the opportunity to have the 'right' pregnancy due to third party negligence. This could occur, for example, during *in vitro* fertilisation following implantation of the 'wrong' embryo. In wrongful conception actions, the losses claimed are for the cost of the unwanted pregnancy and its consequences.

Wrongful birth actions involve a claim on the grounds of the defendant's negligence. These actions include those situations where parents have been deprived of the opportunity to lawfully terminate a pregnancy. A typical example might be where a negligently performed diagnostic ante-natal test (such as an ultrasound scan) fails to detect foetal abnormality. In these circumstances, and where there is evidence that the woman would have sought a lawful abortion, the claim is that the woman was denied the opportunity to terminate the pregnancy due to the negligence of the defendant. In wrongful birth actions, the loss claimed is the cost of the unwanted birth and its consequences.

Kennedy and Grubb (2000) classify wrongful conception as prenatal negligence leading to the birth of a healthy infant, whereas wrongful birth is prenatal negligence leading to the birth of a disabled child. Claims for wrongful conception and wrongful birth include unwanted pregnancies (caused by frustration of parental wishes not to have further children or at least not to have a child at that particular time) or an unwanted birth (e.g. due to an undiagnosed congenital abnormality). The key elements of both actions are prenatal negligence and an unwanted pregnancy or birth. Damages are claimed for that pregnancy, or birth, and consequential losses.

Actions brought by (or on behalf of) the child include prenatal injury actions and wrongful life actions. Prenatal injury actions are brought following a negligent act or omission that occurred before birth and which lead to an injury. The negligent act or omission may have taken place prior to conception, or during pregnancy. Examples include negligent failure to offer contraception (an occurrence before conception), negligent selection of an embryo during *in vitro* fertilisation (an occurrence before implantation), negligent prescription during pregnancy (an occurrence before birth) or negligent delivery (an occurrence during birth).

A wrongful life action is a claim of the child that 'but for' the defendant's negligence, he or she would not have been conceived or born. Claims may relate to situations where negligence occurred prior to conception, implantation or gestation. In a wrongful life action it is claimed that 'but for' the negligence, the wrongful life of that particular child would have been avoided.

5.11 Terminology

The terminology surrounding actions following prenatal negligence can be confusing. Kennedy and Grubb (2000) stress that wrongful birth claims must include the child that is born disabled as a consequence of prenatal negligence. At times the label 'wrongful birth' is used to encompass 'wrongful conception,' and the phrase 'wrongful life' seems to suggest that the claim is to impugn life itself. Distinctions between wrongful birth and conception are founded on different factual bases for the purposes of quantifying damages.

According to Teff (1985b at 425),

> These labels are unfortunate not least in their bizarre, even macabre, overtones…This aside, the terms are neither immediately intelligible nor readily distinguishable from each other. (Although they) signify claims for damages when negligent conduct has resulted in a child being born, they conceal a host of different legal and social implications, depending both on the circumstances leading up to the birth and on its consequences. Thus, both 'wrongful life', 'wrongful birth' and other expressions canvassed by courts and commentators are potentially a source of considerable confusion.

From a conceptual perspective we suggest categorisation of these actions on the basis that some form of prenatal negligence has led to a negative outcome with respect to the pregnancy, which is the foundation of the claim. Thus, the possible options are

(a) Prenatal negligence leading to an unwanted conception
(b) Prenatal negligence leading to an unwanted birth

(c) Prenatal negligence leading to injuries sustained before or at birth
(d) Prenatal negligence leading to impairment in the life of the child

In the above taxonomy, (a) corresponds to 'wrongful conception' and (b) to 'wrongful birth'. Both (a) and (b) are actions brought by parents. However, (c) corresponds to 'prenatal injury' and (d) to 'wrongful life'. Both (c) and (d) are actions brought by (or on behalf of) the child.

5.12 Prenatal negligence leading to unwanted conception (wrongful conception actions)

A wrongful conception action can be brought in tort (usually) or in contract (rarely). In the case of a sterilisation procedure carried out in the private sector, the claimant would have a contract with the private health-care provider (unless the procedure was undertaken as part of an NHS contract). The duty to exercise reasonable care in carrying out the procedure is an implied term incorporated in contract, but there is no implied warranty that sterility will be achieved. In *Eyre v Measday* [1986] 1 All ER 488, the court was not persuaded that the doctor's statement that male and female sterilisation procedures were irreversible, amounted to a guarantee that sterility would be achieved. The Court of Appeal took a similar approach in *Thake v Maurice* [1986] QB 644 in rejecting a claim for breach of warranty.

An action may be brought in tort provided that the requirements of a negligence action (existence of a duty of care, breach of duty and causation) are satisfied. Without doubt, a duty of care would be owed to the patient undergoing a sterilisation procedure, but the extent to which that duty extends to the patient's partner is less apparent. In *Goodwill v British Pregnancy Advisory Service* [1996] 1 WLR 1397, a man's vasectomy spontaneously reversed and his partner became pregnant. She sued the defendant for loss of income and costs for raising the child on the grounds that the defendants owed her a duty of care. The claim was struck out by the Court of Appeal. A duty of care would extend to the partner if that person was within the contemplation of the doctor at the time that the procedure was carried out. This would be reasonable if that person was the patient's partner at the time the procedure was carried out. This was not, however, the situation in *Goodwill*.

A breach of duty might occur if the doctor fails to warn the patient of the (small) risk of reversal following the procedure. This occurred following a vasectomy in *Newell v Goldenberg* [1995] 6 Med LR. However, *Newell* is an old case and clear clinical guidelines now exist with regard to male and female sterilisations which require full and frank disclosure of the risk that the procedure might fail. It therefore seems likely that nowadays an action for failure to warn would be settled out of court.

The third hurdle for the claimant is to prove causation, which can be problematic since conception is caused by sexual intercourse rather than a failed sterilisation. Having unprotected sex would not amount to a new act that breaks the chain of causation, unless the claimant is aware that the sterilisation procedure has failed (*Sabri-Tabrizi v Lothian Health Board* [1998] BMLR 190).

What losses can be compensated for pregnancy and childbirth? Normally these are not regarded as injuries but since pregnancy and childbirth represent risks to health and can be painful, compensation can be sought. An unwanted conception following negligent advice or a negligent sterilisation procedure would be regarded as an impairment suffered by the patient. As Auld LJ stated in *Walkin v South Manchester Health Authority* [1995] 1 WLR 1543 at 1550, 'it seems to me that the unwanted conception, whether as a result of negligent advice or negligent surgery, was a personal injury ... The resultant physical change in her body resulting from conception was an unwanted condition which she had sought to avoid by undergoing the sterilisation operation'. In the situation where a woman carries a pregnancy, compensation can be sought. However, if she terminates the pregnancy, then any claim would be for the cost of the abortion together with a relatively small award for pain and suffering.

5.13 Prenatal negligence leading to unwanted birth (wrongful birth actions)

Claims for wrongful birth are brought by parents of the unwanted child. They cannot be brought by siblings or more remote relatives. These claims can be complicated by application of the Limitation Act 1980.

5.13.1 Birth of a healthy child

The law in this area is now settled following the House of Lords decision in *McFarlane v Tayside Health Board* [2000] 2 AC 59 (see 5.13.1(a)) although prior to *McFarlane* the courts were divided on this issue. In *Udale v Bloomsbury Area Health Authority* [1983] 2 All ER 522, the costs for bringing up a healthy child were not recoverable, although damages for the pain and inconvenience of the pregnancy and childbirth were allowed. The reverse occurred in *Emeh v Kensington and Chelsea and Westminster AHA* [1985] QB 1012 where the Court of Appeal allowed the costs of raising a child and damages for the child's private education. *Emeh* has been overruled by *McFarlane*.

5.13.1(a) McFarlane v Tayside Health Board

Mr McFarlane had a vasectomy following the birth of his fourth child. He was negligently informed that his sperm count was negative, following which Mrs McFarlane became pregnant. The couple brought an action for damages. The majority in the House of Lords allowed Mrs McFarlane to recover general damages for pain and inconvenience of pregnancy and the birth, as well as the financial losses directly attributable to those events (Lord Millett dissenting). The House was, however, unanimous in rejecting the couple's pure economic loss claim for the costs of raising the child.

Lord Steyn's reasons for rejecting the claim were based on distributive justice. In his view the claim would not satisfy the requirements of being fair, just and reasonable since, in his view, if a commuter on the Underground was asked whether compensation equivalent to the cost of bringing up the child until about 18 years should be awarded, the answer would be in the negative. He went on to state (at 81) that

> to explain decisions denying a remedy for the cost of bringing up an unwanted child by saying that there is no loss, no foreseeable loss, no causative link or no ground for reasonable restitution is to resort to unrealistic and formalistic propositions which mask the real reasons for the decision. ...It is my firm conviction that where courts of law have denied a remedy for the cost of bringing up an unwanted child the real reasons have been grounds of distributive justice. That is, of course, a moral theory.

Lord Millett also based his reasoning for rejecting the McFarlane's claim for pure economic loss on moral grounds. He stated that 'There is something distasteful, if not morally offensive, in treating the birth of a normal, healthy child as a matter for compensation. ... In my opinion the law must take the birth of a normal, healthy baby to be a blessing, not a detriment'. In his view, such blessings came with the balance of joy, sorrow and responsibility, and society should regard the birth of a healthy child as beneficial since it would be repugnant to do otherwise. Lords Hope, Clyde and Slynn while expressing themselves in slightly different language nevertheless held that allowing the pursuers to recover economic loss would not be resonant with morality and societal benefit. It would not be fair, just or reasonable to impose the cost of bringing up a child on the negligent clinician. Lord Hope stated that if economic recovery was to be allowed, then 'the pursuers would be paid far too much. They would be relieved of the cost of rearing the child. They would not be giving anything back to the wrongdoer for the benefits ... The logical conclusion, as a matter of law, is that the costs to the pursuers of meeting their obligations to the child during her childhood are not recoverable as damages'. Likewise, in Lord Clyde's view, allowing the pursuers to have the child maintained free of any cost would not align with restitution or an award of damages that would do justice between the parties concerned.

The judgement in *McFarlane* is interesting since on principles of tort there is no reason why economic loss associated with the upbringing of a child should not be recoverable. Yet *McFarlane* blocks this approach principally on grounds of legal policy and the moral acceptability of recovering damages for the costs of raising a healthy child.

5.13.2 Birth of a disabled child

The decision of *McFarlane* is restricted to actionable negligence claims that result in the birth of a healthy child. In *Parkinson v St James and Seacroft University Hospital NHS Trust* [2001] EWCA Civ 113, the Court of Appeal had to consider whether the *McFarlane* principle applied if the child was born disabled. The claim arose following a negligently performed sterilisation operation, following which Mrs Parkinson became pregnant with her fifth child. The couple was already in very strained financial circumstances. The child had significant disabilities that were mainly behavioural in characteristic, although it was accepted that the defendant's breach had not caused the disability. Mrs Parkinson brought a successful action to recover the costs incurred for providing for the child's special needs.

There are at least three relevant issues to be considered: first, the extent to which *Parkinson* can be distinguished from *McFarlane*; second, what constitutes disability; and third, the disability must be a foreseeable consequence of the defendant's negligence.

In *McFarlane* the court dealt with the normal birth of a healthy child and *dicta* suggested that the outcome could have been different in the case of an unwanted child born with a serious disability. In *McFarlane* the benefits of the child's existence had to be balanced against the costs. There is certainly an argument that this ought to be the same irrespective of a child's disabilities since a disabled child will also bring love, pleasure, affection and joy. The approach of the Court of Appeal was not that the life of a disabled child was less valuable, but simply that disabled children cost more. Brooke LJ stated that 'it would not be fair, just and reasonable to award compensation which went further than the extra expenses associated with bringing up a child with a significant disability'. On the principles of distributive justice, ordinary people would consider the law fair to make an award provided that this was limited to the extra expenses incurred that were incumbent upon the disability. A similar view was shared by Hale LJ who felt that whatever the reasonable commuter on the Underground might think of the claim of Mrs McFarlane, it might not be considered unfair or disproportionate if the person who had negligently failed to prevent a further pregnancy was held responsible for the extra costs of caring and bringing up a disabled child. Thus, while the Court of Appeal was bound by *McFarlane*, and the moral basis of its reasoning, it focused on the additional costs associated with the raising of a child with a disability. The law thereby distinguishes between the needs of the ordinary child and the special needs of a disabled child.

Disability was determined by reference to the definition provided by section 17(11) of the Children Act 1989. For these purposes 'a child is disabled if he is blind, deaf or dumb, or suffers from a mental disorder of any kind or is substantially and permanently handicapped by illness, injury or congenital deformity or such other disability as may be prescribed'. In effect, the child's disability has to be of a certain level of seriousness before extra costs are recoverable and minor defects or inconveniences would be excluded. It seems likely that a future court will have to consider the parameters of the concept of 'significant' disability for these purposes.

The Court of Appeal stressed that the disability of the child must be a foreseeable consequence of the negligence. In *Parkinson* the negligence did not cause the behavioural disorder that was the subject of the disability. The child who was conceived just happened to be disabled. However, since there is inevitably some risk that a child will be born with a congenital abnormality, the birth of a disabled child in *Parkinson* was considered a foreseeable consequence of the negligent sterilisation procedure.

> The embryos of Steve and Lucy had negligently not been screened for cystic fibrosis or Down's syndrome.
>
> ▶ What possible actions could be brought by Lucy and Steve? Are these likely to be successful?
> ▶ What possible actions (if any) could be brought on behalf of the twins? Are these likely to be successful?

5.13.2(a) Disability in the neonate

In *Parkinson*, Hale LJ stated that a disability arising from genetic causes or foreseeable events during pregnancy (such as rubella, spina bifida or oxygen deprivation) up until a child is born alive and which has not been caused by an intervening act would be sufficient to found a claim for compensation. The key phrase here is 'up until the child is born alive' which provides a bright line point. However, to what extent could a claim be successful if a child becomes disabled following birth? This was the central issue in *Groom v Selby* [2001] EWCA Civ 1522.

The claimant unwittingly underwent a sterilisation procedure during the very early stages of her pregnancy. Subsequently, and despite reporting symptoms, the pregnancy was not diagnosed until around 13 weeks, following which and after seeing the ultrasound scan, she refused an abortion. It was established that failure to carry out a pregnancy test was a negligent omission that had deprived the woman of the opportunity to terminate the pregnancy. The apparently healthy infant was born 3 weeks premature but 1 month later developed meningitis and frontal brain abscesses. At first instance, the court held that the claimant could recover the costs attributable to raising a disabled child according to *Parkinson*. The defendant's appeal that *McFarlane* ought to apply since the child had appeared healthy at birth was dismissed. The infant's prematurity made her particularly susceptible to meningitis caused by exposure to the bacterium during the process of birth, and the condition had not been caused by any intervening act. In *Parkinson*, Brooke LJ and Hale LJ concurred that the source of the disability must be genetic or have arisen from some intrauterine process before birth. Although many newborns are exposed to bacteria and do not succumb to serious infections, in *Groom* the court considered that the prematurity of the infant had caused its susceptibility to infection. This represented an unbroken chain of causation from the deprivation of the opportunity to abort a foetus, this opportunity being lost by the failure to diagnose the pregnancy at an early stage.

There are at least two important aspects to this decision. First, the infant had been born healthy and on a strict rule of principle, it seems that *McFarlane* ought to apply. Yet, in applying *Parkinson*, the Court of Appeal demonstrates a judicial sympathy towards the claimant with respect to meeting the additional costs likely to be incurred in raising a disabled child. Second, and possibly more problematic, is the view of Hale LJ and Brookes LJ that *Parkinson* also applies to disability caused by an event at birth, and Hale LJ specifically gave the example of oxygen deprivation. The difficulty here is that if this cannot be attributed to the negligence of any second actor, then liability will fall to the first, namely the doctor whose negligence during the prenatal period (e.g. negligent sterilisation or failure to diagnose pregnancy) led to the birth of the unwanted child. An action for brain damage caused by hypoxia at birth can result in a very large claim. On this principle, the practitioner responsible for the index, and perhaps relatively minor, negligent act or omission during the prenatal period could be liable for the additional costs of raising a disabled child, which could be substantial.

5.13.3 The healthy infant born to a disabled mother

Rees v Darlington Memorial Hospital NHS Trust [2003] UKHL 52 concerned a severely visually impaired woman who gave birth to an unwanted healthy infant. Mrs Rees had decided to undergo sterilisation out of concern that she would be unable to adequately care for an infant. The procedure was negligently performed and she later gave birth to a healthy child. The case was appealed to the House of Lords where a bare majority (4:3) rejected her claim with respect to the extra costs for the child (as occasioned by the claimant's disability). She was awarded a conventional sum of £15,000 in recognition of the pain and harm that she suffered.

Rees is an interesting decision in that it adds a gloss to *McFarlane*. The *McFarlane* principle is that no additional costs can be recovered for the birth of a healthy child (resulting from prenatal negligence). The reasoning in *McFarlane* was that the birth of a healthy baby was a blessing and that it would be contrary to public morality to compensate the birth of a healthy child since the parents would experience an incalculable benefit in raising the child. It would be contrary to public policy and the child's parents would be unjustly enriched if all costs for child maintenance were deflected onto the NHS. *McFarlane* has been criticised because it is an exception to the ordinary principles of tort law upon which a claimant should be able to recover the reasonably foreseeable consequences of a doctor's negligence. This compensation would include costs that might be associated with the child's upbringing. However, the gloss that *Rees* adds to *McFarlane* is with respect to the modest 'conventional award' which offers some recognition of the harm that the parent has suffered. *Rees* and *McFarlane* do not sit comfortably together in matters of principle. *McFarlane* represents a clear divergence and exception to tort-based principles. *Rees* is positioned somewhere between the spectrum of recoverable loss on tort principles and *McFarlane*. Lord Steyn (in *Rees*) stated that there was no precedent to make a conventional award and that it was contrary to principle. One explanation for the decision in *Rees* to award a conventional award might be the desire of their Lordships to provide some redress to the parent of a child born as a result of prenatal negligence while not opening the floodgates to the huge costs that might be incurred towards the maintenance of such children.

5.13.4 Should parents be allowed to bring actions?

Fundamental legal and ethical arguments underpin the desirability, or otherwise, of allowing parental redress following the birth of a child, in circumstances where this has been actively avoided and is the result of prenatal negligence.

5.13.4(a) Ethical issues

Prenatal negligence that precedes the birth of an undesired child has the effect of constraining the autonomous decision making of the mother or couple concerned, by depriving them of the opportunity to avoid having a child at a particular point in time. In prenatal negligence situations, the very thing that the claimant sought to avoid actually occurs. For these reasons, from an ethical perspective, failure to award adequate and fair compensation amounts to a denial of individual rights. In *Rees v Darlington Memorial Hospital NHS Trust* [2003] UKHL 52 (at para 70), Lord Millett recognised this in his statement that

> I still regard the proper outcome in all these cases is to award the parents a modest conventional sum by way of general damages, not for the birth of the child, but for the denial of an important aspect of their personal autonomy namely the right to limit the size of their family. This is an important aspect of human dignity, which is increasingly being regarded as an important human right which should be protected by law.

5.13.4(b) The McFarlane rule

The *McFarlane* rule, whereby parents cannot recover damages for the raising of a child born as a result of prenatal negligence, represents an exception to general tort principles. In respect of recovery for pure economic loss, the tests in *Caparo v Dickman* (1990) 2 AC 651 are applied:

(a) the loss should be foreseeable;
(b) there should be a relationship of proximity between the doctor and the patient;
(c) it should be fair, just and reasonable to impose a duty of care in these circumstances.

In *McFarlane*, the birth of the child and the costs of upbringing were foreseeable consequences of the negligent advice that Mr McFarlane received following his vasectomy. Mrs McFarlane herself was not a patient but clearly she was in a sufficiently proximate relationship such that she would be detrimentally affected by the negligent advice. It was on the third limb of the test that the House of Lords felt that it would not be fair, just or reasonable to impose liability on the defendant for the upbringing of a healthy infant.

Several reasons were given for the determination. It was felt that a child was a blessing and that the raising of a child would undoubtedly confer certain benefits. If the claimant was to be allowed to recover damages, then the value of these benefits would need to be offset, which would be an impossible exercise to calculate in monetary terms. The computation would require offsetting a pure economic loss (the costs of raising the child) against the emotional benefit of having that child, a seemingly impossible task to achieve. Furthermore, the very notion of being able to recover in damages for the birth of a healthy child was intuitively wrong. If this was the case, it would have to be a matter of public instinct and Lord Steyn appealed (metaphorically) to the reasonable commuter on the London Underground to canvass public opinion. There was also concern that the potential size of such a claim might be disproportionate to the degree of fault of the wrongdoer. As a matter of policy there was an underlying concern that allowing the claim might open the floodgates, putting further pressure on an already financially strained NHS.

It is interesting that the Court of Appeal adopted a 'moral wrongfulness' approach in determining and awarding the additional costs incurred in raising a child with disabilities. From a moral perspective, a disabled child also brings emotional benefits and drawing a distinction between a normal and a disabled child could be viewed as pejorative. *Dicta* from the House of Lords in *Rees* indicates that *Parkinson* was viewed by their Lordships with some disfavour, and only a bare majority considered *Parkinson* to be good law.

Lord Scott's analysis (in *Rees*) on the distinction between a disabled and a healthy child is of interest. In his view, a distinction must be drawn between the situation where the parents seek advice or services to avoid the conception of a child with a disability (where there is an above-average likelihood of such an occurrence), and where such services are sought simply to avoid conception (as in *Parkinson*). Thus, the distinction drawn was not between a healthy child and a disabled child who is born as a matter of chance, but between a child and another who may have an undesired characteristic or trait, the likelihood of which is already known. On the face of it, this approach seems to be morally more appropriate. It is arguable, however, that parents faced with an undesired child born with a disability (which has occurred purely by chance) are at a greater disadvantage because at best only the cost of bringing up a child was within their contemplation, and not one with a disability.

The recent case of *Farraj v King's Healthcare NHS Trust and Cytogenic DNA Services Ltd (2008)* was a 'wrongful birth' claim that followed the birth of an infant who suffers beta-thalassaemia major, due to the negligent failure to detect the condition on ante-natal testing. The DNA sample was sent to an independent laboratory for culturing, afterwhich the sample was wrongly reported as negative. The claimant's case was that she had been denied the opportunity to have an abortion. At first instance, the judge apportioned liability between the Trust and laboratory. The Court of Appeal allowed the appeal and held the laboratory as 100% liable for the damages and costs of the action. The claimant's cross appeal that the Trust owed them a non-delegable duty of care was rejected on account of the specific facts of the case (see 3.2.4).

5.13.4(c) Other jurisdictions

In *Cattanach v Melchior* [2003] HCA 38, the High Court of Australia dealt with a case with strikingly similar facts to *McFarlane*. The *McFarlane* decision was not followed and in giving judgement, the court was clear that the expenses incurred by the parents arose as a result of the negligent medical advice they received and that there were definite grounds for an award of damages for economic loss.

The *McFarlane* judgement was criticised on the basis that it was a moral assessment concealed in an inarticulate premise dressed up as legal principle and that 'Neither the invocation of Scripture nor the invention of a fictitious oracle on the Underground...authorises a Court of law to depart from the ordinary principles governing the recovery of damages for the tort of negligence'. The court also considered that although calculation of compensation might be difficult it was relatively straightforward in comparison with other judicial exercises.

5.14 Prenatal negligence resulting in injuries sustained before birth

A claim based upon prenatal negligence that results in injuries sustained before birth can be brought by (or on behalf of) the child. The Congenital Disabilities (Civil Liability) Act 1976 ('the 1976 Act') provides a statutory cause of action for a child born after 22 July 1976, and a duty of care is owed at common law to those born prior to that date. The 1976 Act does not impose strict liability and causation can be difficult to establish.

5.14.1 The Congenital Disabilities (Civil Liability) Act 1976

The scope of the 1976 Act is wide and legislates for negligent occurrences during a woman's pregnancy (section 1(2)(b)) as well as occurrences which affected the ability of either parent to conceive a normal child (section 1(2)(a)). Any person (other than the infant's mother) is a potential defendant and will be liable to the child if there is proof of breach of duty to the mother. The duty owed to the child derives from the duty owed to one or both parents even though actionable damage does not need to be suffered by either or both of them (section 1(3)). This section has potential to cause hardship to the child. For example, if a child suffers injuries because of its mother's refusal to undergo an emergency caesarean section despite being warned that the foetus was at risk, the child would have no claim under the 1976 Act. This is because the duty would have been discharged by the health-care advisor, and no cause of action can be brought against the mother in such circumstances. The defences of *volenti non fit injuria* (section 1(6)) and contributory negligence (section 1(7)) apply, both of which can operate to defeat a claim or reduce the award of damages. As the child's action arises through a duty owed to the parents, no liability arises to second- or third-generation claimants. There is no liability for preconception risks if the parent knew of the possibility of the child being born disabled (section 1(4)). The exception is the defendant father who knew of the risk whereas the mother was unaware. The 1976 Act was amended by the Consumer Protection Act 1987 with the effect that it also applies to those whose injuries were caused by defective products.

The statutory standard of care is described in section 1(5). A professional attendant advising or treating the parent of the child making the claim will not be liable if that person took reasonable care having due regard to the then received professional opinion applicable to that particular class of case. The professional will not be answerable only because she departed from approved practice. The section permits *Bolam*-defensible professional discretion and requires that matters are considered in the context of the time that treatment or advice was given.

Section 1(6) allows for exclusion or limitation of liability and section 1(7) for the defence of contributory negligence. Section 4(1) requires that an infant has to be born in order to bring an action, and 'born' means 'born alive'. For these purposes 'disabled' encompasses a range of conditions including 'any deformity, disease or abnormality, including predisposition (whether or not susceptible of immediate prognosis) to physical or mental defect in the future' (section 4(2)(a)).

5.14.1(a) Amendment to the 1976 Act

From recognition of developments in reproductive technologies and the potential for negligence, the 1976 Act was amended by the Human Fertilisation and Embryology Act 1990. Section 1A extends the scope of the 1976 Act to occurrences of negligence during infertility treatments that lead to a child being born disabled. A child disabled by negligent infertility treatment retains a right of action where the sperm or egg donor (who is not the legal parent) has been compromised in his or her ability to procreate a healthy child (section 4(4)(A)).

5.14.2 Maternal immunity

A disabled child has no claim against his or her mother unless the damage was caused by the negligent driving of a woman who was aware that she was pregnant (section 2). The rationale for this exception is on account of compulsory road traffic insurance or the Motor Insurance Bureau that extends to these claims.

The principal reasons for denying a child a course of action for prenatal injury arising from maternal negligence are mainly based on policy. According to McLean (1999), imposition of retrospective liability would mean that all fertile and sexually active women should act at all times as though they were pregnant. Maternal immunity gives precedence to a woman's liberty in priority to the interests of the foetus that she carries.

Fathers do not enjoy similar protection from liability. The Law Commission defended this anomaly on the basis that there were fewer ways in which congenital disabilities could be caused by the father. A child injured following a father's assault on the pregnant mother ought to have a cause of action. Nowadays, however, it is apparent that male behaviours such as smoking and exposure to toxic materials can affect foetal well-being, although an action could only be brought if the father owed a duty of care to the pregnant woman with respect to his exposure to noxious agents, and it is difficult to envisage such circumstances.

5.14.3 Common law

The 1976 Act applies to those born after 22 July 1976 (section 4(5)). The common law applies to those born prior to this date who become aware of their injuries later in life. Since the foetus has no legal personality, and therefore is owed no duty of care, common law actions for prenatal injury are difficult. The courts have adopted the legal fiction that the relationship between the defendant and the unborn claimant was contingent and following birth crystallises into a relationship to be protected by law. In effect this means that duty, breach and causation are contingent factors that crystallise into actual factors at, and after, birth.

The common law right of a live born infant to sue for damage caused by prenatal injuries was established by the consolidated appeal of *Burton v Islington HA* and *De Martel v Merton and Sutton HA* [1993] QB 204. In *Burton* it was alleged that a gynaecologist had negligently performed an operation on the pregnant woman and *De Martel* concerned negligent care at the time of delivery. It was held that a duty of care crystallises at the moment of birth when a child acquires legal personhood and the damage was sustained at the moment that the child inherited the damaged body. All events leading up to the birth were deemed to be links in the chain of causation.

5.15 Prenatal negligence resulting in the birth of a (less than able) child

The essence of a claim under this heading is one of wrongful life, in that 'but for' the negligence of the defendant, the child would not have been born and the damage (being the wrongful life) would not have occurred. Several events might lead to an action being brought under this heading. Negligently performed ante-natal diagnostic tests might mean that a foetal abnormality is not detected, or negligent failure to advise could mean that parents are not aware of a risk of transmitting a genetic disorder. Negligence during assisted conception might lead to implantation of a damaged embryo, leading to the birth of a disabled child.

5.15.1 The 1976 Act

The 1976 Act was based upon the Law Commission Report that had decided against allowing 'wrongful life' actions. Kennedy and Grubb (2000) state that section 1(2)(a) of the 1976 Act provides for the birth of a disabled infant following an occurrence that could have affected parental ability to have a normal and healthy child. On this interpretation negligent genetic counselling of parents might be construed as an occurrence within the 1976 Act, thereby permitting an action on these grounds.

Section 1(A) permits a child born disabled as a result of specified negligent infertility treatment a right of action. Section 1A(1)(b) provides for disability caused by an act or omission during the selection, keeping or use of an embryo outside the body. While in all likelihood such circumstances will fall within prenatal injury actions, a wrongful life action might also lie if it is construed that use of such embryos or gametes was an occurrence that led to the existence of the child.

5.15.2 Common law

The leading authority for wrongful life actions is *McKay v Essex AHA* [1982] QB 1166. Mrs McKay came into contact with rubella when she was less than two months' pregnant. She sought medical advice but due to negligence her samples were mislaid and she was misinformed that she had not contracted rubella and therefore there was no need to consider an abortion. The child was born deaf and partially blind, and brought an action (by her mother) for 'wrongful life' on the grounds that 'but for' the negligence she would not have been born at all.

The Court of Appeal rejected the claim on grounds of public policy and law. First, liability would be contrary to public policy since it would undermine the sanctity of life and devalue the life of a handicapped child. Second, such actions might result in doctors trying to persuade pregnant women to terminate their pregnancies, to avoid potential liability. This again would undermine the sanctity of life because life, even though disabled, would be better than no life at all. Third, calculation of appropriate compensation would be impossible being based upon the difference between existence and non-existence of life.

The Court of Appeal placed great emphasis on the latter issue of measuring damages. According to Stevenson LJ, trying to measure 'loss of expectation of death' required a value judgement where a crucial factor lies altogether outside the range of human knowledge. This sentiment was echoed by Ackner LJ when he asked: 'How can a Court begin to evaluate non-existence, "the undiscovered country from whose bourn no traveller returns?" No comparison is possible and therefore no damage can be established which a Court could recognise.' Griffiths LJ concurred that assessment of damages was an insurmountable problem and was the most compelling reason to reject the claim. Nonetheless, in many civil actions, calculation of general damages can be complex and at times is based upon a convenient fiction.

The two policy grounds for rejecting the claim, namely the sanctity of life and difficulty of assessing damages, have been criticised. It has been said that the Abortion Act 1967 provides legislative support for lawful termination of pregnancy, and therefore providing a woman with a choice to abort cannot be considered contrary to public policy. Furthermore, on exactly the same grounds and facts, a court would be able to assess damages payable to Mrs McKay for negligent ante-natal care. Mason (2007) considers that judicial hostility towards claims of this nature is chiefly caused by use of the label 'wrongful life.' In his view, it is the characterisation of life as being 'wrongful' that evokes emotion, incredulity and judicial hostility.

Wrongful life claims have been permitted in some jurisdictions such as France and the Netherlands. There are two principal strategies for justifying this. The first is one of corrective justice whereby a wrong has been done and which ought to be remedied. From an ethical standpoint this seems a more acceptable approach than that where it is regarded that it is sufficient to justify holding the defendant liable to pay damages that are better directed towards the economic costs of raising the child. In any event, the mother may have an action on grounds of wrongful conception or wrongful birth. An alternative approach would be to consider a compensation scheme to provide redress for such actions of negligence.

C Assisted reproduction

This section considers the law and ethics that underpin treatment of the infertile. The law is governed mainly by the Human Fertilisation and Embryology Act 1990 (the 1990 Act). The Human Fertilisation and Embryology Act 2008 is largely an amending statute and includes new provisions that pertain to parenthood. A fundamental question concerns the legitimacy of state regulation for the control of infertility treatment, since generally the law does not interfere with the procreative liberty of those who are fertile. There are substantial human rights implications to much of this topic.

5.16 Ethics

Moral and ethical influences are apparent in this area and have, at times, provoked strong and polarised views. There is considerable public concern about the possibility of reproductive cloning, stem cell research, chimeras and sex selection of embryos.

Individual perspectives often reflect religious, cultural, philosophical and sociological views.

A key issue at the heart of many controversies centres on the notion of reproductive autonomy and the extent of the individual's right to exercise self-determined choice about procreation. According to Dworkin, reproductive autonomy is necessarily 'embedded in any genuinely democratic culture' (Dworkin, 1993). Reproductive autonomy is principally a negative right that operates to protect the individual against State interference and restrictions. It is not necessarily a positive right to have State provision of resources or the means by which to have, or avoid having, children.

The extent of personal autonomy is inevitably constrained by the autonomous rights of others, and is influenced by economic and social factors. It could be argued that interference with access to infertility treatment violates reproductive autonomy, since restrictions can lead to involuntary childlessness. Involuntary childlessness represents the physical inability to fulfil a person's desire to have a biologically related child, and it is a condition that can have devastating psychological and emotional effects. Successful use of assisted reproductive technologies can help to overcome physical inabilities, although these technologies can potentially be used by the fertile, for example, to satisfy the desire to create a particular kind of child, or family.

The ethical issues at the heart of using assisted reproductive techniques evidence a tension between the concepts of 'dignity as constraint' and 'dignity as empowerment' (Beyleveld and Brownsword, 2001). The dignity as constraint position rejects practices that are contrary to human dignity, irrespective of their possible beneficial outcomes. This position opposes the use of gametes, surrogacy and techniques that permit selection of future children. In comparison, the concept of dignity as empowerment is based on autonomy and encompasses right-based arguments. This perspective supports exercise of informed choice that should be respected. From this position, use of assisted reproductive techniques and genetic technology are morally permissible.

A further tension arises on account of access to treatment and globalisation. Individuals with the requisite knowledge and resources may travel thousands of miles to access cutting-edge technology that may not be available in their country of origin. This can lead to the occurrence of reproductive tourism, a morally dubious situation.

Rights-based arguments pervade the area of exercise of reproductive freedom. Article 8 of the European Convention, for example, delineates a right to privacy and respect for one's family life. Article 12 contains a right to 'marry and found a family' which may well be relevant. However, Articles 8 and 12 are 'qualified' rather than 'absolute' rights meaning that the State has considerable latitude to provide justifications for their denial. The common law authorities also indicate that reproduction is an area that Member States are typically granted a significant 'margin of appreciation'.

5.17   Assisted reproductive procedures and technology

According to NICE, infertility is defined as the 'failure to conceive after frequent unprotected sexual intercourse for one to two years in couples in the reproductive age group' (NICE, 2000). Infertility is not uncommon and affects around one in six couples at some point during their reproductive lives. Use of assisted reproductive techniques is rising and *in vitro* fertilisation accounts for approximately 1:80 births in the United Kingdom. A range of procedures and techniques are available to treat male and female infertility.

5.17.1 Male infertility

Artificial insemination by husband or partner (AIH) involves semen from a woman's husband or partner being injected into the woman's uterus. The technique is used when it is believed that the chance of conception might be raised by concentration of sperm. To a large extent, AIH has been superseded by intracytoplasmic sperm injection (see below). A child conceived by this process would be the natural child of both parents and treatment does not require a licence from the Human Fertilisation and Embryology Authority.

A related technique is that of cryopreservation where sperm is frozen and stored for later use using AIH. This treatment may be used in situations where the man is to undergo therapy, such as chemotherapy, that could result in permanent sterility. If the man dies prior to usage of the sperm, questions arise as to the legality of its posthumous use and ownership (5.21.1).

Artificial insemination by donor (AID) is another method used for male sterility, or where the male partner is a known carrier of a genetic disorder. This procedure may also be used for women without a male partner or as part of a surrogacy arrangement. As its name implies, sperm from a donor is artificially inseminated.

Intra-cytoplasmic sperm injection was introduced in 1992 and involves injection of a single sperm into an ovum under *in vitro* conditions. The technique is a highly effective and revolutionary treatment for male infertility and sub-fertility.

5.17.2 Female infertility

The development of *in vitro* fertilisation has allowed many infertile couples to have children. Essentially, the procedure requires preliminary hormonal stimulation of the woman's ovaries to produce multiple ova which are harvested and fertilised outside the body using sperm from a partner, or donor. Following fertilisation the zygotes are transferred to the uterus, or cryopreserved for later use. Since *in vitro* fertilisation procedures usually involve the creation of several embryos, a contentious ethical issue concerns the fate of those that are not used for implantation and this has been perceived as legitimate grounds for opposing the practice. Since *in vitro* fertilisation can also be used to avoid transmission of genetic disorders, concerns have been raised about the inherent value of life, discrimination and eugenics particularly with respect to wasted embryos.

A dispute arose following *in vitro* fertilisation treatment in *Leeds Teaching Hospitals NHS Trust v A* [2003] EWHC 259. Mr and Mrs A, a white couple, received treatment at the same time as a black couple, Mr and Mrs B. Mr B's sperm was mistakenly used to fertilise ova from Mrs A who subsequently gave birth to mixed race twins. The issue concerned fatherhood and whether Mr A could acquire fatherhood by the process of adoption. In giving judgement, Elizabeth Butler-Sloss P stated that this was 'not a sperm donor case and should not be treated as such when considering the position of the twins. To refuse to recognise Mr B as their biological father is to distort the truth about which someday the twins will have to learn through knowledge of their paternal identity'. She ruled that Mr A should be able to acquire fatherhood by adoption and that by doing so the twins would remain in a loving, stable and secure home while retaining the advantage of preserving the reality of their paternal identity.

Gamete intrafallopian transfer is a technique that involves the collection of ova, as with *in vitro* fertilisation. However, the ovum and sperm are injected into the uterine tubes so that the process of fertilisation occurs within the woman's body (rather than *in vitro*, or outside the body).

Donations of ova are required by women with ovarian failure, or for those with serious hereditary conditions. The donor is given hormonal stimulation prior to the harvest of ova which are fertilised using *in vitro* techniques and transferred to the uterus of the infertile woman. The woman who gives birth to the child is the child's mother (section 27(1) of the 1990 Act). The preferred method of acquiring ova is altruistic donation. Drugs such as clomifene may be used to stimulate production of ova, and drugs containing follicle stimulating hormone and luteinising hormone may be prescribed.

In vitro maturation involves harvesting immature ova from unstimulated ovaries and maturing them *in vitro* prior to fertilisation by intra-cytoplasmic sperm injection. The advantage of this method is that it is safer, cheaper and quicker, particularly for women who may be infertile due to a common cause known as polycystic ovary syndrome.

5.17.3 Infertility of both partners

Infertility in male and female partners has been treated by embryo donation. An embryo (e.g. spare embryos from *in vitro* treatments) can be cryopreserved for later use or donated. The 1990 Act allows for variation or withdrawal of consent for the use or storage of an embryo. This provision was challenged in *Evans v Amicus Healthcare* [2004] EWCA Civ. 727. The claim failed at first instance and on subsequent appeal to the Court of Appeal, the European Court of Human Rights and also on appeal to the Grand Chamber.

5.18 The overarching regulatory framework

Louise Brown was the first 'test tube' baby born in 1978. Her birth fuelled considerable debates about the legitimacy of infertility treatments. In 1982 a major public enquiry was led by Mary Warnock with the aim of reviewing developments in assisted conception and to consider policies and safeguards that ought to be applied in the public interest. The main recommendation was that formal regulation was desirable and necessary to ensure safe and ethical use of assisted reproductive techniques and research using human embryos.

The 1990 Act established the legal framework for the regulation of infertility treatment and research. The 1990 Act has been subject to piecemeal amendment by legislation such as the Human Fertilisation and Embryology (deceased fathers) Act 2003 and the Human Fertilisation and Embryology Authority (disclosure of donor information) Regulations 2004. A major review of the 1990 Act commenced in 2004 and culminated in the Human Fertilisation and Embryology Act 2008 (HFEA, 2008).

5.18.1 The Human Fertilisation and Embryology Act 1990

The 1990 Act was intended to promote safe and ethical application of infertility treatment and embryo research. It includes prohibitive and permissive elements and identifies procedures that are lawful subject to conformity with specific requirements such as licensing. The 2008 Act amends many of the provisions of the 1990 Act as well as the Surrogacy Arrangements Act 1985. Aspects of surrogacy regulation are now subsumed within the 1990 Act.

The 2008 Act is intended, amongst other matters, to ensure that the creation and use of all *in vitro* human embryos are subject to regulation, to ban sex selection for non-medical reasons, to retain the duty to take account of 'the welfare of the child' when providing fertility treatment, but without specific reference to 'the need for a father'. The scope of legitimate embryo research has been clarified such as the regulation of embryos which include human and animal material. The 2008 Act is in three parts: Part I deals mainly with amendments of the 1990 Act; Part II with the determination of parenthood and same sex couples and Part III includes general provisions and operates to amend the Surrogacy Arrangements Act 1985. The majority of the provisions of the 2008 Act came into force in October 2009.

5.18.1(a) Rationale for the 2008 amendments

The need for the 2008 Act arose following introduction of some of the more controversial aspects of infertility treatment many of which could not have been envisaged when the 1990 Act came into force. Ethical concerns regarding reproductive technologies have tended to revolve around the perceived modification and commercialisation of the reproductive process. Partly in response to such concerns, as well as in anticipation of a major review, several public enquiries and consultation exercises took place. One example was the Sperm, Egg and Embryo Donation Review which included the selection and screening of donors, limitations on the use of donated gametes and embryos, and also legitimate payments that can be given to donors.

5.18.2   The Human Fertilisation and Embryology Authority

The 1990 Act established the Human Fertilisation and Embryology Authority (HFEA) as a statutory independent regulator (section 5). The body corporate meets several times a year and has power to grant and withhold licences, issue mandatory directions (section 23) and by section 25 publish a Code of Practice. Its principal functions are to regulate treatments that use gametes and embryos, to monitor treatment and research, to issue licenses and set standards for clinics and treatment centres. The HFEA provides guidance for professionals, researchers and patients and operates subcommittees such as the Clinical Advances Advisory Committee and the Ethics and Law Advisory Committee. It is responsible for advising the Secretary of State for Health on specific issues within its regulatory remit and the need for new primary legislation.

The HFEA publishes regular policy reviews on areas of contemporary public and professional interest and importance. The Code of Practice (8th edition) operates as guidance for the conduct of licensed organisations. Failure to comply with the Code is not an offence but can be taken into consideration when considering the renewal or revocation of a license (section 25(6)). A principal benefit of the HFEA has been the potential to respond rapidly to technological developments without the need to resort to primary legislation. By way of illustration, the early success of the technique of intra-cytoplasmic sperm injection provided the impetus for the HFEA to set up a working group to look at new developments in reproductive technology, the outcome being that additional safeguards were introduced to the licenses of existing centres to enhance safety and efficacy. More recently, definitive evidence showed that the established practice of transferring multiple embryos during *in vitro* fertilisation served to dramatically increase the risk of harm to women and foetuses because of the tendency to produce multiple pregnancies. This practice was popular as a means of enhancing the likelihood of success. The HFEA formulated a strategy of avoidance by disseminating up-to-date information to licensees and stakeholders.

The HFEA has considerable regulatory powers over embryo research and assisted fertility treatment. Despite the system of licensing, publication of directives and the Code of Practice, mishaps and negligence do occur as illustrated by the negligent implantation of a couple's last viable embryo into another woman, and an ovum negligently fertilised using the 'wrong' sperm. The HFEA is an expensive form of regulation and has been criticised for being insufficiently responsive to societal opinion. Despite this, it is still perceived as a model system by much of the international community.

As part of a range of reforms intended to curb public spending and avoid duplication of services, the Department of Health in its review of arm's length bodies has announced that the HFEA is to be abolished and its core functions transferred between the Care Quality Commission, the Health and Social Care Information Centre and a proposed new research regulator. However, if human embryo research and fertility treatments have unique status on account of their controversial ethical underpinnings, it is arguable that general regulatory and informative bodies will not be able to offer the same specialist regulatory response as the current regulatory system that has received global acclaim.

5.18.3 The EU Tissues and Cells Directive

The EU Tissues and Cells Directive 2004/23/EC was brought into force by the Human Fertilisation and Embryology (Quality and Safety) Regulations 2007. These Regulations amended the 1990 Act and introduced additional requirements for licensed organisations involved in the donation, procurement, testing, processing, storage and distribution of gametes and embryos. All centres that deal with assisted conception have to demonstrate compliance with the Regulations. Previously unregulated assisted conception services (such as Gamete Intra Fallopian Transfer) and the purchase of fresh sperm for insemination are now subject to regulation.

5.18.4 Licensing

A key function of the HFEA is to control the activities of licensed clinics and research centres engaged in assisted reproductive technologies and research. The need for control is justified on several grounds. First is the potential risk to the woman on account of treatments such as hormonal therapy. Second is the legitimate public interest in embryo research and the *in vitro* creation of early human life. Third, the HFEA relies heavily on expert opinion provided by a range of medical professional bodies which has to be collated to form a unified framework of best practice.

The HFEA can grant four types of licence (section 11 of the 1990 Act):

(a) for treatment services;
(b) for non-medical fertility services, such as those provided for the purpose of assisting women to carry children, but that are not specifically medical, surgical or obstetric services;
(c) storage of gametes and embryos; and
(d) research using embryos.

On receipt of an application for a licence, an inspection team visits the premises and prepares a report. Licences are usually granted by a panel of the HFEA, or in more complex cases by a committee. Licences for treatment and storage tend to be approved for a maximum of 5 years, although shorter periods may be granted to permit greater scrutiny and oversight. Licensed centres are encouraged to report incidents and near-misses to the HFEA, and a feedback system is in place to permit learning from these events by the issue of anonymised alerts to all licensed centres. These give notification of the risk and aim to reduce the possibility of recurrence.

An application for a licence must designate a responsible individual to supervise the activities authorised by the licence and ensure compliance with the conditions of the licence (section 16(2) of the 1990 Act). Licenses may be revoked or varied (section 18) and procedures exist for refusing, revoking or varying a licence (section 19). If an application is unsuccessful, the applicants may appeal to the HFEA's independent Appeals Committee.

5.18.4(a) Judicial review

The HFEA is a public body and its decisions are subject to challenge by judicial review. Conditions imposed by the HFEA must be 'Wednesbury reasonable' in that decision-making committees must have taken into account relevant factors and have disregarded irrelevant considerations. A decision of Wednesbury unreasonableness is a determination that no reasonable body could have come to the same decision (Associated Provincial Picture Houses v Wednesbury Corporation [1948] 1 KB 223). The HFEA must not fetter its discretion and must be ready to make an exception where justified.

An application for judicial review was brought by a 46-year-old woman with respect to HFEA guidance that 'no more than three eggs or embryos should be placed in a woman regardless of the procedure used' (R (on the application of Assisted Reproduction and Gynaecology Centre) v Human Fertilisation and Embryology Authority [2002] EWCA Civ. 20 at para 65). According to the Court of Appeal, the HFEA

> is open to challenge by way of judicial review if it exceeds or abuses the powers and responsibilities given to it by parliament; but where, as is manifest here from an examination of the facts, it considers requests for advice carefully and thoroughly, and produces opinions which are plainly rational, the court, in our judgment, has no part to play in the debate and certainly no power to intervene to strike down any such decision. The fact that the appellants may disagree with the Authority's advice is neither here nor there.

This ruling appears to indicate the Court's unwillingness to interfere with a decision of the HFEA provided that due process has been followed, and it appears unlikely that the court would substitute its own judgement in place of that of the Authority.

5.18.4(b) Activities outside a HFEA licence

Not all reproductive activities are subject to control by the HFEA. One example is the prescription of medication that causes hyperovulation. Even more significant is that the jurisdiction of the HFEA does not extend to the provision of assisted conception services in other jurisdictions. This situation, in the context of a profit-generating market, means that British citizens who have the resources can access services abroad that they cannot readily obtain in the United Kingdom. According to Brazier (1999b at 166),

> The most profound change in regulating reproductive medicine since Warnock is…the dramatically increased role of commerce. Warnock based its recommendations…on the supposition that fertility services would be integrated into the NHS…yet debate on commodification and commercialisation is at the forefront of debate today. A fertility 'industry' has developed to provide treatment on a profit-making basis both to British citizens and 'procreative tourists', escaping more prohibitive regimes elsewhere in Europe.

It seems arguable, therefore, that challenges such as these make it impossible for an organisation such as the HFEA to adequately regulate assisted reproductive technologies.

5.18.5 Confidentiality

The 1990 Act requires high levels of confidentiality to be maintained by service providers particularly with respect to personal data pertaining to gamete and embryo donors. Section 31 of the 1990 Act imposes a statutory obligation on the HFEA to keep a register of information from licensed centres regarding the provision of treatment services to individuals. Licences are required to deliver information to the HFEA on donors, recipients, treatment services and children born subsequent to treatment. Disclosure of information is governed by special rules and is subject to the requirements of section 33A.

Following implementation of the Disclosure of Donor Information Regulations 2004 (implemented in April 2005), a noticeable dip occurred in the number of donors and several sperm banks had to close. In countries such as Sweden and the Netherlands, the number of donors initially dropped following implementation of similar legislation, but then rose again following an intensive publicity campaign. A change in donor characteristics also became evident, with a greater proportion of older married men choosing to donate, rather than impoverished students. Data from the HFEA indicates that since February 2009, donation rates have almost returned to normal.

The original anonymity provisions of the 1990 Act were so stringent that it was virtually impossible to use information from the HFEA register for purposes of research. This was predicted to have detrimental effects on longitudinal epidemiological research into the outcome and health consequences of reproductive technologies. The processing of protected information for purposes of medical research is now permitted if the Secretary of State considers this necessary or expedient in the public interest, or for improvements in patient care (section 33D(1) of the 1990 Act).

5.18.6 Conscientious objections

A conscientious objection clause permits individuals with ethical objections to opt out of participation in licensed activities under the 1990 Act. This has not been amended by the HFEA 2008. For legal proceedings, the burden of proof lies with the person seeking to rely on the conscientious objection clause (section 38(2)). It seems likely that this provision extends to nursing staff and laboratory technicians but whether it would apply to administrators is unclear and might depend upon the court's interpretation of the term 'participating'. The Code of Practice 2010 (paragraph 29.9) states: 'A staff member's views about the lifestyle, beliefs, race, gender, age, sexuality, disability or other perceived status of a patient, patient's partner or donor should not affect that individual's treatment or care.' It is therefore arguable that a conscientious objection against treatment of gay couples or single women would not fall within the auspices of the conscientious objection clause.

The Code of Practice (2010) requires the person responsible for the licensed activities to be familiar with relevant equality legislation, and states: 'The person responsible should satisfy themselves that the staff member has a conscientious objection to providing a *particular licensed activity* [our emphasis], and is not unlawfully discriminating against a patient on the basis of their race, disability, gender, religion or belief, sexual orientation or age' (paragraph 29.11).

5.19 Access to treatment

A pertinent issue for those seeking infertility treatments is access to, and availability of, services and the extent to which these should be available on demand with costs borne by the NHS. Infertility treatments are notoriously expensive and often several cycles may be required. Although section 3 of the National Health Service Act 2006 imposes a duty on the Secretary of State for Health to provide services for the diagnosis and treatment of 'illness', it is questionable whether infertility can be legitimately classified as such. This is relevant in that it determines whether an individual has a *legal* right to NHS care (see 2.6.1). Those with sufficient financial resources can access the private sector and treatment abroad.

5.19.1 Welfare of the child

A controversial aspect of the 1990 Act in its unamended form was section 13(5) which provided that 'A woman shall not be provided with treatment services unless account has been taken of the welfare of any child who may be born as a result of the treatment (including the need of that child for a father), and of any other child who may be affected by the birth'. This statutory obligation was criticised by many who felt that the provision unfairly discriminated against women without male partners, even though single women and lesbian couples are not prevented from adopting children. Furthermore, same-sex couples can enter into civil partnerships and acquire the same legal rights as married couples.

5.19.1(a) Amended section 13(5) requirements

Section 14(2) of the 2008 Act has amended section 13(5) of the 1990 Act by replacing the requirement to consider 'the need of that child for a father' with 'the need of that child for supportive parenting'. This change was intended to remove the potentially discriminatory aspect yet retain the positive welfare safeguard. License holders are required to consider risk factors that might indicate likely risks to the welfare of the potential child although they are not required to be assured of 'ideal' parenting, whatever that might be.

5.19.1(b) Risk assessment for the welfare provision

The Code of Practice (2010, 8th edition) details how section 13(5) risk assessments ought to be carried out. Patients and their partners (where appropriate) are to be assessed fairly, their wishes considered and there should be no discrimination on grounds of gender, race, disability, sexual orientation, religious belief or age. Relevant factors are those likely to cause a risk of significant harm or neglect to any existing child or one born as a result of treatment and include (paragraph 8.10):

    (a) Past or current circumstances that may lead to any child mentioned above experiencing serious physical or psychological harm or neglect, for example:
        (i)   Previous convictions relating to harming children
        (ii) Child protection measures taken regarding existing children, or
        (iii) Violence or serious discord in the family environment

    (b) Past or current circumstances that are likely to lead to an inability to care throughout childhood for any child who may be born, or that are already seriously impairing the care of any existing child in the family, for example:

      (i)   Mental or physical conditions

      (ii) Drug or alcohol abuse

      (iii) Medical history, where the medical history indicates that any child who may be born is likely to suffer from a serious medical condition, or

      (iv) Circumstances that the Centre considers likely to cause serious harm to any child mentioned above.

The above list is not exhaustive and licence holders are permitted some measure of discretion to identify situations that may lead to serious harm to the child. Furthermore, at paragraph 8.11, when considering a child's need for supportive parenting, the concept is explained as being a commitment to the health, well-being and development of the child. The *prima facie* position is the presumption that all prospective parents will be supportive parents in the absence of any reasonable doubt.

5.19.1(c) Limits to the welfare concept

Monitoring compliance with section 13(5) requirements is difficult, if not impossible. Furthermore, the revised section has been criticised as placing an unfair burden on the infertile. Third-party evaluations of the risk factors provided in the Code of Practice have no relevance to fertile persons who intend to become pregnant. The fundamental difference being that the infertile person needs third-party medical assistance in order to become pregnant. However, the extent to which this difference is sufficient to justify what appears to be discriminationary is perhaps questionable. The welfare provision has been criticised for making infertility centres and staff moral arbiters of a provision of illusory value and impossible to implement. While there is a need for a minimum threshold to avoid preventable or serious harm, the welfare provision in its current guise is arguably unjustifiable and at best, mere rhetoric.

In a pre-1990 Act decision, *R v Ethical Committee of St Mary's Hospital (Manchester), ex p Harriet* [1988] 1 FLR 512, judicial review was sought of a doctor's decision to remove a patient from the waiting list for *in vitro* fertilisation. The prospective mother had been rejected as a suitable foster or adoptive parent due to her previous convictions for prostitution. Once this was discovered she was removed from the waiting list. Her application for judicial review failed on the grounds that it could not be suggested that no reasonable consultant could have come to the decision to refuse treatment to the applicant. The criteria were not *Wednesbury* unreasonable. It seems unlikely that the same decision would be reached nowadays given the enactment of the Human Rights Act 1998 and the potential for challenge under Articles 8, 12 and 14 (rights to a private life, to found a family and not to be discriminated against in the exercise of Convention rights).

In *R v Secretary of State for the Home Department, ex p Mellor* [2001] EWCA Civ. 472, a prisoner was prevented from artificially inseminating his wife in order to found a family. The decision was challenged under Article 8 and the Court of Appeal found that the restriction on the prisoner's right was justifiable and proportionate under Article 8(2). Lord Phillips MR stated: 'Imprisonment is incompatible with the exercise of conjugal rights and consequently involves interference with the right to respect for family life under Article 8 and with the right to found a family under Article 12. This restriction is ordinarily justifiable under the provisions of Article 8(2), and '[e]xceptional circumstances may require the normal consequences of imprisonment to yield because the effect of its interference with a particular human right is disproportionate'.

A similar situation arose in *Dixon v UK (Application No 44362/04)* [2007]. Artificial insemination was sought because by the time Dixon would be released, his wife would be 51 years old and her chances of conceiving would be considerably diminished. Their capacity to have a child would therefore be eliminated and not just delayed. The decision not to allow artificial insemination was upheld by the Court of Appeal and also by the European Court of Human Rights. However, the Grand Chamber of the European Court of Human Rights subsequently held that prisoners retained their human rights on imprisonment and any interference had to be justified and proportionate. In the view of the Grand Chamber, the applicant had to demonstrate exceptional circumstances when requesting artificial insemination facilities and the burden imposed was inordinately high because as a starting point the applicant had to demonstrate, as a condition precedent to the application of the policy, that deprivation of artificial insemination facilities would prevent conception altogether. Second, the applicant would need to demonstrate that the circumstances were 'exceptional'. The finding of the Grand Chamber was that in the assessment of the proportionality of the State's interference 'as regards a matter of significant importance for the applicants, must be seen as falling outside any acceptable margin of appreciation so that a fair balance was not struck between the competing public and private interests involved'. The Court of Appeal's justification for the interference of Dixon's Article 8 rights included (amongst others) the public concern that the punitive element of Dixon's sentence had been undermined, that the relationship of the Dixons had not been tested in normal daily life and that there was insufficient provision for the child's material welfare. It is notable that even though these reasons included the welfare of the child, the decision of the Grand Chamber was clear in that the Dixons's individual circumstances with regard to founding a family (which in all probability would not have been possible had they waited for Dixon's release) was a factor of significant weight in appraising the justification of the State's interference and the proportionality of the response.

5.19.2 Counselling

A standard condition of licensing is that patients and their partners (where relevant) are provided with 'suitable opportunities to receive counselling' prior to receiving treatment (section 13(6) of the 1990 Act). According to the Code of Practice (paragraph 3.7), counselling should be clearly distinguished from suitability assessments for treatment, storage or donation of gametes or embryos and from information provision prior to obtaining consent.

Factors and health conditions such as advanced maternal age (over the age of 35), smoking, underweight and obesity can negatively affect the likelihood of a successful outcome. There is no mandatory requirement for counselling, even with regard to the relatively high chance of treatment failure. It is arguable that there is a greater need for counselling in order to make better use of public or private resources.

5.19.3 Financial constraints

Infertility treatments are costly and by way of example a single cycle of *in vitro* fertilisation costs around £4000. The NICE guidelines (NICE, 2004) recommend that infertile couples ought to receive up to three treatment cycles at the public expense. The guidance is relatively narrow and applies to those at the optimum age of fertility (when a woman is between 23 and 39 years) and where there is a recognised cause of infertility of any duration, or alternatively where there is unexplained infertility of at least 3 years' duration. The Health Minister promised that by April 2005 all Primary Care Trusts should offer at least one free cycle of treatment to all eligible persons. A Department of Health survey in March 2009 reported that approximately 30% of Primary Care Trusts funded three cycles of *in vitro* fertilisation, 23% funded two cycles, 25% funded one full cycle and 22% funded one further fresh cycle (Department of Health, 2009b). The wide variations in funding have had the effect of promoting private provision and reproductive tourism.

Lucy was provided with three cycles of *in vitro* fertilisation on the NHS even though she was 45 years of age.

▶ What is the duty of the NHS to fund infertility treatment? To what extent is fertility an 'illness' for the purposes of the NHS Act 2006?
▶ What other options for treatment might be available to Lucy and Steve?

5.20 Use of gametes and embryos

The issues that pertain to consent and the control, storage and disposal of gametes and embryos are regulated by a combination of statute and common law. Several test cases have been brought in to clarify the law.

Valid and effective consent for the storage, use and disposal of embryos and gametes is the cornerstone of the 1990 Act. Consent is governed by the common law and it is a licence condition that the consent requirements in Schedule 3 are abided by (section 12(c)). The principal effect of this duality is that consent for the removal of procreative materials is governed by the common law, whereas consent for storage and subsequent use or disposal is controlled by the 1990 Act. The amending provisions of the 2008 Act require consent to be in writing and signed (Schedule 3, paragraph 1(1)). Similarly, consent can be withdrawn by notice in writing. In certain circumstances, a person may sign on behalf of another in the presence of a witness (Schedule 3, paragraph 1(2)). Schedule 3ZA of the 1990 Act requires counselling to be offered when

(a) A woman or couple seeks treatment with donated gametes or embryos
(b) An individual or couple seeks treatment that creates embryos *in vitro* (includes treatment such as *in vitro* fertilisation but excludes GIFT or intrauterine insemination)
(c) An individual or couple wishes to store their gametes or embryos (subject to exceptions)
(d) An individual or couple seeks to donate their gametes or embryos for the treatment of others
(e) An individual seeks to donate their gametes for the use of non-medical fertility services
(f) An individual or couple seeks to donate their embryos for research or for the training of others for embryological purposes

Guidance for the storage of ovarian or testicular tissue is found in the Code of Practice (2010) and the donor's valid consent is a principal requirement prior to storage and use. The consent of both donors is required for embryos. The HFEA has no power, even if gametes have been lawfully removed, to authorise storage of gametes, or embryos, unless specific consent has been given. The statutory storage period is currently up to 10 years although gametes and embryos can be stored for longer in defined circumstances where specific criteria are met.

5.21 Gametes

Subject to evidence of effective consent (meaning consent given in compliance with Schedule 3 of the 1990 Act that has not been withdrawn), gametes can be used for assisted reproduction during the donor's lifetime, or even posthumously.

5.21.1 Consent to use gametes

Effective consent is required for the use of gametes and pursuant to Schedule 3 of the 1990 Act, consent must be voluntary, informed, in writing and counselling must have been offered. Similarly, consent to storage must be voluntary, fully informed and specify what is to be done following the incapacity or death of the donor.

The posthumous use of sperm was considered by the Court of Appeal in of *R v Human Fertilisation and Embryology Authority, ex p Blood* [1997] 2 WLR 806. The claimant, Mrs Blood, brought an action for judicial review of the HFEA decision to refuse her request to be inseminated using her dead husband's sperm. Prior to his death the couple had allegedly discussed the posthumous use of Mr Blood's sperm, but written consent had not been given in accordance with statutory requirements. Sperm samples had been taken while Mr Blood was comatose and these had subsequently been stored. The law was clear that Mrs Blood could not lawfully use the sperm for treatment in the United Kingdom. She therefore applied for permission to export the sperm to Belgium where treatment would be lawful. She applied for judicial review of the HFEA's decision to refuse her request.

The Court of Appeal held that the retrieval of sperm had been unlawful since the husband had not given consent. On the evidence, sperm retrieval and its subsequent use would not have been in the deceased's emotional, welfare or medical best interests. According to the court, however, despite the unlawfulness of retrieval and storage, the decision of the HFEA was flawed in that the effect of (what is now known as) Article 49 of the EC Treaty had not been taken into account. Under Article 49, Mrs Blood had a right under European law to receive treatment in another Member State, unless denial of access was necessary in the public interest. The Court of Appeal stated that following *Blood* there should be no further cases where sperm was retrieved or preserved without valid consent.

Despite this assurance a broadly similar event was at the heart of *L v Human Fertilisation and Embryology Authority* [2008] EWHC 2159 (Fam), where L's husband had died following routine surgery. The couple had been keen to have a second child and an emergency out-of-hours application was made to the court for the removal and storage of sperm from the deceased's body. The judge declared that this would be lawful after being misinformed that the Human Tissue Act 2004 (which does not apply to gametes) permitted the posthumous retrieval of sperm with the consent of a qualifying relative. Since consent had not been given for the use of sperm for treatment purposes, as required by the HFEA 1990, L applied to the HFEA for permission to export the sperm to a jurisdiction where consent was not a mandatory requirement. The lawfulness of this application was tested.

In the view of the court, storage and use of the deceased's sperm would be unlawful. However, the HFEA had wide discretion to allow export and the applicant could rely upon EC Treaty rights to receive treatment from another Member State. She could also rely on Articles 8 and 12 of the European Convention which would permit export outside the European Union.

Section 39 of the 2008 Act provided that if a man has given effective consent, his sperm may be used, or an embryo transferred, following his death. The man will be treated as the father for birth registration but not for other purposes such as inheritance rights. This also applies where an embryo is transferred after the death of a man who was married, or was in a legal partnership, and who did not provide sperm, provided that effective consent was in place. Again this applies solely for birth registration (section 40 of the 2008 Act). The 1990 Act permits the removal and storage of gametes from those who temporarily lack capacity.

5.21.2 Donor anonymity

Assisted reproductive techniques can involve the use of donor gametes. Until April 2005, gamete donation was anonymous, a situation later challenged on grounds of public policy. Disclosure of genetic origins was considered an overriding duty to children conceived following infertility treatments for psychological and welfare reasons. Furthermore, knowledge of the gamete donor can provide important information about medical histories since genetic variations in the expression of disease is apparent (e.g. coronary artery disease, diabetes and breast cancer). Article 8 of the Convention gives rights to such information as everyone should be able to establish his or her identity as a human being.

In *R (on the application of Rose) v Secretary of State for Health* [2002] EWHC 1593 (Admin), the court stated that it was satisfied that Article 8 of the Convention was engaged in the circumstances of ascertaining donor identity, although on the facts it could not be determined whether a breach of Article 8 had occurred since the government had decided to abolish the regulations of anonymity.

Pursuant to section 31ZB(2) of the 1990 Act, individuals born following anonymous donation can request disclosure of non-identifying information such as the donor's ethnic origin. After the age of 16, persons may apply to the HFEA to ascertain whether they are related to an intended spouse or civil partner. The Code of Practice (2010, 8th edition) states at paragraph 20.7, 'The centre should tell people who seek treatment with donated gametes or embryos that it is best for any resulting child to be told about their origin early in childhood', and at 20.8, 'The centre should encourage and prepare patients to be open with their children from an early age about how they were conceived. The centre should give patients information about how counselling may allow them to explore the implications of treatment, in particular how information may be shared with any resultant children'. Despite these reforms and guidelines, the majority of donor conceived children are not aware of their origins and for this reason the implications of removal of donor anonymity may be of little consequence.

In the United Kingdom, payment of gamete donors is a criminal offence (section 41 of the 1990 Act), although expenses such as travel or time off work up to a modest ceiling may be given. However, one *quid pro quo* is the use of egg-sharing schemes. A woman who requires *in vitro* fertilisation may agree to donate half her eggs retrieved during harvesting, in return for free or reduced fees, for her personal treatment. As such this represents payment in kind. Arguably, this sits uneasily against the prohibition of direct payment, or indeed property rights in gametes. A public consultation of the HFEA is underway to review current policies.

5.21.3 Property rights

In *Yearworth v North Bristol NHS Trust* [2009] EWCA Civ 37, the issue concerned whether stored sperm constituted 'property' for the purposes of a negligence claim. Several cancer victims had stored semen samples prior to receiving chemotherapy that was expected to damage their future fertility. The samples were negligently allowed to thaw and were no longer suitable for use. The claimants sought compensation in negligence and under the law of bailment. The court held that a bailment of the sperm had been made to the hospital which had assumed responsibility for its storage in liquid nitrogen. Since the agreements between the claimants and the hospital for storage were similar to contractual agreements the court held that breach of contract had occurred to the extent that the men were entitled to damages for distress, anxiety and psychiatric injury.

For the negligence claim, the central issue concerned whether the claimants held property rights over their stored sperm. The court held that for these purposes the men had ownership of the sperm which they had ejaculated. The men's right to direct that the sperm was not to be used in a specific way was absolute, as was their right to withdraw their consent to storage at any time up until the maximum statutory storage period following which the sperm would have to be destroyed. Even though the 1990 Act imposed certain duties on the hospital in its capacity as licence holder, no persons other than the claimants had any rights over the samples. For the purposes of negligence the sperm was capable of being property.

5.22 Embryos

An embryo is formed following fertilisation of two gametes: a sperm and an ovum. Storage and use of embryos require effective consent as with storage and use of gametes. Embryos are also used for two other purposes, namely research and pre-implantation genetic diagnosis.

5.22.1 Consent to use

As with gametes, valid consent is required for the use of embryos created *in vitro* and consent may be withdrawn on written request at any stage. Since two donors are involved, matters can be problematic if one donor withdraws consent against the wishes of the other. Schedule 3, paragraph 4 of the 1990 Act provides that embryos must not be used and must be destroyed following withdrawal of consent.

The tragic dilemma that can arise was illustrated in *Evans v Amicus Healthcare* [2004] EWCA (Civ.) 727, a case subsequently heard in the Grand Chamber of the European Court of Human Rights (*Evans v UK* (Application No. 6339/05) (2007)). Ms Evans and her partner Mr Johnson had stored several embryos after Ms Evans was informed that she needed urgent surgery to remove cancerous ovaries. The couple each signed the requisite forms that the embryos would be destroyed if the consent of either was withdrawn. Two years later their relationship ended and Mr Johnson withdrew his consent. Since the embryos represented the only opportunity for Ms Evans to have a genetically related baby, she sought a court order that the provisions of the 1990 Act contravened her Article 8 Convention rights. She failed at first instance, and on appeal.

Although the courts were deeply sympathetic to Ms Evans' desperate situation, they confirmed the 'bright-line' rule that the government had chosen in requiring the continuing need for both partners' consent to embryo use and storage. The Grand Chamber stated that the central dilemma was that it involved a conflict between the Article 8 rights of two private individuals and any decision made would necessarily frustrate the rights of one of them. Even though Ms Evans' contention was that her particular circumstances and infertility meant that her Article 8 rights should prevail, there was no consensus that this ought to be the case.

Evans has been criticised on several grounds. It could be said that the 'bright-line' approach had a disproportionate effect on Ms Evans's Article 8 rights and that this rule ought to allow a degree of flexibility to accommodate individual circumstances. The law gave great weight to Mr Johnson's desire not to become a father, even though this would not have been given had he accidentally fathered a child. Though the bright-line rule may offer a degree of consistency and certainty to clinics, it seems certain that had Ms Evans created embryos with sperm from a donor, then these embryos would have been available for her future use.

The 2008 Act introduced a minor variation to the bright-line rule. Schedule 3(4A) provides that if consent is withdrawn by one party in relation to the use of an embryo, storage will be lawful for a 12-month cooling-off period during which the embryo cannot be used or disposed of without the consent of both parties. It is hoped that this might provide an opportunity to facilitate agreement between the parties.

5.22.2 Research

Scientific research on human embryos has brought major advances to health care, particularly for fertility treatment. Research is necessary to advance knowledge in this area for future therapeutic application. However, it is inevitable that in the process of research a large number of embryos will be used and discarded to gain an understanding of science and in the perfection of interventional technique.

Embryo research is an emotive and controversial topic that attracts significant public interest and concern. The factors that underpin these concerns relate to the moral and legal legitimacy of the status accorded to the embryo as well as to potential future outcomes as research develops. Public apprehension has been heightened by the creation of human–animal hybrids and the finding that induced pluripotential stem cells might offer a way for adult cells to revert to their embryonic health status.

5.22.2(a) Ethical issues

The ethical framework for embryo research was first considered in the Peel Report in 1972, followed by the Warnock Report in 1984 and the Polkinghorne Report in 1989. The latter suggested that since the law in this area was inadequate, ethical principles should be the guide.

The moral legitimacy of the use of embryos for research depends upon the position one takes as to when meaningful life begins and the stage at which a person comes into being. Although the Warnock Committee ultimately rejected the value of personhood theory in its recommendations that embryonic research should be permitted (subject to statutory control and authorisation), nonetheless the personhood concept remains an important cornerstone. This is particularly so since research tends to involve destruction of the embryo. From a moral perspective, therefore, if the embryo is considered a 'person' then its intentional destruction will be murder.

Personhood is recognised as the point or source of moral and legal rights. The existence of such rights bestows an individual's free will, choice and capacity for self-interest. The possession of personhood is a necessary precondition for legal rights and moral status. One perspective is that personhood is conferred at the point at which sentience is acquired which is likely to be toward the end of the second trimester of gestation. At that point, a foetus will acquire at least a minimal interest to the right to avoid painful stimuli.

According to Kuhse and Singer (1990), the minimal characteristic needed to give the embryo a claim to be considered as a person is 'sentience', being the capacity to experience pleasure or pain. Until that point, the embryo has no interests and as with other non-sentient organisms cannot be harmed, at least in any morally relevant way. However, in the process of scientific research an embryo may be damaged and if allowed to further develop, that damage may manifest in the sentient being that it later becomes.

The position of many 'right to life' advocates is that every human life is sacred and that life begins at the moment of conception, after which everyone has a right to be protected by law. These arguments generally emanate from theological philosophy, although Dworkin (1993) asserts that human life is intrinsically valuable and therefore deserves honourable treatment from a secular perspective. He argues that life can become sacred by association or designation and that the belief that human life is inviolable is rooted in two intersecting bases of the 'sacred': natural and human creation.

The moral and ethical arguments around embryo research range from the absolutist sanctity of life position, which prohibits any form of research. The converse position is that an embryo is merely a cluster of cells which until implantation lacks potential for further development, and for this reason there should be no prohibition on research. The middle ground, and perhaps the majority view, is that meaningful life begins at a point beyond the early embryonic stage and possibly on the appearance of the primitive streak, which is an indication of neural tube development or at a time at which rudimentary sentience or brain activity becomes discernible. This approach means that embryonic research is legitimate and permissible since it precedes any stage of meaningful life. According to this view, the onset of human life is a gradual process that develops incrementally throughout gestation. This gradualist approach was adopted by the Warnock Report, which recommended that the embryo had a 'special status' that entitled it to 'some protection in law'.

5.22.2(b) Sources of embryos

For research purposes embryos are obtained from three sources: surplus embryos following *in vitro* fertilisation; interspecies embryos (human–animal hybrids, chimeras) and embryos from cell nuclear replacement.

In vitro fertilisation treatment typically generates surplus embryos which may (subject to consent) be destroyed, cryopreserved, donated to others or used for research. Interspecies embryos may be created and are part-animal and part-human. These are defined in section 4A(6) of the 1990 Act as 'admixed embryos'. The creation of admixed embryos has generated considerable public debate and concern. The creation of a 'true hybrid' is where the ovum and sperm of humans and animals are fused and it remains illegal to implant such an embryo into a woman. The scientific community consider that admixed embryos will facilitate and promote medical research. Ideally, human ova would be used for such purposes. However, their short supply has led researchers to look for alternative options, such as ova from animals. Stem cells harvested from hybrid and chimeric embryos behave essentially in the same way as those from humans.

The third source is cloned embryos created by a technique known as cell nuclear replacement. This involves removing the nucleus of an ovum and replacing it with the nucleus of an adult cell. This is stimulated to undergo cell division, resulting in embryonic stem cells that are grown and extracted for stem cell research. This process creates embryos without the need for fertilisation.

A question arose as to whether or not embryos created by cell nuclear replacement could be regarded as embryos for the purposes of section 1(1)(A) of the 1990 Act. This was the subject of a judicial review in *R (on the application of Quintavalle) v Secretary of State for Health* [2003] UKHL 13, an action brought on behalf of the Pro-life Alliance. If such artificially created embryos did not fall within the statutory definition then these embryos would be unregulated by law. Bruno Quintavalle's action succeeded at first instance, but was overturned by the Court of Appeal and finally dismissed by the House of Lords. Lord Bingham asked (at para 15),

> Does the creation of live human embryos by CNR fall within the same genus of facts as those to which the expressed policy of Parliament has been formulated? In my opinion, it plainly does. An embryo created by *in vitro* fertilisation and one created by CNR are very similar organisms. The difference between them as organisms is that the CNR embryo, if allowed to develop, will grow into a clone of the donor of the replacement nucleus which the embryo produced by fertilisation will not. But this is a difference which plainly points towards the need for regulation, not against it...

Lord Steyn took a purposive interpretation of the statute, saying that it was meant to be protective, and that it would be counter to Parliament's intentions if embryos created in a particular way were excluded. In Lord Millett's view, although the statutory definition described 'a live human embryo where fertilisation is complete', the important words were 'live' and 'human', and fertilisation was just one process that achieved this end. On the other hand animal embryos were not provided for.

The reference to fertilisation has been removed by the 2008 Act amendments and section 1(1) reads, 'In this Act...embryo means a live human embryo and does not include a human admixed embryo'.

5.22.2(c) Statutory control

The overarching statutory control of research in embryos is the 1990 Act which requires the HFEA to regulate the creation, keeping and use of embryos for research purposes. The Human Fertilisation and Embryology (Research Purposes) Regulations 2001 have been revoked by the 2008 Act.

Section 1 of the 1990 Act has been amended by the 2008 Act:

1 Meaning of 'embryo', 'gamete' and associated expressions
  (1) In this Act (except in section 4A or in the term 'human admixed embryo') –
    (a) embryo means a live human embryo and does not include a human admixed embryo (as defined by section 4A(6)), and
    (b) references to an embryo include an egg that is in the process of fertilisation or is undergoing any other process capable of resulting in an embryo.

Section 3 of the Act expressly prohibits the creation, keeping or use of an embryo except in pursuance of a licence conferred by the HFEA. Sections 3(3)(a) and 4A(3) of the 1990 Act provide that research on an embryo may not be carried out after 14 days from the date that the gametes were mixed.

A list of permitted research purposes for which a research licence can be issued was extended by the Human Fertilisation and Embryology (Research Purposes) Regulations SI 2001 No 188 (amended by the 2008 Act) to enable embryos to be created and used for stem cell research for the treatment of a serious disease. The 2008 Act extends such purposes to include *inter alia* research conducted for the purposes of increasing knowledge about serious medical conditions other than disease, and research into the development of treatment for serious medical conditions (Schedule 2).

The creation of embryos specifically for research remains controversial. The Warnock Committee was divided on the acceptability of permitting the creation of embryos with the sole purpose of research, although ultimately the Committee's recommendation was in favour. The 1990 Act allows the creation of admixed embryos subject to a licence from the HFEA. Such embryos may only be created, stored and used under licence subject to the 14-day rule and embryos may not be placed in any woman or animal.

The HFEA's Research Licence Committee has issued three licenses authorising the creation and use of human admixed embryos. The first two licenses were issued in February 2008. These were challenged in *R (on the application of Quintavalle and CLC) v HFEA* [2008] EWHC 3395 (Admin) on the grounds that such embryos could not be described as 'human' and therefore the 1990 Act did not apply. Before the case came to court, Parliament had already enacted the 2008 amendments thereby expressing its intention to permit the creation of admixed embryos for research purposes. The *Quintavalle* application for judicial review to stop the decision to grant the first licences was dismissed as being without merit.

5.23 Cloning

Reproductive cloning is essentially the production of an exact genetic copy of an organism. It occurs in nature in the form of identical twins. In 1997 a sheep known as 'Dolly' was created by fusing nuclear DNA from an adult sheep with an ovum from which the nuclear DNA had been removed. Dolly was not a perfect clone, but was the first reported cloned animal. Therapeutic cloning involves the production of tissues or cells and not the creation of an entire organism. Although similar techniques are used there are substantial ethical and legal differences between them.

5.23.1 Reproductive cloning

The aim of reproductive cloning is the deliberate production of a genetically identical individual. It was considered and rejected in 1999 by the Human Genetics Advisory Commission and HFEA report 'Cloning issues in reproduction, science and medicine' (Cm 4387). The principal argument in favour of reproductive cloning is that it would expand the options available to the infertile and enhance procreative liberty. This could be particularly valuable, for example, if there was a need to duplicate a partner's or an existing child's DNA.

A principal argument against reproductive cloning is an intuitive opposition or revulsion to such a possibility. Cloning has generally met a hostile response because of its unnaturalness and its perception as being on a slippery slope towards creation of artificial human life and eugenic selection of particular traits. There are further arguments that cloning might lead to discrimination against clones, and that random distribution of genetic material will be reduced with consequent reduction in population diversity with negative consequences. Uncertainties remain about the health and life expectancy of cloned organisms and 'Dolly' the sheep died prematurely after developing early onset degenerative disease. Cloning could also make men redundant to the reproductive process.

Several international agreements have condemned the practice of human reproductive cloning, of which the Council of Europe's Convention on Human Rights and Biomedicine (ETS No 164) was the first. Countries that are signatories to the Convention are required to introduce implementing legislation to bring national law into conformity with its doctrine. The World Health Organisation has published its opinion that reproductive cloning would contravene human dignity and is incompatible with protection of human life. The Human Reproductive Cloning Act 2001 created a criminal offence punishable by up to 10 years and section 1(1) stated: 'A person who places in a woman a human embryo which has been created otherwise than by fertilisation is guilty of an offence.' The Act was repealed by the 2008 Act which allows only 'permitted embryos' to be transferred to a woman.

5.23.2 Therapeutic cloning

Therapeutic cloning, which is also known as stem cell therapy, involves the production of cells or tissues for therapeutic purposes (but not intended to be used to create an entire organism). Embryonic stem cells are used to develop cell culture lines. The potential benefits are that cultivation of replacement cells and tissues for degenerative body parts will be possible without risk of tissue rejection or the need for immunosuppressive treatment following transplantation. Embryonic stem cells could provide a virtually unlimited supply of specific cell types for the treatment of diabetes, inherited defects such as hepatic metabolism and for dopamine-secreting neurones in Parkinson's disease.

5.24 Pre-implantation genetic diagnosis

Pre-implantation genetic diagnosis is a technique used to screen embryos to ascertain their tissue type prior to implantation using *in vitro* fertilisation. It was traditionally used to screen embryos for inherited conditions that would cause serious harm to the infant following implantation. A typical example is the X-linked recessive condition known as haemophilia. An X-linked recessive disorder will only manifest in males. Pre-implantation genetic diagnosis to screen out male embryos therefore avoids risk of the disease being manifest (although female embryos could be carriers of the condition).

Pre-implantation genetic diagnosis is an expensive, complex procedure that can only be performed in the laboratory. As its name implies, it is undertaken at the pre-implantation stage and an affected embryo will not be selected for implantation if a particular disorder is identified. This means that a woman will be relieved of the possible decision and trauma of an abortion. Screening procedures such as chorionic villous sampling and amniocentesis also identify genetic disorders but these are post-implantation procedures undertaken during the ante-natal period.

Pre-implantation genetic diagnosis permits detection of gender as well as genetic traits other than those linked to medical conditions. This has raised the spectre that it could be used for eugenic purposes and there has been a call for regulation.

5.24.1 Regulation of pre-implantation genetic diagnosis

Schedule 2 of the 1990 Act provides conditions for which licences may be granted for embryo testing. Schedule 2, paragraph 1ZA(1) states that a licence may be obtained for the following situations (amongst others):

> (c) in a case where there is a particular risk that any resulting child will have or develop –
>   (i) A gender-related serious physical or mental disability,
>   (ii) A gender-related serious illness, or
>   (iii) Any other gender-related serious medical condition,
>
> For such purposes and for establishing the sex of an embryo the HFEA will need to be satisfied that the physical or mental disability, illness or medical condition, is gender-related and that it affects only one sex, or that it affects only one sex significantly more than the other.

In deciding whether screening is appropriate in particular cases, the Code of Practice (2010, 8th edition) states at paragraph 10.6 that the following should be taken into account:

(a) The views of people seeking treatment in relation to the condition to be avoided, including their previous experience
(b) The likely degree of suffering associated with the condition
(c) The availability of effective therapy, now and in the future
(d) The speed of degeneration in progressive disorders
(e) The extent of any intellectual impairment
(f) The social support available, and
(g) The family circumstances of people seeking treatment.

The Code of Practice has delineated these particular conditions because although the 1990 Act refers to a serious mental or physical condition, seriousness is not always easy to define and may be a relative construct. It is difficult to ascertain an arbitrary dividing line between serious and non-serious conditions. Doubt exists, for example, whether being blind or deaf is disabling but this disability may appear relatively less serious to one who has the condition compared to one who does not. Furthermore, the seriousness of the disability might be quite different from the perspectives of two individuals with the same condition. The Code of Practice provides guidance for determining what might be regarded as serious.

A number of diseases are autosomally determined rather than sex-linked. These may increase susceptibility to disease and may have variable penetrance. Individuals with these genotypes might have a greater susceptibility to certain forms of disease in adult life or be more likely to develop a specific disease. As examples, carriers of the BRCA1 and BRCA2 genes have a greater chance of developing breast cancer and ovarian cancer at a relatively young age. Carriers of the gene for Huntingdon's disease (a degenerative neurological disorder) will almost certainly develop this condition during adult life unless they die before the disease manifests. The HFEA undertook a public consultation in 2006 and decided that in principle it would be acceptable to use pre-implantation genetic diagnosis to detect late onset or adult onset conditions. In principle, therefore, screening should be permitted for susceptibility genes. However, in practice it would depend upon the probability of manifestation of the disease. The higher the probability, the greater the chance that pre-implantation genetic diagnosis would be permitted although the exact cut-off might depend upon advances in medical technology.

Section 13(9) of the 1990 Act prohibits the use of screening where prospective parents wish to positively select embryos that are affected by a particular condition, for example, congenital deafness. The prohibition against selection of embryos affected by a particular condition has been criticised by Savulescu (2002 at 772) in that certain 'disabilities' are not that awful and provided that disability is not to such a degree that the child's life is not worth living, then positive selection ought to be permitted since

> reproductive choices to have a disabled child do not harm the child, couples who select disabled rather than non-disabled offspring should be allowed to make those choices…Reproduction should be about having children who have the best prospects. But to discover what the best prospects are, we must give individual couples the freedom to act on their own value judgement of what constitutes a life of prospect.

Lucy is aware of a familial predisposition to a hereditary condition and is assured that pre-implantation screening will be undertaken.

▶ What are the legal and ethical issues that pertain to pre-implantation screening and selection of embryos?
▶ Lucy undergoes prenatal investigations during her pregnancy. What are the key ethical and legal distinctions with those of pre-implantation screening?

5.24.2   Pre-implantation tissue typing

Pre-implantation genetic diagnosis (PGD) is most commonly used to screen embryos for genetic disorders. The technique can also be used to identify healthy embryos that would be a good tissue match to donate stem cells for the benefit of an existing child. The embryo with a good tissue match would be selected for implantation. For example, an existing child might be in need of a bone marrow transplant and if the selected embryo is a good match, then, at the time of birth, umbilical cord blood can be taken and used to treat the sibling.

When this was first considered in 2001, the HFEA decided that tissue typing could be legitimate in circumstances where the child to be born was at risk of suffering from the same genetic disease as the existing child. The HFEA was asked for permission for pre-implantation tissue typing for two couples, the Hashmis and the Whitakers. The Hashmi's son had beta-thalassaemia major and the Whitaker's son had Blackfan Diamond syndrome, both conditions leading to anaemia. Each couple wanted to use pre-implantation tissue typing to select an embryo that would be a good match for the benefit of an existing child. The condition that the Hashmi child was suffering from was genetic but the condition of the Whitaker child had was not inherited. As a result, the Hashmis met the HFEA criteria and screening went ahead, whereas the Whitakers were denied access. An action for judicial review was brought on the grounds that tissue typing was not a 'frequent service' within the HFEA 1990. At first instance the application succeeded but was overturned on appeal. The Court of Appeal decision was upheld by the House of Lords which took a purposive interpretation of the statute and considered that both pre-implantation genetic diagnosis and tissue typing could be lawfully authorised by the HFEA to determine the suitability of the embryo for implantation. The purpose of screening was to help the woman decide whether the embryo was suitable and whether she would bear the child. Lord Browne added the caveat: 'Whereas, however, suitability is for the woman, the limits of permissible embryo selection are for the authority.'

The 2004 guidance of the HFEA altered the criteria for tissue typing. It no longer became necessary for the recipient child's condition to be inherited and it also removed the requirement that cord blood only could be taken. This was based on medical evidence from haematologists who indicated that there may be circumstances where bone marrow transplant might be necessary, and that this procedure in a young child was less intrusive than in an adult.

The 2008 Act has put these reforms on a statutory footing and the 1990 Act states at Schedule 2 paragraph 1ZA(1)(d) that a licence may be granted

> in a case where a person (the sibling) who is the child of the persons whose gametes are used to bring about the creation of the embryo (or of either of those persons) suffers from a serious medical condition which could be treated by umbilical cord blood stem cells, bone marrow or other tissue of any resulting child, establishing whether the tissue of any resulting child would be compatible with that of the sibling...

Schedule 2, paragraph 1ZA(4) specifies that other tissues of the resulting child does not include a reference to any whole organ of the child.

Sheldon and Wilkinson (2004) state: 'Banning the use of PGD and tissue typing to select saviour siblings would lead to the avoidable deaths of existing children. As such, it seems appropriate to assume that the onus of proof rests with the prohibitionists who must demonstrate that these consequences are less terrible than the results of allowing this particular use of PGD...' They argue that a saviour sibling would not be a commodity because the initial reason for having a sibling would be to provide a playmate for the existing child. Furthermore, the saviour sibling would likely benefit from the older sibling's company and derive pleasure from the knowledge that he or she had been instrumental in saving the older sibling's life. However, it cannot be denied that screening to select a saviour sibling would mean that a principal reason (as opposed to the sole reason) would be to act as a saviour for the elder child. Although there might well be psychological benefits for the saviour sibling, there are also risks. These include the possibility of exploitation, of being used as an insurance policy and source of tissue for the other sibling, of being subjected to the harm of testing and harvesting procedures, of being manipulated, pressurised or possibly even forced (Wolf, 2003).

Summary

5.1 The main legal and ethical issues at the beginning of life pertain to abortion, liability for (wrongful) prenatal occurrences and assisted reproduction.

5.2 Abortion is the intentional destruction of a foetus in the uterus or the premature termination of a pregnancy with intent to cause death of the embryo or foetus. The status of the foetus is a central issue at the heart of the abortion debate.

5.3 The year after the Abortion Act 1967 came into force approximately 50,000 abortions were notified, compared to 189,100 in 2009.

5.4 The ethical debate surrounding abortion is between the moral status of the foetus and the competent woman's right to self-determined choice. In England and Wales the foetus has a limited moral status that is proportional to its gestational age. This concept serves as a utilitarian justification for abortion.

5.5 The statutory provisions that pertain to abortion are found mainly in sections 58 and 59 of the Offences Against the Person Act 1861, the Abortion Act 1967 and the Mental Capacity Act 2005 (for those lacking decision-making capacity).

5.6 Grounds for abortion are provided for by the Abortion Act 1967. The majority of abortions are undertaken on the grounds of section 1(1)(a) (the 'social grounds' for abortion) which can be relied upon up to 24 weeks of gestation if the continuation of the pregnancy would involve risk to the woman's health (greater than if the pregnancy were terminated) or risk to the existing children of the woman's family. An abortion can be carried out under section 1(1) (b) to prevent the 'grave permanent physical or mental injury' of the pregnant woman (no time limit is included). Section 1(1)(c) permits a lawful abortion if two doctors concur that continuance of the pregnancy would involve risk to the life of the pregnant woman (greater than if the pregnancy is terminated). Section 1(1)(d) provides that termination of pregnancy is lawful if two doctors are of the opinion formed in good faith that there is a substantial risk that if the infant is born it will be seriously handicapped due to physical or mental abnormalities.

5.7 Multiple pregnancies are a risk to the health of pregnant woman and the other foetuses. This risk can be reduced by 'selective reduction' which is the termination of one or more foetuses of a multiple pregnancy.

5.8 Rarely, following an abortion, the foetus may survive and in theory killing a living abortus could amount to manslaughter, or even murder. To avoid this situation, efforts are made to ensure that the foetus is dead prior to removal in pregnancies of 21 weeks 6 days gestation or more.

5.9 The intrauterine contraceptive device and post-coital pill (which work by preventing implantation of a fertilised ovum) are regarded as contraceptive rather than as abortificent agents.

5.10 Liability for negligent prenatal occurrences is a reproductive or pregnancy-related tort. Actions may be brought by parents for wrongful conception or wrongful birth, or by (or on behalf of) a live born infant for prenatal injury or wrongful life.

5.11 Prenatal negligence may lead to a negative outcome with respect to the pregnancy and can form the basis of a claim in tort. Prenatal negligence may lead to an unwanted conception ('wrongful conception'); an unwanted birth ('wrongful birth'); injuries sustained before or at birth ('prenatal injury'); or a disadvantaged life ('wrongful life').

5.12 A claim for prenatal negligence leading to an unwanted conception (wrongful conception) can be brought in tort (usually) or in contract (rarely). Damages are usually low. Compensation would be for the cost of an abortion (if undertaken) with a relatively small award for pain and suffering.

5.13 A claim for prenatal negligence leading to an unwanted birth (a wrongful birth action) is brought by parents. No claim is allowed for pure economic loss related to the costs of raising a healthy child. In the case of a disabled child, recovery is allowed for costs incurred for providing for the child's special needs.

5.14 A claim for prenatal negligence that results in injuries sustained before birth (a prenatal injury action) can be brought by (or on behalf of) the child under the Congenital Disabilities (Civil Liability) Act 1976. A disabled child has no claim against its mother unless the damage was caused by the negligent driving of a woman who knows that she is pregnant. Fathers are not

Summary cont'd

similarly protected from liability. A claim for injuries sustained at the time of birth is brought under negligence.

5.15 A claim for prenatal negligence leading to impairment in the life of a child is brought by or on behalf of the child on the grounds that 'but for' the negligence of the defendant, the child would not have been born and the damage (being the impairment or 'wrongful life') would not have occurred. Such claims have been rejected on grounds of public policy.

5.16 A key issue at the centre of many of the controversies are based on the notion of reproductive autonomy and the extent of the individual's right to exercise self-determined choice about procreation. Rights-based arguments pervade the area and the law is mainly governed by the Human Fertilisation and Embryology Act 1990 (as amended).

5.17 Infertility is defined as 'failure to conceive after frequent unprotected sexual intercourse for one to two years in couples in the reproductive age group'. A range of medical techniques are available for treating the infertility of men, women and couples.

5.18 The Human Fertilisation and Embryology Act 1990 established the legal framework to regulate infertility treatment and research. The 2008 Act amendments are intended, amongst other matters, to ensure that the creation and use of all *in vitro* human embryos are subject to regulation; to ban sex selection for non-medical reasons; to retain the duty to take account of 'the welfare of the child' when providing fertility treatment, but without reference to 'the need for a father', and to clarify the scope of legitimate embryo research including admixed embryos. The Human Fertilisation and Embryology Authority is a statutory independent regulator for treatments that use gametes and embryos, to monitor treatment and research, to issue licenses and set standards for clinics and treatment centres.

5.19 A central issue for those seeking infertility treatments is access to, and availability of, services and the extent to which these should be available on the NHS. Infertility treatments are notoriously expensive and several cycles are typically required.

5.20 Issues that pertain to consent and the control, storage and disposal of gametes and embryos are regulated by a combination of statute and common law.

5.21 Subject to evidence of effective consent, gametes can be used for assisted reproduction during the lifetime of the donor, or even posthumously. Individuals born following anonymous sperm donation can request disclosure of non-identifying information such as the donor's ethnic origin. After the age of 16, persons may apply to the Authority to ascertain whether they are related to an intended spouse or civil partner.

5.22 Storage and use of embryos require effective consent as with storage and use of gametes. Embryos are also used for research and pre-implantation genetic diagnosis. For research purposes embryos are obtained from three sources: *in vitro* fertilisation, interspecies embryos and embryos from cell nuclear replacement. Embryo research is a controversial topic that attracts significant public interest and concern. Embryo research has brought considerable therapeutic benefits and is governed by statutory regulations and is overseen by the Human Fertilisation and Embryology Authority.

5.23 Cloning is the production of an exact genetic copy of an organism. Cloning can be used for both reproductive and therapeutic purposes. Reproductive cloning is prohibited by law. Therapeutic cloning could potentially be used for treatments of a range of disorders.

5.24 Pre-implantation genetic diagnosis is a technique for screening embryos to ascertain their genotype prior to implantation. It is used mainly to screen for serious sex-linked genetic disorders but can also be used for other inherited conditions that manifest in later life. Pre-implantation tissue typing is a variant and can be used for tissue typing for the purpose of saviour siblings in order to harvest umbilical cord blood or bone marrow.

Exercises

5.1 'The thought that an unborn child might die because a woman chooses a late-term abortion is abhorrent and should be rejected by the law.' Discuss this statement in the context of foetal and maternal rights.

5.2 'The 24 week time limit for an abortion carried out on the section 1(1)(a) of the Abortion Act 1967 is too long in the context of medical developments that allow infants born at 22 weeks to survive.' Critically consider this statement.

5.3 In the event of prenatal negligence the law allows no recovery for pure economic loss with respect to the upbringing of a healthy child. Consider the justification for this in the context of tort-based principles as well as the approach of the courts with respect to a disabled child.

5.4 To what extent do you think the Human Fertilisation and Embryology Act 1990 (as amended) provides true choice and opportunities for assisted reproduction? What improvements, if any, could be made?

5.5 'The dangers and ethical dilemmas posed by embryo research outweigh potential benefits and are not subject to sufficient regulatory control.' Discuss.

Further reading

Beyleveld D, Brownsword R. *Human dignity in bioethics and biolaw*. Oxford University Press, Oxford, 2001

Brazier M. Regulating the reproduction business? *Medical Law Review* 1999; 7: 166–193

Mason JK. *The troubled pregnancy: Legal rights and wrongs in reproduction*. Cambridge University Press, Cambridge, 2007

Sheldon S, Wilkinson S. Hashmi and Whitaker, 'an unjustifiable and misguided distinction'. *Medical Law Review* 2004; 12: 137–163

Woolfe SM, Kahn JP, Wagner JE. Using pre-implantation genetic diagnosis to create a stem cell donor: Issues, guidelines and limits. *Journal of Law, Medicine and Ethics* 2003; 31: 327

Links to relevant websites can be found at: http://www.palgrave.com/law/samanta

Chapter 6 follows overleaf.

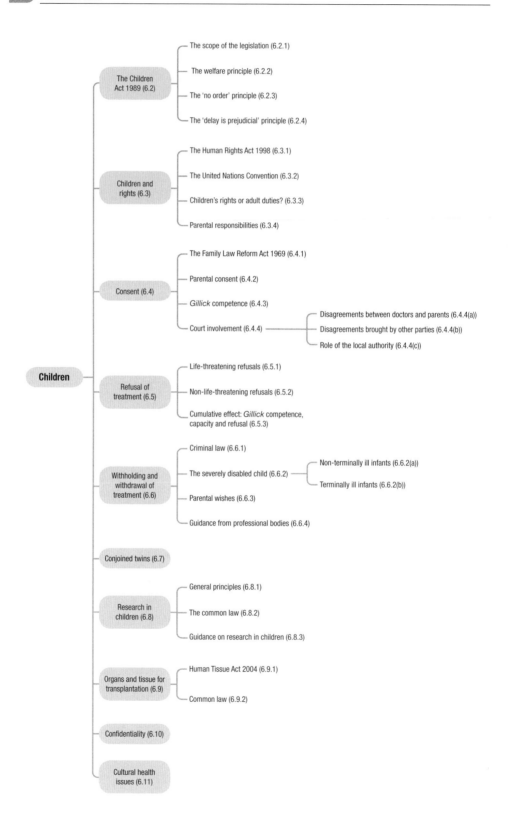

Key Terms

- ▶ **Confidentiality** – a duty owed to a *Gillick*-competent minor subject to certain exceptions.
- ▶ ***Gillick* competence** – a mature minor below the age of 16 who has sufficient maturity and intelligence to fully comprehend proposed treatment and medical advice sufficient to give valid consent.
- ▶ **Parental consent** – the form of consent required in most instances for the treatment of incompetent minors.
- ▶ **Parental responsibility** – a primary claim and responsibility to raise a child.
- ▶ **Statutory consent** – children aged 16 or 17 are presumed capable of consenting to medical treatment, unless there is evidence that they lack capacity (Family Law Reform Act 1969).
- ▶ **The Children Act 1989** – an important statutory source of children's law.
- ▶ **United Nations Convention on the Rights of the Child** – the most authoritative and comprehensive statement of the fundamental rights of children covering civil, political, social, economic, cultural, recreational and humanitarian rights.

Scenario

Rebecca, who is 15 years old, is a high achiever at school. She was born with a congenital heart defect and was advised that the optimum age for surgical correction would be between 14 and 15 years of age. Beyond the age of 16, the benefits of surgery would progressively decline. Rebecca and her parents have recently attended several specialist consultations with regard to her heart condition that, amongst other things, affects her ability to participate in competitive sports. They unanimously believe that surgery is in her welfare and best interests. Until very recently, Rebecca was keen to have surgery.

Two weeks ago, Rebecca announced that she had changed her mind and that she no longer wanted cardiac surgery on the grounds that the risks were too great. She explained that she had undertaken considerable research using the Internet and on balance she no longer felt that the risks could be justified. This decision led to a major row with her parents and during the argument she advised her parents to stop interfering in her life and decisions. She told them that at the age of 14 (while her parents were on holiday and she was staying with her friend Emma), she had consulted her GP and had undergone a termination of pregnancy. Since then she has been receiving oral contraceptives from a family planning clinic and for the last 3 months she has been participating in a clinical research trial for a new oral contraceptive medication.

Her parents are shocked and dismayed and believe that they should have been informed. They are particularly concerned that their daughter is taking oral contraceptives when she has a recognised heart condition. They visit the GP and demand to see her medical records.

Rebecca spends a considerable time helping and supporting her Aunt Alex and Uncle David. Their 9-month-old baby, Jude, was born with a chronic lung condition characterised by respiratory failure. Jude has been admitted to intensive care on several occasions during his short life and has required ventilation during each stay. Jude's life is very fragile. Alex and David are steadfast in their belief that life is sacred and must be protected. They demand that doctors do 'everything possible' to preserve Jude's life, even though his expected lifespan is short and his clinical prognosis is poor. They are extremely distressed when they are told that the hospital considers that no further active intervention should be given if Jude is admitted again with respiratory failure. They seek legal advice.

Jude is shortly readmitted to hospital and on this occasion he is placed on a ventilator. Two days later his condition deteriorates and doctors wish to stop treatment in his best interests. Alex and David are strongly against this decision and protest that Jude has a right to life. They believe that removal of the ventilator will lead to the death of their son.

6.1 Introduction

This chapter considers the application of medical law principles to children. The capacity of children and adolescents with respect to medical decision making is particularly complex, especially when considered in the context of children's rights. The growing recognition that children have rights that need protection has characterised the development of the law and is reflected by the passage of the Children Act 1989. Given the ongoing rights-based discourse in relation to children and the dominance of autonomy-based reasoning in health care, it is critically important to recognise the circumstances whereby some children ought to be able to exercise their self-determined choice and personal rights. Assigning rights to children might give the right to make choices, such as in relation to health-care decisions. However, *exactly* what is required to determine decision-making capacity has not been explicitly defined. If children do not have decision-making capacity, then those with parental responsibility may consent to care and treatment that is in the child's best interests. If no-one has parental authority, then under the Children Act 1989, the court can exercise such power using its wardship or inherent jurisdiction.

A child is normally defined as a person below the age of majority. Section 105(1) of the Children Act 1989 defines a child as a person under the age of 18. The United Nations Convention on the Rights of the Child (UNCRC), which is the most authoritative and comprehensive statement of the fundamental rights of children, states that 'a child means every human being below the age of 18 years unless, under the law applicable to that child, majority is attained earlier' (Article 1). Thus, it is generally accepted that childhood extends from birth (or even before birth in some jurisdictions) to the age of 18. This chapter focuses on health-care decision making as applied from birth to 18 years.

6.2 The Children Act 1989

The Children Act 1989 (the Children Act) is arguably the most important single source of law with respect to children within England. Broadly, the Children Act incorporates matters pertaining to issues regarding minors and to some extent has direct impact on other legislation. Its key principles can influence health-care decision making and it is therefore important to consider briefly some of these issues that may be of relevance.

6.2.1　The scope of the legislation

The Children Act provides a statutory code that governs public and private law that pertains to children. It repealed eight post-war statutes and provides a comprehensive basis for the law that developed piecemeal over several decades. It includes several schedules that provide much of the detail and the Act is considered to be comprehensive and extensive in its reach (Bainham, 2005).

The Act establishes the concept of parenthood as the primary legal status in relation to children. Parental responsibility is the central organising concept and the welfare of the child is the paramount consideration, particularly for dispute resolution in family law. However, the nature of the legal relationship between a parent and a child still to a large part falls to be determined by common law. This is relevant in medical circumstances, for example, when considering whether a child is sufficiently mature to have capacity to make a health-care related decision, particularly if that decision runs counter to parental views. Such predicaments can lead to problematic issues about the ambit of parental responsibility. Part 1 of the Children Act provides a range of fundamental principles that pervade the legislation and which may have implications for medical law.

6.2.2　The welfare principle

Section 1(1) of the Children Act provides:

> When a court determines any question with respect to –
>
> (a) the upbringing of a child; or
> (b) the administration of a child's property or the application of any income arising from it, the child's welfare shall be the court's paramount consideration.

While this provision specifically relates to the upbringing of a child, or a child's property, the welfare principle is central and means that the child's welfare should be the Court's sole concern. This means that when all factors are being considered, such as parental views and relevant information and circumstances, the correct decision will be that which is in the child's welfare or best interests. This principle has overriding significance for health-care decision making in deciding which course of action (or inaction) is appropriate.

Determining the most appropriate course of action is often complicated in that 'best interests' is an inherently vague concept that is unavoidably influenced by the values of the decision-maker. Section 1(3) provides a checklist of factors to be considered as part of this primary determination:

▶ The ascertainable wishes and feelings of the child (considered in light of the child's age and understanding)
▶ The child's physical, emotional and educational needs
▶ The likely effect on the child of any change in circumstances
▶ The child's age, sex, background and any characteristics which the court considers relevant
▶ Any harm which the child may have suffered, or is at risk of suffering

▶ The capability of the child's parents, and of any other person that the court considers relevant, to meet the needs of the child

▶ The range of powers available to the court for the proceedings in question.

As the statutory checklist applies only in contested private proceedings, the range of matters to be considered for determining the welfare of the child provides helpful guidance and has generic application to medical law and health-care decision making for children.

6.2.3 The 'no order' principle

A fundamental assumption that underpins the Children Act is the 'no order' principle. This means that when the court is considering whether or not to make one or more orders with respect to a child, it shall not make that order, or any of the orders, unless it believes that doing so would be better for the child than making no order at all (section 1(5)). The focus of the Act is that orders ought not to be made if they are unnecessary. To some extent, the 'no order' supposition complements the welfare principle as it cannot be in the best interests of a child to make that child subject to unnecessary court orders.

In the context of health-care decision making, court orders are principally considered where the opinion of parents and doctors do not align, such as in the context of withdrawing or withholding treatment.

6.2.4 The 'delay is prejudicial' principle

In any proceedings the court must have regard to the principle that any delay in determining an issue relating to the upbringing of a child is likely to prejudice that child's welfare (section 1(2)). For public law actions, the Children Act provides for a protocol of judicial case management and guidelines have been set in order to reduce delay. In the context of health-care decisions, the prejudicial impact of delay is readily apparent since delay in treatment could endanger the health, or even the life, of the child.

6.3 Children and rights

The concepts of parenthood and childhood are social constructs. A key issue that flows from such a construct is whether children have rights and whether parents have only responsibilities, or perhaps rights and responsibilities. If there is a conflict between the adult and child, then how are the duties of the adult balanced against the rights of the child? Fundamental to this debate is the premise that children do in fact have rights.

In the United States, for example, the Supreme Court in *Re Gault*, 387 U.S. 1 (1967) stated that neither the 14th Amendment nor the Bill of Rights was for adults alone.

6.3.1 The Human Rights Act 1998

The European Convention of Human Rights, the Human Rights Act 1998 and jurisprudence from the European Court of Human Rights operate as an integral part of English law. The convention rights are directly enforceable in the English courts through the Human Rights Act 1998 and the courts are required to consider and apply jurisprudence from the European Court of Human Rights into domestic law.

The key articles that apply to children and their families are Articles 8, 6 and 14. Article 8(1) provides the right to respect for private and family life and underpins the principle of autonomy as the basis of self-determination or self-rule. This has significant implications for children, particularly with respect to the circumstances when a child may consent to treatment and the possible sequelae in the event of treatment refusal. Article 8(2) provides derogation for the exercise of this right in that there shall be no interference by a public authority such that it is in accordance with the law and necessary (amongst other matters) for the protection of health. This derogation forms the basis of action that may be taken in the event of refusal of treatment.

Article 6 provides the right to a fair and public hearing within a reasonable time by an independent and impartial tribunal established by law in the determination of civil rights and obligations. This has potential application in health-care situations for obtaining injunctions to halt proceedings, for example, for decisions to withhold or withdraw life support where there is a difference of opinion between parents and doctors. It would also have application in determining the lawfulness of medical intervention where there is a dispute between parties.

Article 14 confers a general prohibition against discrimination in the delivery of convention rights, although it is not a freestanding provision and is of application to other articles. It provides that discrimination is proscribed on the basis of birth or other status. If childhood is regarded as falling within the category of 'other status', it needs to be considered whether any alternative approach to the legal treatment of children and adults by the State can be justified.

Bainham (2005 at 81) considers it likely that challenges under the European Court of Human Rights will be brought against

> the kinds of paternalistic interventions in relation to adolescents which we have seen in recent years. It may well be that greater State paternalism or protectionism is justified towards children than towards adults but the starting point in future may have to be that children are persons with fundamental rights and the burden will be squarely on those who seek to interfere with these rights.

6.3.2   The United Nations Convention

The United Nations Convention on the Rights of the Child (UNCRC) was ratified by the United Kingdom in 1991. The Convention provides a comprehensive international statement to incorporate the human rights of children from social, economic, cultural and humanitarian perspectives. Ratification of the Convention by national governments signifies their commitment to protect and uphold the rights of children.

The universal aims of the UNCRC are to set an agreed range of standards and obligations for minimum entitlements and freedoms that should be maintained by governments. In its application to clinical decision making and health care, specific articles relate to preventative health care. Article 12 pertains to the need to respect the views of the child and has direct relevance for the need of adults to consider these views in decisions regarding medical treatment and matters of consent. The Convention recognises that the ability of a child to engage in the decision-making process will be dependent upon the child's maturity.

When making treatment decisions about children, the overriding principle is the best interests of the child. This is articulated in Article 3 as follows: 'In all actions concerning children, whether undertaken by public or private social welfare institutions, courts of law, administrative authorities or legislative bodies, the best interests of the child shall be a primary consideration.' Article 6 of the Convention requires the State to recognise every child's inherent right to life and ensure to the maximum extent the survival and development of the child. This provision has evident implications for medical decision making and treatment, but the right to survival may have to be qualified where the quality of life is such that it is not sustainable. The right of the child to express views is contained in Article 12(1). This requires states to 'assure to the child who is capable of forming his or her own views the right to express those views freely in all matters affecting the child, the views of a child being given due weight in accordance with the age and the maturity of the child'. This provision again has relevance for consent to medical treatment by a mature minor.

A primary criticism of the UNCRC lies in the difficulties of enforcing these rights. The principles enshrined in the Convention can have real value only if there is political and resource commitment of governments. Nevertheless, this is an important and authoritative source of rights for children and has a role in extending to children many of the rights enjoyed by adults. It is likely that the UNCRC will influence the development and content of rights for children under other processes. The concept of rights for children appeals to a wider interest in society and recognition that rights pervade continuously into adulthood could enhance respect and fulfilment at all stages of life (Eekelaar, 1992).

6.3.3 Children's rights or adult duties?

The recognition and development of children's rights has been difficult. According to Fortin (2006), very little case law has acknowledged recognisable rights of children under the European Convention even though it is apparent that the Human Rights Act 1998 gives children the same rights as adults. If such rights are more fully acknowledged by the courts it might lead to a shift in thinking in health-care law from that which is based entirely upon the welfare principle to one underpinned by children's rights.

The advent of the Human Rights Act 1998 was expected to effect a sea-change with respect to a rights-based discourse underpinning domestic jurisprudence, with a radically altered stance taken by the court in determining what relates to a child's best interests. Furthermore there might be a reinterpretation of the paramountcy principle with a shift towards a body of rights-based morality in support of such a revision. One evident application lies in consent from a mature minor, but could also extend to the withdrawal and withholding of life-saving treatment in infants and very young children. Another justification to determining the substance of children's rights is that this should be influenced and informed by the UNCRC (Bainham, 2005). This would mean that such rights would be enforceable in the United Kingdom under the Human Rights Act 1998 heralding a shift away from the traditional protectionist stance of English health-care law as applied to children. It remains to be seen, however, how conflicts might be resolved between the exercise of Convention rights of parents and their children.

An alternative approach taken by O'Neill (1988) is that rights for children are best achieved by concentrating on fundamental obligations of adults in society towards children. She argues that many of the rights in international documents are merely manifesto rights that will remain in a vacuum until it is established against whom claims may be lodged on behalf of any particular child. Her view (O'Neill 1988 at 39) is that 'those who urge respect for children's rights must address not children but those whose action may affect children; they have a reason to prefer the rhetoric of obligations to that of rights, both because its scope is wider and because it addresses the relevant audience more directly'.

6.3.4   Parental responsibilities

The statement of parental duties was recognised in the Law Commission working paper (1986, paragraph 7.16) where it was stated, 'Parenthood would entail a primary claim and a primary responsibility to bring up the child. It would not, however, entail parental "rights" as such'. Such a view of parenthood is based on the reciprocity of parents enjoying rights on account of their responsibilities, and their responsibilities because of their rights. The duties and reciprocal rights are referenced by the minimal standard of protecting children from harm.

Parental responsibility clearly extends to giving consent for a child's medical treatment. Section 1(a) of the Children (Scotland) Act 1995 embodies this responsibility as 'to safeguard and promote the child's health, development and welfare'. However, how would this responsibility operate in the event that the child has a view of her own? Furthermore, at what stage would this responsibility terminate?

In *Gillick* (a House of Lords decision that considered whether a minor could consent to receiving the contraceptive pill, discussed at 6.4.3), it was held that a disagreement of a parent and child would be determined by the child's maturity and capacity for decision-making. For parent and child interactions, Lord Fraser took the view that maturity alone was insufficient to justify the provision of contraceptives and he was particularly concerned that medical personnel ought to persuade the girl to involve her parents. The majority in *Gillick* appeared to recognise parental participation in decision-making in line with the approach of a supportive participatory partnership. One approach to *Gillick* might be that parental control is extinguished once children are able to decide for themselves. However, Lord Scarman appeared to acknowledge that parental rights (and by reciprocity, responsibilities) would survive until the child become an adult.

6.4   Consent

Consent is a fundamental principle in medical law and is required to convert what would be unlawful touching into a lawful act. Valid consent is required to respect the patient's right of self-determined choice and represents the basis for co-operative clinical management of a patient. This section considers consent as specifically applied to children.

6.4.1   The Family Law Reform Act 1969

Section 8(1) of the Family Law Reform Act 1969 states:

> The consent of a minor who has attained the age of sixteen years to any surgical, medical or dental treatment which, in the absence of consent, would constitute a trespass to his person, shall be as effective as it would be if he were of full age; and where a minor has by virtue of

this section given an effective consent to any treatment it shall not be necessary to obtain any consent for it from his parent or guardian.

Thus, consent to medical treatment by a child of 16 or 17 is as effective as if it was given by an adult with capacity.

Section 8(2) provides that 'surgical, medical or dental treatment' includes any procedure undertaken for the purposes of diagnosis as well as procedures that are ancillary to any treatment being given. This would include, for example, the administration of an anaesthetic which is necessary for a procedure. The statutory presumption of capacity. This may be rebutted if the 16- or 17-year-old is not able to believe, retain, weigh the information and communicate that choice. In these circumstances, the provisions of the Mental Capacity Act 2005 would apply.

Section 8 specifically applies to diagnosis and treatment but does not extend to consent for purposes such as transplantation or research. Although section 8(1) displaces the need ('it shall not be necessary') for parental consent, section 8(3) states that this does not render ineffective any consent that would have been effective, but for the provision of the Act. This means that the parental right to consent (based upon the reciprocity of parental rights and responsibilities discussed above) is not obviated. The Family Law Reform Act is silent on the capacity of children below the age of 16 as well as on refusals of treatment.

6.4.2 Parental consent

The role of parental responsibilities *vis-à-vis* children's rights has been examined above. Parental responsibility as defined by section 3(1) of the Children Act comprises 'all the rights, duties, powers, responsibilities and authority which by law a parent has in relation to the child and his property'. For the purposes of health care this includes capacity to consent to medical treatment on behalf of a child. By section 2(1), parental responsibility will be shared if the child's mother and father were married to each other at the time of birth. Where the parents were not married at the time of the birth, only the mother automatically has parental rights. The father may acquire parental rights by section 2(2)(b), for example, where the father is registered as such at the child's birth, both parents enter into a parental responsibility agreement or if rights are granted by court order. Parental responsibility may also be acquired by a second female parent, or a step-parent, a person appointed as the child's guardian (section 5(6)), a local authority in receipt of a care order (section 33(3)(b)) or an emergency protection order (section 44(4)(c)). Section 2(7) provides that where parental responsibility is vested in more than one individual, the consent of only one of those persons will be sufficient for the purposes of appropriate medical treatment, subject to specific circumstances where the consent of both parents is necessary. In *Re J (specific issue orders: child's religious upbringing and circumcision)* [2000] 1 FLR 571, Dame Elizabeth Butler-Sloss said that where circumcision was being considered on grounds other than medical necessity, it was important to have the consent of both parents. Likewise, in *Re C (welfare of a child: immunisation)* [2003] EWCA Civ 1148, which involved a dispute between parents as to whether a child ought to receive the measles, mumps and rubella vaccine, the court considered that this was another example of a situation where parental agreement was required.

In emergency situations or where parental consent cannot be obtained, a child will be treated according to the principles of best interests. In the event of a dispute between medical and parental opinion, such as where parents refuse consent on the grounds that in their perception the proposed intervention or care is not best for the child, a court order will be necessary.

6.4.3 *Gillick* competence

The leading case that considered the extent to which doctors can lawfully treat a mature minor without parental consent is *Gillick v West Norfolk and Wisbech AHA* [1986] AC 112. The case commenced as a judicial review brought by Mrs Gillick who was the mother of five daughters under the age of 16. She challenged the Department of Health guidance that allowed doctors to provide contraceptive advice or treatment to girls under the age of 16, in exceptional circumstances, without parental consent and knowledge. Following the local area Health Authority's refusal to assure Mrs Gillick that no such advice or treatment would be given to her minor daughters without her permission and consent, she sought a declaration that the memorandum was unlawful. She lost by a majority of 3:2 in the House of Lords. This case is foundational for determining the competence of mature minors to consent to medical treatment under the age of 16.

The basis of *Gillick* competence is that minors have the capacity to consent provided they have sufficient maturity and understanding to make the decision in question. Parental decision-making rights exist for the best interests of children and these rights diminish as the child approaches maturity. According to Lord Scarman (at 189),

> I would hold that as a matter of law the parental right to determine whether or not their minor child below the age of 16 will have medical treatment terminates if and when the child achieves a sufficient understanding and intelligence to enable him or her to understand fully what is proposed. It will be a question of fact whether a child seeking advice has sufficient understanding of what is involved to give a consent valid in law.

The central issue concerned precisely what needed to be understood such that the threshold of *Gillick* competence could be crossed. In Lord Scarman's view, it was not only sufficient that a minor understood the nature of advice given but also that the minor has sufficient maturity to understand what was involved. In the particular context of contraception, for example, there were other aspects to consider such as moral and family questions, the parental relationship, long-term problems associated with the emotional impact of pregnancy, the risks to health of sexual intercourse and the risks of unplanned pregnancy which contraception may reduce but not eliminate. The onus would be on the doctor to be satisfied not only with regard to the minor's level of understanding of the immediate situation but also the understanding of ancillary matters.

In Lord Fraser's view the mere acquisition of capacity would be insufficient for a doctor to proceed without parental consent. In deciding whether to offer contraceptive treatment and advice to a girl under 16, the doctor should be satisfied on five matters:

(1) that the girl will understand his advice;
(2) that the doctor cannot persuade her to inform her parents or to allow the doctor to inform them that she is seeking advice;
(3) that she is very likely to begin or continue having sexual intercourse with or without contraceptive treatment;

(4) that, unless she receives contraceptive advice or treatment, her physical or mental health, or both, are likely to suffer; and

(5) that her best interests require the doctor to give her contraceptive advice or treatment or both without parental consent.

Lord Fraser strongly advocated parental involvement in that the doctor 'should, of course, always seek to persuade her to tell her parents that she is seeking contraceptive advice, and the nature of the advice that she receives. At least he should seek to persuade her to agree to the doctor's informing the parents'.

The doctor must act in the minor's best interests, and in Lord Fraser's view, there may be circumstances in which the doctor would be a better judge of the medical advice and treatment that may be conducive to the welfare of the minor rather than her parents. In effect, this means that contraceptive advice or treatment may be given if this is considered to be in the minor's best interests and medical judgement would supersede the parents' right to be informed and to consent to their child's treatment. Parental power is not absolute and there are limits to parental authority. According to Lord Scarman, '[p]arental rights are derived from parental duty and exist only so long as they are needed for the protection of the person and property of the child'.

Rebecca is 15 and is considered to be intelligent on the basis of her educational achievements.

▶ Consider these characteristics with respect to Rebecca's maturity and probable level of understanding in relation to her age group.

Rebecca is at the optimal age (from a clinical perspective) to undergo surgical correction of her cardiac defect.

▶ Who can give consent?
▶ Is Rebecca *Gillick*-competent? Consider the extent to which she can give consent for major surgery. Assuming that she is *Gillick*-competent, are her parents also required to give consent?

The extent to which *Gillick* reigns supreme is tempered in that the courts are typically unwilling to find that a mature minor is competent to make a decision if that decision conflicts with the court's interpretation of the child's best interests. In *Re E (a minor) (wardship: medical treatment)* [1993] 1 FLR 386, a devout Jehovah's Witness with leukaemia refused a clinically indicated transfusion of blood and blood products. Despite being 15 years and 9 months, and intelligent enough to make decisions about his welfare, the court held that he lacked sufficient understanding of the full implications of his decision. The courts have also declined to follow *Gillick* in the event of treatment refusal (see 6.5).

In *R (on the application of Axon) v Secretary of State for Health* [2006] EWHC 37 (Admin), the *Gillick* principles were applied in the context of sexual health including abortion. Mrs Axon applied for judicial review of the Department of Health's best practice guidance on the Provision of Advice and Treatment to Young People under Sixteen on Contraception, Sexual and Reproductive Health (Department of Health, 2004). The guidance permitted health-care professionals to give confidential contraceptive, sexual health and abortion services to those under 16 where this was considered to be in the best interests of a competent minor. Although this issue had been considered by the House of Lords in

Gillick, the issue before Silber J was whether service provision was an interference with parental rights under Article 8 of the European Court of Human Rights.

In rejecting the application, Silber J concluded that nothing in the Human Rights Act 1998 required a different approach to be taken from *Gillick*. While recognising that abortion was more intrusive than contraception and raised wider issues, he considered that Lord Scarman and Lord Fraser's reasoning applied to the instant case. Since in the 'overwhelming majority of cases, the best judges of a child's welfare are his or her parents' (Lord Fraser), every attempt should be made to persuade persons under 16 to consult and involve their parents. However, if this failed, advice and treatment could be given without parental knowledge and consent. Without the assurance of confidentiality young people might not seek advice and treatment with significant consequences.

Silber J concluded that health-care professionals are entitled to provide services to mature children provided that certain criteria are met:

(i)   the person under 16 understands all aspects of the advice including all possible adverse consequences that might follow the advice;
(ii)   the medical professional cannot persuade the person to involve his or her parents, or allow the medical professional to inform the parents;
(iii) that, with respect to contraception and sexually transmissible illnesses, the young person is very likely to begin or continue having sexual intercourse with or without contraceptive treatment or treatment for a sexually transmissible disease;
(iv)   that unless the person receives advice and treatment on relevant sexual matters, his or her physical or mental health or both are likely to suffer;
(v)   that it is in the person's best interests to receive advice and treatment on sexual health without parental notification and consent.

According to Silber J, as a matter of principle it was 'difficult to see why a parent should retain an art 8 right to parental authority relating to a medical decision where the young person concerned understands the advice provided by the medical professional and its implications'. This seems to suggest that parents should not retain a right to be involved in medical decision-making where a mature minor comprehends fully the issues involved.

> Rebecca informs her parents of her previous abortion and that since this time she had been taking the contraceptive pill.
>
> ▶ What are the ethical and legal issues here?
> ▶ In the light of *Gillick*, consider these in relation to the termination of pregnancy and the oral contraceptive pill.
> ▶ Should Rebecca's parents have been told, and should they have been involved in the decision?

6.4.4   Court involvement

The court has authority to make proxy decisions under its inherent jurisdiction or wardship authority. Both of these powers derive from the Crown's ancient prerogative as *parens patriae*. The court continues to be in charge of the care of the ward and involved in all important decision making, under its inherent jurisdiction, one-off decisions can be taken. Section 8 of the Children Act 1989 empowers the court to make a 'specific issue order' or a 'prohibited steps order'. A specific issue order determines the legality of a specific matter which has arisen, or may arise, in connection with an aspect of parental responsibility. A 'prohibited steps' order is an order that no step may be taken by those with parental responsibility, unless permission of the court has been obtained. In making such orders, the welfare principle is paramount (section 1(1)) and regard must be had to the checklist provided in section 1(3) of the Children Act.

6.4.4(a) Disagreements between doctors and parents

Decisions about medical care and treatment are based upon the 'best interests' of the child, the notion of which is wider than clinical considerations and includes welfare and psychological factors. The General Medical Council (2007) guidance on the assessment of best interests states that this includes clinical relevance. In addition, other factors to be considered include:

(a) the views of the child or young person, to the extent that these can be ascertained, including previously expressed preferences
(b) the views of those with parental responsibility
(c) the views of those close to the child or young person
(d) the cultural, religious and other beliefs and values of the child or parents
(e) the views of other health-care professionals involved in the care of the child or young person
(f) the option or choice that is least restrictive of the child or young person's future options.

Nevertheless, disagreements may arise between doctors and parents. In *Re C (a child) (HIV test)* [2000] Fam. 48, an HIV-positive mother refused permission for her child to be tested for HIV. The court overruled this objection on the grounds that testing was unequivocally in the child's best interests. In *Re T (a minor) (wardship: medical treatment)* [1997] 1 All ER 906, the Court of Appeal did not authorise a liver transplant that had been refused by parents. The child had already undergone major painful surgery for a life-threatening liver condition at 3½ weeks of age. The child had a poor prognosis, but nevertheless medical opinion was that without a liver transplant he would not live beyond 2½ years. His parents, who were health professionals, had considerable experience with the care of sick children. In addition, the family was living abroad and it would be difficult for them to return to England for the operation. The court held that surgery would not be in the best interests of the child, taking all factors into account. According to Waite LJ, 'in the last analysis the best interests of every child include an expectation that difficult decisions affecting the length and quality of its life will be taken for it by the parent to whom its care has been entrusted by nature'. This authority is one of the very few examples where the courts have declined to follow expert medical opinion, and it is arguable that some of the factors underlying this decision were accorded undue weight (see 6.6.3).

Where disagreement exists between doctors and parents with regard to alternative treatments, the court will heavily scrutinise which option is likely to be in the child's best interests. In *Re MM (medical treatment)* [2000] 1 FLR 224, a disagreement ensued over the type of treatment to be given to a child with immunodeficiency. The child, of Russian origin, had been treated with immunostimulant therapy in Russia. The boy's parents were satisfied with this treatment, whereas the consensus medical opinion was for replacement immunoglobulin administered intravenously to be continued throughout life. During the proceedings, an agreement was reached between the parties with respect to clinical management, and the judge, approving the proposal, indicated that while parental objections had been rational, their preference would have been overridden if necessary since the evidence that immunoglobulin treatment was in the child's best interests was overwhelming. This decision, along with many others, makes the decision in *Re T* appear all the more exceptional.

Disagreements can also occur where parents demand a particular intervention considered to be inappropriate by the clinical team as not being in the child's best interests. One example is where parents request continued ventilation in circumstances where it is not considered medically appropriate.

In *Royal Wolverhampton Hospital NHS Trust v B* [2000] 1 FLR 953, the parents of a 16-weeks premature infant with multi-organ failure favoured continuation of ventilation. The paediatrician considered that this would not be in the child's best interests, and a declaration was granted that the child be treated in accordance with medical opinion. In *Re J (a minor)(child in care: medical treatment)* [1991] 2 WLR 140, a very premature infant with severe and permanent brain damage had been made a ward of court. Medical evidence suggested that further ventilation would be fatal, although he was not dying. The issue before the court was to determine the course of action to be followed in the event of a further respiratory collapse. Lord Donaldson, exercising the court's *parens patriae* jurisdiction, made an order that J should be treated with antibiotics if he developed a chest infection but should not be re-ventilated. He stated that a doctor could not be compelled to act contrary to clinical judgement. Thus, although the court may overrule parental refusal and may declare that treatment or action taken by doctors will be lawful, it is reluctant to mandate that a medical practitioner adopts a course of action that is not considered to be in the best clinical interests of the patient.

A similar approach was observed in *R v Portsmouth NHS Trust ex p Glass* [1999] 2 FLR 905 following a dispute over the care and treatment of a severely disabled 12-year-old boy. His mother wanted her son to receive whatever treatment was necessary to prolong his life, whereas medical opinion was that he should receive palliative care only. Following a complete breakdown of trust between the family and health-care professionals, the boy was given morphine against the mother's wishes.

The mother sought an anticipatory declaration from the court to clarify the course of action to be taken if the boy (who had breathing difficulties) had to be admitted for emergency treatment and a disagreement arose as to the treatment likely to be received. The declaration was refused at first instance and this decision was subsequently upheld by the Court of Appeal on the grounds that it would be inappropriate to dictate in advance the treatment to be given or withheld.

Fundamental disagreements between the medical team and the family can lead to protracted difficulties and have far-reaching negative implications, particularly for chronically ill children who require considerable contact with health-care organisations. In intervening, the courts will consider what is in the best interests of the child and can override parental refusal or consent, or declare that a particular course of action is lawful. The importance of consultation between doctors and parents has been emphasised and the need to reach a consensus wherever possible. However, the European Court of Human Rights in *Glass v United Kingdom* [2004] 1 FLR 1019 underlined that a decision to impose treatment in defiance of a parent's objections constitutes an interference with the child's right to respect for his private life and in particular the right to physical integrity under Article 8 of the European Convention. The imposition of treatment by the medical authorities would violate this right. There is an obligation on health-care authorities to bring serious disagreements to the court, and parents may do likewise. In some instances, disputes can be brought by other interested parties where determination of the welfare of the child is required (see 10.7.2).

6.4.4(b) Disagreements brought by other parties

In *Re B (wardship: abortion)* [1991] 2 FLR 426, B was 12-year-old school girl of average intelligence and maturity who was living with her maternal grandparents. After being informed of the risks of termination and continuance with her pregnancy she requested an abortion, a decision supported by her grandparents and her 16-year-old boyfriend. B was made a ward of court by the local authority, who applied for permission to have her pregnancy terminated, despite maternal objections. The abortion was authorised by the court, applying its wardship jurisdiction, on the grounds that this was in B's best interests.

Re D (a minor) (wardship: sterilisation) [1976] 1 All ER 326, concerned a 11-year-old girl who had behavioural problems and some impairment of intellectual ability. Her parents and doctors agreed that she should be sterilised on the grounds that there was a real risk that she could give birth to an abnormal child that she would be unable to care for. Her educational psychologist applied to have D made a ward of court in order to delay or prevent the sterilisation procedure being carried out. It was held that the decision to carry out a sterilisation procedure on a minor for non-therapeutic purposes was not solely a medical determination. In the circumstances it would not be in D's best interests to carry out surgery at this stage since it was likely that in later years she would be able to reach her own decision.

6.4.4(c) Role of the local authority

The local authority has an important role in the welfare of children if it is likely that a child might suffer significant harm due to a health-related cause. In *Re C (HIV test)* [1999] 2 FLR 1004, the authority obtained a specific issue order that a baby born to a woman with HIV be tested for the HIV virus. The woman had continued to breastfeed the infant against medical advice and both parents were opposed to conventional treatment for the HIV virus. It was held that although parental views were important, these could be overridden in the best interests of the child. The parents' leave to appeal was refused by the Court of Appeal. Butler-Sloss LJ stated: 'I have no doubt at all, for my part, that it is right that this child should have the test done... In my view, the child is clearly at risk if there is ignorance of the child's medical condition... It does not matter whether the parents are responsible or irresponsible. It matters whether the welfare of the child demands that such a course should be taken...' On the face of it, this decision appears to suggest that the welfare principle overrides parental discretion with respect to treatment decisions. However, the circumstances need to be considered in context. This was a situation where the intrusiveness of treatment was very minor compared with the potential benefits. It seems less likely that parental views would be overridden in circumstances where potential benefits are more equivocal or evenly balanced against the level of intrusion.

The local council may also take protective action in child welfare situations. In *Metropolitan Borough Council v DB* [1997] 1 FLR 767, the court had to consider the circumstances whereby a court acting under its inherent jurisdiction could make an order that reasonable force be used to compel a 17-year-old crack cocaine addict to submit to medical treatment. After finding that D lacked decision-making competence, the court authorised doctors to use such reasonable force as was necessary to treat the woman who had very recently given birth.

6.5   Refusal of treatment

A minor between the ages of 16 and 18 is presumed (rebuttable) competent to consent to treatment by statute (see 6.4.1). At common law a minor below the age of 16, who is *Gillick*-competent, may consent to treatment. However, the competent minor's right to refuse treatment is not respected to the same extent.

6.5.1   Life-threatening refusals

An adult with capacity has the right to refuse even life-saving treatment, no matter how irrational that decision may be. This right is respected on the basis of autonomous choice. This principle does not apply to a minor.

Even though a minor may be *Gillick*-competent, or may have reached the age of 16, the right to refuse treatment, particularly for life-threatening conditions, has been rejected by the court principally on the grounds that the child's capacity has to be determined within the context of the particular decision being made. The approach taken is that the graver the decision, the greater the capacity required in order to make that decision. Justification for this principle can be illustrated by several authorities such as *Re S (a minor) (consent to medical treatment)* [1994] 2 FLR 1065, *Re E (a minor) (wardship: medical treatment)* [1993] 1 FLR 386 and *Re L (medical treatment: Gillick competency)* [1998] 2 FLR 810.

In *Re S* a 15-year-old girl suffered from a blood disorder known as thalassaemia. During her life she had undergone multiple blood transfusions which she now refused on the basis of her religious views. It was held that she was not competent to refuse treatment. It was not enough for her to understand that she would die if she did not have the transfusion, but in the view of the court she needed to have a greater understanding of the manner of death and the inevitable pain and distress that would be involved.

In *Re E* a similar approach was taken. The boy, aged 15, suffered from leukaemia and wished to refuse a life-saving blood transfusion on religious grounds. As in *Re S*, the boy understood that death would be an inevitable consequence of his decision. The court found that although E was *Gillick*-competent, he failed to appreciate the full implications of his refusal, including the likely manner of his death and the inevitable extent of his own and his family's suffering.

In *Re L* a girl aged 14 refused a life-saving blood transfusion on account of her sincere and strongly held religious views. In this instance, the court found that she lacked the constructive formulation of her beliefs that typically came with adult experience, because she was still a child. Since her upbringing had been dominated by the Jehovah's Witness congregation, this experience had operated as a profound influence which unavoidably influenced her decision. She lacked sufficient information to be *Gillick*-competent to achieve the level of understanding required to make such a decision. On the facts, treatment would be in her best interests.

The decisions in *Re S* and *Re E* suggest that the requisite degree of understanding required by a mature minor to refuse treatment is set so high that it is virtually unattainable. It could certainly be questioned as to how many adults who refuse treatment in similar circumstances would have a full understanding of the manner of their death, as well as the likely pain and distress caused to themselves and their loved ones. The requirement proposed in *Re L* that the child lacked sufficient information seems dubious in relation to her capacity since capacity is essentially based upon understanding, retaining and weighing the information that is given for the purpose of decision making and should therefore apply equally to consent as well as *refusal* of consent.

The law appears to view the concepts of competence and capacity very differently for adults and children. In *Re R (a minor) (wardship: consent to treatment)* [1992] Fam 11, Lord Donaldson MR stated that *Gillick* competence is a developmental concept that is not lost or acquired on a day-to-day or week-by-week basis. A competent adult has capacity to consent to, or refuse, medically indicated treatment. Capacity in a *Gillick*-competent minor is not viewed in the same way and the functional status of capacity appears to depend upon the potential implications of the refusal. The potential outcome, as far as consent to clinically endorsed treatment is concerned, is likely to be beneficial, whereas the potential outcome following a refusal of treatment is likely to be harmful or at least non-beneficial. In the case of minors, the threshold for the functional capacity test is set far higher.

Another approach taken by the court is one that is more beneficent and protective. In *Re P (a minor)* [2003] EWHC 2327 (Fam), a minor aged just under 17 years (and who therefore had the benefit of the statutory presumption of competence) sought to refuse blood products on religious grounds. The court acknowledged that there would be situations whereby a minor's refusal would be determinative when that minor was approaching the age of 18. This would be particularly apparent where treatment was likely to defer an inevitable death for a matter of only months. Obligatory treatment against a patient's will was to be avoided wherever possible particularly where there was evidence of firm convictions. Nevertheless, the refusal was overriden on the grounds that the decision to treat was in the minor's best interests, as construed in the widest sense. An order permitting the hospital to give blood or blood products was given subject to there being no other appropriate treatment.

Rights-based commentators have argued that if *Gillick* competence and the statutory presumption of competence give effect to autonomy and self-determined choice, then it is difficult to understand why the same principle does not extend to treatment refusal. The judicial approach is based on policy and its inherent role in the protection of minors in that if a particular treatment is necessary for a patient, in this case a minor, then that decision is based on the assumption that it is in the best interests of the patient. In such circumstances it is rational for the law to facilitate treatment provision and allow a *Gillick*-competent child to give valid consent. Equally, the law should be reluctant to allow a child of whatever age to veto treatment (which, since it is medically supported, would be in the minor's clinical best interests), particularly if refusal was expected to lead to permanent injury or death of the child. The clear and consistent policy of the law is protection of the minor (Lowe and Juss, 1993). While this may be understandable to some degree with respect to refusal of life-sustaining treatment, or an intervention to avoid permanent harm, whether this principle can justifiably be extended to discretionary treatment seems less persuasive.

6.5.2 Non-life threatening refusals

The leading authorities that have considered non-life threatening treatment refusals are *Re R (a minor) (wardship: consent to treatment)* [1992] Fam. 11 CA and *Re W (a minor) (medical treatment: court jurisdiction)* [1993] Fam. 64 CA. In *Re R*, a girl aged 15 was in the care of the local authority. Her mental state was characterised by fluctuant violent and suicidal behaviour. During one episode she was detained in a psychiatric unit under section 2 of the Mental Health Act 1983. During a lucid interval, R indicated that she would refuse compulsory administration of anti-psychotic medication. The local authority withdrew its consent and began wardship proceedings, requesting court approval for treatment to be given without her consent. Although it was held that in exercising its wardship authority the refusal of a competent minor could not be overruled. In the circumstances R's mental states prevented her from achieving the required competence. The application was therefore successful.

Re W concerned a 16-year-old girl with anorexia nervosa. She refused treatment and objected to being transferred to a specialist unit that dealt with the treatment of eating disorders. Being over the age of 16, the statutory presumption of capacity applied and she argued that section 8 of the Family Law Reform Act 1969 conferred on her the same right to refuse medical treatment as that of an adult. Her claim was unsuccessful.

In *Re R* the two main issues before the court were whether R was *Gillick*-competent and if so, the extent to which the court had power to override her wishes. On the facts it was held that, R was not *Gillick*-competent. Lord Donaldson made *obiter* comments about what the position might have been had she been judged to be competent. He used a metaphor of keys and locks, stating that consent was a key which would unlock a door (to permit lawful treatment). The *Gillick*-competent child was a key holder, as was the parent of the child, and either of the keys within the context of that metaphor could be used to unlock the door to allow treatment to proceed. What this means, therefore, is that until a child is *Gillick*-competent, the parent has an exclusive right to consent. Once the child attains *Gillick* competence, the parent's right to consent is not extinguished but still exists concurrently and in parallel with the minor's ability to consent. As consent from either source would be sufficient for treatment to proceed, a *Gillick*-competent refusal could be overridden by parental consent. Accordingly, the refusal of the *Gillick*-competent child was an important factor in the doctor's decision as to whether to treat or not. However, this would not prevent the necessary consent from being obtained from another legitimate source.

Later, in *Re W*, Lord Donaldson stated that he regretted his use of the key holder analogy since keys could lock, as well as unlock. He stated (at 78) that his preferred approach would be 'the analogy of the legal "flak jacket" which protects the doctor from claims by the litigious whether he acquires it from his patient who may be a minor over the age of 16, or a "*Gillick*-competent" child under that age or from another person having parental responsibilities which include a right to consent to treatment of the minor'. Thus, the purpose of consent was to make treatment lawful, thereby 'protecting' the doctor. As long as consent was available from one valid sector, that would be sufficient to function as a 'flak jacket'.

In summary, consent to treatment may be obtained from one of several sources: those with parental responsibility; a minor over the age of 16, a *Gillick*-competent child below the age of 16, or the court. If a *Gillick*-competent minor below the age of 16 refuses consent, or if a minor between 16 and 18, who has *prima facie* capacity to consent refuses, then that refusal can be overridden if valid consent is obtained from an alternative source. This position has been criticised on several counts such as rights-based arguments, paternalism and illegitimacy.

From a rights-based perspective, Harris (2003b) argues that in order to give valid consent, an understanding is required of the nature and proposed course of action which includes civil rights and likely consequences. If a person can consent to treatment based upon such understanding, it follows that there ought to be a right to refuse based upon a similar understanding of the consequences of refusal. In fact, the right to refuse is a corollary of the right to consent.

Lord Donaldson's approach to rationalising consent as being necessary to protect those who provide treatment with a defence against a criminal charge has been criticised as an overly restricted view of the requirement which is embedded in fundamental civil rights in that personal integrity ought not to be interfered with without lawful justification, or valid consent. Eekelaar (1993) suggests that Lord Donaldson's primary concern was to minimise the risk of legal action against doctors, rather than to protect the civil liberties of competent minors to the same extent as adults. The court's approach to treatment refusal by minors has been viewed as paternalistic since it does not support autonomous decision-making. The law appears to permit decisions to be taken with respect to treatment by those under 18 only if they know what is 'good for them' as evidenced by their acceptance of the treatment proposed (Elliston, 1996).

The decision of the Court of Appeal in *Re W* binds any court below the Supreme Court and serves to undermine *Gillick*. It is possible that the decision could be challenged in that denial of capacity to a competent minor violates Convention rights such as Article 3 (the right not to be subject to inhuman or degrading treatment), Article 5 (the right not to be deprived of liberty and security of person), Article 8 (the right to private and family life), Article 9 (freedom of religion). Article 14 (the right not to be discriminated against in the enjoyment of the Convention rights) could buttress the impact of the other Articles in determining whether the current common law infringes Convention rights in not respecting a competent minor's refusal to treatment (Hagger, 2003).

> Rebecca has changed her mind about surgery on the grounds that the risks are too great. She has based her refusal on the extensive personal research that she has undertaken.
>
> ▶ Assuming that Rebecca is *Gillick*-competent, can she refuse surgery?
> ▶ If surgery is considered to be life saving, what is the legal status of her refusal? Would there be a difference if surgery was considered to be discretionary?
> ▶ Can treatment be authorised in the event of her continued refusal?

6.5.3 Cumulative effect: *Gillick* competence, capacity and refusal

Consent for treatment may be given by a 16- or 17-year-old by the statutory *prima facie* presumption of competence, or a *Gillick*-competent minor. However, the common law approach is not merely determined according to competence. It is also status and outcome-based.

Capacity is considered to be a status-based criterion since after the age of 18 the court will not overrule a competent patient's refusal, yet below this age a competent minor apparently cannot validly refuse consent. This was starkly demonstrated in

Re E [1993] 1 FLR 386 where a devout Jehovah's Witness and competent minor had his refusal of a blood transfusion overridden on the basis that he did not fully comprehend the implications of this decision. He died after validly refusing a transfusion once he attained the age of 18. It is difficult to imagine the momentous change that transpired on his 18th birthday such that his refusal before that time could be overridden, but not subsequently.

The approach to capacity is also outcome-based. The graver the risks of refusal, the greater the likelihood that refusal will be overridden. This is illustrated by *Re M (medical treatment: consent)* [1999] 2 FLR 1097, where a 15-year-old girl refused consent to receiving a heart transplant to save her life. Her reasons were that she did not wish to take medication for the rest of her life, but more importantly she did not wish to live with another's heart even if this was a potentially life-saving option. She believed that if she was given a transplant she would be different, to the extent that she would rather die. The court acknowledged the gravity of the decision to override M's wishes, but nonetheless authorised the operation as being in her best interests. Bainham (2005) has commented that this serves as the best illustration of the virtually limitless powers of the courts over the fate of children. In this case, there was no express finding of competence or otherwise, but since an emergency decision was necessary, it proceeded on the assumption that it could override the wishes of a competent minor.

Taken together, the decisions of *Gillick, Re R* and *Re W* demonstrate that a degree of caution is required as to when a doctor may proceed solely on the basis of a mature minor's consent under common law. Following *Gillick* it appears that while a doctor should make every effort to persuade a competent minor to acquiesce with parental involvement in decision making, nevertheless the doctor would be acting lawfully in dealing exclusively with the child in circumstances that were appropriately defined. Parental views should not trump the consent of a competent minor.

Re W and *Re R* cast some doubt on the above analysis. Although these decisions were concerned with refusals (rather than consent), it seems that the 'flak jacket' approach permits medical intervention to proceed following authorisation from any one of three sources: the competent minor, the person with parental responsibility, or the court. The refusal of a minor aged 16 or above, or a *Gillick*-competent minor below the age of 16 can be trumped by the consent from any alternative source. Does this mean that consent can be trumped by parental refusal? It also raises the question as to whether parents have the right to be informed of communications between health-care professionals and their children. If the answer is yes, then this immediately conflicts with the child's rights to confidentiality. There are multiple issues that young people might wish to keep from their parents, particularly those that arise from sexual activity (Herring, 1997). Bainham (2005) reports that termination of pregnancy has generated the greatest amount of litigation in the United States (which has not yet ratified the UNCRC). Whereas parents may not have an absolute right to veto an abortion, in some circumstances it can be constitutional for a State to notify parents that such a procedure is to be undertaken on a competent minor or alternatively to obtain judicial authority. In this jurisdiction, *Gillick* and *Axon* appear to preserve the rights of the competent minor to confidentiality provided that attempts have been made to obtain the minor's agreement to parental involvement.

In the United States a number of jurisdictions have adopted what is termed a 'judicial bypass procedure' which attempts to accommodate the interests of parents and adolescents. It is doubtful that judges are best placed to make decisions that are often based on value judgements. Parental involvement may well be beneficial and there would seem to be merit in seeking the middle ground that could incorporate a collaborative approach such as that advocated by the Department of Health (2001c).

Rebecca has a major row with her parents and tells them to stop interfering.

▶ Consider Rebecca's rights. To what extent is parental involvement an interference with her rights? What rights, or possible rights, does Rebecca have?
▶ Consider whether Rebecca has Convention rights (either the European Convention of Human Rights or UNCRC) that might apply in these circumstances.
▶ What are the limits of parental responsibility particularly where there seems to be a significantly detrimental effect of not having surgery?

6.6 Withholding and withdrawal of treatment

Decisions as to whether or not to commence treatment of newborns with serious and life-threatening medical conditions can be difficult and emotive. The common law is considered in the following section.

6.6.1 Criminal law

Failure to provide life-sustaining treatment could, in theory, satisfy the requirements for murder. Although failure to provide treatment would be an omission (rather than an act), it might nonetheless satisfy the *actus reus* for murder in the event of a duty to treat. However, the requisite *mens rea* (being the necessary state of mind for the offence) would also need to be satisfied. In *R v Arthur* (1981) 12 BMLR 1, a consultant paediatrician was charged with the attempted murder of a newborn with Down's syndrome and birth defects. Dr Arthur prescribed 'nursing care only' with the baby kept sedated following the parents' decision that they did not want their baby to survive. The prosecution's case was that the painkillers and decision not to feed the infant was intended to cause death, while the defence argued that the doctor's actions were accepted medical practice and did not amount to the necessary positive act for attempted murder. The forensic evidence was uncertain as to the precise cause of death.

Farquharson J, in directing the jury, said that '[w]here a child gets pneumonia and is a child with an irreversible handicap, whose mother has rejected him, if the doctor said: "I am not going to give it antibiotics", and by a merciful dispensation of providence he dies…it would be very unlikely, I would suggest, that you (or any other jury) would say that that doctor was committing murder'. At the same time he directed that no one, including the doctor, had the right to kill a disabled infant, any more than the right to kill anyone. The jury acquitted Dr Arthur.

Gunn and Smith (1985) have criticised this decision on the basis that there can be liability for omissions where there is a duty to act. The implication from *Arthur* is that the duty owed would seem to be set at a lower threshold for a child with Down's syndrome, compared with an unaffected child and that this creates ambiguity in the extent to which duties of care are owed to disabled infants.

This does not mean that doctors always have a duty to prolong life. If treatment is futile then doctors are entitled to withhold or discontinue treatment. However, doctors must take an objective determination as to what is in the best interests of the child and not be influenced by irrelevant considerations.

6.6.2 The severely disabled child

The Court's approach to the withdrawal or withholding of treatment in a severely disabled child can be illustrated by the following decisions.

6.6.2(a) Non-terminally ill infants

Re J (a minor) (wardship: medical treatment) [1990] 3 All ER 930 concerned a premature infant born at 27 weeks gestation. J was maintained on a ventilator and his condition was characterised by repetitive seizures and respiratory arrests. Medical evidence suggested that J had permanent and severe brain damage on account of his prematurity and would be blind and deaf. His expected prognosis was upper nerve damage with spastic paralysis of his limbs and it was unlikely that he would be able to sit unsupported. He had a limited life expectancy but would be able to feel pain to the same extent as any other baby.

The question before the court was whether or not, in the event of a further respiratory arrest, it would be lawful not to resuscitate him and to withhold artificial ventilation. At first instance Scott Baker J directed that there should be no further ventilation on account of the inevitable distress and limited benefit from the procedure. The Court of Appeal upheld this decision approving a palliative care regime avoiding further hazardous and invasive procedures. In giving judgement Taylor LJ, having taken all the circumstances into account, stated: 'In those circumstances, without there being any question of deliberately ending the life or shortening it, I consider the court is entitled in the best interests of the child to say that deliberate steps should not be taken artificially to prolong its miserable lifespan...'

At least three important points emerge. The first is that in arriving at such a decision, it is the child's best interests that is the paramount consideration and is in essence an application of the welfare principle. The second is that there is no absolute rule that life-prolonging treatment should never be withheld. However, the point at which this decision should be made is difficult to determine since it will almost always be in a child's best interests to continue living. Third, what is the threshold at which it would be in the child's best interests to withdraw or withhold potentially life-sustaining treatment?

In considering the last point, Taylor J (at 945) applied what is known as the 'intolerability test'. He stated:

> I consider that the correct approach is for the court to judge the quality of life the child would have to endure if given the treatment and decide whether in all the circumstances such a life would be so afflicted as to be intolerable to that child. I say "to that child" because the test should not be whether the life would be tolerable to the decider. The test must be whether the child in question, if capable of exercising sound judgement, would consider the life tolerable.

In emphasising the need to assess quality of life from the perspective of the child, rather than the decision-maker, is an application of the 'substituted judgement test'. Bainham (2005) asserts that this equates with the best interests of the child being that which the child would have wished for had he been fully competent. This perception has been criticised on the grounds that it is contrary to the usual application of the welfare principle. It necessarily amounts to a legal fiction since there is no basis upon which supposed views and wishes can be predicted since the infant has never possessed the ability to express such a view.

In these circumstances it seems evident that the court will rely upon two principal factors. First, a balancing exercise will be undertaken to determine the quality of life of that particular child. Second, the decision will be guided by the weight of medical evidence to ascertain whether, on the basis of clinical judgement, life-prolonging treatment should be withdrawn or withheld.

6.6.2(b) Terminally ill infants

Re C (a minor) (wardship: medical treatment) [1989] 2 All ER 782 concerned a terminally ill infant who was made a ward of court following birth. She was born with hydrocephalus, poorly formed brain structure, and expert medical opinion was that the aim of treatment should be to ease suffering rather than achieve a short prolongation of life.

At first instance, Ward J directed the hospital authorities to treat the infant in such a way to allow her 'to die with the greatest dignity and the least of pain, suffering and distress'. The Official Solicitor appealed against these directions that treatment of serious infections and intravenous therapy were not necessary. The Court of Appeal accepted that the purpose of treatment would be to ease suffering rather than to achieve a short prolongation of life. However, it was inappropriate to direct how the infant should be treated. The stance that the hospital should not be required to treat any serious infection or set up an intravenous feeding system was removed and the direction was amended 'to treat the minor to allow life to come to an end peacefully and with dignity'. This decision confirms that there is no absolute right to heroic treatment and that in the instance of a terminally ill child, the court can give broad directions about the general nature of (non) treatment but will leave the detail to health-care professionals.

6.6.3 Parental wishes

Decisions to withhold or withdraw life-saving treatment, particularly for the very young child with congenital disabilities, may be brought to court particularly where there is conflict between those with parental responsibility and clinicians. Parents may insist on life-sustaining treatment against medical opinion, or *vice versa*. A further scenario is where parents and doctors agree that no further intervention should be undertaken but approval is sought in order to declare the course of action as lawful. Each case will turn on its facts, but case law is illustrative of the likely reasoning and approach in these potentially difficult and fraught circumstances.

In *Re B (a minor) (wardship: medical treatment)* [1990] 3 All ER 927, an infant born with Down's syndrome also had an intestinal blockage that could easily be corrected. Successful surgery would mean that her life expectancy would be around 20 to 30 years, whereas without the operation she would die within days. Her parents refused consent on the grounds that it was not in her best interests to survive with her mental and physical conditions. The local authority made the child a ward of court and applied for authorisation for surgery to proceed. At first instance the application was refused in deference to the parents' wishes but this was overturned on appeal.

In giving judgement, Templeman LJ said (at 929):

> I have no doubt that it is the duty of this court to decide that the child must live. The judge [at first instance] was much affected by the reasons given by the parents and came to the conclusion that their wishes ought to be respected. In my judgement he erred in that the duty of the court is to decide whether it is in the interests of the child that an operation should take place.

The decision emphasises two important principles. First, there is no absolute rule that parental wishes must be respected where questions of life and death of their children are concerned. The court, in exercising its wardship jurisdiction, can override parental wishes where this is deemed appropriate. Second, the court has a duty to make a qualitative assessment of the life of the child in the longer term and the interests of the child must be the overriding consideration.

The resurgence of parental rights can be seen in the Court of Appeal decision in *Re T (a minor) (wardship: medical treatment)* [1997] 1 All ER 906 (see 6.4.4(a)), where consensus medical opinion was that a life-saving liver transplant was necessary in the infant's best interests, and against parental objections. The Court of Appeal held that it was not in the best interests of the child for the operation to take place against the wishes of the mother.

Alex and David want everything to be done to save Jude's life and seek advice:

▶ What are the options for Alex and David if they seek a declaration of best interests?
▶ What are the key issues that the court would likely consider?
▶ How is medical opinion weighed against parental wishes? Link this with the prolific case law in this area.
▶ If the court decides in favour of parental views, what can be done to ensure that treatment is carried out?

Consider the similarities in *Re T* and *Re B* above. In *Re T* much persuasive weight was given to parental wishes and it is of note that both parents were health professionals. They were also living in New Zealand and they would have had to return their child to the United Kingdom to allow the transplant to take place. What makes *Re T* controversial is that the Court of Appeal was prepared to make a close association between the interests of the mother and child. It was also prepared to attach significance to the practicalities of care with regard to the child (with respect to returning to the United Kingdom and for post-operative care), yet in *Re B* the court was prepared to state that if necessary, responsibility for substitute care for the child should fall upon the local authority.

Re T represents a rare example of the court rejecting medical opinion in favour of parental refusal. Conflation of maternal interests with that of the child can be contentious as it can relegate the child's interests to a lesser position. Butler-Sloss LJ sought to distinguish *Re T* from *Re B* when she said, 'Unlike the intestinal obstruction of the Down's syndrome baby which could be cured by a single operation, T's problems require complicated surgery and many years of special care from the mother'. Whether this is a convincing argument seems doubtful since parental refusal tends to be overridden if the child's health or life would be at risk by not having proposed treatment (see *Re B* at 6.6.3).

Disputes can arise when doctors consider that life support should be withheld against the wishes of parents. In *Re C (a minor) (medical treatment)* [1998] Lloyds Rep Med 1 Fam Div, a 16-month baby was seriously ill with a fatal condition known as spinal muscular atresia which caused her to stop breathing. Medical opinion was that further ventilation was futile and was not in her best interests. In the event of a further respiratory arrest, additional active resuscitation or re-ventilation would subject the infant to further suffering and was unlikely to help her prognosis. The parents wanted treatment to continue and sought a court order on the grounds of their religious beliefs. In giving judgement, Sir Stephen Brown P stated that he had no doubt that in this desperate situation it was in the best interests of the child that she should be taken off ventilation and that this should not be recommenced in the event of a further arrest. It was a desperately sad situation for all concerned and his decision was one taken with 'grave solemnity' because of sincere parental conviction. Nevertheless, the child's best interests were fundamentally important and while sanctity of life was a central consideration, it was not the paramount determination. The proposed course of withholding aggressive treatment was in the best interests of the child in the context of her prognosis, and for the avoidance of suffering.

The more recent Wyatt litigation, *Re Wyatt (a child) (medical treatment: parents' consent)* [2004] EWHC 2247 (Fam) and *Re Wyatt (No3) (a child) (medical treatment: continuation of order)* [2005] EWHC 693 (Fam) and *Re Wyatt (a child) (medical treatment: continuation of order)* [2005] EWCA Civ 1181, illustrates the judicial approach in two important respects, namely with regard to parental demands for continuation of treatment against medical opinion, and the approach for granting declaratory relief.

Charlotte Wyatt was an extremely premature infant with chronic respiratory and renal problems and profound brain damage. Medical opinion was that further invasive treatment would not be in her best interests and Hedley J concluded: 'I do not believe that any further aggressive treatment, even if necessary to prolong life, is in her best interests.' This is not unsurprising and is similar to the approach taken by Sir Stephen Brown P in *Re C* above. Charlotte's parents returned to court on several occasions, with evidence that their daughter's condition had improved. In the event of a further respiratory collapse they sought confirmation that the previous declaration would be set aside. Hedley J continued to be persuaded by medical opinion that intensive therapy should not be undertaken in the future. The Court of Appeal approved of Hedley J's judgement and also stated that the court should not become embroiled in granting declaratory relief with respect to future anticipatory situations that might never arise. It was misuse of process to use the court as a sounding board for general advice, and judgement was to be delivered with respect to specific situations rather than being anticipatory. On the facts, Charlotte's medical condition had not materially changed and therefore Hedley J's continuation of the declaration was approved. In a fourth hearing, Hedley J considered Charlotte's condition and on the facts was satisfied that it had changed sufficiently for previous declarations with regard to non-treatment to be set aside. A few months later, he was asked to consider the case for the fifth time (by which time Charlotte's parents had separated). There had been a significant deterioration in Charlotte's condition and it was decided in accordance with unanimous medical evidence that should the need arise it would be in the child's best interests that further aggressive intervention (intubation and ventilation) was withheld.

At least two issues of importance emerge from *Wyatt*. In relation to declaratory relief each situation is considered on its own facts at that particular time and declaratory relief should not be of indefinite duration. The second is in relation to parental wishes to continue treatment against medical opinion. In these situations, in considering what lies in the child's best interests, it is likely that the court will give considerable weight to medical opinion in preference to parental views.

An intermediate approach that may be taken is where, against medical opinion, the court specifies that only particular types of non-intervention would be in the child's best interests, and therefore lawful. This approach was apparent in the first instance decision in *An NHS Trust v B* [2005] EWCA Civ 1181 which involved a boy with spinal muscular atrophy. Medical opinion was that it would not be in the child's best medical interests to continue life-prolonging treatment. In applying the welfare principle and determining best interests, Holman J drew up a balance sheet of benefits of treatment compared against the expected burdens of continuing or discontinuing treatment. His conclusion was that despite the disadvantages or burdens, the boy experienced pleasure from certain aspects of life, such as watching television and his relationship with his family. The judge ordered that certain aspects of life-prolonging treatment were to be continued, such as maintaining ventilation, while recognising that more aggressive therapy such as cardiopulmonary resuscitation would not be in the child's best interests and accordingly these should be withheld. A key issue that may lead the court to favour life-prolonging measures lies in the level of awareness of the child and its capacity to gain experiential pleasure. In *Re K (a minor)* [2006] EWHC 1007 (Fam), the ability of the child to gain pleasure from life was virtually non-existent and under these circumstances the court authorised that it was in the best interests to cease providing life-prolonging treatment (in this case, parenteral nutrition).

6.6.4   Guidance from professional bodies

The Royal College of Paediatrics and Child Health (RCPCH, 2004) has provided guidance on the circumstances where withholding or withdrawing life-sustaining medical treatment may be considered. Five situations have been identified:

▶ The 'brain dead' child. The criteria for diagnosis of brain stem death must be agreed by two practitioners. Treatment in these circumstances is considered to be futile and withdrawal of medical treatment is considered appropriate.
▶ The 'permanent vegetative state'. Where it is considered that the child will never regain consciousness it may be deemed appropriate to withdraw or withhold life-sustaining treatment.
▶ The 'no chance' situation where the child has such severe ill-health or disease that life-sustaining treatment merely delays death without real or significant alleviation of suffering.
▶ The 'no purpose' situation where the child may survive treatment. However, the degree of physical or mental impairment is expected to be so great that it would be unreasonable to expect the child to bear it.
▶ The 'unbearable' situation of progressive or irreversible illness where the child and/ or family members consider that further treatment is more than can be borne and they wish to have treatment withdrawn, or withheld, irrespective of medical opinion that there may be some ensuing benefit.

Jude is readmitted to hospital and ventilated. Doctors wish to switch off the ventilator in his best interests after his condition has deteriorated. Alex and David protest vigorously that the baby has a right to life.

▶ What are the baby's rights in these situations?
▶ Does Jude have an Article 2 right to life?
▶ What rights do parents have in such situations and is there infringement of their Article 8 rights?

6.7 Conjoined twins

The Court of Appeal decision of *Re A (children) (conjoined twins: surgical separation)* [2001] 1 FLR 1 raised a myriad of legal and ethical issues. The court was asked to authorise separation of conjoined twins in circumstances that would inevitably lead to the death of the weaker twin, Mary, while allowing the stronger twin, Jodie, a good chance of survival. If surgical separation did not go ahead, it was inevitable that the twins would die. The parents were devout Roman Catholics and refused their consent in the knowledge that separation would inevitably lead to the death of Mary. Surgical separation was authorised at first instance and then again on appeal. The operation went ahead and Mary died. Jodie survived and returned home with her parents to the Mediterranean island of Gozo.

The interest in this case lies in the reasoning and approach taken by the courts in grappling with the thorny ethical and legal issues at the heart of the decision to operate the twins. Surgical separation would inevitably mean the death of one twin and the survival of the other. The first point to consider is, what is the correct principle to apply in the circumstances where the interests of two children conflict and how much weight should be attached to parental views? In terms of the principles to be applied there was an inevitable clash since the best interests of the twins pulled in opposite directions. This meant that the welfare principle could not be viewed as paramount for both children at the same time. The majority in the Court of Appeal adopted a utilitarian approach. Family law considerations are apparent in the judgement of Ward LJ, who stated that to say that welfare is paramount would be a trite observation in these particular circumstances. In his view, to state that the proposed operation would be in Mary's best interests was incorrect. Nor could the court put Jodie's interests as uppermost since this would be contrary to the paramountcy principle with respect to Mary's interests. The stark reality was that the surgical team could save Jodie, whereas Mary was beyond help. Hence he stated (at 50):

> I am in no doubt at all that the scales come down heavily in Jodie's favour. The best interests of the twins is to give the chance of life to the child whose actual bodily condition is capable of accepting the chance to her advantage even if that has to be at the cost of the sacrifice of the life which is so unnaturally supported. I am wholly satisfied that the least detrimental choice, balancing the interests of Mary against Jodie and Jodie against Mary, is to permit the operation to be performed.

There is clearly a tension between such a utilitarian approach and one that emphasises individual human rights or even the paramountcy of welfare of each child. Perhaps this was in the mind of Robert Walker LJ when he took the approach that although surgery would plainly be in Jodie's best interests, it would also be in the best interests of Mary because remaining alive and conjoined would deprive both of bodily integrity and human dignity. The case provides support for the principle that parental views do not hold ultimate sway even though these may be sincerely felt and reasonable in the circumstances. In the final analysis, respecting the religious views of the parents was not of decisive importance.

From the perspective of criminal law, the essential issue concerns the distinction between omissions (such as the withdrawal of life-sustaining treatment) and the positive act of killing. An omission would generally not be unlawful (unless there was a positive duty to treat), whereas a positive act could amount to an unlawful killing. In this case the positive act was surgical separation. In his analysis, Ward LJ started from the *Woollin* principle to consider whether he was satisfied that death or serious harm would be a virtually certain consequence of surgical separation and stated that it was common ground that the death of Mary would result from severance of their conjoined common aorta. His approach to obviating 'murderous intent' upon the surgeons was to resort to the justification of self-defence. His reasoning was that since Mary was reliant upon Jodie's heart and lungs for her survival, continuation of their conjoined state would cause Jodie's heart to fail and lead to her death. Therefore, separation could be rationalised on the basis of representing a form of self-defence for Jodie. He took pains to qualify that such a decision should not become authority for wider propositions and that this particular case had quite exceptional circumstances.

In contrast to Ward LJ's approach of quasi self-defence, Brooke LJ relied on the doctrine of necessity. In his reasoning, Mary was designated for an early death and nobody could extend her life beyond a short span. However, continuation of her life was at the expense of her sister's. In his view, given that the principles of family law pointed irresistibly towards the interests of Jodie, it was necessary to undertake surgical separation.

Ward LJ's comments are of particular interest in that it would have been equally legitimate to comply with parental wishes (as a result of which both twins would have died). This seems to be at odds with the doctrine of necessity because a situation cannot be necessary and yet optional at the same time. Perhaps his comments were founded on giving more consideration to parental views. Gillon (2001b) argues that parental opinion should have been given greater weight as the parents were neither incompetent nor negligent, but they were religious and their reasoning was based upon widely accepted moral analysis. According to Gillon, the court 'should have declined to deprive the parents of their normal responsibilities and rights in order to impose its own preferred resolution of the moral dilemma and should have allowed the parents to refuse medical intervention – while still ruling as it did, that such separation would not have been unlawful had the parents consented'.

Another issue is that of human rights and the extent to which these were engaged and respected, if at all, by the decision. Although the case was decided prior to implementation of the Human Rights Act 1998 nonetheless some arguments were justifiably presented under Convention rights, particularly with respect to the right to life. Article 2 provides that 'Everyone's right to life shall be protected by law' and that 'No one shall be deprived of his life intentionally...' Article 2 therefore poses two obligations, the first being a positive obligation to protect life and the second as a negative obligation not to deprive of life, intentionally. In the court's view, the stronger obligation was the former. In terms of discharging the negative obligation under Article 2, the European Court found that there was already a legal framework against unlawful killing in English jurisdiction.

6.8 Research in children

Clinical research undertaken on minors involves a range of ethical and legal issues, particularly consent to participation. In the event that no standard treatment is available for a seriously ill child and an innovative treatment is available, then subject to the duty of care being satisfied on clinical grounds, participation may be appropriate subject to the course of action being in the best interests of the child and appropriate consent or authorisation being obtained. Participation in clinical research that is of no direct benefit to the child is controversial.

6.8.1 General principles

Children are regarded as a particularly vulnerable group. As such, they need protection and there is an argument that children and infants ought not to participate in clinical research. Although protective, this stance has inevitable negative implications such as stultifying therapeutic developments in paediatric medicine and health care. Physiologically, children are not simply 'small adults' and research findings from studies conducted on adults cannot always be extrapolated to children. Aspirin, for example, has been known to precipitate Reye's syndrome in children with serious results. It is also apparent that diseases can manifest differently in children than in adults. By way of example, lymphoma is a disease that can occur in adults and children but has a completely different clinical course in children when compared to adults. If children with conditions such as this are not allowed to participate in research which aims to develop new and more efficacious therapies, then paediatric medical progress could easily be impeded.

In addition to the potential vulnerability of children who are ill and dependent on their doctor is the potential for a conflict of interest if parents are given inducements to enrol their children into trials. There is no blanket exclusion of persons who are in dependant positions from participating in research and the sixth version of the Declaration of Helsinki, as adopted by the World Medical Association in October 2008, declares that such persons may participate in research provided that an appropriately qualified individual, who is independent of such a relationship, provides consent. A further confounding factor is that if children are not allowed to participate in research, then treatment that is regarded as fairly standard for adults will in fact be innovative for children since the effects of treatment will not have been rigorously assessed in the paediatric age group. Arguably, exclusion of minors could be challenged as discriminatory on the grounds that a child should have more optimised health care based upon an adequate evidence base.

6.8.2 The common law

The courts have yet to address the issue of clinical research in children. Section 8(1) of the Family Law Reform Act 1969 (see 6.4.1) is limited to therapeutic and diagnostic procedures. Although a *Gillick*-competent child may give valid consent to treatment, it remains unclear as to whether a suitably mature minor may consent to clinical research participation.

The authorities of *S v S* [1972] AC 24 and *Simms v Simms* [2002] EWHC 2734 illustrate some of the issues involved. Whilst neither case actually involved research in children, useful analogies can be drawn as to how the common law might approach the question of clinical research in the paediatric age group.

In *Simms v Simms* a High Court declaration was obtained stating that it was lawful to use innovative treatment on a 16- and 18-year-old who suffered from variant Creutzfeldt-Jakob disease. As a result of the condition, the teenagers were terminally ill and exhibited a range of neurological abnormalities. There was no cure or recognised treatment although clinical research studies in Japan had identified a treatment although tests had only been carried out on animals. The treatment had previously been used on humans as treatment for thrombosis. The parents applied for declaratory relief that the teenagers lacked decision-making capacity and that the innovative treatment would be in their best interests in that there was a possibility of unquantifiable benefit and furthermore, there was no alternative treatment available.

The court required that medical care be given in accordance with a responsible and competent body of professional opinion in accordance with the 'Bolam standard', although satisfaction of this requirement for an untried treatment would be difficult, if not impossible. According to Dame Butler-Sloss, 'The "Bolam test" ought not to be allowed to inhibit medical progress ... if one waited for the "Bolam test" to be complied with to its fullest extent, no innovative work such as the use of penicillin or performing heart transplant surgery would ever be attempted'. In declaring that treatment would be in the best interests, the court was prepared to take a flexible approach to innovative therapy.

In *S v S* the House of Lords had to consider the refusal of two mothers to allow their ex-husbands to paternity test their children (during divorce proceedings). The approach taken was that the blood tests would be lawful if these were not against the interests of the children. The House also considered the public interest to see justice being done particularly since the blood tests were minimally invasive. Again, although this case did not involve clinical research, these principles could perhaps be extrapolated to apply to clinical research that is minimally invasive, provided that participation was not against the interests of the child. There might be further justification with respect to the potential benefit that might accrue from such research, with respect to possible direct benefit to the participant as well as indirect benefits gained by enhancement of the medical knowledge base.

6.8.3 Guidance on research in children

The Medicines for Human Use (Clinical Trials) Regulations 2004, Schedule I Part IV deal with conditions and principles that apply in relation to minors and clinical research. These are found at paragraphs 6–10 as follows:

- ▶ The minor receives information according to his or her capacity for understanding of the trial's risks and benefits, and this information to be provided by staff who have experience with children.
- ▶ The explicit wish of the minor to be withdrawn from the clinical trial at any time must be considered by the investigator.
- ▶ That no incentives or financial inducements are given to the minor, or to those with parental responsibility, or the minor's legal representative (except provisions for compensation in the event of injury or loss).
- ▶ That the clinical trial relates directly to a clinical condition from which the minor suffers or the research is of such a nature that it can only be carried out on minors.
- ▶ That there is some direct benefit for the group of patients involved in the clinical trial and which is to be obtained from that trial.

The Clinical Trials Regulations appear to suggest that if research is solely non-therapeutic and not in the child's best interests, then children ought not to be involved unless there is some direct benefit for the child from that particular trial. The Medical Research Council (MRC) 2004, in its guidance on medical research involving children, takes a more flexible approach and provides that since the benefits of research are unpredictable, the investigator needs to be satisfied that the research is not contrary to the child participant's interests. A similar approach is taken by the Royal College of Paediatrics and Child Health (RCPCH) (2000) which states that a research procedure which is not intended to be of direct benefit to the child is not necessarily unethical or illegal. However, valid consent can only be achieved if the risks are sufficiently small so as not to go against the child's best interests. The approach taken by the MRC and the RCPCH is more in line with the reasoning in *S v S* with regard to procedures which, while not directly being of benefit to the child, may be undertaken if they are not against the interests of the child, provided they are minimally invasive and there is another justifiable reason for doing so.

The General Medical Council, in its guidance on research for children (General Medical Council, 0–18 years: guidance for all doctors, 2007) states that research involving children and young people can benefit all children, although they should be involved only when research in adults cannot provide the same benefits. Research can be undertaken 'as long as the research does not go against their best interests or involves only minimal or low risk of harm'. Note that the guidance states that research should not be against the best interests of the child, rather than being in the best interests. The guidance offers examples of minimally invasive procedures, as including blood samples and questionnaires.

The GMC guidance states that prior to involving children in research, necessary approval should be obtained from the relevant research ethics committee, the Medical Research Council or a Medical Royal College. The EU Directive that pertains to the ethical considerations of clinical trials of medicinal products conducted within the paediatric population (EC No 1901/2006) reiterates the need for informed consent from the minor's legal representative and also recommends that the child's assent should be sought. In practice, in addition to obtaining relevant approval for such research, consent from the parent or representative will be required as well as the child's agreement, and in some cases it may even be necessary (dependent upon the degree of risk and level of invasiveness) to obtain judicial authorisation.

Rebecca informs her parents that she has been participating in a clinical trial.

▶ Consider the possible ethical and legal issues of participation.
▶ Can her parents prevent her from participating?
▶ Have the clinical trial investigators committed an offence?

6.9 Organs and tissue for transplantation

As a general tenet, parents have power to consent to treatment of a therapeutic nature whereas it is doubtful if they can consent to non-therapeutic procedures unless this is in the child's best interests. However, some interventions that are non-therapeutic, such as research, may still be undertaken provided that this is not against the child's interests.

Particularly difficult issues can arise in circumstances where it is envisaged that a child might become a living organ donor. Donation may be justified on an altruistic basis in that it is of benefit to other children. However, this must be balanced against the fact that it may have no direct benefit to the child who is undergoing that procedure. Furthermore, with regard to organ transplantation, the harvesting of organs may be hazardous and uncomfortable.

6.9.1 Human Tissue Act 2004

Section 1 of the Human Tissue Act 2004 requires 'appropriate consent' to be obtained for the storage or use of material taken from a living person for the purpose of transplantation. If a child lacks capacity, or does not want to make a decision, then appropriate consent can be obtained from a person with parental responsibility, (section 2(3)). According to the Codes of Practice, Code 1 (which pertains to consent) states that provided that children are competent, they can provide appropriate consent. The Code also outlines a summary of the *Gillick* competence test. Code 2, which pertains to organ donation, tissues and cells, provides that children can be considered as living organ donors in exceptional and rare circumstances. If the child is competent the decision to consent must be made by the child, and it is good practice to consult the person with parental responsibility (paragraph 33). Donation must also be approved by a panel of at least three members of the Human Tissue Authority. This situation is at odds with the common law whereby a child's refusal to treatment can be overridden by those with parental responsibility. This is perhaps rationalised on the grounds that once tissue has been removed, its storage and use could be construed as being less harmful than the effects of refusal of therapeutic treatment. However, this is not to underplay the potential adverse effects of the surgical procedure used for removal.

Where the child has died, organ retrieval is lawful under section 2(7) which provides:

Where the child concerned has died ... 'appropriate consent' means –

(a) if a decision of his to consent to the activity, or a decision of his not to consent to it, was in force immediately before he died, his consent;

(b) if paragraph (a) does not apply –

(i) the consent of a person who had parental responsibility for him immediately before he died, or

(ii) where no person had parental responsibility for him immediately before he died, the consent of a person who stood in a qualifying relationship to him at that time.

However, in the case of a deceased child, the appropriate consent provision would apply only if there was evidence that the child had been *Gillick*-competent and had previously consented to (or refused) organ retrieval.

6.9.2 Common law

There is no relevant case law in this jurisdiction addressing living organ donation from children. Section 8(1) of the Family Law Reform Act 1969 is specifically limited to therapeutic and diagnostic procedures, and the capacity to consent to transplantation was not considered in *Gillick*.

In *Re W* (see 6.5.2) in the Court of Appeal, *obiter* comments were made on the legality of using a child as a donor, although these remarks failed to clarify the position. One view from these comments is that *Gillick* competence may extend to donation of blood or organs, although this was contradicted by later statements which seem to suggest that as far as the donor is concerned, donation does not constitute treatment or diagnosis. It is unlikely that any practising clinician in this jurisdiction would involve a child as a living donor and if an unavoidable need did arise, then it is almost certain that a court application would be made to determine the legality of such an action.

There is United States case law that addresses child organ donation. In *Hart v Brown* [1972] 289 A 2d 386 (Connecticut Supreme Court), the view of the court was that the psychological benefits to the donor from donation to her identical twin sister and the outcome, namely the survival and companionship that would ensue, would justify the risk of donation. Guidance from the General Medical Council (0–18 years: guidance for all doctors, 2007 at para 41) states:

> The Human Tissue Act 2004 and Human Tissue (Scotland) Act 2006 were passed following inquiries into the storage of children's organs and tissue without the proper consent. The Acts make consent central to the lawful storage and use of children and young people's organs and tissue, and to the removal of such material after death. The Human Tissue Authority regulates and issues codes of practice on activities covered by the Act in England, Wales and Northern Ireland. Scottish ministers have those powers in Scotland.

6.10 Confidentiality

If *Gillick* is viewed as a mechanism for the mature minor to exercise autonomy on the basis that the child is capable of making decisions about medical treatment, then it follows that that child is entitled to medical confidentiality. *Gillick* provides authority that a duty of confidentiality is owed to the mature minor, as affirmed in *Axon*. The extent of the duty will depend upon the nature of the treatment in that the child's capacity to consent will depend upon his or her understanding of that particular treatment.

Another perspective is Lord Donaldson's flak-jacket approach of legal immunity being conferred with consent to treatment (see 6.5.2). From this perspective, the child's consent operates as protection for the doctor in order to proceed with therapeutic treatment or intervention. Confidentiality, in this context, may be maintained in good faith and operates to protect the doctor as well as the child. However, there is no duty on the doctor to maintain confidentiality and he would not be in breach of the duty of care if he later chose to disclose matters to those with parental responsibility. This is because the child's consent is not based upon exercise of the child's autonomy but instead provides legal immunity with respect to providing treatment. Nevertheless, deliberately breaching the confidentiality of the child serves no useful purpose because with confidentiality comes trust and young people might not be inclined to seek medical care and advice if they feel that they cannot have trust in their doctor.

The General Medical Council guidance emphasises the need to attempt to share information with the consent of the child: an explanation should be given as to why a doctor might need to share information and ask the child for their anticipatory consent to do so. Of course, information would be shared without consent in certain circumstances, such as in the public interest, when required by law, where disclosure is in the best interests of a child who may not have the maturity or understanding to make a decision about disclosure, to protect the child from harm or in the case of a child who lacks capacity.

It is tempting to consider confidentiality as having two characteristics. The positive aspect is that the doctor must respect the confidence of the *Gillick*-competent child, whereas the negative aspect provides that the doctor may respect such confidence. The negative aspect can be justified on the basis that *Gillick*-competent confidence represents merely a flak jacket that is available for legal immunity for treatment decisions.

The positive aspect of confidentiality may apply to contraceptive advice to girls under the age of 16 (as in *Gillick*) and to abortion (as in *Axon*). Abortion and contraceptive advice could be classified as 'special' in that they are both strongly underpinned by elements of public policy, namely the avoidance of teenage pregnancy. In the United States, the constitutional right to privacy was considered in the context of abortion in *Bellotti v Baird* 443 US 662 (1979). A statute that required parental consent before a minor could be entitled to an abortion was considered and the court was asked to strike it down. It was held that a statute that allowed an external agency to have a veto could not be constitutional. However, in this particular instance it could be constitutionally valid only because 'every pregnant minor is entitled in the first instance to go directly to the court for a judicial determination without parental notice, consultation or consent' for the purpose of proving herself sufficiently mature to take a decision, in which case the court will automatically uphold her autonomy. In Montgomery's analysis (1987 at 102), this

> position is similar to that which now prevails in English law. It differs in that the person who must decide whether the minor is sufficiently mature to take her own decision is, in this country, a doctor and not a judge... Translated into the English context, this would mean that a minor is entitled to approach his or her doctor to have that person determine her capacity to consent to the medical procedures without her parents being informed. If she is found not to have that capacity, she must choose between not receiving the treatment or telling her parents, but that is her choice, not the doctor's.

What would be the outcome if parents requested access to the medical records of their children, as opposed to asking the doctor for details of their child's treatment? The General Medical Council guidance (paragraph 53) states: 'Young people with capacity have the legal right to access their own health records and can allow or prevent access by others, including their parents. [There is a qualification that in some circumstances disclosures may be made without consent.] In Scotland, anyone aged twelve or over is legally presumed to have such capacity. A child might of course achieve capacity earlier or later'. At paragraph 54, the guidance states that parents should be allowed access to their child's medical records if the child or young person consents or lacks capacity and disclosure does not go against the child's best interests. However, if the records contain information given by the child in confidence, then normally disclosure ought not to occur without the child's consent.

Rebecca's parents consider that they should have been informed about her abortion. They visit the General Practitioner and demand to see her medical records.

- ▶ Does the General Practitioner owe Rebecca a duty of confidentiality?
- ▶ In the circumstances should her parents have been informed?
- ▶ What are the limits of confidentiality within a medical situation in a *Gillick*-competent child?
- ▶ Did her friend Emma have a duty to inform the parents?
- ▶ Can parents demand to see medical notes?

6.11 Cultural health issues

Ritual circumcision is an irreversible procedure and involves modification of the external genitalia usually for non-therapeutic purposes, such as religion or culture. Female circumcision is prohibited by section 1 of the Female Genital Mutilation Act 2003. However, male circumcision is not prohibited, and can be undertaken for religious or cultural reasons, if both parents consent.

In *Re J* [1999] 2 FLR 678, the child's mother was a non-practising Christian. The father was a non-practising Muslim and the mother objected to circumcision of their son, against the father's views. The Court of Appeal supported the mother's objections as there was no medical reason for circumcision and also on the grounds that the mother had primary responsibility for the child. In *Re S (children)* [2004] EWCA Civ 1257 the circumcision of an 8-year-old boy who had been brought up according to his father's Jain faith was not held to be in the boy's best interests. The parents had separated and the mother wanted the boy circumcised according to her Muslim faith. The Court of Appeal held that circumcision would not be in the boy's best interests. Although the Muslim religion favoured circumcision by the age of 10 years, there was no upper age limit and the child could make a decision for himself once he attained *Gillick* competence.

The Human Rights Act 1998, Article 9 (freedom of religion) may be relevant and directly engages in a situation such as this where the child is being actively reared in a religion where circumcision is the norm. In *Re S* (above) the court stated that the child had been ambivalent about his religion and was not old enough to decide or understand the long-term implications, particularly whether the child wished to practice Jainism when he matured. Each case will turn on its facts and the engagement of Article 9(1) is subject to the qualification in 9(2) as being necessary in a democratic society. The guidance provided by the General Medical Council (paragraph 35) is that in assessing the best interests of the child, the doctor 'should consider the religious and cultural beliefs and values of the child or young person and their parents as well as any social, psychological and emotional benefits. This may be relevant in circumcision of male children for religious or cultural reasons...' However, medical interventions in children that are of non-therapeutic value will continue to remain problematic with respect to their validity, particularly if their justification is founded on cultural norms and compounded by disagreement between parents.

Summary

6.1 Clinical decision-making for children and adolescents must be viewed in the context that children have rights as well as the growing dominance of autonomy-based reasoning in medical law. This is particularly important for competent minors who may be able to give consent themselves. In other circumstances, parents can provide the requisite consent, or the court can exercise such power under the Children Act, through wardship or exercising its inherent jurisdiction.

6.2 The Children Act 1989 is the most important single source of child law. It is underpinned by the principles of 'welfare', 'no order' and 'delay is prejudicial'. While the statute applies mainly to the upbringing of a child and dealings regarding the child's property, its principles are generic and extend to health-care decision making.

6.3 Children have rights under the Human Rights Act 1998. An authoritative and comprehensive statement of fundamental rights of children is contained in the United Nations Convention on the Rights of the Child. (UNCRC). Although ratified by the United Kingdom, its substantive provisions do not form part of English law. Articles 8, 6 and 14 of the European Convention have particular relevance to health-care decision-making in children.

Summary cont'd

6.4 Section 8 of the Family Law Reform Act 1969 provides a statutory right to consent to medical treatment for minors aged 16 or over. Those with parental responsibility for the child have power to consent to the child's medical treatment and provided that both parents have parental responsibility, either would normally be able to give valid consent. At common law, a child below 16 may consent to clinically indicated treatment if he or she has sufficient understanding and intelligence to fully understand the proposed treatment (*Gillick* competence). The court can authorise a course of action or medical treatment undertaken by doctors as being lawful and can also override parental refusal to treatment, in the best interests of the child.

6.5 Refusal of treatment by a minor aged 16 or 17, or by a *Gillick*-competent minor below the age of 16, or not bonding and treatment may proceed lawfully if valid consent is obtained from a person with parental responsibility, or if authorised by the court.

6.6 Withholding or withdrawing treatment (that may result in the death of a child) could amount to a charge of murder or manslaughter. Doctors need to carefully consider treatment that is in the best interests of the child, having regard to professional guidance as well as clearly documenting their reasons. In situations of doubt or disagreement between parties, a declaration order should be sought. The common law suggests that where the child may have a serious disability or an extremely poor prognosis, then the court is inclined towards authorising palliative care rather than aggressive intervention. In deciding whether to authorise non-intervention or continue life-prolonging treatment, the court will determine what lies in the best interests of the child and medical opinion will generally be given considerable weight. The Royal College of Paediatrics and Child Health provides guidance for situations where it may be ethical and legal to consider withholding or withdrawing life-sustaining medical treatment in children.

6.7 The conjoined twins' case presented a range of ethical and legal challenges. When the welfare of two children was considered simultaneously, the court adopted a utilitarian approach. From a criminal law perspective, the positive act of surgery that led to the death of one of the twins was justified on the grounds of quasi self-defence and necessity, thereby avoiding a possible charge of homicide.

6.8 Children are vulnerable subjects for the purpose of clinical research. Participation may be allowed if the research provides direct benefit to the child or, if there is no direct benefit, provided it is not against the child's interests and has minimal risks. In all forms of research in children, appropriate ethical approval must be sought, along with consent from the parents or legal representative, as well as the child's agreement.

6.9 Parental consent regarding organ removal or organ donation from a child poses problematic issues because the procedure is hazardous and may not be of direct clinical benefit to the child. The Human Tissue Act 2004 applies to retrieval of organs from the dead child. There is no case law in this jurisdiction that addresses the issue of the child as a living donor.

6.10 A duty of confidentiality is owed to the *Gillick*-competent child. In sharing information, a participative approach should be sought and the child's consent should be obtained. However, information can be shared without consent in certain circumstances which (amongst others) include the public interest, disclosures by law if non-disclosure is not in the best interests of the child, and protection from harm.

6.11 Non-therapeutic intervention, such as ritual male circumcision, is permitted on religious and cultural grounds provided that it is in the best interests of the child.

Exercises

6.1 'The Children Act 1989 is an important and significant piece of legislation for children, yet it does not go far enough since it does not positively support children's rights.' Discuss this statement in the context of the Act and whether rights for children are justified.

6.2 In *Gillick*, Lord Scarman stated: 'I would hold that as a matter of law, the parental right to determine whether or not their minor child below the age of 16 will have medical treatment terminates if and when the child achieves a sufficient understanding and intelligence to enable him or her to understand fully what is proposed.' Consider whether the judgement in *Gillick* truly upholds this statement.

6.3 'But enter now Lord Donaldson. He had clearly taken against *Gillick* and decided that he was going to provide a gloss on it.' Consider the gloss provided by Lord Donaldson with respect to refusal of treatment by a competent minor (in *Re R* and *Re W*) and whether such a 'gloss' is justified.

6.4 In deciding whether to withdraw or withhold treatment in children with serious disability or who are terminally ill, the court bows to medical opinion rather than giving force to parental wishes. Discuss.

6.5 Critically consider the role of non-therapeutic interventions in children.

Further reading

Bainham A. *Children, the modern law* (3rd edn). Jordan Publishing, Bristol, 2005

Eekelaar J. White coats or flak jackets? Children and the courts again. *Law Quarterly Review* 1993; 109: 182–187

Fortin J. Accommodating children's rights in a post Human Rights Act Era. *Modern Law Review* 2006; 69: 299–326

Hagger L. Some implications of the Human Rights Act 1998 for the medical treatment of children. *Medical Law International* 2003; 6: 25–51

Herring, J. Children's abortion rights. *Medical Law Review* 1997; 5: 257

Links to relevant websites can be found at: http://www.palgrave.com/law/samanta

Chapter 7 follows overleaf.

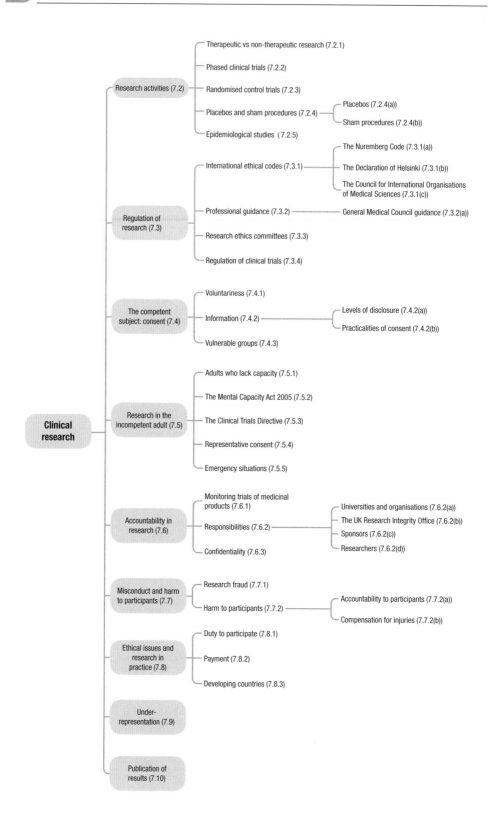

Clinical research

Key Terms

- ▶ **Clinical research** – aims to ascertain the efficacy and safety of medicines and interventions used in clinical practice.
- ▶ **Consent for research** – is required prior to participation and a competent subject must give valid consent that is voluntary and based upon sufficient information, and can be withdrawn at any stage and for any reason.
- ▶ **Representative consent** – consent to participate in a clinical trial by a person who lacks decision-making capacity is by proxy through an authorised representative.
- ▶ **Research accountability** – the governance framework for clinical research that ensures maintenance of ethical and legal standards in order to protect participants.
- ▶ **Research activity** – spans a range of actions including data collection and analysis, laboratory experiments and clinical trials in humans.
- ▶ **Research ethics committees** – professional and lay members who advise on the extent to which research proposals meet established ethical standards and criteria.
- ▶ **Research regulation** – is by the general law, and more specifically by the international ethical codes, the Medicines for Human Use (Clinical Trials) Regulations 2004 and guidance from the professional bodies.

Scenario

A pharmaceutical company approaches Dr Jones, a rheumatologist, to take part in a Phase III placebo-controlled randomised clinical drug trial of a new medication for the treatment of arthritis. He is informed that it would be a short trial to run over eight weeks. In recognition of his support he has been promised a sum of money by way of donation to his departmental research fund for every patient who completes the trial. He is also informed that research participants would receive a 'token' of appreciation.

Dr Jones immediately asks his registrar Dr Yin (who is eager to add to his research based publications) to commence recruitment at the clinic scheduled for the following morning. Jenny, a registered nurse who is a recent immigrant from Nigeria, agrees to participate after Dr Yin explains the protocol. An article has recently appeared in a leading medical journal which indicates that particular caution must be exercised when administering medication that contains compounds present in the trial medication in black persons due to a possible deficiency of an enzyme 'nephrotransferase' which can predispose those with the condition to renal problems.

Jaswinder, a longstanding patient of Dr Jones, is keen to participate even though a recent stroke has affected his decision-making ability. At present, Jaswinder is an in-patient on the rheumatology ward waiting for assessment of his chronic bone condition. Dr Yin enters him into the study. Three days prior to completion of the study a nurse informs Dr Yin that Jaswinder wishes to withdraw from the trial and that he has stopped taking the medication. Dr Yin informs the nurse that Jaswinder should continue in view of the trial's imminent completion.

Following completion of the trial Dr Yin takes the data and trial records home for consideration and analysis. During the weekend he discusses the results with a friend who works as a statistician at another university. They analyse the data. Dr Yin writes an article which is subsequently submitted for publication with his own and Dr Jones's names and their affiliations.

7.1 Introduction

Clinical research is a vital precursor to medical progress and for establishing the safety and effectiveness of clinical interventions. Its aim is to generate new knowledge and understanding for the benefit of society. This widely perceived advantage has to be weighed against potential detriments such as increased health risks that research subjects could be exposed to as a result of participation. A classic illustration is provided by Edward Jenner, who in 1796 injected an 8-year-old boy with cowpox, a disease similar to small pox but relatively less virulent. Some months later the boy was inoculated with smallpox. Happily, the boy survived, and this forerunner of clinical research was the first scientific attempt to investigate the basis for vaccination against smallpox. As recognised by Brazier (2008) 'no modern ethics committee would have sanctioned such an experiment. Consider the case – the experiment used a child subject who was too young to consent for himself in non-therapeutic research where there was a high risk of death or disfigurement. The "exploitation" of James Phipps undoubtedly saved the lives of some of us who are reading this'.

Clinical research offers considerable benefits to society and yet it nonetheless raises questions as to whether societal interests can ever justify the potential disregard of the rights and dignity of individual research subjects. History reveals that participants have been included in clinical research without their knowledge or consent, a situation widely considered to be ethically unacceptable. The notorious *Tuskegee Study of Untreated Syphilis in the Negro Male,* which ran from 1932 to 1974, raised precisely these issues. The study involved a narrative recording of the natural history of untreated syphilis, a potentially fatal disease known to cause damage to the heart, brain, eyes and bones. Participants were informed that they suffered from 'bad blood' which at that time was a euphemism for a range of conditions including anaemia, syphilis and fatigue. They were not informed of the true nature of the study, which was to observe the natural progression of the disease with the overall intention of justifying future treatment programmes. Participants were subjected to regular examinations and investigations and treatment was withheld, even after penicillin became widely available and was accepted as the treatment of choice (Jones, 1981). A pure deontological approach in these circumstances would oppose such research on the grounds that participants were treated merely as a means to an end. Such actions are inherently wrong irrespective of beneficent intentions or positive consequences of research, such as the advancement of knowledge. An extreme teleological, more consequentialist, approach might argue that the overall benefits justify the means, particularly since the intention of this particular study was to support effective treatment programmes for the benefit of future populations.

The apparent ethical tensions that underpin clinical research can pervade more extensively than the anticipated societal benefit in respect of the risks that the subject might be exposed to. Further confounding factors may enter the equation such as potential benefits for the principal investigator, the research team, and sponsors of commercial research projects. The researcher might well have self-interest in completing and publishing positive research outcomes as a means of enhancing a career and reputation. The imperative to achieve goals in the pursuit of the researcher's personal interests might lead to a situation whereby the interests of others assume less importance. Sponsors of research, such as pharmaceutical companies, have a vested interest in generating profits for shareholders, a feature that could provide a further incentive to carry out research with possibly less regard for participants.

Clinical research needs to be undertaken within a robust governance framework that encompasses accountability, openness, honesty, values and respect for those taking part. Participants need sufficient information prior to recruitment, as well as at all stages of the project, to ensure the continued validity of their consent. Central aspects of this topic include consent, confidentiality and human rights issues. Regulatory and legislative reforms such as the European Clinical Trials Directive, the Human Tissue Act 2004 and the Mental Capacity Act 2005 exert considerable influence, as has the central role of Research Ethics Committees (RECs). The ethical and legal aspects of embryo research and children as research subject are considered in chapters 5 and 6, respectively.

7.2   Research activities

Clinical research spans a range of activities and includes clinical drug trials, non-interventional studies (such as those based upon questionnaires and interviews) and epidemiological or population-based studies drawn from clinical data and records. Key issues include the therapeutic versus non-therapeutic divide, and the particular ethical and legal issues that arise in the conduct of clinical research that includes a placebo control in the study design.

7.2.1   Therapeutic versus non-therapeutic research

A key distinction at the heart of legal and ethical debates is whether clinical research can be classified as either therapeutic or non-therapeutic. Verdon-Jones and Weisstub (1998) state that 'the classification of an experiment as either therapeutic or non-therapeutic would profoundly affect the legal and ethical restrictions that apply; a high standard must be met before an experiment should be classified as therapeutic'. For research to be classified as therapeutic some form of benefit to the participant is required, which must be likely, or reasonably foreseeable to occur as a consequence of involvement. If no such benefit is apparent then research is categorised as non-therapeutic. While this classification is significant, distinct categorisation may be difficult in clinical environments and there is frequently much blurring and overlapping of this division. In fact, whether any randomised controlled trial (RCT) can ever really be categorised as therapeutic is perhaps questionable.

7.2.2 Phased clinical trials

The initial stages of pharmaceutical product development are carried out on animals. These tests are necessary to establish the drug's efficacy and baseline safety profile. Once these preliminary investigations are complete, human trials can begin.

The first stage of a study involving humans is known as a Phase I trial and this acts as a bridge between pure scientific research and clinical practice. The intention is to test the drug in a small group of healthy volunteers, or even patients, to study its pharmacokinetics, namely the way in which drugs are absorbed and excreted by the body, as well as the side effects, if any, associated with increasing dosages. Phase I is a precursor to the subsequent phases of the study. Phase II involves controlled testing of the drug on a small group of patients with the condition under study. Participants receive trial medication with a view to further evaluate its effectiveness, side effects and risks. Phase III clinical trials involve controlled and uncontrolled trials in larger groups of subjects who take the drug under medical supervision and for extended periods of time, to enable researchers to gain a deeper understanding of the medication's effectiveness and safety. If the new drug passes these stages satisfactorily, it can be licensed and marketed but should still be monitored in order to obtain further data, particularly in respect of safety data and optimal usage. This is sometimes called Phase IV, or post-marketing surveillance.

Phase I trials, although of no therapeutic value to healthy volunteers, are an essential prerequisite to testing on patients. Recently, some of the problems and possible dangers of first-in-man trials became acutely apparent. A Phase I clinical trial was conducted to test a monoclonal antibody, TGN1412; a compound expected to have therapeutic benefits for a range of conditions such as rheumatoid arthritis, leukaemia and multiple sclerosis. The trial took place at a Phase I Unit at Northwick Park Hospital on eight healthy male volunteers. Although preliminary animal studies had failed to reveal adverse effects, the results of the trial were catastrophic. All six men who received the active drug (rather than the two who received the placebo control) suffered life-threatening multiple organ failure. Although all survived, one volunteer has been diagnosed with early onset lymphoma (cancer of the immune system). In the subsequent enquiry and report into the incident (The Expert Scientific Group on Phase One Clinical Trials, Final Report, 2006), the company disclosed that TGN1412 has the capacity to bind to the cell surface of T lymphocytes, causing more cells to be created. It claimed that the trial medication had been extensively tested on rabbits and monkeys and that no drug-related deaths had occurred despite administering doses of up to 500 times the amounts administered in the Phase I trial. However, in pre-clinical tests, two monkeys had experienced a temporary increase in the size of lymph nodes, but the drug company had not considered this to be a drug-related side effect. The Report recommended that for subsequent Phase 1 trials careful consideration must be given to the route of administration of drugs under investigation and that any intravenous infusions are to be given slowly so that these can be stopped if necessary. Administration of drugs should be sequential to reduce risk by allowing observation of participants and intervention where required.

7.2.3 Randomised control trials

The randomised control trial is widely regarded as the gold standard for determining efficacy and safety in clinical research. In an RCT, participants are randomly allocated to either the active arm or the control arm of a study. Those in the active arm receive the compound being studied, whereas the control group receives either a placebo or the best currently available treatment. The purpose of random allocation is to allow the researcher to observe whether any clinically significant benefit is apparent in the active arm. Many RCTs are 'double blinded' meaning that neither the participant nor the researcher is aware of whether the participant is receiving active treatment or not. In some circumstances double blind studies are not possible and single blind designs are used. In single blind designs only participants are unaware of whether they are in the experimental, or control, arm of the study. The purpose of 'blinding' is to minimise any observer or participant bias and to counteract any confounding of the results by the so-called placebo effect (see 7.2.5).

There are two key ethical dilemmas in placebo controlled RCTs. The first occurs on random allocation of participants into either the control or active arm of the study. By definition those ascribed to the placebo arm receive no active medication. This situation conflicts with the doctor's primary duty to offer every patient the best clinical treatment for his or her condition. Furthermore, patients allocated to the active arm will receive medication of unknown efficacy and side effects, which again presents an ethical dilemma for the clinician, since the purpose of conducting a research trial is to determine the therapeutic value of the trial intervention as opposed to giving best therapeutic care to any individual patient. For studies controlled against the best available treatment this dilemma is reduced, but only for those patients allocated to the control arm of the study. For this reason there is a strong argument for separating the therapeutic and research agendas of clinicians and researchers wherever possible.

There is an argument that an RCT can be considered ethically sound only in circumstances of true equipoise, that is to say genuine uncertainty on the part of the researcher about which treatment is best. True equipoise requires the researcher to have no preference of treatment during the course of the trial. London (2001 at 312) states that the

> requirement that equipoise exists as a necessary condition for the moral acceptability of the clinical trial comparing these interventions is motivated by two interlocking ideas. First, when equipoise obtains it is morally permissible to allow an individual's medical treatment to be assigned by a random process because there is no sufficiently credible evidence to warrant a judgement that one intervention is superior to the other(s). Second, clinical trials that are designed to break or disturb equipoise provide information that will enable the medical community to improve its existing clinical practices.

The point here is that whilst equipoise might be apparent at the start of an RCT this situation might well change during the course of the study. Clinical equipoise could be disturbed on account of empirical observation, or even an intuitive hunch, both of which would arguably oblige the researcher to prematurely terminate the study, or perhaps offer the superior treatment to all those enrolled. This situation can present serious ethical obstacles for the continuance or completion of an RCT which is an essential precursor to publication and dissemination of scientifically valid conclusions. This ethical dilemma might be resolved by the perception that clinical equipoise is met where genuine uncertainty exists among the clinical community as a whole, and not necessarily on the part of any individual researcher.

Further issues can arise as to when, if at all, a trial should be stopped prior to its planned completion. Clearly, one example would be where significant adverse effects become apparent during the course of a trial such that continuation cannot be justified. More problematic is where early evidence suggests that those allocated to the treatment arm are obtaining a significantly better therapeutic result. This creates a tension between what is regarded as the patient's overall best interests and the need to ascertain rigorous and statistically significant evidence for the benefit of society as a whole. Early closure of a trial is likely to detrimentally affect the validity of the study results and ultimately impede medical progress and knowledge.

> Dr Jones, a clinician, has been invited to recruit his patients into a placebo controlled clinical drug trial.
>
> ▶ What are the potential ethical dilemmas raised in this situation?
> ▶ To what extent can informed consent operate to mitigate the effects of this dilemma?

The second central dilemma regarding RCTs is that of consent: to what extent can participants receive information to ensure that their consent is real and valid. Due to the nature of an RCT a patient cannot be informed whether he or she will be allocated to the active arm of the trial since this knowledge could invalidate the results due to the placebo effect. Furthermore, if the starting point is clinical equipoise then genuine clinical uncertainty exists and it is therefore impossible to provide full information in respect of risks and benefits as is normally required. The essential nature of consent from a legal as well as ethical basis is explored in 7.4.

7.2.4 Placebos and sham procedures

The placebo effect is a non-specific benefit that participants might experience and is not directly related to the drug or intervention being tested. The word 'placebo' is sometimes referred to as a 'sugar pill'. The term can also be used to describe an intervention or even surgical procedure. For example, a typical placebo 'sham' procedure would involve the exact same anaesthetic agent (if used), the same physical aspects (such as cutting of skin or injection) but no active compound would be given, or intervention carried out.

The placebo effect is a recognised phenomenon that around a third of all patients will show a therapeutic response after receiving placebo therapy. It is also possible for placebos to cause adverse effects, known as 'nocebos'. The incidence of nocebos is thought to reflect the patient's expectation of anticipated side effects. The mechanism of placebo activity remains largely unknown. In an RCT a new medication or procedure has significant benefits only if its therapeutic effects are statistically and significantly superior to placebo treatment.

7.2.4(a) Placebos

A clinical research trial of a new drug or intervention needs a comparator to test its efficacy and justify its use. In circumstances where no established treatment is available, use of a placebo control may be unavoidable. However, the extent to which placebo use can be justified on ethical grounds where an effective treatment already exists is questionable, even though the trial medication might eventually prove to be more effective, or have fewer side effects.

In research trials on participants with minor conditions, use of a placebo control might be ethically acceptable. Guidance from the Royal College of Physicians (2007, paragraph 6.13) suggests that the use of a placebo control in headache research could be justifiable:

> A protocol that requires a patient to wait two hours after the study medication before taking their usual medication if needed would expose the patient to, at worse, two hours of unrelieved headache. This constitutes inconvenience and discomfort but is unlikely to cause serious or irreversible harm.

The argument used by the Royal College of Physicians is that no serious or irreversible harm is likely to ensue in the context of minor conditions. The added caveat is that participation is voluntary and consensual and the subject is free to withdraw from the study at any time and for any reason whatsoever. For the headache trial described above, the participant could legitimately withdraw at any point, including during the two-hour waiting period.

A placebo-controlled trial deprives those in the control arm of the study of receiving appropriate treatment. The Declaration of Helsinki requires those in the control group to be given the best currently available intervention. However, an ethical 'blanket ban' is not imposed on placebo use. The Declaration states (paragraph 32) that

> the benefits, risks, burdens and effectiveness of a new intervention must be tested against those of the best current proven intervention, except in the following circumstances:
>
> ▶ The use of placebo, or no treatment, is acceptable in studies where no current proven intervention exists; or
> ▶ Where for compelling and scientifically sound methodological reasons the use of placebo is necessary to determine the efficacy or safety of an intervention and patients who receive placebo or no treatment will not be subject to any risk of serious or irreversible harm.

Extreme care is required before using a placebo control for an RCT. From a deontological perspective use of a placebo is wrong since it denies effective treatment being given to a patient who has a legitimate right and expectation to be treated. Although there is an assumption that a placebo-controlled trial is scientifically superior than one controlled against the best effective treatment, there are inherent weaknesses in this approach. A placebo control will not reveal the merits of a treatment relative to other available known interventions. From a health-care perspective this is particularly important since it is unlikely that any new treatment could acquire clinical credibility if not compared against the best available care.

7.2.4(b) Sham procedures

The so-called sham surgery is an operative procedure which (unbeknown to the participant) omits an aspect considered to be therapeutically necessary. The ethical issues that surround sham surgery, or sham procedures, are more acute and controversial due to their intrusiveness. Compared with the use of placebo medication, sham procedures typically conflict with the ethical principle of non-maleficence. The Nuremberg Code states that research ought to avoid the infliction of unnecessary mental or physical suffering, and that the degree of risk to which participants are exposed to ought to commensurate with the humanitarian importance of the subject of the research. Sham surgery has been undertaken as part of a clinical trial which employed foetal tissue grafting for patients with Parkinson's disease. The placebo-controlled study took place in the United States and 40 patients were recruited. All participants, who were anaesthetised, had tiny holes drilled into their foreheads and half of them received foetal tissue grafts (the active limb) while the others received nothing (the control limb undergoing sham surgery). Two-thirds of the patients who received transplants began to produce dopamine (the missing neurochemical in Parkinson's disease) compared to three in the control group (Clark, 2002).

The results of the above study suggest that foetal tissue grafting in Parkinson's disease is effective. It has been argued that unless surgical techniques are tested rigorously, future patients may be exposed to ineffective, unsafe surgical techniques, and a placebo controlled trial helps to prevent this. Furthermore, if a new surgical technique is found to be ineffective (compared with a placebo), then this intervention should not be undertaken. Knowledge of lack of efficacy saves resources, unnecessary pain, suffering and iatrogenic harm. A tension again arises between the utilitarian viewpoint and the deontological approach that goes against sacrificing or putting at risk the interests of a few for societal benefit. Use of sham interventional procedures or surgery can perhaps only be justified where risk to participants is carefully balanced against the potential for a beneficial outcome. They must be rigorously justified and extra care must be taken to ensure that participants are fully aware that the procedure and its inherent risks might well offer no possibility of improving their condition since the experimental treatment could be ineffective and even if it is effective, the participant might be allocated to the placebo arm of the study.

7.2.5 Epidemiological studies

Epidemiological and public health studies are designed to elucidate the occurrence and distribution of diseases and health-related conditions in populations. These studies are used to ascertain the prevalence and distribution of medical conditions and in doing so, test hypotheses that deal with suspected causes and possible risk factors for diseases. The overarching goal of this type of research is improvement of public health.

Properly anonymised information such as that which would be useful for prevalence and incidence studies of disease can be disseminated freely and is not necessarily regarded as confidential (*R v Department of Health ex p Source Informatics Ltd* [2000] 1 All ER 786). Anonymous information falls outside the restrictions of current data protection legislation. However, certain techniques commonly employed for data anonymisation typically make use of codes, or details, that allow subsequent tracing of individuals. This is to prevent data being skewed, for example, by individuals inadvertently being counted twice. Furthermore, patients might need to be followed up in order to monitor disease progression, and for this reason access to personal identifiable information might be necessary. For these reasons data protection, confidentiality and the potential need for consent are central and controversial issues for certain types of epidemiological research. Studies of this nature that investigate prevalence, incidence and disease progression within populations have been justified on utilitarian grounds in that the public benefit overrides individual rights of privacy and confidentiality; however, such arguments do not hold sway in other areas of law. Typical justifications for this position are that the practicalities of obtaining valid consent prior to collection of patient data from records would stifle research because of resource issues and the practical constraints of contacting possibly hundreds and thousands of individuals. Since the intention of such studies is to elicit an enhanced understanding of disease and not to feed back results to individuals, researchers typically do not seek patient consent prior to inclusion. Such studies do, however, require full NHS Research Ethics Committee approval prior to commencement, unless the study falls within the clinical audit exception.

7.3 Regulation of research

The regulatory framework that governs clinical research is a complex of statute and common law against a backdrop of international ethical codes and professional guidance.

7.3.1 International ethical codes

Several key principles emanate from a range of international ethical codes that govern research involving human participants. The first overarching requirement is that the research protocol has received the prior approval of a Research Ethics Committee. The second imperative is the need for the participant's free and informed consent (which can be withdrawn at any time and for any reason). The risks and benefits of the study must be made known to participants and be proportionate to the anticipated positive outcomes of the research. The study must be terminated if risk of injury or death becomes apparent during the course of the study, and since the purpose of research is to benefit the wider society it is necessary that research findings are disseminated and that subjects have access to information following completion.

7.3.1(a) The Nuremberg Code

During the Second World War a range of atrocities were inflicted on prisoners of concentration camps in the name of medical research. Prisoners were kept outdoors without clothing in freezing conditions for several hours at a time, or immersed in tanks of iced water, to study the effects of hypothermia. Others were infected with malaria, typhus and smallpox and subjected to high doses of radiation to evaluate the effects of these noxious agents on the human body. These violations were to lead to the war trials and subsequent conviction of many who had conducted such 'research'.

Following these trials the Nuremberg Code of 1947 was created as a means of protecting people from similar abuse in the future. The Code is a set of ten principles and forms the basis of contemporary regulation of medical research in its emphasis on the need for informed consent, absence of coercion, the need for robust, well-designed protocols underpinned by beneficent principles. Research must only be carried out if necessary and where outcomes are anticipated to yield beneficial effects for society. Wherever possible, experiments on humans need to be designed and based upon preliminary findings of animal studies as informed by the existing knowledge base. Research must be conducted to avoid unnecessary physical and mental suffering and injury, and the level of risk must be proportionate to the anticipated benefits. Studies should be conducted by appropriately qualified and experienced persons. Proper preparation is necessary to anticipate and prevent injury, disability and death, using appropriate skill and care at all stages of study design and performance. Participants can withdraw at any time and the study must be terminated if there is reason to believe that there is a risk of injury, disability or death to participants. The Code is the basis of all contemporary guidelines as well as the Declaration of Helsinki.

7.3.1(b) The Declaration of Helsinki

The Declaration of Helsinki was adopted by the World Medical Association in 1964 and provides ethical principles that govern medical research. The Declaration has been revised on several occasions to incorporate advances in technology (World Medical Association, 2008).

The overriding principles include the need to minimise risk and safeguard participants. Protecting confidential personal information is paramount. A research protocol is required and must be submitted for independent consideration, comment, guidance and approval prior to study commencement. Research on humans should only be conducted by individuals with appropriate training and qualifications. All participants must give voluntary, informed consent and the researcher must act to protect the life, health, dignity and integrity. Although the Declaration does not have force of law it is considered to be of fundamental importance to clinical research and consequently these principles have been embodied in professional guidance and law.

7.3.1(c) The Council for International Organisations of Medical Sciences

In addition to the Nuremberg Code and Declaration of Helsinki, guidance from the Council for International Organisations of Medical Sciences (CIOMS) has been influential. CIOMS is an international, not-for-profit organisation established jointly by the World Health Organisation and UNESCO. The organisation publishes the *International Ethical Guidelines for Biomedical Research Involving Human Subjects* (CIOMS, 2002) as well as specific guidelines for the conduct of research undertaken on participants of the developing nations and how the Declaration of Helsinki can be applied given the socio-economic circumstances, laws and regulations of these communities. The overriding principle is that researchers and research projects, no matter how well intentioned, should leave that community in a better, or at least the same, position as before the research commenced.

7.3.2 Professional guidance

Guidance for the conduct of medical research is produced by the professional regulatory bodies as well as the Royal Colleges. It reflects and is based upon the overriding principles of the International Codes and provides direction for professionals on translating the Codes into contemporary clinical research practice. Professional directions and publications operate at the level of direction, as opposed to law, although failure to follow professional guidance (without considered and legitimate reason) might found the basis of an action in negligence on grounds that the practitioner failed to meet the requisite standard of care according to the *Bolam* standard (see 3.3.1).

7.3.2(a) General Medical Council guidance

The General Medical Council (2002) sets out principles of ethical conduct and requires the investigator to be satisfied that the research is not contrary to the interests of the participant. The guidance emphasises the need to:

- ▶ obtain prior research ethics approval;
- ▶ conduct research in an ethical manner;
- ▶ ensure that patients or volunteers understand the basis of participation;
- ▶ record participants' consent;
- ▶ respect participants' right to confidentiality;
- ▶ ensure that risks do not outweigh potential benefits;

▶ complete research projects (unless evidence exposes risks that require study termination on safety or other grounds). Results should be recorded and reported accurately, and disseminated widely.

7.3.3 Research ethics committees

Research Ethics Committees (RECs) play a central role in the regulation of clinical research and their function is to advise on the extent to which a research proposal meets established ethical standards and criteria. NHS research has long been subject to scrutiny by RECs which became formally established in 1991. A fundamental change occurred in 2000 when the Central Office of Research Ethics Committees (COREC) was set up, and the Department of Health published *Governance arrangements for NHS Research Ethics Committees* in 2001 (GAfREC). COREC was replaced by the National Research Ethics Service (NRES) which is part of the National Patient Safety Association (NPSA) in 2007. A recent review of arm's length bodies by the Department of Health has been undertaken as part of the wider reforms outlined in the White Paper, 'Equity and excellence'. The Department of Health in 'Liberating the NHS: Report of the Arm's Length Bodies Review' found duplication of services in that a range of arm's length bodies share responsibility for the regulation and governance of clinical research. The Academy of Medical Sciences has been asked to conduct a review of the situation to assess the potential for these functions to be transferred to a single regulator. Applications for research studies are currently submitted centrally to a national database known as the Integrated Research Application System (IRAS) following which the study is reviewed by a local REC. For studies that involve no material ethical issues, a fast-track procedure is available and involves scrutiny by a subcommittee of two nationally experienced ethical advisers.

The principal responsibility of the REC is to ensure that research involving human subjects is underpinned by ethical standards. The constitution of the NHS REC comprises 6 to 12 persons; one-third of them are lay members with a balance of age and gender mix. Expert members must have expertise in several areas: methodological and ethical experience in clinical and non-clinical research including qualitative and quantitative research methods; in relation to a range of clinical practice, including primary and secondary care; in respect of statistical methodology and process relevant to research and pharmacy (Grubb, 2004).

Lay members are expected to bring relevant life experience to decision making together with opinion of experts. Due to their wide area of expertise, the REC is regarded as being well placed to assess the ethical standards upon which the research is based as well as to assume a monitoring function. In practice it is the sponsor of the research who has overarching responsibility for the monitoring role. According to NRES procedures (2008) although the principal REC is not required to monitor the conduct of the research proactively, it should keep the ethical opinion under review.

The Declaration of Helsinki requires that clinical research involving humans is conducted only if the importance of the research question outweighs any inherent risks. A principal criterion that the REC is expected to assess is the balance of risks and inconveniences against the benefits for society, present and future. As expected, the boundaries are blurred as to the precise level of risk that participants can legitimately be exposed. Guidance of the Royal College of Physicians (2007) states that there are three main categories of clinical research: those that convey (a) minimal risk; (b) less than minimal risk or (c) more than minimal risk. Minimal risk includes complaints such as headaches and tiredness; one example of a less than minimal risk is the provision of a urine sample. More than minimal risk includes those instances where risk is still small in comparison to potential benefits. Research Ethics Committees are expected to consider the potential for risk, even in projects regarded as comparatively risk-free, such as questionnaire-based research or focus group studies. In these contexts it is still possible for risk of harm to be identified. Questionnaires, for example, might provoke anxiety or worry and similarly focus group studies if facilitation is insensitively handled in respect of participants' personal experiences and perspectives. The extent to which these criteria can be controlled for, or even evaluated, from the IRAS form is perhaps limited.

> Dr Jones is keen to commence patient recruitment as soon as possible. Assuming that the trial has been considered by an NHS REC, what are the key issues that will be examined?

7.3.4 Regulation of clinical trials

Clinical drug trials are the most common form of medical research and are also the most stringently regulated. The Clinical Trials Directive (2001/20/EC) was intended to harmonise regulation and performance of clinical trials across Member States. The Directive was transposed into domestic law by the Medicines for Human Use (Clinical Trials) Regulations 2004 (the Regulations) and relates specifically to clinical trials that test the safety or efficacy of pharmaceuticals. The Regulations aim to safeguard the rights and safety of participants in clinical drug trials and require sponsors to design, conduct and report clinical trials according to principles of the International Conference of Harmonisation for Good Clinical Practice (ICHGCP). The Regulations define a clinical trial as: any investigation in human subjects, other than a non-interventional trial, intended to discover or verify the clinical, pharmacological or other pharmacodynamic effects of one or more medicinal products, to identify any adverse reactions to one or more such products, and/or to study absorption, distribution, metabolism and excretion of one or more such products, with the object of ascertaining the safety or efficacy of those products (Regulation 2). The Regulations do not apply to non-interventional studies such as research involving medical devices, nutritional supplements or surgical procedures.

The Regulations require an independent and objective ethical review prior to commencement. Schedule 1 describes the basis of the requirement for Good Clinical Practice (GCP) underpinned by the principles of the Declaration of Helsinki. The overarching philosophy is that the rights, safety and well-being of trial subjects are paramount and that the research being contemplated is underpinned by good pre-trial data. Careful monitoring of trials is required with termination in the event of unacceptable side effects. Trials must be supervised by appropriately qualified persons and accurate data recording and storage is necessary to protect the confidentiality of participants.

The overarching focus of the Regulations is valid consent as governed by the common law. Detailed advice on the requirements for valid consent for research purposes requires recourse to professional guidance such as those produced by the National Research Ethics Service (2008), the Medical Research Council (2004), the General Medical Council (2008) and the Royal Colleges.

The government agency responsible for ensuring the safety of medicines and medical devices, the Medicine and Healthcare Products Regulatory Agency, has power to suspend or terminate a clinical trial where there are doubts about the conduct, safety and scientific validity of the trial, or that a trial is not being conducted in the way it was originally planned. These powers are supported by criminal sanctions, and sponsors and researchers are required by law to report actual and suspected serious adverse events.

> Dr Jones and his registrar are keen to commence the clinical trial as soon as possible. No information is given about preliminary authorisation:
>
> ▶ Consider the preliminary requirements that would be necessary prior to recruitment.
> ▶ What research governance issues will apply?

7.4 The competent subject: consent

Valid consent is an essential legal and ethical prerequisite to participation in clinical research, as reflected in the international ethical codes, research governance and current law. For these purposes consent must be based upon sufficient information and must be given voluntarily. Special account is often required for prospective participants who are competent to decide, but might be classified as being vulnerable due to the existence of special circumstances. Whilst valid consent is the cornerstone of legitimate clinical research it is arguable whether real consent can ever truly be given in research situations due to the necessary and inherent uncertainty and lack of knowledge that exists at the start of any project.

7.4.1 Voluntariness

Participation in clinical research requires that the informed competent person does so voluntarily. Furthermore, the Declaration of Helsinki requires that the subject is 'informed that he or she is at liberty to abstain from participation in this study, and that he or she is at liberty to withdraw his or her consent to participation at any time. The physician should then obtain the subject's freely given consent, preferably in writing'. The voluntariness of the subject's consent is central to lawful participation. In the absence of valid and informed consent Article 3 of the European Convention (the prohibition of the imposition of torture, and inhuman and degrading treatment) could be invoked as well as the Article 8 (right to privacy). These rights are in addition to any other causes of action that could be apparent.

7.4.2 Information

Sufficient information is the cornerstone of valid consent for research to the same extent as for other types of clinical care. Research participation raises unique and difficult issues that need to be overcome to ensure that consent is valid, informed and freely given.

It remains debatable as to how much information can and should be given by the research team, as well as the potential obscurity of the meaning of 'information' in this particular context. Thornton's (1994) perspective is that it is impossible for a researcher to give sufficient information in these circumstances and consent, at best, can be only partly informed. This view seems reasonable when one considers that at the beginning of a trial only limited information is available, which is why the trial is being carried out. If a true state of equipoise is to exist, then by necessity there are gaps in the knowledge which one hopes would be addressed on completion of the trial. It is salutary to note that an empirical study to consider research participants' perceptions of information found that 94% of participants were happy with the amount information provided (Ferguson, 2002). Around 50% believed they understood 'all' the information provided while 49% of the rest felt that they comprehended 'most' of the information given. It should be noted, however, that these findings relate to patients' perceptions of their understanding and the extent to which such beliefs correlate with their actual understanding is perhaps questionable.

7.4.2(a) Levels of disclosure

The Canadian court in *Hallushka v University of Saskatchewan* [1965] 53 DLR (2D) 436 felt that broad disclosure of information was necessary for volunteers in clinical trials: 'the subject of medical experimentation is entitled to a full and frank disclosure of all the facts, probabilities and opinions which a reasonable man might be expected to consider before giving his consent. It has been suggested that such an approach should be employed in relation to both patients and volunteers'.

A similar approach to information disclosure was apparent in Lord Woolf's formulation of the 'prudent patient' standard. In *Pearce v United Bristol NHS Trust* [1999] PIQR 53 (CA) it was held that 'if there is a significant risk which would affect the judgement of a reasonable patient, then in the normal course it is the responsibility of the doctor to inform the patient of that significant risk, if the information is needed, so that the patient can determine for him or herself as to what course she should adopt'.

Although Lord Woolf's statements were in relation to the standard in negligence, this principle seems to have been adopted by the General Medical Council (2002) guidance that states 'You must ensure that any individuals whom you invite to take part in research are given the information which they want or ought to know, and that it is presented in terms and a form that they can understand.' Although most would agree that researchers should tell subjects about the risks involved and provide them with information, grey areas remain. Notable examples include the absence of information typically given to participants about compensation for the researcher for carrying out the study, as well as the underlying motivation for the research.

7.4.2(b) Practicalities of consent

The General Medical Council guidance (2002) states: 'Giving the information will usually include an initial discussion supported by a leaflet or sound recording, where possible taking into account any particular communication or language needs of the participants. You must give the participants an opportunity to ask questions and to express any concerns that they may have.' However, a difference exists between providing information and ensuring that participants actually understand the information given. Ensuring that patients understand can be complex, particularly where prospective participants are also patients. Patients typically have an expectation of a therapeutic alliance with their doctors who provide care that is in their clinical best interests. It is therefore essential that the distinction between the research imperative (which is to provide an answer to the research question on a scientific basis) and the therapeutic imperative (which is to provide clinical care for the patient) are distinguished. This concept can be difficult to convey and may adversely affect the understanding of patients who are participants if there is an expectation that research is being conducted as therapy. Charuvastra and Marder (2008) state that in the context of obtaining consent for a research project, the patient participant is likely to be influenced by his surroundings and in particular where this is a hospital or medical centre. The patient's evaluation of the researcher's intention might be influenced by any previous therapeutic relationship. This situation, termed the 'therapeutic misconception' is even more likely if the patient knows the person who is suggesting the research and has previously received care from that person.

Schedule 1 of the Regulations requires that informed consent is formally recorded by signature on a written consent form. If the participant is unable to write, consent should be given in the presence of at least one witness, and oral consent should be recorded subsequently. However, irrespective of the evidential value of a signed document, consent is an ongoing and continual process. Participants must be informed throughout the study of facts that become apparent, as well as their right to withdraw at any time. In the event of unfavourable preliminary or interim results these must be communicated, even where disclosure might trigger withdrawal from the study. Understandably, this requirement can create tensions between the researcher's duty to provide information to participants and the imperative to complete the study to ensure substantive and meaningful results for the benefit of society and medical progress.

7.4.3 Vulnerable groups

Certain categories of competent adults could be perceived as being vulnerable in the context of their relationship with the researcher. The archetypal situation is the patient who feels a sense of gratitude to the medical team, or individual doctor previously involved in his or her clinical care. If such persons are invited to participate in a study they might feel disinclined to refuse on account of their subjective moral obligation founded on gratitude, or possibly concern that refusal might compromise their future care. Those who have experienced a therapeutic association might find it difficult to fully comprehend the concept of random allocation and the need for a control, whether placebo or standard therapy. Featherstone and Donovan (2002) suggest that even where trials are wholly explained using comprehensible language, subjects might not always understand the full implications of randomisation and the need for a control. Trial participants need to be informed that in the research setting, the standard doctor–patient relationship is altered once randomisation and blinding of the trial begins.

Other potentially vulnerable groups are employees, nurses or junior doctors. If a prospective participant is in a dependent relationship with the researcher then consent needs to be obtained with particular caution. If that subject is to be recruited into the study, then it is better that consent is sought by an individual who is completely independent of this relationship (Declaration of Helsinki, 2008). Likewise, guidance from the General Medical Council (2002) reiterates that extreme caution is necessary to ensure truly valid consent to make certain that no actual or implied coercion exists with such participants.

Special care is also required when recruiting prisoners as research participants. The Royal College of Physicians guidelines (2007) state that prisoners should not be recruited into studies where non-detained persons could be used. The prison environment creates a real constraint that can impede the ability of prisoners to make truly voluntary decisions to participate. The guidelines identify specific types of study which may be legitimately undertaken using prisoners as participants such as the causes and effects of incarceration, research on practices which have the intent and probability of improving the health and well-being of prisoners and studies of prisons as institutional organisations.

Jenny is a recently appointed nurse on the ward. She agrees to participate in the trial:

▶ What are the potential hurdles to obtaining valid consent from Jenny?
▶ Are there any particular safeguards that need to be included to ensure that her consent is valid?

7.5 Research in the incompetent adult

Research participation by adults who lack capacity is undoubtedly contentious since informed consent cannot be given. In fact, the Nuremberg Code appears to prohibit inclusion of such participants. The Declaration of Helsinki permits participation provided that proxy consent is obtained in accordance with the law of the applicable jurisdiction. However, failure to include subjects in this category would likely jeopardise existing and future patients from the possibility of improved care due to advancements of pharmacology and medical science.

7.5.1 Adults who lack capacity

Several categories of individuals are unable to give valid consent to participate in medical research, such as incapacitated and unconscious adults. These persons are vulnerable due to their inability to exercise autonomous choice and are therefore deserving of special protection. However, if research is not carried out on adults who lack decision-making capacity this will prevent advances in the treatment of conditions that affect this sector of the population. Avoidance of research that involves subjects who cannot consent means that these groups will have access only to treatments tested on those unaffected by such conditions, which might have implications for safety and efficacy.

The need to include vulnerable groups in research was recognised by the Declaration of Helsinki which approves such research if it is necessary to 'promote the health of the population represented by the potential subjects. The research cannot instead be performed with competent persons and the research entails only minimal risk and minimal burden' (WHO, 2008). The courts have also indicated that they are prepared to take a broader view of experimental therapy on incompetent adults. In *Simms v Simms and an NHS Trust* [2002] EWHC 2734 the administration of experimental therapy upon two patients suffering from Creutzfeldt-Jakob disease was authorised by the Court of Appeal.

Therapeutic treatment of adults who lack decision-making capacity is legitimised by the concept of best interests or the doctrine of necessity (section 5 Mental Capacity Act 2005). Application of the best interests approach might extend to participation of the adult who lacks capacity in circumstances where there is an expectation of benefit for the subject. In situations where the anticipated benefit is for society in general, sanctioning participation can be more problematic. The Law Commission (1995, paragraph 6.29) stated that participation in non-therapeutic research by those who lack capacity is likely to be unlawful since 'his or her participation, and the procedure cannot be justified on the doctrine of necessity, then any person who touches or restrains that patient is committing an unlawful battery. The simple fact is that the researcher is making no claim to be acting in the best interests of that individual person and does not therefore come within the rules of law set out in *Re F'*. Lewis (2002) argues that this approach ought to be reviewed on several counts. Notwithstanding actual therapeutic benefits, other advantages may be apparent such as positive caring or social relationships. Such perceived advantages have previously been used for judicial authorisation of a bone marrow transplant from a mentally incompetent adult (*Re Y (adult patient) (transplant; bone marrow)* (1996) 35 BMLR 111). A utilitarian reason for carrying out non-therapeutic research on participants who lack decision-making capacity is to develop better therapeutic and clinical care for this category of persons, or more generally for societal benefit.

Grubb (2004: 879) states that there are difficulties 'in ascertaining an effective and coherent theoretical basis for the decision regarding the inclusion of mentally incompetent adults in clinical trials'. Nevertheless it seems difficult to justify the imposition of a blanket ban on participation by those who lack capacity. The Law Commission (1995, paragraph 6.34) proposed the introduction of certain safeguards. A notable recommendation was that a research committee for mental incapacity should be established and that the lawfulness of non-therapeutic research should be considered by this committee. The following criteria would need to be satisfied: (a) that it is desirable to provide knowledge of the causes of treatment or the care of people affected by the incapacitating condition with which any participant is or may be affected; (b) that the objective of the research cannot be effectively achieved without the participation of persons who are or may be without capacity to consent and (c) that the research will not expose a participant to more than negligible risk, will not be unduly invasive or restrictive of a participant and will not unduly interfere with a participant's freedom of action or privacy. Treatment of the incapacitated person is governed by the Mental Capacity Act 2005, which provides for participation in research.

7.5.2 The Mental Capacity Act 2005

The Mental Incapacity Bill lacked provisions to allow incapacitated persons to participate in clinical research. Following considerable evidence for its inclusion presented by the Royal Colleges and interested groups (such as the Alzheimer's Society), the Joint Select Committee agreed that provisions were required.

Sections 30 to 34 of the Mental Capacity Act 2005 apply to clinical research that:

- is 'intrusive' in that it is of a type that the researcher would need to obtain valid consent if the person had capacity (section 30(2))
- commenced on or before 1 October 2007
- is not a clinical trial subject to the provisions of the Medicines for Human Use (Clinical Trials) Regulations 2004 (section 30(3))
- involves persons over 16 years who lack capacity to consent
- will be carried out in England and Wales
- has been approved by an appropriate body (section 30 (4)) and is carried out in compliance with section 32 and section 33

The MCA requires the research to be of potential benefit to the participant and such benefit to be proportionate to any apparent burdens that might be caused by participation (section 31(5)(a)). Alternatively, the research must be intended to provide knowledge of the cause, care or treatment of those with the same, or similar, condition, provided that the risk of participation is negligible and will not interfere with the subject's freedom of action, privacy or be unduly invasive (section 31(6)). Before any decision is made to include the person who lacks capacity the researcher must take reasonable steps to consult an unpaid carer or any other person interested in the participant's welfare (section 32(1),(2)). If it transpires that the person would have been unlikely to agree to participate, then these views should be respected (section 32(4)), on the grounds that the interests of the individual outweigh those of society and science (section 33(3)).

7.5.3 The Clinical Trials Directive

The Clinical Trials Directive (the Directive) specifically provides for those who lack capacity to participate in clinical trials. The Directive was intended to align with the laws and regulations that pertain to the conduct of clinical drug trials in Member States. Article 5(e) of the Directive requires that incapacitated adults should only be included if 'such research is essential to validate data obtained in clinical trials on persons able to give informed consent or by other research methods, and relates directly to a life-threatening or debilitating clinical condition from which the incapacitated adult concerned suffers'. Furthermore, the Directive requires that trials have been 'designed to minimise pain, discomfort, fear and any other foreseeable risk in relation to the disease and developmental stage; both the risk threshold and the degree of distress have to be specially defined and constantly monitored'. In the context of incapacitated subjects the Directive requires consent for research from a person acting as the representative of the prospective participant.

7.5.4 Representative consent

Schedule 1 of the Medicines for Human Use (Clinical Trials) Regulations 2004 (the Regulations) requires that if a person cannot give consent to participate in a clinical trial, then consent must be obtained from that individual's legal representative, who is independent of the research team and is required to act on the basis of the subject's presumed wishes. The Regulations require that proxy consent is first sought from a representative who has a close relationship to the individual. If no representative is willing or available to assume this role, then consent can be sought from the person's doctor unless that doctor is involved with the conduct of the trial, which would disqualify the doctor from providing consent. Persons involved with the conduct of the trial could include the sponsors of the trial, any person employed, engaged or acting under arrangements with the sponsor, an investigator, a health professional who is a member of the investigator's team and any other person who provides health care under the direction or control of the sponsor or investigator. If the doctor is unable or unwilling to act as proxy then a person nominated by the doctor may give consent, or a health service organisation might have a list of suitable persons who could be approached to give consent on behalf of the incapacitated person. The legal representative is expected to ensure that the trial is regularly re-evaluated from the perspective of the subject's continued participation.

A professional representative (such as the person's general practitioner) who is not involved with the clinical care of the person may consult appropriate others to reach a decision regarding trial participation. Exhaustive enquiries are not required, although if a valid and applicable advance refusal exists then this ought to be regarded as definitive evidence of the presumed will of the subject.

Schedule 1 of the Regulations also includes details and principles that apply to adults who lack capacity and their participation in clinical trials. The incapacitated adult must be given information about the trial according to the prospective participant's level of comprehension, including the trial's potential risks and anticipated benefits. The refusal to participate in, or withdraw from a clinical trial, by a subject who is able to form an opinion must be carefully considered by the investigator. No incentives or financial inducements can be given either to the subject or to the legal representative. A further requirement is an expectation that the product being tested will have a beneficial effect on the subject. The right to withdraw from a trial is important and the General Medical Council (2002, paragraph 49) emphasises the need to consider and ensure that the participant's rights to withdraw from the research is respected at all times.

The category of adults who lack capacity is wide and includes the permanently insensate who are unaware of their existence, such as patients in a vegetative state, and those who, towards the lower end of the spectrum, have relatively minor cognitive impairment. The breadth of this spectrum can be problematic. The General Medical Council guidance (2002) stresses the need to respect the participant's rights to withdraw which should engage at any sign of distress, pain or indication of refusal. However, those who lack capacity might not have the ability to communicate their wishes. Section 33(2) of the Mental Capacity Act 2005 states that:

> Nothing may be done to, or in relation to, him in the course of research –
>
> a) to which he appears to object (whether by showing signs of resistance or otherwise) except where what is being done is intended to protect him from harm or to reduce or prevent pain or discomfort, or
> b) which would be contrary to –
>   i) an advance decision of his which has effect, or
>   ii) any other form of statement made by him and subsequently withdrawn' (of which the researcher is aware).

This provision reinforces the view that cognisance must be taken of the incapacitated subject's wishes. Since the majority of research is regarded as intrusive, it is unlawful to conduct research without consent and prior approval of the study by an appropriate body such as a REC. Research that is unduly invasive or restrictive, or does not have the potential to be of benefit for the incapacitated person, would not comply with the Regulations.

The need to show benefit is widely construed and encompasses an incapacitated person's previous wishes and feelings, including whether participation might have provided some benefit had the person retained decision-making capacity. The concept of benefit could, for example, include altruistic benefits and previously held utilitarian beliefs. Section 32(2) Mental Capacity Act 2005 requires the researcher to take reasonable steps to identify an individual who has an interest in the incapacitated person's welfare and who is willing to be consulted as to whether the person would have been likely to participate had that person retained capacity.

The protection offered by the Mental Capacity Act 2005 for the incapacitated person participating in research appears more robust and rigorous when compared to the Regulations. The fundamental difference is that the Act requires evidence of a previous indication by the incapacitated person either to participate or to refuse to take part in research, and which evidence should be decisive. In comparison the Regulations require that participant's unwillingness must merely be taken into account.

Jaswinder, who is keen to participate in the trial, has a condition that has affected his ability to make decisions. Assuming Jaswinder lacks capacity:

▶ Consider the circumstances by which he could legitimately be included in the trial (in law and ethics).
▶ Jaswinder wishes to stop taking the trial medication. To what extent can Jaswinder withdraw from the trial a) assuming he is competent b) if he is found to lack decision-making capacity?

7.5.5 Emergency situations

Safe and effective treatment of emergency and critical illnesses such as strokes, cardiac arrests and arrhythmias means that clinical research must be carried out on those who suffer such conditions. The 2004 Regulations required that written consent was given by a legal representative prior to participation, a situation that could potentially prevent many from inclusion due to the short time frame available for contacting the legal representative. While this position might be regarded as ethically sound and protective of vulnerable people's rights, it nonetheless could inhibit research into cardiopulmonary resuscitation and critical care. The Declaration of Helsinki (2000) permits research into emergency conditions without the need to obtain prior consent provided that participants give consent (by self or proxy) as soon as they are able to do so.

The 2004 Regulations have since been amended by the Medicines for Human Use (Clinical Trials Amendment No. 2) Regulations 2006 (SI 2006/2984) to better align the Regulations with the Mental Capacity Act 2005 for the purposes of research into emergency conditions on those who lack capacity. The 2006 Regulations provide that patients may be entered into a trial prior subject to consent from a legal representative under the following circumstances:

1. the treatment is required urgently;
2. urgent action is required due to the nature of the trial;
3. it is not practicable to obtain informed consent from a legal representative;
4. the procedure under which the action is taken has been approved by a research ethics committee.

General Medical Council guidance (2002) reflects the law and provides that:

> in an emergency where consent cannot be obtained, treatment can be given only if it is limited to what is immediately necessary to save life or avoid significant deterioration in the patient's health. This may include treatment that is part of a therapeutic research project, where the risks of the new treatment are not believed to exceed the known risks of standard treatment. If, during treatment, the patient regains capacity, the patient should be told about the research as soon as possible and their consent to continue should be sought.

7.6 Accountability in research

Most clinical research involves an element of risk not only in respect of safety of participants but also for return of investment of time and money. Proper governance and accountability are essential to make certain that research is carried out with integrity and in accordance with contemporary standards to protect participants and ensure the validity of results.

7.6.1 Monitoring trials of medicinal products

The Clinical Trial Directive triggered the statutory inclusion of a range of accountability provisions for the governance of clinical drug trials. The Regulations provide the statutory foundation for incorporating 'Good Clinical Practice' for the commencement and continuance of clinical trials (Regs 2, 28, 29, 30 and Schedule 1). Good Clinical Practice incorporates a range of requirements such as reporting, amendments to the trial protocol, dealing with infringements, the appeals procedure, provision of information to participants and the responsibilities of the research team. Similarly, Good Manufacturing Practice (GMP) standards require that investigational medications are manufactured to appropriate high standards (Regulations 36–46, Schedules 7 and 8).

The Regulations permit inspections by the Licensing body, the Medicines and Healthcare Products Regulatory Agency (MHRA), against internationally accepted standards of GCP and GMP in order to identify non-compliance. The MHRA has powers of enforcement to be used for persistent misconduct or suspected fraud.

Amendments to the trial protocol may be required, for example, on account of safety reasons. A substantial amendment is one which is likely to affect to a significant degree the safety, physical or mental integrity of the subjects, the scientific value of the trial, the conduct or management of the trial or the quality or safety of any investigational product used in the trial. Notice of the amendment needs to be sent to the relevant licensing authority, as well as to the REC. Responses should state whether the amendments are accepted or rejected.

Regulation 12 requires that every clinical trial must be approved by a REC and authorised by the MHRA. In addition to having a detailed remit for licensing medicines, the MHRA has power to suspend or prohibit a trial either wholly or at a particular site. The grounds for doing so include the belief that conditions set out in the original request are no longer satisfied or, where there are doubts regarding the conduct of the trial (whether in respect of safety or any other way by which the scientific validity of the study could be affected). Regulations 32–35 require that serious adverse events and suspected unexpected serious adverse events are recorded and reported to the MHRA. Trial sponsors are required to inform all investigators who are responsible for the conduct of the trial about such events; in addition these need to be entered onto a central European database established under Article 11 (i) of the Clinical Trials Directive (Regulation 34). The database is designed to facilitate communication about trials of medicinal products between Member States and it allows events to be reviewed, to generate statistics and to disseminate information to enhance patient safety. Notification is subject to strict time limits.

Infringement of the trial protocol may lead to suspension or termination of the trial by the MHRA. Sponsors may appear before the Licensing Authority or a nominated person following rejection of a request for authorisation, failure to obtain an amendment or termination of a trial. Representations can be made to the appropriate committee which makes a decision and provides a report, although the MHRA is not bound by the report.

Regulations 49 and 50 operate to create criminal offences punishable by imprisonment. These are offences of strict liability, although Regulation 51 amounts to a due diligence defence where there is evidence that a person took all reasonable care and caution to avoid commission of an offence.

7.6.2 Responsibilities

Responsibility for ensuring the integrity and accountability for clinical research is shared by many organisations and individuals, including employers, commercial and academic sponsors and individual researchers. Shared responsibility ensures conduct within a governance framework that protects participants and can provide redress should harmful effects occur as a result of the research.

7.6.2(a) Universities and organisations

The framework for research governance requires employing organisations to ensure that researchers understand and are able to discharge their responsibilities. Employers must support staff and hold them to account over the conduct of research. Universities must ensure compliance with relevant employment, health and safety legislation and codes of practice and ought to have provisions for dealing with non-compliance and misconduct, as well as having a structure by which complaints can be used as a learning exercise. Systems must be in place to detect and address fraud, and mechanisms are required to compensate those negligently harmed through research activities.

Health and social care organisations also have responsibilities. These must be aware of the research currently undertaken and that patients, users and carers are provided with adequate information about the research process. The chief executive of the organisation is accountable for quality and governance in research. Health and social care professionals should retain responsibility for the care of patients when recruited into studies. They have a duty to satisfy themselves that the research has been duly approved by the appropriate bodies, prior to commencement.

7.6.2(b) The UK Research Integrity Office

The UK Research Integrity Office is an independent advisory body established in 2006 to promote robust governance and conduct of research and disseminate good practice for the avoidance of research misconduct. The Office provides confidential and expert advice on specific cases although it is not a regulatory body and has no formal legal powers. Its advice is not mandatory but reflects best practice in the conduct of research and addressing instances of misconduct. It publishes a *Code of Practice for Research: Promoting good practice and preventing misconduct*.

7.6.2(c) Sponsors

Sponsors have a direct responsibility for research, and since April 2004 all research studies must have an identifiable research sponsor. A sponsor is the individual (or body) who assumes ultimate responsibility for the initiation, management and financing (or arranging the initiation, management and financing) for that particular trial (or research project). Sponsors have a duty to ensure that arrangements are in place for the management and monitoring of the study, as well as safety and accountability.

Any organisation that provides research funding is responsible for ensuring the proper use and allocation of funds and that value for money has been obtained. A body wishing to fund research and collaborate with the NHS must be willing to undertake the responsibilities of research sponsor, or to collaborate with another organisation to meet these requirements. If the funder feels unable to take on sponsorship responsibilities, then a precondition of funding is that another body accepts the role.

7.6.2(d) Researchers

Researchers are responsible for the day-to-day management of research projects. They follow agreed protocols, assist health-care professionals, provide appropriate care and supervision of research subjects, act as custodians of confidential data, report adverse drug reactions and report matters via the appropriate channels.

Since research may be carried out by several researchers these activities need to be supervised and coordinated by a 'principal investigator'. Responsibilities of the principal investigator include ensuring that research is conducted according to Good Clinical Practice and that the dignity, rights, safety and well-being of participants are maintained and prioritised. The principal investigator must ensure that members of the research team are appropriately qualified and have received adequate training according to their roles.

7.6.3 Confidentiality

The obligation to safeguard the confidentiality of research subjects is strengthened by statutory provisions such as the Data Protection Act 1998 and Article 8 of the European Convention. The research governance framework requires the protocol to include details of those who will have access to participants' data samples. The protocol also requires details of the measures to be taken to maintain the confidentiality and security of personal data, data anonymity and process to be used (if appropriate) and the purposes for which information will be used.

Data on research subjects is typically made anonymous as part of the study design. This process can be problematic in certain circumstances such as in relation to the participant who wishes to exercise discretion as to whether personal data can be used subsequently in further research projects. This situation is particularly relevant to an individual's data stored on genetic databases used for major population studies (see 11.6).

In certain circumstances statutory exceptions permit disclosure of personal data for research purposes. The National Cancer Registry, for example, collates data from several regional cancer registries. Section 251 of the National Health Services Act 2006 enables the Secretary of State to make regulations to permit processing of patient information for medical purposes as considered necessary in the interests of patient care and the public interest. While this provision may facilitate transfer of information within scientific communities and provide societal benefit, it provides an exception to the principle of confidentiality.

Disclosure in the public interest, and in breach of confidence, ought to be rare and dependent upon the absolute necessity of its use, its sensitivity in respect of an identifiable individual and the importance of the proposed research project for which disclosure is sought. It is generally accepted that if research gives rise to information that could be relevant to the current and future health or quality of life of a participant, then such information ought to be offered. Disclosure could be problematic if the individual is entrusted with information that they would otherwise not wish to know, and may lead to further issues if this is included in the medical record. There is an argument that this information is of value only if it is of immediate clinical relevance, and that its value in respect of longer-term health issues is doubtful and may have negative connotations. A typical example is disclosure of genetic susceptibility to disease that is likely to manifest many years after the culmination of a particular research study.

It is generally held that anonymous patient information can be legitimately used without further consent in certain circumstances (*R v Department of Health XP Source Informatics* [2001] All ER 786). While this principle is relevant for certain forms of research, such as epidemiological research, it is questionable whether it can legitimately be extended to include genetic material. The Medical Research Council (2001) suggests that under such circumstances, a two-stage process ought to be applied. First, consent is necessary for the initial use of material and then further consent should be sought for its storage and subsequent use in research studies (paragraph 3.2). McHale (2004), as well as Kaye and Martin (2000), suggest that the legal and ethical issues are considerably more complex, particularly for large databases, such as the UK Biobank (a collaboration between the Medical Research Council, Wellcome Trust and the Department of Health), which include the genetic information of a population of 500,000 persons between the ages of 45 and 69. Problematic issues can be apparent with large and comprehensive databases of genetic information in respect of the validity of initial consent and whether this is sufficient for subsequent use of sensitive personal data. The boundaries of consent in these circumstances are unclear and ambiguities exist about the secondary use of information, potentially on a very broad scale (see 11.6.4).

> On completion of the trial Dr Yin takes the study data home for purposes of analysis. He subsequently discusses the results with an individual who is unconnected with the study:
>
> ▶ Consider the ethical and legal issues that arise.

7.7   Misconduct and harm to participants

Research misconduct, whether fraudulent or negligent, has significant negative consequences for the research community. The potential damage to reputations, participants, careers and public trust and confidence is enormous. Research misconduct has been widely defined by the Medical Research Council (1997) as the 'fabrication, falsification, plagiarism or deception in proposing, carrying out or reporting results of research or deliberate, dangerous or negligent deviations from accepted practices in carrying out research. It includes failure to follow established protocols if this failure results in unreasonable risk or harm to humans ... and facilitating of misconduct in research by collusion in, or concealment of, such actions by others'. It does not include honest error, or poor judgement, unless this is accompanied by the intention to deceive.

7.7.1   Research fraud

Clinical research frequently takes place in pressured and competitive environments and the career prospects of a researcher might depend heavily on project completion followed by publication of positive results. Rennie (1998) asserts that there is a need for a more centralised review of the research process, as well as systems by which editors of scientific journals can identify and manage research fraud. Research misconduct is primarily dealt with through disciplinary action by employers and the regulatory bodies and as yet there is no specific legal regulation.

A recent example of research fraud concerned the supposed link between the measles, mumps and rubella vaccine and autism published by the prestigious medical journal *The Lancet* in 1998. The article was later retracted in 2010 following a ruling by the General Medical Council against some of the researchers involved in the study. Publication of the article in 1998 caused a significant decrease in vaccination rates, and an accompanying rise in reported measles cases. The investigation carried out by the General Medical Council showed (among other things) that preliminary ethical approval of the study had not been obtained, that blood samples were collected from children at a birthday party, all in the presence of competing financial interests of the researchers that were not declared on publication.

7.7.2 Harm to participants

Harm or injury for which compensation may be payable might occur in participants on account of their involvement in clinical research. Although the likelihood of harm is greater where interventions are involved, damage may also occur due to breach of confidentiality, damage to reputation and psychiatric harm in non-interventional studies.

7.7.2(a) Accountability to participants

Legal proceedings may be brought by a trial participant who suffers injury as a result of participating in medical research. An action can be brought under negligence, product liability or criminal liability against those conducting the trial.

In addition to the above, a legal challenge may be brought against a decision made by a REC that gave a favourable opinion prior to study commencement. One possible approach would be for an applicant to bring an action of judicial review of the decision taken by the committee, or its members, on the basis that the committee acted outside their powers or had not reached a decision by due process. Other grounds could be failure to follow the rules of natural justice or for acting irrationally. A problematic issue in respect to bringing other legal proceedings against a committee concerns the legal status of the REC. Under the 2004 Regulations, all RECs must be approved and have a statutory basis (Part 2 and Reg. 12) although the regulatory obligations and extent of its powers remain unclear. Brazier (1990) suggests that individual REC members owe a duty of care to research subjects. Thus, members must seek to understand and take an ethical view of some of the complex issues that pertain to biomedical science, philosophy and statistics. The standard of care to be applied would be that of reasonableness. Nevertheless, establishing liability might be difficult since negligence must still be established on the part of the committee or individual member, as well as proof of causation. Establishing causation could be problematic since damage sustained by a research participant is more likely to be due to the intervention rather than the decision of the committee, notwithstanding 'but for' the favourable opinion, the research would not have taken place. The Department of Health (1991, paragraph 2.11) suggests that there is little chance of a successful claim against a, or individual member, and that any claim for injury would lie principally against the researcher and the organisation in which the research was carried out.

7.7.2(b) Compensation for injuries

It has been argued that those who are injured as a result of research participation ought to be compensated on a no-fault basis. Since the community expects to benefit from research it perhaps seems unfair if participants had to overcome the usual hurdles of negligence liability to receive compensation.

Whilst a no-fault scheme is not in operation, Article 6(h) of the Clinical Trials Directive requires the REC to take into account provisions for the indemnity, or compensation, of participants in the event of injury or death that can be attributed to a clinical trial. Furthermore, Article 6(i) Clinical Trials Directive requires the REC to consider any insurance or indemnity provisions available to cover the liability of an investigator or sponsor. This provision is reflected in Regulation 15 (5) of the Medicines for Human Use (Clinical Trials) Regulations 2004.

The General Medical Council guidance states that doctors ought to provide participants with details of compensation that is available in the event of injury. The Association of British Pharmaceutical Industry recommends that compensation is paid even where the victim cannot prove negligence. However, the victim would still need to establish causation and this may be particularly difficult if the participant's pre-existing medical condition offers an alternative and plausible explanation for deterioration of the participant's condition or apparent injury.

7.8 Ethical issues and research in practice

The ethical conduct of clinical research demands that it is designed and carried out in accordance with robust standards to protect participants, sponsors, institutions and researchers. Particular issues arise on account of the duty to participate in clinical research, whether participants ought to be paid, and the particular dilemmas where research is to be carried out in the developing nations.

7.8.1 Duty to participate

There is no generally recognised duty to participate in clinical research. It could be argued, however, that for research to provide meaningful and valid results there is a moral duty to act as a research subject. In the absence of sufficient and adequate recruitment of participants results are unlikely to be valid and universally applicable to the general population. Clinical research is invariably accompanied by greater or lesser degree of risk and arguably these ought to be applied across society rather than restricted to certain groups, who might otherwise assume a disproportionate burden. Participation could be perceived as a universal duty under a social contract.

Members of society should give serious consideration to an invitation to participate in clinical research (Research Governance Framework, 2005). Many of the benefits of medicine have been achieved through investigation and research. If people wish to accept the benefits of medical care, then it is arguable that a duty to participate is owed in order to generate societal benefits. Involvement in research ought to be viewed in the context of the public interest as opposed to whether any particular individual might acquire a benefit. However, a time lag is inevitable between research studies, publication and translation into therapeutic care.

7.8.2 Payment

The offer of payment for research participants generates strong and polarised opinion. The arguments in favour are that research takes up time, and it may be inconvenient and uncomfortable. Payment, therefore, represents small compensation and also acts as a useful stimulus to ensure the adequate recruitment of subjects to ensure validity. Nominal payment and financial recompense need not necessarily be coercive. Financial compensation can be viewed in a comparable light to the inducement that a critically ill person might receive when participating in research that is believed to offer some very small hope of recovery.

Those against payment tend to argue that the lure of money may prove irresistible (although it is questionable as to whether the relatively small payments on offer could actually be considered an inducement). A moral concern about payment for research is the psychological repugnance of offering monetary reward for an activity that aims to provide an altruistic benefit for society.

Empirical work suggests that payment, as an inducement, might affect the validity of findings in two principal ways. First, Bentley and Thacker (2004) have shown that payment influences respondents' propensity to fail to inform researchers about restricted activities that they have engaged in, and may influence subjects' behaviour in respect of concealing information. As a result, outcomes and results can be distorted. Covert use of alcohol, caffeine, medication and herbal products, for example, may affect the pharmacokinetics of a study. Second, Ferguson (2008) has shown that payment could skew subject selection. For example, three-quarters of Phase I study volunteers (who were paid to participate) were male and aged between 18 and 45 years. A quarter of the participants were students, half of whom were medical students. Therefore, the results obtained may not be of universal application.

Payments of a relatively modest level are considered less likely to be coercive. Lemmens and Elliott (2001), however, argue that this position is less than frank, and that a better approach might be for researchers to employ research subjects. They argue that the current regulatory system is unsafe. Whereas ethical guidelines and regulations ought to protect healthy research subjects from exploitation, the current regulatory regime means that research subjects are barred from receiving a fair and adequate wage. This situation denies participants the ability to obtain the legal resources that are available to other groups of high-risk workers. Research subjects who are employed would benefit from many forms of protection including health and safety legislation.

7.8.3 Developing countries

Medical research studies that include participants of the developing world (including the world's poorest countries) raise a plethora of ethical issues due to the potential vulnerability of participants. If a trial goes wrong in a developed country, the typical response is massive adverse publicity and financially crippling liability for the organisations (sponsor and host) concerned. Hence there may be a temptation to undertake research in poorer countries. Less controversially, recruitment of patients into Phase III and Phase IV studies can be expected to be easier where the condition being examined has greater prevalence. A typical example is treatment for Human Immunodeficiency Virus and Acquired Immune Deficiency Syndrome (AIDS) in Sub-Saharan Africa.

Research subjects from developing nations are a potentially vulnerable population and there is a danger of exploitation on account of several factors. Governments of such countries may be complicit in minimising the obstacles for sponsors of research when planning clinical trials in their countries. Some nations may be reluctant to impose restrictions on human research in the form of legal protection for participants. Governments may be keen to bring medical research to their country but are prevented due to resource constraints and therefore seek to 'facilitate' pharmaceutical companies by subsidising research initiatives. Individual participants might receive comparatively small sums of monetary compensation, which can be considered attractive within impoverished communities. Participation research might also be a way to receive medical care that would otherwise be unavailable. These factors, along with others, raise serious questions regarding the ethical legitimacy of such studies and more particularly in terms of its regulation.

Informed consent within this context can be fraught with difficulties. Whilst in principle informed consent should be obtained from each prospective participant, at least two problems arise. The first concerns the amount of information that is given, and the way it is communicated. Information needs to be understood, and understanding needs to be checked. For populations that may be poorly educated, the extent to which this is undertaken, or even feasible, within the context of large-scale studies seems dubious. The second issue relates to proxy consent being given on behalf of the participant by another, which can be customary in certain cultures. The Nuffield Council on Bioethics (2002, at 6.22) acknowledges that in 'some cultural contexts it may be appropriate to obtain agreement from the community or assent from a senior family member before a prospective participant is approached'. If a prospective participant does not wish to participate then this refusal must be respected. In some patriarchal societies, refusal can be frowned upon, especially if participation is expected to confer financial advantage to a family or community. Whilst the Nuffield Council on Bioethics proposes that in such a situation, the researcher has 'a duty to facilitate the non-participation', this could lead to reprisals for the individual who refuses consent.

A central concern is whether it is ethical to carry out research on populations who are unlikely to benefit from the medication once it is marketed, due to lack of money and health-care infrastructure. The issue that arises is whether researchers have a duty to make treatments available to participants on completion of the trial. It is difficult to envisage how a pharmaceutical company could be expected to assume responsibility for the future health needs of a developing nation although if a trial has had a positive outcome then post-trial access to the medication would seem to be ethically justified. The Declaration of Helsinki states that medical research involving a disadvantaged or vulnerable population can be justified only where there is a reasonable likelihood that the population or community stands to benefit and that arrangements for post-study access for participants are available. On completion of the study, participants should be informed of the outcome and be assured of access to interventions identified by the study as beneficial (Declaration of Helsinki (2008, paragraph 30)).

A further controversy concerns use of placebo controls in circumstances where an effective treatment is available. Two decades ago, subjects from developing countries were dehumanised in clinical trials designed to develop treatment for AIDS. The trials were designed with a placebo control arm. Following the 2008 version of the Declaration of Helsinki, the effectiveness of a new intervention now must be tested against the best current proven intervention (rather than a placebo). The trials were criticised heavily by Laurie and Woolfe (1997 at 853) who stated in strong terms:

> Residents of impoverished post-colonial countries, the majority of whom are people of colour, must be protected from potential exploitation in research. Otherwise, the abominable state of healthcare in these countries can be used to justify studies that could never pass ethical muster in the sponsoring country ... It is time to develop standards of research that preclude the kinds of double standards evident in these trials ... Tragically, for the hundreds of infants who have needlessly contracted HIV infection in the perinatal transmission studies that have already been completed, any such protection will have come too late.

In recognition of his support for the clinical trial Dr Jones has been promised a donation to his research fund for each patient who completes the study. Participants will also receive a 'token' of appreciation:

▶ Does the indirect payment to Dr Jones create a conflict of interests?
▶ Would these gestures fall into the category of financial inducement?
▶ Are participants effectively being paid to participate?
▶ If so, to what extent are these practices unethical and potentially coercive?

7.9   Under-representation

The Research Governance Framework (2005 at paragraph: 2.2.7) states that 'Research, and those pursuing it, should respect the diversity of human society and conditions and the multicultural nature of society. Whenever relevant, it should take account of age, disability, gender, sexual orientation, race, culture and religion in its design, undertaking, and reporting. The body of research evidence available to policy makers should reflect the diversity of the population.'

Despite this overarching principle, several sectors of society remain under-represented in clinical trials. Key examples are women and the elderly, and yet paradoxically, these groups are perhaps the highest users of medication. Concerns about recruiting the elderly tends to revolve around the difficulties of ensuring adherence to research protocols, follow-up difficulties (due to ill health or death) and the tendency of the elderly to have multiple co-morbidities. The elderly can experience adverse effects from medication due to reduced liver and kidney function, and for this reason research studies need to include elderly participants to ensure safe future use. Research Ethics Committees ought to demand justification for the imposition of arbitrary age limits particularly where the trial medication treatment aims to treat conditions that are prevalent in age groups at either end of the spectrum.

Women, particularly those of child-bearing potential, are typically excluded from Phase I trials and under-represented in subsequent studies. One justification is to protect women and possibly the foetus from damage caused by unanticipated side effects and dangers of experimental interventions. If, however, women are not included in research studies, the safety of prescribed medication cannot be assured. Exclusion from clinical trials exposes women to the risks of untested medication, since the physiology of men and women, particularly during the reproductive years, is dissimilar and metabolism and excretion are influenced by factors that include muscle mass, oestrogen and liver function. Fox (1998) criticises this phenomena from a feminist perspective and suggests that it calls 'into question the scientifically dubious practice of marketing drugs and procedures which have been inadequately tested for their impact on women'. While her conclusions are influenced by her feminist views, the under-representation of women in clinical research raises legitimate questions as to the validity and generalisability of therapeutic agents that have been solely tested on men.

Other under-represented groups, particularly in the United Kingdom, are minority ethnic populations. It is estimated that by 2020 the population in the United Kingdom will be around 70,000,000 of which around 50% might be considered of minority ethnic descent and their offspring. Yet clinical research trials seldom include representation from these groups on several possible grounds. People of minority ethnic origin may be hesitant to participate due to cultural reasons. Further obstacles might be linguistic barriers which impact upon information disclosure and the validity of consent. There is a need for initiatives that promote inclusive participation and enhance positive recruitment in order to ensure adequate representation and safe medication.

7.10 Publication of results

Research results that are not published cannot inform and advance scientific knowledge or provide social benefit. However, within the field of medical publication, positive results (that a new treatment works and is of benefit) are much more newsworthy and meritorious of publication than negative results (that the new treatment or intervention is not effective, or is even harmful). However, so-called negative results also add to the corpus of knowledge and can play a valuable role in the design of future studies, as well as the avoidance of unnecessary repetition. Results that are negative, or inconclusive, should be publicly available because they contribute to future research.

Medical and scientific journals are often reluctant to publish negative results. However, the Declaration of Helsinki (2008) states that every clinical trial must be registered in a publicly accessible database prior to recruitment of the first participant. This is reflected in guidance of the Royal College of Physicians (2007) where it recognises that there could have been instances of trials showing negligible benefit of an active drug against a control, or greater than expected adverse effects, being concealed by the pharmaceutical industry 'burying results to protect its own interests or by editorial choice. This distorts the medical literature, impairs meta-analyses and undermines the confidence of doctors and patients alike.' The College has stated that it is important that the REC does all that it can to ensure that publication of negative results is not precluded in advance or otherwise impeded by the sponsors. The College supports the registration of all clinical trials to help to ensure their eventual publication, irrespective of results, and would like to see approval of applications conditional upon such registration. Publication of all results would not only prevent publication bias but assist in the wider analysis of data. It would also, to some extent, remove the perceived pressure on researchers to publish only positive results.

A more problematic issue concerns unethical research and whether this ought to be published. There is an argument that if unethical research produces results that might actually have a benefit, then refusal to disseminate and publicise this information could be detrimental in the longer term with, for example, more suffering than has already occurred. One way forward might be to ensure that the researcher does not benefit from publication and names could be withheld, or the results could be published with a declaration regarding the methodology and that this is not endorsed due to its unethical nature. Alternatively, if unethical research is published, then this could send conflicting messages. The Council for International Organisations of Medical Sciences (CIOMS) suggests that although unethical research should not normally be published, there may be situations where this could have wider health benefits and under these circumstances, publication should be given careful consideration. The advice from CIOMS is that editors should refuse to publish the results of unethical research and should retract any articles that are subsequently found to contain falsified or fabricated data, unless there are very strong and persuasive reasons to do otherwise. Guideline 2 of CIOMS states that such 'sanctions, however, may deprive of the benefit not only the errant researcher or sponsor, but also that segment of society intended to benefit from the research; such possible consequences merit careful consideration'.

Summary

7.1   Clinical research is fundamental to progress in medicine. It benefits of society in general and requires participation of individuals.

7.2   Research activities may take the form of therapeutic or non-therapeutic research, phased clinical trials and randomised controlled trials (RCT). RCTs are the 'gold standard' of medical research, and may be 'double blind' (where neither the participant nor observer knows whether an active or inert compound is being administered), or 'single blind' (where the characteristic is known to the observer but not the participant).

7.3   Regulation of research is governed by international ethical codes, domestic law, the Medicines for Human Use (Clinical Trials Regulations) 2004, guidance from professional bodies and Research Ethics Committees. The governance framework for clinical research aims to ensure that participants are adequately protected.

7.4   Participation in research by a competent subject requires voluntary consent based on sufficient information. Subjects are under no obligation to continue with the research (even if they have given consent) and may withdraw at any time. Particular care is needed when obtaining consent from vulnerable individuals.

7.5   Obtaining agreement for participation by a person who lacks decision-making capacity is governed by the Mental Capacity Act 2005, the Medicines for Human Use (Clinical Trials Regulations) 2004 and guidance from professional bodies. For the purposes of clinical trials, proxy consent is called 'representative consent'.

7.6   Accountability for ensuring and monitoring proper standards in research rests with researchers, the host organisations wherein the research is being conducted and research sponsors. All research data is confidential subject to limited exceptions.

7.7   At times, research may cause harm to participants. Subjects who suffer injuries as a result of participation might claim compensation under insurance policies, or by a legal action.

7.8   A range of ethical issues surround research participation. Payment of subjects is controversial and could be viewed as coercive and militating against truly autonomous participation. Research in developing countries poses potential ethical problems in respect of financial and cultural vulnerability of subjects.

7.9   Women and elderly participants may be under-represented in clinical research. This situation potentially skews the ability to generalise results from research to these patient groups.

7.10 There is an imperative to publish 'positive' or beneficial research outcomes. However, non-publication of 'negative' results may distort the medical literature and impair the conclusions of meta-analyses of clinical trials.

Exercises

7.1 'Participation in clinical research is underpinned by values derived from human rights. A utilitarian approach to research would be more in keeping with the need for developing medical advances in the twenty-first century.' Discuss.

7.2 Consider whether benefits of the current research governance framework outweigh the detrimental effects of hindering research.

7.3 You have an aunt with Alzheimer's disease, but who is otherwise well and content. You have been asked if she could participate in a clinical trial involving a new drug which could benefit patients who have dementia. What issues would you consider in deciding whether she should participate?

7.4 A randomised controlled trial should be allowed to continue to the end as planned, and should not be stopped because of early beneficial effects seen in one limb of the trial. Do you agree and if so, why?

7.5 'Large-scale clinical drug trials in developing countries are ethically justifiable from the perspective of global public health, and should not be subjugated by "vulnerability" arguments.' Critically evaluate this statement.

Further reading

Brazier M. Exploitation and enrichment: the paradox of medical experimentation. *Journal of Medical Ethics* 2008; 34: 180–183.

Featherstone K, Donovan JL. Why don't they just tell me straight, why allocate it? The struggle to make sense of participating in a randomised control trial. *Social Science and Medicine* 2002; 55: 709–719.

Ferguson PR. Clinical trials in healthy volunteers. *Medical Law Review* 2008; 16: 23–51

Gunn MJ, Wong JG, Clare I, Holland AJ. Medical research and incompetent adults. *Journal of Mental Health Law* 2000; 60.

Research Governance Framework for Health and Social Care, Second edition, Department of Health London 2005. Available at http://www.dh.gov.uk/dr_consum_dh/groups/dh_digitalassets/@dh/@en/documents/digitalasset/dh_4122427.pdf.

Links to relevant websites can be found at: http://www.palgrave.com/law/samanta

Chapter 8 follows overleaf.

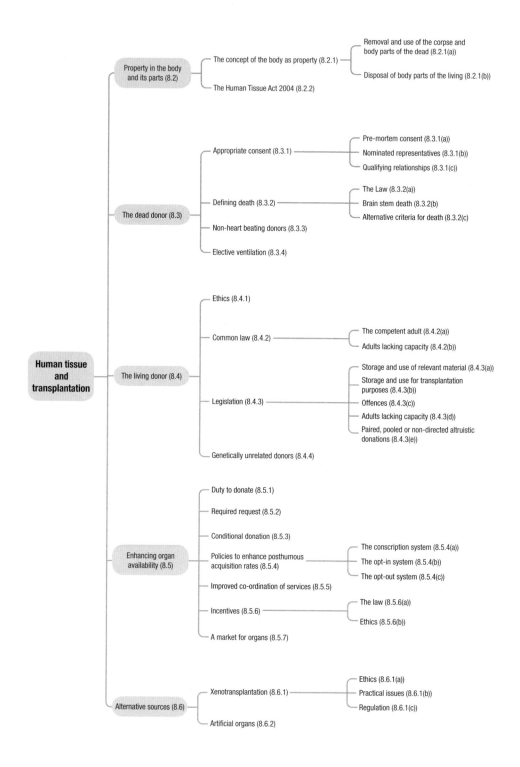

Human tissue and transplantation

Scenario

Jennifer, who was 23, had chronic renal failure and had been on dialysis for 6 years. She was from a mixed race background which meant that, in her particular circumstances, no suitable kidney from a dead donor had been found. Her health was extremely poor and she had been placed on the 'super urgent' waiting list.

Jennifer's sister, Rebecca, offered to donate one of her kidneys. The tissue match was good, though not perfect, which was predominantly why a living organ donation had not previously been undertaken. In view of Jennifer's poor state of health, and her urgent need for a transplant, the Human Tissue Authority authorised the transplant which was successfully performed.

The following year Jennifer's car was involved in a head on collision. She sustained catastrophic head injuries and was transferred to a local intensive care unit. A clinical decision was made that continued life-sustaining treatment would serve no useful purpose and should therefore be withdrawn. Jennifer's parents were informed that she would never regain consciousness and their views were ascertained about organ donation, particularly in view of the dire plight of several persons on the super urgent waiting list. Despite initial reluctance they agreed to donation. The transplant team needed several hours to make preparations and it was therefore decided, with parental agreement, to continue life-sustaining treatment for the time needed to optimise the likelihood of successful transplantation. Jennifer's treatment was withdrawn and five minutes after cardiac arrest she was pronounced dead. Her body was immediately transferred to theatre where her liver was removed and transplanted into a waiting recipient.

8.1 Introduction

The first modern organ transplant took place in Boston, United States, in 1954. Since then transplant surgery has become the optimal therapy for those with organ failure. Figures from NHS Blood and Transplant (2010) indicate that following the first year of surgery 84% of heart transplants are functioning well, as are 94% of kidney transplants (from living donors) and 88% of kidney transplants (from deceased donors). For lung transplants the percentage is 77%.

In order to survive, patients with severe renal failure require dialysis for the remainder of their lives or alternatively, a successful kidney transplant. The average costs for dialysis is in the region of £30,800 per patient per year, notwithstanding the inconvenience and personal costs involved. By comparison, a kidney transplant costs £17,000 per patient per transplant, although additional costs of £5,000 per patient are incurred for immunosuppression and other medication. Following the first year of each successful kidney transplant, a saving of around £25,800 per year is generated and over 10 years the saving to the NHS is around £241,000 (UK Transplant, 2007).

Despite the undoubted fiscal and health benefits of transplantation, a marked shortage of organs is apparent. In April 2009, there were 6,920 people waiting for a kidney transplant (NHS BT, 2010). An important priority, therefore, is to increase the number of organs available for transplantation, either from dead or living human donors, or possibly from other sources. The Organ Donation Taskforce (appointed in 2006) explored the need for statutory reform as well as other ways of increasing organ donation rates without the need for legislative change (Organ Donation Taskforce, 2008).

The law that pertains to organ donation and human tissue in England, Wales and Northern Ireland is mainly governed by the Human Tissue Act 2004 (HT Act 2004), most of which came into effect in September 2006. The HT Act 2004 repealed the Human Tissue Act 1961, the Anatomy Act 1984 and the Human Organ Transplants Act 1984. The statutory framework for Scotland is found in the Human Tissue (Scotland) Act 2006. The HT Act 2004 provides for the storage and use of almost all human tissue apart from human gametes and embryos. The principal driver behind the enactment of the HT Act 2004 was public demand for legislative change following the retained organs scandals reported, for example, at the Bristol Royal Infirmary and Alder Hey Children's Hospital in Liverpool. The reports of the public inquiries that followed revealed evidence of lack of informed consent prior to routine retention of organs and tissues following post-mortem examinations, mainly on young children. The need for valid consent lies at the heart of the principles upon which the HT Act 2004 hinges and the Act encompasses a range of areas such as research, post mortems, anatomy and public display.

The HT Act 2004 also established the Human Tissue Authority (HTA) that subsumes the previous roles of the Inspectorate of Anatomy and the Unrelated Live Transplants Regulatory Authority. The HTA has a statutory function to issue codes of practice and to give practical guidance on the standards expected from those carrying out activities regulated by the HT Act 2004 (section 26(1)). To date there are nine complementary codes which offer guidance rather than a definitive statement of the law on: consent; donation of solid organs for transplantation, post-mortem examination; anatomical examination; disposal of human tissue; donation of allogeneic bone marrow and peripheral blood stem cells for transplantation; public display; import and export of human bodies, body parts and tissue; and research. The HTA also issues licenses to organisations that store human tissue and approves organ and bone marrow donation from living donors, and is one of the competent authorities designated by the EU Tissue and Cells Directive which came into force in April 2006 (the other competent authority is the Human Fertilisation and Embryology Authority, see chapter 5). The Department of Health has reviewed the role of the HTA and is considering the practicalities of sharing some of its core functions between the Care Quality Commission, a new research regulator, and the Health and Social Care Information Centre.

This chapter considers the key legal and ethical issues surrounding organ and tissue transplantation in adults. The EU Directive on standards of quality and safety of human organs intended for transplantation (2010/45/EU) came into force on the 27 August 2010 and must be implemented within 24 months. The Directive provides a minimum standards framework to apply to all Member States providing for all stages of donation to transplantation.

8.2 Property in the body and its parts

Many are surprised to learn that for the purposes of the law a person does not 'own his or her body'. In English law the body and its tissues are not subject to proprietary rights, which typically convey concepts of ownership, control and the right to sell, transfer and destroy.

8.2.1 The concept of the body as property

An in-depth analysis of the body as property has been provided by Beyleveld and Brownsword (2000) who suggest that property rights give 'rule preclusionary' control to individuals in possession. In effect, owners of property have certain *prima facie* rights such that justification for dealing with that property is not required. The rule preclusionary principle is based on the assumption that persons can use their bodies, and exclude others from using it, without specific reason. It therefore follows that the justificatory burden falls upon those who wish to restrict the owner from selling or transferring that property. Assuming that a rule preclusionary right is an interest premised upon rights-based moral theories, the authors argue that since these rights exist over other forms of property, this principle ought to extend over a person's own body and its constituent parts. The body is an entity over which one's legitimate interests extend (arguably the most important entity), and therefore individuals ought to be permitted to do whatever they want with their body without requiring specific justification for each and every purpose.

The rule preclusionary principle seems to be implied in Article 22 of the Convention on Human Rights and Biomedicine (1997) which serves to emphasise the role of consent in relation to property rights in that: 'When in the course of an intervention any part of a human body is removed, it may be stored and used for a purpose other than that for which it was removed, only if this is done in conformity with appropriate information and consent procedures.' A similar principle underpinned by the need for consent of the provider is seen in the Human Fertilisation and Embryology Act 1990 (as amended) for the storage and subsequent use of gametes and embryos. Furthermore, providers of gametes and embryos do not require specific justification for withdrawal of consent to storage and consequent destruction. Although the 1990 Act presupposes 'property' in reproductive materials (for example in *Yearworth* at 5.21.3), this principle is not generally extended to non-regenerative tissues and organs that fall outside its remit.

8.2.1(a) Removal and use of the corpse and body parts of the dead

At common law there is no property in the human body or its parts. This doctrine of uncertain origin is established mainly from nineteenth century authorities. The 'no property' principle has been confirmed in this jurisdiction by the Court of Appeal in *Dobson v North Tyneside HA* [1997] 1WLR 596 and in *R v Kelly* [1998] EWCA Crim 1578.

In *Dobson*, the issue before the court was whether the next of kin had property rights over a deceased woman's brain tissue following autopsy. The deceased had died from brain tumours and the family wished to use the brain tissue as evidence of a health authority's negligent failure to diagnose the condition. The brain tissue had been preserved in paraffin during the post-mortem and sent to the hospital for storage, whereupon it had been disposed of. The family brought an action for failure to retain the deceased's brain. The Court of Appeal held that there was no property in a corpse unless it had undergone a process of work and skill. In the instant case there was no evidence that storing in paraffin was on a par with stuffing or embalming a corpse, and therefore no property rights were found.

In *Kelly*, the Court of Appeal, in upholding the defendant's conviction of theft of body parts from the Royal College of Surgeons, applied an exception to the 'no property' rule. Under this exception, it was held that if a body, or part thereof, acquired special attributes as a result of the application of work and skill (e.g. dissection and preservation techniques) then property rights could be acquired. The case of *Dobson*, where the brain had been stored in paraffin, was distinguished since the anatomical specimens of the Royal College had been carefully preserved for purposes of teaching and exhibition. It should be noted that *Dobson* and *Kelly* concerned tissue removed from deceased persons and different interpretations might ensue where the individual is alive at the time that tissues or organs are removed. The relevance of this distinction can be seen in the following case from the United States.

8.2.1(b) Disposal of body parts of the living

In *Moore v Regents of the University of California* (1990) 51 Cal 3d120, John Moore had been diagnosed with hairy cell leukaemia, following which his spleen was removed as part of the treatment. Unbeknown to him the doctor and a research scientist developed and patented an immortal cell line from his spleen which had a potential market value of around US$3 billion. Moore had given consent for removal of his tissue specifically for the purposes of treatment, and on discovering the sums generated by the cell line, he brought an action to secure a share of the profits. In order to succeed he had to establish that the cells were his personal property. The Supreme Court rejected Moore's claim to property rights on several grounds including one that an extension of the law of property into such an area would hinder research by restricting access to raw materials necessary for medical research. Moore was, however, able to settle his claim out of court since the court ruled that he had a potential action on other grounds, namely that the doctor had failed in the duty of loyalty and truthfulness owed to him, as well as his lack of informed consent. It is doubtful whether the latter grounds would succeed in England and Wales since duties of loyalty and truthfulness tend to be characteristic of a fiduciary relationship, which in this jurisdiction, has not been affirmed between a doctor and patient.

The court's unwillingness to view the body or body parts as property is interesting. One reason might stem from a reluctance to place a monetary value on the body or its parts that would inevitably arise if property rights naturally accrued. This seems particularly likely in a society where there is increasing commercial interest in discarded body parts and tissue. This intrinsic repugnance might stem from the notion of slavery and abhorrence of the notion of buying and selling human beings.

8.2.2 The Human Tissue Act 2004

The HT Act 2004 gives legislative effect to the common law principle that human tissue can become the subject of property by virtue of the application of work and skill. Section 32(9)(c) provides that the offence relating to commercial dealings in body material intended for transplantation excludes 'material which is the subject of property because of an application of human skill'. While in this respect the HT Act 2004 endorses the *Dobson* and *Kelly* principle, it is noteworthy that in *Kelly*, Rose LJ declared that (at paragraph 42)

> The common law does not stand still. It may be that if, on some future occasion, the question arises, the courts will hold that human body parts are capable of being property for the purposes of section 4 (of the Theft Act 1968), even without the acquisition of different attributes... This may be so if, for example, they are intended for use in an organ transplant operation, for the extraction of DNA or, for that matter, as an exhibit in a trial.

This anticipated development can be seen in *Yearworth v North Bristol NHS Trust* [2009] EWCA Civ 37, which concerned the claim of a group of men whose sperm had been negligently destroyed. The Court of Appeal noted that it could take the *Kelly* approach and treat the stored sperm as property on account of the 'work and skill' principle. The court ruled, however, that for the purposes of an action in negligence, the men had ownership of the sperm. This finding was justified on the basis that it had been generated in their bodies alone and ejaculation was for the sole purpose that it would be later used for their benefit. This case represents a subtle and welcome shift in the judicial approach away from the work and skill principle being the only exception to the 'no property in the body' rule.

8.3 The dead donor

The HT Act 2004 requires that 'appropriate consent' precedes the removal, retention and usage of tissue from cadavers for the purpose of transplantation (Section 1 and Schedule 1 Part 1, paragraph 7 HT Act 2004). It is an offence to remove organs or tissue without obtaining appropriate consent (section 5(1)) unless the person removing the material holds a reasonable belief that consent has been given or it is an activity for which consent is not required. Section 5(7) provides that the penalty for conviction is up to 3 years imprisonment, a fine, or both.

8.3.1 Appropriate consent

Sections 2 and 3 expand upon the concept of appropriate consent, and provides a statutory hierarchy of qualifying relationships (discussed below) being those who may give permission for post-mortem organ removal. The Act, however, is silent as to the amount of information necessary to underpin valid consent.

For adults (children are discussed in chapter 6), section 3 provides guidance on the interpretation of the concept of 'appropriate consent' and that this can be obtained in three ways:

3(6) where the person concerned has died ... "appropriate consent" means –

a) if a decision of his to consent to the activity, or a decision of his not to consent to it, was in force immediately before he died, his consent;

b) if –
   (i) paragraph a) does not apply, and
   (ii) he has appointed a person or persons under section 4 to deal after his death with the issue of consent in relation to the activity, consent given under the appointment;

c) if neither paragraph a) nor paragraph b) applies, the consent of a person who stood in a qualifying relationship to him immediately before he died.

Thus, appropriate consent for removal of organs from the deceased can be achieved in any of three ways: the deceased's pre-mortem consent or authorisation; a nominated representative under section 4 HT Act 2004; or else consent can be given by someone in a 'qualifying relationship'.

8.3.1(a) Pre-mortem consent

The deceased may have consented to becoming an organ donor by registration on the NHS Organ Donor Register, or by carrying a donor card, or orally. In these circumstances the medical team would act lawfully in retrieving specified organs. According to the HTA Code of Practice 1 (2009 at paragraph 74) if an adult has given valid pre-mortem consent for post-mortem donation, removal, storage or use of their organs and tissues, then that consent is sufficient in law. Paragraph 75 provides that if those close to the deceased object to donation, they ought to be sensitively encouraged to accept the deceased's wishes and informed that they do not have the right to overrule those wishes. Despite this, paragraph 76 guides health-care staff to consider the potentially negative implications of proceeding with removal where strong opposition exists and as recognised by the Organ Taskforce (2008), clinicians are likely to have some concern that the carrying of a donor card, even where prospective donors have registered their intent, falls short of what is typically regarded as appropriating true consent. Clinical hesitation may be apparent (and perhaps justified) where there has been a considerable delay between the deceased's decision to donate and the occurrence of death, since the passage of time might have influenced the individual's decision. It seems likely that the consent of those close to the deceased will also be sought, and that, in some instances, the deceased's wishes will be vetoed even in the presence of their pre-mortem request.

8.3.1(b) Nominated representatives

Section 4 provides that an adult may appoint a nominated representative to give or withhold consent for post-mortem organ removal (in circumstances where the deceased has made no prior decision). This appointment may be made orally, if witnessed by two persons or in writing with one witness. Appointment of a nominated representative could be a particularly attractive solution in circumstances where no immediate family member is available, or perhaps where the deceased anticipated family disagreement about transplantation. The appointee would be expected to know of the deceased's wishes and express these accordingly. However, an evidential hurdle might be apparent where an oral appointment has been made. Two witnesses would need to affirm that the appointment had been made. If a specific individual has not been appointed, or if the nominated person is unable to consent, then this could be sought from someone in a qualifying relationship (sections 3(7) and 3(8) HT Act 2004).

8.3.1(c) Qualifying relationships

A 'qualifying relationship' is defined in section 27(4) HT Act 2004 and these persons are ranked in hierarchical order: spouse or partner; parent or child; brother or sister; grandparent or grandchild; child of a brother or sister; stepfather or stepmother; half-brother or half-sister; friend of longstanding.

Consent of the highest ranking qualified relative carries most weight, and for those within the same category equal weight is given. If consent is being obtained from persons of the same category, then the consent of any person from that category would suffice. Thus, if a brother and sister are asked and the brother agrees and the sister refuses, then the brother's consent would be sufficient. Section 27 gives statutory guidance for ranking purposes and equality of decisions.

The HTA's Code of Practice 1 (2009) states that great care is required in order to determine whether ignoring a family's strongly held objections might possibly outweigh the benefit of proceeding with organ retrieval. Where there is a discrepancy between the deceased's and family's wishes, the family should be encouraged to move towards the deceased's request, although efforts should be abandoned if the family continues to object (paragraph 99). The Code also provides that a person may be omitted from the hierarchy of those in qualifying relationships where it is not practicable to contact them. Those on the next rung then become the individuals to give appropriate consent.

The Code of Practice 2 states that each case should be considered individually and there may be instances where donation is inappropriate. Thus, whilst relatives are not authorised in law to override the positive wishes of the deceased, in practice they might well continue to do so (Price, 2005). According to figures from the Organ Donation Taskforce 2008, relatives are more likely to support donation if the deceased had previously consented or opted-in for organ donation, and only 10% of families are likely to refuse consent post-mortem in such circumstances compared to an overall refusal rate of around 40%.

Jennifer's name is not on the organ donor register, so following her death her parents are asked for their views. Consider this in respect of:

- Qualifying relationships
- Would it have mattered if Jennifer's name had been on the register?
- Could donation have gone ahead if Jennifer's parents could not be contacted?
- What would be the likely outcome if her parents disagreed?

8.3.2 Defining death

The definition of death is significant since accurate determination of the time of death is essential prior to removing vital organs for transplantation. In the majority of circumstances, diagnosis of death by doctors is a straightforward clinical decision based upon absence of pupillary reflexes, and cessation of respiration and heart beat (absence of neurological and cardiopulmonary function). Waiting for the body to become 'cold, blue and stiff' may be inadequate for retrieval of organs and tissues for transplantation since vascular tissues quickly become unusable. In fact, some organs are only transplantable if taken from a body that is adequately oxygenated at the time of removal. Equally, it is crucial that the intended donor is actually dead prior to removal of vital organs, otherwise a charge in homicide could be brought.

8.3.2(a) The Law

There is no statutory definition of death in the United Kingdom, although section 26(2) (d) HT Act 2004 empowers the HTA to issue a Code of Practice to provide practical guidance and standards for defining death for the purposes of the Act. To date the HTA has not undertaken this role; however a revised guidance titled 'A Code of Practice for the Diagnosis and Confirmation of Death' has been published by the Academy of Medical Royal Colleges in 2008.

The potential difficulty of diagnosing the death of an individual maintained on life support was recognised by the Court of Appeal in *R v Malcherek* [1981] 2 All ER 422 *per* Lord Lane CJ (at 426):

> Modern techniques have undoubtedly resulted in the blurring of many of the conventional and traditional concepts of death. A person's heart can now be removed altogether without death supervening; machines can keep the blood circulating through the vessels of the body until a new heart can be implanted in the patient, and even though a person is no longer able to breathe spontaneously a ventilating machine can, so to speak, do his breathing for him..... There is, it seems a body of opinion in the medical profession that there is only one true test of death and that is the irreversible death of the brain stem, which controls the basic functions of the body such as breathing. When that occurs it is said that the body has died, even though by mechanical means the lungs are being caused to operate and some circulation of blood is taking place.

The benefit of a common law determination is to permit some measure of flexibility sufficient to permit scientific advances that might be constrained by a potentially inflexible statutory definition.

One of the clearest common law endorsements of brain stem death being death for medical and legal purposes is the High Court decision of *Re A* [1992] 3 Med LR 303. *Re A* concerned a 20-month old child who was admitted to hospital with an absence of heartbeat. Several unsuccessful attempts were made to resuscitate the child, following which he was placed on a ventilator. Later, when attempts were made to remove the ventilator, the child emitted gasping sounds although no such response was noted on the following day. The doctor responsible for the child's care considered that the child satisfied the clinical criteria for brain stem death, a finding subsequently confirmed by another consultant. Other possible explanations for the child's condition, such as extreme hypothermia or drugs, had all been excluded.

The court held that the child had been dead since the time the first consultant determined that the criteria for brain stem death had been satisfied. Johnson J found that the clinical criteria for brain stem death had been satisfied and were sufficient for the child to be dead 'for all legal, as well as medical, purposes'.

Re A was a first instance decision later confirmed by the House of Lords in *Airedale NHS Trust v Bland* [1993] AC 789. In *Bland* the court considered the lawfulness of removing nutrition and hydration from an adult in a persistent vegetative state (PVS). According to Lord Keith in 'the eyes of the medical world and of the law, a person is not clinically dead so long as the brain stem retains its function' a position endorsed by Lord Goff and Lord Browne-Wilkinson. While the determination of that case meant that it was lawful to remove nutrition and hydration from a patient in PVS, the House of Lords endorsed the legal position that the definition of death is aligned with satisfaction of the clinical criteria for brain stem death.

8.3.2(b) Brain stem death

Medical progress means that it is possible to successfully resuscitate individuals despite temporary absence of heart and lung function. Patients can be kept alive for considerable periods of time on life support systems that maintain circulatory and respiratory systems, which can make it difficult to determine whether death has occurred. To diagnose the death of a patient on life support, diagnostic tests are necessary to confirm the absence of brain stem reflexes.

Diagnostic clinical tests to confirm brain stem death were laid down in 1976 by the Conference of the Medical Royal Colleges and the Department of Health's revised Code of Practice (1998). The Academy of Medical Royal Colleges (2008) defines death as the irreversible loss of those essential characteristics which are necessary to the existence of a living human person. Death, therefore, is the irreversible loss of capacity for consciousness combined with the permanent loss of capacity to breathe. Irreversible cessation of the integrative function of the brain stem equates with the death of the person. Diagnosis of brain stem death must be made by at least two experienced doctors who are not members of the transplant team in order to avoid any potential conflict of interest that might arise in the context of harvesting organs for transplantation purposes.

Some commentators, however, question whether this standard is appropriate. According to Kerridge *et al.* (2002) the suggestion that the brain stem is the principal regulator of the body is simplistic precisely because brain stem dead patients can be maintained on a ventilator for considerable periods of time. This raises the question as to whether there really is any 'supreme regulator' of the body and therefore the assumption that brain stem death is death of the whole body is perhaps questionable. Others view the concept of brain stem death as nothing more than a convenient fiction created to facilitate organ retrieval and that its rationale would cease to exist if that imperative was removed (Truog, 2007). The White Paper produced by the President's Council on Bioethics provides a comprehensive examination of this controversial subject (2008). Fiction or not, death determined according to brain stem criteria has a pragmatic value since organ retrieval cannot experientially harm a brain dead individual and yet this has the potential to be of immeasurable benefit to the recipient and relatives of the deceased who will have acted in accordance with the altruistic wishes of the dead person.

8.3.2(c) Alternative criteria for death

Some commentators have looked at alternative definitions of death that typically focus on a permanent lack of cognition and higher brain function. These approaches take into account that biological life can be maintained in patients who will never recover. Higher brain function is associated with the personality and conscious awareness whereas the lower brain, namely the brain stem, regulates bodily functions such as respiration. Tännsjö (1999), for example, argues that two separate criteria are required for the definition of death. The first would be used to diagnose that the 'person' has died (meaning that no meaningful conscious awareness is evident), whereas the second would be used to establish that the 'body' as a biological entity has died. If no consciousness or psychological continuity remains, then the individual has died, even though the body, as a biological entity, may continue to exist. The ethical dilemma that arises is at what point should lawful organ retrieval take place – following brain stem death, higher brain death or both? The potential exists to focus on criteria other than brain stem death at least for the purpose of harvesting organs for transplantation.

Patients in a PVS have hearts that continue to beat and typically show diurnal sleep-wake cycles even though they permanently lack higher brain function. Similarly, a very small number of infants are born without a cerebral cortex and major portions of the brain and skull. This condition is known as anencephaly and the majority are stillborn. Those born alive survive only a few days, unless maintained on life support. Although they have functioning brain stems (and are therefore alive for the purposes of the law), they can never achieve consciousness. Due to the acute shortage of infant organs available for transplantation, organs and tissues of anencephalic infants would be particularly valuable, provided that the infant was maintained on a ventilator to ensure that tissues were adequately oxygenated for posthumous removal. From an ethical perspective, the maintenance of life support would be using the infant as a means to an end since the benefit would be solely for a third party (the infant recipient). The Academy of the Royal Medical Colleges states that organs can be removed from anencephalic newborns for purposes of transplantation provided that two doctors, who are not members of the transplant team, agree that spontaneous respiration has ceased (Report of the Working Party of the Conference of Medical Colleges and their Faculties in the United Kingdom on Organ Transplantation in Neonates,1988).

From a philanthropic perspective there is an argument that once death is truly imminent (which is difficult to diagnose with sufficient precision) organs and tissues ought to be available from that point in time, particularly if the intended donor has given informed pre-mortem consent. An even more radical view is that even if death is not imminent, but meaningful life has ceased, then organs should be available from that point in time. This position, however, runs counter to the law since individuals cannot consent to their own death. The utilitarian arguments for harvesting organs from patients in irreversible comas or whose capacity for sentience is irrevocably lost are strong since this would increase the pool of potential organ donors. However, this could have many negative outcomes including mistrust of the medical profession.

Brain stem death criteria as the gateway for organ harvesting could be viewed as precipitating an 'early' diagnosis of death. Brain stem death is not accepted in some jurisdictions as the true determinant of death for legal and medical purposes. Evidence of total brain death, being the complete destruction of the higher brain and the brain stem, is required before death is pronounced. Most United States jurisdictions adopt a whole brain death standard, requiring that *all* functioning of the brain has ceased.

The common law position in this jurisdiction is that patients who satisfy the clinical criteria for brain stem death are considered dead for legal and medical purposes, irrespective of whether the body is maintained on life support. Alternatively, if criteria for brain stem death are not satisfied, a person is alive even though the higher functions of cognitive capabilities are permanently absent.

8.3.3   Non-heart beating donors

Non-heart beating donation or donation after circulatory death, refers to retrieval of organs and tissues from patients diagnosed as dead according to 'traditional' criteria such as permanent absence of cardiopulmonary function. Two distinct types of circulatory death are recognised: 'uncontrolled' and 'controlled'. Uncontrolled donation typically follows the unexpected death of a person whose wishes in respect of organ donation are unknown. The key legal issue in these circumstances is maintenance of the cadaver while consent is sought from the deceased's relatives. In these situations, and dependent upon where death takes place, non-vascular tissues such as corneas and cartilage may be of use, although whole organs are less likely to be of use principally because of hypoxia (lack of oxygen) to the tissues. In health-care situations, provided that consent has been given, once death is confirmed the body can be treated to prevent or reduce deterioration, and in this way vascular organs may be saved. Section 43 of the HT Act 2004 provides specifically for uncontrolled donation and preservation measures that can be taken to preserve organs or tissues being considered for transplantation, until it is established whether consent is available.

In recent years 'controlled' non-heart beating donation (NHBD) has become an important, albeit controversial, source of whole organs and tissues following death diagnosed as the irreversible cessation of heartbeat and respiration. There has been a substantial increase in the number of NHBD from 73 in 2003–2004 to 200 in 2007–2008, and 288 in 2008–2009 (NHSBT, 2010). NHBD can be an option where death follows withdrawal of life-sustaining treatment where this is no longer in the patient's best interests, since continuation would be a battery and trespass to the person (*Airedale NHS Trust v Bland* [1993] AC 789). In these circumstances, and where patients have made known their decision to donate, blood tests are typically performed for virology studies and tissue matching. Furthermore, the decision to withdraw life support treatment may be delayed for a period in order to ensure that the intended recipient is prepared and to allow for co-ordination of the transplant team. The latter, in particular, has attracted concern and criticism though, since blood tests and continuation of care are carried out for the benefit of the recipient rather than the patient concerned. According to Coggon *et al.* (2008) the practice is legitimate on the basis of the interpretation of best interests. Section 4(6) of the Mental Capacity Act 2005 obliges the decision maker to consider a range of factors that include the person's past and present wishes and feelings and, among other things, the beliefs and values that would be likely to influence the patient if he or she were able to make a decision. For this reason, if a patient has made a decision to become an organ donor following death, then ensuring that organs are maintained in an optimal condition would conceivably be in that patient's best interests, provided that this does not involve hastening the patient's death or commencing new active treatment (such as elective ventilation). A withdrawal of treatment decision operates to postpone withdrawal as opposed to commencing new therapy. However, in circumstances where patients have not made known their intention to donate, the best interests argument seems less persuasive. Guidance for health-care teams has been published in 'Legal issues relevant to non-heartbeating organ donation' (Department of Health, 2009).

For NHBD programmes another area of controversy centres on the diagnosis of death on grounds of irreversible cessation of cardiopulmonary function (after a specified period has elapsed which in typical protocols is 5 minutes). Troug, Franklin and Miller (2008) consider that this understanding of death is problematic since 'irreversibility' is the result of a clinical decision not to resuscitate (e.g. on grounds of futility), and yet that same heart (or other major organ) will be expected to fully recommence function following transplantation to the recipient. Although this might be ethical in the circumstances, the authors consider that valid and fully informed consent is the essential precursor to morally acceptable organ donation from the patient, or surrogate decision maker.

In situations of imminent death, further steps could be taken to ensure that organs are maintained in optimal condition for transplantation. This could include initiation of medication to prevent blood clotting by anticoagulant therapy. Clinical decisions such as these are likely to raise issues similar to those of elective ventilation (since treatment decisions would be motivated by enhancing tissue and organ viability rather than by being in the best medical interests of the patient). The Organ Donation Taskforce (2008) recognised that procedures undertaken prior to death aimed to avoid organ deterioration could be expected to raise difficult ethical issues and potentially cause anxiety among staff caring for patients. The Taskforce states that if 'we take registration as a donor to be a valid instance of consent, and further interpret it as a clear statement of an important wish on the part of the patient, we might argue that anything we do to facilitate the patient having that wish fulfilled is in his or her best interests'. The Taskforce added the caveat that in the event of uncertainty about the value of consent, or where wishes are unknown, it is not possible to concede that actions taken to facilitate donation would necessarily be in the best interests of the potential donor. A counter-argument might be that on communitarian principles, once it is known that a patient is not going to recover, and that further treatment is futile, then measures to preserve organs for transplantation might be deemed acceptable. However, rights cannot be discharged on grounds of utility.

Jennifer is unconscious and lacks decision-making capacity. Her doctors have reached a clinical decision that continuation of life-sustaining treatment is no longer in her best interests.

▶ What are the implications of treatment withdrawal?
▶ How are best interests ascertained?
▶ What is the ethical basis for continuing treatment while preparations are made?
▶ On what grounds, if any, can Jennifer's organs be removed after pronouncing her dead and, after 5 minutes, removing her organs?

8.3.4 Elective ventilation

In 1988 the Royal Devon and Exeter Hospital introduced a protocol aimed to facilitate organ removal from patients with fatal conditions who were dying outside of intensive care environments. Once a potential donor had been identified, and with the consent of their relative(s), he or she would be transferred to an intensive therapy unit and placed on life support (elective ventilation) until brain stem death tests were satisfied. Relatives were informed that the patient was not going to recover and they were asked to agree to the transfer to the intensive care unit, as well as to organ donation. The purpose of this exercise was to maximise the likelihood of organs being in a suitable condition for transplantation. The protocol was in operation for 19 months during which the hospital increased the number of organs available for transplant by 50%.

The principal criticism against elective ventilation is that it is not in the best interests of the patient. Mason (1996) states that 'there is no way in which invasive, non-consensual treatment of a dying and incurable patient can be regarded as being in his or her best interests; it follows that elective ventilation must involve an assault or trespass to the person'. He argues that the best interests test must be applied as the ethical parameter. Since there is no benefit to that individual, the person is being used as a means to an end, thereby going against moral and ethical principles based on Kantian imperatives.

The clinicians who developed the Exeter protocol stated that ventilation was commenced following spontaneous respiratory arrest. Ventilation commenced at the moment of death and was continued only until such time as brain stem death could be diagnosed. If this argument is accepted, then this intervention might be regarded as legitimate. If life support starts at the moment of death, arguably a 'best interests' determination will not apply (since the person is no longer alive). Equally the person is not 'dead,' for legal purposes, since brain stem death tests have not been carried out. Whether this is a real argument or simply ethical sophistry is a matter for conjecture. It could be argued that even within this lacuna between life and death there is nonetheless an advantage to an individual's altruistic desires from having organs retrieved for the purpose of donation, if this was their pre-mortem wish. The Mental Capacity Act 2005 requires that actions must be taken in the best interests of the person who lacks capacity. Since the determination of best interests must take into account the past wishes, feelings, beliefs and values of the incompetent person (section 4(6) MCA 2005), it seems feasible that where there is overwhelming evidence of the person's intention to donate, it is possible that the decision maker might reasonably believe that elective ventilation to facilitate organ preservation is in the person's best interests.

Fiscal arguments against elective ventilation tend to focus on scarce health-care resources, such as the limited availability of intensive care facilities and suitably qualified staff. Conversely, the cost effectiveness of successful transplantation in terms of money and quality of life are undoubted. From a communitarian perspective, one could argue that routine salvaging of organs in the absence of registered objections would be of enormous benefit to society as a whole. Arguably, donation is at no cost to the deceased whereas the community as a whole stands to benefit. However, this approach conflicts deeply with individualistic values and rights-based approaches that characterise much of Western society and on balance seems unlikely to receive sympathetic consideration.

The British Medical Association was initially supportive of elective ventilation but later retracted from that position on grounds that too many ethical and practical difficulties existed to recommend a change in the law (BMA, 2000). Similarly, the Academy of Medical Royal Colleges (2008) states that if 'further intensive care is not considered appropriate because it can be of no benefit nor in the patient's best interests, then neither is a continuation of the respiratory support being provided'. Life support should be commenced only if this is for the patient's best interests and not as a means of preserving organ function for the interests of another. Best interests, however, are to be widely construed (section 4 of the Mental Capacity Act 2005) and encompass more than clinical interests.

The protocol is no longer in use. In 1994 the Department of Health stated that elective ventilation for the purpose of transplantation was unlawful, a view later confirmed by a Code of Practice (Department of Health, 1998).

8.4 The living donor

Use of non-vital organs and tissues from living donors confers several advantages over those from dead donors. Tissues and organs are more likely to be useable, and better graft (and patient) survival rates are typically achieved. A range of tissues can be regenerated by the human body, including blood, bone marrow and skin. Segments of liver, as well as lobes of lungs, can be regenerated with the added advantage that the supply of such tissues can continue. From the perspective of the donor several possible disadvantages exist. General anaesthetics and surgery undoubtedly carries some risk, and removal of tissues and organs can lead to death, ill health and long-term complications.

8.4.1 Ethics

Removal of organs and tissues from living donors for transplantation raises a myriad of ethical issues. By its nature, donation is intended for the benefit of someone other than the donor who is necessarily exposed to some degree of injury or harm as part of the process. The extent to which individuals can validly consent to the infliction of personal harm that confers no medical benefit to them is a fundamental ethical dilemma. Those who support rights-based theories and self-determination do not accept that competent persons can commit wrongs to themselves, since 'a wrong' necessarily requires violation of the rights of another. Under this pretext, consent to harming oneself is not considered immoral. Harris (1998), for example, questions why the competent and fully informed adult cannot voluntarily donate even a vital organ, such as the heart, in order to save the life of another if that is what that person wishes to do with his life.

On the other hand, virtue ethicists argue that encouraging self-harm is morally untenable. Elliott (1995 at 93) considers that while the altruistic act of the donor might be laudable, the matter is more problematic for recipients and doctors who perform organ removal from living donors. He states

> Accepting a sacrifice of greater magnitude is not mere passive acquiescence, devoid of any moral import. If I allow someone else to risk his life or health for my sake, I am endorsing his self sacrifice and agreeing to profit by it... If an ailing patient were to take advantage of a healthy donor's self sacrifice, it might well be understandable, but it would not be morally admirable. It would not be the sort of behaviour that we would aspire to and want to encourage.

He further argues that in these circumstances the doctor is a moral agent to be held accountable for his or her actions as opposed to being a passive instrument who acquiesces with the donor's wishes. While one might approve of the altruistic intentions of the donor who voluntarily undergoes harm for another's benefit, this does not extend to the person who inflicts harm on a person for the sake of another. The lack of moral approbation that self-sacrifice cannot be condoned tends to be commensurate with the degree of risk and severity of self-harm. At one extreme is the consensual removal of a vital organ, such as the heart, which would inevitably lead to death, while at the other is the donation of regenerative tissue, such as blood, where the likely consequences are relatively minor.

A pre-requisite to obtaining organs from a person with capacity is valid consent. Despite being non-therapeutic the Law Commission (1995) stated that 'whatever the true legal analysis, there can be no doubt that once a valid consent has been forthcoming, English law now treats as lawful operative procedures designed to remove regenerative tissue, and also non-regenerative tissue that is not essential for life' (at paragraph 8.32). This assertion would also encompass donation of parts of non-renal organs, such as livers and lungs. A key requirement of consent is the need for unbiased information that must precede any decision to donate. Caplan (1993 at 1195) considers that in order to give valid consent,

> a person must have all relevant information and the opportunity to reflect upon and ask questions about the information from those who will provide objective answers. Transplantation centres and other transplantation personnel may face problems in providing 'objective' information to prospective donors because those involved in seeking donors have an inherent conflict of interest. They cannot both advocate for the best interests of patients who need transplants and simultaneously protect the best interests of prospective donors.

Critics of live donation typically express greater concern about donation to family members or spouses since in these circumstances, potential donors may feel subjected to extraordinary and irresistible pressure to volunteer. On this point Beauchamp and Childress (2009) consider that society and health-care professionals ought to start with the presumption that living organ donation is laudable but, nonetheless, discretionary (thereby being supererogatory). Transplant teams need to present their criteria for selecting and accepting living donors to open scrutiny to ensure that their own values about personal sacrifice and risk do not operate as the basis of their judgements.

The ethical debate concerning live donation is heightened in respect of adults who lack decision-making capacity. Article 20 of the European Convention of Human Rights and Biomedicine prohibits donation of non-regenerative organs and tissue from a person who lacks capacity. The donation of regenerative tissue from a person who lacks capacity is permitted only where there is compliance with a range of preconditions prescribed by law. This is also the situation now under Scottish law. These conditions require that there is no other compatible donor who has capacity, that the recipient is a sibling, that donation is likely to be a lifesaving intervention for the recipient, that the potential donor does not object and that authorisation is in writing and granted by a competent body. Although the United Kingdom is not a signatory to the Biomedicine Convention (and therefore the European Convention of Human Rights and Biomedicine does not legally apply), the Convention could still have effect through the Human Rights Act 1998 which gives legislative force to the European Convention of Human Rights.

The ethical dilemmas surrounding organ donation from the living stem from the fact that the procedure is generally perceived to be non-therapeutic to the donor, which brings into question the legitimacy of such procedures. Whilst a plethora of ethical and moral arguments exist against removal of tissues and organs from living donors, these have to be considered in the context of relative risks for the donor. The likelihood of increased mortality from living with one kidney is in the region of 0.03% which is 'equivalent to driving back and forth to work 16 miles a day' (Bloomstein, 1995), and there is a 2% risk that kidney donors will experience major morbidity. Liver donation is accompanied by a slightly higher mortality rate of 0.05% to 0.1% with morbidity rates of 40% to 60% (Neuberger and Price, 2003). Taken in this context, and given the benefits of these practices, it is arguable that, at least from a utilitarian perspective, living organ donation is ethically acceptable.

Article 19 of the European Convention of Human Rights and Biomedicine states that living organ donation is permissible only where there is no suitable organ or tissue available from a deceased person and no other alternative method of comparable effectiveness. Given the shortage of organs and that we are as yet some way from the development and use of artificial organs, it is likely that living donor transplantation will continue for some time. The Law Commission conceded that the ethical principles upon which English law sanctions surgery for organ donation remains, to some extent, problematic. For an operation to be lawful it must be therapeutic and legally justified. If this statement is read disjunctively, as opposed to conjunctively, it perhaps poses less of a problem in respect of translating an ethical basis for removal of organs from living donors.

> Rebecca consents to the donation of one of her kidneys to save the life of her sister. What are the competing ethical arguments that apply to this situation?

8.4.2 Common law

Removal of organs for transplantation from living donors is governed by the common law, although the HT Act 2004 applies to storage and use from the living and the Mental Capacity Act 2005 applies to adults who lack decision-making capacity.

At common law the infliction of serious bodily harm is an offence, even if the individual has given valid consent. An exception is drawn in respect of proper treatment and surgery carried out for therapeutic purposes. By its nature, surgery inflicts 'serious bodily harm' but, because of the legitimate purpose for which it is done, valid consent operates as a defence for the clinician concerned. In the context of living donation, the clinical procedure is carried out for the benefit of a third party, rather than the person donating the organs, which is inherently problematic when viewed in the traditional common law framework.

8.4.2(a) The competent adult

English law does not allow a competent adult to consent to grievous bodily harm (*R v Brown* [1993] 2 All ER 75), or to have death inflicted upon them (as would be the outcome following donation of a vital organ). The exception to this rule is legitimate medical and surgical treatment and once valid consent has been obtained donation of non-essential regenerative and non-regenerative is lawful under the common law. For adults with decision-making capacity, consent must be voluntary and informed.

There is no obligation to donate organs or tissues to another even where this would save the life of a close relative (*St George's Healthcare NHS Trust v S; R v Collins, ex p S* [1999] Fam 26). The likelihood that this reasoning extends to the donation of regenerative tissues, such as bone marrow, can be gleaned from the United States decision of *McFall v Shrimp* (1978) 10 Pa D & C 3d 90. In this case, the Pennsylvanian court refused to require a person to undergo tests to establish suitability to donate lifesaving bone marrow to his cousin. The voluntary and autonomous will of the individual was decisive.

Living donors may be subject to indirect, or even direct, pressure to donate their organs and tissues. Such pressures tends to be subtle and covert, particularly with respect to donation to family members in need. Sauder and Parker (2001) consider that in these situations a prospective donor, particularly a parent or sibling of the prospective recipient, will perceive that their decision to donate is one that they cannot fail to make. Donors report feeling that they had no choice but to donate, and offered their organs willingly and without hesitation, and irrespective of the risks involved in the procedure or its aftermath. In these circumstances decisions to donate hardly seem to represent valid consent and yet society is reluctant to acknowledge the element of duress and on this basis reject the decision to donate. This approach raises several issues.

To what extent should the imminent demise of a son or daughter undermine the validity of a parent's decision to donate an organ and at what point should such pressure amount to undue influence under the law? Whilst potential donors are given a range of information, decisions to donate are often made before that information is received, or properly absorbed, particularly where the prospective donor has witnessed the gradual decline of the intended recipient. The HTA Codes of Practice 1 and 2 offer guidance on the amount of information potential donors ought to receive in order to avoid criminal liability.

8.4.2(b) Adults lacking capacity

In *Re Y* [1997] Fam 110, the lawfulness of performing a blood test and removing bone marrow from an adult Y who lacked capacity was considered in the context of these procedures being undertaken for the treatment and benefit of her sister, who was seriously ill. In giving judgement, Connell J. took the view that if the sister died, this would adversely affect their mother and would potentially and detrimentally deprive Y of her mother's visits. He also took the view that Y's donation of bone marrow would improve her relationship with her sister and that this would further be of benefit to Y. While the judge made it clear that this decision turned on its own facts and should not be regarded as authority for donation of non-regenerative tissue, he was greatly influenced by the fact that marrow is readily replaced and that a healthy individual can donate a considerable amount without long-term consequences.

Nevertheless, the judgement is problematic. To what extent were the perceived benefits for Y real benefits, or merely an artificial construct? Furthermore, although the facts concerned regenerative tissues, it is questionable whether this principle might be extended to non-regenerative organs. There is an argument that *Re Y* might be the start of a slippery slope towards using organs from incapacitated persons for the benefit of others, thereby placing a lesser value on them as persons.

For donation of solid organs, some indication of judicial thinking can be found in the United States authority of *Strunk v Strunk* (1969) 445 S.W.2d 145. In *Strunk*, the Court of Appeal of Kentucky authorised a kidney transplant from a 27-year-old man (with a mental age of 6) to his brother, who was suffering renal disease. Psychiatric evidence suggested that death of his brother would have a profoundly traumatic effect upon the mentally incompetent adult since the brothers shared a very close relationship. Accordingly, the court authorised removal of a kidney from the incapacitated person. In *Strunk*, the court applied (or purported to apply) the 'substituted judgement' test (although the patient had never been competent). In English law, the test to be applied is that of best interests rather than substituted judgement. It would perhaps be possible, however, that a decision-maker acting under the Mental Capacity Act 2005 might hold a reasonable belief that donation from an incapacitated person would be in the best interests of that person, especially if the decision maker took into account previously expressed wishes and feelings (although this might be problematic if the person had never been competent).

The Mental Capacity Act 2005 Code of Practice (2007) requires the prior approval of the Court of Protection for living organ or tissue donation from an adult who lacks decision-making capacity (paragraph 6.18); however to date, no cases have been brought. If similar circumstances arise, however, the court is likely to consider the best interests of the incapacitated person as guided by decided case law, such as *Re Y* and the United States decision in *Strunk v Strunk*.

8.4.3 Legislation

The HT Act 2004 provides the legal framework for the storage and use of organs and tissues for transplantation and research purposes.

8.4.3(a) Storage and use of relevant material

Section 1 requires appropriate consent for the storage and use of 'relevant material' which includes organs, tissues and cellular materials (section 53(1)). It excludes embryos outside the body and hair and nails from a living person (section 53(2)).

8.4.3(b) Storage and use for transplantation purposes

Section 1 requires that 'appropriate consent' precedes the storage or use of relevant material taken from a living person for the purpose of transplantation (section 1(1)(d), 1(f) and Schedule 1).

For a competent adult, 'appropriate consent' means 'his consent' (section 3(2)). If the potential donor is an adult with capacity, only that person can consent. Paragraphs 25 and 30 of the Code of Practice 1 provides that valid consent requires a positive act and must be appropriately informed, voluntary and given by a person with capacity. Paragraph 102 indicates that written consent prior to organ donation represents best practice.

While there is no statutory definition of sufficient information, paragraphs 88–92 provides guidance when informing the potential donor. These include the likely surgical procedures and the medical treatments for the donor and the risks involved. Information should cover the potential advantages for the recipient, and that a positive outcome for the recipient cannot be guaranteed. The donor should be informed that it is an offence to seek or receive payment (section 32) although reimbursement of expenses can be obtained. At present the HTA scrutinizes all living donations, whether donations to complete strangers, or for genetically related donations, and performs psychiatric and clinical assessments.

> To what extent is Rebecca's kidney donation to Jennifer lawful?
> What procedures would be required in order to comply with the provisions of the HT Act 2004?
> What would 'appropriate consent' mean in the circumstances?

8.4.3(c) Offences

Section 33 imposes restrictions on the removal or use of 'transplantable material' from the living. Subsections (1) and (2) makes organ removal in these circumstances a criminal offence, unless no reward has been given and subsections (3) and (5) have been complied with. An offence committed under section 33 is liable on conviction for a term of imprisonment up to 1 year, a fine, or both (section 33(6)).

The Human Tissue Act 2004 (Persons who Lack Capacity to Consent and Transplants) Regulations 2006 (No. 1659) provide for the circumstances whereby certain activities may be undertaken in relation to bodily materials from those who lack decision-making capacity for the purposes of the HT Act 2004. For the purposes of section 33, the Regulations provide the circumstances whereby living donor transplants are permitted. Regulation 10 defines transplantable material as including an organ or part of an organ; bone marrow, and peripheral blood cells.

Several further requirements must be met to avoid an offence under section 33(6). The doctor with clinical responsibility for the donor must have referred the matter to the HTA (Regulation 11(2)), which must be satisfied that no reward has been given (section 32 HT Act 2004), and that removal was consensual or otherwise lawful (Regulation 11(3)). The 'otherwise lawful' clause covers the common law and Mental Capacity Act 2005 requirements necessary for the adult who lacks capacity. Finally, the HTA must have authorised the transplant from the living donor after having taken into account a range of express factors detailed in Regulation 11 (4–10).

8.4.3(d) Adults lacking capacity

With regard to an adult who lacks capacity to consent, transplantable material includes bone marrow and peripheral stem cells, although all proposed transplant procedures are subject to vetting procedures by the HTA and includes psychiatric and clinical evaluations. As with the common law, however, the possibility of using organs from adults who lack capacity has not been ruled out subject to the prior approval of the HTA. Regulation 12 requires a decision to be made by a panel of at least three members of the HTA which reflects the assessment that would be carried out by the court in deciding whether organ retrieval for transplantation is lawful (see *Re Y* at 8.4.2(b)). Donation must be in the incompetent adult's best interests and the person who lacks capacity to consent is deemed to have given consent where the activity is undertaken for a lawful purpose, and the person acting on behalf of the individual reasonably believes that this decision is in that (incapacitated) person's best interests.

Pursuant to the Mental Capacity Act 2005, an intervention will be unlawful unless the decision-maker or proxy, reasonably believes that the intervention is in the person's best interests. The rebuttable presumption is that adults have capacity to consent unless they are unable to reach and communicate a decision due to impaired functioning of the mind or brain such that it renders them unable to understand, retain and weigh the relevant information required to give valid consent (see 4.4.1(a)).

8.4.3(e) Paired, pooled or non-directed altruistic donations

Permission of the HTA is necessary where the donor is an adult with capacity in circumstances of paired donations, pooled donations or non-directed altruistic donations (Regulation 12(4)). Paired donation is a situation where there are two persons in need of an organ and both have a willing donor but these donors are not a blood or tissue match. However, the tissue match corresponds with the other person in need.

Pooled donation relates to a situation where there is a chain of paired donations. The idea is that the organs are pooled so that everyone in the pool receives an organ from a willing donor. Thus, in a paired donation, the organ from a relative of person A (person A being the one who requires a transplant) goes to a stranger and person A receives an organ from someone close to that stranger. In pooled donations, there is a wider catchment of the same principle. Non-directed donation is a situation where a person donates an organ to a complete stranger with wholly altruistic motives. These three forms of live donation did not take place in the United Kingdom prior to enactment of the HT Act 2004.

> One of the difficulties with Jennifer's situation was that her tissue type meant that no suitable organ from a dead donor could be found.
> What measures might facilitate organ availability in these circumstances?

8.4.4 Genetically unrelated donors

The law and public policy have not encouraged donation of organs and tissues by genetically unrelated donors (although this is the norm for blood transfusion and many for bone marrow donors). For genetically unrelated donors, an enhanced degree of altruism is perceived due to the absence of a personal relationship. Nevertheless a degree of scepticism exists on the motivation of donors and the possible connection between donation and commercial interests. In 2008, the World Health Organisation stipulated in its guiding principles on human cell, tissue and organ transplantation that unrelated adult patients may donate organs but that donors should be subject to careful psychosocial assessment.

The Additional Protocol to the Convention of Human Rights and Biomedicine, on Transplantation of Organs and Tissues of Human Origin (2002) states that removal of organs or tissue may be carried out if there is no suitable organ or tissue from a deceased donor and if no alternative effective therapy is available (Article 9). Organ removal may be undertaken where a close personal relationship as defined by law exists between the donor and recipient, thus offering a substantial margin of discretion to Member States in their implementation (Article 10).

Price (2009) considers that, in effect, the HT Act 2004 has abandoned specific *prima facie* restrictions on certain relationships in favour of review of all instances of living organ and tissue donation and enhanced review of contentious forms of donation including altruistic donation between strangers. All living donors and recipients are interviewed by an independent assessor who reports back to the HTA. A panel of at least three members of the HTA makes the final decision in cases involving strangers.

Paired and pooled donations are relatively recent developments and to date have only involved kidneys. Menikoff (1999) argues that paired and pooled donation is in fact a covert form of kidney sale, and that a marked similarity exists between straightforward buying and selling and exchanging that kidney for another. Since neither donor will be willing to donate a kidney unless the other does the same, this transaction is in the form of a true exchange rather than two separate, and unrelated, gifts.

Far less common is non-directed donation, which involves organ donation from a person who has never met the recipient. Sadler (1971) undertook a survey of 22 stranger donations in San Francisco and found that three had underlying psychiatric or personality disorders. Persons wishing to become altruistic donors were almost always considered to be motivated by some form of underlying psychological condition and the practice dwindled in the 1990s. Recent years have witnessed a regenerated interest in the area. In Minnesota, for example, 15% of organ offerees were accepted following full assessment and apparently without ill-effects or negative repercussions (Price, 2009). The NHS Blood and Transplant does not object to the practice provided safeguards are implemented and the procedure is authorised by the HTA. Some members of the Jesus Christians, for example, offer to donate kidneys to strangers in need and some time ago a British member travelled to the United States to donate part of his lung to a young girl (Price, 2009). Altruistic non-directed donation can be viewed as a valuable and selfless gift from a utilitarian point of view. However, it is perhaps questionable whether individuals ought to be allowed to voluntarily assume such risks on grounds of public policy.

A 'domino transplant' involves removal of a transplantable organ from a patient as part of that person's own treatment. A classic example is a person with cystic fibrosis. Although this disease primarily affects the pulmonary system, in surgical terms it is technically simpler to replace the heart and lungs as a unit in those who require a lung transplant from a dead donor. It follows, therefore, that the person's heart (provided this is healthy) could become available for transplantation to another. Domino transplants, however, are not common.

8.5   Enhancing organ availability

The acute shortage of organs available for transplantation leads to tragic outcomes for many of those in need. Numerous ways of addressing the shortfall have been suggested, some of which are highly controversial. Central concerns are based upon the relativity of personal rights (before and after death) compared with the collective rights of others in need. Current law on organ acquisition is underpinned by the need for consent although the extent to which this ought to be the situation is perhaps questionable, particularly where the health, and possibly lives, of others is at stake.

8.5.1   Duty to donate

The moral acceptability, or otherwise, of the removal of organs from the deceased for purposes of donation depends upon the weight attached to the competing interests and rights of the parties involved. Utilitarians might argue for a *prima facie* duty of organ harvesting from the deceased. From this perspective the costs of a compulsory regulatory requirement (the disutility cost) might be deemed relatively low in comparison to the benefits likely to be achieved (the utility benefits). Undoubtedly, the provision of organs from cadavers would benefit potential recipients, although this advantage needs to be counterbalanced against the potential harm incurred to those who conscientiously object on deeply held religious, cultural or other grounds. From a virtue theorist perspective, a virtuous individual would surely save the life of another, especially when this is achieved at little cost to themselves such as by the removal of organs following death.

Even if it is accepted that the deceased or surviving relatives have a moral claim over cadaveric tissue and organs, one approach from the point of view of moral theorists is to consider the comparable costs associated with organ donation. The costs of donating an organ when one is dead are arguably negligible from the perspective of the burden imposed upon the deceased. Arguably, posthumous removal of organs for transplantation from a deceased person should not pose a problem from a moral perspective.

Some ethicists consider that the rights or interests of a deceased person, or those of surviving relatives, can never outweigh the competing interests of those who require lifesaving organs. Harris (2003) asserts a moral justification for automatic and mandatory availability of donor organs for the purposes of saving another's life. He argues that this is at least as compelling as justification for compulsory juror service and forensic post-mortem examinations. The appropriateness of consent as the gatekeeper for deceased donations is questioned, and whether instead there ought to be some form of 'compulsory' system for the routine removal of organs and tissues without the need for consent. Libertarians, by comparison, tend to believe that individuals have interests and rights of control over their own bodies and which continues after death. Irrespective of the needs of others, such rights ought to be respected.

There appears to be strong arguments in support of a public duty on individuals to donate their organs following death. According to Harris (2003) the moral concern of society has tended to focus on the dead, and their relatives and friends, to the detriment of the living who are in need of organs. Since the body cannot remain intact after death, the right to refuse organ retrieval based upon this premise is irrational.

If this line of argument is accepted, namely that a duty to donate exists and that it is irrational not to do so, then organs could be considered to be a public resource. Emson (2003) argues that post-mortem separation of the body and soul means that the individual cannot be reconstituted. The person no longer exists and has no further use for the body. Under this pretext it makes sense to use organs as a vital and potentially lifesaving resource for others. He further argues that it is even more morally objectionable for relatives to deny acquisition of organs from the deceased, since the claim of relatives upon the deceased organs is tenuous and nothing more than a temporary memorial of a loved person who was once alive. McGuinness and Brazier (2008), however, contest arguments that the dead have no interests. They argue that the living retain enduring interests in what happens to their dead bodies, and those of their dead relatives. Arguably, the inherent bond between the individual and his or her body is so close that an interest is sufficient to survive death. From the perspective of self-determination, since competent individuals are permitted to self-govern their lives and refuse intrusion to their bodily integrity (even to the extent of refusing lifesaving treatment), it follows that they should have the right to decide what happens to their organs and tissues following death. As far as relatives are concerned, death is not merely the point at which a switch is turned off. Although death occurs at a distinct point in time, the grieving process is often protracted. Coming to terms with death and the accompanying grief takes time, and mandatory posthumous organ acquisition, although serving a utilitarian objective, is nonetheless contrary to the moral perspective of civilised society.

8.5.2   Required request

Some jurisdictions of the United States have introduced a system of 'required request' in an endeavour to enhance post-mortem rates of organ donation. This system imposes a positive legal duty on health-care staff to make proper enquiries about use of the deceased's organs and tissues for the purposes of transplantation. Opportunities for organ removal are less likely to be overlooked on account of a request not being made.

A potential drawback to this policy is its potential to interfere with clinical discretion and judgement. Relatives of the deceased are likely to be distressed and asking them to authorise organ retrieval might precipitate psychological trauma and harm. Alternatively, if clinical discretion is available, then each situation could be considered on merit. Inevitably, a balance must be struck between avoiding further distress to the grieving, against the possibility of losing a potentially lifesaving organ. Some take the view that the potential for saving the lives of others must take precedence over concerns of upsetting relatives and friends of the newly deceased. Whether the imposition of such a policy would enhance organ acquisition is unclear. The NHS Blood and Transplant (2010) states that although the introduction of such a policy resulted in an increase in acquisition rates, these benefits were not sustained.

8.5.3   Conditional donation

A basic principle of donation from the deceased is that organs are primarily allocated according to clinical need. Part of the remit of the NHS Blood and Transplant is to ensure that donated organs are properly allocated according to priority. If organs cannot be used locally, they are offered nationally according to a points-based system that takes into account blood group, tissue type and geographical location although the criteria vary according to the type of donation.

A controversial situation is where the deceased has agreed to donate subject to satisfaction of specific conditions. In 1998 an unconscious man was admitted to a hospital in Sheffield. His relatives agreed that in the event of his death, his organs could be used for transplantation provided that these were donated to white recipients. His liver was used to save the life of a recipient who would otherwise have died within 24 hours, and his kidneys went to individuals at the top of the waiting list under the renal transplant points system. All the recipients were white. The case generated significant publicity and the Department of Health (2000) set up an investigation into conditional organ donation. The panel concluded that all of the organs had been received by those in greatest need and that in the event allocation would have been the same had the donation been unconditional. The panel recommended that organs should not be accepted with conditions attached and this guidance has since become National Health Service policy. Conditional donation is also unlawful in Scotland (section 49 Human Tissue (Scotland) Act 2006).

There is an argument that if organs subject to conditions are not accepted, then an individual in need might be destined to death on account of a moral objection. For this reason, the moral basis for objecting to conditions has to be balanced against the justification for allowing someone to die on account of this stance. In addition, there is conceivably an inconsistency between the rules that govern living donation and that from the deceased. Living donation is almost always intended for a particular individual, and yet deceased donation must be unconditional. Wilkinson (2003) questions this dichotomy since although a racially motivated condition is difficult to justify, a request that an organ is given to a known individual seems less abhorrent. The principal driver behind the Department of Health's position against conditional donation was that it went against the principle of altruistic donation on the basis of clinical need (and tissue compatibility). However, if altruism forms the legitimate basis of donation then why should this be motivated by the 'greatest need' principle? In its normal interpretation, altruism represents a philanthropic concern for the interests of others, and imposition of a condition will not necessarily violate this principle in the absence of other factors such as deeply seated prejudice.

It appears that proscription of conditional donation is based upon its conflicts with fairness and humanitarian principles of helping those with greatest need. However, a conflict would still be apparent if conditions were attached to the behaviour of potential recipients. To what extent should alcoholics, or former alcoholics, be denied access to liver transplantation on the basis that they contributed to their clinical condition, or perhaps donation ought to be conditional upon undertakings for specific post-transplant behaviour designed to reduce any future lapse. There is no such regulatory policy in England and it is likely that exclusions would be open to challenge under the Human Rights Act 1998 as a potential breach of Article 2 (the right to life), read in conjunction with the right not to be discriminated against under Article 14. Any conditions on recipients could arguably be challenged on grounds of disproportionate invasion of individual lifestyle choice.

The Department of Health has recently announced a change in policy to ensure that in certain circumstances donors may bequeath their organs to family or close friends who are in need of a transplant. Allocation, however, remains subject to clinical priority and those on the super urgent waiting lists retain priority over named individuals.

8.5.4 Policies to enhance posthumous acquisition rates

There are three main policies that govern the posthumous removal of tissues and organs. These are the conscription, opt-in and the opt-out system.

8.5.4(a) The conscription system

A 'conscription' system permits the posthumous removal of organs and tissues without the need for prior consent. Such a system is based on the premise that the rights and legitimate interests of those in need of a transplant outweigh any residual rights of the deceased or surviving relatives. In these circumstances, bodies and body parts are typically perceived as public or state property, and as such can be legitimately used for the benefit of society as a whole on communitarian grounds.

8.5.4(b) The opt-in system

This policy allows the posthumous removal of organs and tissue only with the appropriate explicit consent. A narrow opt-in system is one where only the deceased can decide, whereas a wider opt-in system permits relatives and loved ones to consent to removal of the deceased's organs for transplantation. A variant of an opt-in system could be an obligation to make a formal decision on the issue of organ donation on attaining the age of adulthood; known as 'mandated choice'. However, in order to effectively enforce such a system it would need to be linked to some other condition, for example registration with a general practitioner.

8.5.4(c) The opt-out system

An 'opt-out' system (also known as a 'presumed consent' system) is based on the assumption that everyone is willing to donate their organs unless they register their objections. From an ethical standpoint, there are at least two principal criticisms against this approach. The first is that the public is generally unaware, or may not have sufficient knowledge, about the practice. Therefore merely because a person has not opted out will not necessarily mean that the person is compliant with post-mortem donation. Furthermore, consent in medical law is generally active and positive. For all forms of medical intervention, a person with capacity actively and positively agrees to that intervention. Presumed consent is therefore regarded by some as being no consent at all.

From an ethical perspective there are several potential benefits to be achieved by supporting an opt-out system. It is reasonable to believe that most people would wish to act altruistically and help others by donating their organs after death, yet even amongst of those who are willing to donate, relatively few have registered such a wish or carry donor cards (mainly because of apathy or inertia). If it is accepted that a number of people are willing to donate organs, then there would be good reasons for presuming consent. Using this as the default position would present organ donation in a positive light. Furthermore, moving towards an opt-out system would likely increase the supply of organs for transplantation. Kennedy *et al.* (1998) noted that since presumed consent was adopted in Belgium, organ donation rose by 55% within 5 years, and although citizens who wished to opt out of the scheme could register their objection at any town hall, less than 2% of the population did so.

The presumed consent system has not been adopted in the United Kingdom despite much lobbying in its favour. The Organ Donation Taskforce (2008) felt that the introduction of opt-out legislation would not necessarily increase the availability of organs, and donations might actually decrease. The Taskforce pointed out that although legislation was passed in Spain in 1979 it was only in 1989, when the National Transplant Organisation was founded putting new infrastructures in place, that the organ donor rates began to rise. The Taskforce felt that an opt-out system could potentially erode the trust between clinicians and the families of the deceased at a distressing time, and that this could undermine the concept of a gift freely given, which is recognised as being a key and central principle for donor families and transplant recipients.

Different variations of an opt-out system are apparent. Under a 'hard' opt-out system, organ removal can proceed unless the deceased has registered pre-mortem objections and irrespective of relatives views. In a 'soft' opt-out system, relatives have the right to veto organ removal of organs in the absence of registered objections. Most countries that have introduced an opt-out system have 'soft' versions in place based on the premise that it is ethically inappropriate to proceed with organ removal if this is likely to cause major distress to a first degree relative or long-term partner. However, Gundle (2005) observes that in Austria, where a 'hard' policy exists, donation rates rose from 4.6 donors per million to 27.2 within 5 years and that the number of kidney donations each year now almost equals the number of people on the waiting list.

8.5.5 Improved co-ordination of services

Statistics from the Organ Donation Taskforce (2008) shows the United Kingdom as having one of the lowest rates of donation at around 12.8 per million of the population. By comparison, number of donors per million of the population are 35.1 for Spain, 26.9 for the United States and 23.2 for France. In Spain, following the introduction of a new transplant co-ordinator network in 1990, the system for retrieval of organs has become highly successful. Three major hospitals and intensive care units have a co-ordinating transplant team of medical staff and co-ordinators. This has facilitated effective integration of health-care professionals, who are well-informed about the procedures involved in retrieving and obtaining organs for transplant purposes in intensive care units.

From an ethical perspective, there has been some criticism about this integrated approach. It is possible that boundaries might become blurred between those caring for acutely ill patients and those whose primary objective is to retrieve organs for others. The primary objective of health-care professionals in an intensive care unit is to care for the patient which must always take priority over organ removal for the benefit of others. There is potential for a conflict of interest and from an ethical viewpoint – doctors who are seeking to obtain organs should be different from those involved in the care of patients.

The Organ Donation Taskforce (2008) in recognising the need for an improved system for organ retrieval and donation has proposed several recommendations to improve the co-ordination and retrieval of organs on the part of the NHS. Organ donation must be embraced as a usual, rather than an unusual, event following death and inform end-of-life care discussions when appropriate. Brain stem death testing ought to be a routine feature carried out on all ventilated patients where this is a likely diagnosis, even if organ donation is unlikely to occur. Furthermore, an efficient nationwide network of dedicated teams are required to ensure timely removal of high-quality organs from all heartbeating and non-heartbeating donors, and co-ordinators need to engage with critical care units. The Taskforce recognised an acute shortage of organs from black and minority ethnic populations, and for this reason urgent attention is needed to encourage the promotion of organ donation. It also recommends enhanced recognition of donors to include tributes such as national memorials, local initiatives and personal follow-up of donor families. At present, the Trust where the donor dies organises and pays for retrieval surgery, although the benefit might accrue to a person from a geographically distant area. The Taskforce recognised this as a potential hurdle and recommends that financial disincentives to Trusts facilitating donation should be removed through the development and introduction of reimbursement packages. It was estimated that these recommendations could deliver a 50% increase in organ donation by 2013.

8.5.6 Incentives

Whether or not donors ought to be paid for their organs is a controversial issue. Some argue that payment would offer a practical solution to end the chronic shortage of organs available for transplantation. Others consider this morally abhorrent and socially unacceptable. Payment for transplantable material is an offence, irrespective of whether such material is obtained from the living or dead.

8.5.6(a) The law

The HT ACT 2004 prohibits commercial dealings in human material for purposes of transplantation. Section 32(1) provides that:

'A person commits an offence if he

a) gives or receives a reward for the supply of, or for an offer to supply, any controlled material;
b) seeks to find a person willing to supply any controlled material for reward;
c) offers to supply any controlled material for reward;
d) initiates or negotiates any arrangement involving the giving of a reward for the supply of, or for an offer to supply, any controlled material;
e) takes part in the management or control of a body of persons, corporate or unincorporate, whose activities consist of or include the initiation or negotiation of such arrangements.

The concept of 'reward' is broadly construed and includes financial as well as other material advantages.

Section 32(7) permits reimbursement of expenses incurred in transporting, removing, storing, preparing or preserving controlled material. Section 32(7)(c) allows reimbursement for loss of earnings incurred by the donor who supplies such material. Section 32(3) permits the HTA to exercise its discretion to allow a person to trade in controlled material and would extend, for example, to permitting the National Blood Service to purchase blood from abroad. Section 32(6) extends this permission to commercial tissue banks to receive payments beyond expenses. Section 32(9) exempts from the prohibition of payment for gametes, embryos and tissues that have become the subject of property through the application of work and skill.

Article 8(1) of the European Convention pertains to the right to respect for private and family life. On this principle, it could be argued that the prohibition against selling one's organs violates this right. However, Article 8(2) qualifies this right in that state interference can be permitted where this is in accordance with the law and necessary for the protection of health or morals, or the protection of the rights and freedoms of others, thereby justifying the legislative prohibition.

In addition to the offence that extends over commercial dealings in human tissues and organs, clinicians who are involved in such practices can be subject to regulatory sanctions. Several years ago, doctors who were involved in the Turkish kidney dealing scandal were found guilty of serious professional misconduct by the General Medical Council and their names were erased from the Register for trafficking human organs (Allison, 2002).

8.5.6(b) Ethics

Some commentators believe that payment for organs or transplantable material from the dead ought to be allowed, and that the moral issues of such practice would be less problematic than payment of living donors (Erin and Harris, 2003).

The establishment of a regulatory system to control commercial dealings in transplantable material from the dead would not be straightforward. There are several competing interests, such as those of the seller who would wish to gain maximum fiscal advantage and the interests of potential buyers, who would aim for maximal benefit from reusable organs. Societal interests might strive to achieve a fair and equitable system with protection against monopolisation by the rich.

From a utilitarian perspective some types of commercial dealings in transplantable material would seem to offer a definite benefit for recipients who would stand to gain from a successful transplant. Some variant of a market for organs could conceivably increase the supply. However, commercialisation might result in fewer individuals volunteering to donate for altruistic reasons. From a virtue ethics perspective, a market for organs should be discouraged because philanthropic motivation is more virtuous. Altruism is perceived to be an essential virtue of all superior societies and persons, and the sale of organs runs counter to this principle. However, financial transactions are not always founded upon self-interested motives and could, for example, be motivated by the needs of others, for instance when one family member sells an organ to finance otherwise unaffordable medical care for another family member. Erin and Harris (2003) have proposed a monopsonistic approach to commercialisation of materials from living donors with a single purchaser for the products of several sellers. The purchaser would regulate the subsequent sale of organs to ensure equitable distribution. In the United Kingdom, such a function could conceivably be assumed by the HTA.

Critics argue that offers of reimbursement for organs and tissues from the deceased might not be universally acceptable. Some may be affronted by offers of payment for the organs and tissues of their deceased loved ones. Haddow (2006) carried out empirical research and concluded that there was only a weakly positive response in favour of this approach and found that amongst donor families 16 out of 17 relatives were opposed to financial incentives. The Nuffield Council on Bioethics has launched a public consultation to explore ways to encourage people to become organ donors. Options being canvassed include offers to pay donors' funeral expenses and to prioritise those on the register if ever they need an organ for themselves. Jarvis (1995) considers that since a person's interests in their post-mortem organs are minimal, this represents a highly attractive option, since it guarantees priority inclusion which might save or significantly improve their quality of life. Although many might consider such a reciprocal agreement to be attractive, those who elect not join such a scheme might be regarded as 'blameworthy' compared to those who do. Preferring those who join the scheme means that others might be disadvantaged as far as treatment is concerned. This position runs counter to ethical clinical practice where persons are treated according to need, rather than their blameworthiness.

8.5.7 A market for organs

The commodification or commercialisation of organ transplantation can be rejected in that financial incentives could operate as a form of coercion. Non-financial pressures can also amount to coercion, especially within families where covert pressure can exert considerable psychological and emotional influence. Harvey (1990) considers that one needs to carefully distinguish between the financially vulnerable and those who are not.

However, a market for organs and tissues already exists and trafficking of organs is known to occur. It tends to be the poor and marginalised sections of society who volunteer to donate for relatively small sums. According to Goyal et al. (2002) the majority of donors in India are women. Given the often weak position of women in Indian society, the voluntary nature of such donations seems dubious (Mudur, 2004).

The recognised black market for organs arguably represents the greatest risk. Organ providers are typically given paltry sums and their bargaining position is weakened by the presence of an intermediary. Since organ retrieval is carried out below the law, there is a substantial risk that standards of surgery and care are less than satisfactory. In a study undertaken 40 years ago on the commercialisation of blood donation, Titmuss (1970) suggested that sellers were typically in desperate need of money such as drug addicts, alcoholics and carriers of transmittable disease. Commercialisation could lead to concealment of information leading to risks for recipients. Material incentives continue to be highly controversial although arguably medicine is already highly commercialised to the extent that it is inconsistent not to permit the buying and selling of human materials.

These same arguments could apply to the black market for organs which by its nature would be difficult to monitor and challenge and could readily be dominated by the rich and powerful with potential exploitation of vulnerable persons. Radcliffe-Richards *et al.* (1998) believe that a black market would exacerbate the invidious position of the impoverished who might resort to selling their organs. They consider that poverty leads to a restricted range of opportunities so that organ selling becomes the best option for those in need of money. The only way to reduce this likelihood would be to address the causes of poverty. Since this utopian ideal seems impossible, scope for abuse and exploitation will persist and it is arguable that removal of the prohibition on trade would permit better control, rather than a complete ban.

The crux of the debate is whether there is sufficient ethical, moral and social justification for a blanket ban on a market for organs or whether, all things considered, society should consider ways by which the interests of sellers can be respected and protected. Erin and Harris (2003) argue that buying and selling organs generates substantial hypocrisy with the outcome that everyone receives their dues except the donor. They argue for an ethical market for organs confined to self-governing geopolitical areas and that only residents within that particular union or state could sell into the system and that only they, or their families, would be eligible to receive organs. Under this model a single purchaser should buy and sell every organ and distribute according to the equitable method of clinical need. The principal advantages would be a reduction (and potentially complete end) to exploitation of vulnerable donors who would receive reasonable compensation and knowledge that they had contributed to a system that could offer future benefits to them and their families. Given that a market for organs (of sorts) already exists, it is perhaps sensible to look at ways by which such activities might be harnessed into a regulated framework.

8.6   Alternative sources

There are two principal alternative sources for organs for the purpose of transplantation – other species and artificial engineering.

8.6.1   Xenotransplantation

Xenotransplantation is the transplantation of tissues, cells or organs from one species to another and, in particular, from animals to humans. Although this offers a potential treatment for those with end-stage organ failure, the treatment has shown little success. The major obstacle is that the recipient's immune system tends to reject the transplanted tissue due to immunological responses that cause rejection of the transplant. Certain forms of animal tissue have, however, been used in clinical treatment for some considerable time. Pig heart valves, for example, can be processed so that they act as inert material, and have been used in cardiac valve replacement surgery for several years. However, these techniques are controversial in respect of ethical and practical aspects and the utility of these procedures has been constrained.

8.6.1(a) Ethics

Most work on xenotransplantation has used pig organs and tissues and those of non-human primates, such as chimpanzees. Pigs breed relatively quickly which facilitates harvesting of materials, pig organs are roughly the size of human organs, and for these reasons have been the preferred choice to date.

From an ethical perspective, those of Muslim or Judaic faiths might well refuse such transplants on religious grounds. Similarly, health-care staff might conscientiously object to performing transplants from animals into humans. Research has been undertaken to introduce human genes into pigs in order to rear organs of greater compatibility and the correct size. There are strong ethical concerns as to whether genetic barriers between species ought to be blurred in such a way. The principal concern is that engineering of such creatures that are part human and part non-human animal is unacceptable on account of the moral confusion within our current framework of relationships with non-human animals and hybrids that are in part human (Robert and Bayliss, 2003). While these considerations might seem futuristic in respect of scientific progress, the successful use of pig heart valves has caused little or no concern to date. It is understandable that concerns might be generated if a recipient animal assumed characteristics of possible humanity. As Greeley (2003) explains, single organ xenotransplants into human beings seem unlikely to be heavily controversial. If it were feasible to transplant a chimpanzee brain into a human, then that would undoubtedly cause concern, as would transfer of a large number of animal organs into a human. Greeley suggests that a distinction needs to be drawn between heart valves or skin, and other materials such as brains and gametes.

A further ethical concern focuses on the moral interests of the animals that are used. The fundamental assumption is that it is acceptable to kill another species in order to save human life. The Working Party of the Nuffield Council of Bioethics (1996) states that 'It is difficult to see how, in a society in which the breeding of pigs for food and clothing is accepted, their use for lifesaving medical procedures, such as xenotransplantation, could be unacceptable.' Animal rights activists protest against the use of animals for xenotransplantation, as well as for research, on the basis that rearing and slaughtering animals for these purposes is wrong. Singer (1992) questions the ethics that allow the rearing of sentient animals in confined spaces and little quality of life followed by their slaughter to retrieve their organs, compared with the reluctance to harvest the organs of a person who is not, and never can be, even minimally conscious. He argues that by taking organs from animals, their interests are disregarded and they are ranked as less worthy of concern and respect. Animals, like humans, have qualities of sentience and consciousness and therefore moral standing. He suggests a more effective way to obtain organs is retrieval from persons who are brain dead or cortically dead. This view is shared by Hughes (1998) who says that the capacity for pleasure and pain may vary between species and also within a species. Some individuals will have a lesser degree of sentience than others, or those who may have lost consciousness and their mental capacities may be severely and tragically impaired. If one is prepared to take organs from animals on the basis of limited capacity and sentience, then one should also be prepared to take organs from humans whose capacities are similarly restricted. Against this is the argument that humans are able to form relationships, which include love, attention and devotion, whereas animals appear less capable of such feelings. However, this might lead to the conclusion that if an individual is profoundly incapacitated and has no family or friends, then that person is worthless as a human being, and organs could then be legitimately harvested for the benefit of another.

8.6.1(b) Practical issues

A central difficulty with xenotransplantation is the significantly high risk of tissue rejection as a result of the body recognising foreign tissue. Research into immunosuppressants to reduce this possibility is ongoing, but as yet has been unsuccessful in animal to human transplants. If very high doses of immunological suppressing medication are used (as would be necessary), it can lead to catastrophic complications. Rejection within hours or minutes of the transplant has occurred and is known as hyperacute rejection. One possible way to avoid this is to introduce human genes into the animal's genome, in order to suppress the gene that causes the hyperacute rejection. These transgenic animals then are cloned to increase the supply of suitable organs.

A further latent problem is one of cross-species infection. Relatively harmless viruses, such as the porcine endogenous retrovirus (PERV), which is harmless to pigs, could be incorporated into human cells and mutate into deadly human viruses. Likewise, a variant of Creutzfeldt-Jakob disease (vCJD), which is the human form of bovine spongioform encephalitis (BSE), may cross species and cause deterioration similar to that in Alzheimer's disease. The Nuffield Council of Bioethics (1996) recognised that it is not possible to predict or quantify the risk of the emergence of new human disease. In fact, it might be possible to identify infectious organisms transmitted by xenografting only if this leads to disease in humans and after the event. Xenografts have to be tried in volunteers, but it is questionable whether this is justifiable when the best available treatment is an allograft (human-to-human transplant). A further ethical problem arises in relation to the validity of an individual's consent for acceptance of a xenograft. Barker and Polcrack (2001) recognise significant issues in respect of an individual's informed consent for a potential xenograft. The intended recipient must understand as completely as possible the potential risks to himself or herself, to immediate contacts, and the possible risks to society since the practice could conceivably introduce new or modified pathogens to the human race.

If xenotransplantation becomes accepted as a form of treatment, it will need to be regulated meticulously on a global basis. A person who receives a xenograft in one country may enter another, potentially spreading new pathogens. If potential risks are to be limited there is a need for an accurate, globally maintained register of recipients of xenotransplants and those recipients are likely to require lifelong clinical monitoring and surveillance, which might conceivably extend to future generations.

8.6.1(c) Regulation

Xenotransplantation requires compliance with a regulatory framework. The HT Act 2004 does not extend to this area. Regulation for use of animals is covered by the Animals (Scientific Procedures) Act 1986. Pursuant to the Act, a licence is required for scientific experimental procedures that might cause an animal 'pain, suffering, distress, or lasting harm' (section 2(1)). This applies to 'protected animals' as defined by regulations (sections 1(1) and 1(3)) as 'any living vertebrate, other than man'. A licence will be awarded only if the licencing committee, having listened to the evidence, considers that the likely benefits of the research outweigh the likely adverse effects on the animal (section 5(4)).

It seems unlikely that xenotransplantation would be covered by the Medicines for Human Use (Clinical Trials) Regulations 2004/1031 (as amended) since the Regulations apply to clinical trials of medicinal products. The definition of a medicinal product is wide and includes any substance presented as having attributes for treating or preventing disease, or to be used for restoring, correcting or modifying physiological function in humans by pharmacological or immunological action (Directive 2001/83/EC, Article 1). Williamson, Fox and McLean (2007) doubt that xenotransplants fall within this definition. Part 4 of Annex 1 of the Directive (as amended by Directive 2003/63/EC) provides for advance therapy using medicinal products and includes a specific statement on xenotransplantation medical products. However, a trial that involves only the administration of tissues (except a somatic cell therapy medicinal product) is not considered to be a clinical trial. It therefore appears that whole organ xenotransplants would not fall under the Medicines for Human Use (Clinical Trials) Regulations and therefore not require the prior approval of the Medicines and Healthcare Products Regulatory Agency, the body responsible for regulating medicinal products and medical devices.

Use of animal tissues, or an organ, might be considered to be an innovative therapy to which clinical discretion applies. In *Simms v Simms* [2002] EWHC 2734 (Fam), Butler-Sloss P said, *per curiam*, that in this context 'The *Bolam* test ought not to be allowed to inhibit medical progress since it is clear that if one waited for that test to be complied with to its fullest no innovative work in medicine would ever be attempted.' In her view if there was no alternative therapy available for a progressive and fatal disease, then consideration of experimental treatment with unknown benefits and risks was reasonable. Williamson, Fox and McLean (2007), however, recognise the particular difficulties in calculating the safety risks that (xenotransplantation) poses and particularly since xenotransplantation can transcend regulatory borders.

The UK Xenotransplantation Interim Regulatory Authority (UKXIRA) was founded in 1997 as an oversight body. It was disbanded in 2006, partly because it was felt that the system of research ethics governance would operate as a sufficient safeguard. The Department of Health (2006) document 'Xenotransplantation Guidance' reported the Government's support for exploring the potential for clinical implementation of xenotransplantation in a cautious fashion using appropriately approved clinical trials. In these circumstances, if the xenogeneic product is genetically modified, the clinical investigators require prior ethical approval from the Gene Therapy Advisory Committee. Any proposal for a clinical trial of a xenogeneic medicinal product also requires Medicines and Healthcare Products Regulatory Agency approval in respect of safety, quality and efficacy. Such proposals must also be submitted to a Recognised Research Ethics Committee (REC). The language of the guidance appears unambiguous in the context of medicinal products and the debate essentially concerns whether a whole and unmodified xenogeneic organ is captured by the definition. Irrespective of this point, it is unlikely that a clinical trial would go ahead without appropriate REC approval, failing which there would undoubtedly be public opprobrium and regulatory sanctions levied against the investigators. While it is possible that a single instance of xenotransplantation might fall under the *Simms v*

Simms principle of clinical discretion, it seems unlikely that a trial would receive the accedence of a REC.

8.6.2   Artificial organs

Medical devices have been used for many years and include kidney dialysis machines, pacemakers, ventilators and hip and knee prostheses, amongst many others. Artificial organs, however, are still a long way from being used in routine clinical practice.

Artificial organs represent a future treatment option for those who currently need a transplant due to organ damage or failure. The development of artificial organs is being explored through the use of tissue engineering. This uses a combination of cells and a delivery system to generate tissue for the organ that needs replacing. Sources of cells include stem cells that are pluripotent and undifferentiated, and either embryonic or adult stem cells, as well as differentiated or tissue-specific cells (which could be obtained from an individual or another species). A major persistent problem with transplantation is the body's immune reaction which tends to reject the transplant. However, depending upon the degree of synergy between the cells used and the patient's own cells, the immune response generated after a transplant using stem cells would be comparatively less.

Artificial organs and related devices are regulated under the Medical Devices Regulations 2002/618 as amended by the Medical Devices (Amendment) Regulations 2007/400. These provisions implement Council Directive 90/385/EEC and Council Directive 93/42/EEC which cover active implantable medical devices. Tissue engineered products, however, fall outside the medical device regulations. The Advanced Therapy Medicinal Products (ATMP) Regulation 1394/2007 seeks to cover the area between a medicinal product and a medical device such as tissue engineered products. The Medicines and Healthcare Products Regulatory Agency regulates ATMPs.

If a tissue engineered product is derived from human cells or tissues, it would fall under the Tissue and Cells Directive as implemented (in part) by the Human Tissue (Quality & Safety for Human Application) Regulations 2007/1523. The Quality & Safety Regulations require a licence from the HTA for testing, processing, storing and distributing, as well as acquiring human tissues and cells intended for transplantation. The Medicines and Healthcare Products Regulatory Agency and the HTA have a joint policy by which medicinal products and ATMPs fall under the Quality and Safety Regulations for the purposes of donation, procurement and testing of tissues and cells, and come under the remit of the HTA. The subsequent stages, which include manufacture, storage and distribution, are regulated by the Medicines and Healthcare Products Regulatory Agency.

Summary

8.1   There are great clinical benefits from organ transplantation. The Human Tissue Act 2004 is the legislative framework in this jurisdiction that governs the removal, storage and use of human tissue. The Human Tissue Authority has a statutory function to issue codes of practice to give practical guidance on the standards expected from those carrying out activities regulated by the Act.

8.2   In law there is no property in the dead body or its parts. An exception to the 'no property' rule might be on the basis of the application of work and skill principle in *Dobson* and *Kelly* and in

Summary cont'd

section 32(9)(c) of the HT Act 2004. The courts have shown a reluctance to rule that the body or body parts may be owned.

8.3 The standard recognised at common law and in clinical practice as definitive for the diagnosis of death is the irreversible cessation of the integrative function of the brain stem. This is called brain stem death. Pursuant to section 1 of The Human Tissue Act 2004, no organ or tissue can be taken from the deceased without appropriate consent. Appropriate consent can be provided by the deceased's pre-mortem consent or authorisation, or through an appointed person under section 4 of the Act, or through the consent of a qualifying relative. Anyone who takes organs without appropriate consent commits an offence.

8.4 A competent living donor must give valid consent. Valid consent requires a positive act and must be appropriately informed and voluntary. Written consent prior to organ donation represents best practice. It is a criminal offence to take organs from a living person for the purpose of transplantation unless the requirements of the HT Act 2004 are fulfilled. Organs from adults who lack capacity would have to be approved by a panel of at least three members of the HTA.

8.5 A range of initiatives have been used to try and enhance the number of organs available for transplantation. An 'opt-out' system (also known as a 'presumed consent' system) is based on the assumption that everyone is willing to donate their organs unless they object and register this choice. In England and Wales the Organ Donation Taskforce 2008 has rejected a 'presumed consent' model. However, the Taskforce has recommended a number of operational changes in order to enhance the retrieval of organs. Commercialisation or trafficking in organs is proscribed by law and constitutes a criminal offence.

8.6 Xenotransplantation is the transplantation of tissues, cells or organs from one species to another, and requires compliance with a regulatory framework which is covered by the Animals (Scientific Procedures) Act 1986. There is a risk of zoonosis (transmission of animal diseases to humans), as well as a high risk of immune-induced organ rejection. Artificial organs represent a treatment option for the future, and are being explored through the use of tissue engineering. Artificial organs and related devices are regulated under the Medical Devices Regulations.

Exercises

8.1 What has the Human Tissue Act 2004 achieved in respect of facilitating organ donation for the purposes of transplantation? Why do you think the Act did not adduce the principle that material from humans could *never* be stored or removed without valid consent?

8.2 'If competent individuals are morally the rightful owners of their bodies, even to the extent of refusing life-sustaining medical treatment, then such persons ought to be able to dispose of their bodies or body parts as they see fit.' Discuss this statement.

8.3 Permitting the sale of organs is a pragmatic approach to the current, almost universal, shortage of organs available for transplantation. Furthermore, advances in medical technology have made outcomes from transplantation hugely successful. Given these factors, is there any justification for refusing a market for organs in modern society?

8.4 The moral debates about organ donation will soon be defunct since artificially created organs and tissues will become a reality. Do you agree with this statement?

8.5 Failure to adopt a presumed consent strategy for organ donation in the United Kingdom has been a retrograde step for society. Critically comment on this statement.

Further reading

Erin CA, Harris J. An ethical market in human organs. *Journal of Medical Ethics* 2003; 29: 137–138

Kerridge IH, Saul P, Lowe M, McPhee J, Williams D. Death, dying and donation: organ transplantation and the diagnosis of death. *Journal of Medical Ethics* 2002; 28: 89–94

Nuffield Council of Bioethics. *Animal to human transplants: the ethics of xenotransplantation.* Nuffield Council of Bioethics, London, 1996

Organ Donation Taskforce. *The potential impact of an opt-out system for organ donation in the UK: An independent report from the Organ Donation Taskforce.* Department of Health, London, 2008

Price D. The Human Tissue Act 2004. *Modern Law Review* 2005; 68: 798–821

Williamson L, Fox M, McLean S. The regulation of xenotransplantation in the United Kingdom after UKXIRA: legal and ethical issues. *Journal of Law & Society* 2007; 34: 441–464

Links to relevant websites can be found at: http://www.palgrave.com/law/samanta

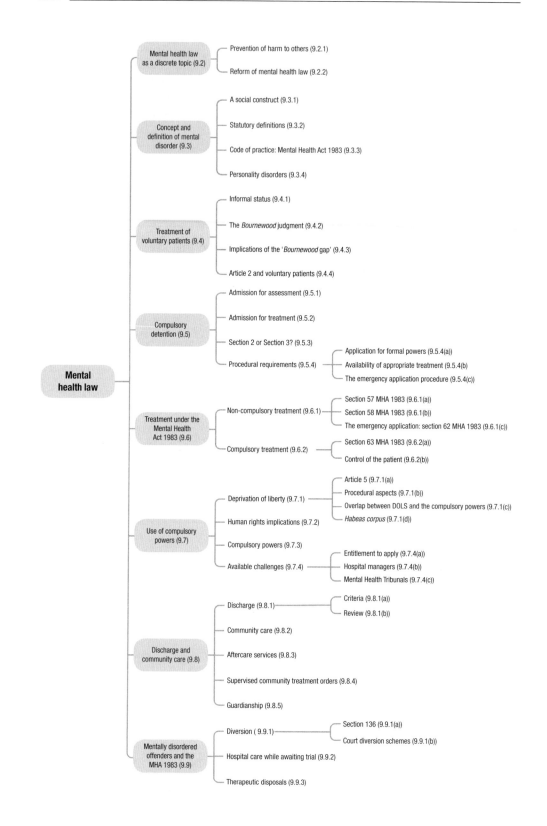

Key Terms

- ▶ **Compulsory detention** – a person with a mental health disorder detained under sections 2, 3 and 4 of the Mental Health Act 1983 for assessment and treatment.
- ▶ **Compulsory treatment** – can be given on statutory grounds even if there is refusal of consent.
- ▶ **Deprivation of liberty procedure** – provisions of the Mental Capacity Act 2005 that are intended to safeguard the rights of persons with mental disorder who lack capacity.
- ▶ **Diversion** – the process whereby certain offenders with mental disorders are identified and treated by the health and social services as opposed to being subject to the Criminal Justice System.
- ▶ **Enforced treatment** – compulsory treatment for mental health disorders justified by statutory powers.
- ▶ **Informal patient** – a person with a mental health disorder who does not resist hospital admission for treatment (also known as a voluntary patient).
- ▶ **Mandatory criteria for discharge** – provided by section 72 of the Mental Health Act 1983 with regard to detention under section 2 or section 3 of the Act.
- ▶ **Mental disorder** – any disorder or disability of the mind.
- ▶ **Mental health law** – the civil aspects that pertain to the detention and treatment of those with mental disorders.
- ▶ **Mental health tribunal** – a first-tier tribunal that has a role and remit through judicial process to oversee issues of detention and consider the discharge of patients with mental health disorders.
- ▶ **Non-compulsory treatment** – treatment that requires consent and a second opinion, or treatment that requires consent or a second opinion.
- ▶ **Supervised community treatment orders** – an initiative to ensure that patients with mental disorder receive supervised treatment in the community rather than in hospitals.
- ▶ **Treatment under the Mental Health Act 1983** – treatment pursuant to the provisions under sections 57, 58 and 63 of the Mental Health Act 1983.

Scenario

Jake, who is 35, has a history of bipolar disorder characterised by episodes of severe depression. His medical records state that he has a mental disorder and it is apparent that he has been receiving treatment for his condition for some time. On occasion Jake has been admitted to hospital for stabilisation although he is usually compliant and attends hospital when advised to do so.

The recent news of his mother's death has led to a rapid deterioration in his mental state and he self-admits for treatment. During his stay Jake remains unstable and becomes violent on one occasion. Following an altercation with a nurse over his treatment, Jake attempts to leave the ward. There is no doctor in the hospital, so a member of the nursing team temporarily restrains Jake even though it is felt that he has decision-making capacity.

The general practitioner attends within the hour and a decision is made to detain Jake to enable treatment to be given. The consensus is that Jake ought to receive electroconvulsive therapy (ECT). Jake refuses ECT in the belief that he will lose his memory. Despite his objections Jake is forcibly restrained and given ECT. Because of his behaviour, Jake is placed in seclusion.

Although there is an initial improvement in Jake's condition, further treatment, such as intense psychotherapy for a dissociated personality disorder, is considered necessary. He is unhappy about his continued detention and asks to see his solicitor.

Jake's solicitor considers that his client's case should be put before a tribunal as soon as possible and an application is made. Jake's case is heard in eight weeks. The tribunal orders his discharge, with care in the community. This, however takes a further four weeks before it can be implemented.

Following discharge Jake remains reasonably well, although his condition tends to deteriorate especially after meeting up with friends who have 'bad habits'. His doctor feels that he ought to be readmitted to prevent contact with these individuals.

9.1 Introduction

This chapter examines mental health law principally in respect of the civil aspects of detention and treatment for mental disorders. The potential defences against liability for offences, on grounds of mental disorder, such as unfitness to plead, insanity, automatism and diminished responsibility will not be considered. The overlap between civil aspects and criminal disposal options for those with mental disorders is considered against the backdrop of the Mental Health Act 1983 (MHA 1983).

9.2 Mental health law as a discrete topic

The consent of a competent adult is a necessary prerequisite for health care and treatment. Those who lack decision-making capacity can lawfully be given treatment in their 'best interests' subject to the Mental Capacity Act 2005. The mental health legislation provides for individuals with mental disorder of a sufficient degree. Those with mental disorder, who also lack capacity, could be subject to both statutory frameworks.

Mental health law is distinct from other areas of medical law since it permits the detention and compulsory treatment of those suffering from mental disorders who may, or may not, have decision-making capacity. For this reason, patients detained under the MHA 1983 are in a unique situation compared to other patients. First, they may not have agreed to be admitted to hospital. Second, they may be in good physical health and third, they may not be in a position to self-discharge from care. As a result, involuntary detention and treatment has the potential to be challenged under the European Convention of Human Rights, most notably Article 5 which provides that:

(1) Everyone has the right to liberty and security of person. No one should be deprived of his liberty save in the following cases and in accordance with a procedure described by law:...

(e) the lawful detention of persons for the prevention of the spreading of infectious diseases, of persons of unsound mind, alcoholics or drug addicts or vagrants.

Although mental disorders are not specifically mentioned in Article 5, the phrase 'unsound mind' has been interpreted to extend to those with mental disorders and human rights challenges have been brought.

The involuntary detention of those with mental disorders is perceived to be necessary to permit treatment to be given. Even if the individual is competent, detention and treatment without consent might be necessary to protect them against self-harm, or for the protection of others.

9.2.1 Prevention of harm to others

The belief that patients with mental disorders have to be detained against their will has been criticised by academic commentators, as succinctly summarised in the report of the Royal College of Psychiatrists (2004). Amongst the statistics quoted, the College states that for each citizen killed by a mentally ill person, 10 are killed by corporate manslaughter, 20 by others who are not mentally ill, 25 by passive smoking and 125 by NHS hospital acquired infections. With regard to homicide it appears that between 2000 and 5000 people would need to be detained in order to prevent a single murder. According to the College, the mental health legislation is unlikely to have any significant effect on homicide or suicide rates and that the starting point for risk-reduction strategies is to ensure that patients are able to access adequate psychiatric and counselling services.

Further empirical evidence in support of these findings comes from the MacArthur Project in the United States (Monahan *et al.*, 2001). This was a prospective study that involved 939 people who were divided into five risk categories and their behaviour was monitored over a year. Sixty-three persons were designated to the high-risk category, 48 of whom demonstrated violence during the follow-up period. In total, 176 individuals in the study committed violent acts. The conclusions were that of the high-risk group, approximately one in four did not commit any violent offence. This means that on a risk-stratification basis, one-quarter of detainees from the high-risk group were detained unnecessarily. Furthermore, of the total number of violent offenders, the majority (128 out of 176) were from lower-risk categories, and predictors of violent behaviour, especially in lower-risk categories, were not at all reliable. The study concluded that detention of those with mental health problems is an unsophisticated and potentially inadequate means of preventing future violent acts and is not necessarily the best way of preventing harm to others. Notwithstanding these findings, there is a persistent public perception that mentally ill patients, particularly those who have already committed violent acts, are likely to offend.

9.2.2 Reform of mental health law

Recent years have witnessed a sustained impetus for change to mental health law, driven primarily by human rights jurisprudence and challenges brought under

Article 5 of the European Convention, particularly in respect of the deprivation of liberty of the mentally ill. Since implementation of the Human Rights Act 1998 in October 2000, any primary legislation that is inconsistent with the Convention may receive a declaration of incapability (section 4 of the Human Rights Act 1998). In *R (on the application of H) v Mental Health Review Tribunal, North and East London Region* [2001] EWCA Civ. 415 an application for incapability was made in relation to sections 72 and 73 of the MHA 1983. By means of a fast-track procedure for preventing legislation that is incompatible with the Convention, ministers are empowered to make a remedial order by way of statutory instrument (section 10 of the MHA1983). The error in the instant case was rectified by a remedial order (Mental Health Act 1983 (Remedial) Order 2001 SI 2001 No. 3712) and operated to reverse the burden of proof at tribunal, in that the grounds for continued detention, as decided by a tribunal, mirror those requirements for the first point of detention. Evidence that the grounds have been met will rest with the detaining authority. The further impact of human rights on mental health law is considered below.

A significant driver for change has been the shift in societal attitudes towards the incarceration of those considered to be mentally ill. The end of the nineteenth and early part of the twentieth century saw a massive increase in the number of institutionalised mentally ill persons, as evidenced by the plethora of gothic-style hospitals built specifically for these purposes (many of which have since been redeveloped for other uses). The second half of the twentieth century witnessed a dramatic shift towards deinstitutionalisation and care in the community. Keown *et al.* (2008) has shown the sharp reduction in psychiatric hospitals and an increasing number of patients being admitted to psychiatric wards in general hospitals. Nowadays there is clear recognition that the mentally ill must be protected from abuse and neglect with enhanced protection of the socioeconomic needs of those cared for in the community with improved access to necessary support services being an urgent objective (Stavert, 2007). In line with societal and parliamentary recognition, several reforms have been made to this area. The Mental Capacity Act 2005 has established a new Court of Protection with jurisdiction over the affairs (health, welfare and financial) of patients who lack capacity, including those who are mentally ill.

The Mental Health Act 2007 was brought into force incrementally, with key features coming into effect in November 2008. These reforms introduced significant change to the MHA 1983 and the Mental Capacity Act 2005. The Mental Health Act 1983 Code of Practice provides guidance on the application and interpretation of the mental health legislation and while there is no absolute duty to comply with the Code, all those who work with the Act must have regard to the guidance and departure may give rise to legal challenge. The Code of Practice came into effect in November 2008.

9.3 Concept and definition of mental disorder

Diagnosis of physical illness typically depends upon the existence of a set of symptoms and clinical signs that corroborate positive investigations such as blood tests, imaging (x-rays, scans) or tissue diagnosis following biopsy. Mental illness is often distinct in that investigations are seldom of benefit since there is no definitive investigation, or test, to confirm the presence or absence of disorder. In certain circumstances the mental health legislation provides statutory justification for those with mental disorder to be detained for compulsory treatment. This has considerable implications for civil liberties and it is therefore crucial that a patent and circumscribed definition exists for mental disorder, and that an accurate diagnosis can be made.

9.3.1   A social construct

Commentators, such as Thomas Szasz, have denied the existence of mental disorder *per se* and regard illness as being wholly physical. This reflects his view that the classification of mental illness is a political mechanism used to control variation and deviations within the spectrum of human behaviour. According to Szasz (1984):

> The term 'mental illness' is a metaphor. More particularly, as this term is used in mental hygiene legislation, 'mental illness' is not the name of a medical disease or disorder, but is a quasi-medical label whose purpose is to conceal conflict as illness and to justify coercion as treatment. ... The expression 'mental illness' is a metaphor which we have come to mistake for a fact. We call people physically ill when their body-functioning violates certain anatomical and physiological norms; similarly, we call people mentally ill when their personal conduct violates certain ethical, political and social norms ...

According to this rationale, since there are no particular laws for those with physical illnesses, there should be no special laws for people with mental illness. In his view mental health law is essentially 'sanitising' legislation which attempts to fit behaviour into a narrow norm and as such ought to be repealed.

Bartlett (2003) considers that compulsory psychiatric treatment is essentially concerned with social control and those with mental illness 'tend to be admitted when their behaviour becomes socially unacceptable; and they are treated until it is no longer unacceptable. Alternatively, they are admitted when they are perceived to be unable to cope or function in society and treated until they can be discharged, able to do so'. In his view, psychiatrists function as agents of social control and the pertinent question concerns the extent to which this can be justified.

9.3.2   Statutory definitions

Section 1(2) of the MHA 1983 provides that for the purposes of the Act, 'mental disorder' means any disorder or disability of the mind; and 'mentally disordered' is construed accordingly. A mental disorder does not include a 'learning disability', although the rider in section 1(2A) qualifies that the learning disability exception is not classified as a mental disorder unless that disability is associated with abnormally aggressive or seriously irresponsible conduct. For these purposes, 'learning disability' means a state of arrested or incomplete development of the mind which includes significant impairment of intelligence and social functioning (section 1(4)). Section 1(3) provides that dependence on alcohol or drugs is not considered a disorder or disability of the mind for the purposes of section 1(2) although it is possible that drug or alcohol dependence may give rise to abnormally aggressive or seriously irresponsible conduct. Individuals who are dependent on alcohol and drugs would not be excluded from the scope of the Act, if they also suffer from a mental disorder, even if that disorder is related to their alcohol or drug use.

The section 1(2) definition of mental disorder is somewhat circular and is intended to ensure that the clinician's discretion to consider whether a patient should be treated under compulsory powers is not fettered, either in the presence or absence of any particular clinical condition or diagnostic label. The Code of Practice (paragraph 3.3) provides examples of conditions that could fall within the statutory definition. These include phobic anxiety disorders, neurotic and obsessive compulsive conditions, eating and post-traumatic stress disorders. The MHA definition is different to the MCA 2005 which describes a person as lacking capacity in relation to a matter if he is unable to make a decision because of 'an impairment of, or a disturbance in the *functioning* of, the mind or *brain*' (emphasis added). The definition in the MHA 1983 clearly excludes disorders of the brain which might be physical and excludes the element of functioning because persons with mental disorder may have capacity (but may still be in need of compulsory detention or treatment for their own safety or for that of others).

Section 1(3) of the MHA 1983 stipulates that persons may not be dealt with under the Act when suffering from a mental disorder by reason of promiscuity, other immoral conduct or sexual deviancy. The reforms introduced by the 2007 Act removed these exceptions. The rationale behind this amendment was the government's belief that this provisions might introduce obstacles against dealing with sex offenders with personality disorders (e.g. those at risk of reoffending or paedophiles). If sexual deviancy did not fall within the mental health legislation, this would prevent the necessary continued detention of such persons. It is unlikely that the terms 'promiscuity' and 'immoral conduct' would have any real relevance in this era, and it is also questionable as to whether the term 'sexual deviancy' is anachronistic and ought to be amended (if the intention is, as above, to keep those at high risk of reoffending for sexual offences within the ambit of the Act).

Jake has been diagnosed with bipolar disorder with severe depression:

▶ Does a diagnostic label necessarily mean that a person has a mental disorder for the purposes of the mental health legislation?
▶ What is mental disorder? How is this defined?

9.3.3 Code of Practice: Mental Health Act 1983

The Code of Practice sets out the principles by which decisions under the MHA 1983 are expected to be made (paragraphs 1.2–1.6). These are: the purpose principle; the restriction principle; the respect principle; the participation principle and the effectiveness, efficiency and equity principle. Satisfaction of the purpose principle requires decisions under the Act to be taken with a view to minimising the undesirable effects of mental disorders and maximising the safety, well-being and recovery of the patient. If action is to be taken without a person's consent, then every attempt must be made to minimise the restrictions applied to that person's liberty having regard to the purposes for which such restrictions are imposed. The respect principle requires that decisions under the Act recognise and respect the diverse needs, values and circumstances of each and every patient, including their race, religion, culture, gender, age, sexual orientation and disability. Wherever possible, the views, wishes and feelings of the patient should be engaged in decision-making and discrimination should be avoided. Patients must be given opportunities to participate in decision-making relative to their circumstances and include the involvement of carers, family members and others who are interested in the patient's welfare. Finally, decisions made under the Act must endeavour to use resources in the most efficient, effective and equitable way to meet the specific needs of patients and achieve the purpose for which the decision was taken.

9.3.4 Personality disorders

The MHA 1983 in its original form included four categories of mental disorder: mental illness; severe mental impairment; mental impairment and psychopathic disorder. The latter was arguably the most controversial classification and described a persistent disorder or disability of mind which resulted in abnormally aggressive or seriously irresponsible conduct. The term 'psychopathic disorder' was removed from the MHA 1983 (following amendment by the Mental Health Act 2007), a move recommended by the Butler Report over 35 years previously.

The Government White Paper 'Reforming the Mental Health Act', that preceded the Mental Health Act 2007, introduced the expression 'dangerous severe personality disorder' (DSPD). Prior to the reforms protection of the public was identified as a key priority of the Government and serious concerns were acknowledged that the existing mental health legislation was inadequate for providing patients with high-quality care and safeguarding the public. The need to satisfy the 'treatability test', that was a mandatory requirement for the compulsory admission to hospital, was almost impossible to satisfy and led to public outcry following the murders of Megan and Lin Russell by Michael Stone.

A key issue for those responsible for the care of persons with serious personality disorders is that the objective of detention is usually for the prevention of harm to others, rather than representing a therapeutic option for the patient. Some paedophiles fall into this category since the condition causes no harm to the offender but instead causes harm to the children who are abused. Paedophiles may be considered untreatable since the condition is a manifestation of their personality rather than an illness. One view is that treatment is necessary to eliminate their tendency to harm others. Despite concerns raised in 'Reforming the Mental Health Act' the draft Bill did not specifically provide for DSPD largely on account of professional objections that the emphasis on detention in the interests of public safety could seriously damage the reputation of psychiatrists.

The World Health Organisation's International Statistical Classification of Diseases and Related Health Problems (ICD–10) contains a definition of 'dissocial personality disorder' (WHO 2007). The *Diagnostic and Statistical Manual* (*DSM–4*) used by psychiatrists, physicians, social workers and psychologists sets out specific diagnostic criteria for the diagnosis of mental illness and antisocial personality disorders. Whether dangerous people with serious personality disorders ought to be classified as mentally ill, or else as recidivists, by the criminal justice is debatable. Psychiatrists have tended to object to categorisation of personality disordered individuals as mentally ill since if such an individual cannot be 'treated' for their condition, then hospital detention is inappropriate. The role of a doctor is to treat the patient rather than operate as a gaoler, but it seems likely that the interface between mental disorder and antisocial behaviour will persist.

The law has its own terminology for mental health issues and in certain circumstances is very different to that used in clinical psychiatry such as the American Psychiatric Association's *DSM–4* and the World Health Organisation's *ICD–10*. However, to some extent, clinical discretion for the purposes of compulsory treatment of mental disorders ought to be facilitated by the amended definition of mental disorder (section 1(2) of the MHA 1983), together with the guidance offered in the Code of Practice.

9.4 Treatment of voluntary patients

Persons with mental disorders may be treated as in-patients without recourse to the statutory powers of detention if they agree voluntarily to be admitted for psychiatric care. Such patients are known as 'voluntary' or 'informal' patients, as distinct from those admitted as involuntary patients in accordance with the mental health legislation. Voluntary admission is provided for in section 131 of the MHA 1983. Anyone who requires treatment for a mental disorder (as defined in section 1(2)) may be admitted informally as a voluntary patient.

9.4.1 Informal status

Pursuant to section 131(1) MHA 1983:

> Nothing in this Act shall be construed as preventing a patient who requires treatment for mental disorder from being admitted to any hospital or [registered establishment] in pursuance of arrangements made in that behalf and without any application, order or direction rendering him liable to be detained under this Act, or from remaining in any hospital or [registered establishment] in pursuance of such arrangements after he has ceased to be so liable to be detained.

The patient admitted in pursuance of section 131 is not subject to the detaining powers of the legislation and, in theory, has the right to leave hospital at any point in time.

Informal admission may arise on account of an individual's willingness to voluntarily seek psychiatric care and treatment. This represents the ideal situation but it is not representative of the reality of most informal admissions. Voluntary patients may agree to admission following coercion from others or they may be admitted on account of acquiescence and their inability to resist. Health-care professionals have been known to give ultimatums to patients: either agree to voluntary admission or be sectioned. Prior to implementation of the Mental Capacity Act 2005 the majority of patients who lacked decision-making capacity (and who did not resist) tended to be admitted and treated in hospital under the common law and without recourse to the compulsory detention procedures of the mental health legislation.

The advantages of informal status are that, in principle, admission and treatment is based upon the mutual agreement of the individual and hospital team. Such spirit of co-operation can be expected to be accompanied by additional advantages, such as the cooperative willingness of the individual to engage with a treatment plan. Perhaps more pragmatically, admission under section 131 avoids time-consuming and expensive procedures that are required for formal admission procedures. For patients, however, informal status deprives them of the range of protective mechanisms and safeguards that are triggered by compulsory admission, such as access to First-tier tribunals (Part 4 of the MHA 1983). To some extent this potential difficulty has been alleviated following the seminal case of HL v United Kingdom [2004] ECHR 45508/99, a decision that led to amendment of the Mental Capacity Act 2005. More fundamentally, voluntary patients may lack sufficient understanding to exercise their rights as informal patients, such as the ability to self-discharge. There is an argument that informal patients are the most vulnerable: as voluntary patients they are denied routine access to the legal safeguards, and yet they may be unable to leave of their own volition.

If voluntary patients wish to self-discharge in circumstances considered inappropriate for their own health and safety, or the safety of others, statutory holding powers can be invoked in certain situations in order to prevent them from leaving hospital. Section 5(4) of the MHA 1983 gives nurses a holding power that can be used once the patient is in hospital. The power can be exercised for up to six hours with no renewal provision, provided that no doctor is available to write a report and the patient appears to be suffering from mental disorder to such a degree that detention is necessary for her own health and safety, or for the protection of others. Section 5(2) of the MHA 1983 provides doctors with a 72-hour holding power to be exercised in circumstances where an informal patient receiving treatment is waiting to be formally detained under section 2 or 3 but the required documentation has yet to be completed. Holding powers are interim measures used for emergency situations to allow additional assessment and dialogue and to complete documentation. They usually precede compulsory detention.

> Jake has been admitted to a psychiatric hospital as a voluntary patient:
>
> ▶ What are the advantages and disadvantages to Jake from being an informal patient?
> ▶ What are the potential advantages and disadvantages of informal status for his carers?

9.4.2 The *Bournewood* judgment

The plight of informal patients and their lack of statutory safeguards compared with the rights of those formally detained arose in *R v Bournewood Community and Mental Health NHS Trust, ex p L* [1998] 3 WLR 107. L was a patient with autism and profound learning disabilities. On a visit to a day centre, he became agitated and was admitted to hospital on an informal basis under section 131 of the MHA 1983. His carers of several years objected to his admission but were denied access on the grounds that L might attempt to leave. The NHS Trust admitted in evidence that if L had attempted to leave he would have been compulsorily detained. The carers appealed against the legality of L's admission and detention in hospital. The Court of Appeal held that the detention had been unlawful, a decision subsequently appealed by the Trust.

The House of Lords considered two central questions: (i) in what circumstances would a person who lacked capacity be considered to be detained in law, and (ii) in what circumstances should a person who lacks capacity be detained under the MHA 1983 as opposed to the common law. The House found that the applicant's initial sedation and admission had been justified on the doctrine of necessity and had been in L's best interests. Since he had been kept in an unlocked ward, his informal admission did not amount to a 'detention.' The European Court of Human Rights (ECHR) (*HL v United Kingdom* [application no. 45508/99] 05.10.2004) was critical of the common law authority that allowed health-care professionals to fully control the liberty and treatment of vulnerable, incapacitated individuals solely on the basis of a clinical assessment. In giving judgment, the court stated that individuals cannot be deprived of their liberty on the basis of unsoundness of mind unless three minimum conditions could be satisfied:

(i) they must be reliably shown to be individuals of unsound mind;
(ii) the mental disorder must be of a kind that warrants compulsory confinement;
(iii) the validity of continued confinement depends upon the persistence of such a disorder.

The ECtHR found a striking lack of fixed procedural rules by which admission and detention of compliant incapacitated persons were conducted, in sharp contrast with the extensive range of safeguards that applied to psychiatric committals under the MHA 1983. The court did not question the good faith of professionals who acted in what they considered to be in HL's best interests. Nonetheless, procedural safeguards were necessary to protect health-care professionals against possible misjudgements and professional lapses.

9.4.3 Implications of the 'Bournewood gap'

In its determination, the ECtHR considered that the lack of procedural safeguards failed to adequately protect voluntary patients against arbitrary deprivations of liberty and failed to comply with the essential purpose of Article 5(1) of the European Convention. This lacuna of statutory safeguards, recognised by Lord Steyn in the House of Lords, has come to be known as the 'Bournewood gap', representing the lack of due process for challenging the detention of compliant incapacitated patients. As a consequence of Bournewood section 50 of the Mental Health Act 2007 Act inserts new sections 4A, 4B and 16A into the Mental Capacity Act 2005. These amendments permit the lawful deprivation of liberty of an individual in a hospital, or care home, in circumstances where a standard or urgent authorisation is in force, or if deprivation of liberty is a consequence of giving effect to an order of the Court of Protection on a matter of personal welfare. Detention must be in the person's best interests and should represent a proportionate response to the seriousness and likelihood of harm being suffered by that individual. The deprivation of liberty provisions apply to those aged 18 or over who lack capacity to consent to treatment and where it is considered necessary to administer treatment for their mental disorder.

> During Jake's voluntary admission he remains unstable and is prevented from leaving the ward:
>
> ▶ Consider the potential ethical and legal issues that arise.

9.4.4 Article 2 and voluntary patients

The Deprivation of Liberty Safeguards Code of Practice (which supplements the Mental Capacity Act 2005: Code of Practice) came into force in April 2009 and is intended to protect the interests of extremely vulnerable persons. The guidance aims to ensure that individuals can be provided with the care that they need while preventing arbitrary decisions that can deprive vulnerable people of their liberty. The safeguards are intended to provide rights of challenge against unlawful detention, and to avoid unnecessary bureaucracy.

The case of *Rabone v Pennine Care NHS Trust* [2010] EWCA 698 concerned a depressed patient who agreed to be admitted to hospital following two suicide attempts. She was considered to be a moderate to high suicide risk and was subject to 15 minute observation during her stay. A few days after admission, a doctor allowed the patient to return home despite serious concerns being raised by her parents. The patient committed suicide the following day. The Court of Appeal found that the obligation to protect life under Article 2 of the European Convention did not automatically engage for voluntary patients with mental disorder.

9.5 Compulsory detention

The principal grounds for compulsory detention in hospital are contained in section 2 (admission for assessment) and section 3 (admission for treatment) of the MHA 1983. The necessary procedural requirements are also provided for by the legislation. The tension between 'legalisation' and 'medicalisation' of the compulsory detention of mentally disordered persons continues to be at the forefront of ongoing debate. Civil libertarians remain concerned that patients may have their liberty sacrificed too easily on the basis of formal detention. There is also a power under section 135 of the Act to apply to a Magistrates Court for a warrant to search for, and remove, patients where there is reasonable cause to believe that they suffer from a mental disorder and are, or have been, ill-treated, neglected or are unable to take proper care of themselves. The warrant allows a constable to attend (accompanied by an approved a mental health professional and a doctor), to enter the property and remove the individual to a place of safety.

9.5.1 Admission for assessment

The purpose of section 2 is to permit the detention of a person in a psychiatric hospital for up to 28 days for the purposes of carrying out a detailed assessment. It is non-renewable. The grounds for admission are that:

(a) the patient is suffering from mental disorder of a nature or degree that warrants detention in a hospital for assessment (or for assessment followed by medical treatment) for at least a limited period; and

(b) the patient ought to be detained in the interests of his or her own safety or with a view to the protection of others.

The procedure for admission requires a formal application to be made to the hospital managers on the written recommendation of an 'approved mental health professional' (AMHP). The patient's 'nearest relative' may make the application, although this is rare and is discouraged by the Code of Practice. If the applicant is an AMHP, then the patient's nearest relative is informed either before or within a reasonable time of making the application. The nearest relative is also informed of the power to discharge the patient (section 23(2)(a) of the MHA 1983). The applicant must have seen the patient within the previous 14 days and the application is certified by two registered medical practitioners each of whom must have examined the patient within the previous 14 days. One of the doctors must be an 'approved doctor' with recognised expertise in mental disorder such as a psychiatrist (section 12 of the MHA 1983). The other doctor will often, but not necessarily, be the patient's general practitioner.

After the end of the 28-day-assessment period the patient must be discharged. Alternatively, the patient can be admitted for treatment (section 3 of the MHA 1983) or remain in hospital as a voluntary patient (section 131). Discharge can be effected by the responsible clinician, the hospital managers or the nearest relative. Section 25 of the MHA 1983 provides the route that needs to be followed by the nearest relative. However, discharge by the nearest relative may be blocked by the hospital managers if the responsible clinician certifies that the patient needs to remain in hospital. Patients admitted under section 2 retain the right to appeal to a First-tier tribunal against their continued detention, although the appeal has to be submitted within the first

14 days of detention (otherwise the right is lost). The tribunal has power to remove the section 2 detention, and hearings are often set up in 7 working days of the appeal being lodged.

The position of patients detained under section 2 and who lack capacity was examined in *R (MH) v Secretary of State for Health* [2005] UKHL 60. The patient, who was admitted for assessment in accordance with section 2, lacked capacity to apply for a tribunal hearing and her detention was extended beyond the 28-day period. The central issue was whether failure to refer a section 2 detention and extend it to beyond the specified period to a tribunal or other court in order to review the merits of detention was incompatible with Article 5 of the European Convention. Although the Court of Appeal found that the statutory provisions was incompatible with Article 5, the House of Lords allowed the Secretary of State's appeal that Article 5(4) required every *sensible* (emphasis added) effort be made to allow such patients access to a tribunal. Although the argument that the right to access a tribunal was illusory for those who lacked the ability to apply, this did not mean that section 2 was incompatible with Article 5. The absence of an automatic referral policy did not represent a breach of a Convention right.

It is apparent that the requirements for section 2 admissions for assessment are less stringent than those required for section 3 admissions. Little statutory guidance is provided on the substantive criteria for admission apart from the requirement that the patient must be suffering from a mental disorder. The mental disorder must be sufficiently severe to warrant detention but no direction is given on the assessment of 'severe'. According to Bartlett (2003) the lack of statutory guidance on the criteria for admission under section 2 in the context of chronic underfunding of psychiatric services introduces standards based upon clinical, rather than legal, norms and represents an indirect form of rationing.

9.5.2 Admission for treatment

The statutory justification for admission to a psychiatric hospital for treatment is provided for in section 3 of the MHA 1983. The duration of detention is six months with possible renewal for a further six months after which annual review cycles come into effect. The grounds for admission for treatment are:

(i) the person is suffering from mental disorder of a nature or degree which makes it appropriate for that person to receive treatment in a hospital; and

(ii) it is necessary for the health and safety of the individual, or for the protection of others, that treatment ought to be given, and it cannot be provided unless he is detained under section 3; and

(iii) appropriate medical treatment is available to the patient.

Section 3(4) was added by the 2007 MHA Act and states that 'appropriate medical treatment' refers to medical treatment which is appropriate to the patient's case, taking into account the nature and degree of the mental disorder and all other circumstances of the situation. The procedural aspects of detention are broadly in line with those for a section 2 admission. The nearest relative is consulted prior to a section 3 admission for treatment, where practicable, and that person has power to veto the decision to admit. However, the nearest relative can be replaced by an 'acting' nearest relative in the event that the nearest relative unreasonably objects to an application for treatment being made (section 29).

Section 3 provides for *parens patriae* and police power admissions. The power of the police and the *parens patriae* jurisdiction of the court is founded on a paternalistic approach to the protection of society and the patient's best interests. Nonetheless, predicting the likelihood of harm, either to the patient or to others, is challenging and there is an argument that there is no proper basis for the detention of persons solely on the basis of the perceived risk to others, since this is principally the role of the Criminal Justice System. A balance needs to be struck between the need to detain in an endeavour to improve or arrest the deterioration of a person's mental health against the need to protect the interests and safety of others. Some commentators believe that detention is justified only in the event of imminent and serious harm to the public.

The compulsory powers of detention may also interface with the Article 2 right to life. In *Savage v South Essex NHS Trust* [2008] UKHL 74 a patient with paranoid schizophrenia was admitted for treatment under section 3 of the MHA 1983, during which she absconded and committed suicide. The deceased's daughter claimed breach of her mother's right to life under Article 2. The Court of Appeal recognised that a duty to take positive steps to prevent a patient with a mental disorder from committing suicide provided that the authorities knew, or ought to have known, that there was a real and immediate risk of suicide. The House of Lords dismissed the appeal and held that the Trust owed a positive 'operational obligation' to protect life under Article 2 towards detained patients with suicidal tendencies.

9.5.3 Section 2 or section 3?

In health-care situations, there might be doubt as to whether an individual ought to be admitted in accordance under section 2 or section 3 of the MHA 1983. Reference is made to this dilemma in chapter 5 of the Code of Practice. The following are considered relevant factors in favour of a section 2 application (which authorises a shorter period of detention) as against a section 3 admission:

- The diagnosis or prognosis of the person's condition is unclear.
- There is a need to carry out an in-patient assessment in order to formulate a treatment plan.
- Judgment is required as to whether the patient will accept treatment on a voluntary basis.
- A decision has to be made as to whether a particular treatment plan, which can only be administered to a patient under Part 4 of the Act, is likely to be effective. The patient, who has already been assessed and detained under the legislation, is considered to have changed since the previous admission and therefore requires further assessment.
- The patient has not previously been admitted to hospital either by compulsion or as an informal patient.

In some situations, a proposed treatment to be administered under the Act may last for less than 28 days. Furthermore, the nearest relative may block an application under section 3 but not under section 2, and a patient detained under section 2 will have quicker access to a First-tier tribunal than a person detained under section 3. These factors, however, should not influence using section 2 in preference to a section 3 application.

9.5.4 Procedural requirements

Some of the procedural issues around compulsory detention under sections 2 and 3 have already been considered. The compulsory detention of individuals represents a fundamental violation of their liberty. Detention must therefore be justified on the basis of clear and defensible criteria, a situation that requires a careful balance between preventing an individual from self-harm and ensuring that treatment can be given, alongside protection of society and the prevention of harm to others.

9.5.4(a) Application for formal powers

Submissions for formal powers of detention under sections 2 and 3 are broadly the same and most applications are brought by the AMHP. The category 'AMHP' was previously the 'Approved Social Worker' but now includes other professionals such as psychologists, occupational therapists, mental health nurses and learning disability nurses. Section 2 of the MHA 1983 requires that the person suffers from a mental disorder of 'a nature or degree that warrants the detention ... for assessment' and under section 3 'which makes it appropriate for him to receive medical treatment in a hospital'. Although both provisions have therapeutic intent, the net cast by section 2 is wider and includes circumstances where an individual 'ought to be so detained in the interests of his own health or safety or with a view to the protection of others'. The scope of section 3 is narrower and states that detention must be '*necessary* (emphasis added) for the health or safety of the patient or for the protection of others'. The section 3 criteria are more stringent than section 2 which is arguably counterbalanced by the shorter period of non-renewable detention of section 2 compared to that of section 3.

Section 11 gives general provisions of application procedures and section 11(4) requires the AMHP to consult with the nearest relative except where consultation is not reasonably practicable or would involve an unreasonable delay. The AMHP may not make a section 3 application where the nearest relative objects to the application being made. Section 26 provides a statutory hierarchy of persons entitled to act as the nearest relative, and the Act gives equal status to homosexual and heterosexual couples. The patient may be discharged by the nearest relative (as well as the registered medical practitioner or hospital manager) but the relative's discharge can be blocked under section 25 of the Act which would consequently lead to a mental health review tribunal hearing. An application for a MHT hearing as well as a hospital manager's meeting can be made at the same time. The timescale for the hospital manager's meeting would normally be fixed within two weeks, which is sooner than that of the MHT.

The compulsory detention of a person in hospital inevitably infringes that person's civil liberties. It is questionable whether formal admission is required solely on the grounds that the patient will not accept treatment in the community (where she is located) as opposed to the need arising on the basis that treatment can be provided only in hospital. Consequently, in some jurisdictions of the United States procedural due process requires a formal hearing by a fair and independent body, which has the hallmarks of an adversarial process and the Criminal Justice System. The advantage of such a process is enhanced protection of civil liberties although this can create barriers to speedy access for assessment, or treatment, of a person's mental health disorder.

9.5.4(b) Availability of appropriate treatment

A major reform of the MHA 1983 (introduced by the MHA 2007) relates to the 'treatability' requirement. The previous law included specific provisions for patients with personality disorders (described as psychopaths) and detention was possible only if treatment was available that was 'likely to alleviate or prevent a deterioration of his condition'. This statutory requirement was problematic for the person diagnosed with an 'untreatable' personality disorder since by definition that person could not be treated, and therefore did not meet the legislative criteria. In order to detain persons with DSPD the treatability requirement had to be revisited as part of the statutory reform.

Much publicity of the treatability requirement followed Michael Stone's horrific murders of Lin Russell and her daughter, Megan. The Chair of the Inquiry, Robert Francis QC, published a reflection entitled 'The Michael Stone Inquiry – a reflection' (2007) which found no evidence to substantiate the assertion that Stone had been denied treatment on the basis that his disorder was untreatable. According to Francis, the perceived difficulty in relation to dangerous personality disordered individuals who had not been convicted of an offence was an artificial construct. In his opinion, 'assenting powers and obligations under the Criminal Justice Act 2003 provide a more fruitful means of reassuring the public' since indefinite detention can be imposed (although only for those individuals previously convicted of an offence). However, in practice it seems unlikely to present a difficulty since it is unlikely that there are many persons known to the statutory agencies that are so dangerous and yet have not yet been convicted of any serious offence. Mr Stone certainly had more than one conviction.

The test for treatability is no longer one that is 'likely to alleviate or prevent a deterioration of his condition' which in effect required clinical prediction of whether treatment would be effective for a particular individual. The 'treatability test' has been replaced with 'availability of appropriate treatment' which requires only that treatment is available irrespective of whether the individual accepts it. References to appropriate medical treatment for a person suffering from a mental disorder are to 'medical treatment which is appropriate in his case, taking into account the nature and degree of the mental disorder and all other circumstances of his case' (section 3(4) of the MHA 1983). The test of availability extends to remands to hospital for treatment (section 36) and renewals of civil detention (section 20).

Section 145(1) of the MHA 1983 states that medical treatment includes nursing, psychological intervention and specialist mental health habilitation, rehabilitation and care, most of which require the co-operation of the patient and are typically used for those with personality disorders. Section 145(4) clarifies that 'Any reference to medical treatment, in relation to mental disorder, shall be construed as a reference to medical treatment the *purpose* (emphasis added) of which is to alleviate, or prevent a worsening of, the disorder or one or more of its symptoms or manifestations.' The key difference between the definitions is the new inclusion of the word 'purpose' compared with the previous word 'likely'. The Code of Practice (paragraph 6.4) notes that 'purpose' is not the same as 'likelihood'. Medical purpose may be aimed at the alleviation or prevention of deterioration of a mental disorder even though it cannot be predicted whether any particular effect is likely to be achieved by that intervention.

Jake's general practitioner attends the hospital within the hour and a decision is made to detain Jake to enable treatment to be given:

▶ What formal procedures have to be followed for Jake to be detained in hospital?
▶ What are the available safeguards for Jake?

9.5.4(c) The emergency application procedure

Section 4 of the MHA 1983 provides for admission to hospital for assessment in cases of emergency. This is known as the emergency application and is resorted to only in circumstances of urgent need rather than convenience. The application of an AMHP or nearest relative requires the recommendation of a single doctor and detention is authorised up to 72 hours. The criteria are analogous to those of section 2 in circumstances of urgent necessity but where a section 2 application would involve an undesirable delay.

The emergency admission procedure can be used for the purpose of assessment. Treatment may not be given following a competent patient's refusal to consent during this period. However, a section 4 admission may be used as a pathway to a section 2 admission. Under section 4, discharge is required at the end of the 72-hour period or alternatively an individual may remain in hospital as an informal patient, or, depending upon the assessment, a section 3 admission may be invoked.

An inherent danger of the section 4 provisions is the potential for abuse as an easy route to a hospital admission, following which continued detention can be facilitated. However, it appears that admissions under section 4 have declined and a possible explanation for this is the development of more robust community-based care structure.

9.6 Treatment under the Mental Health Act 1983

A general principle of common law is that an adult with capacity has the right to refuse medical treatment for any reason whatsoever. Competent patients, including those admitted under the Mental Health Act, can consent to treatment. Treatment decisions for those who lack decision-making capacity are made in accordance with their best interests in compliance with the Mental Capacity Act 2005. The position for incompetent persons admitted under the mental health legislation is different in that the aim of treatment is to improve the mental health and safety of the patient and general public. Part 4 of the MHA 1983 pertains to consent for treatment and provides the circumstances where patients admitted to hospital with mental disorders can be given treatment without their consent even if the patient actively refuses (section 63 of the MHA 1983).

The MHA 1983 provides statutory justification for two types of treatment: non-compulsory and compulsory. The 'non-compulsory' treatments are subject to statutory safeguards such as the consent of the competent patient, and formal second opinion procedures. The provisions for compulsory treatment are such that these can be commenced even where there is a competent refusal on the part of the patient.

9.6.1 Non-compulsory treatment

Non-compulsory treatment requires the patient's consent *and* a second opinion or, alternatively, consent *or* a second opinion. The competent patient who is detained consents to treatment under the common law. The MHA 1983 provides that certain forms of treatment for mental disorder are subject to special safeguards, such as neurosurgery for mental disorder, hormone therapy, electroconvulsive therapy and the administration of medication.

Non-compulsory forms of treatment mean that the competent patient with a mental disorder has power to refuse such treatment in accordance with sections 57 and 58. These sections are distinguished from section 63 (see 9.6.2(a)) which permits compulsory administration of treatment in certain circumstances even to the competent patient who objects. Although the powers in sections 57 and 58 are referred to as non-compulsory powers, a competent refusal is effective only for treatment under section 57. The patient being treated in accordance with section 58 may make a competent refusal, although this can be overridden if the treatment is deemed 'appropriate' (see 9.6.1(b)).

9.6.1(a) Section 57 MHA 1983

Section 57 of the MHA 1983 pertains to neurosurgery or the surgical implantation of sex hormones and requires the consent of the patient and the agreement of a doctor appointed to give a second opinion. The doctor must consult two others who have been involved in the patient's care, one of whom should be a nurse. Neurosurgery is rare and during the period between 2005 and 2007, the Mental Health Act Commission (the regulatory body that preceded the Care Quality Commission) reported receiving seven applications of which five were approved. Section 57 also provides justification for implantation of hormones designed to control the male sex drive and, once again, is highly unusual in modern clinical practice. The test of capacity for section 57 is whether the patient is capable of understanding the nature, purpose and potential effects of treatment. Hormonal treatment can be given under compulsory powers of detention and is usually administered as hormone analogues, tablets or by injection. If treatment needs to be continued beyond three months, it is usually implemented using powers under section 58.

9.6.1(b) Section 58 MHA 1983

Section 58 essentially pertains to administration of medication for mental disorder that requires the patient's consent or a second opinion. Medicines may continue to be given for longer than 12 weeks to a competent patient who objects. Compliance with the section requires the patient's consent *or* a second opinion. Section 58 is usually used for the administration of psychiatric medicines for periods beyond three months. Section 58(3)(a) states that subject to section 62 (see 9.6.1(c)) the patient should have consented 'to that treatment and either the approved clinician in charge of it or a registered medical practitioner appointed for the purposes of this Part of this Act by the regulatory authority has certified in writing that the patient is capable of understanding its nature, purpose and likely effects and has consented to it'.

Alternatively, section 58(3)(b) permits treatment on the grounds that 'a registered medical practitioner appointed as aforesaid (not being the responsible clinician or the approved clinician in charge of the treatment in question) has certified in writing that the patient is not capable of understanding the nature, purpose and likely effects of that treatment, or being so capable has not consented to it but that it is appropriate for the treatment to be given'.

Under section 58 the registered medical practitioner must consult two others who have been professionally involved with the patient's medical treatment. One of these persons must 'be a nurse and the other neither a nurse nor a registered medical practitioner, and neither shall be the responsible clinician or the approved clinician in charge of the treatment in question' (section 58(4)(a)(b)). The consultation requirement provides a statutory safeguard to protect detained persons in a vulnerable position. Provided that these provisions have been complied with, medication can be given even if the competent patient objects to such treatment.

Section 58 decisions could be open to challenge under human rights law. In *R (on the application of Wooder) v Feggetter* [2002] EWCA Civ. 554 the Court of Appeal held that in the context of the Human Rights Act 1998, and in fairness to the patient, a second opinion doctor who sanctioned the provision of such treatment would be violating the autonomy of a competent adult patient. It was held that the second opinion doctor should therefore give written reasons for the opinion when certifying that a patient ought to be compelled to receive treatment under section 58. These reasons should be disclosed to the patient unless this was likely to cause serious harm to the physical or mental health of the patient, or any other person.

For the patient who lacks capacity, treatment can be administered (for periods longer than three months) as long as the statutory safeguards are met and that such treatment is considered to be appropriate. The section 58 standard is lower than the 'best interests' standard of the Mental Capacity Act 2005 that is used when treating patients who lack capacity and where there is no need to invoke the MHA 1983.

Electroconvulsive therapy (ECT) cannot be given to a competent patient who refuses treatment (section 58A). If the patient consents, and is over the age of 18, this must be certified by the registered medical practitioner after consultation with two others who have been professionally involved in the care of the patient, one of whom is a nurse and the other neither a nurse nor registered medical practitioner. ECT cannot be administered contrary to an advance refusal of treatment or against the direction of a donee of a Lasting Power of Attorney, although ECT treatment can be given in an emergency (section 62 of the MHA 1983).

The Code of Practice recognises that many of those who are alleged to have given consent to treatment may not in fact have done so, either due to lack of informed consent or due to unrecognised lack of mental capacity. The issue of capacity to consent was considered in *R (on the application of B) v S and others* [2006] EWCA Civ 28. The patient with bipolar disorder had been detained under the MHA 1983 and had the capacity to consent to treatment. It was held that the fact that a patient was competent and refused treatment was a factor to be taken into account by the registered medical practitioner and others professionally involved in the patient's care, but it was not determinative as a bar to treatment. Treatment that was a medical or therapeutic necessity could be provided and it was not necessary to show that treatment was necessary for the protection of the patient or public.

The applicant's case was that section 58 was incompatible with Articles 3 and 8 of the European Convention. Section 58 provided justification for the compulsory treatment of patients with capacity who actively objected without specifying precisely the circumstances whereby a competent refusal could be overridden. These circumstances included where treatment was necessary to protect the public from serious harm or where failure to treat would result in serious harm to the patient's health. The patient refused to acknowledge his mental disorder and there was a divergence of psychiatric opinion as to whether the patient had decision-making capacity. The Court of Appeal found that the trial judge had been correct to conclude that capacity was not the critical factor in determining whether treatment could be administered without consent (where it was for medical or therapeutic necessity). It was held that the 1983 Act provided for an integral package of detention and treatment with restrictions designed to ensure that treatment of the individual was justified. The objective of detention in a mental health hospital is rehabilitation of the patient. This militated against the suggested threshold approach that treatment without consent could only be justified if treatment was necessary to prevent the patient causing serious harm to others, or to protect the patient from serious harm. The judge had been correct to find that the proposed treatment was in the patient's best interests and was a medical necessity. The imposition of treatment was in accordance with the law and did not infringe the patient's Convention rights. In situations where detention is disputed, the mental health tribunal is the appropriate arena for adjudication.

Jake is given ECT despite his objections:

▶ What statutory category of treatment applies?
▶ What are the requirements for treatment under section 58A?
▶ To what extent can use of restraint and force be used if required?

9.6.1(c) The emergency application: section 62 MHA 1983

Section 62 provides for urgent treatment in that sections 57 and 58 do not need to be satisfied before any treatment is given:

a) which is immediately necessary to save the patient's life; or
b) which (not being irreversible) is immediately necessary to prevent a serious deterioration of his condition; or
c) which (not being irreversible or hazardous) is immediately necessary to alleviate serious suffering by the patient or
d) which (not being irreversible or hazardous) is immediately necessary and represents the minimum interference necessary to prevent the patient from behaving violently or being a danger to himself or to others.

In effect, the section 62 provisions mean that all treatments covered by sections 57 and 58 can be provided (in an emergency) without a second opinion, or the patient's consent. Section 62(1A) provides that ECT can be given without consent where it is necessary to save life, or prevent a serious deterioration in the health of the patient.

The MHA 1983 includes special safeguards for patients receiving treatments such as neurosurgery, surgical implantation of hormones, ECT and long-term administration of medication. It is, however, noteworthy that certain forms of invasive therapy such as force feeding and seclusion have not been included as worthy of enhanced protection.

9.6.2 Compulsory treatment

It is central tenet of law that medical treatment must be preceded by valid consent unless an exemption applies under the MHA 1983, the MCA 2005 or the common law. In the absence of justification, an action could be brought in battery or negligence. Many patients to whom Part 4 of the MHA 1983 applies will consent to treatment, and in these circumstances recourse to the compulsory powers is unnecessary.

9.6.2(a) Section 63 MHA 1983

Section 63 of the MHA 1983 states: 'The consent of a patient shall not be required for any medical treatment given to him for the mental disorder from which he is suffering, not being a form of treatment to which sections 57, 58 or 58A above applies, if the treatment is given by, or under the direction of, the approved clinician in charge of the treatment.' In effect, treatment can be given to a patient to whom Part 4 of the Act applies, even if that patient is competent and actively objects. The powers of this section are wide. An important distinction between section 63 and the non-compulsory powers of treatment (sections 57, 58 and 58A) is that section 63 does not require an independent second opinion.

The practitioner in charge of the patient's care and treatment under the MHA 1983 is termed the 'approved clinician', who could be a doctor, social worker, psychologist, occupational therapist, mental health nurse or learning disability nurse. The revised definition of 'medical treatment' under the 1983 Act includes nursing, psychological intervention, specialist mental health rehabilitation and care (section 145 of the MHA 1983).

Compulsory treatment may be required in a small number of cases in order to preserve life or restore a patient's cognitive abilities to the extent that the person may meaningfully engage in active psychotherapy or behaviour modification programmes. The Code of Practice recognises that compulsory administration of treatment is an infringement of Article 8 of the Convention and as such must be proportionate and in accordance with the law. It is also possible that treatment could represent an infringement of Article 3 unless treatment can be shown to be a therapeutic necessity.

In *Herczegfalvy v Austria* (1992) 15 EHRR 437 it was held that in the context of Article 3, a treatment that is therapeutically necessary cannot be considered inhuman or degrading. In order to justify treatment by compulsion, a range of factors need to be taken into account, some of which were considered in *R (on the application of N) v M* [2003] 1 WLR 562. The factors considered relevant by the Court of Appeal were: the certainty that the patient had a treatable mental disorder; the seriousness of that disorder; the severity of the risk posed to others; the likelihood that the proposed treatment would alleviate the condition; the expected benefit of treatment and the likelihood and potential severity of adverse consequences for the patient caused by the treatment.

Since the definition of medical treatment is extensive, much depends upon the interpretation given to the concept of 'mental disorder'. If this is interpreted widely, there is a possibility that competent patients could be forced to accept treatment that has little bearing on their mental state. For these reasons the interpretation of section 63 is of paramount significance.

In *R v Broadmoor Special Hospital Authority, ex p S, H and D, The Times*, 17 Feb 1998 it was held that detention for treatment necessarily implies control for that purpose. Although the statute was silent on the necessary requirements of control, it could include the power to restrain patients, to use seclusion and to deprive them of their personal possessions for their safety and that of others. It could also extend to the frequency and number of visits made to them. Section 63 validates treatment 'for mental disorders from which he is suffering', which can be widely interpreted and encompasses a range of procedures. Force feeding has been authorised by the courts in several cases such as *Re KB (adult) (mental patient: medical treatment)* [1994] 2 FCR 1051, *B v Croydon HA* [1995] Fam 113 and *R v Collins, ex p Brady* (2000) 58 BMLR 173. In the view of the court, medical treatment is looked at from a holistic perspective as reinforced by the wide definition of section 145(1) that extends to care, habilitation and rehabilitation. Section 63 could extend to the administration of non-consensual nasogastric tube feeding in the specific circumstances of the aforementioned cases.

Force feeding of patients has been severely criticised on grounds that forcibly inserting a nasogastric tube against a competent patient's wishes is as intrusive as ECT or the use of long-term medication, both of which are subject to the special safeguards of a second opinion (section 58 of the MHA 1983). Lewis (1999), for example, considers that force feeding crushes the patient's will and personal identity and is the very antithesis of what a successful therapeutic treatment regime ought to be.

Section 63 was given an even more expansive interpretation and extended to authorisation of a caesarean section (*Thameside and Glossop v CH* [1996] 1 FCR 753). In *Thameside and Glossop*, a non-consensual caesarean section was authorised as treatment for schizophrenia on the grounds that achieving a successful outcome of pregnancy was a necessary aspect of the overall treatment of her mental disorder. This judgment has been criticised on the basis that the interpretation of section 63 was excessively wide. A more restrictive approach was taken by the Court of Appeal in *St George's Hospital v S* [1998] 3 WLR 936 where a pregnant woman with mental health problems refused consent to a caesarean section. In this case, the Court of Appeal determined that a woman detained under the Act for a mental disorder could not be forced to undergo medical procedures that were unconnected with her mental condition unless she lacked capacity to consent to such treatment.

In *R (on the application of B) v Ashworth Hospital Authority* [2005] UKHL 20 the issue concerned whether a section 63 application could extend only to treatment of the mental disorder which initially justified the patient's detention. In this case, the applicant had been detained for schizophrenia but while in hospital had also developed a psychopathic disorder. A decision was taken to transfer him to a ward that provided for patients with the latter condition. The House of Lords rejected the applicant's case that transfer had been unlawful on the basis that this was not the mental disorder that had justified his detention. Although it could be accepted that patients who were detained for compulsory treatment were a vulnerable group who deserved protection against forcible acceptance of inappropriate treatment, the House of Lords nevertheless justified their decision on several grounds. First, psychiatry is not an exact science and an initial diagnosis was unlikely to be definitive. Second, it could at times be difficult to disentangle the presenting characteristics of a condition from those of an underlying personality trait and the principal aim of treatment was to treat the patient as a whole. Third, once a person's liberty was withdrawn for the purposes of treatment, it would be unreasonable to dwell on the semantics of the classification of psychiatric disorders and yet not provide the necessary treatment. A potential problem with this decision, however, is that the second condition for which the treatment is being instituted may not always be one which would have justified detention and treatment in the first place.

Jake's carers consider that psychotherapy and behavioural therapy is required as treatment for a dissociated personality disorder:

▶ Is this a form of compulsory treatment? What are the statutory requirements?
▶ Is this treatment for a disorder that is different to the original condition for which he was admitted?
▶ Is psychotherapy a form of treatment?
▶ What are the limits of section 63 requirements? What are the criticisms of this?

9.6.2(b) Control of the patient

Following admission of an involuntary patient in accordance with the mental health legislation, day-to-day control of the patient lies with the responsible clinician. Responsibility for care is typically shared by a team but the final decision on matters such as permission to dine in a public area, to have escorted walks, and permission for overnight leave, lies with the responsible clinician.

Restraint, whether verbal or physical, may be used where immediate control is required to manage a dangerous situation by limiting the patient's freedom. Such control is used to end, or significantly reduce, any danger to the patient or others and is applied for no longer than necessary. Some of the reasons for implementing restraint include physical assault, threatening or destructive behaviour, non-compliance with treatment, risk of physical injury by accident and extreme and prolonged overexertion leading to physical exhaustion. In deciding whether to restrain a patient, a range of factors need to be taken into account, such as the need for an individual care plan, the patient's physical condition, the environment of the ward or unit and the need to maintain adequate staffing levels.

The Code of Practice states that legitimate restraint can be justified but it remains an emergency measure. Restraint by tying is specifically prohibited, and where physical restraint is used, this must be duly recorded. Restraint should be subject to minimum force and applied for only as long as necessary. The Code states that staff should not slap, kick, punch or use neck holds, and they should be mindful of excessive weight being applied to areas such as the stomach and neck since this could lead to injury and possibly death.

Seclusion is defined in the Code of Practice (paragraph 15.43) as 'the supervised confinement of a patient in a room, which may be locked. Its sole aim is to contain severely disturbed behaviour which is likely to cause harm to others'. Paragraph 15.45 provides that:

> Seclusion should not be used as a punishment or a threat, or because of a shortage of staff. It should not form part of a treatment programme. Seclusion should never be used solely as a means of managing self-harming behaviour. Where the patient poses a risk of self-harm as well as harm to others, seclusion should be used only when the professionals involved are satisfied that the need to protect other people outweighs any increased risk to the patient's health or safety and that any such risk can be properly managed.

Seclusion of an informal patient should be taken as an indicator of the need to consider a formal detention (paragraph 15.46). Hospitals should have clear written guidelines as to the use of seclusion. These guidelines should be taken into account to ensure the safety and well-being of the patient, that the patient receives the care and support necessary during and after seclusion and to distinguish between seclusion and behaviour modification therapy, such as 'time out'. A suitable environment for the use of seclusion is required to respect the patient's dignity and physical well-being. Set requirements are necessary for recording, monitoring and reviewing the use of seclusion and follow-up plans (paragraph 15.47).

Patients subject to seclusion should be reviewed every two hours by two nurses, one of whom was not involved in the decision to seclude, and every four hours by a doctor. A formal multidisciplinary review is completed by a consultant or a senior doctor, nurse or other professional who is not involved in the incident which led to the seclusion. Specific conditions are required for the seclusion room such as safety and security, privacy, the ability to observe and absence of items that could harm the patient.

It should be sufficiently furnished, lit, ventilated and quiet but not soundproofed, with a mechanism to call for attention by the patient.

In *R (Munjaz) v Mersey Care NHS Trust* [2005] UKHL 58 the seclusion policy of the hospital was reviewed. The policy was found to require far fewer medical reviews of the secluded patient than was recommended by the Code. This was apparent after the first twelve hours and, in particular, after the first seven days. It was held that the Code provided essential reference guidance for those who applied the Act and that departure needed to be supported by cogent reasons. If seclusion is properly applied, it would not be contrary to Articles 3, 5 or 8 of the European Convention.

> Jake is placed in seclusion. What are the legal and ethical issues that engage?

9.7 Use of compulsory powers

The powers that permit compulsory treatment of a patient (treatment provided against a competent refusal) conflict with the general law of consent for treatment. Not only do the compulsory powers infringe the autonomous rights of individuals, but they also amount to deprivation of liberty. For this reason, robust mechanisms are required to ensure that powers are used legitimately and that rights of challenge are available to patients subject to the compulsory powers of the MHA 1983.

9.7.1 Deprivation of liberty

The detention and compulsory treatment of a person with a mental disorder necessarily amounts to the deprivation of liberty of that individual. This raises several issues.

9.7.1(a) Article 5

Article 5 of the European Convention states that everyone has a right to liberty and security of person, and that no one should be deprived of liberty except in accordance with a procedure prescribed by law. The derogations include the lawful detention of persons of unsound mind (including alcoholics, drug addicts or vagrants). In the *Winterwerp Case* (1979) 2 EHRR 387 the ECtHR found three necessary preconditions to the detention of a person of unsound mind. A person could not be detained by reason of unsound mind unless:

(i)   he was reliably shown to be of unsound mind by objective medical opinion,
(ii) the mental disorder was of a kind or degree to warrant compulsory confinement,
(iii) continued confinement was dependant on the persistence of the disorder.

9.7.1(b) Procedural aspects

The Mental Capacity Act 2005, deprivation of liberty procedure applies when a person is deprived of his or her liberty. The distinction between restraint and deprivation of liberty is narrow and the crucial concern is not whether a person has been incarcerated or restrained, but whether that person was free to leave, as illustrated by *JE v DE* [2006] EWHC 3459 (Fam). In *JE*, Munby J. stated that the essential issue was whether the individual was, or was not, free to leave.

In addition to determining whether a patient is free to leave, the overall circumstances of the case need to be taken into account in terms of distinguishing between restriction of liberty and deprivation of liberty. In *LLBC v TG* [2007] EWHC 2640 (Fam), the overall circumstances pointed to a restriction of liberty rather than deprivation. This was because the family of TG (who was restrained) was able to visit him on an unrestricted basis and were entitled to remove him from the care home to go on outings. Furthermore, the premises was a care home where ordinary restrictions of liberty applied and TG himself was personally compliant and expressed himself to be happy in that environment. Under the circumstances, Munby J came to the conclusion that having had regard to all the relevant circumstances of the case, TG's placement in the care home fell short of deprivation of liberty.

The Mental Capacity Act: Deprivation of Liberty Safeguards (DOLS) Code of Practice (2008) provides a non-exhaustive list of factors that might be relevant in identifying whether steps taken are more than restraint and amount to a deprivation of liberty (paragraph 2.5). These include:

- Using restraint, including sedation, to admit a person to an institution where that person is resisting admission.
- Staff exercising complete and effective control over the care and movement of a person for a significant period.
- Staff exercising control over assessments, treatment, contacts and residence.
- A decision taken by the institution that the person cannot be released into the care of others or permitted to live elsewhere unless staff consider it appropriate.
- Refusal of a request by carers for a person to be discharged.
- The person is unable to maintain social contacts because of restrictions placed on their access to others.
- The person loses autonomy because of continuous supervision and control.

The Mental Health Act 2007 amended the MCA 2005 to make provision for the lawful deprivation of liberty for those with mental disorders who lack capacity. In these circumstances, detention must be in their best interests and the six requirements of schedule 1A Part 3 of the MCA 2005 must be complied with:

- The person must be 18 years old or over.
- The person must suffer from a mental disorder within the meaning of the MHA 1983.
- The person lacks capacity in relation to the question whether he should be accommodated in hospital or a care home for the purpose of receiving care or treatment.
- Deprivation of liberty must be in the person's best interests and necessary to prevent harm to that person. Deprivation of liberty is a proportionate response to the likelihood and seriousness of that harm.
- The person must be eligible to be detained under the Act and not be subject to restrictions on their freedom in the community.
- There must not be a valid and applicable advance refusal of the treatment for which deprivation of liberty is sought.

The MCA 2005 procedure requires that deprivation of liberty is in the individual's best interests, necessary to protect the person from harm, and represents a proportionate response. There is also a duty to appoint a representative, and an IMCA must be appointed (if no one is able to act) to represent and support the person who lacks capacity in all matters including using an organisation's complaints procedures and for making an application to the Court of Protection. Authorisation for deprivation of liberty is by a supervisory body and applications must be made to the NHS body responsible, which is usually the Primary Care Trust or hospital where the individual is being treated. Authorisation lasts for a 12-month period subject to review by the Court of Protection.

9.7.1(c) Overlap between DOLS and the compulsory powers

The mental health legislation and the Mental Capacity Act 2005 provide statutory regimes for the civil detention of persons with mental disorder. Although the powers and objectives of the two regimes are different, significant overlaps exist. In certain circumstances a choice between regimes might be available for those caring for persons who lack capacity between the MCA 2005 deprivation of liberty procedures (DOLS) and the compulsory detention regimes of the MHA 1983. The DOLS procedure cannot be relied upon if the person who lacks capacity objects to admission or treatment, or where a donee of Lasting Power of Attorney or Court Appointed Deputy objects to admission or treatment. The existence of a valid and applicable advance decision would also operate to prevent recourse to the DOLS regime.

If the person with mental disorder lacks capacity the MHA 1983 regime provides the statutory safeguard of review by tribunal. However, these safeguards might be of limited benefit for those who lack the ability to exercise their legal rights. In any event, a DOLS admission requires routine and independent assessment of the person's best interests.

9.7.1(d) Habeas corpus

Habeas corpus is a common law prerogative writ that goes back to the thirteenth century. It requires the production before the court of an individual who has been restrained and the writ is directed at the person who has custody of that individual. *Habeas corpus* results in an order of release through the civil courts and the burden of proof (for the continued detention) is on the detaining authority on the basis that the individual's liberty has been taken.

A modern day example of the use of this power is provided by *Re S-C (mental health patient: habeas corpus)* [1996] 1 All ER 532. *Habeas corpus* is likely to remain a remedy of last resort and judicial review is likely to remain the mechanism of choice for challenging an unlawful detention. In *Gorshkov v Ukraine* [2005] ECHR 67531/01 it was held by the European Court that Article 5(4) contains a guarantee that a patient detained compulsorily for psychiatric treatment would have the right to seek judicial review of detention.

9.7.2 Human rights implications

The compulsory detention and treatment of patients with mental disorders has undoubted implications for the potential infringement of human rights and contravention of the European Convention of Human Rights. Of particular relevance are Article 5 (the right to liberty and security of person), Article 8 (the right to respect for private and family life) and Article 3 (the right not to be subjected to torture or to inhuman and degrading treatment or punishment). The impact of Article 5 on the deprivation of liberty is considered above.

The potential engagement of Article 8 as a right to be free from non-consensual medical treatment was considered in *X v Austria* (1980) 18 DR 154. The European Commission stated that 'compulsory medical intervention, even if it is of minor importance, must be considered an interference with this right'. However, the derogation offered by Article 8(2) permits non-consensual treatment if it can be shown that it is necessary in a democratic society for the protection of health. If medical treatment is a necessary and proportionate response, violation of Article 8 will not occur (*R (on the application of N) v M and others* [2002] EWCA Civ 1789).

The courts have had to consider whether Article 3 has been breached following administration of non-consensual treatment. No derogation is permitted from Article 3 even if justified on grounds of public health, safety or national security. The concept of inhuman and degrading treatment is interpreted to provide the widest protection from abuse, although the touchstone for inhuman treatment is 'if it reaches a level of gravity involving considerable mental or physical suffering', and for degrading it is 'if the person has undergone humiliation or debasement involving a minimum level of severity' (*Ireland v United Kingdom* 25 Eur Cr HR (1978) at 162). The ECtHR's deference to mental health establishments in respect of Article 3 jurisprudence is exemplified by *Herczegfalvy v Austria* in that whilst the court would reach the definitive decision, it was for the medical authorities to decide on the therapeutic methods to be used on the basis of 'medical necessity' as 'convincingly shown'.

The meaning of medical necessity and the standard of proof to be applied was considered in *R (JB) v Haddock* [2006] EWCA Civ 961. The Court of Appeal held that medical necessity is a value judgement to be made by a court in reliance on the available medical evidence. The court resisted expressing the burden of proof in forensic terms and stated that if it was to be described as such, it would amount to no more than the balance of probabilities of the likelihood of therapeutic benefit.

Bartlett (2007) has criticised the decision in *Haddock* on the grounds that uncertainty is relied upon as the basis for restricting the protection conferred by human rights legislation for the involuntary treatment of patients with mental disorders. He contends that non-consensual treatment should, at the very least, be justified on solid and objective foundations such as evidence-based practice. This seems an entirely justifiable observation, although even in optimal clinical practice, definitive medical evidence is often difficult to establish, not only in respect of the practicalities of conducting trials but also for the measurement of specific outcomes. For certain conditions, therefore, the medical evidence base will inevitably be grounded on smaller studies that may not offer a randomised control element.

The second limb of the *Herczegfalvy* requirement is that it must be convincingly shown that medical necessity exists. In *R (on the application of N) v M and others*, the court essentially applied the *Bolam* test and held that where there is a responsible body of opinion to support the provision of treatment this will be relevant to the question of whether it is in the patient's best interests, or medically necessary, but no more than that.

Jake is unhappy about his continued detention and asks to see his solicitor who looks at options for discharge:

▶ What options should be considered?
▶ Has Jake been deprived of his liberty and human rights?
▶ How can Jake's detention be challenged?
▶ What are the roles of the hospital manager and MHT?

9.7.3 The compulsory powers

Recent evidence has shown that the use of compulsory powers is increasing, and with a higher representation of black people. Keown *et al.*, (2008) have shown an approximately 20% increase in involuntary admissions between 1996 and 2006. Although there has been a reduction in admissions for depression, learning disabilities and dementia, the involuntary admission of persons with psychotic disorders and substance misuse has increased.

Afro-Caribbean black individuals are more likely to be admitted involuntarily, compared with other ethnic groups (Audini and Lelliott, 2002). Several reasons for this anomaly have been proposed such as lack of awareness of mental health disorders combined with inability to access services. The outcome being more advanced problems that ultimately require more coercive treatment. In order to break the cycle, it has been suggested that black and minority ethnic groups should be provided with better and more effective information about mental health disorders and available treatments. This could be facilitated by means of more active community engagement. Furthermore, services need to be aware of specific cultural issues to ensure appropriate and responsive service provision.

9.7.4 Available challenges

A patient who is subject to the compulsory powers of the MHA 1983 (except for guardianship) has the right under Article 5(4) to challenge the use of compulsory powers in the courts and the Mental Health Tribunal (MHT). The MHT is a 'public authority' for the purposes of the Human Rights Act 1998 and must act in a way that is compatible with the Convention.

9.7.4(a) Entitlement to apply

A patient admitted for assessment under section 2 of the MHA 1983 can apply for review by a MHT within 14 days of admission. A patient admitted for treatment in accordance with section 3 of the MHA 1983 can seek review by an MHT within six months of admission, and thereafter once during every renewal cycle. The nearest relative may apply for a tribunal hearing within 28 days of an objection to a request to discharge the patient.

9.7.4(b) Hospital managers

Hospital managers have a duty to ensure that detained patients understand how the MHA applies to them following detention. This includes being informed of hospital managers' power to discharge most detained patients, which is in addition to the right to apply to the MHT. The MHA 1983 does not identify specific criteria to be used when considering discharge but the key concern is whether the grounds for continued detention can still be met. Hospital manager review meetings must be conducted fairly and reasonably and in accordance with the law. A managers' meeting is usually set within two to three weeks of application, compared with a possible delay of six weeks to convene a tribunal hearing. For this reason, detained individuals may wish to apply for review using both options.

Not all detained persons will be in a position to exercise their right to apply for review of their continued detention. In these circumstances, if a detained individual has not applied for a review to a tribunal in the first six months of detention and renewal under section 3 is envisaged, then section 68 requires hospital managers to make a reference to the MHT. A similar duty applies under section 19 following a transfer to guardianship if no appeal has been brought in the first six months and a renewal is envisaged. The duration of authority for detention of a patient is renewable and statutory safeguards exist through the hospital managers for removal of the section, and referral to a MHT (section 20 of the MHA 1983).

Section 68 of the MHA 1983 requires the hospital manager to refer a patient detained for assessment or treatment to a MHT within six months of the initial day of detention, or following the day on which they were detained after transfer from guardianship. The referral period is the same for all patients, whether detained for assessment or treatment, and applies irrespective of whether detention is being reviewed.

9.7.4(c) Mental Health Tribunals

The Mental Health Review Tribunal service was established by the Mental Health Act 1959 with the duty to consider the continued need to detain a patient under the Act. Since then the tribunal service has been affected by the MHA 1983, as amended by the Mental Health Act (Patients in the Community) Act 1995, the MHA 2007 and the Tribunals, Courts and Enforcement Act 2007. The most significant changes have followed decisions of the ECtHR.

Major changes to the tribunal system were introduced following the Leggatt Report which was commissioned in 2000. At the time of the review there were around 70 administrative tribunals although only 20 of these heard more than 500 cases each year and the quality of service provision was variable. The objective of the review was to recommend a system that was independent, coherent, cost-effective and user friendly. The Leggatt recommendations have been implemented by the Tribunals, Courts and Enforcement Act 2007.

Following implementation of the Tribunals, Courts and Enforcement Act 2007 in November 2008, the Mental Health Review Tribunal became part of the First-tier tribunal in the Health, Education and Social Care Chamber administered by the Ministry of Justice. This Act also introduced an Upper tribunal for appeals on points of law and judicial review.

The Mental Health Tribunal (MHT) hears applications and references for persons detained under the MHA 1983. The First-tier tribunal makes decisions to discharge, corrects and re-classifies decisions, reviews cases and can set aside decisions or grant permission to appeal to the Upper-tier. The substantive powers of the MHT are provided by the MHA 1983. The First-tier tribunal has jurisdiction for England. There is a separate Mental Health Review Tribunal for Wales and another for Scotland.

For a tribunal hearing relevant reports are prepared, usually by the responsible clinician and the AMHP. This may include a formal nursing report. Information is shared with the detained party and their legal representative. Section 2 hearings are generally set within seven days of the appeal being made and it is therefore a rapid procedure. An application must be made within fourteen days of the detention. With regard to section 3, the timescale is closer to six weeks before the date is set, and for forensic sector hearings, dates can run from two to three months.

In England, the mental health tribunal procedure is governed by the First-tier Tribunal (Health Education and Social Care Chamber) Rules 2008 SI 2008 No. 2699. The tribunal doctor completes a preliminary attendance for the detained party prior to the hearing itself. This is usually a day or two prior to the hearing, or early on the day of the hearing. The findings of the preliminary discussion are disclosed at the start of the tribunal hearing. The detained party may invite relevant individuals to the hearing (e.g. close family members or friends), and the right to cross-examine other parties at the hearing exists through the solicitor. At the conclusion of the hearing a verbal decision is provided to the detained party. The procedure requires a follow-up by a written decision sent out to all parties within a reasonable period.

In England, for the financial year 2008–2009 the total number of days that the judiciary sat to consider applications was 19,964. Of these applications 14,998 final determinations were made of which 14% of decisions went in favour of the applicant.

9.8 Discharge and community care

Once a person has been detained, continuation of detention must be justified. There is an imperative to review and possibly discharge with treatment continued in the community.

9.8.1 Discharge

Discharge criteria are contained in section 72 of the MHA 1983 (with regard to unrestricted cases) and section 73 (for restricted cases). The MHT retains a general discretion in all civil cases. The standard of proof is on the balance of probabilities that the individual is not mentally disordered, or sufficiently disordered to warrant detention in hospital, or that the detention for treatment is not necessarily in the interests of the individual's health or safety, or for the protection of others.

9.8.1(a) Criteria

Section 72(1)(a) provides that where an application is made to a tribunal by, or for, a patient detained under the Act, the tribunal has a duty to discharge if not satisfied that:

- the patient is suffering from mental disorder of a nature or degree which warrants his detention in hospital for assessment; or
- detention is justified in the interests of his own health or safety or for the protection of others.

The tribunal must also discharge the patient if it is not satisfied that:

- the patient is suffering from mental disorder or from mental disorder of a nature or degree which makes it appropriate for him to be liable to be detained in hospital for medical treatment; or

▶ detention is necessary for the health and safety of the patient or for the protection of others that he should receive treatment; or
▶ that appropriate medical treatment is available for him; or
▶ in the case of an application by the nearest relative following the exclusion of a discharge order, that the patient would be likely to act in a manner dangerous to himself or others, if released (section 72(1)(b)).

Even if the above criteria are not met, the tribunal nevertheless has discretion to discharge non-restricted patients, although the tribunal must provide reasons for exercising its discretion.

In considering whether continued detention is justified, there are two factors of key importance:

(a) the 'nature or degree' of the mental disorder which warrants detention; and
(b) the standard of proof required for assessing whether grounds for detention exist at the time of the hearing.

The meaning of the 'nature or degree' requirement that warrants detention was considered in *R v Mental Health Review Tribunal for the South Thames Region, ex p Smith* [1998] 47 BMLR 104. The court held that for these purposes the terms 'nature or degree' were disjunctive. A person might be detained on the grounds of their mental disorder which was of a sufficiently serious nature to warrant detention in hospital, even though at the time of review they were not suffering to a degree that warranted detention. This interpretation has been criticised by Bartlett and Sandland (2007), who argue that this approach permits detention when a person's disorder is of a nature, but not of a degree, sufficient to justify detention. In their view this interpretation falls outside the spirit of the European Convention and that in order to be Convention-compliant, the words ought to be read conjunctively as 'nature *and* degree'.

For the purpose of reviewing the lawfulness of detention, the standard of proof to be applied is the civil standard. In *R (on the application of N) v Mental Health Review Tribunal (Northern Region)* [2005] EWCA Civ 1605 the Court of Appeal confirmed the standard to be applied gave sufficient flexibility to recognise that the more serious an allegation, the stronger the evidence required for proof on the balance of probabilities.

The principal question for the tribunal is whether grounds for continued detention exist at the time of the hearing. In *R (on the application of Care Principles Ltd) v Mental Health Review Tribunal* [2006] EWHC 3194 (Admin), Collins J explained as follows: 'The question before the Tribunal is: is the detention proper now? The burden is upon the hospital or those who seek his continued detention, to establish that that detention is necessary and within the terms of the Act. It is always necessary for any such detention to be justified. The standard required is the balance of probabilities.' In our view, therefore, the determination of whether detention is justified at the time of the hearing required the tribunal to take the following into consideration:

▶ the nature and severity of the mental disorder,
▶ whether treatment was in the interests of the patient's health or safety, or the protection of others,
▶ consideration of the evidence on the balance of probabilities, applying a flexible standard that requires more robust evidence for more serious allegations.

9.8.1(b) Review

Detention under section 2 automatically lapses after 28 days unless the person is formally detained under section 3. For detention under section 3, a hospital manager has a duty to refer the case to a MHT after six months and thereafter every three years (section 68).

Article 5(4) of the Convention entitles those deprived of their liberty to take proceedings against the lawfulness of detention, and this must be decided speedily by a court. Whilst there is no definition of 'speedy', in the context of mental health, a range of factors might precipitate delays, including the preparation of reports, scheduling of hearings or even on account of less-than-effective case management. Many of these hurdles are fuelled by inadequate resources, although a defence to a breach of Article 5(4) may not be offered by lack of resources or administrative issues (*R v Mental Health Review Tribunal, ex p KB* [2002] EWHC 639 (Admin) and *R v Mental Health Review Tribunal, ex p B* [2002] All ER (D) 304.

Each application must be judged on its merits. The routine hearing of cases following a set number of weeks after an application has been made, without consideration of individual circumstances, will breach Article 5(4) (*R (on the application of C) v Mental Health Review Tribunal* [2002] 1 WLR 176). A decision taken by an MHT to discharge a patient cannot be overridden by re-sectioning that patient on account of a disagreement between the detaining body and the Tribunal. In *R v East London and the City Mental Health NHS Trust, ex p von Brandenburg* [2003] UKHL 58, a patient's discharge that had been ordered by a tribunal had been deferred in order to find suitable accommodation. The responsible clinician (at that time known as a Responsible Medical Officer) arranged for the patient's readmission under section 3 of the MHA 1983, and judicial review of this decision was sought. Lord Bingham stated that an approved mental health professional (AMHP) (at that time known as an Approved Social Worker or ASW) 'may not lawfully apply for the admission of a patient whose discharge has been ordered by the decision of a mental health review tribunal, of which the ASW is aware unless the ASW has formed a reasonable and bona fide opinion that he has information not known to the tribunal which puts a significantly different complexion on the case as compared with that which was before the tribunal'. Thus, if after the tribunal hearing the patient's mental state deteriorates to present a degree of risk or requires treatment or supervision then the AMHP may properly apply for admission of the patient subject to receiving required medical support.

9.8.2 Community care

There is an increasing trend away from in-patient care of the mentally disordered to what is known as 'care in the community'. There is a need, therefore, to consider the extent to which the required degree of control and supervision might be provided for those who are cared for and treated in the community.

9.8.3 Aftercare services

Section 117(2) of the MHA 1983 provides that a Primary Care Trust and the local social services authorities have a duty to co-operate with relevant agencies for the required aftercare service provision. These services could involve medical treatment, assistance with accommodation, education and training.

R v Ealing District Health Authority ex p Fox [1993] 1 WLR 373 provides authority for the duty to provide aftercare services following discharge. It was stated that a 'district health authority's duty under section 117 of the MHA 1983 is to provide aftercare services when a patient leaves hospital, and acts unlawfully in failing to seek to make practical arrangements for aftercare prior to that patient's discharge from hospital ...' However, Lord Phillips in *R v Camden and Islington Health Authority ex p K* [2001] EWCA Civ 240 stated that although section 117 imposes on health authorities a duty to provide aftercare facilities, 'the nature and extent of those facilities must, to a degree, fall within the discretion of the health authority, which must have regard to other demands on his budget....' In the view of Lord Phillips, there was no justification for interpreting section 117 so as to impose an absolute obligation on health authorities. If, after taking all reasonable endeavours to provide care and treatment in the community, the health authority was unable to do so, then in his Lordship's view, continued detention of the patient in hospital did not violate the right to liberty conferred by Article 5.

The scope of the duty to plan with regard to section 117 and its potential discharge was examined in *R v MHRT ex p Hall* [1999] All ER (D) 935. The issue concerned the anticipatory steps that ought to be taken prior to a tribunal hearing in order to comply with a decision to discharge. It was felt that appropriate professionals and agencies should have met prior to the hearing to facilitate the provision of suitable aftercare arrangements. This would ensure that discharge arrangements were available in readiness for a potential discharge.

The need to monitor aftercare provision supplied in accordance with section 117 was addressed in *R (B) v Camden LBC* [2005] EWHC 1366. The court held that the monitoring arrangements under section 117 engaged after a person had ceased to be detained and had left hospital. It was, however, unrealistic to expect the authorities implementing statutory aftercare provisions to act without having first explored resource issues. The principle that emerges is that a discussion about aftercare requirements should take place prior to a tribunal hearing so that these measures can be practically implemented as soon as the tribunal (potentially) has ordered a discharge.

> Jake's solicitor makes an application for a hearing before a MHT which is heard in eight weeks. The tribunal orders discharge with care in the community which takes a further four weeks before implementation:
>
> ▶ Would this delay satisfy the requirements for a 'speedy' review?
> ▶ What are the duties of the authorities to instigate community care under section 117?

9.8.4 Supervised community treatment orders

A significant reform introduced by the MHA 2007 is the new and detailed provisions that pertain to supervised community treatment orders (SCTOs). The purpose of a SCTO is to ensure that a patient receives treatment in the least restrictive environment while at the same time being subject to supervision. This was intended to end the 'revolving door problem', used to describe the situation whereby patients with mental illness were admitted to hospital, treated, and stabilised. Once discharged into the community, failure to comply with treatment regimes tended to destabilise their condition resulting in readmission.

Section 17A of the MHA 1983 authorises a responsible clinician to make a SCTO on the written agreement of an AMHP provided that the following criteria in section 17A(5) are met:

a) the person is suffering from mental disorder of a nature or degree which makes it appropriate for him to receive medical treatment;
b) it is necessary for his health or safety or for the protection of other persons that he should receive such treatment;
c) subject to his being liable to be recalled, such treatment can be provided without his continuing to be detained in a hospital;
d) it is necessary that the responsible clinician can exercise power of recall;
e) appropriate medical treatment is available for him.

The power of recall that can be exercised by the Responsible Clinician is provided for in section 17A as follows:

▶ the patient requires medical treatment in hospital for his mental disorder; and
▶ there would be a risk of harm to the health or safety of the patient or to other persons if the patient were not recalled to hospital for that purpose.

If the patient is recalled, treatment can be given without consent and the person may be detained up to 72 hours, after which he can be discharged but will continue to be subject to the SCTO. If a person refuses to comply with the SCTO, this can be revoked and the person can become a detained patient. The Responsible Clinician also has power to impose conditions (section 17B(2)) if these are deemed necessary or appropriate, for the following reasons:

▶ to ensure that the patient receives medical treatment,
▶ to prevent risk to the patient's health or safety,
▶ the protection of others.

The power to impose conditions is wide and the Mental Health Act Code of Practice (paragraph 25.33) offers guidance. Conditions should be kept to a minimum and be the least restrictive of the person's liberty, and have a rationale linked to one or more of the purposes of the conditions. They should be clearly and precisely expressed.

If the patient fails to comply with a condition this may be taken into account by the Responsible Clinician in deciding whether to recall the patient. The conditions imposed should not constitute a deprivation of liberty, but if they do, the Code of Practice allows for the deprivation of liberty under DOLS to coexist alongside SCTOs.

Following discharge Jake remains reasonably well. However, his condition tends to worsen especially after meeting up with friends who have 'bad habits'. His doctor feels that he ought to be readmitted to prevent contact with these individuals:

▶ Is there an SCT in place? Should there be one?
▶ Is the doctor the responsible clinician? What are the powers of the responsible clinician?
▶ What powers do responsible clinicians have for imposing conditions and restricting friends? What is the guidance of the Code of Practice on this? Is there a restriction in Jake's liberty by imposing conditions?

SCTOs were intended to be an innovative way of treating patients' mental disorder without recourse to hospital detention. However, the system has been criticised in that SCTOs emphasise the administration of medication. Concerns have also been raised that SCTOs could operate as a hazard and disincentive for patients to seek help. They may also erode the relationship of trust between the patient and psychiatric services.

9.8.5 Guardianship

The principle behind guardianship is to permit patients to receive care for their mental disorder in the community without recourse to compulsory powers. Section 7 of the MHA 1983 provides that a guardian may be appointed on the recommendation of two doctors and an application by the patient's nearest relative or an AMHP. The conditions for guardianship are that the patient is over the age of 16 and is suffering from a mental disorder of a nature or degree that warrants reception into guardianship, which is necessary in the interests of the patient, or for the protection of others.

The guardian has a range of statutory powers such as deciding where the patient should live, ensuring that the patient attends hospital for treatment and having access to the patient's place of residence (section 8 of the MHA 1983). The guardian does not have power to compel a patient to receive treatment, and guardianship is an option to be considered for patients who are relatively compliant.

9.9 Mentally disordered offenders and the MHA 1983

An issue of major significance is the care and treatment of mentally disordered offenders and an overlap exists between the mental health-care services and the Criminal Justice System. Thus, although a distinction exists between the Criminal Justice System and health care, that distinction becomes somewhat blurred in the context of offenders with mental disorders.

9.9.1 Diversion

Various agencies associated with the Criminal Justice System encourage the use of mechanisms to 'divert' mentally disordered offenders and suspects into the mental health system. This means that in certain circumstances offenders are not prosecuted, imprisoned or punished, but instead are subject to care and treatment by the health care and social services sector. Diversion may take place when an offender is proceeding through the Criminal Justice System but is remanded into hospital care or given medical treatment for a mental disorder while under bail conditions. Diversion may also occur at the sentencing stage where the court imposes a therapeutic disposal of the offender, thereby avoiding a custodial punishment.

9.9.1(a) Section 136

Section 136 of the MHA 1983 provides that a constable may remove to a place of safety any person found in a place to which the public have access, who appears to be suffering from a mental disorder and is in immediate need of care or control, provided that removal is thought necessary in the interests of the person, or for the protection of others. No statutory form needs to be completed and this can be used even if the person in question has, or may have, committed an offence.

The person may be detained in place of safety for up to 72 hours for the purposes of enabling an examination to be carried out by a registered medical practitioner and an interview to be conducted by an AMHP. The place of safety could be residential accommodation for the mentally disordered provided by the local authority, a private or voluntary residential or nursing home, a hospital or police station.

The ultimate decision of whether to initiate diversion at this stage is at the discretion of the constable. One of the obstacles to achieving this is the difficulty of accurately identifying those who may be in need of treatment whilst in police custody. A number of initiatives to facilitate the process of diversion have evolved, including the presence of a community psychiatric nurse at police stations to undertake a preliminary screen for mental disorders and where necessary to arrange for care to be provided where required.

9.9.1(b) Court diversion schemes

Some of the forms of court diversion schemes that are available include the presence of community psychiatric nurse in court, psychiatric assessment teams in courts or police stations, panel schemes, community mental health teams linked to the court and stand alone consultant-led teams. These systems could be highly effective in facilitating the diversion of mentally disordered offenders in the Criminal Justice System where appropriate, provided that such initiatives are properly constituted and resourced and have effective links with other organisations, such as social care, probation and health organisations.

The Centre of Public Innovation's 'Review into the current regime of court liaison in diversion schemes' indicated that funding arrangements negatively impacted on the scheme's activities (Nacro, 2005). The project sought to identify innovative ways to promote collaboration working within Care Services and the National Offender Management Service. One conclusion was that integrated funding, supported by strengthened liaison, was critical to the success of such a scheme, as was good communication and service integration to meet individual's needs. Robust diversion schemes require good relationships between the police, probation, primary care, housing agencies, bail hostels, prison teams and social services. Diversion schemes have been reported to work well in other jurisdictions, particularly within the Magistrates' Courts of South Australia (The Courts Administration of South Australia, *Magistrates Court; Court Diversion Programme, 2005*).

9.9.2 Hospital care while awaiting trial

Section 48 of the MHA 1983 permits the Secretary of State to direct that a person remanded in custody be transferred to a psychiatric hospital. Reports are required from at least two registered medical practitioners to confirm that the person suffers from a mental disorder of a nature or degree that makes detention in hospital appropriate for medical treatment, and that appropriate treatment is available for him.

Section 35 of the MHA 1983 provides for remanding an accused to hospital for a report on his mental condition. This provision was relied upon 145 times from 2007 to 2008. Section 36 permits remand to hospital for treatment and was used 17 times from 2007 to 2008. Section 35 powers can be exercised by a magistrates' court or the Crown Court, whereas section 36 is exercisable only by the Crown Court.

Sections 35 and 36 provide an opportunity for a person who has been brought before a court to be examined and treated in hospital for a period of 28 days with further 28-day review periods up to a maximum of not more than 12 weeks before the court makes a final decision as to disposal. If a mental disorder is diagnosed by two registered medical practitioners one of whom is approved under section 12 of the MHA 1983, the magistrates or the Crown Court may impose a section 37 hospital order rather than a remand order under section 35. In effect, a hospital order means that an accused individual with a mental disorder will be detained in hospital rather than in custody.

Section 35 does not permit treatment without consent, unless the patient lacks capacity, in which case he may be treated in his best interests in accordance with the Mental Capacity Act 2005. However, a section 37 order can be made without convicting the offender and without his consent, provided the court is satisfied that the accused committed the offence. Furthermore, following a section 37 order, the person can be subject to the powers of compulsory treatment under Part IV of the MHA 1983. Compulsory and non-consensual treatment can be given following a section 36 order, although section 36 is exercisable by the Crown Court only.

9.9.3 Therapeutic disposals

The court has a variety of therapeutic disposals available to deal with mentally disordered offenders as opposed to imposing a custodial sentence. Hospital orders are permitted under section 37 of the MHA 1983. Section 37(2)(A) provides that before making a hospital order, the court must be satisfied on the written or oral evidence of two registered medical practitioners (one of whom must be approved) that the defendant is suffering from a mental disorder of a nature or degree which makes it appropriate for him to be detained in hospital for treatment and that appropriate medical treatment is available for him. There are two main differences between the hospital order and civil admission for treatment: first, the patient cannot be discharged by his nearest relative, who must apply to a MHT; second, the offender (although he can appeal against the order) has no right to apply to a MHT within the first six months of admission.

The hospital order may be made with restrictions under section 41 of MHA 1983 (a restriction order). Restriction orders have to be made by the Crown Court and are used to impose special restrictions on the offender discharged from hospital. The purpose of a restriction is to protect the public and predictions as to future dangerousness may not always be accurate. Thus, in practice, restriction orders last for a prolonged period of time and also result in patients being detained for much longer periods in hospitals.

Summary

9.1 In this chapter mental health law covers civil aspects governed by the Mental Health Act (MHA 1983).

9.2 The principal difference between mental health law and the general law is that those with mental health disorders may be detained and given treatment against their will. Compulsory powers have been justified on the principle that detention and treatment is required in certain circumstances to prevent self-harm and harm of others.

9.3 The statutory definition of a mental disorder is any disorder or disability of the mind. Dependence on alcohol or drugs is excluded (unless there is an associated mental disorder,

Summary cont'd

even if this is directly related to the dependence). A person with learning disabilities will be excluded unless that person is abnormally aggressive or displays seriously irresponsible conduct. The statute does not define specific disorders.

9.4 Informal or voluntary patients are those who voluntarily agree to hospital admission for care. The lack of process for challenging the detention of those who are compliant and incapacitated was identified as the *Bournewood* gap. Measures are now in place to provide a mechanism by which deprivation of liberty can be authorised, as well as safeguarding the interests of such patients.

9.5 Compulsory detention under the MHA 1983 is provided for by section 2 (admission for assessment), section 3 (admission for treatment) and section 4 (emergency admission for assessment). Strict procedural rules must be followed and the duration of detention under each section is different. An application for these sections can be made by the nearest relative or an AMHP. Major reform to the MHA 1983 was introduced by the Mental Health Act 2007 in terms of the 'treatability' of mental disorder. The emphasis now is on the purpose of treatment to alleviate or prevent deterioration rather than the likelihood of such alleviation or prevention.

9.6 Powers for non-compulsory treatment are found in sections 57 and 58 of the MHA 1983. Treatment under section 57 requires consent and a second opinion and applies to procedures such as neurosurgery and surgical implantation of sex hormones. Section 58 treatment requires consent or a second opinion and applies to administration of medication beyond 12 weeks and electroconvulsive therapy (ECT). This is provided for by section 58A and may not be given to a patient (with capacity) who refuses consent. The powers for compulsory treatment arise from section 63 which may be given even if a competent patient objects. A second opinion is not required.

9.7 Enforced detention for treatment of persons with mental health disorders deprives them of their liberty and may infringe Article 5 rights. A person of unsound mind can only be detained if there is objective supporting medical evidence, and if compulsory confinement is warranted on account of the persistence of that disorder. Enforced detention and compulsory treatment may also infringe Article 3, which protects against inhuman or degrading treatment. Article 3 would not be infringed if such treatment is a medical necessity convincingly shown to exist. The principal right of challenge against enforced detention is an application to the Mental Health Tribunal, which utilises the judicial process. Hospital managers may review detention with a view to having the section removed.

9.8 Section 72 of the MHA 1983 provides for the mandatory discharge of a patient under certain circumstances. In addition, it provides the MHT with discretionary powers to discharge. Continued detention of a patient needs to be justified on the nature or degree of the mental disorder which warrants detention, treatment that is in the interests of the patient's own health or safety or with a view to the protection of others. The burden of proof rests on the detaining authority and the evidence is judged by the civil standard on the balance of probabilities. Once an application for review has been made, this should be undertaken speedily. Applications that are not considered on individual merits, or that are delayed due to lack of resources or administrative reasons, are likely to breach Article 5. Following discharge, health authorities have a duty to provide necessary aftercare and provisions. Supervised community treatment orders permit treatment in the community, which is a less restrictive environment compared to detention in hospital, while at the same time maintaining an element of supervision of the patient.

9.9 Offenders with mental health disease may be 'diverted' from the Criminal Justice System and treated by the health and social services. Diversion can occur at the early stages of the criminal process while offenders are awaiting trial, or through sentencing as a therapeutic disposal.

Exercises

9.1 What changes have been made by the reforming statute of the Mental Health Act 2007 to the Mental Health Act 1983? What do you consider to be the advantages of these changes?

9.2 'A supervised community treatment order is employed to keep patients with mental disorder out of hospital, mainly because of resource implications'. Critically discuss this statement.

9.3 'It is possible to treat a mentally disordered patient even if he is competent to refuse such treatment. This exception to the principle of autonomy is justified'. Critically discuss this comment.

9.4 It has been argued that the general public needs protection from those from persons with mental disorders. What are the arguments for and against this statement?

9.5 The decision-making capacity of individuals with mental disorder is justifiably ignored. Such persons can be formally detained, supervised and given treatment, and there is no regard to the human rights implications of such an invasion. Consider the above in the context of contemporary mental health law in England and Wales.

Further reading

Bartlett P. A test of compulsion in mental health law: capacity, therapeutic benefit and dangerousness as possible criteria. *Medical Law Review* 2003; 11: 326–352.

Bartlett P and Sandland R. *Mental health law: policy and practice* (3rd edn). Oxford University Press, Oxford, 2007.

Keown P, Mercer G, Scott J. Retrospective analysis of hospital episode statistics, involuntary admissions under the Mental Health Act 1983, and number of psychiatric beds in England 1996–2006. *British Medical Journal* 2008; 337: 1837.

Stavert J. Mental health, community care and human rights in Europe: still an incomplete picture? *Journal of Mental Health Law* 2007; 182.

Szasz T. Law, liberty and psychiatry: an enquiry into the social uses of mental health practices. Routledge and Keegan Paul: London, 1984.

Links to relevant websites can be found at: http://www.palgrave.com/law/samanta

Chapter 10 follows overleaf.

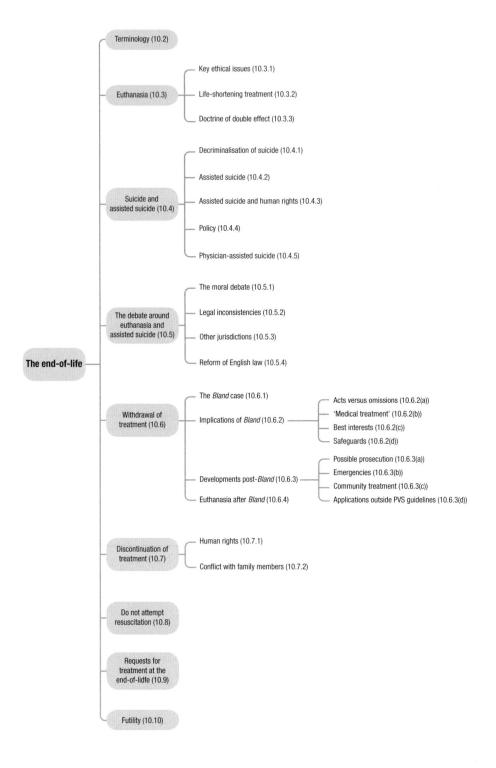

The end-of-life

Key Terms

- **Active euthanasia** – is brought about by a positive act on the part of the agent (usually a health-care professional).
- **Assisted suicide** – assisting or encouraging another to commit, or attempt to commit, suicide.
- **Do not attempt resuscitation** – a clinical direction that cardiopulmonary resuscitation is not to be attempted.
- **Doctrine of double effect** – an ethical principle that distinguishes between intended ('desirable or good') outcomes of clinical interventions and any unintended, yet foreseen, ('undesirable or bad') side effects of the same.
- **Euthanasia** – bringing about the death of a patient in the context of a terminal or incurable illness in the belief that death is of greater benefit than life in those circumstances.
- **Futility** – the argument used to justify withdrawal of active treatment of patients with a very poor clinical prognosis.
- **Involuntary euthanasia** – euthanasia carried out against the wishes of competent person.
- **Non-voluntary euthanasia** – euthanasia without the consent, or objection, of a person.
- **Passive euthanasia** – euthanasia brought about by an omission on the part of an agent (usually a health-care professional).
- **Physician-assisted suicide** – where a doctor (acting in a professional capacity) assists a patient to commit suicide.
- **Suicide** – death caused by the direct or indirect effect of the victim's act or omission.
- **Voluntary euthanasia** – euthanasia carried out at the competent patient's request.

Scenario

Lilly is 62 and has a chronic, progressive neurological disorder. Although competent, she is completely dependent on others for her physical needs. Lilly wishes to travel to Switzerland with her nephew in order to end her life. Her husband is not aware of these intentions.

Whilst arrangements are made for the journey, Lilly suffers a stroke that leaves her even more disabled than before, but she retains decision-making capacity. She is admitted to hospital where she repeatedly asks the clinical team to allow her to die and, in fact, makes specific and repeated requests for lethal medication. She is in some pain, although this is not a prominent concern. A junior registrar is very moved by her condition and considers giving her intravenous potassium chloride (which would cause cardiac arrest) or commencing a morphine drip (which would alleviate her pain but might also lead to respiratory depression and stop her breathing).

Lilly remains in hospital and develops pneumonia that leads to cardiac arrest. After she is resuscitated she remains deeply unconscious due to severe brain injury. She is totally dependent upon mechanical ventilation. Despite all clinical efforts her condition deteriorates and her doctors wish to switch off the ventilator in her best interests. Her husband vigorously protests.

10.1 Introduction

Dying is an inevitable part of life and death comes to us all. The actual process of dying, however, remains cloaked in mystery since no empirical data exists apart from knowledge gleaned from 'near death experiences'. Furthermore, there is a marked paucity of thanatological research that might assist with the development of a principled construct about the process. Perceptions on dying tend to be personal, cultural or influenced by religious or secular beliefs.

Legal issues that pertain to death, dying and end-of-life decision-making have assumed considerable importance in recent years on account of several developments including the demographic shifts that typify Western societies, such as the preponderance of an ageing population. Improvements in public health and medicine mean that people tend to survive longer than ever before. Advances in medical technology, such as advanced life support indicate that, theoretically, it is possible to keep seriously ill individuals alive for considerable lengths of time. These changes have brought significant societal transformations in perceptions and attitudes towards death. While the death of an individual may have profound and lasting effects on family and friends, these events tend to be of lesser significance for society than in previous decades. The aspirations of modern, secular societies tend to eschew relationships of dependency in the campaign to live a good life. The ascendancy of autonomy as representing the moral ideal means that individuals have expectations of having a 'good death'. The media has done much to shape societal thinking on the way that euthanasia and assisted suicide is depicted, and has been instrumental in generating the often strongly held views on these matters.

This chapter examines the key legal and ethical issues at the end-of-life. As a general tenet, the law prohibits killing. Nonetheless, allowing a person to die as a result of withdrawing or withholding treatment may, in some therapeutic situations, be the correct clinical, ethical and legal decision.

10.2 Terminology

A useful starting point is to consider a few terms that are commonly encountered in this topic as well as fundamental principles of law.

The word 'euthanasia' literally means a 'good death' according to its Grecian roots, and by this definition euthanasia would seem to be an uncontroversial ideal to be aspired to by all. A more modern definition is 'the act or practice of putting painlessly to death, especially in cases of incurable suffering' (*The Chambers Dictionary*, 2003). In common parlance 'euthanasia' is used to describe 'mercy killing', or 'assisted dying', and refers to clinical decisions taken by health-care practitioners that have the effect of shortening the lives of patients, and which are carried out in the belief that death would be preferable to the patient.

Euthanasia is classified according to patient factors and distinctions are drawn between voluntary, involuntary and non-voluntary euthanasia according to whether the patient seeks death, lacks decision-making capacity or whose wishes are ignored in the decision-making process. Voluntary euthanasia describes that which is carried out at the request of the patient, or with her consent. Involuntary euthanasia is where euthanasia is performed against the wishes of a competent patient. Non-voluntary euthanasia is where death is brought about to a person who lacks the ability to consent or object, or alternatively, is carried out on a competent person who has no opportunity to consent or object.

Euthanasia can be further divided according to the conduct of the doctor and whether an act or omission was the operative cause of death. Active euthanasia entails a positive act on the part of the doctor, or health-care professional. An example of active euthanasia is where a doctor deliberately injects a patient with a lethal medication which causes the patient's death. No matter how beneficent the motive, active euthanasia is murder (*Airedale NHS Trust v Bland* [1993] AC 789). Passive euthanasia entails an omission by the practitioner that leads to the patient's death, for example where a doctor withdraws life-sustaining treatment. In certain circumstances, passive euthanasia will not be unlawful. The crux of the distinction is between killing and letting a person die.

The term 'suicide' is used to describe death caused as a result of a direct, or indirect, positive act or omission of the victim herself and represents 'self-murder'. The fundamental distinction between suicide and euthanasia is that suicide describes death caused by the person's own conduct, whereas death caused by the conduct of another represents euthanasia. Assisted suicide is where another individual, such as a spouse or a friend, helps the person to commit suicide. Physician-assisted suicide refers to the situation where a doctor assists the patient to commit suicide. While the distinction between euthanasia and assisted suicide might appear discrete, there can be very considerable overlap, and it is not always obvious exactly where the boundary lies and to some degree such classifications are arbitrary.

10.3 Euthanasia

Under the jurisdiction of England and Wales, a doctor who deliberately ends the life of a patient will be subject to the criminal law on a charge of murder. For the purposes of the law, the fact that the doctor's motives were altruistic and that the patient had given consent and wished to die are irrelevant. If the patient is known to suffer from a terminal condition or pre-existing illness, and dies following a deliberate act of a doctor, it might be difficult to establish on evidential grounds that it was the doctor's conduct, rather than the pre-existing illness, which actually caused the patient's death. As far as causation is concerned, the doctor's conduct must have 'contributed significantly' or have been a 'substantial cause' of death, but does not necessarily need to be the sole reason for the death.

Compassionate motives do not provide a defence to a criminal charge of murder. A friend or relative responsible for the death of a loved one may have the plea reduced to manslaughter on the grounds of diminished responsibility. It also appears unusual for cases of mercy killing to be prosecuted. Between 1982 and 1991, only 24 such cases came before the court, of which only one resulted in a murder conviction. Of the remainder, 16 were reduced to manslaughter convictions and 3 received custodial penalties (Herring, 2008).

There is no special defence for a doctor who performs active euthanasia on a patient although it appears that juries and the judiciary tend to be sympathetic towards doctors who have acted on compassionate grounds. In *R v Arthur* (1981) 12 BMLR 1, Farquharson J, directed the jury to think long and hard before deciding that a doctor of eminence had adopted such standards to amount to committing a crime. Likewise Dr Moore, prosecuted for the murder of George Diddle, an 85 year old man suffering from bowel cancer, was cleared by the jury. Dr Moore was described as being a man of excellent character, having no previous convictions and who had gone out of his way to care for his patient. The jury was asked to consider that it might be ironical that a doctor who took time off in his day to attend to a dying patient ended up on such a charge (Dyer, 1999). All of these illustrations, however, are taken from a pre-Dr Shipman era, and the extent to which uncritical sympathies persist remain to be seen.

10.3.1 Key ethical issues

Supporters of euthanasia tend to be of the belief that a slow, painful death is an intolerable and inhumane situation to be avoided wherever possible. On this basis, persons with decision-making capacity ought to receive assistance to end their lives at a time and place of their choosing. Opponents argue that legalisation of euthanasia would mean that some lives would be judged as just not worth living, which is inherently repugnant as an ethical concept. To better understand some of the reasoning behind these perspectives, it is necessary to consider the moral arguments that underpin such viewpoints.

Proponents of euthanasia argue for protecting the dignity of those who are dying. As death becomes imminent a person will lose control, physically and mentally. The inevitable loss of decision-making capacity means that a person will, for a shorter or longer period, come to be dependent on others. This inevitability is heightened for those destined for a protracted and painful death and which for some will preclude dying with dignity. The opportunity to choose the time of death by euthanasia is viewed by some as allowing a person to die before this stage is reached.

Recognition and protection of human dignity is widely perceived as a core value of humanity and is a fundamental principle underlying all societies. Some proponents of euthanasia consider that if one is to give real meaning or value to the concept of dignity, particularly at the time of death, then euthanasia ought to be lawful. In addition to arguments underscored by dignity is the need to prevent the cruelty of a slow and painful death. Viewed in these terms, euthanasia represents an act of compassion and change in the law could bring comfort and reassurance to the terminally ill, safe in the knowledge that if pain and suffering become too acute, relief is available. From this perspective, legalisation of euthanasia serves to empower the dying person.

Opponents of legalisation tend to assert that effective palliative care and pain management offers an acceptable alternative to euthanasia. Adequate care and pain relief at the end-of-life ensures the preservation of human dignity and safeguards the intrinsic worth of humanity which would be eroded by allowing any person to be killed at the hand of another. Amarasekara and Bagaric (2002) argue that although allowing patients to die in pain against their wishes is undignified, killing a person can hardly represent respect or value for human life and could be seen as the very antithesis of respect for dignity.

Proponents of euthanasia believe that the right to choose euthanasia ought to be supported on the basis of autonomy. If the law supports the right of competent individuals to refuse even life-saving treatment, no matter how unreasonable that decision might be, then why deny access to euthanasia? Dworkin (1993) considers that all individuals will have their own view as to what amounts to a good death and if that perspective entails dying before life becomes painful and undignified, then that preference ought to be respected. Mandating that a person must die in any other way, on account of the subjective beliefs of others, is nothing but tyranny. In arguing for protection of the interests of individuals, Dworkin distinguishes between two types of interests. Critical interests are those that make life meaningful and are based upon determinations of what makes life worthwhile according to personal values and aspirations. Experiential interests are those that pertain to quality of life and from which a person experiences pleasure, or freedom from pain. According to Dworkin, critical interests are of fundamental importance and are pre-eminent in making life meaningful. The manner in which a person dies might be of critical interest to an individual, and on this basis if euthanasia offers the means for having a 'good death' then this choice ought to be respected. Dworkin qualifies his liberal ideas by suggesting that euthanasia ought to be an option available only for those predicted to die within a short, and foreseeable, time.

Opponents of euthanasia challenge the autonomy argument on several grounds, and the principles or values used to counterbalance autonomy can be persuasive. Critics argue that autonomy must be weighed against the interests of society as a whole, as illustrated by the poet John Donne that 'No man is an island, entire of itself; everyone is a continent, a part of the main'. The exercise of autonomy by one individual might have profound implications for society in that assisted dying could have detrimental effects on the lives of others. For example, if active euthanasia became an end-of-life option, then the elderly might feel pressurised into making such a choice due to perceived coercion rather than making a voluntary and autonomous choice. Furthermore, exercise of autonomy needs to be balanced against the sanctity of life principle, and there are moral grounds for arguing that death through choice ought not to be permitted since this violates the moral tenets that life is of the highest value. It has been argued that those who request euthanasia are likely to be influenced by their belief that their lives are worthless on account of depression, and often tragic and difficult life events and illness. They might not be aware of all treatment options and in fact once these have been explored may well change their minds and demonstrate a fervent wish to continue living. Death is inexorable and if such persons had been allowed to choose death, there would be no retreat from that position. The counterargument is that euthanasia must be subject to robust control, as already evident in some jurisdictions (see 10.5.3).

Opponents of euthanasia may base their opposition on the grounds that human life is sacred, as buttressed by the view of Western religions that people are created in God's image. The sanctity of life principle accords the highest value to all human life and in equal measures across all human beings. Killing is inherently wrong and the sanctity of life principle is inviolable as a cornerstone of relationships between individuals, as well as the bond between the individual and society. Accordingly it is God's law that life should not be taken and that death should occur naturally. In refusing to violate this principle, one respects the individual in the most fundamental way. To do otherwise, it is argued, commodifies human life in a way that is repugnant. Opponents of the inviolability of life doctrine tend to distinguish between that which makes life valuable and a living body. Technically a person with severe neurological compromise could be maintained on a life-support machine almost indefinitely. The body would be 'living' although no sentient life would be evident. The development of criteria for death, such as brainstem death (see 8.3.2(b)) has arguably simplified the approach to be taken in practical terms to define where the line lies between a 'living body' and 'life'.

Although the principle of sanctity of life is well recognised and pervasive, it is not absolute. Supporters of autonomy and the sanctity of life may equally accept that competent persons may refuse treatment that could save their lives. Dworkin (1993) argues that the value of life could be conceptually construed as lying within three domains: subjectively (from the perspective of the person himself or herself), instrumentally (for the value of that life for society and others) and intrinsically (which is the inherent value of life in itself). All these components are important in themselves and whether one opposes or supports euthanasia depends upon the relative weight that is placed upon the intrinsic value of life as balanced against subjective and instrumental values.

It is also apparent that individual perceptions and attitudes can alter with age and it is these individual values that in the long analysis contribute to societal ideals. Surveys and public-opinion polls on euthanasia reveal interesting trends. The House of Lords Select Committee in 2005 reported that the Voluntary Euthanasia Society survey showed that 47% of the population would be willing to assist others to take their own lives in the event of terminal illness or unbearable suffering. Likewise, Park (2007) found that 80% of the population stated that the law should allow a doctor to end someone's life at that person's request if that individual suffered a painful and incurable illness. However, a smaller percentage (45%) was also in favour of euthanasia if the illness was not considered to be terminal. The British Attitudes Survey found (perhaps unsurprisingly) that those who did not regularly subscribe to a religion were more likely not to oppose euthanasia. The study by Chapel (2006) is one of very few empirical studies undertaken at the time of death. This small-scale, qualitative study ascertained the views of those who were close to death and concluded that the majority were in favour of allowing euthanasia, particularly if the condition was terminal and accompanied by intractable pain.

10.3.2 Life-shortening treatment

Active euthanasia is a crime in the United Kingdom and the case of *R v Cox* (1992) 12 BMLR 38 illustrates the approach of the law towards a doctor who commits the offence by administering life-shortening treatment.

Dr Cox was a consultant rheumatologist who for several years had treated his 70-year-old patient, Mrs Boyes, for rheumatoid arthritis. Mrs Boyes was terminally ill with multiple-organ impairment. Evidence was available that she had repeatedly asked Dr Cox, and other health-care professionals, to end her life as her pain was unbearable and she considered that her life was no longer worth living. Her pain could not be controlled using conventional pain-management techniques. In response to her repeated requests, Dr Cox administered a lethal dose of potassium chloride which led to cardiac arrest and death.

Since the body of Mrs Boyes was cremated shortly after her death, it was not possible to establish definitively that the administration of potassium chloride was either the sole cause, or had contributed significantly, or had been a substantial cause, of her death. As a result, Dr Cox was charged with *attempted* murder and convicted. In his summing up to the jury, Ognall J stated that it is never lawful to use drugs with the primary purpose of hastening the moment of death. Potassium chloride had no analgesic or curative properties and even a single ampoule was enough to cause death. On the evidence, Dr Cox had injected two ampoules.

Unlike murder, attempted murder carries no mandatory sentence. Dr Cox was convicted and given a 12-month suspended sentence. At the subsequent disciplinary hearing of the General Medical Council the outcome was that he was allowed to continue to practise subject to conditions being imposed upon his registration. The relatively lenient penalty and regulatory sanction appear to indicate a sense of sympathy for the motives of his actions.

Although the legal position on active euthanasia is clear, a doctor may in certain circumstances provide treatment that has the side effect of hastening death (see 10.3.3). The Voluntary Euthanasia Society (2003) survey of over 1000 doctors practising in the United Kingdom found that 40% of respondents had been asked by patients to help them die and 55% of doctors held the view that euthanasia ought to be legalised. An earlier study by Ward and Tate (1994), in their survey of some 400 English doctors, found that 9% had taken active steps to hasten the death of patients who had requested euthanasia and 32% had in some way complied with such a request from a patient.

10.3.3 Doctrine of double effect

The doctrine of double effect draws a distinction between the intended results of a treatment or intervention and those consequences that are merely foreseen, yet unintended. Essentially, when an action has two recognised effects one of which is intended and desirable and the other which is unintended and undesirable, then in certain circumstances that action will be morally acceptable (see 1.8.2).

Four conditions must be satisfied in order for an act with a double effect to be morally justified:

▶ the action itself must not be (regardless of its consequences) inherently wrong;
▶ the good effect must not be achieved through the means of the bad effect;
▶ the intention must be solely to produce the good effect;
▶ a proportionate and favourable balance must exist between the beneficial and detrimental effects of the action.

In end-of-life decisions the doctrine tends to be applied to the administration of pain-relieving medication, (such as those derived from opium), which are known to have two principal effects. The ability to control pain and suffering represents their beneficial and desirable action, while the potential side effect of respiratory depression, which can hasten death, is an undesirable effect. Administration of opium-based pain relief is, however, in certain circumstances considered morally and clinically appropriate. The intended effect of administering the medication is to relieve suffering; the decision as to the amount to be given must be proportionate to the level of pain, and the effect that the medication is likely to have upon breathing is an undesired and unintended side effect, rather than a means of achieving the beneficial effect of pain relief. Alternatively, if administration of pain-relieving medication was given with the intention of killing the patient then this would not be morally permissible according to the doctrine. Whilst killing the patient would most certainly relieve the patient's pain, the beneficial intention of pain relief would be achieved by means of the undesirable effect.

In *R v Adams* [1957] Crim LR 365, Dr Adams was charged with administering a fatal dose of heroin and morphine to an elderly patient who was incurably ill. In his famous direction to the jury, Devlin J stated that 'If the first purpose of medicine, the restoration of health, can no longer be achieved, there is still much for the doctor to do and he is entitled to do all that is proper and necessary to relieve pain and suffering even if the measures he takes may incidentally shorten life.' This principle was echoed by Lord Goff in *Airedale NHS Trust v Bland* [1993] AC 789 when he stated that 'a doctor may, when caring for a patient who is, for example, dying of cancer, lawfully administer painkilling drugs despite the fact that he knows that an incidental effect of that application will be to abbreviate the patient's life'. The law therefore may avoid infraction of the principle of the avoidance of killing, by means of the doctrine of double effect.

The doctrine has its origins in the moral theology of the Roman Catholic Church and is subscribed to and defended by supporters of the sanctity of life principle. However, the 'good' and 'bad' effects demand that the principle can only be applied with reference to the relative positions of these terms. Within end-of-life decision-making it can be applied to a patient's reason for refusing life-sustaining treatment (thereby accelerating his or her own death). Refusal of treatment with a view to committing suicide would violate the sanctity of life principle whereas refusing treatment for any other reason, but without intending to die even in the full knowledge that refusal will hasten death, does not breach the sanctity of life according to the doctrine.

Thus, for the patient who experiences great pain and suffering and who is expected to die imminently, administration of sufficient therapeutic quantities of morphine-based analgesics would seemingly satisfy the four conditions even where it is recognised that death is likely to be hastened as a result of administration. Adequate symptomatic relief would seem to be a proportionate response in the circumstances. Hence, the perception that the doctrine of double effect is in fact euthanasia by stealth that is used by doctors to practice covert active euthanasia (National Council for Hospice and Specialist Palliative Care Services, 1997). This could also account for the high proportion of respondent doctors (in the surveys cited above) who stated that they had performed euthanasia. Although the doctrine has been used by the courts, and is widely recognised, tensions exist in the moral arguments as well as in the interpretation of the central notion of 'intention'.

From a moral standpoint a central requirement for the legitimate application of the doctrine is that the doctor's intention is solely to achieve the good effect. A key issue is the conceptual distinction drawn between 'intention' and 'foreseeing a virtually certain consequence' of the action to be undertaken. These arguments were developed by John Finnis and John Harris in 'Euthanasia examined' (Keown, 1995). Finnis takes an extremely narrow view of the concept of intention. As an example, he cites a British climber in the Andes who finally cuts the rope on which his friend was dangling, lest he himself be dragged over the precipice. Later he found, to his great delight, that the friend he had thought certain to be dead, had fallen into deep snow which had broken his fall and, as a result, he was unharmed. According to Finnis, the side effect (of causing injury or death of the friend) is in the first place unintended. Second, the climber did not calibrate or adjust his plans to achieve the side effect (since his intention had been to save himself). Therefore the conceptual difference between the intended effect and the unintended side effect carries significant moral weight. Harris rejects this argument on the grounds that an individual is morally responsible for what he or she knowingly and voluntarily brings about, irrespective of whether the consequences were intended or not. Thus, Harris, arguing from a utilitarian perspective, holds that moral culpability attaches to a virtually certain consequence that follows from an intended result.

Another problematic issue lies in reconciling the narrow construction of intention in the doctrine of double effect compared with the interpretation of intention in criminal law. In *R v Woollin* [1999] 1 AC 82 the House of Lords stated that if 'the defendant recognised that death or serious harm would be virtually certain (barring some unforeseen intervention) to result from his voluntary act', then the jury 'may find it easy to infer that he intended to kill or do serious bodily harm, even though he may not have had any desire to achieve that result'. Essentially, therefore, on the *Woollin* construct the jury is entitled to infer that intention encompasses directly intended consequences, as well as those that are subjectively recognised by the defendant as virtually certain consequences of the conduct. Viewed from this perspective intention, as within the doctrine of double effect, seems to sit uneasily with the *Woollin* decision. An alternative approach was apparent in the Court of Appeal decision in *Re A (children) (conjoined twins: surgical separation)* [2000] 4 All ER 961, where reconciling *Woollin* with the principle of double effect was left unresolved and justification of the act that accelerated death was based upon the doctrine of necessity.

Following her stroke, Lilly retains decision-making capacity. Although she experiences some pain, this is not a prominent feature. A junior registrar considers giving her intravenous potassium chloride (which would cause cardiac arrest) or commencing a morphine drip (which would alleviate her pain but might also lead to respiratory depression and arrest):

▶ Consider the ethical and legal issues of the doctor's decision to administer potassium chloride. Could this decision be justified on the grounds of double effect?
▶ Consider the ethical and legal issues of the doctor's decision to administer morphine. To what extent, if any, could this decision be justified on the doctrine of double effect?
▶ Is there anything that can be done to help Lilly?

The junior doctor decides to administer a morphine infusion and Lilly dies peacefully three hours later:

▶ What are the potential legal implications for the junior doctor?
▶ What are the potential ethical and professional regulatory consequences?

10.4 Suicide and assisted suicide

Suicide has been decriminalised by section 1 of the Suicide Act 1961. However, assisting in the suicide of another remains a crime and is punishable by up to 14 years of imprisonment. It is unusual for a crime to be committed by assisting in an activity that in itself is not criminal, and the case for the continued criminalisation of assisted suicide remains controversial.

10.4.1 Decriminalisation of suicide

Section 1 of the Suicide Act 1961 states that:

> The rule of law whereby it is a crime for a person to commit suicide is hereby abrogated.
> Section 2 pertains to criminal liability for complicity in another's suicide and provides that:

> 2(1)   A person ('D') commits an offence if –
>   (a) D does an act capable of encouraging or assisting the suicide or attempted suicide of another person, and
>   (b) D's act was intended to encourage or assist suicide or an attempt at suicide.
> 2(1A) The person referred to in subsection (1)(a) need not be a specific person (or class of persons) known to, or identified by, D.
> 2(1B) D may commit an offence under this section whether or not a suicide, or an attempt at suicide, occurs.
> 2(1C) An offence under this section is triable on indictment and a person convicted of such an offence is liable to imprisonment for a term not exceeding 14 years.

Section 2 was amended by section 59 of the Coroners and Justice Act 2009 which came into force on 1 February 2010. These amendments have replaced the substantive offence of aiding, abetting, counselling or procuring suicide and the separate crime of attempt with a single offence described in modern language. The purpose of these changes is to improve public understanding of the law and to clarify that the law extends to online actions.

No changes have been made to section 1 of the Suicide Act 1961. The decriminalisation of suicide means that even if a person's intention to commit suicide is known, the court has no power to interfere with that decision. The case of *Re Z* [2004] EWHC 2817 concerned a woman with an incurable and progressive condition, cerebellar ataxia. She wished to end her life at Dignitas in Switzerland, a decision supported by her husband. The local authority sought to restrain Mr Z from removing his wife from its care. Headley J (at paragraph 12) rejected the claim and ruled that although the local authority had a duty to inform the criminal authorities about Z's intention, it did not extend beyond that. He stated:

> Section 1 of the Suicide Act 1961 abrogated the rule that made suicide criminal. It did not make suicide lawful, much less did it encourage it; it simply removed suicide from being punishable as a criminal act. It follows inevitably that our law does not penalise the decision of a competent person to take their own life. Moreover nor does the law prohibit them from so doing.

The basis of this decision is founded on autonomy and human freedom which, if it is to have any real meaning, must in the context of section 1 of the 1961 Act, involve the right of a competent person to commit suicide even though this decision may be considered as unwise or bad in the opinions of others. Thus, although suicide is no longer a criminal act, assisting someone to commit suicide remains an offence.

10.4.2 Assisted suicide

Section 59 of the Coroners and Justice Act 2009 amends section 2 of the Suicide Act 1961. Section 2, now provides for a single offence of encouraging or assisting suicide and will apply where an individual carries out an act that is capable of intentionally encouraging or assisting another to commit, or attempt to commit, suicide. The person committing the offence need not know the other person, or even be able to identify them. This change has been made to extend the scope of the offence to websites and publications that promote suicide.

Section 2A(1) provides that a person who arranges for another to carry out an act capable of encouraging or assisting suicide, or the attempted suicide of another, will be liable for the offence if the victim carries out that act. This means that if A arranges for B to supply lethal medication to C with the intention that C will use the medication to commit suicide, although B may have physically supplied the medication to C, A will also be liable for the offence.

Section 2A(2) provides that an act can be capable of encouraging or assisting suicide even if the circumstances are such that it was impossible for that act to have encouraged or assisted. This provides for the situation where pills (believed to be lethal) are provided with the intention that they will assist another to commit suicide, but in fact the pills are harmless. This extends to the situation where lethal pills are sent with the intention that the person receiving the pills will commit, or attempt to commit, suicide but the pills are never received.

Section 2A(3) clarifies that acts capable of encouraging or assisting the commission or attempt to commit suicide include threatening another person, or putting pressure on another to commit, or attempt to commit, suicide. Performing an act capable of encouraging or assisting suicide is insufficient and the act must be done with the intention of encouraging or assisting. Proceedings under section 2(1) can only be brought by or with the consent of the Director of Public Prosecutions (section 2(4)).

The new provisions are intended to capture the behaviours of encouraging or assisting suicide, or attempted suicide, previously provided for by the phrase 'aiding, abetting, counselling and procuring'. The court's interpretation of the previous provision can be illustrated by *Attorney General v Abell* [1984] 1 All ER 277. The defendants had been members of the Voluntary Euthanasia Society and had published a booklet entitled *A Guide to Self-Deliverance*. This contained a section that set out the reasons why one should think twice before contemplating suicide and another section which described five separate methods by which suicide could be committed. Evidence was available that following distribution 15 suicide cases could be linked to publication of the booklet within the first 18 months. In a further 19 cases, evidence was available that the deceased had been a member of the Society, or at least had corresponded with the Society. The Attorney General sought a declaration that future supply of the booklet would amount to an offence under section 2(1) of the 1961 Act. Woolf J, in giving judgment, determined that the booklet, which included information on methods, could be expected to encourage suicide, and that distribution could be an offence. However, before an offence could be established it would have to be proved that:

(a) the booklet was intended to be used by someone contemplating suicide and the contents were intended to assist that person;
(b) the booklet was distributed in the knowledge that the recipient planned to read it and use it, and
(c) such a person was assisted or encouraged by reading the booklet to attempt or commit suicide.

While this judgment provides clear guidance, it appears to restrict the application of section 2(1) of the 1961 Act. Given the amendments of the Coroners and Justice Act 2009 and the new sections 2A(1)(2) and (3), it is likely that the new offence of encouraging or assisting another to commit, or attempt to commit, suicide would cast the net more widely to establish an offence of assisted suicide.

Scotland has no specific provisions on assisted suicide which could lead to potential uncertainty, although a person assisting another to commit suicide could be charged under homicide laws.

10.4.3 Assisted suicide and human rights

Although competent individuals may take their own lives without State interference (section 1 of the Suicide Act 1961), this right does not extend to those unable to commit suicide independently. Those unable to take their own lives, on account of disability or for any other reason, cannot lawfully obtain assistance in order to do so. This apparent anomaly was challenged on the grounds of human rights in *R (Pretty) v Director of Public Prosecutions* [2001] UKHL 61.

Diane Pretty was paralysed from the waist down on account of motor neurone disease, a terminal neurological condition. Her prognosis was poor due to the progressive and degenerative nature of her illness. Due to her disabilities she was unable to take her own life and asked the Director of Public Prosecutions (DPP) for assurance that her husband (if he assisted her to die) would not be prosecuted. This was refused. She subsequently challenged this decision, as well as section 2(1) of the Suicide Act 1961 on the grounds that her convention rights had been infringed. Her claim was rejected by the High Court and on appeal to the House of Lords.

Two principal issues considered by the House of Lords (amongst other matters) was the power of the DPP to undertake not to prosecute in advance of a proposed suicide and the compatibility of section 2(1) of the Suicide Act 1961 with the European Convention in respect of Articles 8 and 14. Articles 2, 3 and 9 were also considered.

With regard to the extent of the DPP's discretion, Lord Steyn stated (at paragraph 65):

> The DPP may not under s2(4) exercise his discretion to stop all prosecutions under s2(1). It follows that he may only exercise his discretion, for or against a prosecution, in relation to the circumstances of a specific prosecution. His discretion can therefore only be exercised in respect of past events giving rise to a suspicion that a crime under s2(1) has been committed. And then the exercise of this discretion will take into account whether there is a realistic prospect of securing a conviction and whether a prosecution would be in the public interest.

In essence, the House of Lords refused to provide a guarantee against prosecution before a crime had taken place. Tur (2003) argues that section 2(4), which allows prosecution only after an assisted suicide has taken place, requires that a person knows in advance if a course of conduct will attract criminal sanctions. He stated (at 3):

> There is something fundamentally wrong in saying to someone like Diane Pretty 'well, you have had a miserable time and morally we quite see that you should be allowed the assistance you seek in ending your own life, but you know, the greater good of society requires that you should continue to suffer for fear of being a bad example – hard cases make bad law'. Morally, society simply should not use someone like Diane Pretty as a means only and not as an end in herself.

In *Re Z* Headley J recognised that it might not always be in the public interest to prosecute someone who has contravened section 2(1) since 'Parliament recognises that although an act may be criminal, it is not always in the public interests to prosecute in respect of it.' With regard to the compatibility of section 2(1) and convention rights, the House of Lords considered the decision of the Supreme Court of Canada in *Rodriguez v Attorney General of Canada* [1994] 2 LRC 136. The facts of the case were strikingly similar to those of *Pretty*. The appellant, who had a similar condition to Mrs Pretty, sought an order to allow her doctor to set up a means by which she could end her life at a time of her own choosing. Although suicide is not a crime in Canada, section 241(b) of the Criminal Code was very similar to the original section 2(1) of the Suicide Act 1961. Mrs Rodriguez challenged section 241(b) under the Canadian Charter of Rights and Freedoms and lost to a majority of 5:4 in favour of upholding the Canadian Criminal Code. Likewise, the House of Lords found no incompatibility of section 2(1) with convention rights. In considering Article 8, Lord Bingham stated: 'I would for my part accept the Secretary of State's submission that Mrs Pretty's rights under article 8 are not engaged at all.' Mason and Laurie (2006) have criticised the argument that Article 8 was inapplicable on the basis that the concept of autonomy, as generally understood, concerns and includes decisions about dying. Since dying is part of life (even if death in itself is not) it is difficult to understand or imagine how some decisions about the nature of one's death could have nothing to do with the exercise of self-determined choice. However, Lord Bingham qualified his argument by stating: 'If, however, that conclusion is wrong, and the prohibition of assisted suicide in section 2 of the 1961 Act infringes her convention right under article 8, it is necessary to consider whether the infringement is shown by the Secretary of State to be justifiable under the terms of article 8(2).' Lord Bingham added that if Article 8 had been engaged, then criminalisation of assisted suicide would be justified under Article 8(2) as seeking to protect the rights of vulnerable persons. In his words: 'It is not hard to imagine that an elderly person, in the absence of any pressure, might opt for a premature end to life if that were available, not from a desire to die or a willingness to stop living, but from a desire to stop being a burden to others.'

Article 2 was considered not to protect the right to self-determined choice in respect of decisions of life and death. Instead, Article 2 enunciates the principle of the inviolability of life and guaranteed, subject to the statutory qualification, that no one should be intentionally deprived of his or her life. Article 3 was dismissed because Mrs Pretty's treatment did not meet the required level of severity to be considered torture on account of the availability of symptomatic care. Likewise, it was not credible to suggest that the State was inflicting inhuman or degrading treatment since Mrs Pretty's suffering arose from her clinical condition. Article 8 was dismissed in that this right did not pertain to the manner by which a person wished to die, and Article 9 was considered not to provide persons with the right to perform any act according to any belief that they might hold. Article 14 was inapplicable since Mrs Pretty had no convention rights to which she could attach her claim for discrimination in the exercise of that right.

Pretty v UK (2002) 35 EHRR 1 was the first case on which the ECtHR had to determine an issue on which the House of Lords had previously delivered a judgment based on the Human Rights Act 1998. In upholding the reasoning of the House of Lords the ECtHR allowed a considerable margin of appreciation to municipal jurisdiction to determine this controversial matter. The ECtHR acknowledged the tension in that a competent person could refuse treatment which could result in her death, and that it would not be unlawful for an able-bodied individual to take her own life. The issue before the court was that a competent woman asked for assistance in committing suicide since she was unable to perform the act for herself. In delivering judgment, the ECtHR stated: 'The applicant was prevented by law from exercising her choice to avoid an undignified and distressing end to her life which potentially constituted an interference with her right to respect for private life. It followed that article 8 was engaged.'

The ECtHR recognised that the principle of autonomy engaged in the context of assisted suicide. The court also referred to *Rodriguez* (see above) and the Supreme Court's recognition that the prohibition on assisted suicide could contribute to stress and prevent an individual from managing her own death, thereby depriving her of autonomy which would need to be justified under the principles of fundamental justice.

The dissonance between the competent person's right to refuse life-saving treatment and the prohibition against a competent person receiving assistance to commit suicide has been succinctly stated by Pattinson (2006) in that 'placing a pill on Mrs Pretty's tongue is *legally* distinguishable from turning off Ms B's ventilator at her request. Both lead to death, but the first is legally prohibited (if the pill has no palliative effect) and the second is legally required (as the doctor has a legal obligation to comply with a valid request that treatment be withdrawn)'. Whether this distinction is morally defensible remains (at least for the time being) controversial.

10.4.4   Assisted suicide policy

The *Purdy* litigation has compelled the Director of Public Prosecutions to publish the Assisted Suicide Policy. Ms Purdy has progressive, multiple sclerosis, a condition for which there is no known cure. She believes that there will come a time when she feels that her existence would be such that she may wish to end her life, but is concerned that at that stage she would be unable to do so without assistance from others. In particular, she anticipates that she might wish to travel to a country that permits assisted suicide accompanied by her husband. Ms Purdy's fundamental concern is that her husband will be at risk of prosecution under section 2(1) of the Suicide Act 1961 on his return and on these grounds asked for clarification of the Director of Public Prosecutions' criteria as to whether a prosecution would be brought. In particular, she sought clarification of what represented 'assistance' for these purposes: would this include helping another to book a flight, driving them to the airport, or accompanying them on a final journey to a jurisdiction that permitted assisted suicide? She argued that if she knew these criteria in advance then her husband could consider this before making a commitment to assist with travel plans or accompanying her to another jurisdiction. Without this knowledge, she might feel compelled to make the journey at an earlier stage, so that she could travel alone. This predicament, she argued, was state interference with her human rights. She applied for judicial review of the Director of Public Prosecution's failure to set out guidance as to when a prosecution for aiding and abetting suicide would ensue.

Pursuant to the Prosecution of Offences Act 1985, the Director of Public Prosecutions has a duty to issue guidance for Crown Prosecutors on the principles to be applied to determine whether proceedings for crimes should be brought. At first instance the claim failed. The Divisional Court held (following *Pretty*) that Ms Purdy's Article 8 rights did not engage and even if they did, then interference was justified under Article 8(2).

Ms Purdy's appeal to the Court of Appeal was dismissed (*R (Purdy) v Director of Public Prosecutions* [2009] EWCA Civ 92). The court held that it was bound to follow the House of Lords' decision in *Pretty*, notwithstanding the inconsistency between this and the subsequent judgment of the European Court (in respect of the engagement of Article 8). The court expressed sympathy for the dreadful predicament of Ms Purdy and her husband, but according to the court, what the appellant sought was 'the nearest thing possible to a guarantee that if the circumstances … come to pass, and her husband assists her suicide when she is no longer able to end her own life by her own unassisted actions, he would not be prosecuted'. However, prior to the appeal being heard the Director of Public Prosecutions had published a detailed account of the rationale for the decision not to prosecute the parents of Daniel James. Daniel James was a 23-year-old man who had been seriously injured in a rugby accident and following which he had been accompanied by his parents to receive assistance with his suicide at a Dignitas clinic. In the view of the court, the general guidance on this matter, together with the more specific reasons provided by the Director of Public Prosecutions following the death of Daniel James, constituted sufficient information to enable Ms Purdy's legal advisers to assess the likelihood of prosecution if her husband was to assist with her suicide.

Ms Purdy contended she was not asking for her husband be granted a guarantee of immunity from prosecution. What she sought was the information she required in order to make a decision which affected her private life, as there were already a number of people who had made the journey to countries where assisted suicide was lawful, and those who had provided assisted had not been prosecuted. This meant that the right to respect for private life under Article 8 of the convention is engaged. She argued that having regard to section 2(4) of the 1961 Act, it was clear that Parliament had not intended that all those who might be guilty of an offence under section 2(1) of the Act should be prosecuted for the offence. Clarification was required as to the circumstances when it would be in the public interest for a prosecution to be brought against those who had rendered assistance. She successfully appealed to the House of Lords (*R (on the application of Purdy) v Director of Public Prosecutions* [2009] UKHL 45) which held that the issue was directed to section 2(4) of the 1961 Act and the way in which the DPP could be expected to exercise discretion. On the question of discretion the following factors came into play: consistency of practice; prevention of abuse which might result in vexatious private prosecution; to enable mitigating factors to be taken into account and to provide central control in this area of law. Consistency of practice was particularly important in the Purdy's case where the question was whether Ms Purdy's husband would be subject to prosecution if he assisted her to travel to another jurisdiction where assisted suicide was lawful. The House of Lords held (following *Pretty*) that Article 8 could be engaged and therefore any justifiable derogation under Article 8(2) had to satisfy the tests of accessibility and foreseeability. The Code for the Crown Prosecutors (which gave general guidance on prosecution and was a valuable safeguard for the vulnerable) nevertheless fell short in this regard where the offence was one of aiding and abetting the suicide of a terminally ill or severely and incurably disabled person who wished for assistance to travel to a place where assisted suicide was lawful. The Director of Public Prosecutions was therefore obliged to clarify the relevant factors as to whether to prosecute in this special and defined set of circumstances to ensure predictability and consistency of decision-making.

Following *Purdy*, the Director of Public Prosecutions was required to promulgate an offence-specific policy to identify the facts and circumstances that would lead to prosecution. This was published on 25 February 2010 (available at http://www.cps.gov.uk) and identifies 16 public interest factors in favour of prosecution being where the victim:

- was under the age of 18,
- lacked decision-making capacity,
- had not reached a voluntary, settled and informed decision to commit suicide,
- had not clearly and unequivocally communicated a decision,

- did not seek assistance from the suspect personally,
- was physically able to undertake the act herself.

Where the suspect:

- was not wholly motivated by compassion,
- pressurised the victim to commit suicide,
- did not take reasonable steps to ensure the absence of any form of pressure,
- had a history of violence or abuse against the victim,
- was unknown to the victim and encouraged or assisted the victim to commit, or attempt to commit, suicide,
- provided encouragement or assistance to more than one victim who were unknown to one another,
- was paid by the victim,
- was acting in the capacity as a doctor, nurse, health-care professional or professional carer,
- was aware that victim intended to commit suicide in a public place
- was acting in the capacity of a person involved in the management, or as an employee, of an organisation which allows others to commit suicide.

The six public interest factors that militate against prosecution are where the:

- victim had reached a voluntary clear, settled and informed decision,
- suspect was wholly motivated by compassion,
- actions of the suspect were only of minor encouragement or assistance,
- suspect had sought to dissuade the victim,
- actions of the suspect could be characterised as reluctant encouragement or assistance in the face of a determined wish on the part of the victim to commit suicide,
- suspect reported the victim's suicide to the police and fully assisted with enquiries.

Lilly is competent but physically dependent on others for her needs. She is unable to commit suicide and wishes to travel to a jurisdiction that permits assisted suicide. Her nephew has agreed to travel with her:

- Consider the moral arguments for and against assisted suicide. Which is the most persuasive?
- What are the potential legal implications for Lilly's nephew?

10.4.5 Physician-assisted suicide

Physician-assisted suicide refers to the direct or indirect assistance of a doctor intended to enable a patient to end his or her own life. This will involve providing a patient with medication, or a prescription for medication, in sufficient quantities to cause death. From one perspective, such an action is not morally wrong since the supplier of drugs has merely provided the means to commit suicide and has not been the direct cause of death, as compared to the doctor who injects a competent patient with a lethal compound at the patient's request. In certain circumstances, however, the boundary between physician-assisted suicide and voluntary active euthanasia is virtually indistinguishable. Beauchamp and Childress (2009) assert that some physician-related activities are ethically justified in assisted dying, whereas others are not.

Dr Jack Kevorkian, a Michigan pathologist, designed a suicide machine to help terminally ill patients to end their own lives. One such patient was Janet Adkins, a 54-year-old woman with early-stage Alzheimer's disease, who retained decision-making capacity. Dr Kevorkian commenced an intravenous infusion with normal saline, a non-lethal fluid. A machine was attached that enabled the self-injection of a lethal cocktail of drugs to be administered on the flick of a switch by the patient. Many commentators have condemned Kevorkian's actions out of concern about physician-assisted suicide, the potential for abuse and lack of control and accountability, arguing that permitting doctors to lawfully assist suicide would represent the start of a slippery slope leading to involuntary and non-voluntary euthanasia.

The lack of organised facility for assisted suicide by physicians is seen by some as a deplorable gap in our society. According to this perspective, urgent policy must be developed to ensure robust safeguards and accountability structures can be put in place underpinned by public and parliamentary consultation and scrutiny. A bright line would need to be apparent in respect of justified and unjustified physician assistance. However, the extent to which a public consensus will readily be achieved on this highly controversial topic seems questionable, particularly in a society that is seemingly evenly divided with strongly held views.

Beauchamp and Childress (2009) consider the following criteria to be justifiable bases for physician-assisted suicide:

- ▶ A voluntary request by a competent patient.
- ▶ Evidence of an enduring doctor and patient relationship.
- ▶ Mutual and informed decision making by patient and physician.
- ▶ Supportive and critical probing of the patient's decision to commit suicide.
- ▶ The patient's considered rejection of alternatives.
- ▶ Evidence of structured consultation with other parties.
- ▶ A patient's continued expression of preference for death.
- ▶ Unacceptable suffering by the patient.
- ▶ Use of painless and comfortable methods.

In this context, physician-assisted suicide could perhaps be viewed as part of the continuum of medical care. A physician's primary duty is the care and safety of all patients. However, not all medical conditions can be 'cured', yet there is far more that a doctor can do, such as relieving pain and suffering. For patients with terminal conditions and intractable pain medical care could arguably extend to the relief of distress and suffering that can only be brought about by death. At the very end-of-life in circumstances of zero prognosis there is perhaps little moral distinction between a clinical response that facilitates death by the easing of pain and suffering, and one that alleviates pain and suffering by hastening death. Respect for autonomy and beneficence, underscored by an ethic of care and compassion, offers a strong basis for recognising that physician-assisted suicide may have a legitimate position in contemporary society.

10.5 The debate around euthanasia and assisted suicide

The debate around euthanasia and assisted suicide essentially hinges on whether such practices represent 'killing' or not. Jurisdictions that regard such practices as falling within special categories of death have tended to legalise assisted death whether in the form of euthanasia or assisted suicide, most often within carefully circumscribed parameters. Such practices tend to remain illegal in jurisdictions that consider euthanasia or assisted suicide as being akin to killing. An alternative to either legalisation or continued criminalisation has been proposed by Huxtable (2007) who considers that:

> Open acceptance that euthanasia is a particular type of killing, subject to particular moral norms which are themselves the source of much conscientious competition, must be a move in the right direction...The first, central reform is that the law ought explicitly to recognise mercy killing as an offence, which is also available as a partial defence to other homicide charges.

Viewed from this perspective, there could be a focus on moral causes that precede any killing as well as specific circumstances which could offer a defence against the crime. This represents a compromise position. The key concerns of proponents and opponents in this debate have been well rehearsed by countless distinguished philosophers and commentators. The following section aims to give a flavour of the central arguments.

10.5.1 The moral debate

The principal argument against euthanasia and assisted suicide is that of respect for the sanctity of life. Proponents of this belief argue that there is something inherently wrong with killing a human being that goes against respect for the person, a view shared by several faiths that treat human life as sacred. While the inevitability of death is accepted, it is held that a moral duty exists to conserve human life wherever, and whenever, possible.

The sanctity of life principle derives from the concept that man is created in the image of God. How pervasive this view is in Britain is unclear, particularly on account of the growing trend towards secularism. Scientific advances in medical technology, genetic engineering and an understanding of the universe appear to be demystifying the 'wonder of creation'. Religious arguments are, however, persuasive and strongly supported by those who espouse a theological stance. However, for some, the universality of religious belief within a secular society is unconvincing. Otlowski (2000 at 216) states:

> Religion is a matter of personal commitment, and objections to active voluntary euthanasia based purely on religious views should not dominate the law, nor impinge on the freedom of others. Whilst the convictions of believers must obviously be respected, it must be recognised that in a pluralistic and largely secular society, the freedom of conviction of non-believers must also be upheld.

Proponents of assisted dying do not seek to impose their beliefs on others. They ask instead that assisted dying be available to those wish to exercise this choice in circumstances of terminal illness, intractable pain or extreme distress at the end-of-life. This compares with those who argue against legalisation since they are stating that not only do they themselves not wish to access this choice but that access to assisted dying should be denied to all.

One argument against legalisation of euthanasia is the potential risk of abuse, particularly for elderly citizens who might feel duty bound to seek death. There could be several subtle, and perhaps none too subtle, drivers behind perceived coercion including avaricious relatives, limited health-care resources and a person's subjective sense of not wishing to be a burden on others. These pressures need not be overt and might operate as subtle influences that affect personal choice. When patients consider themselves to be in helpless situations and feel ambivalent as to whether they live or die, an inclination towards requesting assisted death could be engineered without recourse to blatant coercion. Well-meaning and discreet suggestion could influence vulnerable persons and even subconscious suggestions such as gestures, tone of voice and changes in expression might coerce a susceptible person to choose death. The motives of others need not always be base, or consciously manipulative. For example, a quick release from suffering might be tempting to a patient who is depressed and frightened, and who might have received a bad prognosis regarding an illness (Kass and Lund, 1996). Whether a ban on euthanasia can adequately protect vulnerable individuals seems dubious. Competent patients can refuse life-saving treatment and passive euthanasia can occur by withdrawal of treatment or by the legitimate use of analgesics at the end-of-life, all of which could have the effect of hastening death.

Since the outcome of euthanasia will be the patient's death, which is irreversible and affords no opportunity for correcting any error, it would be vital that any request for euthanasia is voluntarily made. Concerns have been raised that requests for euthanasia are often made by the clinically depressed, a condition that frequently accompanies the terminal stages of illness. Wolf (1998) argues that a strong link exists between clinical depression and requests for assisted death, a correlation that is stronger than between requests for euthanasia in the context of chronic pain. A patient who requests assisted death might instead be seeking relief from their depression or pain, both of which could be treatable conditions. In Wolf's view, terminal patients 'are quite unlike independent rights bearers freely negotiating in business transactions. Instead, they are profoundly dependent, often at the mercy of health-care professionals, for everything from toileting to life-saving care, and may be experiencing too much pain, discomfort or depression to make independent and truly voluntary decisions'. There is also the argument that end-of-life care has advanced considerably in recent years. Palliative care can offer better and more optimised pain control and symptom relief than ever before. These benefits and developments ought to militate against the need for legalisation of assisted dying. While this is undoubtedly true, even optimal palliative care will not negate the mental anguish that some experience towards the end of their lives. There are inherent limitations of palliative care for relief of suffering and even the very best of care might not address aspects such as loss of autonomy, loss of control of bodily functions and subjective loss of dignity. For some, even the best palliative care cannot effectively control their pain (House of Lords Select Committee on Assisted Dying, 2005). A further argument advanced by opponents of assisted dying is that legalisation could represent the beginning of a slippery slope. According to this argument, allowing voluntary euthanasia will inevitably progress to other less-acceptable practices, on account of a progressive desensitisation of society leading to blurring of the boundaries between voluntary, non-voluntary and involuntary euthanasia. Proponents of the slippery slope principle contend that legalising voluntary euthanasia will make involuntary killing more likely and there is some evidence from other jurisdictions that hints that this might well be true. The Dutch experience suggests that non-voluntary euthanasia is practised and condoned in The Netherlands (Keown, 1995). Despite this, some commentators consider that even if there is evidence of unacceptable instances of euthanasia, absolute prohibition may not present the optimum regulatory response. Distinguishing between acceptable, and unacceptable, practices in situations that lie in the middle of the slippery slope, rather than at the polar ends, will always be difficult. This is the typical 'grey area problem' that becomes apparent whenever any attempt is made at regulatory reform. In these circumstances, it is not obvious that 'a blanket ban' is the best response to concerns about a practice's potential for leading to a related, though unacceptable, end point.

According to Jackson (2004) if circumstances can be envisaged whereby euthanasia might be considered legitimate, a complete prohibition to prevent its use in some less-compelling circumstances is an overly blunt approach to regulation, especially since the consequences for those who do merit access to euthanasia will be a protracted, painful or possibly intolerable death. According to this view, it seems more logical to put in place regulations that strictly confine access to those whose circumstances comply with specific criteria, rather than to impose a blanket ban.

Proponents of legalisation for assisted dying frequently base their view on what is perhaps their strongest argument, which is respect for autonomy. Death marks the end-of-life and is relevant to us all. Accordingly, those who are at the ends of their lives ought to have control over how they die. The knowledge and accompanying assurance that assisted death exists as an option can provide considerable comfort and peace of mind. Knowledge that euthanasia is prohibited could for some cause extreme distress on account of the perceived loss of control over one's autonomous being. Legalisation of euthanasia would safeguard choice at the end-of-life. It must be recognised, however, that this choice is different from the autonomous refusal of treatment which must be respected by health-care practitioners. The choice of lawful euthanasia would not compel a doctor to follow this course of action which could be refused on the grounds of it being incompatible with the doctor's duty of care or the doctor's conscientious objection. The right that would ensue from legalisation of euthanasia would not be the right to compel a doctor to assist a patient, but rather the right to lawfully seek help from a willing doctor. An analogy can be drawn with abortion. An abortion carried out in compliance with the Abortion Act 1967 will be lawful, although a woman cannot compel a doctor to carry out an abortion (section 4 of the Abortion Act 1967).

The legal and ethical position in respect of euthanasia and assisted suicide is inconsistent and unclear. In certain circumstances it can be lawful to withdraw life-prolonging treatment, yet it is not lawful to give an injection that would produce a quick and painless death. This anomaly has been summarised by Frey (1998) in that: 'Withdrawing feeding tubes and starving the patient to death is permissible, supplying the patient with a pill that produces death is not. Yet both sorts of assistance assuredly produce death, and both sorts involve the patient and doctor acting together to produce that death.' It therefore seems little short of incredible that a patient who is terminally ill and on life support could result in such a moral transformation. In both cases, steps are taken that will assuredly produce death, and death will be certain. In both cases, the patient's death is intended. Therefore, there is an argument that they ought to be considered as equivalent.

A further reason for opposing legalisation of assisted dying is that this is already happening in any event. Magnusson (2004) conducted anonymous interviews with doctors, nurses and therapists working with patients with HIV and AIDS in Sydney, Melbourne and San Francisco. The results indicated that doctors were providing covert assistance to patients to assist their dying but little was known as to how this was being done. There seemed to be no consistency in approach and most instances seemed to reflect random decision-making. Magnusson observed (at 441):

> For me, the most striking feature of these accounts was the way they (healthcare professionals) portrayed the absence of norms or principles for deciding when it was appropriate to proceed. One doctor injected a young man on the first occasion they met, despite concerns from close

friends that the patient was depressed...In another case, a patient brought his death forward by a week so as not to interfere with the doctor's holiday plans.

Similar opinions have been voiced by Baron (1997). An article in the *Journal of the American Medical Association* (1996) indicated that physicians in Washington committed acts of physician-assisted suicide in numbers comparable to those in The Netherlands. In response, Baron states (at 15):

> It is an open secret that such technically illegal practices take place but prosecutions, and disciplinary actions involving them, have thus far been almost non-existent...Potential abuses are left completely without internal or external checks, and such a regime encourages the view that medical personnel may safely consider themselves 'above the law'. Patients are also denied the equal protection of the law.

Observations such as these, and others, have been given as the basis for adopting a pragmatic approach towards the legalisation of assisted dying so that appropriate checks and balances can be put in place. Criminalisation of assisted dying imposes a prohibition for opponents as well as advocates. Ideally, legalisation of assisted dying would permit choice for those who wish to end their lives. At the same time, regulation must provide a robust framework to protect the vulnerable and prevent potential abuse.

10.5.2   Legal inconsistencies

The principal objections to legalisation of assisted dying are based upon the need to avoid killing (see 10.5). This is primarily a deontological principle and can conflict with consequentialist ideologies of beneficence and non-maleficence.

In law a distinction is drawn between what is lawful and what is not by relying on the concepts of active killing versus letting die, and direct effects versus indirect effects. The law proscribes an act that leads to killing yet letting die by way of omission (withholding or withdrawing treatment) may be lawful. Likewise, the administration of a drug such as morphine will be unlawful if the intention is to kill the patient, although administration of the same drug with the intention of relieving pain, but having a foreseeable effect of causing death, might not be unlawful.

Is there really a valid distinction between active killing and letting die? Some argue that on the basis of intuition, such a distinction can be made. This instinctive response, however, could be on account of the way we have come to regard them as different. Furthermore, active killing is illegal whereas foregoing treatment might, in certain circumstances, be considered legal. However, the fact that one is legal and the other is not does not necessarily establish that a moral distinction exists between the two. Consequentialists argue that a difference exists between killing and letting die, and that the consequences to society will be far worse if active killing is permitted, and hence active killing is proscribed by law. Likewise, the distinction between death as a direct intended effect, and death as an indirect and merely foreseen effect, can be viewed as nothing more than prevarication. Within the notion of the doctrine of double effect, the unintended and undesirable effect is morally tolerable. An inherent and central notion of the doctrine is the character and the intention of the person who performs the act. Thus, if one maliciously took advantage of the severe pain of a patient and gave an unacceptably high dose of morphine, risking death, then that would be morally unacceptable. However, if the person performing the act did so without malice and for the intention of pain relief (nevertheless risking death or killing), then that action might be morally acceptable.

The distinctions drawn between killing and letting die are morally obscure. Beauchamp and Childress (2009) state that in ordinary language, 'killing is a causal action that brings about death, whereas letting die is an intentional avoidance of causal intervention so that disease, system failure, or injury causes death'. They assert that killing extends to the animal and plant world and that in neither ordinary language nor the law does the word killing entail an act that is necessarily wrongful or criminal. In their opinion conventional definitions are unsatisfactory and the meanings of 'killing' and 'letting die' are vague and inherently contestable, a view seemingly shared by Lord Goff in *Bland* [1993] 1 All ER 821 when he stated that 'it can be asked why, if the doctor, by discontinuing treatment, is entitled in consequence to let his patient die, it should not be lawful to put him out of his misery straight away, in a more humane manner, by a lethal injection, rather than let him linger on in pain until he dies'. Furthermore, it remains unclear as to what aspects of behaviour constitute an act and what represents an omission. Would, for example, the act of switching off a life-support machine represent an act (flicking the switch) or an omission (withdrawal of treatment)? One view is that stopping a ventilator is not an act of killing, but represents a clinical decision taken by a doctor to let nature take its course (Williams, 1978). This appears to be the better view since spontaneous respiration can occur.

The distinction between a directly intended effect and one that is merely foreseen can be problematic. In fact such a distinction can be artificial and to some extent depends upon semantics. Harris (1985) provides the example of a group of pot-holers who are trapped and their only means of escape entails moving a boulder which will inevitably crush one person to death. He states that the situation could be equally accurately described in two ways: 'intending to make an escape route, foreseeing that this will kill someone', or 'intending to make an escape route by killing someone'. In the first statement, the intention is making the escape route, and killing the person is merely a foreseen consequence. According to the current intention and foreseeability notion, this represents a morally acceptable situation. In the second statement, the intention is to make an escape route as a direct consequence of killing someone, since the escape route cannot be made unless someone is killed. The killing would therefore be part of the intention of the escape route. This position would be immoral. It seems illogical to determine morality in such a way. An alternative perspective is that the totality of consequences determines whether an action or choice is morally good rather than intention and foreseeability. If the overall consequences are 'good', then the action is deemed morally acceptable even though there may be other specific foreseeable consequences that would not be morally acceptable in their own right. Thus, in the scenario of administering escalating doses of opiate-based analgesics to a terminally ill patient, the overall good is that the patient is kept comfortable and free of pain. This would be morally acceptable even though the foreseeable consequence of death would, on its own, be considered unacceptable.

Aside from the basic distinction between an act and omission a second distinction further complicates the ethics of the care of the dying. The question arises as to whether it is morally worse to withdraw treatment once it has begun than to avoid commencing treatment at all. The law regards stopping treatment as being equivalent to not starting it, and withdrawing treatment is morally comparable to withholding, and not as an act of killing. Veatch (2003) explains this from the standpoint of autonomy and asserts that from a clinical perspective it makes no sense to draw distinctions between what is derived from autonomy as being a negative right and what is considered to be based on positive rights. Stopping treatment is morally (and legally) required on the basis of autonomy following withdrawal of consent to treatment. Stopping treatment is the equivalent of not starting it. Therefore, in end-of-life decision-making, it would seem prudent to follow a policy of attempting a treatment with later withdrawal if this is found to be ineffective. Withdrawal is (as with the example of switching off a ventilator) a decision not to strive any longer and hence is akin to withholding.

10.5.3   Other jurisdictions

It is worth examining what happens in those jurisdictions where assisted dying is accepted by the law. The Netherlands, for example, has overt legalisation whereas assisted suicide is tolerated in Switzerland. Different jurisdictions will inevitably have different cultural, religious and societal attitudes that are not necessarily directly translatable to the United Kingdom. Nevertheless, the lessons learnt and experiences of these jurisdictions are invaluable for contemporary debates on assisted dying.

In 2002, The Netherlands legalised adult euthanasia under the Termination of Life on Request and Assisted Suicide (Review Procedures) Act 2001, which amends the penal code of The Netherlands (Article 293) to permit euthanasia (which encompasses assisted suicide):

(1) Any person who terminates another person's life at that other person's express and earnest request shall be liable to a term of imprisonment not exceeding twelve years or a fifth category fine.
(2) The act referred to in the first subsection shall not be an offence if it is committed by a physician who fulfils the due care criteria...and if the physician notifies the municipal pathologist of this act.

This fundamental change in law followed public debate and landmark decisions of the Supreme Court such as the *Schoonheim* case and the *Chabot* case.

Until 1990, doctors in The Netherlands had a duty to report cases of euthanasia and assisted suicide to the police who would then conduct an investigation. Now, however, such cases are conducted by a committee who need to be satisfied that the requisite criteria have been fulfilled and are only notified if the committee concludes that the doctor did not fulfil the due care criteria. The due care criteria are set out in section 2 of the Termination of Life on Request and Assisted Suicide (Review Procedures) Act and came into force in April 2002. These require that the physician:

▶ was satisfied that the request for euthanasia by the patient was voluntary and well-considered;
▶ held a conviction that the patient's suffering was lasting, hopeless and unbearable;
▶ had informed the patient about his or her situation and the prospect of improvement;
▶ shared a conviction, with the patient, that the patient's suffering was hopeless;
▶ had consulted at least one other independent physician, who has seen the patient and given a written opinion on the requirements of due care;
▶ has terminated the life or assisted in a suicide with due medical care and attention.

The Act provides for advance requests for euthanasia. Children over the age of 12 may be entitled to euthanasia or assisted suicide. For those between 12 and 15 years, parental consent is required and for those aged between 16 and 17 years, parents should be consulted but they do not have the right to veto the child's wishes.

Approximately 140,000 people of the 16,000,000 population of The Netherlands die each year and there are around 9700 requests for euthanasia. Of these, about 4000 receive some form of assistance in dying, and euthanasia accounts for 2.5% of all deaths in The Netherlands compared to assisted suicide which accounts for 0.2% of deaths (House of Lords Select Committee, 2005).

Some commentators have expressed grave reservations about the Dutch system (Keown, 2002; Finnis, 1998). Concerns have tended to focus on evidence that some doctors ignore the formal guidance for euthanasia as well as the apparent low levels of reported cases which, for some, implies that non-voluntary euthanasia also occurs. This evidence is used as the basis of allegations that in The Netherlands euthanasia is increasingly resorted to, rather than being used as a last resort. This is seen as evidence of the slippery slope pertaining to abuse of the system. Undoubtedly, evidence that lives have been curtailed for non-competent persons, or for others who are competent but have not consented or been given an opportunity to object, raises serious moral and ethical concerns. According to Griffiths (1995) legitimate medical practice has involved the administration of high doses of analgesics or withdrawal of life-prolonging treatment in patients where the remaining life expectancy is exceptionally short. He considers that there is no evidence that the frequency of such behaviour in The Netherlands is any greater than that found elsewhere. The only difference is that such practices are more open and widely acknowledged.

In the United States while euthanasia remains illegal, physician-assisted suicide is lawful in three States, subject to specific criteria. The first State to legalise physician-assisted suicide was the State of Oregon. The Death with Dignity Act 1994 provides that a doctor may comply with a competent terminally ill patient's voluntary request for prescription of drugs that would end the patient's life in a humane and dignified manner. The following factors need to be fulfilled:

- The person must be a resident of the State of Oregon.
- The person must make an initial request followed by a formal written request.
- There must be a 15-day-cooling-off period followed by a repeated oral request.
- A further 48 hours must elapse between repeating the request and prescribing the drug.
- The request must be witnessed by two people, in addition to the doctor, one of whom should not be a relative or an employee of the institution.
- The patient should notify the family.
- A second doctor should confirm the diagnosis that the patient is competent and is acting voluntarily.
- If there is any suggestion of depression or psychiatric disorder, then appropriate referral to a psychiatrist should be made.
- The patient should have received complete information about the prognosis, or alternative treatments, as well as the availability of palliative care.

In 2009, the Oregon Department of Human Services (http://www.oregon.gov/DHS/ph/pas/index.shtml, 2010) reported that 95 prescriptions for lethal medication were written under the Act, of which 53 were used by patients to end their lives. Thirty patients died from their underlying condition and 12 were alive at the end of 2009. The commonest medical condition of those who requested physician-assisted suicide was terminal cancer (79.7%). The majority of participants were white (98.3%) and well educated (48.3% held a bachelor's degree). The median age was 76 years old, and 98.3% of patients died at home. Most had some form of health insurance (98.7%) and the main reasons for wanting to end their lives was loss of autonomy, loss of dignity and not being able to do the things that made life enjoyable. To date it appears that the system of physician-assisted suicide in Oregon has not been abused, although lack of any reporting requirements perhaps casts doubt on this conclusion.

The State of Washington also permits physician-assisted suicide in certain circumstances. The Washington Death with Dignity Act Initiative 1000 was brought into force in 2008 and permits Washington residents, who are competent adults with less than six months to live, to request lethal doses of medication with which to end their lives. The Washington State Department of Health (http://www.doh.wa.gov/dwda/) reported that in the first nine months following the passage of the Act, 63 terminally ill patients received lethal medication. Thirty-six patients died as a result of ingesting the medication and three patients experienced complications while taking the drugs.

Physician-assisted suicide is legal in the State of Montana, according to a trial court decision in 2008 (*Baxter* v *Montana*, Decision and Order, Cause No. ADV-2007–787, Mont. 1st Jud. Dist. Ct., 12/5/08). The Attorney General's subsequent appeal to the Supreme Court affirmed the ruling, but it failed to determine if the State's constitution actually guaranteed the right to assisted dying (*Baxter v Montana*, DA 09–0051, 2009 MT 449, MT Sup. Ct., 12/31/09).

In 2002, Belgium became the second European country after The Netherlands to legalise voluntary euthanasia. Euthanasia is to be used as a last resort and the decision-making process involves not only the patient and doctor but also the family and nursing team to permit detailed review of the underlying reasons for the patient's request. Euthanasia is permitted subject to satisfying residence criteria, review by the Belgium Federal Control and Evaluation Commission and requires the agreement of two doctors that the patient is in a 'medically futile condition of constant and unbearable physical or mental suffering that cannot be alleviated, resulting from a serious and incurable disorder caused by illness or accident' (Article 3, 2 (1)).

In Switzerland, assisted suicide is legal under Article 115 of the Swiss penal code which came into force in 1942. It is a criminal offence only if the motive of the assistant is 'selfish'. The penal code does not give a special status or protection to doctors. Several organisations that offer assistance to patients who wish to commit suicide will help only Swiss nationals. Dignitas, a smaller organisation, assists non-residents as well. Active euthanasia is a criminal offence.

In March 2009, Luxembourg became the third European country to decriminalise euthanasia. Patients who are terminally ill can receive voluntary euthanasia with the approval of two doctors and after satisfying a panel that this is necessary for the avoidance of suffering.

10.5.4 Reform of English law

Several attempts have been made to introduce change to English law to permit assisted suicide and voluntary euthanasia. To date, these have all been unsuccessful. The Euthanasia (Legislation) Bill 1936 was intended to permit voluntary active euthanasia for persons over the age of 21 who were suffering an incurable and fatal illness accompanied by severe pain and included several safeguards designed to prevent abuse. An application needed to be signed in the presence of two witnesses followed by submission to a referee, who would interview the patient and other interested parties to ensure that euthanasia represented the patient's voluntary wish. The matter would then be referred to a court which would consider the case and, if satisfied, issue a certificate to authorise a doctor to perform euthanasia in the presence of an official witness. The Bill was defeated 35 votes to 14.

In 1969, the Voluntary Euthanasia Bill was put forward, but this too was defeated. Under the Bill euthanasia would be lawful if carried out by a registered medical practitioner, or a nurse acting under the doctor's direction. The patient, being over the age of 21 and certified by two doctors as suffering from an incurable condition that was expected to cause the patient severe distress, would make a statutory declaration requesting euthanasia. The request had to be made between 30 days and 3 years prior to the procedure being performed.

More recently in 2004, Lord Joffe introduced the Assisted Dying for the Terminally Ill Bill with the aim of legalising physician-assisted dying. The Bill was scrutinised by the House of Lords Select Committee on Assisted Dying and the report was published in 2005. The Committee took into account contemporary developments, such as the legislation in Oregon, the Netherlands and Belgium. The report indicated that there should be a distinction between euthanasia and assisted suicide so that these issues could be addressed independently and there should also be provision for compulsory psychiatric assessment. The report suggested that a new bill be put forward addressing these issues and for further subsequent scrutiny.

A third version of Lord Joffe's Bill focused solely on permitting assisted suicide and included a range of formalities and procedural safeguards. An individual person would need to sign a declaration requesting assisted suicide, witnessed by two individuals, one of whom should be a solicitor or public notary. The patient must have been asked to inform the next of kin and should be confirmed as having decision-making capacity. The patient should be terminally ill, with a progressive and irreversible disease with death being expected within six months. The patient would need to be suffering unbearably as a result of pain and distress. A further requirement was that full information had been given about disease prognosis and alternative approaches including the availability of palliative care. The requirements were modelled upon the Oregon approach. The Bill would also have set up a monitoring commission to maintain records of all instances of assisted dying. The Bill was introduced in the House of Lords in 2006 and was defeated.

Despite several attempts to legalise assisted dying in the United Kingdom, none have been successful. Arguably, the most positive move in favour of a change in the law has been the recently published guidance by the Director of Public Prosecutions in respect of the factors to be taken into consideration in deciding whether to prosecute a non-health-care professional following an assisted suicide, as a result of *Purdy*.

A Member of the Scottish Parliament (MSP) introduced the End of Life Assistance (Scotland) Bill (SP Bill 38) in January 2010. If enacted, the Bill would have allowed certain persons including those whose lives had become intolerable through terminal illness to seek medical assistance in dying. The Scottish Parliament disagreed to the general principles of the Bill on 1 December 2010.

10.6 Withdrawal of treatment

Active euthanasia is a criminal offence; however, in certain circumstances passive euthanasia might be lawful, for example, in the context of treatment withdrawal. Drawing a clear distinction between these situations is problematic and remains fraught with pertinent legal and ethical issues. The leading authority is the House of Lords' decision of *Airedale NHS Trust v Bland* [1993] AC 789 which concerned withdrawal of treatment from a patient in a persistent vegetative state (PVS).

Patients in PVS are permanently unconscious following serious brain injury. The heart continues to beat and the brainstem (responsible for core cardiovascular and respiratory functions) continues to function. Patients in a PVS may exhibit normal diurnal variations in terms of sleeping and waking patterns and some even appear to smile or frown. Because these functions are predominantly dependent upon brainstem connections, as opposed to higher cortical functioning, it is believed that those in a PVS are unable to see, hear, taste, smell or feel pain. The Royal College of Physicians (1996) states that the diagnosis of PVS can be made when a patient has been in a continuing vegetative state following head injury for more than twelve months, or following other causes of brain damage for more than six months. It has, however, been disputed whether the label 'permanent' is appropriate since there have been reported incidents of recovery following a diagnosis of PVS although this is rare and patients typically retain limited cortical function. Although patients in PVS may not be terminally ill, health professionals are not obliged to continue treating, feeding and hydrating a patient in a PVS, indefinitely.

10.6.1 The *Bland* case

Anthony Bland was a victim of the Hillsborough football stadium disaster of April 1989. As fans poured into the stadium after the start of a match, hundreds were crushed, 95 died, and Anthony was badly injured and suffered severe brain damage leading to a PVS. For over three years Anthony was fed through a nasogastric tube, his bladder was emptied by a catheter and he required supportive treatment (such as antibiotics for infections).

At the time of the disaster Anthony Bland was 17 and had not expressed any preferences as to how he would wish to be treated if he was in a PVS. Medical opinion held that he had suffered catastrophic and irreversible damage to the parts of his brain responsible for consciousness and that there was no hope of recovery. With the agreement of family and strong medical support, a court declaration was sought that his doctors might lawfully discontinue all life-sustaining treatment (including, where required, termination of ventilation, nutrition and hydration by artificial means), as well as discontinuing and subsequently withholding all treatment except symptomatic relief that would allow him to die with dignity. The trial judge granted the declarations, a decision subsequently upheld by the Court of Appeal and the House of Lords. Anthony Bland might have lived for decades in a PVS. However, he died much earlier from dehydration following the (lawful) removal of the nasogastric tube that provided him with artificial nutrition and hydration.

The House of Lords was unanimous that the principle of the sanctity of life was an important, though not absolute, criterion. Their Lordships accepted that withdrawal of artificial nutrition and hydration constituted an omission, rather than an act.

Furthermore, since prolonging Anthony Bland's life was no longer in his best interests, his doctors were no longer under a duty to provide treatment to prolong his life, and withdrawal of treatment could not constitute the *actus reus* for murder. Lord Browne-Wilkinson and Lord Lowry suggested that if continued treatment was not in Anthony Bland's best interests, then the doctor might be under an obligation to cease further treatment.

10.6.2 Implications of *Bland*

The decision in *Bland* poses a range of ethical and legal dilemmas such as what constitutes futility, the differentiation between active medical treatment and basic care and how and where the line ought to be drawn on a principled basis between active and passive euthanasia. Some of the implications of *Bland* are considered below.

10.6.2(a) Acts versus omissions

The majority in the House of Lords (Lords Browne-Wilkinson, Lowry and Mustill) accepted that the doctor's intention in withdrawing artificial nutrition and hydration was to bring about Anthony Bland's death and terminate his life. The withdrawal of the nasogastric tube could be characterised as an act which would be problematic since this arguably satisfied the *actus reus* of murder. It was therefore crucial to characterise this as an omission. Lord Goff relied on the reasoning of Professor Glanville Williams that the basis for what a doctor does when he switches off a life-support machine is in substance not an act but an omission to struggle to preserve life. Furthermore, such an omission would not represent a breach of the doctor's duty since there is no obligation to continue to provide futile medical care. Lord Goff stated (at 866):

> I agree that the doctor's conduct in discontinuing life support can properly be characterised as an omission. It is true that it may be difficult to describe what the doctor actually does as an omission, for example where he takes some positive step to bring the life support to an end. But discontinuation of life support is, for present purposes, no different from not initiating life support in the first place. In each case, the doctor is simply allowing his patient to die in the sense that he is desisting from taking a step which might, in certain circumstances, prevent his patient from dying as a result of his pre-existing condition; and as a matter of general principle an omission such of this will not be unlawful unless it constitutes a breach of duty to the patient.

Lord Goff makes clear two distinctions. First, he distinguishes between the physical 'act' of discontinuing life support from a 'positive step' to bring life support to an end. While both may lead to the same end, namely the death of the patient in this instance, there is a difference between the two. The first might impact upon an attitude or emotional disposition towards the action whereas the second relates more to the ultimate end of that action. Although, from an orthodox perspective, motives are irrelevant to criminal responsibility, the motive of an attitude or emotional disposition may be relevant in the context of denying responsibility, resulting in a situation whereby the ends justify the means; for example, self-defence or the use of life-shortening pain relief at the very end-of-life. Second, Lord Goff emphasises that an omission will not be unlawful unless it constitutes a breach of duty owed to the patient. If it is no longer in the best interests of the patient to continue treatment, then no duty to continue treatment exists for the doctor. This situation is potentially capable of moral and legal justification. These two points taken together provide a *justificatory* rather than an excusatory reason for accepting the categorisation of withdrawal of treatment as an omission under such circumstances.

Despite the reliance upon the acts and omissions distinction, Lord Mustill (at 887) expressed disquiet:

> The conclusion that the declarations can be upheld depends crucially upon a distinction drawn by the criminal law between acts and omissions... The acute unease which I feel about adopting this way through the legal and ethical maze is I believe due in an important part to the sensation that however much the terminologies may differ the ethical status of the two courses of action is for all relevant purposes indistinguishable.

In Lord Mustill's view, such a distinction was dubious and simply served to emphasise the distortion of a morally and intellectually misshapen legal structure.

10.6.2(b) 'Medical treatment'

A distinction is often made between 'ordinary' and 'extraordinary' treatment. Ordinary treatment typically refers to those activities and care regimes considered to be basic and essential levels of care. Failure to provide basic care, such as nutrition, hydration and assistance with personal hygiene could attract legal sanction whereas no similar duty would be likely to extend to the provision of medical treatment that was not clinically indicated. In *Bland*, the application of the health-care organisation was for withdrawal of nutrition and hydration that was delivered to the patient by way of a nasogastric tube. Lords Keith and Lowry considered ANH to be medical treatment and, similarly, Lord Goff regarded this as part of the patient's medical care. Finnis (1993) argues that this distinction is dubious, and he questions whether 'spoon feeding' would be classed as medical treatment since this arguably also provides artificial nutrition and hydration, since the patient does not feed herself. Keown J (1997) suggests that while the insertion of a gastrostomy tube will require a minor operation (and would therefore legitimately be classed as a medical procedure), insertion of a nasogastric tube being the passage of a soft tube down a patient's nose ought not to be viewed in the same way. A further and primary question concerns what the artificial nutrition and hydration is supposed to be treating. Great weight was placed in *Bland* that tube feeding was regarded as medical treatment, although the alternative view, and certainly one shared by many nurses, is that tube feeding is nothing more than basic care. This being the case, the only reason to categorise tube feeding as 'medical treatment' would be so that it could be lawfully withdrawn.

An issue that remains, although perhaps not germane to the *Bland* situation, is whether artificial ventilation could be regarded as extraordinary care within the *Bland* distinction. In *Nancy B v Hotel Dieu du Québec* (1992), 86 DLR (4th) 385 (Que. SC), judicial approval was given for the withdrawal of such treatment in these situations. Furthermore, in the United States case of Karen Quinlan, withdrawal of ventilation did not lead to her death and she lived on (*Re Quinlan* 70 NJ 355 A2d 664 US 922 (1976)).

10.6.2(c) Best interests

The decision as to whether to withdraw artificial nutrition and hydration from Anthony Bland was determined according to whether withdrawal would be in his best interests. For Lord Mustill the distressing truth was that the proposed course of action was not in the best interests of Anthony Bland because he had no best interests of any kind. According to Lord Hoffman it would be demeaning to the human spirit to say that because one is unconscious there was no interest in personal privacy and dignity, or in how one might live or die. On these grounds there was a recognisable interest that Tony had in the manner of his life and death. What remains unclear, however, is that even if it was in his best interests that treatment was discontinued, was it really in his interests to let him die slowly from starvation and dehydration rather than quickly by lethal injection?

The majority of the court in *Bland* concurred that what amounted to best interests was to be determined by reference to the *Bolam* standard. However, once a patient has lost all capacity for consciousness (and who had not made his or her previous wishes known), then the only way to determine best interests was to impose an objective opinion by reference to broader connotations of what is good and what is bad. For these purposes it remains unclear as to why this should entirely depend upon the *Bolam* test. While a reasonable body of medical opinion should almost certainly carry some weight as being one component in the decision-making process, it should not necessarily be the ultimate deciding factor. The (unattractive) truth is that in such circumstances any decision is likely to incorporate a quality of life opinion and that in certain circumstances the quality of an individual's life may be considered to be such that it is not worth living. This perspective runs counter to the concept that human life is intrinsically valuable and when a decision has to be made independently of the patient's own terms of reference, an external agent is required to make that judgment as to the worth of what remains of that life.

In Lord Browne-Wilkinson's view, it would be unlawful to persist with treatment if such treatment was not in the patient's best interests. According to his Lordship (at 883):

> In my judgment it must follow from this that if there comes a stage where the responsible doctor comes to the reasonable conclusion (which accords with the views of a responsible body of medical opinion) that further continuance of an intrusive life support system is not in the best interests of the patient, he can no longer lawfully continue that life support system: to do so would constitute the crime of battery and the tort of trespass to the person.

It therefore appears that prolongation of life, for example, at relatives' requests, but where this is not in the patient's best interests, would be unlawful. Furthermore, exactly what would constitute 'intrusive' and 'life-support system' remains open to debate and discussion.

10.6.2(d) Safeguards

As a matter of good practice, Lord Browne-Wilkinson in *Bland* advised that doctors 'would be well advised in each case to apply to the court for a declaration as to the legality of any proposed discontinuance of life support where there has been no valid consent by or on behalf of the patient to such discontinuance'. While not all their Lordships were explicit on this point, the use of a declaratory procedure was considered to be advisable, at least until a body of precedent had built up. This approach was considered to be justifiable for the protection of vulnerable patients, medical staff and for the reassurance of society.

In addition, Lord Goff identified four additional safeguards:

▶ Every effort should be made to rehabilitate the patient for at least six months following the injury.

▶ The diagnosis of irreversible PVS should not be confirmed until at least twelve months after the injury. Any decision to withhold life prolonging treatment to be delayed during that period.

- The diagnosis of the treating clinician to be confirmed by two independent doctors.
- Great weight should be given to the wishes of the patient's immediate family.

In *Bland* the Law Lords clearly indicated that there was a need for these issues to be considered by Parliament. In Lord Mustill's view: 'The whole matter cries out for exploration in depth by Parliament and then for the establishment by legislation not only of a new set of ethically and intellectually consistent rules, distinct from the general criminal law, but also of a sound procedural framework within which the rules can be applied to individual cases. The rapid advance of medical technology makes this an ever more urgent task, ...' In 1994, a House of Lords Select Committee on Medical Ethics reported on euthanasia (paragraphs 106 and 237, House of Lords paper 21-I, 1994). The select committee recommended that a definition of PVS be drawn up as well as a code of practice for the management of PVS patients. It did not, however, recommend a change in the law to permit euthanasia.

10.6.3   Developments post-*Bland*

The *Bland* decision was the forerunner for several subsequent dilemmas to be considered by the court, as detailed below.

10.6.3(a) Possible prosecution

The proceedings in *Bland* took the form of an application for a judicial declaration which, if obtained, would have the effect of averting any subsequent prosecution for the specific issue considered. The Practice Note of the Official Solicitor, Declaratory Proceedings: Medical and Welfare Proceedings for Adults who Lack Capacity [2006] 2 FLR 373 provides guidance on the procedural aspects for referring cases to seek a declaration.

Following *Bland* a minister, the Reverend Morrow, attempted to initiate criminal proceedings for murder against the doctor who had clinical responsibility for Anthony Bland. In *R v Bingley Magistrates' Court, ex p Morrow*, April 13, 1994, QBD this application was refused, and a subsequent application for judicial review of the magistrates' decision was rejected. The court followed Lord Goff's statement that a civil declaration would preclude subsequent prosecution.

10.6.3(b) Emergencies

In *Frenchay Healthcare NHS Trust v S* [1994] 2 All ER 403, S was deeply unconscious following a severe brain injury that had followed a massive drugs overdose. He was diagnosed as being in a PVS and had been fed by nasogastric tube, followed by a gastrostomy tube. The gastrostomy tube disconnected and required urgent replacement to ensure his continued survival. His doctors sought a declaration that reinsertion would not be in his best interests which was granted at first instance. The Official Solicitor lost the appeal but due to pressures of time he was unable to adduce independent medical evidence to oppose the application. In the Court of Appeal, *Frenchay* was distinguished from *Bland* in that the application required an urgent decision because the tube had been dislodged, and it was also apparent that the diagnosis of PVS was not as conclusive as it had been in *Bland*. The court took the view that in an emergency such as this, it was not possible to comply with all of the guidelines set out in *Bland*. This decision seems problematic on two counts: first, the diagnosis of PVS may not always be clear.

Following publication of guidance of the Royal College of Physicians (1996), however, diagnosis should now be more consistent. Second, the tube needed to be replaced as an emergency. Arguably, one approach might have been to replace the tube in the interim to allow the Official Solicitor to argue his case, particularly since the decision concerned a life and death decision.

10.6.3(c) Community treatment

In *Swindon and Marlborough NHS Trust v S Guardian*, 10 December 1994 (Fam Div), a 48-year-old lady was cared for at home, principally by her family. She was in a PVS and at intervals required periods of care in hospital. She was fed by means of a gastrostomy tube. A minor surgical procedure was required to reinsert a new tube (since the previous had become blocked) and an application was made to the court for an order that it would be lawful not to pursue further treatment. The application was granted and the trial judge clarified that in a situation where the person was cared for at home, such proceedings should be brought either by the hospital (involved in the care of the patient) or the GP to avoid the burden being brought upon the family.

10.6.3(d) Applications outside PVS guidelines

In *Frenchay* (see 10.6.3(b)) the court granted an application not to reinsert a feeding tube in a patient where the diagnosis of PVS was uncertain. Further cases reflect a similar judicial willingness to approve withdrawal of treatment for diagnoses that fell outside professional guidance. In *Re D (medical treatment)* [1998] 1 FLR 411 the court permitted a departure from the safeguard that required a period of at least 12 months to elapse after the initial injury prior to making the diagnosis of PVS. Following an accident in September 1995 D sustained a brain injury and in March 1996 was diagnosed as being in a PVS. The hospital sought a declaration that it would be lawful not to reinsert the nasogastric tube which had become dislodged. The Official Solicitor opposed the declaration as medical evidence indicated that she fell outside the guidelines for definitive diagnosis of PVS. For example, she showed nystagmus (involuntary eye movements) to ice water testing and at times was able to track moving objects. However, notwithstanding that the criteria were not entirely satisfied, the judge accepted that there was no evidence of meaningful life and that it was not in her best interests to have her body kept alive. Likewise, in *Re H* [1998] 2 FLR 36, H had suffered very serious brain damage following a road traffic accident. She had been kept alive using artificial nutrition and hydration and although a clinical psychologist reported that she occasionally tracked objects and could at times be aroused by clapping, the court was satisfied that although the guidelines were not met, H was in a PVS and it was in her best interests to withdraw life-sustaining treatment.

The safeguard that required the clinical diagnosis of PVS to be agreed by two independent doctors was weakened in *Re G (Adult incompetent: withdrawal of treatment)* (2002) 65 BMLR 6, where the court was content to rely on the evidence of one expert witness alone. The final safeguard articulated by law at Goff in *Bland* (see above) that great weight should be given to the wishes of the immediate family was ignored in *Re G (Persistent Vegetative State)* [1995] 2 FCR 46, where the court held that the mother's objections should not operate as a veto and granted a declaration in support of discontinuing life-sustaining treatment.

Taken together, this tranche of authorities following *Bland* demonstrate a judicial willingness to incrementally extend the boundaries whereby withdrawal of treatment is regarded as lawful in those in a PVS or 'PVS-like' condition.

10.6.4   Euthanasia after *Bland*

Active euthanasia remains illegal yet passive euthanasia, such as within the *Bland* context, is not unlawful. The principal driver for the House of Lords' decision in *Bland* was that Anthony Bland had lost sentience and had no further interest to protect or promote (according to the majority). This approach is, of course, anathema to those who believe that full moral status ought to be accorded to any individual who is alive. According to Finnis (1995), Anthony Bland in a PVS was in a profoundly disabled state: 'He has lost the capacity (ability) to think and feel – but not the humanity, the human life, which until death goes on shaping, informing and organising his existence towards the feeling and thinking which are natural to human life…' As can be seen from some of the post-*Bland* decisions above, in juridical practice patients who lack certain capacities appear to be afforded a diminished right to life, in that treatment may be withdrawn resulting in their death.

Price (2009) states that 'quality of life evaluations are integral and unavoidable elements of end-of-life decision-making, and that in lieu of extreme retrenchment by way of the SOL [sanctity of life doctrine] or the continued arbitrariness generated by the AOD [acts and omissions doctrine], the progressive jurisprudential logic of incrementalism is inescapable and inexorable'. In Price's view, the suffering paradigm is compelling and relief of suffering by assisting a person to die can be seen as an extension of the duty of care owed to such patients. If indeed one were to expound such a view, then compassionate considerations would be crucial (and indeed to some extent are used) in justifying specific instances of euthanasia as well as for sustaining the policy frameworks whereby the acts and omissions distinction is entrenched. Following *Bland*, futuristic paradigms for euthanasia may be based on quality-of-life assessments, which in turn depend upon a range of pragmatic factors, and it is likely that incrementalism will relentlessly shift the boundary between what is and what is not acceptable. If a futuristic paradigm is expected to hold a firm and acceptable status, then this would need to be based on clearly articulated tenets with principled constraints to prevent abandonment and erosion of values as currently understood and cherished.

Lilly suffers a cardiac arrest and severe brain injury and requires mechanical ventilation to survive. Her prognosis is very poor and her doctors wish to withdraw treatment in her best interests. Her husband vigorously protests:

▶ Advise the doctors who are unsure as to whether they ought to obtain a declaration of best interests prior to withdrawal of treatment.
▶ Consider the arguments for treatment withdrawal on the grounds of acts and omissions, best interests, futility, sanctity of life, resource allocation and human rights
▶ Lilly's husband cannot accept that treatment is likely to be withdrawn. Consider the ethical and legal arguments that pertain to these circumstances

10.7   Discontinuation of treatment

Bland was a pre-Human Rights Act 1998 decision. Furthermore, the application for treatment withdrawal was supported by relatives. This section considers whether discontinuation of treatment is in accordance with the Human Rights Act 1998, as well as the potential for conflict with relatives.

10.7.1 Human rights

Compatibility of the Human Rights Act 1998 and treatment withdrawal was considered in *NHS Trust A v M; NHS Trust B v H* [2001] 1 All ER 801. At the time of the hearing, Mrs M had been in a chronic vegetative state for over three years following a cardiorespiratory arrest while under a general anaesthetic. Mrs H suffered anoxic brain damage following a cardiac arrest and had been diagnosed as being in a PVS for around nine months at the time of the hearing. In granting the declarations sought, Butler-Sloss LJ considered that it would be lawful to withdraw artificial nutrition and hydration since it was not in the best interests of either patient for treatment to continue. She considered, in particular, whether withdrawal of artificial nutrition and hydration in these circumstances would violate a patient's right to life (Article 2) or amount to inhuman and degrading treatment (as prohibited by Article 3). She concluded that withdrawal of artificial nutrition and hydration was compatible with Convention rights.

The starting point for the analysis was that the patient in a PVS is alive and therefore Article 2 would engage. The issue concerned the extent to which the withdrawal of treatment, which resulted in the shortening of the patient's life, would be in breach of Article 2. In considering the scope of Article 2, Butler-Sloss LJ took a narrow approach consistent with that of Robert Walker LJ in *Re A* [2000] 4 All ER 961. In *Re A*, Robert Walker LJ stated: 'The Convention is to be construed as an autonomous text, without regard to any special rules of English law, and the word "intentionally" in article 2(1) must be given its natural and ordinary meaning. In my judgment the word, construed in that way, applies only to cases where the purpose of the prohibited action is to cause death.' Article 2 imposes a negative obligation on the State to refrain from taking life intentionally. According to Butler-Sloss although withdrawal of ANH might intentionally hasten death, breach of an individual's Article 2 right to life would need to be caused by a deliberate act, as opposed to an omission. Furthermore, the responsible decision of a medical team would not amount to intentional deprivation of life by the State since the patient's death would be the result of the illness or injury from which the individual suffered, which could not therefore be described as a deprivation. Her analysis reaffirmed the House of Lords' decision in *Bland* that an omission to provide medical treatment would be incompatible with Article 2 only if the circumstances were such as to impose a positive obligation on the State to take steps to prolong that patient's life. A responsible (and *Bolam* compliant) medical decision to withhold treatment where this would have no beneficial clinical effects would not violate the negative obligation imposed by Article 2.

Article 2, however, also includes a positive obligation to take adequate and appropriate steps to safeguard life. Following *Osman v UK* [1999] 1 FLR 193, the applicant would have to show that the authorities did not do all that could be reasonably expected to avoid a real and major risk to life in order to demonstrate a breach of the positive obligation of Article 2. Therefore, a positive obligation to provide life-sustaining treatment would extend to those circumstances where according to a responsible body of medical opinion such treatment was in the best interests of the patient, but not if such treatment would be futile. This again, is consistent with the approach in *Bland*.

The view that a decision to withhold treatment would comply with the convention, provided that it satisfies the *Bolam* test, has been criticised. Grubb (2000) considers that the effect of Butler-Sloss LJ's analysis is that the convention is seen as a floor, rather than a ceiling, for the protection of individual human rights. As a result the impact of

Article 2 on treatment limiting decisions will be minimal, such that the lawfulness of decisions will continue to be governed principally by medical opinion according to the *Bolam* standard.

With reference to Article 3, Butler-Sloss concluded that this was inapplicable on two counts. First, a measure or intervention considered to be a therapeutic necessity could not be regarded as inhuman or degrading. Withdrawal of treatment from a patient in a PVS, in accordance with a responsible body of medical opinion, would be in the best interests of the patient which in turn would create a therapeutic necessity. Second, Article 3 would not apply since engagement required the victim to be aware of the inhuman and degrading treatment. This view has been criticised by Keown (2001) who questions why it is not inhuman or degrading for a doctor to subject an insensate patient to a lingering death from dehydration if a doctor does so to end a life no longer considered to be worth living. It is of interest that this echoes Lord Browne-Wilkinson's opinion in *Bland* where he indicated his support for removal of the tube because the tube, by itself, could not cause death nor, by itself, could it sustain life. His Lordship stated (at 885), however, that

> the conclusion I have reached will appear to some to be almost irrational. How can it be lawful to allow a patient to die slowly, though painlessly, over a period of weeks from lack of food but unlawful to produce his immediate death by a lethal injection, thereby saving his family from yet another ordeal to add to the tragedy that has already struck them? I find it difficult to find a moral answer to that question.

In *R (Burke) v GMC* [2004] EWHC 1878, Munby J also criticised the argument that Article 3 did not apply to those who are unaware of inhuman or degrading treatment, or in a state of physical or mental suffering, and suggested that this interpretation would circumvent the Convention's emphasis on protection of the vulnerable.

10.7.2   Conflict with family members

Conflict with family members can proceed to human rights challenges as evidenced by the *Glass* litigation. David Glass was a severely disabled 12-year-old boy who contracted several infections following surgery. Clinical staff considered him to be terminally ill and wished to administer diamorphine to alleviate his distress, an action strongly opposed by his mother. Nevertheless, an infusion was commenced without her consent. There was considerable bad feeling between the family members and clinical staff that resulted in several violent outbursts. Subsequently a 'do not resuscitate' order was placed in the boy's notes without consulting the family. The boy survived and was discharged into the care of his general practitioner. Subsequently the Trust wrote stating that it would be more appropriate for the boy to be treated at another hospital if further hospitalisation was required. The mother (on behalf of her son) applied for judicial review of this decision and sought a declaration on the lawfulness of the decision regarding withdrawal of life-saving treatment. Her application was dismissed at first instance and it was held that it would be inappropriate to grant relief as it would be difficult to frame a declaration in respect of a hypothetical situation. The Court of Appeal also refused the application and the family appealed to the ECtHR.

In *Glass v UK* [2004] 1 FLR 1019, the European Court ruled that the decision to override the mother's objection to the proposed treatment in the absence of court authorisation was in breach of her Article 8 rights. The court was critical of the Trust's decision not to seek a declaration from the High Court, particularly since there was little doubt that the proposed action would be unacceptable to the mother. The onus was on the trust to take the initiative. The ECtHR ordered compensation to be paid in respect of non-pecuniary damages as well as costs, although the complaint regarding the 'do not resuscitate' notice in the child's records without his mother's knowledge or consent was not separately examined.

The *Glass* litigation highlights several points. First, NHS bodies need to be mindful of the need to refer cases to the court in the event of dispute or conflict about treatment regimes. Given the level of disagreement between the family and the hospital in this case, it is striking that this had not occurred. Second, it serves to highlight the role of parents, professionals and the court with regard to discontinuation of treatment. Although this particular case concerned a dependent child, the principle is that family members' views need to be given due consideration. In the event of disagreement a declaration should be sought.

10.8 Do not attempt resuscitation

Cardiopulmonary resuscitation is a potentially life-saving intervention. However, in some therapeutic situations a decision may be taken that this would not be clinically indicated in the event of a cardiac or respiratory arrest, particularly if such a course of action is considered to be futile. These anticipatory clinical decisions are known as 'do not attempt resuscitation' (DNAR) orders and were previously known as 'do not resuscitate' (DNR) orders. By their nature, DNAR orders are considered appropriate for those patients in whom resuscitative interventions is not expected to be successful, such as those who are terminally ill and those with multiple co-morbidities. Patient interest groups, such as Age Concern, have expressed disquiet about DNAR orders and the potential for reduced quality of clinical care based upon ageism and discrimination (Age Concern, 1999). Despite considerable media attention, DNAR decisions and policies have received scant judicial or legislative consideration.

One dispute that did reach the courts was *Re R (Adult: medical treatment)* [1996] 2 FLR 99. R was a 23-year-old man with learning difficulties and cerebral palsy and described as being in 'a low awareness' state. He was entirely dependent upon others for his care and medical opinion was that it was in his best interests to let nature take its course if and when a life-threatening crisis intervened. As a result, it was determined that in the event of a cardiac arrest he should not be resuscitated. The staff caring for R challenged this order and sought judicial review, claiming that the DNAR (at that time DNR, and hereafter referred to as a DNAR) policy was irrational and unlawful because it allowed treatment to be withheld based upon an assessment of the patient's quality of life. The trust's application for a declaration that its actions were lawful was upheld.

Sir Stephen Brown was satisfied that, in the circumstances, the DNAR order would be lawful. The judge commented on the fact that the Trust had used the phrase 'because of an unacceptable quality of life' in the determination of whether a DNAR order should be made. This wording was at variance to that current guidance at that time (a joint statement of the British Medical Association and the Royal College of Nursing, 1993) which provided that a DNAR order might be considered where successful cardiopulmonary resuscitation is likely to be followed by a length and 'quality of life which would not be acceptable to the patient'. The key point here is that the quality of life is considered from the perspective of what is acceptable to the patient and is therefore indicative of the need for an active partnership between the carers and the patient in reaching the decision. From the perspective of the health-care team, a decision for a DNAR order may be reached on several grounds: resuscitation efforts and subsequent care can be very costly; the success rate is very low; it is an invasive procedure and not without potential risks and complications. Guidance from the Resuscitation Council (UK) 'Decisions relating to cardiopulmonary resuscitation: A joint statement from the British Medical Association, the Resuscitation Council (UK) and the Royal College of Nursing' (October, 2010) provides that decisions on resuscitation must be made on the basis of individual patient assessments. Where no explicit decision has been made, the presumption should be in favour of resuscitation, although if this would not be likely to restart cardiac and respiratory function (on grounds of futility) it should not be attempted. A valid and applicable advance decision refusing resuscitation should be respected. Since DNAR orders can be a potent source of misunderstanding amongst health-care practitioners, patients and their relatives, sensitive and appropriate communication is strongly recommended to engage all interested parties in the decision-making process. It has been suggested that the acronym AND should be used ('allow natural death') to dispel misunderstandings caused by use of the supposedly more emotive term DNAR. There are strong arguments for closer scrutiny of DNAR orders so that the current uncertainty can be resolved on a principled basis to ensure that 'competent patients are not subject to arbitrary decision-making with regard to resuscitation... It would be banausic for the medical profession to ignore sentinel raw feelings. The patient's perspective in the right to self-determination is key to patient-centred clinical care, within the context of modern professionalism' (Samanta and Samanta, 2007). The shift urged in the more recent Resuscitation Council guidance (2007) is a welcome development in respect of more engaged participation of patients in decision-making.

10.9 Requests for treatment at the end-of-life

It is axiomatic that competent individuals may refuse any form of treatment, even if this leads to their death. There are also continuing and heated debates, inside and outside the courts, rehearsing the right to assisted dying. One in particular, however, concerned the 'right to live' in the context of a request for end-of-life treatment. In *R (on the application of Burke) v General Medical Council* [2004] EWHC 1879 Mr Burke was fully competent and had been diagnosed with a progressive degenerative neurological disorder that would inevitably lead to serious disabilities. He sought judicial assurance that at the end of his life he would be given appropriate hydration and nutrition until his death occurred by natural causes. The history of the disease was such that he was likely to lose decision-making capacity at the time that death became imminent, and his concern was that medical staff would take a decision that withdrawal of nutrition and hydration was in his best interests. He contended that the General Medical Council guidance on good practice in decision making with regard to withholding and withdrawing of life-prolonging treatment was incompatible with his Convention rights and sought declaratory relief. At first instance, Munby J found in his favour and made a series of pervasive declarations. He ruled that the emphasis in the General Medical Council guidance was principally on the right of the competent patient to refuse, rather than receive, treatment. According to Munby J the guidance did not acknowledge the heavy presumption in favour of life-prolonging treatment in its failure to require Trusts to obtain prior judicial sanction for the withdrawal of artificial nutrition and hydration in circumstances other than PVS. Buttressing his analysis on a rights-based discourse, he concluded that the General Medical Council guidance could be in violation of the European Convention, and in particular Articles 2, 3 and 8.

The decision was appealed, and reversed, by the Court of Appeal (*R (on the application of Burke) v General Medical Council* [2005] EWCA Civ. 1003). In the view of the court Mr Burke's concerns were groundless. According to Lord Philips (at paragraph 34):

> No such difficulty arises, however, in the situation that has caused Mr Burke concern, that of the competent patient who, regardless of the pain, suffering or indignity of his condition, makes it plain that he wishes to be kept alive. No authority lends the slightest countenance to the suggestion that the duty on the doctors to take reasonable steps to keep the patient alive in such circumstances may not persist.

Their Lordships neatly circumvented Mr Burke's concern that in his closing days, when he might be unable to communicate his wishes (thereby being classed as lacking decision-making capacity under the Mental Capacity Act 2005) and yet not being completely insensate, he did not want to die of starvation and dehydration. The Court of Appeal was highly critical of the approach of Munby J and concluded that he had misstated the law. The *Glass* decision was considered by the Court of Appeal and concluded that this did not amount to a significant and important change in English law. According to the Court of Appeal 'the court does not "authorise" treatment that would otherwise be unlawful. The court makes a declaration as to whether or not proposed treatment or the withdrawal of treatment will be lawful'.

Munby J's decision was powerfully rights-based and patient-centred, characterising him as a new model judge (Montgomery, 2006). The tension between his judgment and that of the Court of Appeal illustrates the difficulty in rationalising respect for autonomy with discretion in clinical decision-making and serves to reaffirm judicial orthodoxy. While it might be good practical sense for doctors to have some leeway recognised in law for when a patient demands resources which cannot be justified (Gurnham, 2006), the principle seems to push too heavily for decisions that pertain to nutrition and hydration at the very end-of-life, which is arguably nothing more than humane treatment. Furthermore, it was highly likely that the Court of Appeal's disagreement with Munby J regarding when judicial authorisation should be required in terms of withdrawing treatment at end-of-life will create an inconsistency and arbitrariness in non-PVS cases.

From one perspective, the appellate decision in *Burke* is disappointing, and arguably 'the Court of Appeal has lost the potential opportunity to resolve other key concerns regarding decision-making at the end-of-life. Munby J's judgment at first instance has raised a number of issues germane to death, dying and clinical practice in a rights-based culture. Some of these legal and ethical matters are likely to be revisited in the courts again' (Samanta, 2005).

10.10 Futility

The concept of futility is, on occasion, used to justify selective non-treatment of those who are extremely unwell and for whom the clinical prognosis is very poor. Assessment as to whether an intervention might be futile will be relevant in the care of neonates and others who lack decision-making capacity for decisions to withhold or withdraw treatment, or not to commence resuscitation. The implications of deciding that an intervention is futile can be of fundamental importance to the subsequent care of the patient and yet the concept has received protracted criticism on account of insufficient uniformity (Beauchamp and Childress, 2009).

Medical futility can broadly be categorised into 'physiological' and 'qualitative'. Physiological futility describes the circumstances where the intended intervention has a high probability of failing to achieve its physiological objective. In essence, this is a technical medical decision to be determined by doctors. Qualitative futility is a more nebulous concept based upon a projection of the anticipated consequences of the intervention and whether those consequences will be acceptable to the patient. The balance between the anticipated burdens of the intervention, its potential benefits and the acceptability of the patient's quality of life following the intervention will all underpin any such judgement. The Appleton Consensus, which aimed to provide international guidance for decisions to forego medical treatment, identified three areas of central importance: the consequences for the patient that are deemed unacceptable to medical professionals; consequences for the patient that are deemed unacceptable by the majority; the burdens of the proposed intervention considered by the medical profession to outweigh its possible benefits (Stanley, 1989). Thus, physiological futility implies a situation where a proposed medical intervention will not prolong the patient's life. Qualitative futility (also known as normative futility) refers to the situation whereby although life may be prolonged, that life would not be considered 'worthwhile' on the grounds that the burdens of treatment would outweigh its potential benefits or alternatively where the quality of life following the intervention would be so diminished that the quality of life would be unacceptable.

While there is no universally accepted definition of futility, Jecker and Pearlman (1992) identify four main themes in being treatment that:

- is either useless or ineffective;
- fails to offer a minimum quality of life or modicum of medical benefit;
- cannot possibly achieve the patient's goals and
- does not offer a reasonable chance of survival.

Gillon (1997) argues that the term futility is, in itself, ambiguous with pejorative undertones, and suggests that the value of any specific intervention should be assessed. Even from this perspective, however, the debate continues as to whether futility ought to be considered principally from the patient's perspective, the physician's perspective or from that of any other. Gillon proposes the expression 'non-productive treatment' as an alternative, and arguably less pejorative, term.

From the clinical perspective, there are difficulties with the need to be 'certain' that an intervention would be futile. Medicine is not an exact science and even a highly skilled and experienced clinician cannot predict individual patient prognoses with absolute certainty. Clinical evidence is not based upon mathematical evaluation and even if an intervention is shown to be beneficial in terms of statistical significance there will be patients within that (intervention) group who will not achieve clinical benefit and vice-versa. Therefore, what may be of very limited value in one situation might well be of considerable benefit in another very similar patient. It seems unconvincing to suggest that doctors should unilaterally take decisions regarding futility of potentially life-sustaining treatment. Youngner (1988) states that all opinions on benefits of treatment are value judgements which should rightly belong to the patient or his surrogate.

Arguably, the doctor–patient relationship only permits doctors to make decisions that pertain to technical and clinical matters, and not about quality of life. The complexity of human nature, values, the framework and beliefs of patients and their surrogates are inherently integral to a decision of quality of life in respect of what would be acceptable to an individual patient.

A further concern about futility determinations is that this can be used to disguise difficult resource allocation decisions, in that patient's treatment may be considered to be 'futile' in the context of constrained resources. An offshoot of this argument is that the concept of futility will eventually become redundant because medical care will unavoidably become restricted by financial resources. Life-sustaining treatment is costly for health-care systems and uses significant manpower and medical resources. From a utilitarian approach, these factors need to be taken into account to determine whether to offer treatment in certain circumstances, particularly if the predicted outcome is poor.

Perhaps the greatest value of futility is that it serves as a concept to justify curtailment of officiously striving to keep alive. Doctors have no duty to treat patients where the disease or condition is such that there is virtually no chance of success and that some patients will die irrespective of what is done. Taken within this fatalistic paradigm, the concept of futility can be used sensitively in end-of-life decisions to allow patients to die with dignity.

Summary

10.1 End-of-life decision-making has gained prominence in recent years due to a range of factors, which include shifting social attitudes, technological advances that can prolong life and media coverage of controversial issues at the end-of-life, such as euthanasia and assisted suicide.

10.2 Euthanasia, or 'mercy killing', is the deliberate bringing about of death (by a health-care professional) in the presence of incurable and painful disease. Euthanasia can be voluntary, involuntary, non-voluntary, active or passive. Suicide is death which is a direct or indirect result of a positive or negative action taken by the victim. Assisted suicide is where someone assists the person to commit suicide and physician-assisted suicide is where the assistant is a physician acting within his or her professional role.

10.3 A doctor who performs an act leading to euthanasia to comply with a competent patient's wishes commits voluntary active euthanasia. Euthanasia is unlawful in this jurisdiction and there is no defence, although there may well be a degree of public sympathy. The doctrine of double effect which distinguishes between intended good consequences and unintended bad consequences of an action is used in end-of-life decisions as a moral justification for a medical intervention that might hasten death.

10.4 Suicide has been decriminalised by the Suicide Act 1961. Assisting someone to commit suicide, however, remains a criminal offence and carries a mandatory sentence of imprisonment up to 14 years. The Coroners and Justice Act 2009 amends the law by setting out a single offence to apply where a person performs an act capable of encouraging or assisting another person to commit, or attempt to commit, suicide and intends his or her act to so encourage or assist. The *Pretty* litigation has shown that the European Court of Human Rights recognises the inconsistency between assisted suicide and the fact that a competent individual may refuse even life-saving treatment, and

Summary cont'd

that legalised assisted suicide would be compatible with the Human Rights Act 1998. Following the *Purdy* litigation, the Director of Public Prosecutions has published the Assisted Suicide Policy which lists the factors to be taken into account when considering prosecution.

10.5 The moral debate that surrounds assisted dying (euthanasia and assisted suicide) revolves around the sanctity of life principle (favoured by opponents) and individual autonomy (favoured by proponents). While both euthanasia and assisted suicide are proscribed by law, withdrawal or withholding treatment from a terminally ill patient, or providing a patient with escalating high doses of painkillers (which may lead to death), might not be illegal. The latter, as undertaken by doctors, has been justified on the distinction between killing and letting die, and the doctrine of double effect. Whether a moral distinction can be made is perhaps doubtful. Legalisation of assisted dying has been introduced in The Netherlands (euthanasia and physician-assisted suicide), in Oregon (physician-assisted suicide) and Belgium (euthanasia). There have been a number of attempts over the years to legalise assisted dying within English law but to date these have been unsuccessful.

10.6 The application in *Bland* was for a declaration that it would be lawful to discontinue artificial nutrition and hydration in a patient in a PVS. The application was allowed. The decision confirmed the existence of the distinction between an act and an omission in English law as the basis of culpability. The House of Lords also held that withdrawal of treatment would not be a culpable omission if it was in the patient's best interests. Artificial nutrition and hydration was held to be medical treatment and not simply basic care. Following *Bland* a spate of decisions has shown a judicial willingness to approve withdrawal of treatment in cases that fall outside strict PVS guidelines.

10.7 Discontinuation of treatment in a patient who is insensate is compatible with Articles 2 and 3 of the European Convention of Human Rights. In the event of disagreement between family members and the medical profession with regard to discontinuation of treatment, there is potential for engagement of the Human Rights Act 1998. In the event of such disagreement, it is advisable that a court declaration is sought.

10.8 Do Not Attempt Resuscitation orders are issued when cardiopulmonary resuscitation is not to be attempted in the eventuality of a cardiac or respiratory arrest. This decision is usually based on a quality-of-life evaluation and has come under scant judicial consideration. In theory, such orders should be issued on a collaborative decision-making basis between health-care professionals and the patient.

10.9 Requests for treatment, including artificial nutrition and hydration at the end-of-life are not legally enforceable. Treatment decisions will be dependent upon what is regarded as clinically indicated at that particular time.

10.10 Futility is a concept used to justify the selective non-treatment of patients who have an extremely poor clinical prognosis. The concept of futility encompasses both physiological and qualitative elements. Qualitative futility is inevitably accompanied by an assessment of the projected quality of life following the intervention by balancing the burdens and benefits of the proposed intervention, and the impact of the subsequent acceptability of the quality of life.

Exercises

10.1 'The ban on assisted suicide is ineffective, discriminatory and not aligned to modern thinking.' Critically evaluate this statement in the light of the current legal framework in England and Wales.

10.2 'Although euthanasia is a criminal offence, euthanasia by the "back door" is tolerated by the law in certain circumstances.' Critically evaluate this statement in the light of the current legal framework in England and Wales, and comment upon the ethical dilemmas that are raised.

10.3 To what extent, if at all, has the Human Rights Act 1998 impacted upon the discontinuation of treatment at the end-of-life?

10.4 Discuss the justification of the position taken by English law with regard to requests for treatment at the end-of-life and the 'right to live'.

10.5 'Futility is simply a pragmatic decision to withhold selectively the treatment of patients who have an extremely poor clinical prognosis.' Discuss this statement in the context of who decides futility.

Further reading

Chapel A, Ziebland S, Macpherson A, Herxheimer A. What people close to death say about euthanasia and assisted suicide: a qualitative study. *Journal of Medical Ethics* 2006; 32: 706.

Dobson R. Guidelines ignored on resuscitation decisions. *British Medical Journal* 1999; 319: 536.

Finnis JM. Bland: crossing the rubicon. *Law Quarterly Review* 1993; 109: 329.

Grubb A. The incompetent patient (adult): *Bland* & the Human Rights Act 1998. *Medical Law Review* 2000; 342.

Gurnham D. Losing the wood for the trees: Burke & the Court of Appeal. *Medical Law Review* 2006; 14: 253.

Links to relevant websites can be found at: http://www.palgrave.com/law/samanta

Chapter 11 follows overleaf.

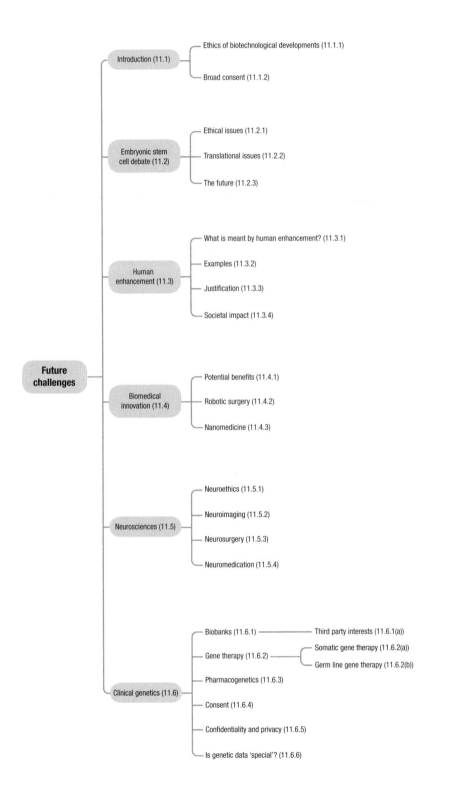

Future challenges

Key Terms

- ▶ **'Automatic escalator'** – bioethical justification to pursue and promote new technology despite potential moral costs.
- ▶ **'Hopeful principle'** – an ethical justification based upon a strongly polarised optimistic attitude to future biotechnological developments.
- ▶ **'Precautionary principle'** – if an action or policy has suspected risks for health or the environment in the absence of scientific certainty the burden of proof that it is not harmful falls to the individual, or body taking that action, or introducing that policy.
- ▶ **Biobank** – a storage facility for biological samples and data from these samples including images and scans.
- ▶ **Biomedical innovation** – new technologies for the delivery of health care.
- ▶ **Broad consent** – general consent given for the use of personal data and biological samples for use in future research in circumstances where the specifics are unknown.
- ▶ **Gene therapy** – a therapeutic remedy of a defect in a person's genetic makeup by the introduction of external genetic material to replace the person's own defective DNA.
- ▶ **Human enhancement** – efforts to permanently, or temporarily, improve the human mind, body or its capabilities using biotechnological methods.
- ▶ **Nanomedicine** – the application of nanotechnology to health care in the form of diagnosis, drug delivery and therapy.
- ▶ **Nanotechnology** – controlling and manipulating matter on a very small scale.
- ▶ **Neuroethics** – the study of the ethical, social and legal issues pertinent to actual or expected advances in neurosciences.
- ▶ **Robotic surgery** – robot-assisted surgery using remote-controlled arms to facilitate procedures that are minimally invasive.
- ▶ **Slippery slope** – a moral argument that seeks to persuade individuals not to take a certain action in the belief that this will lead to unintended negative consequences due to intrinsic momentum.

11.1 Introduction

Much technological advancement has occurred in health care, particularly in respect of diagnostic and therapeutic regimes. The overarching legal and ethical framework plays an ever greater role in the development of science as applied to medicine and its application, for example, in developing an infrastructure for the regulation of new technologies and the protection of intellectual property rights. It is therefore fundamentally important that the interaction between law and the developing biotechnologies facilitates innovation whilst safeguarding against potential harm. New developments and opportunities in medicine invariably create tensions over resources and distribution. Early stage science, and in particular medical science, raises protracted ethical, moral and social debate.

11.1.1 Ethics of biotechnological developments

From an ethical perspective, it has been suggested that the drive to promote medical advancement has led to the creation of new bioethical principles. From the development of environmental ethics came the notion of the 'precautionary principle'. This provides that if an action or policy is suspected of having negative consequences for the public or environment, and in the absence of a consensus that the action is harmful, the burden of proof that the action is not harmful falls to those seeking to carry out the action. The slippery slope argument describes a similar precautionary perspective in the belief that one small movement or action along a certain pathway is likely to cause a significant and undesirable impact on account of intrinsic momentum. Supporters of technological advancements tend to refer to the 'hopeful principle' and the 'automatic escalator principle' (Holm and Takala, 2007). By way of example, a popular conception is that medical innovation and biomedical technologies will present cures for conditions such as cancer and Parkinson's disease. As a consequence of disease eradication, life expectancy is expected to be enhanced in terms of quantity and quality. Similar claims are made in respect of gene therapy and stem cell research. Stem cell research, for example, brings hope that damaged parts of the body can be regenerated without the challenges of tissue rejection and lack of supply that has prevented the widespread use of organ and tissue transplantation. The optimistic ethical attitude towards such developments operates as follows: the cure for cancer is a good thing; genetic research might facilitate this cure; therefore the conclusion, on the basis of the 'hopeful principle', is that genetic research should be promoted, even though this might not eventually lead to a cure for cancer. The underlying assumption is that an unspecified array of genetic research initiatives should be encouraged in the hope of finding a cure for cancer.

The 'hopeful principle' has been criticised in that some actions will invariably have negative outcomes and that in striving to achieve what is best, all manner of bad consequences might result. Furthermore, while the intention is to advance medical care there will be certain aspects that can never be controlled by biomedical advancement. If the 'hopeful principle' is taken to an extreme degree, then this could theoretically lead to exploitation of the environment with detrimental effects. It has been argued that a particular problem of the 'hopeful principle' is that the paramount solution presented represents only one possible way of achieving 'happiness'.

The second emergent bioethical principle in relation to new technologies is the 'automatic escalator principle', which works as follows: there are moral costs associated with promoting a new technology (e.g. embryonic stem cell research); however, the new technology will lead to the eradication of countless diseases and serve to enhance the collective moral good; we should therefore pursue and promote the new technology despite its moral costs. This principle has been criticised on two grounds. First, the development of new technology may be accompanied by other developments that might have a negative moral effect. By way of example, although the creation of a saviour sibling might be ethically permissible, a designer baby might not (see 5.24.2). Second, the aim achieved by technology might have been accomplished by other ways that have less erosive moral effects. On this basis, Holm and Takala (2007) argue that while these emergent doctrines could facilitate a beneficial outcome in overall terms, caution is required.

On the assumption that the ethical basis for the development of biotechnologies is accepted, a further hurdle remains. New developments must be shown to be safe and effective and this can be achieved only by way of empirical assessment and clinical research trials ultimately carried out on human subjects. Consent is the standard way to protect human research subjects and represents a practical ethical tool that is used to make clinical research morally acceptable. It seeks to legitimise new biomedical inventions for human use and protects participants. However, for new technologies the provision of information sufficient to allow the individual to reach an informed choice may be difficult, if not impossible. Thus, although an individual might be competent and voluntarily agree to participate, full appreciation of the implications of an intervention might not be possible. Moreover, a policy that is too restrictive in its requirement for consent could impede the development of possibly useful innovations. One potential way around this quandary is to seek to obtain 'broad consent'.

11.1.2 Broad consent

Broad consent (or general consent) refers to the authorisation by a competent person to a range of options that are specified in broad terms only. It tends to be used when it is difficult to envisage all possibilities and future opportunities for research. General consent has been used for biobanks projects, for personal data and biological sample storage and for research involving new biotechnological developments (see 11.6.4). The principal arguments against broad consent is that it may not adequately protect the rights of research subjects and does not provide sufficient information to permit adequately informed choice for valid consent. Hansson (2006), however, argues that broad consent can be ethically justified for the purposes of innovative research projects provided that robust mechanisms are in place for the safe and secure handling of personal information; that donors of biological samples have the right to withdraw from participation at any time; and that future uses and amendments to the study protocol receive the prior approval of an independent ethics review board. This perspective contrasts with the Declaration of Helsinki that mandates that research involving human subjects should be conducted only if the importance of the objective outweighs the intrinsic risks to individual participants, and that the well-being of the subject takes precedence over the interests of science and society. Hofmann (2009) cautions against over-zealous promotion of research with new biotechnological developments since the combination of risk and information ignorance can be perilous. Sound legal frameworks underpinned by firm ethical foundations are central considerations for the regulation of biotechnological developments. The challenge is to develop substantive regulatory regimes that protect individual participants and societal interests while allowing scientific advancement. Regulation must be balanced to facilitate the development of biomedical interventions, while protecting personal well-being to maintain an adequate moral framework for society.

11.2 Embryonic stem cell debate

New biotechnology creates fertile ground for raising a host of ethical, legal and policy issues. A dramatic illustration was the reaction to discoveries about embryonic stem cells which are the precursors of all cells in the human body. The interplay between science, law and ethics is apparent and the embryonic stem cells story has implications for other scientific developments. A symposium held in Texas in May 2009 that brought together scholars from law, science, medicine and bioethics to investigate these interactions. An overview has been provided by Robertson (2010). The key issues that emerged provide examples of how biotechnological advances might affect the interplay between medicine, science, law and ethics.

11.2.1 Ethical issues

A central concern of the delegates at the symposium in Texas (11.2) was the view that human embryos ought not to be destroyed as a means of obtaining stem cells for therapeutic research, a view grounded on religious doctrine and biology. According to this perspective, the human embryo, even in the first week of development, is a potential person and part of the continuum of human existence. Since all humans have inherent and inalienable rights, it is argued that the sacrifice of even pre-implantation embryos in order to harvest stem cells represents an example of ethics running amok.

An alternative view derives from the Rawlsian doctrine that in matters of constitutional essentials and basic justice, citizens have an obligation to put aside their religious and political principles in favour of that which is more widely accepted (Rawls, 2005). According to Rawls no reasonable political system would ban abortion since the relative moral significance of early human life is not equivalent to the importance of a woman who wishes to terminate an unwanted pregnancy on the basis of her personal autonomy. Applying the same principle, an early *ex-utero* embryo cannot have the degree of moral importance sufficient to restrict potentially lifesaving stem cell research. Furthermore, there is a view that favours use of surplus embryos generated from *in vitro* fertilisation for the purposes of research but not those embryos created solely for this purpose. The rational basis for such a distinction is perhaps questionable.

If one considers that an early embryo is a right-bearing entity or has at least an intermediate status, then there is no logical basis to distinguish between the use of surplus embryos for research with those created solely for this purpose, unless this distinction is founded upon the specific *intention* of making use of embryos only for research purposes. There is an argument that creating embryos solely for research purposes is to use them as a means to an end for the benefit of others, thereby violating the Kantian imperative to use beings as ends in themselves (see 1.4). However, it seems doubtful that embryos are rational beings since they are not (at least according to prevailing evidence) agents with desires and purposes of their own. Although an embryo may have potential to become a person, moral rights should be grounded in the actual properties of a being and would become relevant at the time when the embryo becomes a person. However, proponents of the sanctity of life doctrine argue trenchantly that the status of personhood is established at the point of fertilisation. According to this view, whether fertilisation occurs in, or outside, the uterus is irrelevant.

To understand the development of neurologic and other acute symptoms such as pain, it is necessary to inject embryonic stem cells into animals since such research cannot be performed ethically on humans. However, injection of embryonic stem cells into mice or primates raises further moral issues. As these animals have had their status enhanced from non-human to 'human-animal' (because of the presence of human cells), this situation could be perceived as carrying out research on beings or entities that have human characteristics. There is certainly an argument that there ought to be policies in place to restrict such actions, either by regulatory prohibition or through limitations on funding. From one perspective, abortion is immoral yet public policy does not restrict this. A similar argument could be applied to research using chimeras (organisms that have two or more genetically distinct cells). Even if there is a view that such research is 'immoral' due to the genetically 'enhanced' status of animal subjects, this in itself would not necessarily justify a policy that bans such research, bearing in mind the potential societal benefits.

11.2.2 Translational issues

A key feature of the embryonic stem cell debate has been the translation of basic science into its clinical application, which in itself opens up a challenging set of ethical and legal issues on account of the unique nature of stem cells and the risk that these might develop in unanticipated ways. The moral issues that accompany stem cell research have tended to be considered against theoretical frameworks, even though specific dilemmas need to be resolved against specific clinical contexts such as disease causation, its prognosis, the types of cells, the injection site, the availability of alternate therapies, details about control groups, placebos and subject selection. The key to biotechnological developments is their application in practice and one approach would be to carry out integrated scientific and ethics review at national and local or institutional levels. New developments can generate significant hopes for improved treatment avenues with prospects of major breakthroughs. However, frontier research is bedevilled with challenges, not least being the lack of information of potential risks. The acclaimed trial of embryonic stem cells for the treatment of victims of trauma-induced spinal cord injury was based on data from treating experimentally injured rats, which demonstrated the potential for re-myelinisation of the spinal column thereby restoring motor function. Caution needs to be exercised in extrapolating results from rats to humans, and there is a need for clear evidence of, amongst other matters, minimisation of tumour producing side-effects.

Obtaining valid consent in pioneering research can be challenging, and in the event that information is limited recourse is often made to broad consent (as discussed above). While consent based upon sufficient information is an important aspect of health care, the patient with no, or few other, options might well be willing to accept possibly unknown risks for the possibility of a better outcome.

Whilst any model for the regulatory oversight of biological technologies needs to be robust and rigorous, it nonetheless needs to be tailored to the risks and personal implications for those who participate. Requirements for regulatory oversight and co-ordination are likely to be crucial aspects of allowing innovative therapies to proceed, although there is arguably a need for interim steps of control. Personal professional innovation can be an important stage in the development of any new technique or therapy and the use of a more formal clinical trial model for novel developments may not be feasible. Health-care professionals need to be aware of the innovative nature of some aspects of professional practice and that such therapies and decisions will inevitably be made on a case-by-case basis. Thus, use of embryonic stem cell therapy in certain situations might be ethically acceptable if such use is intended to benefit a competent patient who is as fully informed as possible under the circumstances.

11.2.3 The future

In its infancy embryonic stem cell research tended to generate (inflated) promises about economic benefits as well as concerns that research might contribute to reduced co-operation between scientists with increased secrecy amongst researchers driven by commercial factors. However, it is apparent that these concerns are unfounded and were initially overstated. Moreover, the medical benefits from embryonic stem cell research have been slow in forthcoming and the anticipated commercial benefits have not yet materialised. This could lead to an erosion of public confidence and reduce the will to justify public expenditure in this area, particularly in the contemporary constrained fiscal environment.

Intellectual property rights represent a further factor for this type of research. Pioneers will typically attempt to claim protection for their ideas, and patent rights are necessary to promote the development and application of science. However, such property rights can prevent others from accessing or exploiting an invention on account of substantial charges and licensing fees. The private sector is driven by a profit-orientated approach that sometimes sits uneasily with public sector values. The sectors have potential to collaborate and provide mutual support. Thus, the use of patents in the private sector might potentially fill a gap that seems likely to arise in public sector funding.

Embryonic stem cell research is still a long way from any major breakthrough or directly applicable therapy. There is a view that the ethical debates around the topic ought to transcend the moral arguments that pertain to destruction of embryos and instead address larger questions of social justice. To what extent should society be indulging in high level expenditure for biotechnological advances when many individuals could benefit from the same funds spent on disease prevention and better delivery of care? Can spending enormous sums on cutting-edge research be justified when equivalent funds spent on more fundamental interventions would offer a more reliable and immediate benefit for many more. The economic arguments need to be rehearsed not only in advanced societies but also between the wealthy and developing nations. Critics of those who plangently disclaim the benefits of biotechnological innovations argue for a nuanced and muted discourse that focuses on larger issues of social justice. As stem cell therapies migrate into clinical use, they will undoubtedly be accompanied by resource allocation issues, access to treatment and insurance coverage. Those with sufficient means are likely to be first to benefit and an apparent divide between the private and public sectors seems likely. It is inevitable that geographical divides will become apparent in that certain forms of therapy will be unavailable in some nations. This may promote health tourism, as already seen with infertility treatment and cosmetic surgery. A risk also remains that unscrupulous organisations or individuals might try to profit from untested claims about treatment efficacy. There is some evidence that this already happens as evidenced by the GMC finding that a doctor had exploited vulnerable people with multiple sclerosis with the bogus promise of a stem cell therapy cure (Dyer, 2010). The wider social implications, if such treatments do fulfil their expectations, are legion and it remains to be seen how these evolve with time.

What is the trajectory for the future of embryonic stem cell research? There appear to be three possible answers. The first is that it may provide unrivalled therapeutic opportunities and could represent a victory over ill health. The second is that this may be a journey going nowhere and the highly inflated claims fizzle into insignificance. The third, and perhaps most likely outcome, is that some therapeutic benefit is achieved for presently intractable conditions. The larger questions of ethics, regulation and cost to society, as well as their justification, need further debate.

Embryonic stem cell research has been considered in the public and scientific communities for at least a decade and is used as an illustrative paradigm for some of the legal, ethical and social conundrums that biotechnological innovations can present.

11.3 Human enhancement

The quest of men and women to achieve superior mental and physical capabilities has been relentless since time immemorial. Traditionally, efforts have been to develop the mind through education and disciplined thought and the body by exercise and training. Nowadays, several emergent technologies show potential to improve human ability and potential beyond the norm. Recently the US National Science Foundation funded a 3-year research project to examine the ethics of human enhancement technologies, as well as the underlying moral and social consequences of such innovations (Allhoff, 2010).

11.3.1 What is meant by human enhancement?

Human enhancement is concerned with boosting physical and mental capabilities beyond the statistical range of normality for the functioning of an average human being. The difference between enhancement and therapy is nuanced and indefinite. A superficial distinction is that therapy aims to alleviate compromised health conditions and tries to reconfigure the human status from a reduced one back to normality. Enhancement, by comparison, seeks to improve the human condition beyond the norm. However, contemporary medicine does not always seek to achieve curative goals and includes, for example, palliative care, treatment of infertility, obstetrics and cosmetic surgery. In some circumstances a single therapeutic intervention can be used as a treatment as well as enhancement. Thus, steroids may be used as mainstream treatment for inflammatory disease, whereas they may also be used to promote extreme muscular development by weight trainers, a situation that would seem to fall into the category of enhancement. Likewise, corrective contact lenses for myopia is considered therapeutic since the intention is to produce normal vision, as compared with electronic versions to provide the wearer with enhanced night vision, which would represent enhancement. One starting point for considering human enhancement is the dichotomy between natural and artificial. The natural or latent ability of an individual is based upon a teleological premise that this is a God-given goal or limit. Artificial intervention can be regarded as a form of enhancement but the line between what is acceptable as an artificial intervention is open to debate.

From an extreme perspective is the view that the wearing of clothes, or the use of tools or for that matter a car to travel from one place to another can all be regarded as forms of human enhancement, although these are usually considered to be part of normal life. If tools, such as cars and computers, are not recognised as human enhancement, this then raises the question as to why anything else should be considered to be so. The primary purpose of most commonplace inventions and devices is to improve the quality of life. Enhancements are often perceived to be something that gives an individual an advantage over others, yet it would certainly seem that use of a computer for educational means in an affluent society provides an advantage over those in less-developed societies who do not have computer access.

Enhancements, as with all new technologies relevant to human life, raise moral and ethical issues. However, at what point does normal technological progress as applied to everyday life become an enhancement? It seems likely that 50 years ago the popular view might have been that using a computer for educational purposes would be 'unfair' and would confer some cognitive advantage for preparing for examinations. The line between an enhancement and what is not remains fuzzy. However, from an ethical perspective this alone is insufficient reason to dispense with a distinction on account of the long-term potential effects amidst the moral, social and ethical conundrums.

11.3.2 Examples of enhancement

To date, enhancements have been directed mainly towards cognitive and physical performance in the drive towards increased productivity, creativity and happiness. By way of example Ritalin, a medication used to treat attention deficit disorder, can be used by others purportedly to boost concentration powers for examination preparation. Likewise, the use of beta-blockers may help slow the heart rate and reduce anxiety in situations for those who require high levels of attention, such as professional golfers and competitive darts players. Future technology might permit computer chips to be implanted directly into the brain, thus giving constant access to information as well as previously unimagined information processing powers. Use of anabolic steroids to enhance physical performance is well recognised, as is the possibility of innovative contact lenses to enhance vision beyond normal capabilities. Research is being undertaken in warfare technology and the development of battle suits that are flexible and which can, when required, harden to create splints or a tourniquet for fractured limbs. Further studies are being conducted into the use of 'respirocytes' which are artificial red blood cells capable of holding reservoirs of oxygen. These could be useful not only for victims of respiratory arrest or breathing difficulties, but also in healthy athletes to boost performance. Anti-ageing medication might permit the extension of life by years through rejuvenation of the body and mind. The latter is particularly contentious in respect of its moral and ethical implications, and the potential long-term effects for society.

If enhancements are considered morally and ethical acceptable, then to what extent should 'de-enhancement' be allowed. For example, some individuals (with a psychological disorder known as apotemnophilia) seek amputation of one or more healthy limbs on account of their illness. Deaf parents may specifically seek to have deaf offspring, selected following pre-implantation genetic diagnosis (see 5.24). Such procedures are currently considered unacceptable, on the basis that they are counterintuitive to contemporary thought, yet is the amputation of a healthy limb so very different from gender reassignment surgery?

11.3.3 Justification

Proponents of human enhancement, such as Harris (2007) and Savulescu (2001), consider that persons have a moral obligation for permitting its development and use. Competent persons are free to determine what they wish to do with their bodies, provided that others are not harmed by their actions, subject to certain limitations. They assert that regulation of enhancement technology infringes the fundamental ability of how individuals choose to live their lives. There is, however, a counter-argument that cognitive enhancements may in fact operate to constrain personal autonomy. A mechanism that enhances by mood alteration would be expected to alter the processes of reasoning and decision-making. Under such circumstances it is questionable as to whether individuals would be acting under their own free will. An alarming corollary could be the introduction of neural devices implanted into the brain so that the individual can be controlled, whether by the State or another. Under these circumstances self-determined choice would be constrained considerably.

The potential harm that could accrue from enhancement therapy is unknown. First, harm might be caused to the individual. It remains unknown about the long-term effects and health risks that might ensue. For example, there is some evidence that high dose steroids used for muscle enhancement can have long-term adverse effects. Although risks might not be readily apparent until better evidence is available, nonetheless it seems reasonable and prudent to have some clarity on the risks and expected benefits. The law is well settled that while consent may validate certain forms of medical intervention, a public interest limitation exists.

The assumption that enhancement affects only the individual concerned also seems dubious. To some extent each and every individual has an impact upon the society in which he or she lives. For example, if superhuman strength and stamina was developed, what would be the assurance that that person would not run amok causing public disruption. While this can happen at any time, even without enhancement (e.g. gratuitous shootings and killing of innocent people), nonetheless a societal responsibility remains to ensure a level of checks and balances, particularly if enhancement is artificially induced. While autonomy is used to justify enhancement strategies, some activities may harm others, either actually or statistically. The unbridled and irresponsible use of mental enhancement could put others in dangerous circumstances with resultant harm. Even if it is accepted that the potential for harm is so small as to be practically negligible, accumulated individual choice may lead to aggregation of harm. As with any innovation, once the technology is embraced by society, the harms previously considered negligible might assume far greater significance.

We live in a competitive world. Parents might perceive a pressure or obligation to enhance their children on account of the natural desire to do what is best. A tension could be created between parental rights and responsibilities and the ethics of enhancing incompetent minors. Enhancement of children could lead to permanent alterations that might curtail a child's future choices and opportunities. Will there be a future expectation, for example, that children should receive enhancements, either for their bodies or their minds, or both, so that they achieve their full potential. Furthermore, would children be supportive of such interventions once they reach maturity?

Parents often aspire to give their children an edge in society. Such practices are already evident, for example, with the funding of private tuition, sports coaching and music lessons. However, future parents might feel pressure to enhance their child's physical attributes, or to surgically implant devices to boost intelligence and memory. For many, these possibilities run counter to intuitive reasoning and common morality. The question that arises is should it be prevented, and if so, how?

Another problematic issue with regard to children relates to the concept of 'de-enhancement' (see 11.3.2). One example is provided by that of the deaf community which has developed a complex visual form of communication and culture. There is debate as to whether the treatment of deafness is therapeutic or not. A number of deaf people are of the view that the status of their children would be undermined if their deafness was to be removed (since they would not function completely within the deaf community). Treatments, such as the insertion of cochlear implants, are therefore rejected alongside other attempts to overcome the condition, which according to that frame of reference would be considered to a de-enhancement. Situations have arisen where deaf parents have been permitted to deliberately select embryos using *in vitro* fertilisation techniques with the intention of producing deaf babies. These situations raise a host of moral and ethical issues.

If enhancements were freely available, then how would access to treatment affect obligations and rights? A ubiquitous 'natural right' is that of the right to liberty which encompasses free choice in the pursuit of happiness. It could be argued that the right to access enhancement therapy derives from the right to pursue happiness. However, rights are subject to qualifications. Although the right to liberty is fundamental, it is necessarily restricted by the rights and interests of others. If, in fact, there is a right to enhancement it seems most likely that this would be qualified and justified on grounds of health, knowledge and social acceptability. It is possible that some personal enhancement may in fact constrain individual rights. The situation of Oscar Pistorius, the South African sprinter, provides a case illustration. Although Oscar underwent a bilateral leg amputation as a child he is a successful athlete and runs on artificial legs. He missed the qualifying time for the 2008 summer Olympics by three-quarters of a second. There is an argument that his artificial legs, which provide considerable spring and do not require a blood supply, gave him an advantage to the extent that he should not compete with non-disabled runners. Others might argue that he should be allowed to compete. The limits and territorial lines that demarcate such rights are bound to shift as enhancements develop and society begins to accept such change. The normative acceptance of enhancement by society is likely to justify conferment of rights.

11.3.4 Societal impact

The purpose of enhancement is supposedly to achieve a good, or at least better, life. What actually constitutes a good life, however, varies between individuals and according to personal perception. Arguably, a good life will encompass certain core characteristics such as happiness, pleasure, personal autonomy and good health, along with the knowledge and security that one has sufficient freedom, resources and opportunities to achieve personal goals. Human enhancements seem to promise to assist. However, due to perceived similarities of human drives and ideals, it is possible to some extent to predict what is likely to maximise happiness amongst societies. If enhancements promote diversity such predictions might be more difficult. By nature, humans are social animals and prefer to live in groups and communities. The achievement of social harmony in a diversely enhanced population could be a significant challenge with implications for public policy.

Enhancements that lead to significant increases in life expectancy could impact upon publicly funded services, pensions and life insurance particularly if life was considerably extended and particularly on account of population density and natural resources. Looking to the future, technologies that allow underwater or high-altitude living, would necessitate the need for new institutions to govern the change in lifestyle. Other possibilities include social disruption due to neural implantation technology that allows better data processing and retention that would consistently outstrip the abilities of unenhanced candidates.

Given the potential impact of enhancements what should be the policy view for such technology? At the extremes would be a full ban or no restrictions at all. The likelihood is that policy will fall somewhere between with a framework of principled and ethical regulation. Technological developments might have unforeseen consequences and these need to be met with an anticipatory and measured response to establish policies and minimise potential deleterious effects. Equally, new technologies may bring considerable benefits to be harnessed for optimal use. Formulating and justifying a policy-based approach is critical and can be best achieved by collaborative international efforts of governments, lawyers, scientists and ethicists. The arguments that accompany human enhancement ethics are set to continue in the attempt to establish cogent policy.

The law of England and Wales has previously responded positively to the challenges and opportunities of new interventions. One illustration has been the regulation of human reproductive technologies and embryo research, a model that has received global acclaim. Human enhancements would seem to raise issues of fairness and equity of access in that those with sufficient means are likely to be first in line to receive those technologies predicted to offer significant advantages. A flexible and public supported regulatory mechanism will be essential.

11.4 Biomedical innovation

Biomedical innovations involve the development of new technology for the provision of health care and are subject to principal challenges of cost and regulation. Some of these challenges are considered below.

11.4.1 Potential benefits

Since the early part of the twentieth century, biomedical innovations such as medication, medical devices and procedures, in the context of public health and environmental improvements have been the primary reason for the increase in longevity. The archetypal example is the development of antibiotics used to control bacterial infection. Whereas previously patients with infections would have had a high chance of death, the advent of antibiotics meant that even severe infections could be controlled and overcome. Equally, technology has meant that health-care expenditure has grown exponentially and the likelihood is that demographic, social and economic forces will create new priorities with an emphasis on value-enhancing developments that improve the quality of life (Fuchs, 2010). Whereas in the early periods of biomedical innovation, most of the gains in life expectancy were realised before the age of 65, now almost 80% of gains are realised at the age of 65 years or older. Several factors are responsible and include a decline in the death rates of younger persons and the demographic shift in the population with an increasing cohort above 65 years (Fuchs, 2010). Consequently, there is an expected shift in emphasis onto innovations that enhance the quality, rather than the quantity, of life.

From an ethical perspective, there is a need to balance progress achieved at any cost against value conscious advancements. It seems unlikely that any economy can sustain developments that ignore cost. The problematic issue of paying for high value advances in quality of care for the entire population would be easier to address if some of the resources used for developing marginal advances were reallocated to the development of innovations to reduce the cost of care. Such changes would involve policy development at national level.

11.4.2 Robotic surgery

One example of new technology and its attendant costs is seen with robotic surgery, which allows surgeons to work from a console by operating remote-controlled 'arms'. This technique facilitates the performance of laparoscopic, or 'key-hole' surgery, which in turn is associated with shorter hospital stays and reduced post-operative pain, risk of infection and the need for blood transfusion. The technology has been developed recently in the United States and Europe mainly for surgical treatment of localised prostate cancer (Hu, 2009).

Robotic surgical systems have high start-up costs and expensive maintenance. Surgeons must perform a large number of procedures to become proficient. The economic analysis for robotic surgery for localised prostate cancer has been examined by Barbash and Glied (2010). Drawing from a large nationwide database, the authors found that between 2005 and 2008, the number of hospital discharges for prostatectomy increased by more than 60% in the United States. The authors conclude that this pattern suggests that robotic technology may have contributed to the substitution of surgical treatments for non-surgical treatments for localised prostate cancer, and this may have increased both the cost and volume of cases treated surgically. Looking at the evidence in respect of outcomes, robotic technology has been accompanied by some short-term benefits but may not have improved patient outcomes, or quality of life, in the longer term. The authors predict that if robot-assisted surgery for localised prostatic cancer were to completely replace conventional surgery, this would generate an additional $1.5 billion in health-care costs, and if the fixed and maintenance costs of the robots were included, then the total is likely to be greater than $2.5 billion dollars.

It is therefore crucial that comparative effects of biomedical innovations are assessed to facilitate informed decision-making. Those funding the costs of innovations need information to facilitate pragmatic choices about funding further developments. In considering biomedical innovations, a future challenge for health-care systems will be to balance the benefits of technological developments against potential increases in costs.

11.4.3 Nanomedicine

The development of new health-care technology can create new legal challenges to be positioned within a regulatory framework. One example of such a challenge has been the development of a regulatory framework for nanomedicine.

Nanomedicine is the application of nanotechnology (the control and manipulation of matter on an atomic or molecular scale) for health-care purposes such as diagnostics, drug delivery and therapy. To date the most significant medical application involves the use of biosensors and molecular imaging to diagnose and deliver drugs to specific sites without recourse to invasive techniques. This technology offers considerable potential for improving health-care delivery even though it remains in its infancy.

Nanomedicine is a vast field of study and includes *in vivo* and *in vitro* diagnostics and targeted therapy delivery. As an example, nanotechniques can be used for comprehensive laboratory testing of a single drop blood. This reduces the need for venepuncture and permits efficient testing. Nanotechnology in the area of pharmaceuticals may help to accurately deliver therapeutic molecules to targeted sites, for example, a carrier placed on the shell of a nanomolecule could be targeted specifically to the site of cancerous cells. Better precision in respect of delivery promises greater efficacy and fewer side-effects compared with other routes of administration. For diagnostics, nanotechnology has been used with ultrasound for greater precision using miniaturised imaging systems. This could facilitate the early detection of disease with potentially less invasive early treatment.

Nanomedicine offers immense potential but is accompanied by risks. There is a need for early identification of potential safety concerns to permit recognition, avoidance and resolution. The European Group on Ethics in Science and New Technologies undertook an ethical review of nanomedicine to facilitate appropriate ethical review of proposed projects involving nanoscience and nanotechnology (Commission of the European Communities, 2005). Some of the key findings are summarised by McHale (2007).

One uncertainty that was identified in the report was the lack of a clear legal definition for nanomedicine and its pervasive reach. This means that developing a holistic regulatory approach could be problematic and regulation at European level could arise in the context of nanotechnology being used for different purposes, such as whether it was to be used for pharmaceutical delivery, or as a medical device. The implications are that it may not be possible to introduce an over arching regulatory regime and that perhaps the optimal approach would be achieved through specific developments and derived from existing structures and frameworks.

A second concern was in respect of safety. The long-term effects of nanoparticles on human health, or the ecosystems, are unknown. Since there is the possibility that particles may leak or that spillage may occur, there could be possible threats to individuals and the environment. There is also the possibility of risks from nanomedicines that cross the blood-brain barrier. These real or perceived dangers could lead to diminution of public confidence. Public trust could be bolstered by interdisciplinary research into the ethical, legal and social implications of nanotechnology, as well as transparency in respect of the potential challenges posed by this new technology. Such transparency would also facilitate the consent process.

Concerns were also expressed about the possibility of nanotechnology-based tests becoming available through Internet sales, as well as intellectual property rights which could, in theory, hinder developments for therapeutic use. Initiatives should be encouraged to exchange information between researchers in different Member States and to create databases for the scientific application of nanomedicine, as well as for potential ethical, legal and social implications. The challenges for developing a regulatory framework become all the more acute when considering potential overlaps between medical and non-medical use, in that these may shift from being purely therapeutic to those intended for enhancement. In the context of assisted reproduction, pre-implantation genetic diagnosis can be used for the positive and negative selection of potential embryos, a controversial situation that has generated considerable debate. Use of nanotechnologies for enhancement could raise the same, or even more, ethical quandaries than other forms of enhancement. The use of nanoscale brain implants may go beyond therapeutic use, which could give rise to issues of autonomy, integrity and personhood and require considered public debate. Biomedical innovation needs to be developed within a regulatory framework that balances the demand for innovative technology against potential ethical, legal and social implications.

11.5 Neurosciences

Some of the most innovative work in recent years has been within the field of clinical neurosciences involving psychiatry, neurology and neurosurgery. Significant advances in this area have been accompanied by ethical concerns. Neuroethics is the study of the ethical, social and legal issues that emerge from actual and expected advances in neuroscience. Glannon (2006) and Takala (2010) provide an insight for analysis in this area.

11.5.1 Neuroethics

Neuroethics is a developing field and linked to progress in respect of neuroimaging and psychosurgery, as well as electrical and magnetic stimulation of the brain. Most authors in this area consider that the issue of moral responsibility is the most challenging and important area for philosophical neuroethics. The issue of moral responsibility in innovative technology is not new and has been considered by several commentators in the areas of genetic testing, pre-implantation genetic diagnosis and the positive or negative selection of embryos. However, understanding how the brain works takes this challenge a step further by raising concerns of freewill and the potential implications for autonomy, legal liability and culpability. Chemical attempts to enhance cognitive functioning draw attention to core philosophical problems of the mind, thinking, freedom and determination. The link between freewill, biochemistry and physiology at cellular level in the neurosciences is interesting. A fundamental question concerns whether determinism at the neurobiological level is the same as determinism at the level of cognition. If the two are not equivalent, then developments in neurosciences can be used only to provide empirical evidence of what is, and as such cannot be used to invalidate the concept of freewill. What seems more problematic, however, is the degree to which synchronicity at the two levels imply that cognitive determinism is a function of molecular biology, and how this relates to our deeply rooted concept of independent thought and freewill.

11.5.2 Neuroimaging

Neuroimaging in the way of computer tomography, magnetic resonance imaging, functional magnetic resonance imaging, positron emission tomography and single photon emission computer tomography have done much to reveal the neurobiological basis for mental activity as well as brain disorders. Brain imaging studies have shown that some violent people have diminished activity in the prefrontal region of the brain, while there is increased activity in the amygdala, which is the most important region of the limbic system and regulates emotions. This has been shown with positron emission tomography and functional magnetic resonance imaging scans that measure the rate of glucose uptake by brain cells. The prefrontal cortex, amygdala and other interacting brain regions control interacting cognitive and emotional systems. In addition, it is believed that a person acts freely and is morally responsible for her behaviour barring evidence of compulsion, coercion or ignorance of her actions. However, neuroimaging that demonstrates an overactive amygdala often correlates with heightened negative emotions such as fear and anger. These findings beg the question as to the extent to which neurobiological conditions will prevent a person from acting freely and being morally responsible for her behaviour? Furthermore, would this (or should this) be acceptable as a legal defence for violent behaviour? Neuroimaging also shows that there are several areas of the brain that regulate information storage and the retrieval of memory. In the main, this involves the hippocampus and neocortex. Negligent acts or omissions that result in harm to others may be due to damage or dysfunction of these areas and the question arises as to whether neuroimaging evidence could be used as a defence. Some argue that neuroimaging provides only empirical information about the brain and its physiological functioning, and it would be too far reaching to assert that neuroimaging should be the basis of a normative claim about how people ought to behave.

11.5.3 Neurosurgery

Selective MRI-guided stereotactic techniques (that allow accurate three-dimensional positioning) have been instrumental in improving the safety and efficacy of brain surgery and related interventions. Dysfunction in the anterior part of the cingulate gyrus (part of the brain) has been implicated as a cause for patients who are obsessed with contamination evidenced by a compulsion to continually wash their hands. The same part of the brain plays a role in modulating pain sensation. Cingulotomy has been used as a surgical procedure to treat severe obsessive compulsive disorders with some success. Likewise a subcaudate tractotomy and limbic leucotomy have been used to treat severe anxiety disorders. However, the risk of permanent damage to the brain circuits with potentially adverse psychological effects cannot be ignored and it is questionable as to whether valid informed consent can be obtained from patients considering such procedures. Patients might consent to treatment in a desperate bid for relief of symptoms, for example, those in chronic pain might be willing to undergo a cingulotomy. Furthermore, such patients may well have impaired competence and what is even more problematic is that the dysfunctional region of the brain that is the target for the intervention may be the cause of that person's competence. On account of the potentially serious changes to thought and behaviour that might follow surgery, it seems sensible approval of the Clinical Ethics Committee and a judicial declaration of best interests.

11.5.4 Neuromedication

Another interesting area is the use of drugs designed to enhance cognition and mood. One example is modafinil, which was approved for the treatment of narcolepsy (a chronic sleep disorder) and is now prescribed to treat sleep apnoea (a sleep disorder characterised by abnormal pause in breathing during sleep) and shift work sleep problems. While modafinil has definite benefits for these conditions, the drug is also used to promote alertness in those without clinical conditions. The drug can be used to enhance alertness and allow functioning at a high cognitive level despite sleep deprivation. Another area relates to memory storage and expediting memory retrieval, which is done through modulation of a protein called cyclic AMP response element-binding protein. Experimental work is underway to develop drugs aimed to enhance this protein (the so-called smart drugs). Some argue that cognitive enhancement and memory development drugs would be beneficial as this could bring all the advantages of a heightened intelligence leading to improvements in income, well-being, education and employment. However, there is no guarantee that these drugs would be used in a beneficial way. Even if the risks of psychopharmacological enhancement were minimal, the potential for altered personality raises metaphysical questions, and whether alteration would affect the whole concept of 'self' and personality.

Advances in neurosciences raise a myriad of issues. There is a need to carefully consider the potential benefits against possible harm. The number of emerging ethical issues from clinical neuroscience certainly merit wider public debate.

11.6 Clinical genetics

The human genome project was an international collaborative effort to identify and map the genes and chemical base pairs that make up human DNA. The project completed in 2003. Whilst every individual has a unique gene sequence, the data obtained from the project offer a frame of reference for future studies that look at individual variation. The conclusions drawn followed meticulous analysis of biological samples donated by many volunteers. Whilst these findings will be invaluable for future medical science and its application, it is evident that the majority of diseases are the result of a complex interplay of genetic predisposition, lifestyle and environmental factors. Causative factors include variables such as diet, exercise and smoking, exposure to infectious agents and environmental hazards.

The introduction and development of genetic tests and screening has generated protracted debate on account of a range of legal, ethical and social challenges and opportunities. The storage of genetic data in biobanks has lead to public inquiries and debates on questions of ownership, consent and privacy. Novel applications of genetic science include gene therapy and pharmacogenetics which promise to take treatment of hereditable conditions to a new level, and the development of more efficient and cost-effective therapies. The availability of direct-to-consumer genetic screening tests carry the advantage of widening access, but is accompanied by challenges such as social injustice, the potential for harm and issues of confidentiality and privacy. Data protection concerns, in particular, are considered by some to be unique on many grounds. First, test results might well have implications that extend beyond the person being tested, for example, to blood relatives and also communities. Second, genetic information may have implications for future generations. Third, genetic results might predict the likelihood of future ill health and predisposition to disease in those who are currently well.

At present, the most prevalent use of medical genetics is in the field of diagnosis and screening. Very few diseases can be accurately classified as being monogenetic (due entirely to the presence or absence of a specific gene or base pair) and most genetic conditions are caused by a combination of predisposition and the influence of environmental factors.

11.6.1 Biobanks

A biobank is a storage facility for biological samples, data from these samples, images and scans. They can also include databases of samples that contain human genetic material and, for this reason, are sometimes referred to as 'genetic databanks'. Biobanks are prevalent throughout the world and range from large-scale epidemiological initiatives, such as the DeCODE in Iceland, the UK Biobank, the Estonia Genome Project and the Public population Project in Genomics in Canada, to purpose built facilities and even the refrigerators of individual researchers. The UK Biobank was launched in 2006 to collect biological samples and lifestyle and clinical data from half a million people aged between 40 and 69 years. It aims to provide a biomedical research database to improve the prevention, diagnosis and treatment of conditions such as diabetes, cancer, heart disease and dementia.

11.6.1(a) Third party interests

It is not inconceivable that the enormous repository of personal, clinical and genetic information on the epidemiological databases would be of value to third parties such as insurers and employers. Marketers and advertising companies could well share that interest, as might organised crime syndicates. From a utilitarian perspective, the moral worth of an action is assessed according to its social utility (as balanced against its potential for harm). According to this ethos, in principle, there ought to be no harm to an individual from donating information or samples to a database that is expected to contribute to the greater good by advancement of medical science. The potential for harm, however, emanates from potential infringement of confidentiality and privacy. For these purposes, Häyry and Takala (1998) suggest that risk of harm can be understood in two ways. First, personal and sensitive data can be released by accident or technical mishap, and this possibility can be predicted and controlled by appropriate governance structures. The second is the potential for abuse and commercial exploitation which is arguably a factor that is more difficult to manage. In fact, at this present time we do not know the exact harms that could be caused by the misuse of such data.

Genetic information, as with all other clinical data, is likely to be of interest to insurers for actuarial assessments. A contract of insurance is one of utmost good faith, meaning that all parties must fully disclose all material facts; otherwise the contract could be avoided at a later date. In the context of genetic screening and tests, these would need to be disclosed alongside any other clinical history. The Science and Technology Committee (1995) expressed concern that this requirement might influence people to avoid being tested, even in circumstances where screening might well be advantageous to them.

11.6.2 Gene therapy

Gene therapy refers to the therapeutic remedy of a defect in a person's genetic makeup and involves the introduction of external genetic material to replace the patient's own defective DNA. Vectors (transfer agents such as viruses) can be used to introduce new genetic material into the nuclei of the patient's cells. Alternatively, strands of pure DNA can be introduced directly into cell nuclei, as can DNA that has been chemically processed to enhance the delivery of replacement DNA. To date, no single method of gene transfer has been perfected and combination methods are being developed.

In 1990 a 4-year-old girl diagnosed with an immune deficiency disorder was the first patient to receive an approved gene therapy in the United States. The results were temporary, but effective. Nine years later, however, gene therapy research suffered a major setback following the death of 18-year-old Jesse Gelsinger who died while participating in a gene therapy trial. Jesse, who had a sex-linked genetic disease of the liver, died of multiple organ failure four days after receiving an injection of a viral vector that carried a corrective gene.

To date, gene therapy is being investigated as a possible treatment option for conditions such as Parkinson's disease and cancers such as malignant melanoma. The conditions that might be most suited to gene therapy appear to be those caused by single gene mutations, such as cystic fibrosis, muscular dystrophy and specific blood disorders.

Possible applications of gene therapy are not limited to the restoration of health for those who are ill and it seems possible that genetic technology might be used to enhance capabilities such as physical prowess, cognitive skills or for mood enhancement. The extent to which these types of enhancements could lead to happier, more fulfilled lives is not yet clear. There are two main subgroups of gene therapy: somatic gene therapy and germ line (or reproductive) gene therapy.

11.6.2(a) Somatic gene therapy

Somatic gene therapy involves the transfer of therapeutic genetic material (DNA) into a patient's body tissues and cells. Since the reproductive cells are not modified by the treatment, any therapeutic effects will be restricted to that patient alone. New characteristics are not expected, nor intended, to be transmitted to future generations.

11.6.2(b) Germ line gene therapy

Germ line gene therapy involves modification of the cells that produce sperm or ova. Therapeutic genetic materials are introduced to the patient's germ cells using DNA from external sources. The implications are that any change will have the potential to be transmitted to future generations, with the benefit that hereditary disease might be counteracted. Many jurisdictions expressly prohibit this application for humans on account of the profound ethical and societal issues on eugenic grounds.

Gene therapy is still experimental. The effects of DNA transfer are unknown and even if the target disease can be eradicated it is not clear whether defects could be transmitted to the embryo and future generations. The ethical dilemmas stem from the potential for gene therapy to be used for the eugenic alteration of future individuals, communities and possibly entire populations.

If effective, and safe, gene therapy might represent an expensive therapeutic option that is divisive of societal equality with access to care being circumscribed according to personal or national economic circumstances. An alternative perspective is that individuals have always striven to improve their physical and mental condition using any means available at that particular time. From the rigorous personal training and mental preparation evident in the film *Chariots of Fire* where an affluent Cambridge student was able to pay for the services of a professional coach, to the more recent enhancement techniques offered by nutritional science, evidence-based training regimes and pharmacological interventions. Genetic enhancement might represent the next, and perhaps inevitable, progression.

11.6.3 Pharmacogenetics

Patients respond very differently to the administration of medicine, and individual variability explains why some patients, though not all, suffer serious adverse events, and also why few medications are effective for everyone. Individual variability might not be evident during clinical trials and may manifest only once the drug is released to the public. Individual genetic makeup can partly explain idiosyncratic response since DNA is the template for the manufacture of enzymes responsible for the absorption, metabolism and excretion of medication. An abundance of enzymes involved in the metabolism of medication will tend to reduce its effects whereas reduced metabolism might lead to serious side-effects due to the build-up of toxins. Pharmocogenetics is the study of how individual genetic variation affects response to medication and offers the potential to enhance the safety and effectiveness of drugs, notwithstanding that other variables such as age, gender, diet and interaction with other medication will also explain individual response. Once again, like other genetics related topics, pharmacogenetics raises legal, ethical and social issues that impact in particular upon research, consent and the use and storage of samples and sensitive personal information.

Pharmacogenetic testing, if reliable, may help identify those most likely to benefit from particular treatments, which could be invaluable for the purposes of resource allocation, a factor of even greater significance in the current climate. Enhanced predictability of drug response might lead to significant savings on drug budgets. However, exclusive focus on economic rationales might mean that those affected by rare genetic conditions could be excluded from treatment with all the attendant moral implications. Genetic characteristics and variations are more prevalent in certain populations, and efforts would be required to ensure that this does not lead to racial stereotyping and prejudice. Pharmaceutical companies might be incentivised on economic grounds to concentrate their efforts on those drugs proven to be effective for large markets with the effect of reducing the availability of those proven to be effective for small numbers only.

11.6.4 Consent

Valid consent as underpinned by sufficient information is founded on the Kantian aim of protecting personal dignity and the need to treat each individual as an end in themselves, rather than as a means to an end. However, respect for self-determined choice, as evidenced by valid consent, can seriously impede the progress of clinical research that aims to promote the common good of society, as opposed to individual need. For the purposes of clinical research, and particularly for population-based biobank projects, a tension exists between public and private interests. Sutrop and Simm (2009) suggest that individual centred priorities ought to be replaced, or at least complemented, by collective values and public interests.

According to the Nuffield Council on Bioethics (2003), it is arguable that voluntary consent cannot truly be obtained in the context of clinical trials or in therapeutic practice. If genetic profiling is required for enrolling into a project, particularly if that study offers the only way to access a particular medication, then that patient might feel compelled to consent. Although the possibility of perceived coercion could extend to any participant enrolled in a clinical trial, in the event that no therapeutic alternative exists these concerns might be particularly acute, and especially where personal genetic material is involved on account of societal perception and concern.

A further quandary is whether limits ought to be applied to the uses to which samples containing genetic materials can be put, since there might be types of research that the participant would not wish to contribute. For these purposes a distinction is sometimes drawn between 'primary' and 'secondary' use of data. Primary use refers to application of information for the main purpose for which the data was collected and secondary use is for purposes other than these. Principle 2 of the Data Protection Act 1998 further consolidates this distinction in that 'Personal data shall be obtained only for one or more specified and lawful purposes, and shall not be further processed in any manner incompatible with that purpose or those purposes'. This statutory requirement might operate to inhibit legitimate genetic research, unless valid consent has been given. Related concepts include 'narrow' and 'broad' consent. Broad consent implies that the patient agrees that their sample may be used for a variety of future purposes and not restricted to those that are apparent at the commencement of the study (see 11.1.2). According to Hanson *et al.* (2006) broad consent is acceptable for secondary use of biological samples because of the considerable public benefit in the context of low risk. It arguably respects autonomy and is consistent with current practices. Narrow consent refers to consent being given specifically for the purposes of the instant project and without more. While broad consent can be invaluable for researchers, and ultimately for the public benefit, issues remain where samples and information can be traced back to participants. According to Hoffman (2009), broad consent for biobank projects can hide significant ethical challenges and can jeopardise public trust in clinical research. He suggests that notions of consent such as broad, blanket or future consent are inherently misleading and that the requirement ought to become 'broad authorisation' which avoids false justification. The Nuffield Council (2003) in its recommendations states that a two-stage process can be used: first, consent should be obtained for the instant study; and second, consent should be sought for the purposes of future research studies. In this way, subjects will retain some modicum of choice and control.

The need to secure valid consent based upon sufficient information can seriously hamper clinical research that aims to promote the common good, and particularly the need to obtain informed consent prior to the re-use of biological samples. For genetic studies, further complexities include the extent to which one can truly consent to the use of personal genetic information since the privacy of blood relatives and future offspring might well be involved. Invariably, these individuals will not have consented, and eliciting consent might be impossible. The extent to which data is anonymised will affect the type of consent required.

11.6.5　Confidentiality and privacy

Genetic tests that reveal the interconnectedness of blood relatives, communities and even entire populations operate to challenge fundamental rights of individuals, such as privacy, confidentiality and ownership. The success of large-scale biobank projects depends upon public acceptance and participation which could be disadvantaged by widespread concern. For epidemiological studies designed to maximise the common good of society, traditional rights-based discourse rooted in liberal individualism and respect for autonomy necessarily gives way to communitarian ideals. Since genetic characteristics are typically shared by others, the consequences of predicting predispositions to ill health will be relevant to others.

The extent to which individual's rights of privacy might be at risk depends upon the extent to which identifying information can be traced back to the individual. For example, many so-called anonymisation procedures use coding regimes that permit samples to be traced to back to named individuals in certain circumstances.

National epidemiological databases are necessarily staffed by large workforces all of whom have legitimate access to vast amounts of de-personalised, albeit sensitive data. Digital storage and access means that complex analyses can be conducted at speed by research teams. Despite rigorous procedural safeguards, such as the use of quasi-identifiers, designed to protect participants' anonymity, the extent to which true anonymity can be guaranteed is questionable, and there is concern about the potential for abuse and misconduct. Quasi- identifiers are personal variables that, although not unique to any single individual, can identify participants when considered in conjunction with other quasi-identifiers. Typical examples include dates of birth, death and specimen collection and locations such as postal codes and referring general practitioners. Biobanks also collect data on marital status, ethnicity, profession, income and gender.

Further dilemmas can present as to whether information that might be of clinical relevance to an individual research subject ought to be conveyed back to the participant concerned.

11.6.6 Is genetic data 'special'?

There is a common perception that genetic information is fundamentally different from other types of personal data on the basis that this is uniquely identifying and predictive of individual susceptibility to disease and ill health. However, not all genetic data is diagnostic of individuals or their blood relatives, and in any event, routine investigations such as blood tests, cholesterol and tests for infection can yield highly predictive information without the need for special rules. According to the Nuffield Council on Bioethics (2003), there is no reason to assume that genetic information is qualitatively exceptional compared with information gleaned from other diagnostic tests: it is the implications of that information which is key. While genetic tests can reveal significant personal information and susceptibility to future ill health, the same might be said of other non-genetic tests.

The Human Genetics Commission has recommended that stricter regulations are imposed to govern the accessibility of direct-to-consumer genetic tests. A blanket prohibition has been rejected, however, on account of individual rights to receive personal information without state interference, unless this is necessary for protection from harm. Knowledge of one's own genetic constitution and possible predispositions can have profound implications. The concept of benefit is interpreted differently when considered from the perspective of individuals compared with that of communities. It is widely perceived that communitarian benefits of mass population screening can be invaluable to drive public health campaigns for the prevention of conditions of multi-factorial aetiology, such as diabetes, cardiovascular disease and cancer.

Summary

11.1 Biotechnological developments involve an interaction between law and biomedical innovation. This provides an ethical and regulatory framework for new developments. The rapid advancement of biomedical technology and its (potential) practical application has brought new bioethical challenges.

11.2 Innovative technology is accompanied by an interplay of law, ethics and science. A paradigmatic case is the creation, research and use of human embryonic stem cells. Challenging issues arise from the ethical bases of such procedures, commercialisation, intellectual property rights and the social justification of high level expenditure in a limited area. In addition, translating basic research into clinical application can be beset with difficulties particularly in respect of conducting appropriate clinical trials and obtaining valid consent from research subjects. The embryo stem cell controversy illustrates some of the key features that surround the ethical and legal debates that may arise from cutting-edge biotechnological innovation.

11.3 Human enhancement involves any kind of activity undertaken to improve the mind and body and to enhance well-being. Enhancements are likely to trigger public debate of ethics, law and public policy. An impressive range of technologies, such as drugs (steroids and Ritalin), visual enhancement, and neuro-enhancement by microchip technology, is driving the urgency of this debate. It seems likely that these technologies will be freely available in the future and a robust regulatory framework will be required.

11.4 Biomedical innovations involve new technology for the delivery of health care. Two principal future challenges include costs and regulation. Robot-assisted surgery involving remote-controlled robotic arms for minimally invasive procedures have been adopted in the Unites States and Europe. The costs of technology are substantial and while there are short-term benefits, there is currently no compelling evidence that this has improved patient outcomes or quality of life in the longer term. Nanomedicine involves the use of nanotechnology for health care. This could be used for diagnostics as well as targeted delivery of pharmaceuticals. A number of legal and ethical challenges will be involved in developing a robust regulatory framework.

11.5 Recent advances in neurosciences such as neuroimaging, psychosurgery and psychopharmacology have potential benefits and harms. Key issues in neuroethics involve moral responsibility and freewill, informed consent and the effect of neuromodulation on personhood. These emerging issues create new challenges at the interface of law, medicine and ethics.

11.6 A biobank is a storage facility for biological samples, data from these samples, images and scans. They can also include databases of samples that contain human genetic material and for this reason are sometimes referred to as 'genetic databanks'. Biobanks are prevalent throughout the world. Gene therapy refers to the therapeutic remedy of a defect in a person's genetic makeup and involves the introduction of external genetic material to replace the patient's own defective DNA. If effective, and safe, gene therapy might represent a unique therapeutic option for the future.

Exercises

11.1 What are the main ethical and legal challenges for the future of medical law? Consider this within the paradigm of the debate around embryonic stem cell therapy.

11.2 'Human enhancement should be allowed and deserves protection as a human right under Article 8 of the European Convention of Human Rights.' Consider this statement in the context

Exercises cont'd

of autonomy and the degree to which infringement should be allowed on the basis of public policy.

11.3 Discuss the key challenges of biomedical innovation and the development of new technology in health care.

11.4 'The brain can reveal the mind and affect personal identity, freedom of thought and other aspects of ourselves.' Discuss this statement in the context of advances in neuroscience.

11.5 Critically analyse the principal issues that could impact upon the development of a substantive ethical and legal framework for the regulation of biobanks and gene therapy.

Further reading

Allhoff F, Lin P, Moor J, Weckert J. Ethics of human enhancement: 25 questions and answers. *Studies in Ethics, Law and Technology* 2010; 4: 1–39

Commission of the European Communities. Nanosciences & nanotechnologies: an action plan for Europe 2005–2009. Commission of the European Communities, Brussels, COM 243, 2005. Available at http://ec.europa.eu/research/industrial_technologies/pdf/nano_action_plan_en.pdf

McHale JV. Regulating nanotechnology: New legal challenges? *Eurohealth* vol.13, no. 2, 4–6

Robertson JA. Law, science and innovation: Introduction to the Symposium. *Journal of Law, Medicine and Ethics* 2010; 38: 175–190

Savulescu J. Procreative beneficence: Why we should select the best children. *Bioethics* 2001; 15: 412–426

Sutrop M, Simm K. Public and private interests in the genomic era: A pluralist approach, in *Ethics, Law and Society*, vol. IV, Gunning J, Holm S, Kenway I (eds). Ashgate, Surrey, 2009

Links to relevant websites can be found at: http://www.palgrave.com/law/samanta

Bibliography and further reading

Association of the British Pharmaceutical Industry 2009. Community prescribing in the UK. Available at http://www.abpi.org.uk

Academy of Medical Royal Colleges 2008. A code of practice for the diagnosis and confirmation of death. Available at http://www.aomrc.org.uk

ACC 2009. Annual Report. Available at http://www.acc.co.nz

Additional Protocol to the Convention of Human Rights and Biomedicine, on Transplantation of Organs and Tissues of Human Origin (2002). EU Council of Europe Convention. CETS No 186

Age Concern. *Turning your back on us – older people and the NHS.* Age Concern, London, 1999

Allhoff F, Lin P, Moor J, Weckert J. Ethics of human enhancement: 25 questions and answers. *Studies in Ethics, Law and Technology* 2010; 4: 1–39

Allison R. Doctor in organs sale scandal struck off. *The Guardian*, 31.08.2002

Amarasekara K, Bagaric M. *Euthanasia, morality and the law.* Peter Lang, New York, 2002

Appelbaum PS, Lidz CW, Meisel A. *Informed consent: Legal theory and clinical practice.* Oxford University Press, Oxford, 1987

Audini B, Lelliott P. Age, gender and ethnicity of those detained under Part 2 of the Mental Health Act 1983. *British Journal of Psychiatry* 2002; 180: 222

AvMA 2011. Implementation of patient safety alters: Too little too late. Available at http://www.avma.org.uk/data/files/patient_safety_alerts_report_feb_11.pdf

Bainham A. *Children, the modern law* (3rd edn). Jordan Publishing Ltd, Bristol, 2005

Barbash GI, Glied SA. New technology and healthcare costs–the case of robot-assisted surgery. *New England Journal of Medicine* 2010; 363: 701–704

Barker JH, Polcrack L. Respect for persons, informed consent and the assessment of infectious disease risks in xenotransplantation. *Medicine, Healthcare and Philosophy* 2001; 4: 53–70

Baron C. Physician-assisted suicide should be legalised and regulated. *Boston Bar Journal* 1997; 41: 15

Bartlett P. A test of compulsion in mental health law: Capacity, therapeutic benefit and dangerousness as possible criteria. *Medical Law Review* 2003; 11: 326–352

Bartlett P. *Blackstone's guide to the Mental Capacity Act 2005* (2nd edn). Oxford University Press, Oxford, 2008

Bartlett P. A matter of necessity? Enforced treatment under the Mental Health Act. *Medical Law Review* 2007; 15: 86–98

Bartlett P, Sandland R. *Mental health law: Policy and practice* (3rd edn). Oxford University Press, Oxford, 2007

Beauchamp TL, Childress JF. *Principles of biomedical ethics* (6th edn). Oxford University Press, Oxford, 2009

Bentley JP, Thacker PG. The influence of risk and monetary payment on the research participation decision-making process. *Journal of Medical Ethics* 2004; 30: 293–298

Beyleveld Deryck, Brownsword Roger. My body, my body parts, my property? *Healthcare Analysis* 2000; 8: 87–99

Beyleveld D, Brownsword R. *Human dignity in bioethics and biolaw.* Oxford University Press, Oxford, 2001

Bloomstein JF. The use of financial incentives in medical care: The case for commerce in transplantable organs, in *Justice in healthcare: Comparative perspectives,* A Grubb, MJ Melham (eds). John Whiley, Son, 1995

Boseley S. 40,000 drug errors logged in a year. *The Guardian* 11.08.2006

Botros S. An error about the doctrine of double effect. *Philosophy* 1999; 74: 71–83

Brazier M. Liability of ethics committees and their members. *Professional Negligence* 1990; 6: 186

Brazier M. Liberty, responsibility and maternity. *Current legal problems* 1999a; 52: 359–391

Brazier M. Regulating the reproduction business? *Medical Law Review* 1999b; 7: 166–193

Brazier M, Miola J. Bye Bye Bolam: A medical litigation revolution? *Medical Law Review* 2000; 8: 85–114

Brazier M, Cave E. *Medicine, patients and the law*. Penguin, London, 2007

Brazier M. Exploitation and enrichment: The paradox of medical experimentation. *Journal of Medical Ethics* 2008; 34: 180–183

British Medical Association 2000. Organ Donation in the 21st century: Time for a consolidated approach. British Medical Association, London

British Medical Association 2009. The Confidentiality and Disclosure Health Information Toolkit. Available at http://www.bma.org.uk/images/confidentialitytoolkitdec2009_tcm41-193140.pdf

The British Medical Association and The Law Society 2009. Assessment of Mental Capacity: A practical guide for doctors and lawyers (3rd edn). Law Society publishing, London

Buchanan A. Medical paternalism. *Philosophy in Public Affairs* 1979; 7: 49

Buchanan AE, Brock DW. *Deciding for others: The ethics of surrogate decision-making*. Cambridge University Press, Cambridge, 1989: 62–63

Buller T. Competence and risk relativity. *Bioethics* 2001; 15: 93–109

Caplan AL. Am I my brother's keeper? *Suffolk University Law Review* 1993; 27:1195

Capron AM. Informed consent in catastrophic disease research and treatment. *University of Pennsylvania Law Review* 1974; 123: 340 (at 4116–4117)

Case P. Confidence matters: The rise and fall of informational autonomy in medical law. *Medical Law Review* 2003; 11: 208–236

Chambers Dictionary (9th edn). 2003

Chapel A, Ziebland S, Macpherson A, Herxheimer A. What people close to death say about euthanasia and assisted suicide: A qualitative study. *Journal of Medical Ethics* 2006; 32: 706

Charuvastra A, Marder SR. Unconscious emotional reasoning and the therapeutic misconception. *Journal of Medical Ethics* 2008; 34: 193–197

Chief Medical Officer 2003. Making amends: A consultation paper setting out proposals for refining the approach to clinical negligence in the NHS. Available at http://www.dh.gov.uk

Christian Witting. National Health Service rationing: Implications for the standard of care in negligence. *Oxford Journal of Legal Studies* 2001; 21: 443

Clark PA. Placebo surgery for Parkinson's disease: Do the benefits outweigh the risks? *Journal of Law, Medicine and Ethics* 2002; 30: 58

Clouser KD, Gert B. A critique of principlism. *Journal of Medicine and Philosophy* 1990; 15: 219–236

Coggon J, Brazier M, Murphy P, Price P, Quigley M. Best interests and potential organ donors. *British Medical Journal* 2008; 336: 1346

Commission of the European Communities. Nanosciences and nanotechnologies: An action plan for Europe 2005–2009. Brussels: Commission of the European Communities, COM 243, 2005. Available at http://ec.europa.eu/research/industrial_technologies/pdf/nano_action_plan_en.pdf

Conference of Medical Colleges and Faculties of the United Kingdom, working party on organ transplantation in neonates. DHSS, London, 1988

Conference of the Medical Royal Colleges 1976, Code of Practice 1983 and 1998. Available at http://www.dh.gov.uk

Courts Administration of South Australia, Magistrates Court; Court Diversion Programme, 2005. Available at http://www.courts.sa.gov.au

Council for International Organisations of Medical Sciences 2002. International ethical guidelines for biomedical research involving human subjects. Available at http://www.cioms.ch

Council of Europe 2008. Access to safe and legal abortion in Europe. Resolution 1607

Cox J, King J, Hutchinson A, McAvoy P. *Understanding doctors' performance*. Radcliffe Publishing, Oxford, 2006

Declaration of Helsinki 2008. Ethical principles for medical research involving human subjects. Available at http://www.wma.net

Department of Health 1991. Guidelines in local research ethics committee. Available at http://www.dh.gov.uk

Department of Health 1994. Identification of potential donors of organs for transplantation. NHS Executive HSG (94) 41

Department of Health 1998. A code of practice for the diagnosis of brain stem death – including guidelines for the identification and management of potential organ and tissue donors. Available at http://www.dh.gov.uk

Department of Health 2000a. An investigation into conditional organ donation: the report. Available at http://www.dh.gov.uk

Department of Health 2000b. An organisation with a memory: Report of an expert group on learning from adverse events in the NHS. The Stationery Office, London. Available at http//:www.dh.gov.uk

Department of Health 2001a. Good Practice and Consent. Available at http://www.dh.gov.uk

Department of Health 2001b. Governance arrangements for NHS Research Ethics Committees in 2001 (GAfREC)

Department of Health 2001c. Seeking consent: Working with children. Department of Health. Available at http://www.dh.gov.uk

Department of Health 2001d. Reforming the mental health act. Available at http://www.webarchive.nationalarchives.gov.uk

Department of Health 2003a. *Confidentiality: NHS Code of Practice*. Department of Health, London

Department of Health 2003b. Maintaining high professional standards in the modern NHS: A framework for the initial handling of concerns about doctors and dentists in the NHS. Available at http://www.dh.gov.uk

Department of Health 2004. Best practice guidance for doctors and other health professionals on the provision of advice and treatment to young people under 16 on contraception, sexual and reproductive health. Available at http://www.dh.gov.uk

Department of Health 2005a. Creating a patient-led NHS. Department of Health, London

Department of Health 2005b. Research governance framework for Health and Social Care. Available at http://www.dh.gov.uk/

Department of Health (DH 080205), Available at http://www.dh.gov.uk/en/Publicationsandstatistics/Publications/PublicationsLegislation/dh080205

Department of Health 2006a. Our health, our care, our say (Department of Health)

Department of Health 2006b. Integrated governance handbook. Available at http://www.dh.gov.uk/

Department of Health 2006c. Xenotransplantation Guidance. Department of Health, London. Available at http://www.dh.gov.uk

Department of Health 2008a. High quality care for all: NHS next stage review final report. Available at http://www.dh.gov.uk/

Department of Health 2008b. Our NHS, our future: Next Stage Review leading local change. May 2008. Available at http://www.dh.gov.uk/publications

Department of Health 2009a. Legal issues relevant to non-heartbeating organ donation. Available at http://www.dh.gov.uk/

Department of Health 2009b. Regulated fertility services: A commissioning aid. (June 2009). Available at http://www.dh.gov.uk/

Department of Health 2010a. Abortion Statistics 2009. Department of Health, London, 2010a. Available at http://www.dh.gov.uk/

Department of Health 2010b. *Equity and excellence: Liberating the NHS.* Available at http://www.dh,gov.uk

Department of Health 2010c. The NHS Constitution for England. Available at http://www.dh.gov.uk

Dobson R. Guidelines ignored on resuscitation decisions. *British Medical Journal* 1999; 319: 536

Donaldson LJ. Doctors with problems in an NHS workforce. *British Medical Journal* 1994; 3081: 277–1282

Dresser R. Missing persons: Legal perceptions of incompetent patients. *Rutgers Law Review* 1994; 46: 609

Dworkin R. *Life's Dominion: An argument about abortion, euthanasia and individual freedom.* Knopf, New York, 1993

Dyer C. British GP cleared of murder charge. *British Medical Journal* 1999; 318: 1306

Dyer C. Stem cell therapy doctor struck off by GMC. *British Medical Journal* 2010; 341: c5410

Eekelaar J. The importance of thinking that children have rights. *IJLF* 1992; 6: 221

Eekelaar J. White coats or flack jackets? Children and the courts again. *Law Quarterly Review* 1993; 109: 182–187

Elliott C. Doing harm: Living organ donors, clinical research and the tenth man. *The Journal of Medical Ethics* 1995; 21: 91–96

Elliston S. If you know what's good for you: Refusal of consent to medical treatment by children, in S McLean (ed), *Contemporary Issues in Law, Medicine and Ethics.* Ashgate, Dartmouth, 1996

Emson HE. It is immoral to require consent for cadaver organ donation. *Journal of Medical Ethics* 2003; 29: 125–127

Encouraging or assisting suicide: The implementation of Section 59 of the Coroner's and Justice Act 2009. Available at http://www.justice.gov.uk/

Erin CA, Harris J. An ethical market in human organs. *Journal of Medical Ethics* 2003; 29: 137–138

Ethical considerations for clinical trials of medicinal products conducted with the paediatric population (EC No 1901/2006)

Faden RR, Beauchamp TL, King NMP. *A history and theory of informed consent.* Oxford University Press, Oxford, 1986: 306–307

Fagerlin A, Schneider C. Enough: The failure of the living will. *Hastings Centre Report* 2004; 34: 30

Fann R, Teo J. Consent to medical treatment. *Journal of Medical Ethics and Philosophy* 2004; 29: 139

Featherstone K, Donovan JL. Why don't they just tell me straight, why allocate it? The struggle to make sense of participating in a randomised control trial. *Social Science and Medicine* 2002; 55: 709–719

Ferguson PR. Clinical trials in healthy volunteers. *Medical Law Review* 2008; 16:23–51

Ferguson PR. Patients' perceptions of information provided in clinical trials. *Journal of Medical Ethics* 2002; 28: 45

Ferner RE. Medication errors that have led to manslaughter charges. *British Medical Journal* 2000; 321: 1212–1216

Finnis J. The rights and wrongs of abortion: A reply to Judith Thomson. *Philosophy and Public Affairs* 1973; 2: 117–145

Finnis JM. Bland: Crossing the rubicon. *Law Quarterly Review* 1993; 109: 329

Finnis J. Misunderstanding the case against euthanasia: Response to Harris's first reply, in *Euthanasia examined*, Keown J (ed). 1995

Finnis J. Euthanasia, morality and the law. *Leola Los Angeles Law Review* 1998; 1: 1465

Finucane PM, Bourgeois-Law GA, Ineson SL, Kaigas TM. A comparison of performance assessment programmes for medical practitioners in Canada, Australia, New Zealand and the United Kingdom. *Academic Medicine* 2003; 78: 837–843

Forster AJ, Murff HJ, Peterson JF, Gandhi TK, Bates David Waller. The incidence and severity of adverse events affecting patients after discharge from hospital. *Annals of Internal Medicine* 2003; 138: 161–167

Fortin J. Accommodating children's rights in a post Human Rights Act Era. *Modern Law Review* 2006; 69: 299–326

Foster C. It should be, therefore it is. *New Law Journal* 2004; 154: 7151

Fox M. Research bodies: Feminist perspectives on clinical research, in S Sheldon, M Thomson (eds), *Feminist perspectives on healthcare law.* Cavendish, London, 1998

Francis RQC. The Michael Stone Enquiry—a reflection. *Journal of Mental Health Law* 2007; 15: 41

Frey RG. Distinctions in death, in J Dworkin, RG Frey, S Bok (eds), *Euthanasia and physician-assisted suicide: For and against.* Cambridge University Press, Cambridge, 1998

Fuchs VR. New priorities for future biomedical innovations. *New England Journal of Medicine* 2010; 363: 704–706

General Medical Council 1998. Seeking patients' consent: The ethical considerations. GMC, London.

General Medical Council 2002. Research: The role and responsibilities of doctors. GMC, London.

General Medical Council 2007. 0–18 years: Guidance for all doctors. Available at http://www.gmc-uk.org

General Medical Council 2008. GMC Consent: Patients and doctors making decisions together. Available at http://www.gmc-uk.org

General Medical Council 2009. Confidentiality. GMC, London

Gentleman D, Easton J, Jennett B. Brain death and organ donation in a neurosurgical unit: Audit of recent practice. *British Medical Journal* 1990; 301: 1203

Gewirth A. The community of rights. University of Chicago Press, Chicago, 1996

Gilligan C. *In a different voice.* Harvard University Press, Massachusetts, 1982

Gillon R. Medical ethics: Four principles plus attention to scope. *British Medical Journal* 1994; 309: 184

Gillon R. Futility—too ambiguous and pejorative a term. *Journal of Medical Ethics* 1997 December; 23(6): 339–340

Gillon R. Imposed separation of conjoined twins—moral hubris by the English courts? *Journal of Medical Ethics* 2001a; 27: 3–4

Gillon R. Is there a "new ethics of abortion"? *Journal of Medical Ethics* 2001b; 26 (Suppl 2): 5–9

Glannon W. Neuroethics. *Bioethics* 2006; 20: 37–52

Good Medical Practice (GMC, London, 2001) para 9

Government White Paper 'Reforming the Mental Health Act'. Available at http://webarchive.nationalarchives.gov.uk

Goyal M, Mehta RL, Schneiderman LJ, Segal AR. Economic and health consequences of selling a kidney in India. *Journal of the American Medical Association* 2002; 288: 1589–1593

Greeley HT. Defining chimeras .. and chimeric concerns. *American Journal of Bioethics* 2003; 3: 17–20

Green S. Coherence of medical negligence cases: A game of doctors and purses. *Medical Law Review* 2006; 14: 1

Griffiths J. Assisted suicide in the Netherlands: The Chabot case. *Modern Law Review* 1995; 58: 232–248

Grubb A. The incompetent patient (adult): *Bland* and the Human Rights Act 1998. *Medical Law Review* 2000: 342

Grubb A. Consent to treatment: The competent patient, in A Grubb, J Laing (eds), *Principles of medical law*, (2nd edn). Oxford University Press, Oxford, 2004, 131–203, at 200)

Grubb A. (ed.) *Principles of Medical Law* (2nd edn). Oxford University Press, Oxford, 2004

Grubb A, Laing J. *Principles of medical law.* Oxford University Press, Oxford, 2004

Gundle K. Presumed consent: an international comparison and possibilities for change in the United States. *Cambridge Quarterly of Healthcare Ethics* 2005; 14: 113

Gunn M, Smith MJ. Arthur's case and the right to life of a Down's syndrome child. *Criminal Law Review* 1985; 705

Gunn M. The meaning of incapacity. *Medical Law Review* 1994; 2: 8

Gunn MJ, Wong JG, Clare ICH, Holland AJ. Decision-making capacity. *Medical Law Review* 1999; 7: 296–306

Gurnham D. Losing the wood for the trees: Burke and the Court of Appeal. *Medical Law Review* 2006; 14: 253

Haddow G. Because you are worth it? The taking and selling of transplantable organs. *Journal of Medical Ethics* 2006; 32: 324–328

Hagger L. Some implications of the Human Rights Act 1998 for the medical treatment of children. *Medical Law International* 2003; 6: 25–51

Hansson MG, Dillner J, Bartram CR. Should donors be allowed to give broad consent in future biobank research? *Lancet Oncol* 2006; 7: 266–269

Hare RM. Abortion and the golden rule. *Philosophy and Public Affairs* 1975; 4: 201–222

Harris J. *The value of life: An introduction to medical ethics*. Routledge, London, 1985

Harris J. *Clones, genes and immortality: Ethics and the genetic revolution*. Oxford University Press, Oxford, 1998

Harris J. Organ procurement: Dead interests, living needs. *Journal of Medical Ethics* 2003a; 29: 130–134

Harris J. Consent and end-of-life decisions. *Journal of Medical Ethics* 2003b; 29: 10–15

Harris J. *Enhancing Evolution: The Ethical Case for Making Better People*. Princeton University Press, Princeton, 2007

Harvey J. Paying organ donors. *Journal of Medical Ethics* 1990; 16: 117–119

Hayry M. Neuroethical theory. *Cambridge Quarterly of Healthcare Ethics* 2010; 19: 165

Healey P, Samanta J. When does the "Learning curve" of innovative interventions become questionable practice? *European Journal of Vascular and Endovascular Surgery* 2008; 36 (3): 253–257

Healthcare Commission. Responses to the Healthcare Commission Consultation and Complaints. 2004, Healthcare Commission. Available at http://www.cqc.org.uk/redirection.html

Herring J. Children's abortion rights. *Medical Law Review* 1997; 5: 257

Herring 2008 *Medical Law and Ethics*. Oxford University Press, Oxford

HFEA Code of Practice (8th edn) 2008. Available at http://www.hfea.gov.uk

High quality care for all. Available at http://www.nrls.npsa.nhs.uk/resources/collections/never-events/

Her Majesty's Treasury 2007. 2007 Pre-budget report and comprehensive spending review. Available at http://www.webarchive.nationalarchives.gov.uk

HM Treasury. Budget Report, June 2010. Available at http://www.hm-treasury.gov.uk

Hofmann B. Broadening consent—and diluting ethics? *Journal of Medical Ethics* 2009; 35: 125–129

Holm S, Takala T. High hopes and automatic escalators: A critique of some new arguments in bioethics. *Journal of Medical Ethics* 2007; 31: 1–4

House of Commons Public Accounts Committee 2009. Reducing healthcare associated infection in hospitals in England: 52nd report of session 2008/09. Available at http://www.publications.parliament.uk/

House of Lords Select Committee (2005) on the Assisted Dying for the Terminally Ill Bill. *House of Lords*. TSO, London, 2005

HTA 2004 Code of Practice. Code of Practice 2 (donation of solid organs for transplantation) Available at http://www.hta.gov.uk

HTA Code of Practice 1 2009. Available at http://www.hta.gov.uk

Hu JC, Gu X, Lipsitz SR. Comparative effectiveness of minimally invasive versus open radical prostatectomy. *Journal of the American Medical Association* 2009; 302: 1557–1564

Hughes J. Xenografting: Ethical issues. *Journal of Medical Ethics* 1998; 24: 18

Human Fertilisation and Embryology Authority 2006. Choices and boundaries. Available at http://www. hfea.gov.uk

Huxtable R. *Euthanasia, ethics and the law: From conflict to compromise*. Routledge-Cavendish, Abingdon, 2007

Jackson E. Whose death is it anyway? Euthanasia and the medical profession. *Current Legal Problems* 2004; 57: 415

Jackson E. Degendering reproduction. *Medical Law Review* 2008; 16: 346–368

Jarvis R. Join the club. *Journal of Medical Ethics* 1995; 21:199

Jecker NS, Pearlman A. Medical futility: Who decides? *Archives of Internal Medicine* 1992; 152: 1140–1144

Jones J. *Bad blood: The Tuskegee syphilis experiment*. The Free Press, New York, 1981

Jones M. The *Bolam* test and the responsible expert. *Tort Law Review* 1999; 7; 226–250

Judicial Studies Board 2010, Guidelines for the Assessment of General Damages in Personal Injury Cases. 10th edn

Kass LR, Lund N. Physician-assisted suicide, medical ethics and the future of the medical profession. *Duquesne Law Review* 1996; 35: 395

Kaye J, Martin P. Safeguards for research using large scale DNA collections. *British Medical Journal* 2000; 321: 1146

Kennedy I. *Treat me right*. Oxford University Press, Oxford, 1991

Kennedy I, et al. The case for presumed consent in organ donation. *The Lancet* 1998; 351: 1650–1652

Kennedy I, Grubb A. *Medical Law* (3rd edn). Butterworths, London, 2000

Keown J (ed). *Euthanasia examined*. Cambridge University Press, Cambridge, 1995

Keown J. Euthanasia in the Netherlands: Sliding down the slippery slope? in *Euthanasia examined*. Cambridge University Press, Cambridge, 1995a

Keown J. Restoring moral and intellectual shape to the law under *Bland*. *Law Quarterly Review*. 1997; 113: 482–503

Keown J. Dehydration and human rights. *Cambridge Law Journal*. 2001; 60: 53

Keown J. *Euthanasia, ethics and public policy: An argument against legalisation*. Cambridge University Press, Cambridge, 2002

Keown J. Morning after pills, miscarriage and muddle. *Legal Studies* 2005; 25: 296–319

Keown P, Mercer G, Scott J. 2008. Retrospective analysis of hospital episode statistics, involuntary admissions under the Mental Health Act 1983, and number of psychiatric beds in England 1996–2006. *British Medical Journal* 2008; 337:1837

Kerridge IH, Saul P, Lowe M, McPhee J, Williams D. Death, dying and donation: Organ transplantation and the diagnosis of death. *Journal of Medical Ethics* 2002; 28: 89–94

Kirklin D. The role of medical imaging in the abortion debate. *Journal of Medical Ethics* 2004; 30: 426

Kuhse H, Singer P. Individuals, humans and persons: The issue of moral status, in P Singer et al (eds), *Embryo experimentation*. Cambridge University Press, Cambridge, 1990

Kuhse H, Singer P. Bioethics: An anthology. Helga Kuhse, Peter Singer (eds). Blackwell, Oxford, 2006

Law Commission. Family law review of child law: Custody Number 96. 1986 HMSO. Available at http://www.lawcommission.wordpress.com/1986/10/01/00001

Law Commission 1995a. Consent and the criminal law (law com no. 139, 1995)

Law Commission 1995b. Report on mental incapacity (Law Commission No 231)

Law Commission (1997) Aggravated, Exemplary and Restitutionary Damages (Law Commission No 247), London HMSO

Learning from Bristol: The report of the public enquiry into children's heart surgery at the Bristol Royal Infirmary 1984–1995 CM 5207 2001. Available at http://www.bristol-enquiry.org.uk/

Lemmens T, Elliott C. Justice for the professional guinea pig. *American Journal of Bioethics* 2001; 1: 51–53

Lesser H. The patient's right to information, in Margaret Brazier, Mary Lobjoit (eds), *Protecting the vulnerable: Autonomy and consent in healthcare.* Routledge, London, 1991

Lewis P. Feeding anorexic patients who refuse food. *Medical Law Review* 1999; 7: 21–37

Lewis P. Procedures that are against the medical interests of incompetent adults. *Oxford Journal of Legal Studies* 2002; 22: 575–618

Lloyd Thomas AR, Fitzgerald M. Reflex responses do not necessarily signify pain. *British Medical Journal* 1996; 313: 797–798

London AJ. Equipoise and international human subjects research. *Bioethics* 2001; 15: 312–332

Lovell MA, Mudaliar MY, Klineberg PL. Intrahospital transport of critically ill patients: Complications and difficulties. *Anaesthesia and Intensive Care* 2001; 29: 400–405

Lowe N, Juss S. Medical treatment—pragmatism and the search for principle. *Modern Law Review* 1993; 56: 865–872

Lurie P, Woolfe SM. Unethical trials of interventions to reduce perinatal transmission of the Human Immunodeficiency Virus in developing countries. *New England Journal of Medicine* 1997; 337: 853–856

Magnusson RS. Euthanasia: Above ground, below ground. *Journal of Medical Ethics* 2004; 30: 441–446

Mason. Contemporary issues in organ transplantation, in S McLean (ed), *Contemporary issues in law, medicine and ethics.* Dartmouth, Aldershot, 1996: 117–141

Mason JK, Laurie G. Mason and McCall-Smith's law on medical ethics. Oxford University Press, Oxford, 2006

Mason JK. *The troubled pregnancy: Legal rights and wrongs in reproduction.* Cambridge University Press, Cambridge, 2007

McCarthy D, Blumenthal D. Stories from the sharp end. Case studies in safety improvement. *Millbank Quarterly* 2006; 84: 165–200

McDonagh EL. My body, my consent: Securing the constitutional right to abortion funding. *Albany Law Review* 1999; 62: 1057

McGuinness S, Brazier M. Respecting the living means respecting the dead too. *Oxford Journal of Legal Studies,* 2008; 28(2): 297–316

McHale JV. Regulating genetic databases: Some legal and ethical issues. *Medical Law Review* 2004; 12: 70

McHale JV. Regulating nanotechnology: New legal challenges? *Eurohealth* 2007; 13(2): 4–6

McLean S. *Old law, new medicine.* Pandora, London, 1999

McNaughton D. Consequentialism, in *Routledge Encyclopaedia of Philosophy,* E Craig (ed). London, Routledge, 1998

Medical Research Council 2001. MRC Human tissue and biological samples for use in research—operational ethical guidelines. MRC Ethics series, 2001

Medical Research Council 2004. Medical research involving children. Medical Research Council. Available at http://www.mrc.ac.uk/

Medical Research Council 2007. Medical Research Council ethics guide: Medical research involving adults who cannot consent. Medical Research Council. Available at http://www.mrc.ac.uk

Menikoff J. Organ swapping. *Hastings Centre Report* 1999; 29: 28–33

Mental Health Act 1983 Code of Practice. Available at http://www.dh.gov.uk

Michalowski S. Advance refusals of life-sustaining medical treatment: The relativity of an absolute right. *Modern Law Review* 2005; 68: 958

Mill, John Stuart. *On Liberty* (first published 1859). Watts and Co, London, 1929

Monahan J, Steadman HJ, Silver E, Appelbaum P, Clark-Robbins P, Mulvey EP, Roth LH, Grisso T,

Banks S. Rethinking risk assessment: The MacArthur study of mental disorder and violence. Oxford University Press, Oxford, 2001

Montgomery J. Confidentiality and the immature minor. *Family Law* 1987; 10: 101

Montgomery J. Rhetoric and Welfare. *Oxford Journal of Legal Studies* (1989); 9: 395

Montgomery J. Law and the demoralisation of medicine. *Legal Studies* 2006; 26: 185

Morris A. Spiralling or stabilising? The compensation culture and our propensity to claim damages for personal injury. *Modern Law Review* 2007; 70: 349

Morrison D. A holistic approach to clinical and research decision-making. *Medical Law Review* 2005; 13: 45

Mudur G. Kidney trade arrest exposes loopholes in India's transplant laws. *British Medical Journal* 2004; 328: 246

Mulcahy L. Mediating medical negligence claims: An option for the future? HMSO, London, 1999

Mulcahy L. Disputing Doctors: The socio-legal dynamics of complaints about doctors. Open University Press, Buckingham, 2003

Nacro. Multi-agency partnership working and the delivery of services to mentally disordered offenders—key principles and practice. Nacro, London, 2005

Najarian JS, Chavers VM, McHugh LE, Matas AJ. 20 years or more of follow up of living kidney donors. *The Lancet* 1992; 340: 807–810

National Audit Office. *A safer place for patients: Learning to improve patient safety.* National Audit Office, London, 2005

National Council for Hospice and Specialist Palliative Care Services (1997). *Voluntary euthanasia: The Council's view.* NCHSPCS, London, 1997

National Institute for Health and Clinical Excellence (NICE, 2004) Fertility: Assessment and treatment for people with fertility problems, 2004. Available at http://www.nice.org.uk/

National Patient Safety Agency. *Achieving our aims: Evaluating the results of the pilot 'Clean your hands' campaign.* NPSA, London, 2004

National Patient Safety Agency 2004. Seven steps to patient safety: A guide for NHS staff. Available at http://www.npsa.nhs.uk/sevensteps

National Research Ethics Service (2008) Medicines for human use (Clinical Trials Regulations) 2008: Informed consent in clinical trials. Available at http://www.nres.npsa.nhs.uk

NCAS (2009) *The first eight years.* NCAS, London, 2009

Nelson JL. *Hippocrates' maze: Ethical explorations of the medical labyrinth.* Roman and Littlefield, New York, 2003

Neuberger J, Price D. The role of living liver donation in the United Kingdom. *British Medical Journal* 2003; 327: 676–679

Newdick C. *Who should we treat?* Oxford University Press, Oxford, 2005

NHS Blood and Transplant 2010. Monthly statistics. Available at http://www.organdonation.nhs.uk/

NHS Information Centre, July 2007. Community care statistics. Available at http://www.ic.nhs.uk/

NHS Information Centre, 2010. Community care statistics. Available at http://www.ic.nhs.uk/

NHSLA 2008. Reports and Accounts 2008. Available at http://www.nhsla.com/publications

NHSLA 2010. Reports and Accounts 2010. Available at http://www.nhsla.com/

Novack DH. Changes in physicians' attitudes towards telling a cancer patient. *Journal of the American Medical Association* 1979; 241: 897–900

NRES 2008. Standard operating procedures for RECs in the UK. Available at http://www.nres.npsa.nhs.uk

Nuffield Council of Bioethics 1996. Animal-to-human transplants: the ethics of xenotransplantation. Available at http://www.nuffieldbioethics.org/

Nuffield Council of Bioethics 2002. The ethics of research related to healthcare in developing countries. Available at http://www.nuffieldbioethics.org.uk

Nuffield Council on Bioethics 2003. Pharmacogenetics: Ethical issues. Available at http://www. nuffieldbioethics.org/

Oken D. What to tell cancer patients: A study of medical attitudes. *Journal of the American Medical Association* 1961; 175: 1120–1128

O'Neill O. Children's rights and children's lives. *Ethics* 1988; 98: 445

Oregon Department of Human Services http://www.oregon.gov/DHS/ph/pas/index.shtml (2010)

Organ Donation Taskforce 2008. Department of Health, London, 2008. Available at http://www.dh.gov.uk

Organ Donation Taskforce. Organs for transplants: A report from the Organ Donation Taskforce Department of Health, London, 2008. Available at http://www.dh.gov.uk

Organ Donation Taskforce. The potential impact of an opt-out system for organ donation in the UK: An independent report from the Organ Donation Taskforce. Department of Health, London, 2008. Available at http://www.dh.gov.uk

Organ Donation Taskforce. UK Transplant 2008. Available at http://www.dh.gov.uk

Otlowski M. *Voluntary euthanasia and the common law.* Oxford University Press, Oxford, 2000

Our NHS, Our future: NHS next stage review. Department of Health, 2008. Available at http://www. dh.gov.uk/

Palmer K. *NHS reform: Getting back on track.* King's Fund, London, 2006

Parfit D. *Reasons and persons.* Oxford University Press, Oxford, 1984

Park A. *British Attitudes Survey.* National Centre for Social Research. 2007

Parliamentary and National Health Services Ombudsman (2005) NHS funding for the long term care of elderly and disabled people (TSO)

Pattinson SD. *Medical law and ethics.* Sweet and Maxwell, London, 2006

President's Council on Bioethics. *Controversies in the Determination of Death.* President's Council on Bioethics, Washington, D.C.: 2008

Price D. The Human Tissue Act 2004. *Modern Law Review* 2005; 68: 798–821

Price D. *Human tissue for transplantation and research: A model legal and ethical framework.* Cambridge University Press, Cambridge, 2009a

Price D. What shape to euthanasia after *Bland*? Historical, contemporary and futuristic paradigms. *Law Quarterly Review* 2009b; 125: 142–174

Quigley M. A NICE fallacy. *Journal of Medical Ethics* 2007; 3: 465

Radcliffe-Richards J, Daar AS, Guttmann RD, Hoffenberg R, Kennedy I, Lock M, Sells RA, Tilney N. The case for allowing kidney sales. International Forum for Transplant Ethics. *The Lancet* 1998; 351: 1950–1952

Rawlins M. National Institute for Clinical Excellence and its value judgements. *British Medical Journal* 2004; 329: 224

Rawls J. *A Theory of Justice.* Harvard University Press, Harvard 2005

Raymont V, Bingley W, Buchanan A, David AS, Hayward P, Wessely S, Hotopf M. Prevalence of mental incapacity in medical in-patients and associated risk factors: Cross sectional study. *The Lancet* 2004; 364: 1421–1427

RCPCH 2004. Royal College of Paediatrics and Child Health. *Withholding or withdrawing life-sustaining treatment in children: A framework for practice.* Royal College of Paediatrics and Child Health, London, 2004

Rennie D. Education and debate. Dealing with research misconduct in the UK. *British Medical Journal* 1998; 316: 1726–1733

Research Governance Framework for Health and Social Care. Department of Health, London, 2001. Available at http://www.dh.gov.uk

Resuscitation Council (UK). Decisions relating to cardiopulmonary resuscitation, a joint statement with the British Medical Association, the Resuscitation Council (UK) and the Royal College of Nursing. 2001. Available at http://www.resus.org.uk/pages/dnar.htm

Resuscitation Council Guidance 2010. Resuscitation Guidelines. Available at http://www.resus.org.uk

Robert JS, Bayliss F. Crossing species boundaries. *American Journal of Bioethics* 2003; 3: 1–13

Robertson J. Second thought on living wills. *Hastings Centre Report* 1991; 21: 6

Robertson JA. Law, science and innovation: Introduction to the Symposium. *Journal of Law, Medicine and Ethics* 2010; 38: 175–190

Royal College of Gynaecologists. *The care of women requesting abortion: Evidence-based clinical guidelines No 7*, Royal College of Obstetricians and Gynaecologists, London, 2004

Royal College of Obstetricians and Gynaecologists (RCOG) 1996. *Termination of pregnancy for foetal abnormality in England, Wales and Scotland.* RCOG, London, January 2006

Royal College of Paediatrics. Child health: Ethics Advisory Committee guidelines for the ethical conduct of medical research involving children. *Archives of Disease in Childhood* 2000; 82: 177–182

Royal College of Paediatrics and Child Health 2004. Withholding or withdrawing life sustaining treatment in children: A framework for practice (2nd edition). Available at http://www.rcpch.ac.uk/Publications/

Royal College of Physicians, Royal College of Physicians Working Group. The persistent vegetative state. *Journal of the Royal College of Physicians of London* 1996; 30: 119–121

Royal College of Physicians 2007. *Guidelines on the practice of ethics committees in medical research with human participants.* Royal College of Physicians, London, 2007

Royal College of Psychiatrists. *Evidence submitted to the Joint Committee on the draft Mental Health bill.* RCP, London, 2004

Royal College of Surgeons 2002. Good surgical practice

Sadler H. The living genetically unrelated kidney donor. *Semin Psychiatry.* 1971; 3: 86

Safer Healthcare. Available at http://www.saferhealthcare.org.uk/

Safer Patients Safety Initiative (The Health Foundation) Available at http://www.health.org.uk/

Samanta A, Samanta J, Gunn M. Legal considerations of guidelines: Will NICE make a difference? *Journal of the Royal Society of Medicine* 2003; 96: 133

Samanta A. Death, dying and the doctor: A dilemma at the bedside. *Contemporary issues in law* 2005; 7: 211–241

Samanta A, Samanta J. The Human Rights Act 1998—why should it matter for medical practice? *Journal of the Royal Society of Medicine* 2005; 98: 404–410

Samanta A, Mello MM, Foster C, Tingle J, Samanta J. The role of clinical guidelines in medical negligence litigation: A shift from the *Bolam* standard? *Medical Law Review* 2006; 14: 321–366

Samanta A, Samanta J. Do not attempt resuscitation orders: The role of clinical governance. *Clinical Governance, An International Journal* 2007a; 13: 215–220

Samanta A, Samanta J. Safer patients and good doctors: Medical regulation in the 21st century. *Clinical Risk* 2007b; 13: 138–142

Samanta J. Lasting powers of attorney for healthcare under the Mental Capacity Act 2005: Enhanced perspective self-determination for future incapacity or a simulacrum? *Medical Law Review* 2009; 17(3): 377–409

Samanta J, Healey P. Calling time on abortion—a hopeful beginning or an untimely end? *Contemporary Issues in Law* 2005; 7: 281–300

Sauder R, Parker NS. Autonomy limits: Living donation and health-related harm. *Cambridge Quarterly of Healthcare Ethics* 2001; 10: 399–403

Savulescu J, Momeyer RW. Should informed consent be based upon rational beliefs? *Journal of Medical Ethics* 1997; 23: 282–288

Savulescu J. Procreative beneficence: Why we should select the best children. *Bioethics* 2001; 15: 412–426

Savulescu J. Deaf lesbians, designer disability and the future of medicine. *British Medical Journal* 2002; 325: 771–773

Scally G, Donaldson LJ. Clinical governance and the drive for quality improvement in the new NHS in England. *British Medical Journal* 1998; 317: 61–65

Science and Technology Committee 1995. Human Reproductive Technologies and the Law. 5th Report. Available at http://www.publications.parliament.uk/

Sen A. *On ethics and economics*. Basil Blackwell, Oxford, 1987

Sheldon S. Multiple pregnancy and reproductive choice R v Queen Charlotte Hospital, Professor Philip Bennett, North Thames Regional Health Authority and Socoal Services of Brentford and Hounslow LBC, ex parte Philys Bowman. *Feminist Legal Studies* 1997; 5(1): 99–106

Sheldon S. A responsible body of medical men skilled in that particular art…rethinking the *Bolam* test, in S Sheldon, M Thompson (eds), *Feminist perspectives on healthcare law*. Cavendish, London, 1998

Sheldon S, Wilkinson S. Hashmi and Whitaker: An unjustifiable and misguided distinction. *Medical Law Review* 2004; 12: 137–163

Sherwin S. Feminism in biocthics, in Susan Woolf (ed), *Feminism and Bioethics*. Oxford University Press, Oxford, 1996

Singer P. Xenotransplantation and speciesism. *Transplantation Proceedings* 1992; 24: 728–732

Singer P. *Practical ethics* (2nd edn). Cambridge University Press, Cambridge, 1993

Smith R. All changed, changed utterly. *British Medical Journal* 1998; 316: 1917–1918

Smith R. The failings of NICE. *British Medical Journal* 2000; 321: 1363

Stanley JM. The Appleton Consensus: Suggested international guidelines for decisions to forego medical treatment. *Journal of Medical Ethics* 1989; 15(3): 129–136

Stauch M. Pregnancy and the Human Rights Act 1998, in Garwood-Gowers A, Tingle J. (eds). *Healthcare law: The impact of the Human Rights Act 1998*, Cavendish Publishing, London, 2001

Stavert J. Mental health, community care and human rights in Europe: Still an incomplete picture? *Journal of Mental Health Law* 2007; 16: 182

Stern K. Advance directives. *Medical Law Review* 1994; 2: 57–76

Sumner LW. Rights, in *The Blackwell Guide to Ethical Theory*. Hugh LaFollette (ed). Blackwell Publishers, Malden, Massachusetts, 2000

Sutrop M, Simm K. Public and private interests in the genomic era: a pluralistic approach, in J Gunning, S Holm and I Kenway (eds), *Ethics, Law and Society* Volume 4. Ashgate, Farnham 2009

Syrett K. Impotence or importance? Judicial review in an era of explicit NHS rationing. *Medical Law Review* 2004; 67: 289

Szasz T. Law, liberty and psychiatry: An enquiry into the social uses of mental health practices Routledge and Keegan Paul, London, 1984

Takala T. Guest editorial: Introduction to philosophical issues in neuroethics. *Cambridge Quarterly of Healthcare Ethics* 2010; 19: 161–163

Tam BC, Knowles SR, Cornish BL, Fine N, Marchesano R, Etchells EE. Frequency, type and clinical importance of medication history errors at admission to hospital: A systematic review. *Canadian Medical Association Journal* 2005; 173: 510–515

Tännsjö T. Two concepts of death reconciled. *Medicine, Healthcare and Philosophy* 1999; 2: 41–46

Teff H. The action for "wrongful life" in England and the United States. *International and Comparative Law Quarterly* 1985a; 34: 423–441

Teff H. Consent to medical procedures: Paternalism, self-determination or therapeutic alliance. *The Law Quarterly Review* 1985b; 101: 432–453

Teff H. The standard of care in medical negligence—moving on from *Bolam*? *Oxford Journal of Legal Studies* 1998; 18: 473–484

The Expert Scientific Group on Phase One clinical trials: Final report. 2006. Available at http://www.dh.gov.uk

The National Health Service (General Medical Services) Regulations 1992 SI 1992/635 Schedule 2, para 4 (H)

The new NHS: Modern, dependable (1997) Department of Health. Available at http://www.dh.gov.uk/

Thompson, Barber, Schwartz. Adherence to advance directives in critical care decision-making: A vignette study. *British Medical Journal* 2003; 327: 1011

Thomson JJ. A defence of abortion. *Philosophy and Public Affairs* 1971; 1: 47

Thornton H. Clinical trials: A brave new partnership? *Journal of Medical Ethics* 1994; 20: 19

Titmuss RM. The gift relationship: From human blood to social policy. George Allen and Unwin, London, 1970

Truog RD. Brain death—too flawed to endure, too ingrained to abandon. *Journal of Law, Medicine and Ethics* 2007; 35(2): 273–281

Tur R. Legislative Technique and Human Rights: the sad case of assisted suicide. *Criminal Law Review* 2003; 3–12

UK Transplant 2005. Available at http://www.uktransplant.org.uk

UK Transplant 2007. Available at http://www.uktransplant.org.uk

UK Transplant 2008. Transplant activity in the UK 2007–2008 and the cost effectiveness of transplantation (UK Transplant, 2007). Available at http://www.uktransplant.org.uk

US Government Printing Office. Trials of war criminals before the Nuremberg Military Tribunals under Control Council Law No 10. US Government Printing Office, Washington, DC.: 1949

Veatch RM. *The Basics of Bioethics* (2nd edn). Prentice Hall, New Jersey 2003

Vehmas S. Parental responsibility and the morality of selective abortion. *Ethical Theory and Moral Practice* 2002; 5: 463–484

Verdon-Jones S, Weisstub D. Drawing the distinction between therapeutic research and non-therapeutic experimentation: Clearing a way through the definitional thicket, in David N Weisstub (ed), *Research on human subjects: Ethics, law and social policy*. Elsevier, Oxford, 1998: 88–110

Vincent C. Why do people sue doctors? A study of patients and relatives taking legal action. *The Lancet* 1994; 343: 1609–1613

Voluntary Euthanasia Society. *Public opinion*. Voluntary Euthanasia Society, 2003

Ward B, Tate P. Attitudes amongst NHS doctors to requests for euthanasia. *British Medical Journal* 1994; 308: 1332

Warren MA. On the moral and legal status of abortion. *The Monist* 1973; 1: 43–61

Welfare decisions for adults who lack capacity (2010) 2 FLR 158

Wilkinson TM. What's wrong with conditional organ donation? *Journal of Medical Ethics* 2003; 29: 163–164

Williams G. *Textbook of criminal law*. Stevens, London, 1978

Williamson L, Fox M, McLean S. The regulation of xenotransplantation in the United Kingdom after UKXIRA: Legal and ethical issues. *Journal of Law and Society* 2007; 34: 441–464

Wilson J, Tingle J (eds). Clinical risk modification: A route to clinical governance. Oxford, Butterworth, Heinemann, 1999

Witting C. National Health Service rationing: Implications for the standard of care in negligence. *Oxford Journal of Legal Studies* 2001; 21: 443

Wolf SM. Pragmatism in the face of death: The role of facts in the assisted suicide debate. *Minnesota Law Review* 1998; 82: 1063

Wolf SM, Kahn JP, Wagner JE. Using preimplantation genetic diagnosis to create a stem cell donor: Issues, guidelines and limits. *Journal of Law, Medicine and Ethics* 2003 31: 327–339

Woolf Lord. Access to Justice: Final report of the Lord Chancellor on the civil justice system. HMSO, London, 1996

Woolf Lord. Are the courts excessively deferential to the medical profession? *Medical Law Review* 2001; 9: 1–16

Woolfe SM, Kahn JP, Wagner JE. Using pre-implantation genetic diagnosis to create a stem cell donor: issues, guidelines and limits. *Journal of Law, Medicine and Ethics* 2003; 31: 327

World Health Organisation (2005). World Alliance for Patient Safety. Available at http://www.who.int/

World Health Organisation (2007). ICD-10 F60.2. Available at http://www.who.int

World Health Organisation. Guiding principles on human cell, tissue and organ transplantation (updated edition). Geneva, World Health Organization, 2008. Available at http://www.who.int/transplantation/TxGP08-en.pdf

World Medical Association. Declaration of Helsinki: Ethical principles for medical research involving human subjects (2008). Available at http://www.wma.net

Wyatt J. Medical paternalism and the foetus. *Journal of Medical Ethics* 2001; 27: ii18–ii20

Youngner S. Who defines futility? *Journal of the American Medical Association* 1988; 260: 2094–2095

Youngner SJ, Lewandowski W, Macleish DK. Do Not Resuscitate orders—the incidence and implications in a medical intensive care unit. *The Journal of the American Medical Association* 1985; 253: 54–57

Index